SQL/400

Developer's Guide

PAUL CONTE • MIKE CRAVITZ

A Division of
Penton Technology Media

221 E. 29th Street • Loveland, CO 80538 USA
(800) 650-1804 • (970) 663-4700 • www.29thStreetPress.com

Library of Congress Cataloging-in-Publication Data

Conte, Paul, 1948-
SQL/400 developer's guide / by Paul Conte and Mike Cravitz.
p. cm.
Includes bibliographical references (p.) and index.
ISBN 1-882419-70-7
1. IBM AS/400 (Computer)--Programming. 2. SQL (Computer program language) 3. Database design. I. Cravitz, Mike, 1946- II. Title.
QA76.8.I25919 C64 2000
005.75'65--dc21
00-010108

29th Street Press® is a division of
Penton Technology Media
Loveland, Colorado USA

This book was printed and bound in Canada.

ISBN 1-882419-70-7

2004 2003 2002 WL 2 1 10 9 8 7 6 5 4 3

To my wife, Janice,
whose patience and support are a part of every book I write.

— Paul Conte

To Philip and Becky.
And to Kerrie, who always believed in me.

— Mike Cravitz

Acknowledgments

Producing a successor to *Database Design and Programming for DB2/400* that would provide comprehensive and updated coverage of SQL/400 and DB2 UDB for AS/400 was a daunting project. SQL/400 and UDB/400 are enormously broad and challenging technical subjects, and we could never have accomplished the task of boiling the relevant information down to a comprehensible guide without the help of a number of other people.

We benefited greatly from our frequent discussions with Kent Milligan, who is one of IBM's UDB/400 experts in the AS/400 PartnerWorld for Developers organization. Kent contributed an enormous amount of time answering our questions and bringing to bear the combined knowledge of many of IBM's UDB/400 developers. We very much appreciate Kent and other IBM developers' help. Of course, we take responsibility for any errors that may remain in the final version.

Our editor, Katie Tipton, glued the whole project together from early planning through publication with unflagging enthusiasm, encouragement, patience, and a deft editing hand. Whenever the work remaining to be done seemed more than we could accomplish in the allotted time, Katie found just the right calm and coaxing voice to keep us moving ahead.

Several other people had a hand in shaping the book. Jan Hazen, the 29th Street Press AS/400 textbook manager, provided valuable feedback from instructors so we could organize the content most effectively. Bernie Cinkoske, assistant professor at Ivy Tech State College in Indiana, offered helpful suggestions on our manuscript as well as her encouragement for the project. Martha Nichols did all the production work for the book in record time and with incredible precision. Mike Friehauf designed the cover, and Kathy Wong provided administrative assistance. And, once again, Paul's wife Janice kept her good humor and provided support and advice as he typed away evenings and weekends. We're grateful to you all for your help and patience.

This book is built on the foundation of *Database Design and Programming for DB2/400*, and thus credit is also due the people who worked on the original volume. We want to thank again Trish Faubion, Dave Duke, Dave Bernard, Janice Weinberg, Penny Ellis, Ted Tucker, Bryan Meyers, Julian Monypenny, Dan Riehl, Frank Soltis, Carol Ramler, Sue Romano, Carol Woodbury, John Broich, Mark Anderson, John Fulton, Jon Paris, John Morris-Reihl, Sharon Hamm, Jan Caufman, and the many others who helped on *Database Design and Programming for DB2/400* and who have contributed to our continued education about the AS/400 and UDB/400.

There are also many editors, technical editors, and other staff of Duke Communications who have helped with earlier articles on topics covered in this book. Thanks to all of you for your help getting it right.

Finally, we'd like to renew our thanks to the many AS/400 programmers with whom we've spoken or corresponded over the years for their observations, tips and techniques, stimulating questions, and encouragement. We hope all of you take pleasure in being a part of this book.

Table of Contents at a Glance

Table of Contents

Preface

By many measures, including number of units sold and customer satisfaction ratings, IBM's AS/400 is the most successful business computer ever developed. One reason for that success is the system's integrated database management system, known as DB2 Universal Database for AS/400 (UDB/400). UDB/400 provides a highly functional, efficient, and reliable system for storing and manipulating large volumes of data and is the foundation for most of the business applications that run on the AS/400. SQL/400 is IBM's strategic language for defining and manipulating UDB/400 databases,[1] and in the past few years, many organizations have adopted it for their application development. For that reason, it's no overstatement to say that a well-designed database and a solid understanding of SQL/400 are prerequisites for top-quality AS/400 application software.

This book provides that understanding to students and practicing programmers. Once you master the topics covered in *SQL/400 Developer's Guide*, you'll be able to design and create *professional-level* databases for real applications. A professional application developer requires skills in several areas, among them:

- modeling the system[2]
- designing the system implementation
- implementing the system's database and software

In other words, you need to understand a system from the user's point of view, design a suitable system conceptually, and then implement it with the tools at hand. You can't neglect any of these areas and expect much success.[3] That's why this book gives developers extensive advice on database *design* as well as *programming* — the application development world doesn't need more "hacks" who charge into projects with a little knowledge of syntax and not much more.

Of course, pure theory alone isn't enough either. Ultimately, somebody has to create the database tables and application programs that constitute a system. You'll find that if you get a good education in basic design and programming principles, along with some practical coding knowledge, the implementation part gets much easier as you gain more experience. Modeling and design, on the other hand, remain challenging throughout a developer's career because the world is both complex and rapidly changing. In the long run, modeling and design skills are the most difficult to master; but you have to start somewhere, and our experience teaching and "mentoring" new programmers suggests that most people find it easier to learn something tangible — like how to create a database table — before they get too deeply into conceptual areas. So this book starts with SQL/400 basics — by the end of Chapter 3, you'll know how to use the Create Table statement to create a table to hold data, and by the end of Chapter 8 you'll know almost all the basic ways you can set up and use various kinds of SQL objects.

1 For many years, IBM used the proprietary Data Description Specifications (DDS) language to define AS/400 databases and used proprietary extensions to RPG and Cobol I/O statements to manipulate database files. Since V4R1, however, IBM has concentrated almost all of its database development efforts on SQL. Because SQL is a universally supported industry standard for relational databases, you can expect SQL to remain IBM's focus.

2 Another common term for this part of the process is "systems analysis." We prefer "modeling" because it captures both the *analysis* and the *synthesis* aspects of the process.

3 Of course, many other associated skills are required: Project planning, quality assurance, and a certain amount of "political savvy" are all important for a developer.

At that point, you'll be "armed and dangerous" and ready for the second part of the book, which explains how to use SQL in high-level languages, such as RPG IV and ILE COBOL/400. This part of the book also covers a variety of more advanced topics that are essential for professional-level applications. The third part of the book covers data modeling and database design. This may be the final part in the book, but it's crucial to successful database development. We'll preview the content of each section of the book in a moment, but first let's go over where this book fits into your education.

The broad subject of application development can be sliced several ways. We've already suggested that there's theory and practice — this book is practical, but it includes one chapter on the relational database model, which is the conceptual foundation of both UDB/400 and widely used data modeling and design techniques. The discussion of the relational model minimizes formal mathematics and emphasizes the model's "intuitive" nature, which is one of its great strengths. Another split is high-level language programming (e.g., RPG IV, ILE COBOL/400, or C++) versus database programming. Both types of programming are essential to application development, of course. This book concentrates on database programming — most importantly on using SQL/400 — but includes an entire section on accessing the UDB/400 database from HLL programs. We urge the reader to pursue comparable courses (or books) on HLL design and programming in conjunction with the use of this book. The annotated bibliography in the appendices includes a number of highly recommended books about HLL programming.

As with any topic, database material can range from introductory level to advanced. We've tried to write this book so that anyone with at least some familiarity with computers and programming finds it accessible. On the other hand, we haven't shied away from challenging material when we thought it was important to help the reader become a *professional-level* developer. This shouldn't be your first book about computers or programming, although it may be the first book you've read that concentrates on database issues. For college-level Information Systems or Applied Software Development programs, this book should work well for a course (or sequence) that requires at least one HLL programming course as a prerequisite. Naturally, the pace of instruction can be significantly faster if the book is used in an upper-division course, as opposed to early in the student's exposure to software development. (Instructors should note that this book isn't intended to provide comprehensive enough treatment of relational database theory or UDB/400 system internals to be used as the only text for in-depth courses on those topics. See the annotated bibliography for books that cover these topics in more detail.)

For programmers — or readers who want to become programmers — who aren't enrolled as students, we recommend that you have a fairly good knowledge of at least one programming language and at least a superficial exposure to the AS/400. Naturally, having an AS/400 available to try out solutions to exercises will be a big advantage. This is an ideal book for programmers coming from other database platforms, such as Oracle, Microsoft's SQL Server 2000, or other versions of DB2 (e.g., on IBM mainframes). If that's your situation, you should be able to blast through most of the chapters and get a very rapid start with UDB/400.

This is a textbook, not a technical reference manual. However, we've tried to provide numerous examples, tables, appendices, and detailed technical explanations so that no AS/400 manuals are necessary to create, manage, and use UDB/400 tables and other objects. Fortunately, the AS/400 provides extensive online, CD-ROM, and Web-based help for SQL statements and CL commands. With this text and online resources, you should be able to perform almost any UDB/400-related task without too much trouble. For many AS/400 development groups, copies of this book can serve in place of additional copies of IBM's database-related manuals.

Finally, there's the mix of personal opinion and technical fact that goes into any book. While this book is packed with facts, it also offers some opinions and recommendations on various design and programming techniques. In our experience, the most capable developers *think* about why they do things the way they do. Over time, this attitude leads to improvement; and after 10 years' experience, the developer who's been paying attention will have far surpassed the developer who kept doing the same thing over and over — whether from ignorance, superstition, or habit. We've tried to pass along the results of some of our own observations — for instance, about the importance of a consistent and meaningful approach to table and column names. Every one of these opinions is debatable, but we've spared you lengthy arguments for our point of view. Wherever we make a recommendation, consider it, and if you think of a better solution, use it instead. Hopefully, some of our "tips" will save you time and headaches as you accumulate experience.

On a technical note, this edition is based on Version 4 of UDB/400 and AS/400 HLLs. If you're using an earlier release, you may find that your system doesn't support some of the functions used. Because of the rapid development of UDB/400 and the unavoidable span of releases that any edition of a text covers, we've targeted the most recent release available at the time of publication.[4]

A Closer Look at the Contents of This Book

The book is divided into three major parts, as well as a collection of appendices.

Part I introduces UDB/400 and covers the core SQL/400 statements. SQL is the industry-wide standard for relational database access, including remote access via IBM's Distributed Relational Database Architecture (DRDA), Microsoft's Open Database Connectivity (ODBC), and Java Database Connectivity (JDBC). Today, *database* programming on the AS/400 — and all other major servers — means *SQL* programming.

IBM — and the rest of the computer industry — is putting most of its database development efforts into SQL. A professional application developer will require SQL skills to further his or her career on the AS/400, as well as on other platforms. SQL is an extensive topic, so this part of the book concentrates on the SQL statements themselves, leaving until Part II the way that SQL statements are used in HLL programs. Chapter 1 provides a clear explanation of the AS/400 architecture and where UDB/400 and SQL/400 fit in. Chapter 2 introduces SQL, as well as the Interactive SQL (and other) features that let you execute SQL statements. Chapters 3 through 8 explain SQL's Data Definition Language (DDL) and Data Manipulation Language (DML) statements in depth. Chapter 9 covers AS/400 security along with the related SQL statements. The nine chapters in this part should be studied in sequence, and they're all necessary for a student to write SQL-based applications. SQL also is directly based on the relational model, so the material covered in Chapter 18 is very helpful and might be read before beginning this part.

Part II covers SQL/400 programming in high-level languages. Most AS/400 applications will include many RPG IV or ILE COBOL/400 programs that include database access, so this part of the book provides extensive examples in these two languages, including two complete sample programs that illustrate all the major programming techniques necessary for a production application. C/C++ programmers will also find this part helpful because the principles of embedded SQL programming are explained adequately for use with any HLL language.

Chapters 10, 11, and 12 form the core of this topic, and Chapters 14 and 15 integrate the information into two complete examples written in RPG IV and ILE COBOL/400, respectively. Chapter 13 is a long chapter covering many important topics. The "Host Structures" section describes a valuable

4 At the time of publication, the current release was V4R5.

programming technique that's used in the examples in Chapters 14 and 15. This is the only essential section to cover in Chapter 13 before proceeding to the examples. The other topics in Chapter 13 can be selectively included in an academic course. Professional AS/400 developers will find this chapter one of the richest mines of information and advice that goes well beyond the basics. We encourage special attention to the "Transaction Integrity and the Commit and Rollback Statements" section, which explains an underused — and critical function — provided by UDB/400 for robust applications.

Chapter 16 covers a wide variety of advanced database programming topics — including trigger programs and distributed database access — that a professional developer ultimately must master. In an academic curriculum, this chapter can be left to the student to pursue or included in an upper-division elective.

Part III covers database modeling and design. This material is based on the relational database model and provides both an introduction to that model and a description of how it can be used as the foundation of a design process.

Part III provides the reader with important foundation concepts for understanding why the designers of UDB/400 (and other relational database management systems) set things up the way they did; as a consequence, this section also gives the reader a better grasp of how to use UDB/400 effectively. In addition, this section teaches how to model and design application databases. Students shouldn't get too far in their study without understanding the topics covered in this part of the book.

To fit chapters into different curriculum plans, Chapter 18 on the relational database model may be presented as an independent topic. Chapters 19, 20, and 21, which go into specific modeling and design techniques more extensively, require a firm grasp of the relational model and should be taught only after Chapter 18 (or the student gets an equivalent foundation from another course). If chapters need to be pruned to fit course constraints, Chapter 20 on entity-relationship diagramming or Chapter 21 on physical database design could be left to a later course or self-study.

The **Appendices** provide reference material to enable the reader to use UDB/400, and related OS/400 development tools, in a classroom or production environment. They include concise references for the most frequently used SQL statements. A condensed guide to database-related commands is also provided. Two short appendices instruct the reader in the use of the AS/400 Programming Development Manager (PDM) and the Source Entry Utility (SEU) — tools used to work with AS/400 objects and source code. We've included an extensive annotated bibliography, which readers can use to expand their knowledge of UDB/400, database design, and other software development areas. Instructors may want to explore some of the recommended books for additional material for their course syllabus. A glossary recaps the important terms used in this book, for easy lookup.

The three parts of the book are designed to fit comfortably (for the student and instructor) into a two-course sequence. Parts I and III as the first course provide the student a mix of SQL coding details and more general design principles and practices. In this first course, the instructor can pick and choose the topics from Chapter 8 (advanced DML statement features) and Chapter 9 (security). From our own experience, most students will find this approach easier to digest than cramming all the basic and advanced SQL and UDB/400 programming into a single course. It also provides an effective mix of tangible and conceptual so the student is better prepared to tackle advanced topics. The second course can provide a thorough treatment of SQL/400 programming, including embedded SQL in HLL programs and selected additional and advanced topics from Chapters 8, 9, 13, and 16.

An instructor's guide is available to those instructors who adopt this text for classroom use. The guide includes answers to the exercises as well as some additional notes on the topics covered in each chapter of the text. The guide includes a CD with source files for the examples and exercises.

As a final introductory comment, let us say that in our own careers, database design and programming have frequently been the pivotal areas that determined the success of major application development projects. Unfortunately, these skills are often neglected in the training of business programmers. Fortunately for the reader, people who have these skills are in high demand and are usually well compensated. If you learn the material in this book, you can expect to be ahead of the pack in finding interesting and well-paying jobs. On a personal note, we've also found that the early stages of data modeling are especially challenging and fun. We hope a little of both comes through in this book.

Paul Conte
Eugene, Oregon

Mike Cravitz
Long Beach, California

Chapter 1

Introduction to UDB/400, the AS/400's Integrated Database

Chapter Overview

This chapter introduces the concept of a database and describes DB2 Universal Database for AS/400 (UDB/400), the database management system that runs on the AS/400. You'll get a general idea of how the AS/400 and its operating system, OS/400, are architected. You'll also get an overview of UDB/400 physical and logical files and how they are used with Structured Query Language (SQL).

Databases and Database Management Systems

This book teaches you how to use **Structured Query Language**, or **SQL**, which is a computer language used to define and manipulate databases. A **database** is a set of computer files for storing information that's used by a business or other organization. A typical business might keep information about customers and their orders, suppliers of materials, and employees who work for the company. Storing this type of information in computer files enables easy retrieval and updating as well as flexible analysis of the raw data to produce management reports, such as sales trends or average employee-benefit costs.

Of course, how "easy" and "flexible" it is to work with the data is determined largely by how well the database has been set up and by the capabilities of the **database management system** (**DBMS**), which provides the software to store and update database contents. In this chapter, we look at the building blocks of **DB2 Universal Database for AS/400**, or **UDB/400**, the DBMS that runs on IBM **AS/400** computer systems. In subsequent chapters, we'll explore how to use SQL to create and manipulate a UDB/400 database.

UDB/400 is an integrated part of **OS/400**, the AS/400's operating system[1], which means that you don't have to buy UDB/400 as a separate software product and that any AS/400 application you write can take advantage of UDB/400 features. UDB/400 is also the *only* relational DBMS that runs on the AS/400.[2]

Figure 1.1 shows a simplified view of how UDB/400 fits into the AS/400 architecture.

1 Technically, OS/400 is the services layer of the AS/400's operating system. The System Licensed Internal Code (SLIC) layer provides the operating-system kernel, including the hardware-management functions of the operating system.

2 Unlike with other operating systems, such as AIX on IBM's RS/6000 or Microsoft's Windows 2000 on Intel processors, you can't run a third-party relational DBMS (e.g., Oracle) on an AS/400. Although, technically, a relational DBMS vendor could port its product to the AS/400, competing with UDB/400 would be hard because UDB/400 comes free as part of the AS/400's operating system and is highly integrated with other AS/400 functions.

Figure 1.1
UDB/400 and the AS/400 Architecture
(indicates OS/400)

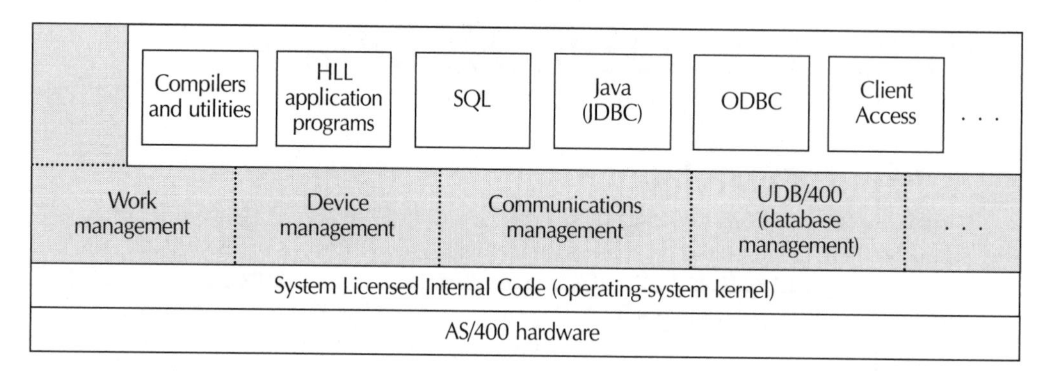

As you can see, UDB/400 provides a DBMS layer that all **high-level language** (**HLL**) programs (i.e., RPG IV, Cobol, C/C++, and Java) use to access application data stored in UDB/400 files. You can also see that all utilities and remote applications — for example, a Java applet running in a Web browser and using Java Database Connectivity (JDBC) or a Windows application running on a PC and using Open Database Connectivity (ODBC) — must go through UDB/400 to access the AS/400 database. This integrated, uniform interface provides a high degree of consistency and control for AS/400 application developers.

If you're familiar with other operating systems and DBMS products, you'll find that UDB/400 has features of both conventional operating systems' file-management facilities and relational DBMS products. For example, like a conventional file-management facility, UDB/400 lets you use built-in HLL input/output (I/O) operations, such as Cobol's Read and Write verbs, to access data. Like other relational DBMS products, UDB/400 lets you access the same data using SQL. This "dual" nature of UDB/400 is even expressed in the nomenclature: UDB/400 documentation for conventional file access uses the terms "file," "record," and "field," while documentation for SQL access uses the comparable terms "table," "record," and "column," respectively.

In this chapter, we look briefly at both sides of UDB/400, considering it as a conventional file system and as an SQL-based relational DBMS. The remainder of the book concentrates on just the SQL perspective. At the end of this chapter (page 20), you'll find a list of additional resources you can use to learn more about other aspects of UDB/400.

The AS/400 Integrated File System (IFS)

The UDB/400 database is arguably the most important and widely used way to store data on an AS/400, but it's not the only way. Everything stored on an AS/400 is stored in the AS/400's **integrated file system** (**IFS**). The IFS is organized as a hierarchical directory structure that includes 11 distinct file systems, as depicted in Figure 1.2.

Figure 1.2
AS/400 Integrated File System (IFS)

Directory	File system
/	**"Root" file system** Contains DOS-, Windows-, and OS/2-based files and directories
/QDLS	**Document Library Services file system** Contains document library objects (DLOs) and folders
/QFileSvr.400	**OS/400 File Server file system** Provides access to other file systems that reside on remote AS/400s
/QLANSrv	**OS/2 Warp Server for AS/400 file system** Contains files shared with the OS/2 Warp Server for AS/400 licensed program
/QNetWare	**NetWare file system** Contains files for a local or remote Integrated Netfinity Server for AS/400 running Novell NetWare
/QNTC	**Windows NT Server file system** Contains files for a local or remote Integrated Netfinity Server for AS/400 running Windows NT
/QOpenSys	**Open Systems file system** Contains Unix-based files and directories
/QOPT	**Optical file system** Contains stream files stored on optical media
/QSYS.LIB	**Library file system** Contains AS/400 libraries and other types of AS/400 objects
/mounted-name	**Network file system** Any mounted network file system (NFS) that's exported by an NFS server
/user-defined	**User-defined file system** Contains user-defined and -managed file system(s)

One of these file systems, QSYS.LIB, contains **record-structured files** managed by UDB/400, as well as other types of OS/400 objects. These record-structured files can contain text, numeric, and other forms of data and can be read and updated by HLL programs and SQL. As a shorthand, we use the term "QSys files" to mean those database files in file system QSYS.LIB. Creating and manipulating QSys files with SQL is the main focus of this book.

The "root" file system in the IFS provides a Windows-like directory structure for **stream files** — that is, files that contain a sequence (or stream) of bytes that aren't organized by the operating system into separate records, as the bytes in QSys files are. Like QSys files, stream files can contain text or numeric data, but stream files are not the main database files used by UDB/400.

Files in the root file system and some of the other non-QSYS.LIB file systems can be accessed by PCs and other computers connected to the AS/400; for the most part, these files have specialized purposes not directly related to UDB/400. As you'll see in Chapter 3, however, UDB/400 files can reference the contents of files in the non-QSYS.LIB file systems[3], typically for image files and other types of data managed by non-AS/400 applications. You can learn more about the IFS and its file systems by consulting the resources listed at the end of this chapter.

OS/400 Objects, Libraries, and User Profiles

Because UDB/400 is an integral part of OS/400, it helps to have a general understanding of how OS/400 is organized and where UDB/400 fits in. Everything in the OS/400 operating system, including the database, is organized as **objects**. OS/400 identifies more than 80 types of objects that can be stored in the QSYS.LIB file system, including libraries, programs, database files, display and printer files, user profiles, message queues, SQL packages, and so forth.[4] OS/400 also has a few object types for files outside the QSYS.LIB file system, but these object types aren't of central importance in developing typical AS/400 business applications. In the following discussion, we concentrate just on QSYS.LIB objects and, most important, on database files, which are what most AS/400 applications use.

Like other operating systems (e.g., Unix), OS/400 stores program instructions, application data, and other system components on disk, loading them into main memory as needed. But, unlike most other operating systems, OS/400 doesn't let you get at the bytes on disk or in memory directly. Instead, you must always use specific commands or other system interfaces that are valid for each type of object. For example, you can't execute a database file or perform a file-update operation on a program object.[5] The system prevents any attempt to use an invalid operation on an object altogether rather than let it proceed and possibly cause damage or produce undesirable results. This protection is uniform across all AS/400 operations, including user commands, application code, and operating-system operations. Object encapsulation is so integral to the AS/400 that there are no "back doors" that a system programmer can use to subvert the integrity of an OS/400 object.[6] As we progress through UDB/400's capabilities, you'll learn about various types of OS/400 objects and the way to use them.

3 With Version 4 Release 4 (V4R4), UDB/400 introduced the "datalink" feature to allow a database file (i.e., one in the QSYS.LIB file system) to contain a Universal Resource Locator (URL) reference to a stream file in one of the other file systems.

4 Object-oriented (OO) languages, such as Java and C++, are now widely used, and OO databases are becoming more common. You may wonder how these relate to OS/400. Like OO languages, OS/400 organizes everything into objects of different types, which have restricted interfaces. The details of how an object, such as a file, carries out its operations is encapsulated in the object implementation, hidden from the application programmer. However, application programmers can't create new OS/400 object types in the way they can create new object types in most OO languages; essentially, only IBM can do that for OS/400.

UDB/400, which is part of OS/400, is generally considered a relational DBMS, not an object-oriented DBMS. Object-oriented databases are designed to store irregular, complexly structured data, such as the engineering plans for an airplane. Relational databases are a good fit for table-oriented data but need some additional features to handle the types of data for which object-oriented databases are typically used. With V4R4, IBM has added many of these additional features, including support for complex and large objects. We cover these features in Chapter 3.

5 Most other operating systems treat everything on disk as a "file" and let you attempt nonsensical operations, such as executing a file that contains data instead of instructions. These operating systems may offer some protection by setting file attributes (e.g., "executable"). But you can still create a file with the "executable" attribute that contains data instead of instructions. With OS/400, it's impossible to change an object's type (e.g., from *File to *Pgm), so you can't have the wrong type of contents in an object. As we mentioned, OS/400 doesn't generally distinguish among file types for files stored outside the QSYS.LIB file system, and thus utilities and applications can use system interfaces to directly modify the byte-level contents of most files outside QSYS.LIB. All AS/400 programs and all UDB/400 database files, however, must exist in QSYS.LIB, and, as a result, OS/400 protects the integrity of these objects based on their specific object type.

6 Obviously, anyone with physical control of an AS/400's hardware can use extraordinary means to mess with the operating-system code, but the point is that the AS/400 prevents the typical byte-level modifications to operating-system code that are possible on most other systems.

QSys Objects, Libraries, and User Profiles

OS/400 controls how you use an object by storing some descriptive information with the actual content of the object. Figure 1.3 depicts the storage layout (disk or memory) for an OS/400 object.

Figure 1.3
OS/400 Object Storage Layout

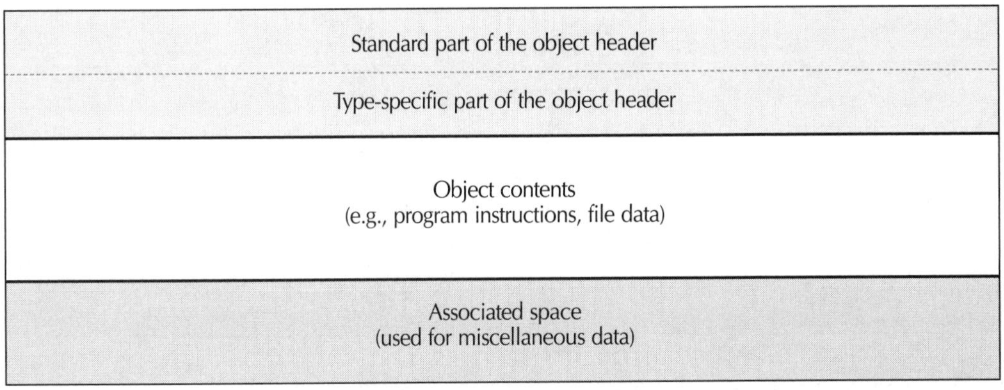

Standard part of the object header
Type-specific part of the object header
Object contents (e.g., program instructions, file data)
Associated space (used for miscellaneous data)

As you can see, all objects have a header, object-specific contents (e.g., program instructions, file data), and an area known as the associated space, where system or user programs store miscellaneous data related to the object.

The object header has a standard part and a type-specific part. All objects in the QSYS.LIB file system include at least the following information in the standard part of their header:

- the name of the library that contains the object
- the object's name
- the object's type
- the object's subtype
- the name of the user profile that owns the object

An AS/400 **library** is an object that contains other objects. Think of an AS/400 library as a Unix or MS-DOS directory or a Windows 9*x*/NT folder; the only difference is that you can't generally nest AS/400 libraries as you can directories or folders — that is, a library can't contain another library object. There's one exception to this rule, however — the QSys library, which contains all other library objects in the QSYS.LIB file system (as well as some additional objects).[7] As a result, QSYS.LIB is organized as shown in Figure 1.4.

7 The other IFS file systems use their own respective approaches to directories or folders and do not use OS/400 library objects. When the AS/400 was first introduced, it had no IFS, and the entire system was contained in the QSys library. To provide file support for applications ported from Unix and Windows systems, IBM introduced the IFS and the additional file systems. However, the QSYS.LIB file system remains the "native" AS/400 environment.

Figure 1.4
QSYS.LIB File System Organization

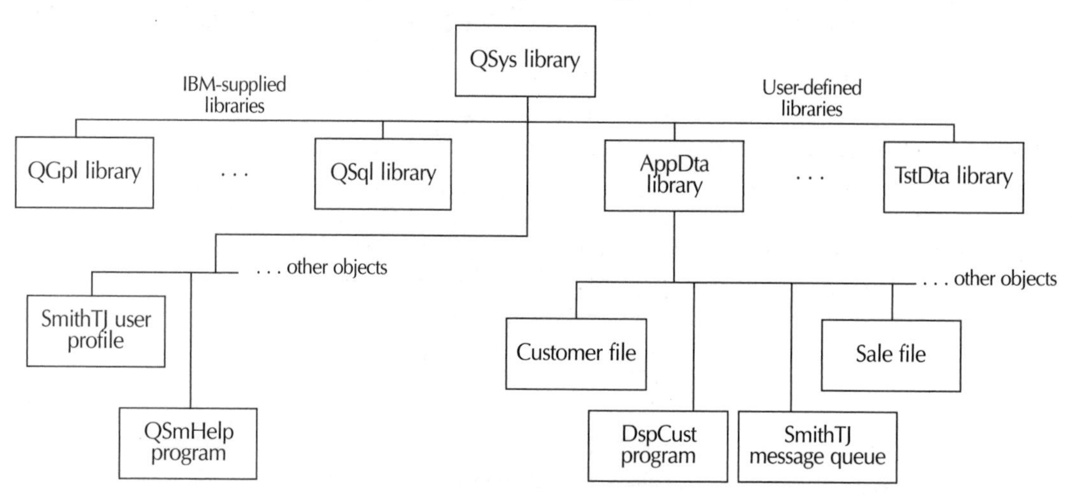

In the discussion that follows, we'll consider only QSys objects — that is, those objects contained in library QSys or in one of the libraries contained in QSys. (QSys objects are simply those objects in the QSYS.LIB file system.)

QSys object names are generally up to 10 alphanumeric characters, beginning with a letter or a national character (e.g., $, #, @ in the United States). Thus, Customer might be the name of the customer master file object, and AppDta might be the name of the library that contains your application database files. A QSys object's **qualified name** is the combination of the name of the library that contains the object and the object's unqualified name, separated with a forward slash (/). For example, AppDta/Customer would be the qualified name of the customer master file if the file were stored in library AppDta.

We've already touched on the notion of object type, and in QSys each object type is designated by a special value, such as *Pgm for program or *File for file. Some object types are further broken down into subtypes. The *File object type, for instance, includes physical files, logical files, printer files, display files, and communications files — all of which are kinds of record-oriented sources or targets for external program data. In the rest of this chapter, we generally use the simple term "file" when it's clear from the context that we're talking about a physical or logical file. When it's necessary to refer to another specific type of file, we use an unambiguous term, such as "printer file."

A QSys object is uniquely identified by the combination of its qualified name and its object type, which means OS/400 allows only one object on an AS/400 that has a given combination of library name, object name, and object type. As a result, you can have a Customer *File object in the AppDta library and another Customer *File object in the TstDta library, but you can't have two files with the same name in the same library. You can have two objects with the same name in the same library as long as they aren't the same type, but this practice is not a wise one, because of the potential for confusion. In general, you should give unique names to all the objects in the same library, regardless of their types.

Each QSys object is owned by a **user profile** — another type of AS/400 object. Each user profile stores information about a system user, including the user's name, password, and authority to access data or use system functions. Whenever you sign on, you supply a user profile name and password, and this lets OS/400 control your use of the system, including access to the database.

Chapter 9 covers database security in more detail; the main things to know as you learn about creating and accessing database files are that each file object has a user profile designated as its owner and all access to the database is controlled based on the authority granted to one or more user profiles.

Files, Record Formats, and Members

Let's recap a couple of fundamental points we've covered: Everything on the AS/400 is stored in one of the 11 IFS file systems, and file system QSYS.LIB is where UDB/400 database file objects are stored. In simple terms, a **database file** object is a named collection of **records**. In the typical example depicted in Figure 1.5, the Customer file would contain a record for each of the company's customers.

Figure 1.5

Sample Customer File Contents

Fields

CustID	Name	ShipLine1	ShipCity	ShipState	Status	Discount
10001	Ajax Plumbing	12 Main St.	Seattle	WA	A	0.01
10002	Sherod Sign Co.	576 Pearl St.	Eugene	OR	X	0.00
10003	Picante Software	132 E. Broadway	Portland	OR	A	0.15
10004	Cobblestones	340 Willamette St.	Seattle	WA	B	0.07
10005	Kinetic Bagel	501 6th Ave.	Seattle	WA	C	0.02
10006	Full City Coffee	11 Monument Ave.	Richmond	VA	X	0.10
10007	Zenon's Cafe	6 Ventura Blvd.	Loveland	CO	C	0.15
10008	Bubba's Grill	491 High St.	Denver	CO	A	0.00
10009	The West Bros.	2601 Stratford Rd.	Portland	OR	A	0.02

Records

A record is a collection of **fields**, which are named items of data — such as CustID (customer ID) and Name (customer name) — that represent attributes of some item (e.g., a customer) of interest to the organization. (In a moment, you'll see how UDB/400 uses database files to implement SQL tables.) Your applications store business data in records in database files and subsequently read and update those records as needed.

An OS/400 file object contains the object-header information we discussed previously. For files, this header is often referred to as the **file description** and includes a description of the file's **record format** — the byte-by-byte layout of all the fields in the file's records.[8] (Some kinds of logical files, which we discuss in the next section, have multiple record formats.) Figure 1.6 depicts a simple record format for the Customer file, along with a sample record.

8 You can create a UDB/400 file that contains simple fixed-length records without any field definitions. This type of file has a single character field with the same name as the file. This type of file is referred to as a **program-described file** because you must explicitly code the file's record layout in any HLL program that uses the file. Program-described files are not very common any more in AS/400 business applications and cannot be created with SQL. The types of files that we discuss in this book (those that do have field descriptions) are known as **externally described files** because they have definitions that are external to the HLL programs that use the files.

Figure 1.6

Record Format for the Customer File

Field name	Data type	Length or precision	Decimal positions	Start position	Size (in bytes)	Usage	Column heading
CustID	Integer	9	0	1	4	In/Out	Cust. ID
Name	Character	30	n/a	5	30	In/Out	Customer Name
ShipLine1	Character	100	n/a	35	100	In/Out	Customer Shipping Line 1
ShipCity	Character	30	n/a	135	30	In/Out	Customer Shipping City
ShipState	Character	2	n/a	165	2	In/Out	Cust. Ship. State
Status	Character	1	n/a	167	1	In/Out	Cust. Sts.
Discount	Packed decimal	3	2	168	2	In/Out	Cust. Disc.

Sample record with starting positions of each field:

10001	Ajax Plumbing	12 Main St.	Seattle	WA	A	0.01
1	5	35	135	165	167	168

The record format is how your applications know where specific elements of data should be placed in a record that's to be added to the file or where specific elements of data should be retrieved from a record that's been read from the file. Once you've defined the record format for a file, your applications can reference all fields by their field names (e.g., Status); you don't have to worry about specific byte locations or other low-level storage details.

You can organize the data in a particular file into one or more file **members**, each with its own member name.[9] Single-member files are the most common organization you'll encounter in AS/400 applications, and typically the one member has the same name as the file (and, of course, holds all the file's data). When you use SQL to create a UDB/400 file, the file *always* has a single member with the same name as the file.

Although multimember files are not commonly used with SQL applications, it's not uncommon to encounter older AS/400 applications that use multimember files and access these files with conventional HLL I/O statements (rather than SQL). One example of how a multimember file might be

9 Members can be added to or removed from a file at any time; you don't have to specify a fixed number of members when you create a file. If a file has multiple members, they all have the same record format.

Members are not a type of AS/400 object; they are a component of a file object, just like record formats and access paths. The earlier statement that everything in the OS/400 operating system, including the database, is organized as objects may seem a little confusing in this light. The statement is true, but there are further degrees of organization *within* various types of objects.

used is to store sales data in a file named Sale with one member for each year (e.g., Sale1999, Sale2000, and so on). UDB/400 provides features that let an application specify which file member should be used when the application is run. Thus, an application to display sales data could be run on the data for any particular year, just by specifying which file member to use.

Despite the fact that you can't *create* a multimember file with SQL, you can use SQL to *access* any member of an existing multimember file. In a typical SQL application, however, you would normally partition data by using multiple (single-member) files rather than multiple members. For example, you might have files named Sale1999, Sale2000, and so forth. The effect is more or less equivalent to using multimember files.

Physical and Logical Files

As we mentioned earlier, there are two types of UDB/400 files:

- physical files
- logical files

You store application data in **physical files**. This is where the actual bytes are that represent numbers, text, and other kinds of information. UDB/400 takes care of low-level details such as reading and writing disk sectors. Application programs and database utility programs see the data in a physical file member as a sequence of records, as in Figure 1.7.

Figure 1.7

Record Placement in a UDB/400 Physical File Member

Relative record number (RRN)	"Deleted record" flag	Contents
1		Record for customer number 10004
2	On	(No record)
3		Record for customer number 10007
4		Record for customer number 10001
. . .	. . .	. . .
(Highest RRN)		Record for customer number 10009

Each record occupies a unique location in a member, and the records are not necessarily in any order based on their content. A record's location is identified by its **relative record number** (**RRN**), which starts at 1 for the first record in the member and increases by 1 for each location. When you delete a record, UDB/400 sets on an internal "deleted record" flag in the record's location. When you insert a new record, UDB/400 puts it either in the first available location with a "deleted record" flag set or after the last record in the file. As more space is needed for additional records, UDB/400 dynamically expands the file member size.

A physical file always has just one record format, and all records in the same physical file (regardless of how many members the file has) have the same record layout. For many business applications, all the fields in a record will have a fixed length, and the resulting record layout consequently has a fixed length as well. UDB/400 also supports variable-length fields and records, a topic we'll take up in Chapter 3.

Logical files provide an alternative way to access data in one or more physical files. You can use a logical file to

- select a subset of the records in a physical file (e.g., only customers in Seattle)
- combine the records from multiple physical files (e.g., combine sales records from a file for the year 1999 with records from a file for the year 2000)
- select a subset of the fields in a physical file's record format (e.g., only the name and status of customers)
- combine ("join") related records in two or more physical files (e.g., combine detailed customer data with each of the sales records for the customer)
- provide an index so records can be efficiently retrieved in a particular order (e.g., by customer name)

Figure 1.8 provides a conceptual view of the relationship between a logical file and a physical file.

Figure 1.8
Relationship Between Logical and Physical Files

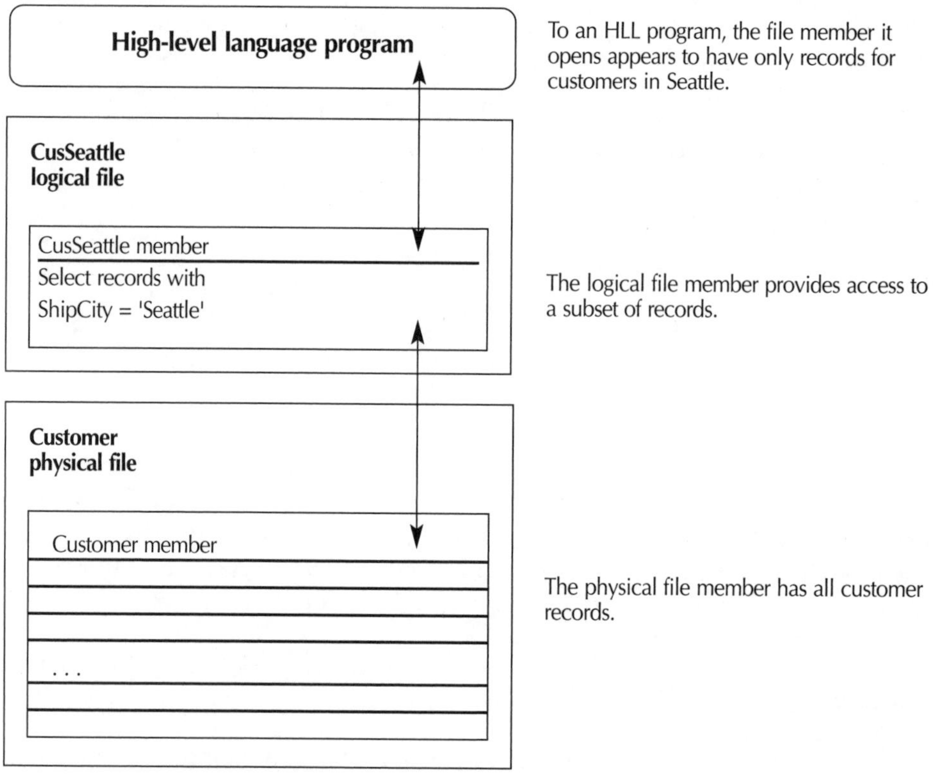

It's important to understand that logical files have no data in them; data is always stored in physical file members. Logical files do have members, however. For each logical file member, you specify which physical file member (or members) it spans.

Logical files also have record formats. Although most logical files have a single record format, logical files can have multiple formats. Multiformat logical files aren't widely used any more, and SQL doesn't support them, so we don't cover them in this book. Subsequent chapters describe the relationship between logical and physical files in more detail — in particular, the relationship between SQL views (which are logical files) and tables (which are physical files).

File and Field Descriptions

One thing that distinguishes UDB/400 from a traditional operating-system file-management facility is that every UDB/400 file object contains a description of itself. The file description includes the following items:

- file name
- file subtype (physical or logical)
- record format (or formats)
- access path description (discussed in the next section)
- list of members

When you compile an AS/400 HLL program, the compiler reads the file descriptions for any files you declare in your programs. AS/400 HLLs have extended I/O-related statements or functions that take advantage of the fact that the compiler has this file information. For example, you don't have to declare a record layout in your RPG input specifications or your Cobol Data Division — with the appropriate file declaration in your program, the compiler automatically generates RPG or Cobol source code for the file's record layout. As another example, the compiler can automatically use the correct fields for keyed record access (e.g., by customer ID) based on the key field (or fields) you define for a file. In addition, utility programs (e.g., report generators) can use file descriptions to determine a file's layout and keyed sequence (if any) without requiring the end user to enter anything other than the file's name.

One of the most useful parts of the file description is the record format, which stores the following information for each field in the record:

- name
- data type (e.g., binary, character, packed-decimal number)
- length (for binary and character fields) or precision and scale (i.e., number of digits and decimal positions, for numeric fields)
- starting position in the record (the first field starts at position 1)
- size (number of bytes occupied in the record)
- usage (whether the field can be used for input, output, or both types of access)
- an optional column heading
- an optional text description of the field

A file's descriptive information is actually stored in *two* places: the file object's header and the **SQL catalog**, which is a set of system files. The SQL catalog is the ANSI-standard means of storing descriptions of database objects and was added to UDB/400 several releases after the AS/400 was first introduced. In case you're wondering, this is the reason UDB/400 supports two, somewhat redundant, mechanisms to store a file's descriptive information. UDB/400 makes sure that no matter how you create or change a file definition, consistent information is maintained in both places.

Access Paths and Indexes

So far, we've seen that UDB/400 stores data as a sequence of records in a physical file. UDB/400 also provides a variety of ways to access records. The two most important concepts are

- the type of access path
- the access method

An **access path** describes the order in which records can be retrieved. There are two types of UDB/400 access paths: arrival-sequence access path and keyed-sequence access path.

An **arrival-sequence access path** is the order of records as they're stored in the database (i.e., by relative record number).

Note

"Arrival sequence" is a bit of a misnomer because a new record can be inserted in a "deleted record" location that has a lower RRN than a record that "arrived" earlier. The term originated before the AS/400 supported reusing deleted-record locations and has hung on. The Cobol language uses a more descriptive term — "relative" file organization — for this type of access.

A **keyed-sequence access path** is the order of records based on ascending or descending values in one or more **key fields** that you specify when you create a physical file or when you create a keyed logical file based on the physical file. UDB/400 also supports access paths that select a subset of the records in a physical file. For example, an access path might include just those customer records with a ShipCity value of "Seattle". Internally, UDB/400 maintains one **index** per file member for any physical or logical file that has key fields, as well as for some logical files that specify record selection. Internal indexes are stored as part of an OS/400 file object. The file description includes the index description, if the file has an index.

In simple terms, an index includes an entry for each record in the file, and each entry has the record's key-field value (or values) and RRN. UDB/400 stores index entries in a way that makes it very fast to look up a key value and then use the associated RRN to retrieve the record. UDB/400 can also step through an index in order of the key values, using the series of associated RRNs to retrieve records in key sequence.[10]

As you might expect, your programs can always use an arrival-sequence access path to access records in a physical file; no special coding is required when you create the file. You can also define one keyed access path as part of a physical file, and UDB/400 will create an index for each member of the physical file. (Note that the definition of the keyed access path is the same for all a physical file's members, but each member has its own index.)

Using logical files, you can have multiple access paths for the same data in a physical file and, thus, can access it in various ways. Each logical file can have one keyed access-path definition. So, for example, if you wanted to retrieve customers in order by name or by address, you could use two log-

10 With V4R4, UDB/400 introduced an Encoded Vector Index (EVI), which uses a bitmap rather than the type of index structure used by other keyed access paths. EVIs are primarily used for very large files to speed record selection on fields that have a relatively small number of different values.

ical files (assuming you didn't use either of these fields for the physical file's keyed access path, which would eliminate the need for one of the logical files). Like physical files, each logical file member has its own internal index, if the file has a keyed access path. Using SQL, you aren't required to create an index to retrieve records in a particular order. If no appropriate index exists, UDB/400 will either create a temporary index or sort the records on the fly.

You can read and write UDB/400 data with either the **sequential access method** or the **direct access method**.[11] With sequential access, your program essentially performs a series of "read next record" operations to retrieve records. If you use an arrival-sequence access path, your program receives records in their physical order (UDB/400 automatically skips "deleted record" locations). If you use a keyed access path, your program receives records in the order defined by the key fields. With direct access, you specify either an RRN or a specific key value, and UDB/400 returns the specific record you've identified (if one exists, of course).

As you insert, delete, or update records in a physical file member, UDB/400 maintains the necessary entries in any indexes that exist for keyed access paths (this includes logical file members over the physical file member). Although you can tune database performance by choosing from several alternative methods of index maintenance, in general your applications can count on all keyed access paths reflecting the current contents of the database.

Creating Files

The AS/400 provides three main ways to create UDB/400 files:[12]

- execute an SQL Create statement
- use the Client Access Express Operations Navigator utility
- enter Data Description Specifications (DDS) in a source file member and execute an OS/400 command to compile the source into a file object

Creating Files with SQL

With SQL, you can use the following statements to create and revise UDB/400 files:

- Create Table
- Create View
- Create Index
- Alter Table
- Comment On
- Label On

Figure 1.9 shows an SQL Create Table statement to create a Customer table.

11 Direct access is often referred to as "random access" — but there's usually nothing random about it.

12 There's actually a fourth OS/400 method you can use to create database files. The Interactive Data Definition Utility (IDDU) is a carryover from IBM's System/36 computer and exists on the AS/400 to aid migration of System/36 applications. IDDU isn't intended for new AS/400 applications.

Figure 1.9
SQL Create Table Statement

```
Create Table AppDta.Customer
  ( CustID     Integer              Not Null
                                    Primary Key,
    Name       Char    (  30 )      Not Null,
    ShipLine1  Char    ( 100 )      Not Null,
    ShipCity   Char    (  30 )      Not Null,
    ShipState  Char    (   2 )      Not Null,
    Status     Char    (   1 )      Not Null,
    Discount   Decimal (   3, 2 )   Not Null
                                    Default 0.0
               Constraint DiscountCk Check ( Discount >= 0.0 ) )
```

In standard SQL terminology, a **base table** (or simply **table**) is the database object that actually contains the data. In UDB/400, an SQL table is a single-member physical file. An SQL **view** provides an alternative way to access data in one or more tables and in UDB/400 is a single-member logical file. An **SQL index** provides a keyed access path that can be used to improve data-access performance. In UDB/400, an SQL index is also a single-member logical file. (Chapter 3 explains in more detail how SQL tables, views, and indexes correspond to physical and logical files.)

The Create View and Create Index SQL statements create the respective objects. You use the Alter Table statement to change a table definition; to change views and indexes, you simply re-create them. The Comment On and Label On statements let you add comments and labels for tables, views, and indexes.

Consistent with the table-oriented terminology, SQL refers to records as **rows** and to fields as **columns**. Figure 1.10 shows a conceptual perspective of an SQL table.

Figure 1.10
An SQL Table

Columns

CustID	Name	ShipLine1	ShipCity	ShipState	Status	Discount
10001	Ajax Plumbing	12 Main St.	Seattle	WA	A	0.01
10002	Sherod Sign Co.	576 Pearl St.	Eugene	OR	X	0.00
10003	Picante Software	132 E. Broadway	Portland	OR	A	0.15
10004	Cobblestones	340 Willamette St.	Seattle	WA	B	0.07
10005	Kinetic Bagel	501 6th Ave.	Seattle	WA	C	0.02
10006	Full City Coffee	11 Monument Ave.	Richmond	VA	X	0.10
10007	Zenon's Cafe	6 Ventura Blvd.	Loveland	CO	C	0.15
10008	Bubba's Grill	491 High St.	Denver	CO	A	0.00
10009	The West Bros.	2601 Stratford Rd.	Portland	OR	A	0.02

Rows

Not surprisingly, this looks just like the table-like presentation of the Customer physical file in Figure 1.5, except for the use of "Columns" and "Rows" instead of "Fields" and "Records." Once we dive into SQL in the next chapter, we'll generally use the table-oriented terminology. In this chapter, we've mostly discussed the underlying AS/400 and UDB/400 architecture using file-oriented terminology because the AS/400 was originally designed with file objects, and the file-oriented terminology is still used today by many OS/400 Control Language (CL) commands and much of the documentation. Even when you're working with SQL, it's important to understand UDB/400 file concepts.

You can enter SQL statements in several ways. If you have the **DB2 Query Manager and SQL Development Kit for AS/400** (**SQL Development Kit** for short) product installed, you can execute SQL statements either interactively using the **Interactive SQL** (**ISQL**) utility that comes with the SQL Development Kit or as **embedded statements** compiled into an HLL program (again using a feature of the SQL Development Kit). The latter approach presents an interesting aspect of UDB/400's support for SQL. Although you must buy the SQL Development Kit to get the interactive SQL interface and the facility that lets you embed SQL statements in HLL programs, *all* AS/400s include in UDB/400 the ability to run compiled HLL programs that were created using embedded SQL. You do not need the SQL Development Kit product on an AS/400 just to run an application that uses SQL.

Creating Files with Operations Navigator

Beginning with V4R4, IBM's Client Access Express AS/400-to-PC connectivity product also provides a Windows-based tool, Operations Navigator, that has a graphical interface for creating new database objects. Figure 1.11 shows a sample Operations Navigator New Table dialog box.

Figure 1.11

Operations Navigator New Table Dialog Box

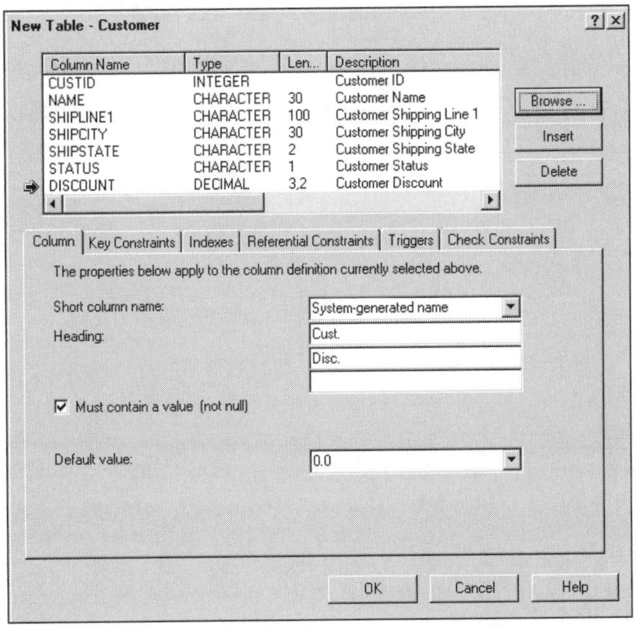

We cover Operations Navigator features in a bit more detail in Chapter 2.

Creating Files with DDS

When the AS/400 was first introduced, IBM provided the proprietary **Data Description Specifications** (**DDS**) language to, as its name suggests, describe file data. You use a source code editor, such as

Source Entry Utility (**SEU**) (covered in Appendix D), to enter DDS statements into a source file member.[13] Figure 1.12 shows some of the DDS source code for the Customer physical file.

Figure 1.12

DDS for the Customer Physical File

```
* - - - - - - - - - - - - - - - - - - - - - - - - - - - - - - - - - - - -
* File name............. CUSTOMER
* Format name........... CUSTOMERR
* Key field(s).......... CUSTID
* Unique/duplicate key.. Unique
* File type............. Physical
* Purpose............... Customer records
* Author................ Paul Conte
* Date.................. 01/01/2000
* - - - - - - - - - - - - - - - - - - - - - - - - - - - - - - - - - - - -

                                           UNIQUE

              R CUSTOMERR                  TEXT( 'Customers' )
*               ==============================================================
                CUSTID          9B 0       COLHDG( 'Cust.'
                                                   'ID' )
*               --------------------------------------------------------------
                NAME           30A         COLHDG( 'Customer'
                                                   'Name')
*               --------------------------------------------------------------
                SHIPLINE1     100A         COLHDG( 'Customer'
                                                   'Shipping'
                                                   'Line 1' )
*               --------------------------------------------------------------
                SHIPCITY       30A         COLHDG( 'Customer'
                                                   'Shipping'
                                                   'City' )
*               --------------------------------------------------------------
                SHIPSTATE       2A         COLHDG( 'Cust.'
                                                   'Ship.'
                                                   'State')
*               --------------------------------------------------------------
                STATUS          1A         COLHDG( 'Cust.'
                                                   'Sts.')
*               --------------------------------------------------------------
                DISCOUNT        3P 2       COLHDG( 'Cust.'
                                                   'Disc.' )
*               ==============================================================
              K CUSTID
```

The syntax of DDS is fairly simple. Each line is split into a number of fixed-width columns. The last column (positions 45–80) provides a free-format area where you can place keyworded entries. You can learn about DDS facilities to define physical and logical files by consulting the resources listed at the end of this chapter.

After you've entered the DDS to define a file, you execute one of the following OS/400 CL commands to create the file object:

- CrtPf (Create Physical File)
- CrtLf (Create Logical File)

13 UDB/400 further categorizes physical files into data files and source files. **Data files** are the ones you create for your applications (in other words, any type of physical file except a source file). **Source files** are physical files with three specific fields: source sequence (SrcSeq), source date (SrcDat), and source data (SrcDta). You store DDS, HLL, SQL, and other source code in source files. The SEU editor, the HLL compilers, and several other AS/400 utilities are designed to work with source files. You create a source file with the CrtSrcPf (Create Source Physical File) CL command, which creates the file with the required fields — no DDS is necessary to create a source file.

Figure 1.13 illustrates the process of creating a new file object from DDS. To change an existing file definition, you edit its DDS source and then execute a ChgPf (Change Physical File) command.

Figure 1.13
Creating a UDB/400 Physical File from DDS

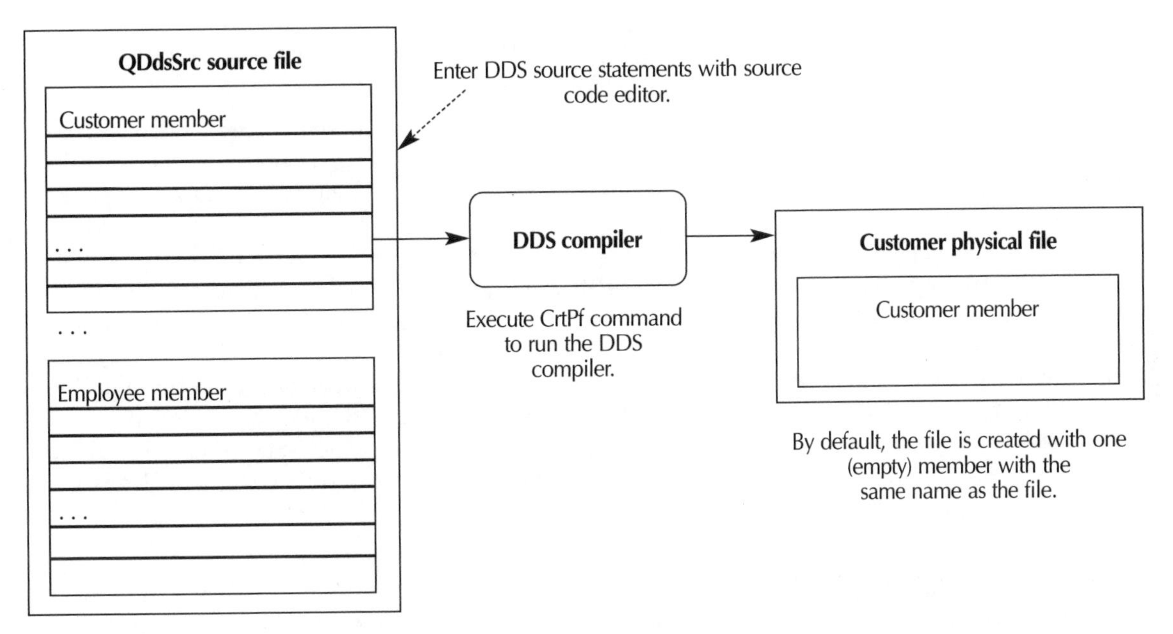

Most AS/400 development installations also have the IBM Application Development ToolSet product installed, which provides a utility known as **Programming Development Manager (PDM)**. PDM provides a list-based, interactive interface for working with AS/400 libraries, objects, and source file members. PDM options are available to simplify execution of the CrtPf and CrtLf commands. Appendix C provides an introduction to PDM.

Whether you create a database file with SQL, Operations Navigator, or DDS, you get the same type of OS/400 object — a physical or logical file.[14] What's more, you can create a file with Operations Navigator or DDS and then read and update the contents with SQL or create a file with SQL or Operations Navigator and read and update the contents with built-in HLL I/O operations. Because UDB/400 includes as part of the "native" file support features that SQL requires, there is no need to add a separate DBMS layer just to support applications written with SQL.

Accessing Files from HLL Programs

When you want to access UDB/400 data, your application performs three steps:

- opens a physical or logical file member
- processes (reads, inserts, updates, or deletes) records in the file member
- closes the file member

14 There are actually some file attributes that are set differently depending on which method you use to create a file. However, the OS/400 object types are the same, and you can generally use files created with any of the three methods interchangeably.

In some cases, you use explicit HLL statements, such as Open and Close in RPG or Cobol, to open and close a file member. In other cases, such as with RPG's built-in cycle, the HLL runtime does this for you automatically.

Note

In HLL terminology, you "open a *file,*" which in UDB/400 means you open a file member. In this book, the two expressions are equivalent unless otherwise noted.

Many types of SQL statements — for example, some forms of the Update statement — open and close the appropriate file member implicitly. SQL also provides a construct known as a **cursor**, which your application opens and closes explicitly, again with the result that a file member is opened and closed.

Whether you open a file member implicitly or explicitly, UDB/400 creates a temporary internal control structure known as an **open data path** (**ODP**), which your program uses to access the records in a file member. UDB/400 uses information from the file description (e.g., the record layout and access path description) to set up an ODP. Then, during your program's execution, HLL or SQL run-time routines and UDB/400 use the ODP for purposes such as keeping track of your position in the file and locking records to avoid conflicting updates by multiple users. To understand some of UDB/400's more advanced features, you need to understand the role of ODPs; however, for most of the topics covered in this book, the ODP is taken for granted, and we can treat UDB/400 files as if HLL and SQL operations operated on them directly, rather than through the ODP.

Chapter Summary

A database is a set of computer files used to store business information. A database management system (DBMS) is the system software for creating database files and updating their contents. DB2 Universal Database for AS/400 (UDB/400) is the AS/400's integrated DBMS and is part of OS/400, the AS/400's operating system.

Everything stored on an AS/400 is stored in the AS/400's integrated file system (IFS), which is organized as a hierarchical directory structure that includes 11 distinct file systems. The QSYS.LIB file system contains all AS/400 programs and the database files used by UDB/400.

Everything in OS/400 is an object. More than 80 OS/400 object types exist, including programs and database files. An object contains a header and the actual content (e.g., program instructions, file data) of the object. OS/400 lets you use objects only through commands or other system interfaces that are valid for the specific type of object. Library objects (which are used only in the QSYS.LIB file system) contain other types of OS/400 objects, except other library objects. User profile objects own objects. In the QSYS.LIB file system, an object is uniquely identified by its library name, object name, and object type.

Two types of UDB/400 database file objects exist: physical files, which contain data, and logical files, which provide alternative ways to access data in physical files. File objects contain a file description, which includes the record format (or formats) of the records in the file. The record format describes the type, length, and other attributes of the fields in a record. The data in a physical file is organized into one or more members, all of which have the same record format. Logical files also have members; each logical file member provides access to the data in one or more underlying physical file members.

UDB/400 has two types of access paths: arrival sequence, which orders records by their relative location in a physical file member, and keyed, which orders records by values in the records' key fields. You can read and write records sequentially (in order of the access path) or directly (by specific relative record number or key value).

You can create database files using SQL statements, Operations Navigator dialog boxes, or Data Description Specifications (DDS). Files created in any of these ways can generally be used interchangeably.

SQL uses a table-oriented terminology to describe database objects. A table contains data, a view provides an alternative way to access data in one or more tables, and an index provides a keyed access path that can be used to improve data-access performance. On the AS/400, when you create an SQL table, UDB/400 creates a physical file; for a view or SQL index, UDB/400 creates a logical file.

To access UDB/400 data from a high-level language (HLL) program, you open a file member, process the records, and then close the file member. When you open a file member, UDB/400 creates an open data path (ODP) that your program and UDB/400 use to keep track of the file position and other runtime information.

Key Terms

access path
arrival-sequence access path
AS/400
base table
column
cursor
Data Description Specifications (DDS)
data file
database
database file
database management system (DBMS)
DB2 Query Manager and SQL Development Kit for AS/400 (SQL Development Kit)
DB2 Universal Database for AS/400 (UDB/400)
direct access method
embedded statement
externally described file
field
file description
high-level language (HLL)
index
integrated file system (IFS)
Interactive SQL (ISQL)
key field
keyed-sequence access path
library
logical file
member
object
open data path (ODP)
OS/400
physical file
program-described file
Programming Development Manager (PDM)
qualified name
record
record format
record-structured file
relative record number (RRN)
row
sequential access method
Source Entry Utility (SEU)
source file
SQL catalog
SQL index
stream file
Structured Query Language (SQL)
table
user profile
view

Additional Resources

The following references provide more information about topics covered in this chapter. See Appendix E for descriptions of these and other resources mentioned in this book.

For information about the AS/400's integrated file system (IFS):

Integrated File System Introduction

For information about Data Description Specifications (DDS) and other non-SQL topics related to UDB/400:

Database Design and Programming for DB2/400

DB2 UDB for AS/400 Database Programming

OS/400 DDS Reference

Exercises

1. List several advantages of using a database. Are there any disadvantages?
2. Why do you think the designers of OS/400 made everything an "object"? Do you think OS/400 objects make programming easier or harder? Do you think OS/400 objects will affect performance?
3. What is the IFS? Which part of the IFS is the most important for applications that use the UDB/400 database?
4. What is an OS/400 library? What are the disadvantages to the OS/400 restriction that you can't nest libraries? Are there any advantages to this approach? *(Hint: Consider how Unix and DOS implement searches for executable and non-executable files.)*
5. Why do you think OS/400 considers as "files" all of the following: database files, display files, printer files, and communications files? Do you think OS/400 allows the same set of file operations for all types of files?
6. What are the two types of database files, and what are their respective purposes?
7. What are the three types of SQL objects (discussed in this chapter) used to contain or access data? How does each correspond to a particular type of database file?
8. What part of a file describes the arrangement of the fields in the file's records? What advantage does this offer to application programmers? To nonprogrammers?
9. Draw a "box" diagram that shows the relationship of the following: library, file, member, record, and field.
10. What is an RRN? How does UDB/400 use it?
11. What are key fields? Give at least two important uses of key fields.

12. Give several possible ways you might want to access the data in a customer master file (e.g., accessing only customers in Seattle).
13. When would you use sequential access? When would you use direct access? Would you ever use both in the same program?
14. List several things you think UDB/400 might use the ODP for.
15. Describe three ways to create a database file. Do you think a physical file must exist before you can create a logical file over it? (In SQL terms, do you think a table must exist before you can create a view over it?) Why or why not? *(Note: You'll find the answer in Chapter 6.)*

Chapter 2

Introduction to SQL on the AS/400

Chapter Overview

In this section of the book, we cover the nonprogramming aspects of Structured Query Language (SQL), an industry-standard language for defining and manipulating data contained in a relational database. This chapter introduces DB2 UDB for AS/400 SQL — "SQL/400" for short — and covers the RunSqlStm (Run SQL Statement) command, Interactive SQL (ISQL), and the SQL catalog. You will learn to use ISQL, which lets you enter nearly all the available SQL statements interactively. We also introduce IBM's Operations Navigator graphical interface, particularly as it relates to SQL/400.You will see that the SQL catalog consists of a set of useful SQL views that provide information about your database.

Introduction to SQL

An IBM research lab developed Structured Query Language (SQL) in the 1970s to explore an implementation of the relational database model.[1] Since that time, SQL has become a widely used language that's included in most relational database management systems (DBMSs), including IBM's family of DB2 products. Several national and international standards organizations have published SQL standards, which the major relational DBMSs, including UDB/400, follow for their versions of SQL.[2]

The official name of the UDB/400 implementation of SQL is DB2 UDB for AS/400 SQL. Throughout this book, we use the term "SQL" when discussing SQL in general (including DB2 UDB for AS/400 SQL) and use "SQL/400" when discussing DB2 UDB for AS/400 SQL specifically.

Learning SQL has many advantages. On the AS/400, the language provides some important database capabilities not available through Data Definition Specifications (DDS) and built-in HLL I/O operations. Because SQL is an industry standard, programming skills in SQL can also be used with many other relational databases, including Microsoft SQL Server, Oracle, and DB2 on other platforms (e.g., IBM mainframe databases, AIX, Microsoft Windows NT). This commonality also makes SQL a valuable cross-platform tool, especially with distributed database facilities, such as IBM's Distributed Relational Database Architecture (DRDA), Java Database Connectivity (JDBC) for Java applications,

1 The original language was SEQUEL — Structured English Query Language — developed in 1974 by D.D. Chamberlin of IBM's San Jose lab. This lab developed several more versions of SEQUEL, and the language was renamed SQL in 1977 when it was included in IBM's System R relational database management system (DBMS) prototype. In 1979, the first major commercial implementation of SQL was included in Relational Software, Inc.'s Oracle DBMS. The first version of SQL that was available for IBM's midrange computers was Advanced Systems Concepts' Sequel/38 product for the System/38 (the predecessor of the AS/400); Advanced Systems Concepts' Sequel/400 is still available on AS/400s. In 1988, IBM announced SQL/400 for the AS/400. IBM now uses the product name DB2 UDB for AS/400 SQL instead of SQL/400.

Due in part to the language's original name (SEQUEL), SQL for some time was usually pronounced "sequel." In recent years, especially among IBMers in the AS/400 community, the favored pronunciation is "S-Q-L" (the three letters) to avoid confusion with products whose names contain "sequel" (e.g., Advanced Systems Concepts' Sequel/400).

2 As of release V4R4, SQL/400 met most of the entry-level requirements of the following standards:

- International Standards Organization (ISO) 9075-1992, Database Language SQL
- American National Standards Institute (ANSI) X3.135-1992, Database Language SQL

and the Open Database Connectivity (ODBC) interface between Microsoft Windows platforms and other operating systems.

SQL includes **Data Definition Language (DDL)** statements to create database objects based on the relational model covered in Chapter 18. SQL also includes **Data Manipulation Language (DML)** statements to retrieve and update the contents of a database. Figure 2.1 lists all the available SQL/400 statements, including DDL, DML, and other categories.

Figure 2.1
Available SQL/400 Statements

Data Definition Language
- Alter Table
- Comment On
- Create Alias
- Create Collection
- Create Distinct Type
- Create Index
- Create Schema
- Create Table
- Create View
- Drop Alias
- Drop Collection
- Drop Distinct Type
- Drop Index
- Drop Package
- Drop Schema
- Drop Table
- Drop View
- Grant
- Label On
- Rename
- Revoke

Data Manipulation Language
- Commit
- Delete
- Insert
- Lock Table
- Rollback
- Select
- Set Path
- Set Transaction
- Update

Embedded Cursors
- Close
- Declare Cursor
- Fetch
- Open

Dynamic SQL
- Describe *statement*
- Execute
- Execute Immediate
- Prepare

Programming
- Begin Declare Section
- Call
- Create Function
- Create Procedure
- Declare Procedure
- Declare Statement
- Declare Variable
- Describe Table
- Drop Function
- Drop Procedure
- End Declare Section
- Free Locator
- Include
- Select Into
- Set *host-variable*
- Set Option
- Set Result Sets
- Values Into
- Whenever

Distributed Database
- Connect
- Disconnect
- Release
- Set Connection

Stored Procedure Language
- Begin...End
- Case
- Declare Condition
- Declare Handler
- Declare *variable*
- For
- Get Diagnostics
- GoTo
- If
- Leave
- Loop
- Repeat
- Resignal
- Return
- Set
- Signal
- While

We look closely at most of the DDL statements in Chapters 3 through 6; however, for now a simple example provides a preview of what SQL looks like. The following statement creates a simplified base table to contain customer data. (In SQL terminology, a **table** is an object, made up of columns and rows, that stores data. A **base table** is a named, persistent object created with the Create Table statement. A **result table** is an unnamed, temporary set of rows that the DBMS generates from one or more base tables during database retrieval or update operations. In this book, we use the term "table" to mean "base table" when the context makes it clear that the term refers to a permanent object.)

```
Create Table Customer
     ( CustID    Dec(    7, 0 ) Not Null,
       Name      Char(  30    ),
       ShipLine1 Char( 100    ),
       ShipCity  Char(  30    ),
       ShipState Char(   2    ),
       Status    Char(   1    ),
  Primary Key( CustID ) )
```

The Customer table created by this statement can be used to store information about customers. Each customer-related item, such as Name, listed in the Create Table statement defines a table **column**. In UDB/400, when you create an SQL base table, you create an AS/400 physical file object. A base table's columns are simply fields in the file's record format. As you will see in subsequent chapters, you can generally use SQL/400 tables and views interchangeably with physical and logical files created from DDS. There are some important differences, however, and we will look at those aspects of SQL/400 tables and views, too.

As we mentioned, SQL also includes statements to manipulate data in tables. For example, the following SQL statement inserts a customer's data into the table created above:

```
Insert Into Customer
 Values ( 10001,
         'Ajax Plumbing',
         '12 Main St.',
         'Seattle',
         'WA',
         'A' )
```

Each value supplied on the Insert statement corresponds positionally to a column in the Customer table. This Insert statement adds a new **row** to the Customer table. Recall from Chapter 1 that an SQL/400 row in a table is just a record in a file.

Note

If you're wondering how you can write application programs with Insert statements that handle a variety of customers and not just specific customers (e.g., Ajax Plumbing), don't worry — SQL/400 provides many features (which we cover in Part II) that let you use SQL to write complete RPG IV, ILE COBOL/400, and other HLL programs, as well as SQL Procedure Language (SPL) procedures. There's lots more flexibility than these first examples show.

As these simple examples suggest, SQL provides statements that can be used to create tables and **views** (the SQL counterpart to OS/400 logical files). SQL also provides statements to read, insert, update, and delete individual rows within a table or view.

If this were all SQL did, its only claim to fame would be that it's a widely adopted standard for database definition and manipulation. But SQL also lets you manipulate *sets* of rows. For example, the following statement changes the status of all customers in Seattle that currently have a status of X:

```
Update  Customer
  Set   Status   = 'B'
  Where ShipCity = 'Seattle'
    And Status   = 'X'
```

The Where clause selects only those rows that satisfy the specified condition, and the Set clause assigns the new value to the Status column in the selected rows. This statement can be entered interactively (using various UDB/400 tools), but, more important, it can also be placed in an HLL program and can use program variables for the values of the city and the old and new status. This capability provides powerful set-at-a-time data manipulation that's not found in conventional HLLs' database access. For example, without SQL, both RPG IV and ILE COBOL/400 would require a read-write loop to carry out what SQL can do with a single Update statement.

Another significant feature of SQL is the capability to define very complex views. Views are implemented as OS/400 logical files (OS/400 sets an attribute that identifies such logical files as SQL views). Views don't store data but provide an alternative way to access data in one or more underlying base tables. Views can select a subset of a base table's rows or can be defined with a subset of a base table's columns. Views can also derive new columns from other columns. SQL views have a rich language for expressing both row selection and column derivation.

As we mention in Part III, SQL is also a good starting point for expressing many of the definitions, manipulations, and integrity constraints you need to document in the logical data modeling and physical database design stages of a project. When you use SQL as a design language, you can extend it with your own notation to cover conditions that aren't directly supported by any actual SQL implementation. Then, when you implement tables, views, and application programs, you can use the various techniques suggested in Chapters 19–21 to handle those cases in which SQL/400 (or the DBMS facility you use) provides no direct implementation of your pseudo-SQL design specification. Even though pseudo-SQL as a design language doesn't eliminate implementation challenges, it provides a very capable language for clearly expressing many database design concepts.

Entering SQL/400 Statements

You can use a variety of means to enter SQL statements on the AS/400, but for production development, you generally use one of following:

- the RunSqlStm (Run SQL Statement) CL command
- the Interactive SQL (ISQL) facility
- AS/400 Operations Navigator

RunSqlStm and ISQL are part of IBM's DB2 Query Manager and SQL Development Kit for AS/400. IBM provides Operations Navigator as part of Client Access Express for Windows (IBM's primary AS/400 PC connectivity product). We'll discuss the RunSqlStm command first. Subsequent sections cover ISQL and Operations Navigator.

Using RunSqlStm to Enter SQL/400 Statements

The RunSqlStm command processes the SQL statements contained in a source member, as in the following example:

```
RunSqlStm  SrcFile( appsrc/sqltblsrc )
           SrcMbr( customer )
```

In this example, the CUSTOMER source member might contain a Create Table statement to create a base table. Putting SQL statements — especially statements to create production tables and views — in a source member is a good idea because you can subsequently revise and/or rerun the commands without having to re-create them. You can put one or more SQL statements in a source member by saving the session log from an interactive SQL session (as we discuss later). You can also enter SQL statements in a source file member using a source code editor, such as Source Entry Utility (SEU). (For those not already familiar with SEU and OS/400 source files, Appendix D provides an introduction.)

Not all SQL statements can be executed with the RunSqlStm command. However, the most useful DDL statements to code in a source member — Create, Label On, Comment On, Drop, Grant, and Revoke — can be executed with RunSqlStm. You can also run Insert, Update, and Delete — but not Select — with RunSqlStm.

If you code multiple SQL statements in a source member, the RunSqlStm command requires you to end each statement with a semicolon (;). Note also that you can code comments in a source member that's subsequently processed by the RunSqlStm command. To code a comment, begin the comment with two adjacent dashes (--) and use the rest of the line for the comment, as in the following example:

```
-- This is a comment in a RunSqlStm source member
```

Using Interactive SQL

IBM's SQL Development Kit product includes a facility known as **Interactive SQL**. ISQL lets you enter nearly all SQL/400 statements interactively. Using ISQL, you can create collections, tables, views, user-defined functions, distinct types (also called user-defined types), and other SQL objects. You can also retrieve and display, print, or store data from the database. With proper authority, you can also add new rows and update or delete existing rows in database tables.

ISQL provides comprehensive online help and is documented in the AS/400 manual *DB2 UDB for AS/400 SQL Programming*. To run ISQL, you enter the StrSql (Start SQL) command. You can press the F4 key to be prompted for the StrSql command parameters shown in Figure 2.2.

Figure 2.2
StrSql Command Prompt Screen

```
                    Start SQL Interactive Session (StrSql)

Type choices, press Enter.

Commitment control . . . . . . . COMMIT          *NONE
Naming convention  . . . . . . . NAMING          *SYS
Statement processing . . . . . . PROCESS         *RUN
Library option . . . . . . . . . LIBOPT          *LIBL_____
List type  . . . . . . . . . . . LISTTYPE        *ALL
Data refresh . . . . . . . . . . REFRESH         *ALWAYS_
Allow copy data  . . . . . . . . ALWCPYDTA       *YES____
Date format  . . . . . . . . . . DATFMT          *JOB
Date separator character . . . . DATSEP          *JOB
Time format  . . . . . . . . . . TIMFMT          *HMS
Time separator character . . . . TIMSEP          *JOB__
Decimal point  . . . . . . . . . DECPNT          *JOB___
Sort sequence  . . . . . . . . . SRTSEQ          *JOB______
  Library  . . . . . . . . . . .                 __________
Language identifier  . . . . . . LANGID          *JOB___
Program language . . . . . . . . PGMLNG          *NONE
SQL string delimiter . . . . . . SQLSTRDLM       *QUOTESQL

F3=Exit   F4=Prompt   F5=Refresh   F12=Cancel   F13=How to use this display
F24=More keys
```

These parameters set the session attributes for the ISQL session that's started. For example, if you want to use a dash (-) for a date separator, you can specify that in this StrSql command. You can also change the session attributes during a session, as we discuss later.

When you start an ISQL session, you see the statement entry display, shown in Figure 2.3.

Figure 2.3
ISQL Statement Entry Display

```
                          Enter SQL Statements

Type SQL statement, press Enter.
===> Create_Table_Customer_____________________________________________
     __(_CustID_____________Dec(____7,_0_)_Not_Null,___________________
     _____Name______________Char(__30_____)_Not_Null,___________________
     _____ShipLine1_________Char(_100_____)_Not_Null,___________________
     _____ShipLine2_________Char(_100_____)_Not_Null,___________________
     _____ShipCity__________Char(__30_____)_Not_Null,___________________
     _____ShipState_________Char(___2_____)_Not_Null,___________________
     _____ShipPostalCode1_Char(__10_____)_Not_Null,___________________
     _____ShipPostalCode2_Char(__10_____)_Not_Null,___________________
     _____ShipCountry_______Char(__30_____)_Not_Null,___________________
     _____PhoneVoice________Char(__15_____)_Not_Null,___________________
     _____PhoneFax__________Char(__15_____)_Not_Null___________________
     _______________________________________With_Default_'_',__________
     _____CreditLimit_______Dec(_7,_0_____)_With_Default_Null,_________
     _____EntryDate_________Date____________Not_Null,___________________
     _____Primary_Key(_CustID_)_)______________________________________

                                                                  Bottom
F3=Exit   F4=Prompt   F6=Insert line   F9=Retrieve   F10=Copy line
F12=Cancel            F13=Services     F24=More keys
```

This screen is a free-format display that lets you enter SQL/400 statements. The example shown in Figure 2.3 was entered directly (without prompting) to provide an easily read sample. You don't have to align elements of SQL statements, as we've done in this example; however, doing so makes it easier to spot syntax errors when they occur.

As you enter statements, ISQL retains them in a session log. You can page up to view previous statements. By placing the cursor on a statement and pressing F9, you can copy a previously entered statement to the statement input area of the display, where you can edit the statement (if desired) and re-execute it. By default, when you exit a session, ISQL saves the log and restores it the next time you run ISQL. Thus, unless you take some action such as clearing the session log (which we discuss later), your previously entered statements are available across multiple sessions.

When you're working in the statement entry display, the following function keys are available:

Function key	Description
F1	Help
F3	Exit ISQL
F4	Prompt statement
F6	Insert a blank line after the line on which the editing cursor is positioned
F9	Retrieve the previous statement or the statement on which the cursor is positioned
F10	Copy the line on which the editing cursor is positioned to the next line
F12	Exit ISQL (same as F3)
F13	Display Session Services menu (discussed later)
F14	Delete the line on which the cursor is positioned
F15	Split the line at the current cursor position; the contents of the line from the cursor position to the end of the line are moved to the next line

continued

continued ...

Function key	Description
F16	Display a collection selection list
F17	Display a table and view selection list
F18	Display a column selection list
F24	Toggle the command keys that are listed at the bottom of the display

For many statements, you'll find ISQL's prompting facility helpful, especially if you're just learning SQL. To request prompting for a statement, enter the beginning of the statement (e.g., Create Table) and press F4. If you're not sure of the statement name, press F4 on a blank line to get a list of SQL statements from which you can select a statement to prompt.

When you prompt a statement, ISQL presents a display such as the one for the Create Table statement shown in Figure 2.4.

Figure 2.4

ISQL Statement Prompting

```
                     Specify CREATE TABLE Statement

 Type information, press Enter.

   File . . . . . . . . . .   Customer__________      Name
     Library  . . . . . . .    __________             Name, F4 for list

 Nulls:  1=NULL, 2=NOT NULL, 3=NOT NULL WITH DEFAULT

 Field               FOR Field        Type            Length      Scale  Nulls
 CustID__________    __________       Dec________     ________7    0_      2
 Name____________    __________       Char_______     _______30    __      2
 ShipLine1_______    __________       Char_______     ______100    __      2
 ShipLine2_______    __________       Char_______     ______100    __      2
 ShipCity________    __________       Char_______     _______30    __      2
 ShipState_______    __________       Char_______     ________2    __      2
 ShipPostalCode1_    __________       Char_______     _______10    __      2
                                                                        More...
   File CONSTRAINT  . . . . . . . . . . . .   Y      Y=Yes, N=No
   Distributed File . . . . . . . . . . . .   N      Y=Yes, N=No

 F3=Exit   F4=Prompt                F5=Refresh   F6=Insert line    F10=Copy line
 F11=Display more attributes        F12=Cancel   F14=Delete line   F24=More keys
```

You enter the appropriate column names or other parts of the statement into entry fields of the prompt. For most entries that require a table, view, or column name, you can put the editing cursor in the entry field and press F4 to display a list of available tables, views, or columns. You can then select one of these for the entry.

To retrieve data, you enter a Select statement (as described in Chapters 5 and 8). ISQL presents the retrieved columns and rows in a rudimentary display as shown in Figure 2.5, which is the result of entering the following Select statement:

```
Select    *
  From    AppDta.Employee
  Order By EmpID
```

Figure 2.5
ISQL Output Display for Select Statement

```
                                Display Data
                                                Data width . . . . . . :      79
Position to line  . . . . .  ______          Shift to column  . . . . . .  ____
....+....1....+....2....+....3....+....4....+....5....+....6....+....7....+....
 Employee    First                    M  Last                          Manager
 ID          Name                     I  Name                          Employee
                                                                       ID
 104,681     Barb                     L  Gibbens                        898,613
 191,944     Hunter                   F  Thompson                       707,504
 212,333     Heide                    J  Smith                          898,613
 227,504     Greg                     J  Zimmerman                      668,466
 234,876     Rick                     O  Millhollin                     709,453
 400,301     Raplh                    S  Sport                          898,613
 567,909     Ralph                    H  Peck                           707,504
 598,213     Sybil                    M  Taylor                         668,466
 668,466     Dave                     R  Bernard                        709,453
 707,504     Bill                     R  Dutcher                        668,466
 767,424     Alfred                   W  Harris                         688,466
 812,213     Joe                      L  Cone                           898,613
 898,613     Trish                    S  Faubion                        668,466
 899,001     Rick                     D  Castor                         898,613
                                                                       More...
F3=Exit      F12=Cancel      F19=Left      F28=Right      F21=Split
```

You can page up and down in this display or use the Position to line entry field to display a particular row as the top row. The positioning options are T (for top, or first, row), B (for bottom, or last, row), or a number (e.g., 20). You can use the scalar functions listed in Chapter 5's Figure 5.6 (page 89) (e.g., SubStr) to improve the formatting of the displayed output somewhat, but ISQL displays are meant for ad hoc retrieval, not for frequently run queries where formatting is more important.

By changing the session's Select output attribute before executing a Select statement, you can redirect the retrieved rows to a printer file or to a new or existing database file. We discuss changing the session's Select output attribute later.

By default, when you start an ISQL session, the processing mode is *Run, which means ISQL actually executes any statements you enter. You can specify the StrSql command's Process(*Syn) parameter (or change the session's processing attribute, as we describe later) so that ISQL will only syntax check statements and won't actually run them. This setting lets you use ISQL to construct SQL statements that you then put in a source file member, either for later execution with the RunSqlStm command or for use as embedded SQL statements in an HLL program.

Another level of statement checking is available if you specify Process(*Vld). With this session setting, ISQL syntax checks the statement and also verifies that all referenced tables and columns exist. The *Vld setting provides an appropriate level of checking for DML statements that use existing tables and views, while *Syn is appropriate when some of the referenced objects don't yet exist.

When you use ISQL to check statements that will be embedded in an HLL language, you should also specify an appropriate PgmLng parameter value for the target programming language. For RPG IV and RPG/400, specify *Rpg; for ILE COBOL/400, specify *Cbl.

Saving Statements to a Source Member

To save a statement to a source file member, enter the statement and, if necessary, revise it so it's syntactically correct and (optionally) validity checked. Then press F13 to display the ISQL Session Services menu (Figure 2.6).

Figure 2.6

ISQL Session Services Menu

```
                    Interactive SQL Session Services

Select one of the following:

     1. Change session attributes
     2. Print current session
     3. Remove all entries from current session
     4. Save session in source file









Selection
     4

F3=Exit      F12=Cancel
```

Enter option 4 to bring up the display in Figure 2.7.

Figure 2.7

Save ISQL Session to Source File Display

```
                         Change Source File

Type choices, press Enter.

  File . . . . . . . . .   sqlsrc____     Name
    Library  . . . . . .     appsrc____   Name
  Member . . . . . . . .   crtcust___     Name, *FILE, *FIRST

  Option . . . . . . . .   1              1=Create new file
                                          2=Replace file
                                          3=Create new member
                                          4=Replace member
                                          5=Add to member


  For a new file:
    Authority  . . . . .   *LIBRCRAUT     *LIBRCRTAUT, *CHANGE, *ALL,
                                          *EXCLUDE, *USE,
                                          authorization list name

    Text . . . . . . . .   Create Customer table___________________________


F3=Exit      F5=Refresh      F12=Cancel
```

Here, you can enter a source file and member name into which the current session log is saved. You can subsequently execute the saved statements in the source member using the RunSqlStm command or use SEU (or another editor) to copy the saved statements to a source member for an HLL program.

To clear statements you don't want to save, select option 3 from the Session Services menu. Be aware that this option clears all statements, so be sure you don't clear statements you'll want to retrieve or save later.

Changing Session Attributes

You can change session attributes — such as the commitment control level, the processing option for statements, and the date and time formats and separator characters — by selecting option 1 from the Session Services menu. Choosing this option brings up a multipage prompt display (Figures 2.8A–2.8C) that you can use to change session attributes.

Figure 2.8A

ISQL Change Session Attributes Display, Page 1

```
                      Change Session Attributes

Type choices, press Enter.

  Statement processing . . . . .   *RUN         *RUN, *VLD, *SYN
  SELECT output  . . . . . . . .   1            1=Display, 2=Printer
                                                3=File
  Commitment control . . . . . .   *NONE        *NONE, *CHG, *CS, *ALL, *RR
                                                *NC, *UR, *RS
  Date format  . . . . . . . . .   *ISO         *JOB, *USA, *ISO, *EUR, *JIS
                                                *MDY, *DMY, *YMD, *JUL
  Date separator . . . . . . . .   '/'___       *JOB, '/', '.', ',', '-'
                                                ' ', *BLANK
  Time format  . . . . . . . . .   *ISO         *HMS, *USA, *ISO
                                                *EUR, *JIS
  Time separator . . . . . . . .   ':'___       *JOB, ':', '.', ','
                                                ' ', *BLANK
  Data refresh . . . . . . . . .   *ALWAYS_     *ALWAYS, *FORWARD
  Allow copy data  . . . . . . .   *YES_____    *YES, *OPTIMIZE, *NO
  Naming convention  . . . . . .   *SYS         *SYS, *SQL

                                                             More...
F3=Exit   F4=Prompt   F5=Refresh   F12=Cancel
```

The SELECT output entry field on the Change Session Attributes display is where you can direct rows retrieved by the Select statement to a printer or database file instead of to the display. If you enter a 3 (File) in this field and press Enter, you see a display like the one in Figure 2.9 (page 34).

Figure 2.8B

ISQL Change Session Attributes Display, Page 2

```
                          Change Session Attributes

Type choices, press Enter.

  Commitment control . . . . . .   *NONE          *NONE, *CHG, *CS, *ALL, *RR
                                                  *NC, *UR, *RS
  Date format  . . . . . . . . .   *ISO           *JOB, *USA, *ISO, *EUR, *JIS
                                                  *MDY, *DMY, *YMD, *JUL
  Time format  . . . . . . . . .   *ISO           *HMS, *USA, *ISO
                                                  *EUR, *JIS
  Data refresh . . . . . . . . .   *ALWAYS_       *ALWAYS, *FORWARD
  Allow copy data  . . . . . . .   *YES_____      *YES, *OPTIMIZE, *NO
  Naming convention  . . . . . .   *SYS           *SYS, *SQL
  List of libraries  . . . . . .   *LIBL_____     Name, *LIBL, *USRLIBL
                                                  *ALLUSR, *ALL, *CURLIB
  List type  . . . . . . . . . .   *ALL           *ALL, *SQL
  Decimal point  . . . . . . . .   *PERIOD        *PERIOD, *COMMA, *JOB,
                                                    *SYSVAL

                                                                     More...
 F3=Exit   F4=Prompt   F5=Refresh   F12=Cancel
```

Figure 2.8C

ISQL Change Session Attributes Display, Page 3

```
                          Change Session Attributes

Type choices, press Enter.

  List of libraries  . . . . . .   *LIBL_____     Name, *LIBL, *USRLIBL
                                                  *ALLUSR, *ALL, *CURLIB
  List type  . . . . . . . . . .   *ALL           *ALL, *SQL
  Decimal point  . . . . . . . .   *PERIOD        *PERIOD, *COMMA, *JOB,
                                                    *SYSVAL
  Sort sequence  . . . . . . . .   *HEX______     Name, *JOB, *JOBRUN
                                                  *LANGIDUNQ, *LANGIDSHR
                                                  *HEX
  Language identifier  . . . . .   ENU____        Name, *JOB, *JOBRUN
                                                  F4 for Prompt

                                                                      Bottom
 F3=Exit   F4=Prompt   F5=Refresh   F12=Cancel
```

Figure 2.9
Specifying the Output Database File for Select Statements

```
                         Change Session Attributes

 Type choices, press Enter.

   Statement processing . . . . .   *RUN           *RUN, *VLD, *SYN
   SELECT output  . . . . . . . .   3              1=Display, 2=Printer
                                                   3=File
   Output file:
     File . . . . . . . . . . . .   empltmp___     Name
       Library  . . . . . . . . .     appdta____   Name
     Member . . . . . . . . . . .   empltmp___     Name, *FILE, *FIRST
     Option . . . . . . . . . . .   1              1=Create file
                                                   2=Replace file
                                                   3=Create member
                                                   4=Replace member
                                                   5=Add to member
     Authority  . . . . . . . . .   *LIBCRTAUT     Authorization list name
                                                   *LIBCRTAUT, *CHANGE, *ALL
                                                   *EXCLUDE, *USE
     Text . . . . . . . . . . . .   Temporary copy of Employee table_____________

                                                                    More...
 F3=Exit   F4=Prompt   F5=Refresh   F12=Cancel
```

You use this screen to specify the output file member and various options. Subsequent Select statement output is sent to the specified member and not displayed. A similar option is available to send the output to a printer file.

After making your changes on the Change Session Attributes display, press Enter twice to return to the statement entry display with the new session attributes in effect.

Exiting ISQL

To exit an ISQL session, press F3 or F12. You'll see the Exit display shown in Figure 2.10.

Figure 2.10
Exit ISQL Display

```
                         Exit Interactive SQL

 Type choice, press Enter.

   Option . . . . . . . . .   1        1=Save and exit session
                                       2=Exit without saving session
                                       3=Resume session
                                       4=Save session in source file









 F12=Cancel
```

Normally, you can take the default option (1), which causes ISQL to save your session so it can be reloaded and resumed the next time you run ISQL under the same user profile. If you run simultaneous ISQL sessions at different workstations, each workstation's sessions are saved independently. You can resume the session saved for a workstation only by running ISQL on the same workstation.

The other Exit menu options let you exit without saving the session, resume (return to) the current session, or save the session to a source file member, as described above. Unfortunately, ISQL provides no way to read previously entered and saved SQL statements from a source member, so if you save a session to a source member instead of letting ISQL save the session to its own internal area, you won't be able to reload the log for this session in a future ISQL session.

Operations Navigator

AS/400 **Operations Navigator** (OpsNav) is a graphical interface that lets you manage your AS/400 system from a Windows desktop. In this section, we briefly discuss some of the database functions available through this interface.[3]

With OpsNav, you can create, change, rename, and delete most of the SQL objects you'll learn about in this book. Among the SQL objects supported are collections, tables, views, indexes, distinct types, user-defined functions, and procedures.[4] OpsNav also provides support for journals and journal receivers, which are AS/400 objects used to support transaction integrity.[5]

Figure 2.11 shows an example of what you see after clicking the icon to start OpsNav.

Figure 2.11

OpsNav Starting Point

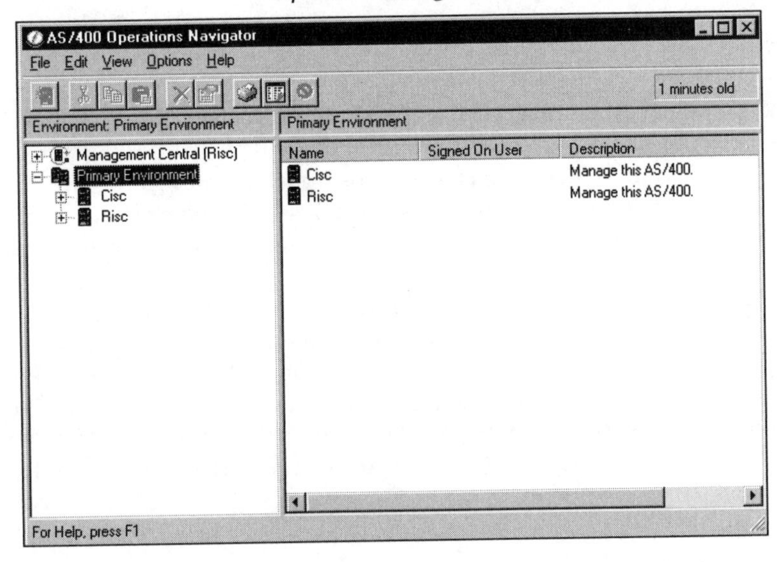

To select an AS/400 system to manage, you click its icon in the left pane of this dialog box. Figure 2.12 shows what the OpsNav dialog box looks like after clicking a system icon (for system Risc, in this case), clicking the plus sign (+) next to the icon to expand the list, and then right-clicking the Database icon to bring up a shortcut menu.

3 For a full discussion of Operations Navigator, visit IBM's AS/400 Information Center Web site at *http://publib.boulder.ibm.com/pubs/html/as400/infocenter.html*.

4 All these objects except procedures are introduced in Chapter 3. We discuss procedures in Chapter 13.

5 Chapter 13 discusses transaction integrity extensively.

Figure 2.12

OpsNav Dialog Box for Managing System Risc

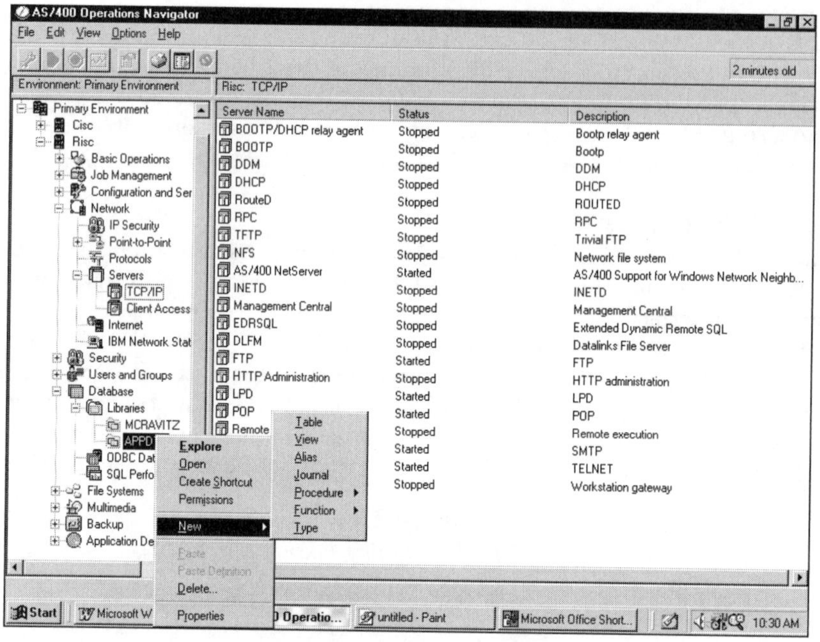

In the figure, the New menu option has been selected. As you can see, this option lets you create new database objects.

OpsNav also provides a Run SQL Scripts dialog box, which is an ISQL-like interface that lets you run SQL commands. In addition, the dialog box lets you key and then save one or more SQL statements into PC files (called SQL Script files). These scripts can then be run at any time from the Run SQL Scripts dialog box.

In general, OpsNav provides a more intuitive interface to use than either the RunSqlStm command or ISQL. For example, OpsNav's New Table definition dialog box features tabs and text boxes that, in essence, prompt you to enter all the information that the SQL/400 Create Table syntax supports. This is an especially helpful type of interface to use for creating new objects when you're first learning SQL. You can use OpsNav's scripting facility to store SQL object-creation commands (e.g., Create Table). Although you can use RunSqlStm for this purpose as well, OpsNav's Run SQL Scripts dialog box is generally less cumbersome to use.

The SQL Catalog

As we described in Chapter 1, an OS/400 physical or logical file object contains descriptive information about the structure of the file. This information includes such things as a description of the file's record format (i.e., field definitions) and a list of the members in the file. Because UDB/400 creates a physical file for an SQL/400 table and a logical file for an SQL/400 view or index, much of the definition of a table or view is stored as part of the database file object. But UDB/400 also has several system dictionary files that store a copy of some of this information, as well as additional information about database files. For example, several UDB/400 system files contain the long names for SQL tables, views, indexes, and packages.

To conform with industry SQL standards, IBM supplies a set of SQL views over the system files with UDB/400. Figure 2.13 lists these views, which are collectively referred to as the **catalog**.

Figure 2.13
SQL/400 Catalog Views

View	Contents
Sql_Languages[1]	Information about supported languages
SysChkCst	Information about check constraints
SysColumns	Information about column attributes
SysCst	Information about all constraints
SysCstCol	Information about the columns referenced in a constraint
SysCstDep	Information about constraint dependencies on tables
SysFuncs	Information about user-defined functions
SysIndexes	Information about indexes
SysKeyCst	Information about unique, primary, and foreign keys
SysKeys	Information about index keys
SysPackage	Information about packages
SysParms	Information about routine parameters
SysProcs	Information about procedures
SysRefCst	Information about referential constraints
SysRoutines	Information about functions and procedures
SysTables	Information about tables and views
SysTypes	Information about user-defined types
SysViewDep	Information about view dependencies on tables
SysViews	Information about view definitions

[1]System name SysLangs

Every AS/400 has one set of these views stored in the IBM-supplied QSYS2 library. The underlying system files (and consequently the views in the QSYS2 library) contain information about all SQL tables, views, indexes, constraints, and packages, as well as non-SQL physical and logical files on an AS/400. Because the catalog views are just like any other SQL view, anyone with the proper authority can retrieve data from the catalog. For example, you can use ISQL or OpsNav to produce a list of all SQL/400 tables on the system by entering the following statement:

```
Select     Sys_DName,
           Name,
           Label
  From     QSys2.SysTables
  Where    Type = 'T'
  Order By Sys_DName,
           Name
```

This statement produces a display like the one shown in Figure 2.14.

Figure 2.14
Sample Output from Querying the SysTables Catalog View

```
                               Display Data
                                     Data width . . . . . . :      75
Position to line  . . . . .  ______ Shift to column  . . . . . .  ____
....+....1....+....2....+....3....+....4....+....5....+....6....+....7....+
SYS_DNAME   NAME         LABEL
APPDTA      BUILDING     Buildings
APPDTA      COURSE       Courses
APPDTA      CUSTOMER     Customers
APPDTA      CUSTOMERBKP  Customers -- Backup copy
APPDTA      CUSTUPD      Customer updates
APPDTA      CUSTUPDBKP   Customer updates -- Backup copy
APPDTA      EMPLOYEE     Employees
APPDTA      PART         Parts
APPDTA      SALE         Sales
APPDTA      SALEITEM     Sale items
APPDTA      SUPPLIER     Suppliers
QSYS2       SQL_LANGUAG
QSYS2       SYSPARMS
QSYS2       SYSPROCS
********  End of data  ********
                                                              Bottom
F3=Exit     F12=Cancel     F19=Left     F28=Right     F21=Split
```

In Chapter 3, you'll learn about SQL collections. For now, it is sufficient to understand that a collection is a container for database objects, such as tables and views. In SQL/400, a collection is an OS/400 library object that is created with the SQL Create Collection statement.

When you use the Create Collection statement, UDB/400 creates a set of catalog views in the new collection that are similar to those in the QSYS2 library, with the exception that a collection will not contain the Sql_Languages, SysFuncs, SysParms, SysProcs, SysRoutines, or SysTypes view. The catalog views in a collection have the same view names and the same columns as those in library QSYS2 but include only entries for objects in the same collection as the catalog. You can query these views to get information about the tables, views, and indexes in a particular collection.

The manual *DB2 UDB for AS/400 SQL Reference* lists all SQL catalog view definitions. You can also display or list the catalog view definitions by entering the following statement in ISQL:

```
Select    *
  From     QSys2.SysColumns
  Where    DbName = 'QSYS2'
    And    TbName Like 'SYS%'
  Order By TbName,
           Name
```

The Where clause selects only rows with a table name that begins with SYS, the common prefix of all the SQL catalog tables.[6] (Don't be concerned if you don't completely understand this Select statement. We cover the Select statement thoroughly later in the book, in Chapters 5 and 8.)

Coding Suggestions

- Use ISQL's prompting facility only until you become comfortable with SQL syntax. After that, it's a good idea to line up similar SQL statement elements vertically, similar to the way it's done

6 The Like 'SYS%' condition matches any character string that begins with SYS and has anything (represented by the % wildcard character) following SYS.

in Figure 2.3. This format makes it easier to correct syntax errors as well as to copy and change a statement from the ISQL log.

- Line up SQL statements used in the RunSqlStm command as suggested above. With RunSqlStm, such alignment is even more critical because source members containing SQL statements to be run with RunSqlStm are typically saved indefinitely as a record of SQL objects created on the system. This record should be as readable and self-documenting as possible.

Chapter Summary

Structured Query Language (SQL) is an industry-standard language for defining and manipulating database objects. SQL/400 is the UDB/400 implementation of SQL. SQL includes a Data Definition Language (DDL) and a Data Manipulation Language (DML).

You can enter most SQL/400 statements interactively using either the Interactive SQL (ISQL) facility or Operations Navigator, or you can embed statements in HLL programs. SQL/400 statements can also be executed from a source file member using the RunSqlStm (Run SQL Statement) command. AS/400 Operations Navigator provides a similar facility, called Run SQL Scripts, that lets you create, execute, save, and later re-execute one or more SQL statements in a PC file.

UDB/400 maintains a set of system files that contain information about all SQL and non-SQL database files on the AS/400. SQL/400 provides a set of views over these files known as the SQL catalog. Each collection also has a similar set of views that include information about only the objects in the collection. You can use SQL/400 (or other means) to query any of the catalog files.

Key Terms

base table
catalog
column
Data Definition Language (DDL)
Data Manipulation Language (DML)
Interactive SQL (ISQL)
Operations Navigator
result table
row
table
view

Exercises

1. Code the RunSqlStm command that will run SQL statements contained in member CRTTBL in source file MYSQLSRC in library MYLIB.
2. When a source member contains more than one SQL statement to be executed by the RunSqlStm command, by what must each statement be terminated?
3. Which AS/400 command is used to start ISQL?
4. Compare and contrast typical usage of ISQL versus RunSqlStm. In other words, under what conditions would you opt to use one rather than the other?
5. What is Operations Navigator?
6. What is the purpose of the SQL catalog?

Chapter 3

Collections, Tables, and Indexes

Chapter Overview

In this chapter, you'll learn how to use several kinds of Create statements to create the basic building blocks of an SQL database: collections, tables, distinct types, indexes, and aliases. We'll also look at the Alter Table statement, which lets you change the definition of a table. In addition, the chapter covers various Drop statements to delete SQL objects.

Creating a Collection

In SQL/400, a **collection** is an object that contains other database objects, such as tables, views, distinct types, indexes, and stored procedures.[1] An SQL/400 collection is implemented as an OS/400 library object, which means that a collection can contain programs, message files, and other OS/400 objects in addition to SQL database objects. (See Chapter 1 if you need to refresh your memory about OS/400 libraries.)

You create a collection using a statement such as the following:[2]

```
Create Collection AppDta
```

This Data Definition Language (DDL) statement

- creates an OS/400 library named AppDta
- creates in the collection a set of SQL views that reference the system catalog tables (discussed in Chapter 2)
- creates an OS/400 journal named QSqJrn and a journal receiver named QSqJrn0001 in the collection. A journal is an AS/400 object that keeps track of all database changes (inserts, updates, and deletes). By default, changes to SQL base tables in the collection are automatically journaled to this journal.

1 SQL also has the concept of a **database** object. With SQL/400, each AS/400 system is a distinct database; that is, on any AS/400, there's always just one SQL database — the entire local system. You can assign the name of this database using the AddRdbDirE (Add Relational Database Directory Entry) command. It follows that an SQL/400 database is a set of collections — the collections that exist on the AS/400.

Note that with some other relational database management systems (RDBMSs), such as DB2 UDB for Windows 2000 Server, a "database" is more like an SQL/400 collection. That is, multiple databases can exist on a single system, and each database can contain tables, views, stored procedures, and other database objects. With these RDBMSs, *non*database objects are typically stored in the operating system's file system, outside the database (or databases). In addition, RDBMSs such as these generally don't support a collection object. Don't be tripped up by the two ways that the "database" construct is used in different RDBMSs.

2 You can also create a collection using the Create Schema statement. Essentially, the Create Schema statement just combines a Create Collection statement and one or more Create Table, Create View, Create Index, Comment On, Label On, Grant, or other statements into a single statement. This can be an efficient way to transmit a single (usually program-generated) SQL statement to create an entire collection and all the SQL objects in it on a remote system. You can execute the Create Schema statement only by placing it in a source file member and executing the RunSqlStm (Run SQL Statement) command.

Once you create a collection, you can create SQL base tables, views, and indexes, as well as other types of OS/400 objects (e.g., non-SQL files and programs) in the collection.[3]

The Create Collection statement has an optional In ASP clause that lets you designate which AS/400 auxiliary storage pool (ASP) OS/400 should use to store any objects created in the collection. If no ASP is specified, the default system ASP is used. ASPs are an AS/400 feature that the AS/400 system administrator can use to set up named groups of disk units. For information about setting up ASPs, see the manual *OS/400 Backup and Recovery*.

Creating a Table

In a relational database, a **base table** contains the actual data. To create a table with SQL/400, you enter a Create Table statement that specifies

- the collection to contain the table (this is optional; if you don't specify a collection, SQL/400 uses an implicit collection[4])
- the table name, which must be different from the name of any other base table, view, index, or non-SQL file in the same collection
- specifications for one or more columns
- an optional primary key constraint
- optionally, one or more unique and/or foreign key constraints
- optionally, one or more check constraints

Figure 3.1 shows the Create Table statement for a more complete Customer table than the one presented in Chapter 2.

Figure 3.1

Create Table Statement for Customer Base Table

```
Create Table AppDta.Customer
     ( CustID     Dec(    7, 0 ) Not Null,
       Name       Char(  30    ) Not Null,
       ShipLine1  Char( 100    ) Not Null,
       ShipLine2  Char( 100    ) Not Null,
       ShipCity   Char(  30    ) Not Null,
       ShipState  Char(   2    ) Not Null,
       ShipPsCd1  Char(  10    ) Not Null,
       ShipPsCd2  Char(  10    ) Not Null,
       ShipCntry  Char(  30    ) Not Null,
       PhnVoice   Char(  15    ) Not Null,
       PhnFax     Char(  15    ) Not Null,
       Status     Char(   1    ) Not Null
                                 With Default ' ',
       CrdLimit   Dec(    7, 0 ) With Default Null,
       EntDate    Date           Not Null,
Primary Key( CustID ) )
```

3 You can create any type of UDB/400 physical or logical file — for example, using Data Description Specifications (DDS) and the CrtPf (Create Physical File) or CrtLf (Create Logical File) CL command — in a collection as long as you don't specify the optional With Data Dictionary clause on the Create Collection statement. The With Data Dictionary clause is provided strictly for compatibility with earlier releases of SQL/400 and generally should not be used because it limits the types of files that can be placed in a collection to physical files with one member or source physical files.

You can also create SQL tables, views, and indexes in a noncollection library created with the CrtLib (Create Library) command. Noncollection libraries don't have the set of views over the system catalog files, however. You also must explicitly create a journal and journal receiver if you want to journal tables in a noncollection library.

4 Later in this chapter, we discuss explicit and implicit qualification of SQL names.

When this statement is executed, SQL/400 creates an externally described physical file object (see Chapter 1 for a discussion of physical files) in the AppDta collection with the following attributes:

- The file is tagged as an SQL table.
- It has a maximum of one member.
- It has no maximum size.
- When a new record is inserted into the file, UDB/400 reuses record locations marked internally as "deleted" (if any).
- Both before and after record images are journaled.
- The file's record format has the same name as the table, and the file has one member with the same name as the table.
- The file has a uniquely keyed access path.[5] As part of the physical file object, UDB/400 creates an internal index on the CustID column, which is the table's primary key.

When the statement is executed, UDB/400 also automatically starts journaling row inserts, updates, and deletes in the table to the QSqJrn journal in the same collection.[6] As you can see in Figure 3.1, the Create Table statement first lists the name of the table to be created and then lists the column and constraint definitions, separated by commas and enclosed in a set of parentheses. In the following sections of this chapter, we explain how to code column definitions. Chapter 4 covers constraints, including primary key constraints, such as the one used on Figure 3.1. In brief, this constraint specifies that no two rows will have the same CustID column value; this column thus serves as a unique identifier for each row.

SQL is a free-format language, and you can use multiple lines for a statement as well as blanks between words. The example shows a coding style that puts each column definition and constraint on a separate line and aligns the similar parts of each column definition. Although this columnar style isn't required, it makes the statement much easier to read than an unaligned stream of text.

SQL isn't case sensitive: "Create Table," "CREATE TABLE", and "CrEaTe TaBlE" are all correct. Be aware, however, that string literals are case sensitive, and 'x' isn't generally treated the same as 'X'. Also, when SQL/400 creates OS/400 file and field names for tables, the names are generally stored in OS/400 system dictionary files (see Chapter 2) as upper case. Thus, if you display a list of the tables in the AppDta collection, the table created by the statement in Figure 3.1 will be listed as CUSTOMER. However, you can still refer to the table as "Customer" or "customer" in SQL statements.

SQL/400 Naming Options

The table name used in Figure 3.1 is a qualified name, which includes the collection name (AppDta) before the unqualified table name (Customer). SQL/400 has two alternative approaches to names, including different syntax rules for qualified names:

- the SQL naming option
- the system naming option

5 The physical file for a base table with no primary key or other constraint does not have a keyed access path, and the file object doesn't have an internal index.

6 If the journal exists. The Create Collection statement automatically creates the QSqJrn journal, but you can delete the journal, or you can specify a noncollection library (without a QSqJrn journal) on the Create Table statement. To control journaling explicitly on SQL/400 tables, you can use the StrJrnPf (Start Journaling Physical File) and EndJrnPf (End Journaling Physical File) commands.

The **SQL naming option** conforms closely to the naming conventions established in several official SQL standards (e.g., the ANSI standard), while the **system naming option** generally follows the rules that apply to OS/400 objects. When you use Interactive SQL (ISQL), execute a RunSqlStm (Run SQL Statement) command, or create an HLL program with embedded SQL, you specify which naming option to use. For example, when you execute a RunSqlStm command, you specify either Naming(*Sql) or Naming(*Sys); if you specify neither, the default is system naming.

With SQL names, you use a period (.) as the separator:

```
AppDta.Customer
```

With system names, you use a slash (/) between the collection name and the table (or other object) name:

```
AppDta/Customer
```

When you specify an unqualified name, SQL/400 determines the implicit collection that qualifies the object based on the naming convention in effect (SQL or system), the type of SQL statement being executed, and several other options you can specify when you execute the statement. Chapter 13 provides more information about the SQL naming convention, which is the one we follow in this book.[7]

Also be aware that SQL has many reserved words, such as Create, Table, and Order, that have special meaning. If you want to use one of these reserved words as the name of a table, column, or other SQL object, you must use quotation marks (") around the name when it appears in an SQL statement. The following example shows how you would code an SQL Select statement that retrieves rows from a table named Order:

```
Select *
  From "Order"
  Where CustID = 499320
```

Column Definitions

On the Create Table statement, you code one or more **column definitions** after the new table name. Each column definition specifies the **column name** and a **data type**. Figure 3.2 shows the data types available with SQL/400. (The "Column Data Types" section later in this chapter discusses these data types in more detail.)

Figure 3.2
SQL Column Data Types

Column data type	Description
String	
Char(*length*)	Fixed-length character string with a length value from 1 to 32766. If *length* is omitted, it defaults to 1.
Graphic(*length*)	Fixed-length graphic string with a length value from 1 to 16383. If *length* is omitted, it defaults to 1.
VarChar(*max-length*)	Variable-length character string with a maximum length (*max-length*) from 1 to 32740.
VarGraphic(*max-length*)	Variable-length graphic string with a maximum length from 1 to 16370.

continued

7 The manual *DB2 UDB for AS/400 SQL Reference* documents the rules for implicit qualifiers for all SQL statements.

Figure 3.2 *Continued*

Column data type	Description
(String)	
Long VarChar	Variable-length character string with a maximum length determined by the amount of space available in the row.
Long VarGraphic	Variable-length graphic string with a maximum length determined by the amount of space available in the row.
Blob(*max-length*)	Binary large object string with a maximum length from 1 to 15728640 bytes. If *max-length* is omitted, it defaults to 1048576 (1 megabyte). The maximum length can be specified as an integer in the allowable range, as an integer from 1 to 15360 followed by K (increments of 1,024 bytes), or by an integer from 1 to 15 followed by M (increments of 1,048,576 bytes). For example, Blob(2M) is equivalent to Blob(2048K) or Blob(2097152).
Clob(*max-length*)	Character large object string with a maximum length from 1 to 15728640 bytes. If *max-length* is omitted, it defaults to 1048576 (1 megabyte). The maximum length can be specified in kilobytes (K) or megabytes (M), as described for the Blob data type.
DbClob(*max-length*)	Double-byte character large object string with a maximum length from 1 to 7864320 bytes. If *max-length* is omitted, it defaults to 1048576 (1 megabyte). The maximum length can be specified in kilobytes (K) or megabytes (M), as described for the Blob data type; however, the maximum length is 7680K or 7M.

Column data type	Description
Numeric	
Decimal(*precision, scale*)	Packed-decimal number. The *precision* value specifies the number of digits and can range from 1 to 31. The *scale* value specifies the number of digits to the right of the decimal point and can range from 0 to the value specified for *precision*. You can use Dec(*p*) for Dec(*p*, 0). You can also use Dec by itself for Dec(5, 0); however, always using an explicit precision with Dec provides clearer documentation.
Numeric(*precision, scale*)	Zoned-decimal number. The *precision* value specifies the number of digits and can range from 1 to 31. The *scale* value specifies the number of digits to the right of the decimal point and can range from 0 to the value specified for *precision*. You can use Numeric(*p*) for Numeric(*p*, 0). You can also use Numeric by itself for Numeric(5, 0); however, always using an explicit precision with Numeric provides clearer documentation.
SmallInt	Two-byte, binary integer
Integer	Four-byte, binary integer
BigInt	Eight-byte binary integer
Real	Single-precision floating-point number
Double	Double-precision floating-point number
Float(*precision*)	Floating-point number; *precision* specifies the number of digits and can range from 1 to 53. The values 1 through 24 specify single-precision, and the values 25 through 53 specify double-precision. You can use Float by itself for a double-precision number.

continued

Figure 3.2 *Continued*

Column data type	Description
Date, Time, and Timestamp	
Date	Date
Time	Time
Timestamp	Timestamp

Column data type	Description
DataLink	
DataLink(*length*)	A datalink that references a nondatabase file. The value *length* must be from 1 to 32718; if omitted, it defaults to 200. A datalink value is an internal representation of a Universal Resource Locator (URL) and an optional comment.

SQL/400 allows the following synonyms for data-type names:

Column data type	Synonym
Char	Character
VarChar	Char Varying
	Character Varying
VarGraphic	Graphic Varying
Blob	Binary Large Object
Clob	Char Large Object
	Character Large Object
Decimal	Dec
Integer	Int
Double	Double Precision

For the VarChar, VarGraphic, Blob, Clob, and DbClob data types, you can optionally specify an Allocate clause after the data type and length. The Allocate clause specifies how many bytes should be reserved for data in the fixed portion of a row's data storage. For example, the column definition

```
PartDesc VarChar( 500 ) Allocate( 50 )
```

specifies that the PartDesc column can contain character strings up to 500 bytes long and that the first 50 bytes are stored in the fixed portion of the row. Values longer than 50 bytes have their first 50 bytes stored in the fixed portion of the row and additional data stored in the variable portion of the row.

Following the data type, you can optionally code either or both of the following clauses:[8]

- `Not Null`
- `Default` *`default-value`*

8 The following optional keywords can also be specified in Char, VarChar, and Clob column definitions to indicate the type of character data contained in the column: For SBCS Data, For Mixed Data, and CCSID. See the *DB2 UDB for AS/400 SQL Reference* for details about these keywords.

In database terminology, null means "no value" or "not known," and a column that is **null-capable** lets you set the column to null, rather than an actual value, as a placeholder to represent one of these meanings. (Chapters 18 and 19 discuss the concept of null in greater detail.) If you specify Not Null when you define a column, the column is not null-capable; otherwise, it is. UDB/400 keeps track of whether a null-capable column is null or not null by setting an associated hidden bit. When the column is null, this hidden bit is 1; when the column has a normal value, this bit is 0. SQL statements can test whether a column is null using the Is Null test described in Chapter 5, as well as set a column null. In Figure 3.1, only the CrdLimit column is defined as null-capable.

The Default clause specifies a default column value, which is used for the column when you insert a row through a view that doesn't include all the underlying table's columns (we discuss views in Chapter 6) or when an explicit value is not provided on an Insert statement (covered in Chapter 7). UDB/400 puts a default value in each column that isn't in the view or the Insert statement's column list. In Figure 3.1, the Status column has a default of blank, and the CrdLimit column has a default of null.

In SQL/400, you can specify the Default keyword with or without an explicit value. The following examples show both alternatives.

```
PersonName   Char ( 30 ) Not Null
                         Default 'no name', ...

PersonName   Char ( 30 ) Not Null
                         Default, ...
```

The table in Figure 3.3 shows the default values SQL/400 assigns to a column depending on the column type, whether a Default clause was specified (with or without an explicit default value), and whether the Not Null clause was specified. Note that SQL/400 does not assign *any* default for a column that specifies the Not Null clause but does not specify a Default clause.

Figure 3.3

Default Values Used in SQL/400 for Various Column Definitions

Column data type	Default keyword specified?	Default value specified?	Not Null specified?	Column's default value
All types	Yes	Yes	Doesn't matter	The value specified
All types	Yes	No	No	Null
Numeric types	Yes	No	Yes	0
Fixed-length string types (Char and Graphic)	Yes	No	Yes	Blanks
Variable-length string types (VarChar, VarGraphic, Blob, Clob, and DbClob)	Yes	No	Yes	Zero-length string
Date, Time, or Timestamp	Yes	No	Yes	Current date, time, or timestamp
DataLink	Yes	No	Yes	A value corresponding to a URL of 'URL' and no comment
All types	No	No	No	Null
All types	No	No	Yes	None

Column Data Types

When a column is stored on disk or in memory, the AS/400 uses one or more eight-bit bytes to represent the value. For example, to represent characters, the AS/400 normally uses the **Extended Binary-Coded Decimal Interchange Code (EBCDIC)** representation, as we describe later. The AS/400 also has several encoding schemes for numeric values, each offering advantages and disadvantages. Although it's useful to know how data is encoded on the AS/400, the more important aspect to understand about SQL/400 column data types is the purpose and relative advantages and disadvantages of each data type. SQL provides data types for character and binary strings, numbers, date and time values, and Universal Resource Locators (URLs) that identify nondatabase files. In the following sections, we look at each of these data-type categories in more detail.

String Data Types

SQL/400 supports both **character** and **binary string data types**. Character string columns are typically used for textual data in applications — names of things, addresses, descriptions, and so on. Many applications also use short character codes in place of longer descriptions; for example, a customer status value of A might mean "active, in good standing." In some cases, codes can save significant disk storage and simplify data entry. The Customer table defined in Figure 3.1 has several character columns.

As we mentioned, the AS/400 normally uses an EBCDIC **single-byte character set (SBCS)** encoding to store characters.[9] Because an SBCS encoding uses one byte of storage for each character, there are 256 possible characters, including the uppercase and lowercase letters, digits, punctuation marks, and an assortment of graphical symbols and control characters. For example, the letter A is represented in the default EBCDIC character set by the eight bits 11000001.

UDB/400 also supports international applications with features for non-English, single-byte character sets and **double-byte character sets (DBCS)**, which use two bytes for each character. One of the supported DBCS character sets is the widely used International Standards Organization (ISO) **Universal Multiple-Octet Coded Character Set 2 (UCS-2)**. You select the character set for a table or specific column by specifying one of the available **Coded Character Set Identifiers (CCSID)**.[10]

The Char column type defines a fixed-length column. Whatever length you specify for the column is the actual length of the character string that's stored in the database, including trailing blanks necessary to pad out shorter values. For example, if you define a column as Char(10) and you attempt to store a value of ABC, the actual value stored will be ABCb̸b̸b̸b̸b̸b̸b̸.

The Graphic column type defines a fixed-length double-byte (i.e., DBCS) character column.

The VarChar column type defines a variable-length character column. For a VarChar column, you specify the *maximum*-length string that the column can hold. A column defined as VarChar(100) can hold strings up to 100 characters long. If you were to store the value ABC in this column, only three characters would be stored. For VarChar columns, UDB/400 also stores the current string length for the column's value — 3 in this example. UDB doesn't store additional blanks to pad VarChar column values.

9 Many other systems, such as Unix and DOS on PCs, use the American National Standard Code for Information Interchange, or ASCII, set of character codes. The AS/400 also provides ASCII support both within UDB/400 and in the integrated file system.

10 *DB2 UDB for AS/400 SQL Reference* lists CCSID values and the associated character sets. This book generally assumes the default USA EBCDIC encoding.

VarGraphic columns are variable-length character strings that use one of the DBCS encodings.[11]

When you use VarChar or VarGraphic, it's usually a good idea to specify the Allocate keyword. As we mentioned earlier, this keyword specifies how much space is reserved within the row for the column, with excess data for any string that's longer than the Allocate value being placed in an overflow area. You can improve SQL performance, particularly for larger tables, by choosing an Allocate length that is greater than the length of most of the values that will be stored in the column. For example, suppose you have a description column defined as VarChar(200) in which roughly 80 percent of your descriptions are 100 or fewer characters in length. In this case, specifying Allocate(100) would be a good choice.

Tip

Don't over-economize when specifying the maximum length for a VarChar or VarGraphic column. Although it's not advisable to greatly exceed the expected maximum size when specifying a length for a VarChar or VarGraphic column, it's better to err on the side of too large rather than too small. Remember, the Allocate keyword (or its default value of 0) is what determines how much space is set aside in each row in auxiliary storage for this type of column. Unless the row is approaching the 32 KByte size limit, you gain little by specifying too small a maximum length.

For example, if you expect most values to be no more than 100 bytes, a few values to be between 100 and 400 bytes, and only an occasional value to be longer than 400 bytes and no more than 500 bytes, you should define the column as VarChar(500) Allocate (100) rather than VarChar(400) Allocate (100). With either alternative, the column will take up 100 bytes of storage in each row, plus any overflow for strings longer than 100 bytes. But only the VarChar(500) alternative lets you store strings longer than 400 bytes without truncating them.

For data that's represented by a string of noncharacter bytes (e.g., a graphical image), you can add the For Bit Data clause to a Char or VarChar column:

```
Photo VarChar( 20000 ) For Bit Data ...
```

The For Bit Data clause tells UDB/400 that the contents of a column should never be interpreted as character data. Among other things, this instruction prevents UDB/400 from attempting to convert the data when it's transmitted to other systems. Note that Char and VarChar columns are limited to a maximum of 32 KBytes, so you may need to use one of the large object data types (discussed next) for binary data.

With SQL/400, you can define columns to hold strings longer than the 32 KByte maximum of Char and VarChar columns. The strings can be binary (the Blob data type), single-byte character (the Clob data type), or double-byte character (the DbClob data type). Large objects can be as much as 15 MBytes in size, making them suitable for large text documents, graphical images, audio data, and other such information. Note that you use the Clob or DbClob data type for character text and the Blob data type for noncharacter data, such as images and audio. When defining a large object column, you specify the maximum length, as in the following example:

```
EmploymentApplication Clob( 1000000 ) ...
```

11 The Long VarChar and Long VarGraphic types are alternatives to VarChar and VarGraphic; for these alternatives, the system calculates the maximum length based on the definition of other columns in the table. In general, Long VarChar and Long VarGraphic are not recommended.

Although you can specify the Allocate keyword for large object columns, in most cases it's best to omit this keyword and let the column assume the default allocation value of 0. With the default allocation, all the object's data is stored in the overflow area. This generally is suitable for the type of data stored in large object columns.

Choosing the Correct String Data Type

To store single-byte character data, use a Char, VarChar, or Clob data type. To store double-byte character data, use Graphic, VarGraphic, or DbClob. And to store binary (noncharacter) data, use Char or VarChar with a For Bit Data clause or use Blob.

To store strings that may be longer than the Char, VarChar, Graphic, or VarGraphic limit (generally 32 KBytes, as shown in Figure 3.2), you must use one of the large object data types (Blob, Clob, or DbClob). As an alternative to storing the data in the UDB/400 database, you can store it in an integrated file system (IFS) file and store a datalink (discussed later) in the database.

For strings that will fit in a Char, VarChar, Graphic, or VarGraphic column, you must decide whether to use a fixed-length string (Char or Graphic) or a variable-length string (VarChar or VarGraphic). The easy category includes those strings that naturally have a fixed length, such as two-character state codes, five-character zip codes, and four-character zip-plus codes.

Other columns are naturally varying in length; name columns and description columns are two examples. If a great deal of variation exists in the lengths of values, variable-length strings may save some disk space, but this often is not a major issue for strings with a relatively small maximum length. Variable-length columns add some processing overhead — how much overhead depends on the number of values that are longer than the allocated space and thus are partially stored in the overflow area. Variable-length columns are more convenient for some string manipulations (as you'll see in Chapter 5) because you don't have to deal with the extra blanks that pad a fixed-length string. The guideline (admittedly, a somewhat arbitrary one) that we generally follow in this book is to specify Char or Graphic for columns whose maximum length is at most 100 and to specify VarChar or VarGraphic for columns whose maximum length is greater than 100.

Numeric Data Types

For **numeric columns**, you have a choice of several data types:

- Decimal (or Dec)
- Numeric
- SmallInt
- Integer (or Int)
- BigInt
- Real
- Double
- Float

Each data type uses a different scheme to store numbers as a series of bytes in the table, and each has its advantages and disadvantages.

Each numeric data type has a **precision** and a **scale**. The precision is the maximum number of digits (including digits to the right of the decimal point). The scale is the number of decimal places. For some column data types (e.g., Decimal), you can explicitly define the precision and scale, while for others (e.g., Integer), the precision and scale are completely determined by the data type.

A Decimal column specifies that numbers are stored in **packed-decimal** format. When specifying Decimal, you generally specify the precision and the scale (if not 0). So to specify a packed-decimal column with a precision of 7 and a scale of 2, you would code Decimal(7, 2) or Dec(7, 2).

A packed-decimal column is implemented by using a *half*-byte (four bits) for each digit and the low-order half-byte (rightmost four bits) of the low-order byte for the sign. The half-byte 1111 is used for positive values, and the half-byte 1101 is used for negative values. Thus, a four-byte packed-decimal field can hold a number up to seven digits long. The number +1234567 would be represented in a Dec(7, 0) column as

```
  1    2    3    4    5    6    7    +
0001 0010 0011 0100 0101 0110 0111 1111
```

Note that this also would be how +12345.67 would be represented in a Dec(7, 2) column because the decimal point is *implicit*, rather than actually stored in the data.

A six-digit number would also require a four-byte packed-decimal field because a field must be an integral number of bytes; in a six-digit packed-decimal field, one half-byte would be unused. Thus, the number –123456 would be represented in a Dec(7, 0) column as

```
  0    1    2    3    4    5    6    -
0000 0001 0010 0011 0100 0101 0110 1101
```

In general, you should declare packed-decimal fields with an odd number for the precision.

Packed decimal has been around for a long time on IBM systems and is both compact and fast to process (on the AS/400). Its main disadvantage is that it's not found on many other systems or as a built-in data type in some widely used languages, such as C/C++ and Java. (IBM's C and C++ compilers for the AS/400 do support packed-decimal fields, and Java has the BigDecimal class. In both languages, however, support for decimal data types is slower than for integer and floating point.) If portability or cross-system data access is a concern, be sure to check on the language and data translation capabilities that will be used.

A Numeric column specifies that numbers are stored in **zoned-decimal** format. The precision and scale are specified the same way as for Decimal columns. Zoned decimal represents a number as one byte (eight bits) per digit. Thus, to hold a seven-digit number, you need a zoned-decimal column that occupies seven bytes. Each byte is simply the EBCDIC character representation of the digit, except the last byte has the high-order half-byte (leftmost four bits) set to indicate the number's sign (1111 for positive, 1101 for negative, or 1110 for unsigned). The number +123 would be represented in a Numeric(4, 0) column as the following four bytes:

```
     0         1         2      +    3
1111 0000 1111 0001 1111 0010 1111 0011
```

The number –123 would be represented in the same column as

```
     0         1         2      -    3
1111 0000 1111 0001 1111 0010 1101 0011
```

Zoned decimal is a legacy of computer punch card days and is not as compact or efficient to process as packed decimal or binary. In general, you should avoid the Numeric column data type.

A SmallInt, Integer (Int), or BigInt column specifies a binary numeric format. A SmallInt column is two bytes and can hold integer values from –32,768 to +32,767. An Int column is four bytes and can hold integer values from –2,147,483,648 to +2,147,483,647. A BigInt column is eight bytes and can hold integer values from –9,223,372,036,854,775,808 to +9,223,372,036,854,775,807. You can't specify a precision or scale for SmallInt, Int, and BigInt columns — both of these attributes are implicit in the data type.

In general, the binary format of integers represents a number as a base 2 value, with one bit used for the number's sign.[12] The value +1234 would be represented in a SmallInt column as

```
0000 0100 1101 0010
```

On the AS/400, negative numbers are represented in binary format using "two's complement" encoding. This approach flips bits for negative numbers and then adds 1, so that –1 is represented by the bit pattern 11111111. This encoding lets the processor perform faster arithmetic. Thus, the value –1234 would be represented in a SmallInt column as

```
1111 1011 0010 1110
```

An Int column would represent +1234 as

```
0000 0000 0000 0000 0000 0100 1101 0010
```

and –1234 as

```
1111 1111 1111 1111 1111 1011 0010 1110
```

Binary fields are compact, and most computer systems and languages support binary values. As we said, SQL/400 BigInt columns can hold values up to approximately ±9 sextillion (a maximum of 19 digits), whereas Decimal columns can hold numbers up to 31 digits long. Also, you can specify a scale for a Decimal column but not for a SmallInt, Int, or BigInt column. Thus, for business applications, the Decimal column data type is a good choice for large numeric fields or those that require precise decimal fraction values (as is often the case in financial applications). The SmallInt, Int, and BigInt column data types are preferable for integers within the supported ranges.

The Real, Double, and Float numeric data types specify a **floating-point** numeric format. Floating point is generally used for scientific or mathematical applications (and by C, C++, and Java programs) and is not very common in AS/400 business applications, although RPG IV and ILE COBOL/400 now include support for floating point. SQL/400 supports **single-precision** (Float(24) or Real) and **double-precision** (Float(53) or Double) floating-point columns. A single-precision column occupies four bytes, and its values can range from approximately 1.2×10^{-38} to approximately $3.4 \times 10^{+38}$. A double-precision column occupies eight bytes, and its values can range from approximately 2.2×10^{-308} to approximately $1.8 \times 10^{+308}$. Although SQL/400 has many variations on how you may specify floating-point types for columns, it's sufficient to use Float(24) for single-precision and Double for double-precision columns.

Date, Time, and Timestamp Data Types

UDB/400 supports special data types for **date**, **time**, and **timestamp** values. For these three data types, you specify the Date, Time, or Timestamp type in the column definition but *not* a length (or number of decimal positions) — the system determines the length of these types of fields.

SQL/400 supports date arithmetic on date columns. You'll learn more about this in Chapter 5. Date columns and date arithmetic can simplify the way many common business applications handle dates.

UDB/400 stores all date fields in the same four-byte *internal* format on disk. When you execute SQL statements or compile a program that contains SQL statements, you specify an *external* format (and in some cases, the separator character) to use. SQL/400 uses this information to translate

12 Our normal numbering system is base 10 — from right to left, the positions in a number represent the number of 1s, 10s, 100s, and so on. In base 2, the positions correspond to powers of 2 — 1, 2, 4, 8, and so on. Both systems, of course, can represent the full range of integers — 1, 2, 3, and so on.

internal values when they're displayed or returned to your program. For example, with ISQL, the StrSql (Start SQL) command's DatFmt and DatSep parameters specify the date format that's used. Figure 3.4 shows the external formats available for date columns in UDB/400.

Figure 3.4
Date Formats Available in UDB/400

Format name	Abbreviation	DatFmt parameter	Field length	Separator	Example
Job Default	—	*JOB	—	—	—
International Standards Organization	ISO	*ISO	10	- (dash)	2000-12-31
IBM USA Standard	USA	*USA	10	/ (slash)	12/31/2000
IBM European Standard	EUR	*EUR	10	. (period)	31.12.2000
Japanese Industrial Standard Christian Era	JIS	*JIS	10	- (dash)	2000-12-31
Unformatted Julian	—	—	7	—	2000366
Julian	—	*JUL	6	DatSep	00/366
Month/Day/Year	—	*MDY	8	DatSep	12/31/00
Day/Month/Year	—	*DMY	8	DatSep	31-12-00
Year/Month/Day	—	*YMD	8	DatSep	00.12.31

For several of the date formats, you can also specify a separator character. The allowable values are slash ('/'), dash ('-'), period ('.'), comma (','), and blank (' ').

Time columns work similarly to date columns. UDB/400 stores time values in three-byte fields internally. Figure 3.5 shows the time formats available in UDB/400.

Figure 3.5
Time Formats Available in UDB/400

Format name	Abbreviation	TimFmt parameter	Field length	Separator	Example
International Standards Organization[1]	ISO	*ISO	8	. (period)	13.01.01
IBM USA Standard	USA	*USA	8	: (colon)	1:01 P.M.
IBM European Standard	EUR	*EUR	8	. (period)	13.01.01
Japanese Industrial Standard Christian Era	JIS	*JIS	8	: (colon)	13:01:01
Hours:Minutes:Seconds	—	*HMS	8	TimSep	13:01:01

[1]This is an earlier version of the ISO format. JIS can be used to get the current ISO format.

For some time formats, you can specify a separator, which can be a colon (':'), period ('.'), or blank (' '). The *USA time format does *not* include seconds (even though the internal storage of the field does).

Timestamp columns use 10 bytes internally. The timestamp data type has a system-defined external format that looks like this:

yyyy-mm-dd-hh.mm.ss.uuuuuu

where *uuuuuu* is millionths of a second. Use timestamps when you need to maintain a precise record of the sequence in which events occur.

Datalink Data Types

Datalink columns are used to hold references to nondatabase files stored in the local integrated file system (IFS), in a remote AS/400's IFS, or in the file system of any attached system (e.g., Windows 2000 Server) that has IBM's DataLink Manager installed.[13] In other words, instead of storing the data in the column itself, you can use a datalink to specify a file location for the value of the column. Columns defined as type DataLink contain a reference to the file (in the form of a URL) and, optionally, a comment. When defining a column as DataLink, you should specify a length large enough to hold the largest expected URL plus any comment you may want to associate with the link. Here is an example:

```
ProductImage  Datalink( 500 ) ...
```

SQL and System Table Names

As we said in Chapter 1, OS/400 object names have a maximum length of 10 characters. SQL table names, however, can be up to 128 characters. Because SQL tables are implemented as OS/400 physical files, each table always has an associated 10-character **system name**. If you specify a table name of 10 characters or less in the Create Table statement, the table's system name is the same as its SQL name. However, if you specify a table name longer than 10 characters, UDB/400 assigns a 10-character system name using the first five characters of your longer name followed by a five-digit sequence number. For example, if you create a table named PartSupplier, UDB/400 will assign a system name such as PartS00001. An SQL statement can refer to a table using either the table's full SQL name or its (possibly shorter) system name.

Because you may work with OS/400 file objects using languages other than SQL (e.g., using CL to perform backup operations), it's preferable to have meaningful system names for all tables. After you create an SQL table (or view or index, as we discuss later), you can use the SQL Rename statement to change the system name. Here's an example of the statements you might use:

```
Create Table PartSupplier ...

Rename Table PartSupplier
  To System Name PartSuplr
```

You can also use the Rename statement to change the SQL name, as in the following example:

```
Rename Table Acct
   To  Account
```

When you create a new table for which you want an SQL name longer than 10 characters as well as a meaningful system name, the best practice is to first create the table with the *system* name and then use a Rename statement to change the *SQL* name:

```
Create Table PartSuplr ...

Rename Table PartSuplr
   To  PartSupplier
   For System Name PartSuplr
```

The advantage of this approach is that PartSuplr is used as the name for the physical file, the physical file member, and the file's record format. Creating the table with the SQL name and then using

13 See Chapter 1 for an explanation of the IFS and the various file systems available on the AS/400. IBM offers DataLink File Managers on all systems for which a version of DB2 Universal Database (DB2 UDB) is available.

Rename to change the system name leaves the file member and record format names as their system-generated names (e.g., PartS00001). Be sure to include the Rename statement's For System Name clause when you follow this practice. Without this clause, the Rename statement will change the system name to a generated name, such as PartS00001.

SQL and System Column Names

In Figure 3.1, we used column names that conformed to the 10-character limit that UDB/400 has for database file field names. As with tables, columns have an SQL name and a system name. If you specify a column name longer than 10 characters, UDB/400 assigns a 10-character system name using the first five characters of the longer name followed by a five-digit sequence number. And, as with table names, it's preferable to use meaningful system names for all columns.[14] The Create Table statement makes it quite easy to explicitly assign system names for one or more columns, using the For clause as shown in Figure 3.6.

Figure 3.6

Create Table with Long Column Names

```
Create Table Customer
     ( CustID                                Dec(    7, 0 ) Not Null,
       CustName               For Name       Char(  30    ) Not Null,
       CustShipLine1          For ShpLine1   Char( 100    ) Not Null,
       CustShipLine2          For ShpLine2   Char( 100    ) Not Null,
       CustShipCity           For ShpCity    Char(  30    ) Not Null,
       CustShipState          For ShpState   Char(   2    ) Not Null,
       CustShipPostalCode1    For ShpPsCd1   Char(  10    ) Not Null,
       CustShipPostalCode2    For ShpPsCd2   Char(  10    ) Not Null,
       CustShipCountry        For ShpCntry   Char(  30    ) Not Null,
       CustPhoneVoice         For PhnVoice   Char(  15    ) Not Null,
       CustPhoneFax           For PhnFax     Char(  15    ) Not Null,
       CustStatus             For Status     Char(   1    ) Not Null
                                                            With Default ' ',
       CustCreditLimit        For CrdLimit   Dec(    7, 0 ) With Default Null,
       CustEntryDate          For EntDate    Date           Not Null,
  Primary Key( CustID ) )
```

For columns with an SQL name of 10 characters or less, you don't have to specify a For clause if you want identical SQL and system names. In SQL statements, you can refer to a column by either the SQL name or the system name.

Descriptive Text and Column Headings

After you create a table, you can define descriptive text and longer comments for the table and its columns. Descriptive text is saved in the SQL catalog and is therefore available to be queried. Moreover, this text shows up with various AS/400 utilities. For example, you see it when prompting (pressing the F4 key) in ISQL. You can also define column headings. ISQL uses column headings when displaying the results of interactive queries.

A Label On statement stores up to 50 characters of descriptive text for a table. The following example adds descriptive text for the Customer table:

```
Label On Table Customer
  Is 'Current and past customers'
```

To add descriptive text for columns, you use the form of the Label On statement shown in Figure 3.7.

14 Among other considerations, non-SQL statements in ILE RPG programs must refer to columns by their system names.

Figure 3.7
Defining Descriptive Text for Columns

```
Label On Customer
  ( CustID              Text Is 'Customer ID',
    CustName            Text Is 'Customer name',
    CustShipLine1       Text Is 'Customer shipping address line 1',
    CustShipLine2       Text Is 'Customer shipping address line 2',
    CustShipCity        Text Is 'Customer shipping address city',
    CustShipState       Text Is 'Customer shipping address state',
    CustShipPostalCode1 Text Is 'Customer shipping address postal code 1',
    CustShipPostalCode2 Text Is 'Customer shipping address postal code 2',
    CustShipCountry     Text Is 'Customer shipping address country',
    CustPhoneVoice      Text Is 'Customer voice phone number',
    CustPhoneFax        Text Is 'Customer Fax phone number',
    CustStatus          Text Is 'Customer status',
    CustCreditLimit     Text Is 'Customer credit limit',
    CustEntryDate       Text Is 'Customer info entry date' )
```

After the table name, there are one or more entries for the column text, separated by commas. Each column text entry has the form

```
column-name Text Is 'text-string'
```

You can also define column headings with SQL/400 as shown in Figure 3.8.

Figure 3.8
Defining Column Headings

```
Label On Customer
  ( CustID              Is 'Cust.                ID',
    CustName            Is 'Customer             Name',
    CustShipLine1       Is 'Customer             Shipping            Line 1',
    CustShipLine2       Is 'Customer             Shipping            Line 2',
    CustShipCity        Is 'Customer             Shipping            City',
    CustShipState       Is 'Customer             Shipping            State',
    CustShipPostalCode1 Is 'Customer             Shipping            Postal code 1',
    CustShipPostalCode2 Is 'Customer             Shipping            Postal code 2',
    CustShipCountry     Is 'Customer             Shipping            Country',
    CustPhoneVoice      Is 'Customer             Phone',
    CustPhoneFax        Is 'Customer             Fax',
    CustStatus          Is 'Cust.                Status',
    CustCreditLimit     Is 'Cust.                Credit              Limit',
    CustEntryDate       Is 'Cust.                Entry               Date' )
```

The Text keyword is not used when defining column headings, and the text string is treated as three 20-character segments. The first 20 characters are used for the first line of the heading; characters 21 through 40 (if present) are the second heading line, and characters 41 through 60 (if present) are the third heading line. You must carefully align the contents of each string to get the right column headings.

SQL also lets you specify longer comments — up to 2,000 characters — for tables, views, columns, and many other SQL objects and their components. Such comments are stored in the SQL catalog, along with descriptive information supplied by Label On statements. To define a comment for a table, you use a Comment On statement such as the following:

```
Comment On Table Customer
        Is 'Customer master file ...'
```

The following examples show how to add comments for a distinct type (covered in the next section) and an index:

```
Comment On Distinct Type CustIdType
  Is 'Customer ID Data Type'

Comment On Index CustNameIdx
  Is 'Index on Customer Name'
```

Figure 3.9 shows a Comment On statement for column comments.

Figure 3.9

Defining Long Comments for Columns

```
Comment On Customer
( CustID                Is 'Customer ID',
  CustName              Is 'Customer name',
  CustShipLine1         Is 'Customer shipping address line 1',
  CustShipLine2         Is 'Customer shipping address line 2',
  CustShipCity          Is 'Customer shipping address city',
  CustShipState         Is 'Customer shipping address state',
  CustShipPostalCode1   Is 'Customer shipping address postal code 1',
  CustShipPostalCode2   Is 'Customer shipping address postal code 2',
  CustShipCountry       Is 'Customer shipping address country',
  CustPhoneVoice        Is 'Customer voice phone number',
  CustPhoneFax          Is 'Customer Fax phone number',
  CustStatus            Is 'Customer status',
  CustCreditLimit       Is 'Customer credit limit',
  CustEntryDate         Is 'Customer info entry date' )
```

Notice the similarity to the Label On statement in Figure 3.7 — except the statement name is different and the Comment On statement doesn't use the Text keyword in the column entries. (This Comment On example uses the same text as the Label On statement in Figure 3.7, but remember that long comments can be up to 2,000 characters while descriptive text is limited to 50 characters.)

Creating and Using User-Defined Types

SQL/400 lets you create a new column data type, known as a **distinct type**, based on one of the built-in data types listed in Figure 3.2.[15] The following statement creates the distinct type CustIdType as equivalent to a Dec(7, 0) data type:

```
Create Distinct Type CustIDType
  As Dec( 7, 0 )
  With Comparisons
```

Once you create a distinct type, you can use it in column definitions:

```
CustID  CustIDType Not Null ...
```

When you use a distinct type to define a column, SQL/400 creates the column using the based-on type — Dec(7, 0) in this example. The Create Distinct Type statement's With Comparisons clause (the default in SQL/400) specifies that you can use equality (i.e., =) and inequality (e.g., <) tests between two columns defined with the same distinct type.[16] SQL/400 generally lets you assign a column with the based-on type to a column with the distinct type — for example, assigning a Dec(7, 0) column to a CustIdType column — and vice versa. However, you can't automatically compare a distinct type to any other type of column except for the same distinct type. For example, you couldn't compare a Dec(7, 0) column to a CustIdType column unless you created your own user-defined

15 UDB/400 creates an OS/400 SQL User-Defined Type (*SqlUdt) object for an SQL distinct type.

16 IBM recommends you code this clause explicitly for compatibility with DB2 implementations on other platforms.

function to do so. (Chapters 8 and 13 discuss user-defined functions.) Nor can you use operations such as addition for numbers or string concatenation for a distinct type, unless you create the appropriate function. (An SQL technique known as "casting" also enables comparison, concatenation, and arithmetic or other operations on distinct types; we cover casting in Chapter 8.)

On the Create Distinct Type statement, you can specify a built-in type and a length, precision, or scale, if appropriate for the built-in type. You can also specify CCSID, For Bit Data, For SBCS Data, or For Mixed Data for any of the character data types (e.g., Char, VarChar, Clob). You can't specify Allocate, Not Null, Default, or any other column attributes; these must be explicitly specified when you code a column definition on the Create Table statement. The implicit default value (as discussed earlier) for a distinct type is the same as for the based-on type.

Distinct types are often referred to as **user-defined types (UDTs)** and serve two main purposes. First, a UDT provides a convenient way to define columns that contain the same kind of data. In the example we've been using, every column that should hold a customer ID can be defined with CustIdType. This use of a UDT improves consistency as well. Second, because of the restrictions in using columns defined with a distinct type, you have tighter control over which operations are valid for columns. For example, SQL/400 won't let you add two columns that are defined with CustIdType — a sensible restriction because customer IDs don't represent quantitative values. For UDTs that do need arithmetic or other operations, you can use user-defined functions, as we mentioned earlier, or casting.

Distinct types provide some of the capabilities of domains as described in Chapter 18. However, because they don't let you restrict which values can be stored in a column, they fall short of implementing the full domain concept. Also, a distinct type can't be based on another distinct type — only on one of the built-in data types. These limitations diminish the usefulness of distinct types; however, distinct types can help standardize the definition of primary key columns, and, when used in conjunction with user-defined functions, they can provide additional flexibility in your database definitions.

Using Standard Data Types

You can improve the consistency of your database and simplify application development by deciding on a set of **standard data types** to be used for column definitions. For example, you might decide to use

```
VarChar(500) Allocate(100)
Not Null
Default
```

as the standard data type for all columns containing descriptions (e.g., of products, courses). You might also decide to use

```
Char(50)
Not Null
Default
```

for columns that store one part of a person's name (e.g., first or last name). To keep track of standard data types, you should establish a data dictionary, either manually or by using a CASE tool[17]. Chapters 19 and 21 provide additional suggestions for using data dictionaries.

17 CASE stands for Computer Aided Software Engineering. CASE tools are often used to define databases logically and sometimes physically (as described in Part III).

For some or all of your standard data types, you might also choose to create SQL distinct types, as described above. However, keep in mind the limitations of distinct types (e.g., you can't specify Not Null) and the fact that you can standardize the data types you use regardless of whether or not you also use distinct types.

Adding, Dropping, or Changing Table Columns

After you create a table, you may need to add or drop (remove) a column or change a column definition. You use the Alter Table statement to do so. The following example shows how to add a column to the Customer table created in Figure 3.1:

```
Alter Table Customer
  Add Discount Dec( 5, 3 ) Not Null
                           Default 0
```

If you use the Not Null clause when you add a new column, you must also specify a Default clause so that UDB/400 can assign the default value for the column in all existing rows. If you don't specify Not Null or a Default clause, the column is set to null in all existing rows. Be aware that under the covers, UDB/400 actually creates a new OS/400 physical file object for the table, copies data from the old file, and then deletes the old file. All related objects, such as views and indexes, are disassociated from the old file and associated with the new file. This process is all handled by UDB/400, but it may take a while and the table may not be available for use during some of this time. (The same process occurs when you drop a column and for many situations in which you change a column definition.)

Here's how you can drop a column:

```
Alter Table Customer
  Drop Discount
```

To change a column definition, you specify any of the column attributes (e.g., data type) that you want to change:

```
Alter Table Customer
  Alter Discount
       Set Default 0.01
```

Any column attributes that you don't specify remain unchanged, and, of course, both new and unchanged attributes must be compatible (e.g., the column's data type and default value).

Creating an Index

Although you don't specify a particular order of rows on either the Create Table or the Create View (discussed in Chapter 6) statement, UDB/400 does use internal **indexes** for efficient row selection and ordering. UDB/400 automatically selects which index (or indexes) to use when a Data Manipulation Language (DML) statement, such as Select, is executed or when an SQL cursor embedded in an HLL program is opened. When you specify a primary, unique, or foreign key constraint (discussed in Chapter 4), UDB/400 creates or shares an internal index as part of the physical file created for a base table. You can create additional indexes using the SQL Create Index statement.

The Create Index statement is fairly simple. You code an index name (which can't be the same name as any base table, view, alias, other index, or non-SQL file in the same collection) and then specify a single base table and the columns over which the index should be created.[18] The following example creates an index over the ShipCity and CrdLimit columns of the Customer table:

18 You can also create an SQL/400 index over a non-SQL, externally described physical file.

```
Create Index AppDta.CustCtyX01
  On Customer
   ( ShipCity,
     CrdLimit Desc )
```

When you create an SQL index, UDB/400 creates an OS/400 logical file with a keyed access path.[19] You *cannot* access an SQL index directly with *any* SQL DML statement. In SQL, indexes are solely for the internal use of UDB/400, and their purpose is generally related to performance.

As the above example shows, you can optionally add the Desc keyword after any column name to specify a descending order. You also can optionally specify Unique or Unique Where Not Null in an index definition:

```
Create Unique Index AppDta.BldRoomX
  On Building
   ( BldName,
     RoomNbr )
```

The Unique keyword enforces unique key values, *including null*, the same way as explained earlier for a base table primary key constraint. If you specify Unique Where Not Null, UDB/400 enforces unique values, *except for null*, as explained in Chapter 4 for unique constraints. In general, you should use a primary key or unique constraint on the Create Table statement for a base table — which causes UDB/400 to create an internal index — rather than create a separate index with Unique or Unique Where Not Null. In UDB/400, independent indexes are primarily useful for two cases:

- unique indexes in addition to the primary key of a base table
- non-unique indexes (as a performance aid)

Note that you can specify only a single primary key constraint for each base table, so if you need to enforce a second *fully* unique key (that is, including nulls) for the table, you need a Create Unique Index statement. Because you can specify multiple unique constraints (which exclude nulls) on a base table, there's little reason to use a Create Unique Where Not Null Index statement in SQL/400. The type of indexes built by the examples discussed so far are called **binary radix tree,** or **b-tree, indexes**. As the name suggests, these indexes use a tree structure to store key values and associated record locations.

You can create another type of index, known as an **Encoded Vector Index (EVI)**. This type of index uses an internal table that maps key values to binary codes and a vector of these codes (one per row in the database table) to identify which records have a particular key value. EVIs can dramatically speed certain types of queries.[20] Here's a Create Index statement for an EVI:

```
Create Encoded Vector Index PartWarehouseIdx
 On Part
  ( WarehouseID )
```

19 For performance tuning, you may want to know that the logical file for an SQL/400 index has attributes that correspond to the MaxMbrs(1) and Maint(*Immed) parameters on the CrtLf command. The logical file has the same record format as the physical file over which it's created. Note that you can change the index maintenance of non-unique indexes to delayed (*Dly) or rebuild (*Rebld) by using the ChgLf (Change Logical File) command.

20 In particular, queries with search conditions where each predicate uses only equal predicates and where the left side specifies column names (e.g., PartColor = 'RED' and PartWhseLoc = 56). See Chapter 5 for a discussion of search conditions and predicates. See the manual *DB2 UDB for AS/400 SQL Programming* for more details about EVIs.

Indexes affect database performance both positively and negatively. In brief, indexes can speed data retrieval, but they may slow updates due to the time UDB/400 spends updating the entries in the index (or indexes) over a base table as rows are inserted, deleted, or updated in the table. UDB/400 is fairly efficient at maintaining indexes, so you don't generally need to worry if you have five or fewer indexes over an active table or 10 to 20 over a less frequently modified table.[21] And, for tables that are primarily read-only, with little update activity, there's not likely to be any significant overhead from having numerous indexes. However, for actively updated tables, you want to avoid an excessive amount of index maintenance, or you may slow down your application's database updates.

Creating an Alias

You can create an alternative name, called an **alias**, for any SQL/400 table or view.[22] Here's an example that creates the PartSuplr alias for a PartSupplier table:

```
Create Alias PartSuplr
   For PartSupplier
```

You might use an alias when you rename an object and still have existing applications that refer to the old object name. You'll also find an alias helpful when you want to use SQL to access an existing OS/400 database file object that has multiple members (as explained in Chapter 1). The following statement creates the SaleJune alias that can be used to reference the June member of the Sale multi-member file — without an alias, there's no way in SQL to directly access a file member other than the first member:

```
Create Alias SaleJune
   For Sale ( June )
```

The optional member name is placed in parentheses immediately after the table (or file) name. SQL DML statements can use an alias anywhere that the corresponding table or view name can be used. For example, the following statement retrieves all rows from the June member of the Sale file, using the SaleJune alias created above:

```
Select *
  From SaleJune
```

Although an alias can be invaluable in certain circumstances, you shouldn't use aliases just to create a variety of different names for the same object. In general, you should use one consistent name for each database table and view.

Dropping Collections, Tables, Distinct Types, Indexes, and Aliases

To delete any of the database objects we've looked at in this chapter, you use one of the following statements:

- `Drop Collection` *`collection-name`*
- `Drop Table` *`table-name`*
- `Drop Distinct Type` *`type-name`*
- `Drop Index` *`index-name`*
- `Drop Alias` *`alias-name`*

21 Keep in mind that these are very approximate rules of thumb. Tuning a database implementation requires an in-depth knowledge of the operating characteristics of the particular release of UDB/400 you're using (performance characteristics can change with each new release) and careful measurement.

22 UDB/400 creates a Distributed Data Management (DDM) file object for an SQL alias.

Caution

Be careful with these statements! Unless you specify the optional Restrict keyword on the Drop Collection statement, all objects in the collection are also deleted. Similarly, without the Restrict keyword, when you drop a table or view, all dependent objects, including views, indexes, and foreign key constraints that reference a table being dropped are also deleted. Here's an example of coding a "safe" Drop Collection statement:

```
Drop Collection AppDta Restrict
```

Before this statement can be executed successfully, you must have dropped all objects from the AppDta collection.

Guidelines for SQL/400 Names

A good **naming convention** for SQL/400 objects goes a long way toward standardizing your database definitions. Table, view, index, column, and other names should meet three criteria:

- They must be syntactically correct.
- They should be consistently formed.
- They should communicate as clearly as possible.

Names should begin with a letter (A–Z) and should use only letters and digits (0–9) in the rest of the name. Avoid national characters (e.g., #, $, and @ in the United States) and the underscore (_) because of international character set conflicts and HLL syntax restrictions. Don't use SQL reserved words (these are listed in an appendix of the *DB2 UDB for AS/400 SQL Reference*).

It's much easier to work with a database if its names follow a regular pattern and use consistent and clear abbreviations. The value of these two principles is easy to see if you consider the problems that arise when names *aren't* formed this way. If you came across the column name CAL1, would you have any idea that it meant "customer address, line 1"? Even if you could guess what the C, A, and L stood for, would you know whether it was a shipping or a billing address? Although a more meaningful name such as ShipLine1 is not completely unambiguous, you have a reasonable chance of comprehending it when you first encounter it. In addition, once you've had a brief period to familiarize yourself with the table definition, you'll find it very easy to follow programs that use this column.

Consistency aids comprehension as well — especially when names must be formed with abbreviations. Consider the frequently occurring need to have a column that stores a count of something (e.g., how many of an item are ordered). If some columns use different abbreviations for "count" — Cnt, Cou, Cn — and others use a variety of abbreviations for "number (of)" — Nbr, No, Num — it becomes difficult to quickly recognize the meaning of a column name, especially when you're working with code that uses the columns. You can avoid this problem by following a simple naming convention, such as:

The term "count" and its abbreviation Cnt are used for columns that store an integral count of some item.

This convention specifies both the term that will be used and its abbreviation.

The people who designed the OS/400 interface studied abbreviations extensively and came up with a simple and effective scheme for creating abbreviations. The two main principles they followed are:

- Whenever possible, use three-letter abbreviations, except for items, such as ID, that have a well-established shorter abbreviation.
- Form a three-letter abbreviation with the first letter of the term and the two consonants that are most prominent in pronouncing the word (e.g., for "number" use Nbr, not Num).

Because system object and column names are limited to 10 characters, you'll inevitably have to squeeze one or more of the abbreviations in a system name. Thus, it's a good idea to develop a list of terms that appear in your applications and two- and three-character abbreviations for each of them. Figure 3.10 provides a partial list of terms that occur in many applications.

Figure 3.10

Sample List of Terms and Abbreviations

Term	Three-character	Two-character	Other	Notes
Address	Adr	Ad	—	—
Amount	Amt	Am	—	—
Application	App	Ap	Aplc	For libraries, such as AppDta and AppSrc
Building	Bld	Bl	Bldg	—
City	Cty	Ct	City	—
Code	Cde	Cd	Code	—
Count	Cnt	Cn	—	—
Country	Cry	Cr	Cntry	—
Credit	Crd	Cr	—	—
Customer	Cus	Cs	Cust	—
Date	Dat	Dt	Date	—
Description	Dsc	Dc	Desc	—
Employee	Emp	Em	Empl	—
Entry	Ent	En	—	—
First	Fst	Fs	First	—
Initial	Inl	In	—	As in middle initial of a name; use Inz for initialize
Initialize	Inz	Iz	—	—
Identifier, Identification	—	Id	ID	Use for unique identifier (e.g., CustId)
Last	Lst	Ls	Last	—
Limit	Lmt	Lm	Limit	—
Line	Lin	Ln	Line	—
Middle	Mdl	Md	—	—
Name	Nam	Nm	Name	—
Number	Nbr	Nb	—	—
Phone	Phn	Ph	—	—
Product	Prd	Pd	Prod	—
Production	Pdc	Pr	Prdc	Don't use Prd, which is for Product
Room	Rom	Rm	Room	Rm is preferred over Rom
Shipping	Shp	Sh	Ship	—
State	Sta	St	State	St is preferred over Sta; avoid ambiguity with St for Status
Status	Sts	St	Status	Avoid ambiguity with St for State
Text	Txt	Tx	Text	—
Total	Tot	Tt	—	—

Create and maintain your own list of terms using a word-processor document or a table. Here are some further naming guidelines:

- If you have only one or two terms in a name and the name can be formed using the full spelling of one or both terms, you can use one or both full terms: Name, Status, ShipState, FileName.
- Within a single table's definition, don't use the full spelling of a term in some column names and its abbreviation in others: not PhoneDay and PhnEvening, but PhnDay and PhnEvening or PhoneDay and PhoneEvn.
- Try to avoid a mix of two- and three-character abbreviations for the same term in the same table: BilLine1 and BilPosCod1, not BillLine1 and BilPosCod1, in the same table.
- When you create a new table, consider the consistency among the column names as a group. Although you may have to vary from your general conventions slightly, it's more important that the column names within a table be as descriptive as possible and consistent among themselves.

Also, most application-oriented names shouldn't include any indication of the table that contains them. For example, in Figure 3.1, we use Name instead of CustName. When Name is defined in the Customer table, it's obvious that Name means "customer's name." If there were a separate Employee table that also had a Name column, it would be clear that Name in that table meant "employee's name."

There's one case in which the column name *should* incorporate some indication of the containing table — a column that serves as a table's primary key. Notice in Figure 3.1 that we followed this convention with the CustID column. The reason for including Cust in the field name is not that ID alone would be an inadequate name within the Customer table itself. Rather, the reason for this explicit indication of the containing file is that a CustID column may also be defined in other tables that have some relationship to the Customer file. For example, a Sale table would normally have a CustID column to contain the customer ID of the customer placing the order. Obviously, it wouldn't be a good idea to use just ID as the name of the customer ID column in the Sale table. (What name would you give the column that contained the order ID?) Because CustID (or a similar name) is the best choice for a column in a table that's related to the Customer table, it's good practice to use the same name in the Customer table itself.

Coding Suggestions

- Store most DDL statements to create production collections, tables, views, indexes, and other SQL/400 objects in source file members, and execute them using the RunSqlStm command.
- Source files are created using a CrtSrcPf (Create Source Physical File) command, such as the following:

  ```
  CrtSrcPf AppDta/SqlClcSrc
  ```

  (Note that you use the slash, or /, character as a qualifier with OS/400 object names.)
- Use a separate source file for different types of SQL objects, and use meaningful source file names, such as the following:
  - SqlClcSrc — SQL statements to create collections
  - SqlTblSrc — SQL statements to create tables and associated indexes
  - SqlViewSrc — SQL statements to create views

- Use the name of the main SQL object (e.g., the table name) you're creating as the source member name.
- Enter a source member description that's the description of the SQL object.
- Place comments at the beginning of your SQL source to describe the object being created.
- Use a consistent order for statements such as Create, Label On, and Comment On in a source member.
- Use spaces, blank lines, and separator line comments to improve the readability of your source code.
- Align column names, data types, compound search conditions, and so on in multiline statements for readability.
- Establish and follow a good naming convention for all SQL names. Review the "Guidelines for SQL/400 Names" section of this chapter for guidelines to follow when setting up a naming standard.
- Use Label On and Comment On statements to add descriptive text and column headings for tables, views, and columns.
- Create tables, indexes, and other SQL objects using meaningful SQL names. If a name is larger than 10 characters, use Rename to create a meaningful system name of 10 characters or less.
- Use the For clause in column definitions as needed to define meaningful system names for columns.
- Use standard column definitions for the same type of column — for example, use Char(50) for all columns that contain descriptive text.
- On the Create Table statement, code the Not Null and Default options for all columns, except columns that should be null-capable.
- Consider update, as well as retrieval, performance implications to decide which indexes to create. In general, indexes speed retrieval while slowing update.
- To simplify object management, create each index in the same collection as the table on which it's based.

Chapter Summary

The Create Collection statement creates an SQL collection, which is an OS/400 library object, to contain SQL tables, views, indexes, packages, and other SQL and non-SQL objects.

The Create Table statement creates a base table, which is a UDB/400 externally described, physical file object. A base table contains the actual data for an application. Data in SQL tables is stored as rows. Each table definition specifies one or more columns, which represent different properties (e.g., customer name) of an application object. Each column has an SQL name and a system name, a data type, and an explicit or implicit size. A column may optionally have an explicit default value. A column can be defined to allow or prohibit the null placeholder.

The Label On and Comment On statements can be used to specify descriptive text for tables, indexes, columns, and other SQL objects and components. You can also use Label On to specify column headings of up to three lines.

The Create Distinct Type statement lets you create a user-defined data type (UDT) based on one of the SQL/400 built-in data types. You can use a distinct type in a column definition.

The Alter Table statement lets you add, drop, or change a base table column.

The Create Index statement creates an SQL index, which is a logical file object with a keyed access path. An SQL index is created over a single base table and specifies one or more key columns. You can also create Encoded Vector Indexes (EVIs) to speed up certain types of queries. In general, UDB/400 uses indexes to improve performance, and SQL DML statements cannot directly use an SQL index to access data.

The Drop Collection, Drop Table, Drop Distinct Type, Drop Index, and Drop Alias statements delete the respective SQL objects and (optionally) all dependent or contained objects.

Key Terms

alias
base table
binary
binary radix tree (b-tree) index
binary string data type
character string data type
Coded Character Set Identifiers (CCSID)
collection
column definition
column name
data type
database
datalink
date
distinct type
double precision
double-byte character set (DBCS)
Encoded Vector Index (EVI)
Extended Binary-Coded Decimal Interchange Code (EBCDIC)
floating point
index
naming convention
null-capable
numeric column
packed decimal
precision
scale
single precision
single-byte character set (SBCS)
SQL naming option
standard data type
system name
system naming option
time
timestamp
Universal Multiple-Octet Coded Character Set 2 (UCS-2)
user-defined type (UDT)
zoned decimal

Exercises

1. Describe the purpose of the following five SQL database objects:
   - collection
   - table
   - distinct type
   - index
   - alias
2. Describe the type of OS/400 object (or objects) created for a collection, a table, and an index.
3. Give one example of the appropriate Create statement to create each of the five SQL database objects listed in Exercise 1.
4. Code the Create Table, Label On, and Comment On statements for a base table to hold the following employee information:

- identification number
- name (last, first, middle initial)
- birth date
- address (street, city, state, postal code)
- identification number of employee's manager
- annual salary
- health-insurance plan (coded)

  Be sure to consider the following:

- appropriate table and column names
- column data types and lengths
- default values
- the table's primary key
- good documentation

5. Code the SQL statement to create a distinct type, and then code a Create Table statement that uses this distinct type in a column definition.
6. Explain the relationship among the following three database items:
   - a base table primary key constraint (specified with the Create Table or Alter Table statement)
   - an SQL Unique index (specified with the Create Index statement)
   - an SQL Unique When Not Null index (specified with the Create Index statement)
7. Code the Create Index statement for an index that SQL/400 can use to improve performance when retrieving rows from the Customer table (Figure 3.1) in order by state (major key) and city (minor key).
8. Give one example of the appropriate Drop statement to delete each of the five SQL database objects listed in Exercise 1.

Chapter 4

Database Constraints

Chapter Overview

In UDB/400, database constraints provide a way to guarantee that rows in a table have valid primary or unique key values, that rows in a dependent table have valid foreign key values that reference rows in a parent table, and that individual column values are valid. In this chapter, you'll learn how to define constraints when you use the Create Table statement and learn details about the data integrity rules that constraints enforce. You'll also learn how to use the Alter Table statement to add and drop constraints for an existing table.

Introduction to Database Constraints

In general terms, database **constraints** are restrictions on the contents of the database or on database operations. As we discuss in Chapter 19, a logical data model documents a variety of constraints, or integrity rules, that reflect an organization's requirements for valid data and valid operations. SQL/400 uses the term "constraint" in a narrower sense that covers four specific integrity rules:

- primary key constraint (to enforce existence integrity)
- unique constraint (to enforce candidate key integrity)
- foreign key constraint (to enforce foreign key, or referential, integrity)
- check constraint (to restrict a column's values; a partial enforcement of domain integrity)

You specify one or more of these constraints when you use the Create Table statement to create a base table. You can also add or drop constraints with the Alter Table statement.

None of the constraints is required, although most base tables will, by design, have a primary key. UDB/400 enforces all four types of constraints when rows in the table are inserted or updated (and in the case of a foreign key constraint, when rows in the parent table are updated or deleted). Once you've defined a constraint for a table, the constraint is enforced for *all* database updates through *any* interface, including SQL DML, HLL built-in I/O operations, Interactive SQL (ISQL) ad hoc updates, and remote access via Open Database Connectivity (ODBC) or Java Database Connectivity (JDBC).

Figure 4.1 shows a Create Table statement that includes all four types of constraints. (This statement includes two check constraints — one as part of the OrderId column definition and one at the end of the statement.)

Figure 4.1
Create Table Statement with Constraints

```
Create Table Sale
  ( OrderID   Dec( 7, 0 ) Not Null
      Constraint SaleOrderIdChk Check( OrderID > 0 ),
    SaleDate  Date        Not Null,
    ShipDate  Date        Default Null,
    SaleTot   Dec( 7, 2 ) Not Null,
    CrdAutNbr Int         Default Null,
    CustID    Dec( 7, 0 ) Not Null,
  Primary Key( OrderID ),
  Constraint SaleCrdAutNbrUK Unique ( CrdAutNbr ),
  Constraint SaleCustomerFK  Foreign Key ( CustID )
    References Customer                  ( CustID )
    On Delete  Cascade
    On Update  Restrict,
  Constraint SaleShipDateChk Check( ShipDate Is Null
                               Or ShipDate >= SaleDate ) )
```

You can specify most constraints either as part of a column definition (e.g., the SaleOrderIdChk constraint in Figure 4.1) or as a separate clause. Our preference is to code within the column definition only those check constraints that reference a single column and to code primary key, unique, foreign key, and multicolumn check constraints after the column definitions.

You can optionally begin each constraint clause with the Constraint keyword followed by a constraint name:

```
Constraint SaleOrderIdChk Check( OrderID > 0 )
```

If you don't specify a constraint name, UDB/400 generates a name when the table is created. A constraint name must be unique within the collection that contains the table.[1] The constraint name can later be used in the Alter Table statement (discussed later) to drop the constraint. Because you don't need a constraint name to drop a primary key constraint with the Alter Table statement (you can specify just the keywords, Primary Key), constraint names are most useful for unique, foreign key, and check constraints. We recommend you specify names for these three types of constraints.

Primary Key Constraints

A primary key serves as the unique identifier for rows in the table. For example, in Figure 4.1, the CustID column is the primary key used to identify customers. The syntax of the **primary key constraint** (following the Constraint keyword and the constraint name, if they're specified) is

```
Primary Key( column-name, ... )
```

Each primary key column's definition must include Not Null. For a table with a primary key constraint, UDB/400 blocks any attempt to insert or update a row that would cause two rows in the same table to have identical value(s) for their primary key column(s). A table definition can have no more than one primary key constraint. Chapter 19 describes how to decide on a table's primary key when you design the table.

1 Note that this requirement means you can't have, for example, two constraints named CustomerFK defined for two different tables in the same collection. As a consequence, we start each constraint name with the table name (or some standard short form that identifies the table); for example, we use SaleCustomerFK for a constraint in the Sale table, and we'd use AcctCustomerFK for a constraint in the Account table.

Unique Constraints

A **unique constraint** is similar to a primary key constraint; however, a column listed in a unique constraint doesn't have to be defined with Not Null. The syntax is similar, but we recommend you always specify a constraint name for a unique constraint:

```
Constraint constraint-name Unique ( column-name, ... )
```

Note that a unique constraint does *not* use the Key keyword, as do primary key and foreign key constraints. In Figure 4.1, the SaleCrdAutNbrUK unique constraint specifies that any *non-null* value for the CrdAutNbr column must be unique. Allowing the CrdAutNbr column to be null and specifying the SaleCrdAutNbrUK constraint together enforce a business rule that some orders (e.g., those paid by cash) may exist without a credit authorization number, but any order that does have a credit authorization number must have a unique value.

A table can have multiple unique constraints; however, the same set of columns (regardless of order) can be listed on only one primary key or unique constraint. For example, it's *not* valid to have the following two constraints on the same table:

```
Primary Key( ColA, ColB ),
Unique     ( ColB, ColA )
```

As is the case for primary key constraints, UDB/400 also blocks any attempt to insert or update a row that would cause two rows in the same table to have identical, non-null value(s) for the column(s) listed in a unique constraint. If any of the constraint columns are null-capable, however, two rows can exist with unique constraint columns set to null. If you need to have a unique constraint enforce the same rules as a primary key constraint (i.e., no identical values for the unique constraint columns), just be sure to code Not Null for the unique constraint columns' definitions.

Foreign Key Constraints

A UDB/400 **foreign key constraint** specifies how records in different tables are related and how UDB/400 should handle row insert, delete, and update operations that might violate the relationship. For example, sales rows are generally related to the customers who place the orders. Although it might be valid for a customer row to exist without any corresponding sale rows, it would normally be invalid for a sale row not to have a reference to a valid customer. With a relational DBMS, the relationship between rows in two tables is expressed by a **foreign key** in the **dependent table**. A foreign key is one or more columns that contain a value identical to a primary key (or unique key) value in some row in the **parent table** (i.e., the **referenced table**).

With SQL/400, we might create the Customer and Sale tables so they have the following partial constraint definitions:

Customer table (parent)

- Primary key column: CustID

Sale table (dependent)

- Primary key column: OrderID
- Foreign key column: CustID

For each row in the Sale table, the CustID column should contain the same value as the CustID column of some Customer row because this value tells which customer placed the order. The purpose of specifying a foreign key constraint is to have UDB/400 ensure that the Sale table never has a row with a (non-null) value in the CustID column that has no matching Customer row.

Because a foreign key is a means of identifying a related row, in general the foreign key column(s) definition should be identical to the definition of the primary key column(s). SQL/400 also lets a foreign key reference the key columns of a unique constraint, rather than the primary key; but unless you have an existing dependent table with columns that reference a unique identifier other than the parent table's primary key, you should define a foreign key constraint to reference the parent table's primary key. Of course, this suggestion implies that you should define a primary key constraint for the parent table before you define foreign key constraints for any dependent tables.

With SQL/400, you specify a foreign key constraint in the *dependent* table. The constraint specifies the foreign key column(s) (in the same table as the constraint) and the column(s) of a primary key or unique constraint in the parent table. The corresponding primary and foreign key columns must have *identical* data type and length or precision.

Consider the Sale table defined in Figure 4.1 that contains rows with information about sales, including a CustID column that contains the customer ID of the customer who placed the order. The Sale table's foreign key constraint, which is

```
Constraint SaleCustomerFK Foreign Key ( CustID )
  References Customer                 ( CustID )
  On Delete Cascade
  On Update Restrict
```

specifies that the CustID column in the Sale table is a foreign key that references the CustID primary key column in the Customer table. With this constraint, UDB/400 does not allow an application to insert a new row in the Sale table unless the row's CustID column contains the value of some existing CustID value in the Customer table. This constraint also blocks any attempt to change the CustID column of a row in the Sale table to a value that doesn't exist in any row in the Customer table. In other words, a new or updated Sale row must have a parent Customer row.

Although the Sale table's CustID column in this example doesn't allow nulls, for a foreign key with one or more null-capable columns, UDB/400 lets a row be inserted or updated in the dependent table if any foreign key column is set to null. The idea behind this aspect of a foreign key constraint is that if you let a foreign key field be null, you're implying it's valid for a dependent row to exist with an unknown parent or that a dependent row may not always require a parent. In most cases, however, you'll find your logical business model dictates that you specify Not Null for foreign key columns, thus requiring that every dependent row have a specific parent row.[2]

The On Delete and On Update clauses determine the rules UDB/400 enforces when an attempt is made to delete or update a parent table row in such a way as to leave dependent table rows that have invalid foreign key references. Both rules apply in those cases in which one or more dependent table rows have a foreign key value that matches the parent key of the parent table row being deleted or updated. The On Delete and On Update rules are intended to prevent "orphan" rows — rows in the dependent table that have a non-null foreign key that doesn't reference an existing parent row.

In the above example, the On Delete clause specifies what action UDB/400 should take when an application tries to delete a row in the Customer table and some row in the Sale table contains the CustID value of the row being deleted. The Cascade action used in this example causes UDB/400 to propagate the delete operation to all Sale rows that have the same CustID as the Customer row being deleted. Thus, any Sale rows for the deleted Customer row will also be deleted automatically.

2 For many cases in which you need to handle dependent rows without a "real" parent row, using a default parent (as we discuss later under the Set Default delete rule) is preferable to using null foreign keys.

The On Update clause in the example specifies what action UDB/400 should take when an application tries to update the CustID value in a row of the Customer table and some row in the Sale table contains the CustID value of the row being updated. The Restrict action used in this example causes UDB/400 to block the update operation and return an error to the application.

If you don't explicitly specify an On Delete or an On Update clause, the default action is the same as with the keywords No Action. The No Action alternative is similar to the Restrict action, but there's a subtle timing difference between Restrict and No Action. With Restrict, the check for an unmatched foreign key occurs *before* an after-delete-event or after-update-event database trigger program is called, whereas with No Action the check occurs *after* an after-delete-event or after-update-event trigger program is called.[3] Chapter 16 covers trigger programs and the sequence of events that occur for database updates involving constraints and trigger programs. Be sure to study this section carefully before deciding whether to use Restrict or No Action.

Also, with SQL/400 set-at-a-time DML statements (discussed in Chapter 7), UDB/400 checks the Restrict rule immediately after *each* row update (or delete) but checks the No Action rule only after statement execution is completed and *all* rows have been updated or deleted. It's possible (although not common) to have an update statement that changes a set of rows' parent key values (e.g., by adding 1 to each parent key value) such that as each row is changed, some foreign key value has no match, but when all the parent rows have been changed, all foreign key values are once again matched. In this situation, specifying On Update (or On Delete) No Action is the appropriate choice.[4]

The On Update clause allows only the two choices: Restrict or No Action.[5] The On Delete clause allows Cascade, Restrict, No Action, Set Default, and Set Null.

When you specify Set Default for the Delete action and you delete a parent row, UDB/400 sets all foreign key columns of dependent rows to their respective default values. If none of the foreign key columns has a default of Null, the parent table must contain a row with a primary key value that's the same as the foreign key column default(s). After the delete operation is completed, the original parent will be deleted and the dependent rows will subsequently reference the "default" parent row.

As an example of how you might use this technique, suppose you want to allow inactive customers to be deleted but you want to keep their old sales information (i.e., rows) for statistical purposes. You could define the default value for the CustID column in the Sale table as 0 and then create one Customer row with a CustID (primary key) value of 0 and some dummy customer name, such as "Placeholder for Deleted Customers". If you specify On Delete Set Default for the previous example's foreign key constraint, when you delete a Customer row, its Sale rows would be updated to have 0 for their CustID (foreign key) value.

3 A trigger program is a program that UDB/400 invokes when a database insert, update, or delete action takes place. Trigger programs can be defined to be invoked at any of six different times: before insert, before update, before delete, after insert, after update, and after delete. In the case of a No Action foreign key constraint, an after-update-event or after-delete-event trigger program could conceivably take action (such as updating or deleting dependent rows) to make sure the foreign key constraint wasn't violated.

4 You can also temporarily disable a foreign key constraint, as we discuss later in this chapter.

5 SQL/400 doesn't provide a Cascade option for the On Update clause as it does for the On Delete clause. If you want to automatically update the foreign key values of dependent rows when you update a parent row, you might consider two techniques to propagate parent key column changes to the foreign key columns in dependent rows. The first approach would be to insert a new parent row with the new parent key values, then update the dependent rows so their foreign keys contain the new parent key value, and then delete the old parent row. Or, you could add an after-update-event trigger to the parent table and have the trigger program change the foreign key values of the dependent rows. This technique can be used with Update No Action, which doesn't check the foreign key constraint until after the after-update-event trigger program is executed.

If any foreign key column is null-capable, another On Delete alternative is Set Null, which causes all null-capable foreign key columns to be set to null.

Additional Foreign Key Constraint Considerations

A dependent table in one foreign key constraint can be the parent table in another foreign key constraint. For example, the Sale table might be the parent table in a foreign key constraint that exists for the SaleItem dependent table. This raises the possibility that a cascaded delete might delete dependent rows that are also parent rows for some other table. For example, if On Delete Cascade were specified for the previous example, deleting a Customer row could delete some Sale rows that were parents of SaleItem rows. If a foreign key constraint for the SaleItem table specifies Restrict or No Action and UDB/400 blocks the deletion of the Sale rows, UDB/400 also blocks the attempted deletion of the Customer row. In general, with On Delete Cascade, if UDB/400 blocks any operation caused by the cascading delete, all operations are blocked.[6] Similar rules apply when Set Default or Set Null is specified and a resulting change in a foreign key value would violate some other constraint.

A foreign key constraint can specify the same table for the dependent and parent tables. Suppose you have an Employee table with an EmpID primary key column and a MgrEmpID column that holds the employee ID for the person's manager. You could use the following to specify the foreign key constraint to express this relationship:

```
Create Table Employee
   ( EmpID     Dec ( 7, 0 ) Not Null,
     MgrEmpID Dec ( 7, 0 ) Not Null,
     other column definitions ... ,
  Primary Key ( EmpID ),
  Constraint EmpMgrFK Foreign Key ( MgrEmpID )
    References Employee           ( EmpID    )
      On Update Restrict
      On Delete Restrict )
```

To handle the case of an employee who had no real manager (e.g., the president of the company), a dummy employee row could be inserted with the name "No manager" and its EmpID and MgrEmpID values set to 0 (or any other value not used by real employees). The MgrEmpID for any employee with no manager could be set to 0 to satisfy the foreign key constraint.

Depending on how you wanted to implement the removal of an employee (who might be a manager), you could add a Default 0 clause to the MgrEmpID column definition and specify On Delete Set Default. Or, you might define MgrEmpID as null-capable and consider a null MgrEmpID to mean "no manager." In this case, you could specify On Delete Set Null to handle the deletion of a manager's row. A final alternative would be to change all the rows for the manager's employees so they had a new, valid MgrEmpID value before you deleted the old manager's row.

A table can have multiple foreign key constraints, including overlapping foreign keys. If a foreign key constraint specifies On Delete Set Default and the constraint's foreign key has a column that's in another constraint's foreign key, deleting a row from the parent table of the first constraint may change the value of a foreign key column in the second constraint. If this happens and the new foreign key value for the second constraint doesn't match a parent key in the parent table of the second constraint, UDB/400 blocks the dependent row updates and the parent row delete.

A table can also be the parent table for multiple foreign key constraints. UDB/400 enforces all constraints when a row in such a table is updated or deleted. The order UDB/400 follows to check

6 UDB/400 may actually perform some of the operations and then use commitment control facilities to roll back (i.e., undo) the operations.

constraints is based on the action specified for each constraint. For an update operation, UDB/400 checks Restrict constraints and then No Action constraints. For a delete action, the order of checking is

- Restrict
- Cascade
- Set Null
- Set Default
- No Action

If any constraints are violated, UDB/400 blocks the operation and ends the constraint checking. See Chapter 16 for more details on the sequencing of constraint checking and trigger programs.

When a foreign key constraint has both On Update Restrict and On Delete Restrict specified, UDB/400 can check the constraint before doing any actual table update or delete operations. With any other rules, UDB/400 must perform some operations, and then, if the constraint check fails, UDB/400 must back out the partial changes to the table(s). As a result, you must journal both the dependent and parent tables in any foreign key constraint other than one with Restrict specified for both the update and delete rules. Both tables must be journaled to the same journal. With SQL/400, the simplest way to ensure that a parent table and its dependent tables are journaled to the same journal is to create them all in the same collection. Note that you don't have to explicitly start commitment control. When necessary, UDB/400 implicitly uses a commitment control cycle to ensure that table changes occur on an all-or-none basis.[7]

Check Constraints

You can define **check constraints** for a table to enforce the validity of column values. Figure 4.1 shows two check constraints:

```
Constraint SaleOrderIdChk Check( OrderID > 0 )
```

which guarantees that the OrderID primary key column is always greater than zero, and

```
Constraint SaleShipDateChk Check( ShipDate Is Null
                                  Or ShipDate >= SaleDate )
```

which guarantees that either a row has no ship date (i.e., the ShipDate column is null, meaning "unknown") or the ship date is on or after the sale date.

A check constraint can compare a column to a constant (such as in the first example), to another column in the same table (such as in the second example), or to an expression (e.g., ColA + 3). UDB/400 checks to make sure a new or changed row doesn't violate any of its table's check constraints before an insert or update operation is allowed. If a check constraint condition evaluates to true, UDB/400 considers the constraint satisfied; if the condition evaluates to false, UDB/400 considers the constraint violated.

As we explain in Chapter 5, SQL conditions such as those used in check constraints can evaluate to true, false, or *unknown*. One way that a condition can evaluate to unknown is when the column is null. For example, the ShipDate >= SaleDate condition is unknown when ShipDate is null. We'll defer further discussion of how a condition can be unknown until we take a more complete look at SQL's "three-valued" logic. For now, it's important to know that when a check constraint condition evaluates

7 Journals were briefly explained in Chapter 3. Recall that they record inserts, updates, and deletes from rows in a table. By default, SQL/400 journals all tables you create. Commitment control is the OS/400 facility that provides for transaction integrity and recovery.

to unknown, UDB/400 considers the constraint *satisfied.* If you want to prevent a null value in a column (and avoid the possibility of an unknown condition), simply add Not Null to the column definition. If you need to test a column for null, use the Is Null or Is Not Null test (explained in Chapter 5), as we've done in the SaleShipDateChk constraint.[8]

A check constraint, such as SaleOrderIdChk above, that references only a single column can be coded as part of the column definition — a coding style we recommend. A check constraint, such as SaleShipDateChk, that references two or more columns in the test must be coded separately from any column definition. We recommend you code multicolumn check constraints after any primary key, unique, or foreign key constraints.

You can combine check constraints for more than one column into a single check constraint, as in the following example:

```
Constraint CustStatusNameChk
  Check ( ( Status =  'A' Or Status = 'I' )
    And   ( Name    <> ' '                ) )
```

However, when UDB/400 detects a constraint violation, it provides only the constraint name — not the specific condition that was violated — in the error message.[9] If this constraint were violated, you couldn't easily determine whether the Status or the Name column was invalid. It's easier to handle constraint violations in your programs if each logical constraint has its own name and separate definition. Although combining constraints provides a small performance gain, the benefit usually is not enough to outweigh the drawbacks.

Adding and Removing Constraints from an Existing Table

After you create a table, you can use the Alter Table statement to add or remove a primary key, unique, foreign key, or check constraint, as the following examples illustrate.

To drop a table's primary key constraint, just specify the Primary Key keywords:

```
Alter Table Sale
  Drop Primary Key
```

To drop a unique, foreign key, or check constraint, you must specify the constraint name:

```
Alter Table Sale
  Drop Constraint SaleCustomerFK
```

To add a new constraint, use the same constraint syntax as in a Create Table statement:

```
Alter Table Sale
  Add Constraint SaleSaleTotChk
      Check( SaleTot >= 0 )
```

Note that you cannot use the Alter Table statement to add any type of constraint unless all the existing rows in the table satisfy the constraint at the time you execute the statement.

8 In the SaleShipDateChk example, we didn't really need to code the ShipDate Is Null condition because the ShipDate >= SaleDate condition evaluates to unknown when ShipDate is null and thus satisfies the UDB/400 requirements for a check constraint. It's much clearer, however, to code an explicit test so anyone looking at the constraint can get a complete picture of the conditions that must be met.

9 The way you obtain this feedback depends on which UDB/400 interface you're using. For example, in ISQL, you place the cursor on the error message and press the F1 (Help) key. The error message details are then displayed with the constraint name.

Foreign Key and Check Constraint States

When you create a new table with constraints, no data yet exists in the table and thus all the constraints can be enabled immediately. When you use Alter Table to add a constraint, the statement succeeds only if all existing rows satisfy the constraint. There are cases, however, when a foreign key or check constraint may exist but not necessarily be fully checked. For example, if you restore a dependent table from backup before you restore the parent table, the foreign key values can't be checked until the parent table is also restored. Also, unlike the Alter Table statement, the AddPfCst (Add Physical File Constraint) CL command lets you add a foreign key or check constraint to a physical file (SQL table or non-SQL file) even when not all records in the file satisfy the constraint. Although these unusual constraint situations are rare and you generally won't have to worry about constraint states, the following information will prove helpful if you encounter a situation where a constraint is in the "check pending" state.

The following chart shows the six possible **constraint states**:

	Disabled	**Enabled**
Defined	1	2
Established — Check pending	3	4
Established — No check pending	5	6

1 = Defined and disabled
2 = Defined and enabled
3 = Established and disabled with check pending
4 = Established and enabled with check pending
5 = Established and disabled without check pending
6 = Established and enabled without check pending

Normally, when you successfully add a foreign key constraint (e.g., with an Alter Table statement), the constraint becomes established and enabled without check pending. From this point on, UDB/400 enforces the constraint. However, if you use an AddPfCst command to define a foreign key constraint for a non-SQL file (either dependent or parent or both) that doesn't yet have a member (see Chapter 1 for a discussion of file members), the constraint is defined and enabled (but not established). In this case, after you add members so that both the dependent and parent files have a member, the constraint becomes established and enabled without check pending.

When a dependent file (again, either an SQL table or a non-SQL file) is restored or the AddPfCst command is used to add a foreign key constraint to a file with existing records, UDB/400 checks to ensure that all non-null foreign key values have a matching parent key value. If the foreign key check is satisfied, the constraint becomes established and enabled without check pending. If there's an unmatched foreign key value, the constraint becomes established and enabled with check pending. Similarly, a check constraint can have a check pending status if you use the AddPfCst command to add a constraint in which there are one or more rows that don't satisfy the constraint.

To remove the check pending status with SQL, you must use the Alter Table statement to remove the foreign key or check constraint, correct the rows in the dependent and/or parent table(s), and then use the Alter Table statement to add the constraint again. SQL/400 provides no explicit way to change the enabled/disabled state of a constraint. However, you can use the ChgPfCst (Change

Physical File Constraint) CL command to change the state of a constraint. For example, you can disable a constraint with a command such as

```
ChgPfCst File( Sale )
         Cst( SaleCustFK )
         State( *Disabled )
```

Using the ChgPfCst command, you can disable a constraint that has check pending, correct the data, and then enable the constraint.

While a foreign key constraint is in the established and enabled with check pending state, *no* I/O operations are allowed on the dependent table and only read (e.g., an SQL Fetch statement) and insert operations are allowed for the parent table. When a check constraint is in the established and enabled with check pending state, insert, update, and delete operations are allowed on the table, but read operations are disallowed. For both types of constraint, when the constraint is in the established and disabled state, all I/O operations are allowed.

Coding Suggestions

- For most tables, define one or more columns as a primary key constraint and use the primary key as the main way you identify rows.
- Code the primary key, unique, and foreign key constraints after all column definitions.
- Code single-column check constraints as part of the column definition.
- Code multicolumn check constraints after the primary key, unique, and foreign key constraints.
- Use the Constraint *constraint-name* option to assign a name to all unique, foreign key, and check constraints; optionally assign names to primary key constraints as well.
- Use a consistent suffix (e.g., PK for primary key, UK for unique, FK for foreign key, and Chk for check constraints).

Chapter Summary

Constraints provide a mechanism to protect data integrity when rows are inserted, updated, or deleted in database tables. UDB/400 supports four types of constraints:

- primary key
- unique
- foreign key
- check

You can define these constraints using the SQL/400 Create Table or Alter Table statement. The Alter Table statement also lets you drop existing constraints.

A table can have one primary key constraint, which defines the set of columns that always have unique, non-null values and thus can be used as the identifier for individual rows in the table.

A table can have multiple unique constraints. Each unique constraint defines a set of columns that must have unique values. Unique constraints allow a column to be null.

A table can have multiple foreign key constraints. Foreign key constraints define a parent-dependent relationship between two tables. A foreign key constraint defines the dependent table's foreign key columns, which reference the parent key (usually the primary key) of the parent table.

Each row in the dependent table must have a foreign key value that is the same as the parent key value in a row in the parent table or that is fully or partially null.

When you define a foreign key constraint, you specify the action UDB/400 should take when an update or delete operation to a parent table row would leave dependent table rows with invalid foreign key values. For an update operation, you can specify No Action or Restrict, both of which block an invalid update, but they differ in when UDB/400 makes the check. For a delete operation, you can specify No Action, Restrict, Set Default, Set Null, or Cascade. The Set Default and Set Null actions set dependent rows' foreign key columns to their default value or null, respectively. The Cascade action deletes matching dependent rows.

A delete action may lead to other constraint checks. UDB/400 uses an implicit commitment control cycle to ensure that all row updates and deletes satisfy the database constraints, or no rows are updated or deleted.

A table can have multiple check constraints. A check constraint is a logical expression that one or more columns within a single row must satisfy. UDB/400 prevents insert and update operations that would violate any check constraints defined for a table.

When you define a new constraint with the Alter Table statement, UDB/400 checks the validity of all existing rows before letting the new constraint be created.

Key Terms

check constraint
constraint
constraint state
dependent table
foreign key
foreign key constraint
parent table
primary key constraint
referenced table
unique constraint

Exercises

1. Show the Create Table statement to create a Loan table with the following columns:
   - LoanID
   - CustID
   - LoanDate
   - ApplicantAge

   Include the following constraints:
   - LoanID is the primary key.
   - Each row must have a unique combination of CustID and LoanDate values.
   - ApplicantAge must not be less than zero.
   - The CustID column must reference a corresponding row in the Customer table. (The Customer table has a CustID column that is its primary key.)

2. Show the Alter Table statement to define a foreign key constraint between the Employee table, which has a DeptID column to identify the department an employee belongs to, and the Dept table, which has a primary key of DeptID. Describe (in general terms) how you would implement the Employee and Dept tables and the foreign key constraint to handle an employee not yet assigned to a department.
3. For the Employee and Dept tables in Exercise 2, describe (in general terms) how you would implement the necessary row updates to handle an organizational change in which a department's name and department ID change, but all employees remain in the department. (It's not necessary to show exact SQL DML statements; we'll cover those in Chapter 7.)
4. Considering the tables in Exercise 2, describe the changes to the database tables and constraints that would be necessary to handle employees who belonged to multiple departments.
5. Show the Alter Table statements to add all necessary primary key and foreign key constraints for the tables in your answer to Exercise 4.

Chapter 5

Select Statement Basics

Chapter Overview

In Chapter 3, you learned how to use SQL's Create Collection, Create Table, and Create Index statements to create fundamental SQL objects. In this chapter, we begin our study of the Select statement, an SQL construct that plays a central role in both Data Definition Language (DDL) and Data Manipulation Language (DML). A limited form of the Select statement (known as a subselect) is used to create views — database objects that provide an alternative way to access underlying data stored in SQL tables. The complete Select statement provides the basis for retrieving data with SQL.

You'll learn about the most commonly used Select statement clauses, including From, Where, Group By, Having, and Order By clauses. We also cover search conditions and introduce predicates, which are used in the Where clause to define a set of rows. In addition, this chapter explains the use of literals, expressions, scalar and column functions, date and time arithmetic, and case expressions.

Introduction to DML

As Chapter 3 explained, SQL lets you define and manipulate data represented in table-like form. SQL base tables contain actual data. The SQL Data Manipulation Language (DML) provides data-manipulation capabilities that include not only row-at-a-time operations but also **set-at-a-time operations**. For example, you can retrieve and display a specific row using a **Select statement** such as the following:

```
Select  *
  From  Customer
  Where CustID = 499320
```

Or, you can retrieve and display a set of rows with this statement:

```
Select  *
  From  Customer
  Where ShipCity = 'Seattle'
```

Both examples retrieve a set of rows; however, if CustID values are unique (e.g., CustID is the table's primary key), the first statement never returns more than one row. (It might return no rows — the empty set — if there's no customer with the specified customer ID value.) The second example might return any of the following results:

- no rows — if there are no customers in Seattle
- one row — if there's exactly one customer in Seattle
- multiple rows — if there are two or more customers in Seattle

As you can see, a set of rows can have zero, one, or more rows. The important point is that SQL has the ability to express conditions (such as ShipCity = 'Seattle') that define a multirow set and then retrieve or update that set in a single statement.

Another important aspect of SQL is that previously defined column names (e.g., ShipCity) are used to identify the specific data that's retrieved, changed, or used in comparisons. With UDB/400, the information about tables and columns, such as a column's name, data type, and size, is stored in the OS/400 file object's header, as well as in the SQL catalog (as we discussed in Chapter 2). These stored descriptions enable SQL database routines to determine how to access the appropriate data without requiring further definition in a utility or HLL program. This same information also supports UDB/400's Interactive SQL (ISQL) facility and the RunSqlStm (Run SQL Statement) command so you can execute SQL DML statements without having to write an HLL program.

Dynamic vs. Static Execution

As we discussed in Chapter 2, you can execute SQL statements in a variety of ways. In this chapter, we look at statements that can be executed dynamically. **Dynamic execution** of an SQL statement means that you construct a statement as a text string and have the SQL routines interpret and execute the text string. Probably the most common way to dynamically execute an SQL statement is to enter it on the ISQL display, as you saw in Chapter 2's Figure 2.3 (page 28). Another means of dynamic execution is to put one or more SQL statements in a source member and process the source member as input to the RunSqlStm command. In Chapter 10, we look at a third method of dynamic SQL statement execution, in which you use HLL string operations to construct an SQL statement in a program variable and use the SQL Execute Immediate statement to execute the string contained in the variable. An important restriction of any dynamic method of execution is that the SQL statement itself can't contain references to HLL program variables.

An alternative way of executing SQL statements — known as **static execution** — lets you code HLL variables within an SQL statement, thus providing the ability to change some of the selection or other values (e.g., customer ID) between subsequent executions of the same statement.[1] Static execution is possible only when an SQL statement is embedded (i.e., coded) in an HLL program and then translated into executable form (i.e., machine language) as part of the program creation process.[2] When the compiled program is run, the translated SQL statement is executed as part of the program's execution. Because an SQL statement that you code for static execution is always translated before execution, you can include HLL variables in a **static SQL** statement — the translation takes care of the steps needed to get a variable's value into the SQL statement when it's executed. We'll defer the details of **embedded SQL** until Chapter 10; however, a simple example will make clear the difference between a dynamic and a static form of an SQL statement.

The following statement shows the second Select example above but uses the SlcCusCity HLL program variable (instead of a literal, such as 'Seattle') to hold the city value used in the Where clause:[3]

1 The use of "static" and "dynamic" to describe the two ways you can execute an SQL statement may seem counterintuitive because static execution is the method that lets you use program variables and perhaps appears to be the more flexible method. With static execution, however, a statement's structure is always the same (i.e., static). The only things that can change between executions of the statement are the values of program variables used in the statement. With dynamic execution, on the other hand, the entire statement can be constructed as a string, and, thus, the structure of the statement is changeable (i.e., dynamic).

Note also that you obviously can change a selection or other value in a dynamically executed SQL statement simply by keying in another statement or constructing a new string in an HLL program. In an HLL program, however, coding dynamic SQL is often more complicated and less efficient than coding a static form of an SQL statement that includes program variables.

2 With embedded SQL, the program creation process involves two steps. The first step is precompilation, which translates embedded SQL statements into HLL Call (and other) statements. The second step is compilation. Chapter 12 explains this process more fully.

3 Note that this example could be used only as part of an embedded SQL cursor, a construct covered in Chapter 11. As you'll see in Chapter 10, the Select Into statement is a similar embedded statement that is not part of a cursor. However, the Select Into statement must never return more than one row, and this example doesn't meet that restriction.

```
Select  *
  From  Customer
  Where ShipCity = :SlcCusCity
```

Notice the colon (:) preceding SlcCusCity — that's what tells the SQL translator that SlcCusCity is a program variable name, not a column name.

Most types of SQL statements can be executed either as a dynamic or as a static statement.[4] It's easier to learn the basics of SQL DML by first using examples without program variables and without worrying about other aspects of embedding SQL statements in an HLL program. So in this chapter, we look at Select statement examples that can be executed dynamically — for instance, by using ISQL. Keep in mind that in most places where we use a literal in an example, the same statement could be embedded in an HLL program using a variable to provide more flexibility.

The four main (non-embedded) DML statements are

- Select — to retrieve rows from one or more tables
- Insert — to add new rows to a table
- Update — to update column values in a table's rows
- Delete — to delete rows in a table

All four statements can be used with base tables or views, although Insert, Update, and Delete require that a view be updatable (i.e., not read only). (We explain views in Chapter 6.) The Select statement can retrieve rows from one or more underlying base tables; however, the Insert, Update, and Delete statements can update only one underlying base table in a single statement.

In this chapter, we introduce the Select statement. We cover Insert, Update, and Delete in Chapter 7.

Retrieving Rows with the Select Statement

The SQL Select statement retrieves rows from one or more tables or views. If you enter a Select statement using ISQL, the results are displayed at your workstation (or printed or written to a database file). To use a Select statement, you list the columns you want in the result, identify the tables and views to access, and specify the selection criteria for returned rows. You also can group and order rows. SQL combines the information you specify on the Select statement with information in the underlying file object headers and catalog to determine what to retrieve and how to carry out the retrieval. The basic structure of a Select statement is

```
Select      select-list
  From      table-list
  Where     search-condition
  Group By  grouping-column-list
  Having    search-condition
  Order By  order-by-column-list
```

Mastering the Select statement, which is powerful and can take quite complex forms, is the key to using SQL successfully. Many of the Select statement's forms are similar to forms of other SQL DML statements, such as Update and Declare Cursor. And, as you will see in Chapter 6, the subselect (which is part of a complete Select statement) is central to defining SQL views.

4 Not all SQL statements can be executed either way, however. For example, the Connect statement can be executed only as a static statement or interactively, through ISQL; the Create Schema statement can be executed only dynamically with the RunSqlStm command.

The next series of examples work through each part of the Select statement. Many of the examples use the four tables shown in Figures 5.1 through 5.3.

Figure 5.1

Sample Customer Base Table

```
Create Table Customer
    ( CustID   Dec(   7, 0 ) Not Null,
      Name     Char( 30    ) Not Null,
      ShipCity Char( 30    ),
      Discount Dec(   5, 3 ),
  Primary Key( CustID ) )
```

CustID	Name	ShipCity	Discount
133568	Smith Mfg.	Portland	.050
246900	Bolt Co.	Eugene	.020
275978	Ajax Inc.	Albany	<null>
499320	Adapto	Portland	.000
499921	Bell Bldg.	Eugene	.100
518980	Floradel	Seattle	.000
663456	Alpine Inc.	Seattle	.010
681065	Telez Co.	Albany	.000
687309	Nautilus	Portland	.050
781010	Udapto Mfg.	Seattle	.000
888402	Seaworthy	Albany	.010
890003	AA Products	Portland	.010
905011	Wood Bros.	Eugene	.010

Figure 5.2

Sample Sale Base Table

```
Create Table Sale
    ( OrderID  Dec(  7, 0 ) Not Null,
      CustID   Dec(  7, 0 ) Not Null,
      TotAmt   Dec( 11, 2 ) Not Null,
      SaleDate Date         Not Null,
      ShipDate Date,
  Constraint SalePK      Primary Key( OrderID ),
  Constraint SaleCustFK  Foreign Key( CustID  )
    References Customer ( CustID )
    On Delete Cascade
    On Update Restrict )
```

OrderID	CustID	TotAmt	SaleDate	ShipDate
234112	499320	35.00	2000-05-01	2000-05-15
234113	888402	278.75	2000-05-01	2000-05-04
234114	499320	78.90	2000-05-03	<null>

continued

Figure 5.2 *Continued*

OrderID	CustID	TotAmt	SaleDate	ShipDate
234115	890003	1000.00	2000-05-04	2000-05-10
234116	246900	678.00	2000-05-04	2000-05-08
234117	133568	550.00	2000-05-05	2000-05-08
234118	905011	89.50	2000-05-05	2000-05-10
234119	499320	201.00	2000-05-05	<null>
234120	246900	399.70	2000-05-06	2000-05-08

Figure 5.3
Sample Employee Base Table

```
Create Table Employee
     ( EmpID     Dec(   7, 0 ) Not Null,
       FstNam    Char( 20    ),
       MdlInl    Char(  1    ),
       LstNam    Char( 30    ) Not Null,
       MgrEmpID Dec(   7, 0 ),
  Constraint EmpPK Primary Key( EmpID ) )
```

EmpID	FstNam	MdlInl	LstNam	MgrEmpID
104681	Barb	L	Gibbens	898613
227504	Greg	J	Zimmerman	668466
668466	Dave	R	Bernard	709453
898613	Trish	S	Faubion	668466
899001	Rick	D	Castor	898613

We begin with an example of the simplest form of Select statement:

```
Select *
  From Customer
```

The asterisk (*) that follows the Select keyword means "all columns."[5] The From clause specifies one or more base tables or views to be used — in this case, the Customer table. You can optionally qualify a table or view name in the From clause with a collection name (e.g., AppDta.Customer). Because in this example no further restrictions are placed on what's retrieved (i.e., there is no Where clause), all columns for all rows are retrieved.

5 The * represents all columns that exist at the time the statement is prepared. When an SQL statement is executed interactively, it's prepared and executed at essentially the same time. However, for static execution, the statement is prepared during the translation step (as part of program creation) and is executed some time later. If a column is added to a table or view after the statement is prepared (e.g., by an Alter Table statement), the new column will not be included in the implicit column list until the statement is prepared again.

Search Conditions and Predicates

The above example retrieves all customers, but suppose you want only the customers from Seattle? You can accomplish this by adding a Where clause to restrict the retrieved rows:

```
Select  *
  From  Customer
  Where ShipCity = 'Seattle'
```

The simplest Where clause contains an SQL **search condition** that is a single SQL **predicate**, as above. All rows for which the predicate is true are retrieved.

When you need to retrieve a single, specific row with a Select statement, you can specify a search condition with a primary key value, as in the following statement:

```
Select  *
  From  Customer
  Where CustID = 499320
```

A Where clause with a primary key column lets you use SQL for single-row operations.

The Where clause also can contain a search condition consisting of two or more SQL predicates connected with And or Or. The following example shows a search condition with the conjunction (i.e., connected by And) of two predicates:

```
Select  *
  From  Customer
  Where ShipCity  = 'Seattle'
    And Discount  > 0
```

To negate a predicate, you can specify the Not logical operator at the beginning of any predicate or before predicates connected by And or Or. To use Not to negate a compound condition, place parentheses around the condition. The following condition is true if ShipCity is not Seattle (and not null) or if Discount is less than or equal to 0 (and not null):

```
Not ( ShipCity = 'Seattle' And Discount > 0 )
```

You can also use parentheses to specify the order of evaluation for a compound condition that has both And's and Or's. In

```
( ShipCity = 'Seattle' Or Discount > 0 ) And TotAmt > 100
```

SQL first evaluates the compound condition ShipCity = 'Seattle' Or Discount > 0. The result of the predicates connected by Or is then And'd with the value of the last predicate, TotAmt > 100. Without parentheses, SQL evaluates negated expressions first, then predicates connected by And, and finally predicates connected by Or. Thus, the example

```
ShipCity = 'Seattle' Or Discount > 0 And TotAmt > 100
```

is evaluated as

```
ShipCity = 'Seattle' Or ( Discount > 0 And TotAmt > 100 )
```

Note that this is not equivalent to the previous example, where we put parentheses around the predicates connected by Or.

An SQL predicate is a logical condition that is true, false, or unknown for a given row. A predicate is unknown if it involves a comparison and one or both of the values being compared is null. (Recall from Chapter 3 that a null-capable column — one defined without the Not Null clause —

may be set to null rather than contain a valid value.) For example, the value of the predicate ShipCity = 'Seattle' is unknown if ShipCity is null. In general, for any comparison

$expression_1 = expression_2$

the result is unknown if $expression_1$, $expression_2$, or both are null. This rule applies whether the comparison operator is not equal, greater than, or any of the other possibilities.

To negate a predicate with Not or to combine predicates with And and Or, SQL uses **three-valued logic** (Figure 5.4) rather than conventional two-valued logic.

Figure 5.4
SQL Three-Valued Logic

p	q	Not p	p And q	p Or q
True	True	False	True	True
True	False	False	False	True
True	Unknown	False	Unknown	True
False	True	True	False	True
False	False	True	False	False
False	Unknown	True	False	Unknown
Unknown	True	Unknown	Unknown	True
Unknown	False	Unknown	False	Unknown
Unknown	Unknown	Unknown	Unknown	Unknown

This somewhat unusual form of logic is necessary to handle a predicate whose value may be unknown.

A Select statement's result table contains only those rows for which the Where clause search condition is true. If the search condition is false or unknown, the row is omitted. So if a row had a null ShipCity column and its Discount column were 0.05, the search condition

```
Where ShipCity  = 'Seattle'
  And Discount  > 0
```

would evaluate to unknown, and the row would not be selected.

In general, a list of the columns you want in the result table follows the Select keyword. As we mentioned earlier, when you specify * following the Select keyword, it means "all columns" in the result table. Rather than specifying *, you can list the columns you want, separated by commas:

```
Select  CustID,
        Name
  From  Customer
  Where ShipCity = 'Seattle'
```

When the select list doesn't include the primary key column(s), the result table may contain duplicate rows. For example, the following Select statement returns one row for each customer:

```
Select  ShipCity
  From  Customer
```

But because only the ShipCity column is in the result table, there may be multiple rows with identical city values. To eliminate duplicate rows from the result table, you can follow the Select keyword with the Distinct keyword, as in

```
Select  Distinct ShipCity
  From  Customer
```

which displays a list of the cities (with no duplicates) in which there is at least one customer.

Literals, Expressions, and Scalar Functions

The select list that follows the Select keyword can also include literals, expressions, functions, and **SQL special registers**.[6] For example, the following Select statement uses both literals and an arithmetic expression to retrieve the result table shown in Figure 5.5:

```
Select  Name,
        ' has a discount of ',
        Discount * 100,
        '%'
  From  Customer
```

Figure 5.5

Sample Retrieval Using Literals and Expressions

```
Smith Mfg.     has a discount of     5.000    %
Bolt Co.       has a discount of     2.000    %
Ajax Inc.      has a discount of     <null>   %
Adapto         has a discount of      .000    %
Bell Bldg.     has a discount of    10.000    %
Floradel       has a discount of      .000    %
Alpine Inc.    has a discount of     1.000    %
Telez Co.      has a discount of      .000    %
Nautilus       has a discount of     5.000    %
Udapto Mfg.    has a discount of      .000    %
Seaworthy      has a discount of     1.000    %
AA Products    has a discount of     1.000    %
Wood Bros.     has a discount of     1.000    %
```

SQL supports standard four-function arithmetic — addition (+), subtraction (–), multiplication (*), and division (/) — as well as exponentiation (**) for numeric values. You can also use addition and subtraction with date/time columns and literals, something we look at in a moment.

The ConCat (or ||) operator can be used to concatenate (join together) two character strings. If an Employee table has three columns — FstNam, MdlInl, and LstNam — to contain different parts of a person's name, the following shows how the parts might be concatenated into a single string:

```
Select FstNam ConCat MdlInl ConCat LstNam
  From Employee
```

Note that this example produces a result table with a single column that is the concatenated result of the three base table columns.

SQL/400 also has a variety of **scalar functions**, listed in Figure 5.6, that can be used in expressions.

6 SQL special registers are predefined values that you specify with the keywords Current Date, Current Path, Current Server, Current Time, Current Timestamp, Current Timezone, and User.

Figure 5.6
SQL/400 Scalar Functions

Data type conversion

Function	Returns
BigInt(*expression*)	Big integer representation of *expression*, which can be a numeric expression or a character expression that represents an integer, decimal, or floating-point number
Blob(*string, max-length*)	Blob representation of a *string* of any type. The optional *max-length* argument specifies the maximum length of the result.
Char(*expression*)	Character string representing *expression*
Clob(*expression, decimal-character*)	Clob representation of a numeric *expression*. The optional *decimal-character* argument specifies either '.' or ',' as the decimal-point character.
Clob(*string, max-length, ccsid*)	Clob representation of a character or graphic *string*. The optional *max-length* argument specifies the maximum length of the result. You can specify the Default keyword for the second argument to use the actual length of a character expression. The optional *ccsid* argument specifies the CCSID of the result.
DbClob(*expression, length, ccsid*)	DbClob representation of a string *expression*. The optional *length* argument specifies the length of the result. You can specify the Default keyword for the second argument to use the actual length of the expression. The optional *ccsid* argument specifies the CCSID of the result.
Decimal(*expression, precision, scale*)	Packed-decimal value representing *expression*. The *precision* and *scale* arguments are optional. The default for *precision* is based on the type of *expression*. The default for *scale* is 0.
Digits(*expression*)	String representing absolute value of *expression*
Double(*expression*)	Double-precision floating-point representation of *expression*, which can be a numeric expression or a character expression that represents an integer, decimal, or floating-point number
Float(*expression*)	Floating-point value representing *expression*
Hex(*expression*)	Hexadecimal value representing *expression*
Integer(*expression*)	Integer value of *expression*, which can be a numeric expression or a character expression that represents an integer, decimal, or floating-point number
Real(*expression*)	Single-precision floating-point representation of *expression*, which can be a numeric expression or a character expression that represents an integer, decimal, or floating-point number
SmallInt(*expression*)	Small integer representation of *expression*, which can be a numeric expression or a character expression that represents an integer, decimal, or floating-point number
VarChar(*expression, max-length, ccsid*)	Variable character string of maximum length *max-length* (or default length) representing *expression*. The second and third arguments are optional. The Default keyword can be specified instead of a *max-length* value. The third argument is an optional CCSID number.

continued

Figure 5.6 *Continued*

Function	Returns
VarGraphic(*expression, max-length, ccsid*)	Variable graphic character string of maximum length *max-length* (or default length) representing *expression*. The second and third arguments are optional. The Default keyword can be specified instead of a *max-length* value. The third argument is an optional CCSID number.
Zoned(*expression, precision, scale*)	Zoned-decimal value representing *expression*. The *precision* and *scale* arguments are optional. The default for *precision* is based on the type of *expression*. The default for *scale* is 0.

Character string

Function	Returns
Character_Length(*expression*)	Length of string *expression*
ConCat(*string-expression*$_1$, *string-expression*$_2$)	Combines two strings. The result is a string consisting of the first argument immediately followed by the second.
Left(*string, length*)	Identical to SubStr(*string*, 1, *length*)
Locate(*search-string, source-string, start*)	Starting position of *search-string* within *source-string*. Searching begins at the *start* position, if specified, or at position 1 if *start* is not specified.
Lower(*expression*)	Lowercase string value in *expression*
LTrim(*string*)	Identical to Strip(*string*, Leading)
Position(*search-string* In *source-string*) or PosStr(*source-string, search-string*)	Position of *search-string* within *source-string*. If not found, returns zero.
RTrim(*string*)	Identical to Strip(*string*, Trailing)
Strip(*string, strip-type, character*)	String with all leading and/or trailing *characters* removed from *string*. The *strip-type* argument is optional and can be B, Both, L, Leading, T, or Trailing; if not specified, Both is the default. The *character* argument is optional; if not specified, the blank character is the default.
SubStr(*string, start-position, length*)	Substring of *string* beginning at *start-position* and having *length*. The *length* argument is optional; default is to end of *string*.
Translate(*expression, to-string, from-string, pad-char*)	Translation of characters in *expression* from characters in *from-string* to corresponding characters in *to-string*, using *pad-char* if *to-string* is shorter than *from-string*
Trim(*string)*	Identical to Strip(*string*, Both)
Trim(*strip-type character* From *string*)	Identical to Strip(*string, strip-type, character*)
Upper(*expression*)	Uppercase string value in *expression*

Numeric

Function	Returns
AbsVal(*expression*)	Absolute value of *expression*
AntiLog(*expression*)	Anti-logarithm (base 10) of *expression*
Ceiling(*expression*)	Returns the smallest integer value that is greater than or equal to *expression*

continued

Figure 5.6 *Continued*

Function	Returns
Exp(*expression*)	Exponentiation; natural logarithm (base e) raised to power specified by *expression*
Floor(*expression*)	The largest integer value that is less than or equal to *expression*
Ln(*expression*)	Natural logarithm (base e) of *expression*
Log(*expression*)	Common logarithm (base 10) of *expression*
Max(*expression*, ...)	Maximum value of set of one or more *expressions*
Min(*expression*, ...)	Minimum value of set of one or more *expressions*
Mod($expression_1$, $expression_2$)	Remainder of $expression_1$ divided by $expression_2$
Power($expression_1$, $expression_2$)	Result of $expression_1$ ** $expression_2$
Round($expression_1$, $expression_2$)	Returns $expression_1$ rounded to $expression_2$ places to the right of the decimal point if $expression_2$ is positive or to the left of the decimal point if $expression_2$ is 0 or negative
Sign(*expression*)	Returns –1 if the *expression* argument is less than 0, 0 if the argument is 0, or 1 if the argument is greater than 0
Sqrt(*expression*)	Square root of *expression*
Truncate($expression_1$, $expression_2$)	Returns $expression_1$ truncated to $expression_2$ places to the right of the decimal point if $expression_2$ is positive or to the left of the decimal point if $expression_2$ is 0 or negative

Trigonometric

Function	Returns
ACos(*expression*)	Arc cosine of *expression* in radians
ASin(*expression*)	Arc sine of *expression* in radians
ATan(*expression*)	Arc tangent of *expression* in radians
ATanH(*expression*)	Hyperbolic arc tangent of *expression* in radians
Cos(*expression*)	Cosine of *expression*
CosH(*expression*)	Hyperbolic cosine of *expression*
Cot(*expression*)	Cotangent of *expression*
Degrees(*expression*)	Number of degrees in an angle expressed by *expression* radians
Sin(*expression*)	Sine of *expression*
SinH(*expression*)	Hyperbolic sine of *expression*
Tan(*expression*)	Tangent of *expression*
TanH(*expression*)	Hyperbolic tangent of *expression*

Date, time, and timestamp

Function	Returns
CurDate()	Current date
CurTime()	Current time

continued

Figure 5.6 *Continued*

Function	Returns
Date(*expression*)	Date represented by *expression*
Day(*expression*) or DayOfMonth(*expression*)	For date and timestamps, day-in-month (1 to 31) part of *expression*; for date and timestamp durations, days (–99 to 99) part of *expression*
DayOfWeek(*expression*)	For date and timestamps, day-in-week (1 to 7) for *expression*
DayOfYear(*expression*)	For date and timestamps, day-in-year (1 to 366) for *expression*
Days(*expression*)	Days from January 1, 0001, to date represented by *expression*
Hour(*expression*)	For time and timestamps, hour-of-day (0 to 24) part of *expression*; for time and timestamp durations, hours (–99 to 99) part of *expression*
Microsecond(*expression*)	For time and timestamps, microsecond-of-second (0 to 999999) part of *expression*; for time and timestamp durations, microseconds (–999999 to 999999) part of *expression*
Minute(*expression*)	For time and timestamps, minute-of-hour (0 to 59) part of *expression*; for time and timestamp durations, minutes (–99 to 99) part of *expression*
Month(*expression*)	For date and timestamps, month-in-year (1 to 12) part of *expression*; for date and timestamp durations, months (–99 to 99) part of *expression*
Now()	Timestamp for current time
Quarter(*expression*)	For date and timestamps, quarter-in-year (1 to 4) for *expression*
Second(*expression*)	For time and timestamps, second-of-hour (0 to 59) part of *expression*; for time and timestamp durations: seconds (–99 to 99) part of *expression*
Time(*expression*)	Time represented by *expression*
Timestamp($expression_1$) or Timestamp($expression_1$, $expression_2$)	Timestamp represented by $expression_1$ (a string representation of a timestamp) or by $expression_1$ (a string representation of a date) and $expression_2$ (a string representation of a time)
Week(*expression*)	For date and timestamps, week-in-year (1 to 53) for *expression*
Year(*expression*)	For date and timestamps, year (1 to 9999) part of *expression*; for date and timestamp durations, years (–9999 to 9999) part of *expression*

Bitwise operations

Function	Returns
LAnd(*expression, ...*)	Bitwise AND of two or more character (byte) string *expressions*
LNot(*expression*)	Bitwise NOT of character (byte) string *expression*
LOr(*expression, ...*)	Bitwise (inclusive) OR of two or more character (byte) string *expressions*
Xor(*expression, ...*)	Bitwise XOR (exclusive or) of two or more character (byte) string *expressions*

DataLink

Function	Returns
DlComment(*expression*)	Comment value, if it exists, from a DataLink
DlLinkType(*expression*)	Link type value from a DataLink

continued

Figure 5.6 *Continued*

Function	Returns
DlUrlComplete(*expression*)	Complete Universal Resource Locator (URL) value from a DataLink
DlUrlPath(*expression*)	Path and file name from a DataLink. When appropriate, the returned value includes a file-access token.
DlUrlPathOnly(*expression*)	Path and file name from a DataLink. Does not include a file-access token.
DlUrlScheme(*expression*)	Scheme from a DataLink
DlUrlServer(*expression*)	Server from a DataLink
DlValue(*location, link-type, comment*)	DataLink formed from a URL string that specifies the *location*, an optional string to specify the *link-type* (must be 'URL'), and an optional *comment* string

***Distributed table*[1]**

Function	Returns
Hash($expression_1$, . . .)	Distributed table partition number for a set of values
NodeName(*table-designator*)	Distributed table name for a row in the *table-designator*
NodeNumber(*table-designator*)	Node number for a row in the *table-designator*
Partition(*table-designator*)	Partition number for a row in the *table-designator*

Miscellaneous

Function	Returns
Coalesce(*expression*, ...) or Value($expression_1$, ...)	First non-null value from list of *expressions*
IfNull($expression_1$, $expression_2$)	Same as Coalesce($expression_1$, $expression_2$)
Length(*expression*)	Length of *expression*
NullIf($expression_1$, $expression_2$)	Returns null if the expressions are equal; otherwise, returns the first expression.
RRN(*table-or-view-name*)	Relative record number of a row in the underlying base table's physical file

[1]Distributed tables are beyond the scope of this book. See the *DB2 Multisystem for AS/400* manual for details.

A scalar function takes one or more arguments that can be literals, column names, or expressions. If a column name is used in a function, the function is applied to the column's value in each row in the result table and produces a value for the same row. The following statement shows how you could use the Strip function (one of the character string scalar functions) to better format the previous example:

```
Select        Strip( FstNam ) ConCat ' '
       ConCat Strip( MdlInl ) ConCat ' '
       ConCat Strip( LstNam )
  From Employee
```

In the example that doesn't use the Strip function, the three parts of the name are concatenated without stripping blanks and without ensuring that at least one blank exists between the parts of the name. With the column definitions in Figure 5.3 (page 85), the resulting strings would look like

```
Dave                RBernard
```

Using the Strip function and concatenating a couple of blank literals, the second example produces strings like

```
Dave R Bernard
```

Date and Time Arithmetic

Another important use of SQL expressions and scalar functions is working with date and time values. Externally, SQL represents date values as character strings containing numbers for the year, month, day, and (in some formats) date separators. When you want to enter a literal date, you code the value as a string. The format of the string depends on the values specified for the DatFmt and DatSep parameters of the StrSql (Start SQL), RunSqlStm, or CrtSql*Xxx* (Create SQL *Xxx*) command.[7] For example, if you specify *ISO format, the following string represents May 1, 2000:

```
'2000-05-01'
```

With *USA format, the proper representation is

```
'05/01/2000'
```

SQL/400 offers some flexibility in the format of date literals and automatically recognizes a literal that's coded in one of the standard formats shown in Figure 5.7.

Figure 5.7
Standard Date Literal Formats

Format name	Abbreviation	Format	Example
International Standards Organization (*ISO)	ISO	*yyyy-mm-dd*	'2000-04-07'
IBM USA Standard (*USA)	USA	*mm/dd/yyyy*	'04/07/2000'
IBM European Standard (*EUR)	EUR	*dd.mm.yyyy*	'07.04.2000'
Japanese Industrial Standard Christian era (*JIS)	JIS	*yyyy-mm-dd*	'2000-04-07'

You can use these formats regardless of the value specified for the DatFmt parameter.

SQL provides date addition and subtraction and date functions. The following example uses the Days function to get the number of days since January 1, 0001, and then uses the difference between the Days value for ShipDate and the Days value for SaleDate to see how long after a sale the order was shipped:

```
Select  CustID,
        OrderID,
        SaleDate,
        ShipDate,
        Days( ShipDate ) - Days( SaleDate )
  From  Sale
  Where ShipDate Is Not Null
```

This Select statement produces the result table shown in Figure 5.8.

7 Review the "Date, Time, and Timestamp Data Types" section of Chapter 3 for information about the available date and time formats and separators. The online help for the StrSql, RunSqlStm, and CrtSql*Xxx* commands also provides detailed information about the allowable values for the DatFmt, DatSep, TimFmt, and TimSep parameters.

Figure 5.8

Sample Retrieval Using Dates and Durations

CustID	OrderID	SaleDate	ShipDate	Days(ShipDate) - Days(SaleDate)
499320	234112	2000-05-01	2000-05-15	14
888402	234113	2000-05-01	2000-05-04	3
890003	234115	2000-05-04	2000-05-10	6
246900	234116	2000-05-04	2000-05-08	4
133568	234117	2000-05-05	2000-05-08	3
905011	234118	2000-05-05	2000-05-10	5
246900	234120	2000-05-06	2000-05-08	2

Notice how for the first row, SaleDate is 2000-05-01 and ShipDate is 2000-05-15, which results in a difference of 14 days between the Days function values for the two columns. If SaleDate were 1999-05-01 (notice the year) and ShipDate 2000-05-15, the difference between the Days value for the two columns would be 380 days (366 + 14).

Note also how the search condition in this example excludes rows with a null ShipDate. Because the Sale table permits the ShipDate column to be null, we must consider the case in which a row has a null ShipDate. For arithmetic expressions, if one of the operands is null, the result of the expression is null. This rule makes sense, as you can see in this example, in which the difference between two dates is obviously unknown if one or both of the dates is unknown (i.e., null). The Is Not Null search condition lets us eliminate the cases where the ShipDate isn't known (e.g., the order hasn't been shipped yet).[8]

As an alternative, you could use the following expression to calculate the difference between two dates as an SQL **date duration** value:

```
ShipDate - SaleDate
```

The result of this expression for sample column values would be

SaleDate	ShipDate	ShipDate - SaleDate
2000-05-01	2000-05-15	14
1999-05-01	2000-05-15	10014 *(1 year, 0 months, 14 days)*

SQL/400 represents a date duration as an eight-digit packed-decimal number in the form *yyyymmdd*, not as a number of days. Be sure you don't get tripped up using a date duration instead of a days duration. You can also add a duration to or subtract a duration from a date. When SaleDate is 2000-05-01, the result of the expression

```
SaleDate + 14 Days
```

is 2000-05-15. The term 14 Days is a **labeled duration**. You can use the following keywords to specify what a duration value represents: Years, Months, Days, Hours, Minutes, Seconds, or Microseconds.[9] To add one year, two months, and 14 days to a date, you would code

```
SaleDate + 1 Year + 2 Months + 14 Days
```

8 Note that SQL requires ColA Is Null or ColA Is Not Null; you can't use ColA = Null or ColA <> Null.

9 The singular form of these keywords is also allowed: Year, Month, Day, Hour, Minute, Second, and Microsecond.

SQL supports time and timestamp columns, literals, and arithmetic in a way similar to what you've seen for date arithmetic. To code a time value with SQL/400's ISO format, you use a string representation such as '13.30.10' for 10 seconds after 1:30 p.m. To use a colon (:) as the time separator (e.g., '13:30:10'), use the JIS format. A time duration is a six-digit packed-decimal number with an *hhmmss* format. You also can use labeled time durations, as in the following expression, which adds labeled-time-duration values to a time column:

```
WrkBgnTime + 1 Hour + 30 Minutes
```

Column Functions

Scalar functions work on values from one row at a time. SQL also has **column functions** that you can specify in a select list to produce a value from a set of rows. Figure 5.9 lists the available SQL/400 column functions.

Figure 5.9
SQL/400 Column Functions

Function	Returns
Avg(*expression*)	Average of non-null *expression* values
Count(*) or Count(*expression*)	Count(*) returns the number of rows in the result table. Count(*expression*) returns the number of non-null expression values.
Count_Big(*) or Count_Big(*expression*)	Same as the Count function except that the result can be greater than the maximum value of a large integer; returns a decimal with precision 31 and scale 0.
Max(*expression*)	Maximum of non-null *expression* values
Min(*expression*)	Minimum of non-null *expression* values
StdDev(*expression*)	Biased standard deviation of non-null *expression* values
Sum(*expression*)	Sum of non-null *expression* values
Var(*expression*)	Variance of non-null *expression* values

As an example, the following Select statement results in a single row with the total number of customers and their average discount:

```
Select 'Average discount for ',
       Count( * ),
       ' customers is ',
       Avg( Discount )
  From Customer
```

The column function Count(*) returns the number of rows in a result table. The column function Avg(Discount) returns the numerical average of the set of non-null values for the specified column.

Be careful when you use column functions with columns that allow null. For example, suppose the Discount column allows nulls and that at least one row in the Customer table has a null Discount column. In this case, the following statement returns surprising results.

```
Select Count( * ),
       Avg( Discount ),
       Sum( Discount )
  From Customer
```

The sum is not equal to the average times the count! The Count(*) function includes all rows, but the Avg and Sum functions ignore rows with a null Discount column.

There are two solutions to this problem. You can use an alternative form of the Count function, which does eliminate rows with a null Discount column:

```
Select Count( Discount ),
       Avg( Discount ),
       Sum( Discount )
  From Customer
```

Or you can use a more general solution — use a Where clause to eliminate rows with null columns before the functions are applied:

```
Select  Count( * ),
        Avg( Discount ),
        Sum( Discount )
  From  Customer
  Where Discount Is Not Null
```

When you use a column function in the select list and you don't specify a Group By clause (discussed later), the column function applies to the entire set of records selected by the Where clause, and the Select statement's result table is always a single row. When you specify a Group By clause, the Select statement's result table contains one row for each group, or — if a Having clause (also discussed later) is also specified — the result table contains one row for each group that satisfies the Having clause's condition, with the column function applied to each row of the group.

If the set of rows to which a column function is applied is empty (i.e., there are no rows), the result of any column function except Count(*) is null. Count(*) returns zero for an empty set.

You can optionally specify the Distinct keyword immediately after the opening parenthesis of a column function to eliminate duplicate expression values (as well as nulls) from the set of values to which the function is applied. The main practical use of this feature is with the Count or Count_Big function to count the number of different values for some column, as in

```
Select  Count( Distinct ShipCity )
  From  Customer
```

which produces a one-row, one-column result table that is the number of cities in which there's at least one customer.[10]

Group By and Having Clauses

You can use the Group By clause to apply column functions to (sub)groups of the rows you select. For instance, the statement

```
Select      ShipCity,
            Count( * ),
            Avg( Discount )
  From      Customer
  Group By  ShipCity
```

returns one row for each group of customers in a different city, as shown in Figure 5.10.

10 Note that you can't use the Distinct keyword with the Count(*) form of the Count function.

Figure 5.10
Sample Retrieval Using Group By Clause

ShipCity	Count(*)	Avg(Discount)
Albany	3	.005000
Eugene	3	.043333
Portland	4	.027500
Seattle	3	.003333

In this example, ShipCity is the **grouping column** that partitions the rows in the Customer table into groups — one group for each different ShipCity value. The column functions Count and Avg are applied to each group in turn and produce one row in the result table for each group. In this example, rows with a null Discount column are intentionally not excluded, letting the result set have a complete count of the number of customers in each city. The average discount is for the customers with a non-null Discount column. For any null-capable grouping column, all nulls are considered in the same (null) group.

Normally, you list grouping columns' names in the select list as well as in the Group By clause so that each row in the final result table has the identifying column value(s) for the group. Any other columns that appear in the select list must be used as arguments of a column function.

You can use the Having clause to restrict rows in the result table after column functions have been applied to grouped rows.[11] The Having clause has a form similar to that of the Where clause, which selects rows before they are grouped. For example, you could enter the following Select statement

```
Select     ShipCity,
           Count( * ),
           Avg( Discount )
  From     Customer
  Where    Discount Is Not Null
  Group By ShipCity
  Having   Avg( Discount ) > .01
```

to retrieve the information shown in Figure 5.11 for cities with an average discount above 1 percent.

Figure 5.11
Sample Retrieval Using Having Clause

ShipCity	Count(*)	Avg(Discount)
Eugene	3	.043333
Portland	4	.027500

The search condition for a Having clause can include grouping columns (e.g., ShipCity) or column functions (e.g., Avg(Discount)).

The grouping clause can also contain an expression, as in this example:

```
Select Day( SaleDate ), Month( SaleDate ), Sum( TotAmt )
  From Sale
  Group by Day( SaleDate ), Month( SaleDate )
```

This Select statement produces the result table shown in Figure 5.12, showing total sales for each day.

11 Although you can specify a Having clause without a Group By clause, this is very unusual.

Figure 5.12

Sample Using an Expression in the Group By Clause

Day(SaleDate)	Month(SaleDate)	Sum(TotAmt)
1	5	313.75
3	5	78.90
4	5	1,678.00
5	5	840.50
6	5	399.70

There's a conceptual ordering to a Select statement that helps clarify when the search conditions of the Where and Having clauses are tested as well as how the other clauses come into play. Each step produces a hypothetical result table from the intermediate result table of the previous step. The steps are as follows:

Step 1. All combinations of all rows from all tables and views listed in the From clause are included in an intermediate result table produced by this step. (If only one table or view is specified in the From clause, the intermediate result table's columns and rows are the same as those in the specified table or view.)

Step 2. If a Where clause is specified, the search condition is applied to each row in the result table produced by step 1. Only those rows for which the search condition is true are included in the intermediate result table produced by this step. (If no Where clause is specified, all rows from the result table produced in step 1 are included.)

Step 3. If a Group By clause is specified, the rows from the result table produced in the previous steps are collected into separate groups such that all the rows in a group have the same values for all grouping columns. (If no Group By clause is specified, all the rows are considered as one group.)

Step 4. If a Having clause is specified, the search condition is applied to each group. Only those groups of rows for which the search condition is true are included in the intermediate result table produced by this step. (If no Having clause is specified, all groups, and rows, from the result table produced in the previous steps are included.)

If a Having clause is specified but no Group By clause is specified, the intermediate result table produced by this step is either empty or contains all rows produced in the previous steps.

Step 5. If neither a Group By nor a Having clause is specified, the intermediate result table produced by this step includes the rows in the result table produced in steps 1 and 2. Each row contains the direct and derived columns specified in the select list.

If either a Group By or Having clause or both clauses are specified, the intermediate result table produced by this step includes one row for each group of rows produced in steps 1 through 4. (If the previous result table was empty, the result table produced by this step is also empty.) Each row contains any grouping columns included in the select list as well as the result of applying any column function(s) in the select list to the group.

Step 6. If the Distinct keyword is specified for the select list, duplicate rows are eliminated in the result table produced in the previous steps; otherwise, all rows are included in the final result table.

Note that although this sequence of steps provides a way to understand the result of a Select statement, it isn't necessarily how SQL/400 actually carries out a Select or other statement. The UDB/400 query optimizer may use a more efficient method to produce the results.

Because you can use either a Where clause or a Having clause to select rows based on the value of a grouping column, you can choose either of the following statements to display the average discount of customers in Portland or Seattle:

```
Select      ShipCity,
            Avg( Discount )
  From      Customer
  Where     ShipCity In ( 'Portland', 'Seattle' )
  Group By ShipCity
```

or

```
Select      ShipCity,
            Avg( Discount )
  From      Customer
  Group By ShipCity
  Having    ShipCity In ( 'Portland', 'Seattle' )
```

Using a Where clause is a clearer way to code this retrieval, and in many cases it performs significantly faster than using the Having clause because UDB/400 can eliminate rows before the grouping step and the calculation of the Avg column function values.[12]

The Order By Clause

You can use the Order By clause to sequence a Select statement's result table before it's displayed.[13] An Order By clause specifies a list of columns with ascending or descending (with the Desc keyword) sequence. For an unnamed column in the result table (e.g., one specified by an expression or a function), you can use a relative column number instead of a column name to specify that the unnamed column is used to sequence the rows. The following statement retrieves shipped orders sequenced by customer ID and, within customer ID, by the number of days (longest interval first) it took to ship the order:

```
Select    CustID,
          OrderID,
          SaleDate,
          ShipDate,
          Days( ShipDate ) - Days( SaleDate )
  From    Sale
  Where   ShipDate Is Not Null
Order By CustID,
          5 Desc
```

In this case, the unnamed fifth column that results from the Days(ShipDate) – Days(SaleDate) expression is used to sequence rows within the same CustID value.

As a more readable alternative to a relative column number, SQL lets you code a name for a derived column by following an expression or function with the As keyword and a column name.[14]

12 Internally, the UDB/400 optimizer tries to move Having conditions to the Where clause when it can. Nevertheless, it's a good idea to code tests in the Where clause when that provides the appropriate selection.

13 Although we cover subselects and views in Chapter 7, be aware that an Order By clause is valid only in a Select statement and is not part of a subselect.

14 You also can use this feature to create a synonym for a named column, but you should avoid a proliferation of synonyms because it leads to less consistent names. Even though you can give a column name to an expression in the select list, SQL/400 doesn't let you use this name in a Where, Group By, or Having clause.

Here's the previous example rewritten to use this technique:

```
Select   CustID,
         OrderID,
         SaleDate,
         ShipDate,
         Days( ShipDate ) - Days( SaleDate ) As DaysToShip
  From   Sale
  Where  ShipDate Is Not Null
Order By CustID,
         DaysToShip Desc
```

Case Expressions

Case expressions provide a multicondition test. The following query produces a table (Figure 5.13) that categorizes sales into small, medium, and large:

```
Select OrderID,
       Case
         When TotAmt <= 100 Then 'Small'
         When TotAmt <= 500 Then 'Medium'
         Else                    'Large'
       End As SaleSize
  From Sale
```

Figure 5.13

Sample Retrieval Using a Case Expression with a Searched When Clause

OrderID	SaleSize
234112	Small
234113	Medium
234114	Small
234115	Large
234116	Large
234117	Large
234118	Small
234119	Medium
234120	Medium

In this example, each When condition specifies a search condition, followed by the keyword Then, followed by a value. For each selected row, the first When condition that's true produces the result. The optional Else clause specifies the result if no prior When condition is true. If none of the When conditions is true and there is no Else clause, the result is null.

You can use a slightly different form of the When clause (called a simple When clause) if you need to test for a set of discrete values. The following Select statement produces a table (Figure 5.14) of customer names and their state:

```
Select Name,
       Case ShipCity
         When 'Portland' Then 'Oregon'
         When 'Eugene'   Then 'Oregon'
         When 'Albany'   Then 'New York'
         When 'Seattle'  Then 'Washington'
       End As CustState
  From Customer
```

Figure 5.14
Sample Retrieval Using a Case Expression with a Simple When Clause

```
Name            CustState
Smith Mfg       Oregon
Bolt Co.        Oregon
Ajax Inc.       New York
Adapto          Oregon
Bell Bldg.      Oregon
Floradel        Washington
Alpine Inc.     Washington
Telez Co.       New York
Nautilus.       Oregon
Udapto Mfg.     Washington
Seaworthy       New York
AA Products     Oregon
Wood Bros.      Oregon
```

You can use case expressions in other Select statement clauses as well. The Select statement

```
Select  *
  From  Customer
  Where Discount >= Case ShipCity
                     When 'Portland' Then .03
                     Else                 .02
                   End
```

produces a result table of customers from Portland that have a discount greater or equal to .03 and customers from all other cities that have a discount greater or equal to .02.

More About Predicates

As you've seen, the Where and Having clauses of a Select statement have a search condition that contains either a single predicate or multiple predicates connected by And or Or. Recall that a predicate specifies a condition that evaluates to true, false, or unknown. SQL has several kinds of predicates, including

- basic predicate
- Null predicate
- Between predicate
- In predicate
- Like predicate
- Exists predicate
- quantified predicate

In this chapter, we discuss basic predicates, Null predicates, Between predicates, In predicates, and Like predicates. We cover Exists predicates and quantified predicates (as well as the use of subqueries with predicates) in Chapter 8.

A **basic predicate** compares two values, using one of the comparison operators listed in Figure 5.15.

Figure 5.15
SQL Comparison Operators

Operator	Meaning
=	Equal
<>	Not equal
<	Less than
<=	Less than or equal
>	Greater than
>=	Greater than or equal

SQL/400 also allows the following equivalent operators:

Operator	Equivalent to
¬=	<>
¬<	>=
¬>	<=

We've already seen several examples of the simpler form of basic predicate, which has the general syntax

$\mathit{expression}_1\ \theta\ \mathit{expression}_2$

where each expression is a column name, literal, or some valid arithmetic, string, or other form of expression and θ is one of the logical comparison operators in Figure 5.15. An example of this type of predicate is

```
Discount > 0
```

In Chapter 8, we'll explain another form of basic predicate that uses a subquery.

Recall that a comparison between two values is unknown if either or both of the values is null. The **Null predicate** provides a way to test for null or not null, using syntax such as

```
Where ShipDate Is Null
```

or

```
Where ShipDate Is Not Null
```

SQL also has some shorthand forms for compound conditions. The **Between predicate** is an alternative to two inequality tests. The search condition

```
Where Discount Between 0.01 And 0.02
```

is equivalent to

```
Where Discount >= 0.01
  And Discount <= 0.02
```

You also can use

```
Where Discount Not Between 0.01 And 0.02
```

which is equivalent to

```
Where Discount < 0.01
   Or Discount > 0.02
```

To simplify a series of equality tests, you can use the **In predicate**. A search condition such as

```
Where ShipCity In ( 'Eugene', 'Portland', 'Seattle' )
```

is equivalent to

```
Where ShipCity = 'Eugene'
   Or ShipCity = 'Portland'
   Or ShipCity = 'Seattle'
```

You also can specify the Not keyword before the In predicate to negate the test. Again, there's a form of the In predicate that uses a subquery — a topic we cover in Chapter 8.

The **Like predicate** provides a rudimentary form of string pattern matching. A Select statement with a search condition such as

```
Select  CustID,
        Name
  From  Customer
  Where Name Like '%Steel%'
```

would display customers containing the string Steel anywhere in the name. The following names would be included:

```
Ajax Consolidated Steel
Portland Steel Yards
Steel Fabricators of the Northwest
John Steeling Grocery Company
Umpqua Steelhead Fly Fishing Guides
```

The expression before the Like keyword must identify a string (e.g., a character column or a string function, such as SubStr). Following the Like keyword, you code a string literal.[15] This string provides the pattern to be matched. In the pattern, you can use the percent character (%) to represent a substring of zero or more occurrences of any character or the underscore character (_) to represent a substring of exactly one occurrence of any character. The following predicate tests for names that are exactly four characters long and end in "ick":

```
Name Like '_ick'
```

This pattern matches Dick, Rick, Mick, and Nick, as well as dick, rick, mick, nick, kick, and !ick. The pattern doesn't match ick (too short), Ricky (too long), or RICK (wrong case).[16]

If you need to match a literal % or _ character, you can optionally define an escape character that's used in the pattern to specify that the escape character and the character following it are to be treated literally as the character following the escape character. For example, the following predicate matches any string that is at least two characters long and has an underscore in the second or later character:[17]

```
Name Like '_%\_%' Escape '\'
```

15 You also can specify the User or Current Server special registers for the pattern, but there's little point in doing so because these two special registers aren't likely to contain any wildcard characters. For embedded SQL statements, you can also use a host variable that contains a string pattern.

16 With SQL/400, you can specify a sort sequence that treats uppercase and lowercase characters as identical for comparison purposes; with this sort sequence, the pattern '_ick' would match the string 'RICK'. The SrtSeq parameter of the StrSql, RunSqlStm, and CrtSql*Xxx* commands specifies the sort sequence.

17 A matching string might also have an underscore in the first character as well as in a later character; thus '_x_' would match the pattern.

The first _ matches any one character. The first % matches zero or more of any character. The _ matches only an _. And the final % matches zero or more of any character.

Coding Suggestions

- Use an As clause to give a meaningful column name to an expression or function in the select list.
- Consider using the SubStr scalar function to shorten long character fields for Select statements entered with ISQL. Also consider using a combination of the SubStr and Digits scalar functions to return only the meaningful part of long numeric fields. These techniques can make the results easier to view.
- Consider null-capable columns when specifying expressions, functions, or search conditions.
- In general, when you specify a Group By clause, include all grouping columns in the select list so that each row in the result table has the identifying information for the group.
- Performance-related suggestions:
  - When possible, use a Where clause rather than a Having clause to select rows.
  - Avoid conversion between different numeric data types in predicates. For example, if a column's data type is Integer, use a comparison such as ColA = 1 rather than ColA = 1.0.
  - If possible, avoid patterns that begin with % or _ in the Like predicate so the UDB/400 optimizer can use an index to select rows.

Chapter Summary

The Select statement retrieves rows from one or more base tables and/or views. The basic structure of a Select statement is

```
Select      select-list
   From     table-list
 [ Where    search-condition      ]
 [ Group By grouping-column-list ]
 [ Having   search-condition      ]
 [ Order By order-by-column-list ]
```

(The brackets, or [ ], indicate clauses that are optional.) The parts of a Select statement serve the following purposes:

Select *select-list*	Specifies the columns in the Select statement's result table
From *table-list*	Specifies 1 to 256 base tables and/or views from which the result table data comes
Where *search-condition*	Specifies a logical condition that must be true for a row to be included in the result table
Group By *grouping-column-list*	Specifies the column(s) whose values are used to group the rows
Having *search-condition*	Specifies a logical condition that must be true for a group to be included in the result table
Order By *order-by-column-list*	Specifies a list of columns with ascending or descending (with the Desc keyword) sequence

The select list for a Select statement can specify either an asterisk (*) — for all columns — or an explicit list of column names, literals, expressions, and scalar or column functions. SQL supports arithmetic, string, and date/time expressions. Scalar functions operate on a single value for each argument, and a value is produced for each row. Column functions operate on a set of values, one value from each selected row.

The From clause can specify one or more tables and views. If multiple tables and views are specified, the Select statement containing the From clause is based on an intermediate table that has all combinations of all rows from the listed tables and views. (This topic is covered in Chapter 8.)

A search condition is a single predicate or multiple predicates connected by the And or Or logical operators. Simple or compound predicates can be negated with the Not operator. A predicate is a condition that's true, false, or unknown. A predicate may be unknown if one or more operands are null. SQL uses three-valued logic to combine predicates (see Figure 5.4). A row is selected only if the search condition is true for the row.

Case expressions provide multicondition tests. The first condition that is true (if any) produces the case expression's result value. If no condition is true, the value associated with the optional Else clause produces the result value. If no condition is true and there is no Else clause, the result is null.

There are several kinds of predicates. The ones discussed in this chapter are

- basic predicate — a comparison between two expressions
- Null predicate — tests whether an expression is null
- Between predicate — tests whether an expression is within a range of values
- In predicate — tests whether an expression is in a set of values
- Like predicate — a string comparison using pattern matching

When a Group By clause is specified, the final result table consists of one row for each group. All rows in a group have the same value(s) for the specified grouping column(s). The result table columns can include the grouping column(s) and any column functions.

The search condition of a Having clause is applied either to each (sub)group of rows — if a Group By clause is also specified — or to the entire set of rows in the intermediate result table — if a Group By clause is not specified. The final result table includes only those rows for groups for which the Having clause's search condition is true.

Key Terms

basic predicate
Between predicate
case expression
column function
date duration
dynamic execution
embedded SQL
grouping column
In predicate
labeled duration
Like predicate
Null predicate
predicate
scalar function
search condition
Select statement
set-at-a-time operation
SQL special register
static execution
static SQL
three-valued logic

Exercises

1. Show the Select statement to retrieve the entire Employee table (all rows and columns).
2. Show the Select statement to retrieve from the Customer table in Figure 5.1 the customers in Eugene who haven't yet been assigned a discount (i.e., their discount is unknown).
3. Show the Select statement to retrieve customers that have a name ending in "Inc." and with "Oregon" anywhere in the name.
4. Show the Select statement to retrieve a list of the different discount rates assigned to any customer. For this retrieval, do the following:
   - Eliminate duplicate discount values from the list.
   - Calculate the percent discount from the fractional value.
   - Include the text "percent" following the values.
5. Show the Select statement to retrieve the minimum and maximum customer discount and the difference between them for each city. Include the city name in your retrieval. What will be the result if all customers in a particular city have an unknown (i.e., null) discount?
6. Modify the Select statement you created for Exercise 5 so that a city must have different minimum and maximum discounts to be included in the result table.
7. Show a Select statement that displays the customer name and the following:
   - 'Deep Discount' if the customer's discount is greater than .03
   - 'Medium Discount' if the customer's discount is less than or equal to .03 and greater than .01
   - 'Small or no Discount' for all other customers
8. Using the following partial definition for a Student table, code the Select statement necessary to display all rows:

```
Create Table Student
  ( StudentID Dec(  7, 0 ) Not Null,
    Year      Char( 1    ) Not Null,
    Primary Key ( StudentID ) )
```

   For each row, show the student ID and a second character string column consisting of the following:
   - 'Lower Division' if Year = 'F' or '2'
   - 'Upper Division' if Year = 'J' or 'S'
   - 'Graduate Student' for all other Student rows

Chapter 6

Views

Chapter Overview

Chapter 3 explained how to use SQL DDL to create collections, tables, and indexes. This chapter explains how to create views, another fundamental database object. We build on the discussion of the subselect — a form of Select statement — that we introduced in Chapter 5 because subselects are a central part of a view definition.

Creating a View

A **view** is an object that appears like a table to application programs but doesn't contain any data. Instead, a view is defined over one or more base tables and provides an alternative way to access the data in the underlying base tables. You can use SQL views to

- select a subset of the rows in a base table
- include only a subset of a base table's columns
- derive new view columns based on one or more underlying base table columns
- join related rows from multiple base tables into a single row in the view

Views provide a way to simplify, as well as restrict, access to data. For example, to provide a view that contains only customers with a credit limit of at least 5000, you would execute the following statement:

```
Create View CustCrd As
  Select  *
    From  Customer
    Where CrdLimit >= 5000
```

Once you created this view, you could use it just like a table in other SQL statements. For example, you could execute the following Update statement to change the Status column for the selected rows:

```
Update CustCrd
   Set Status   = 'B'
 Where ShipCity = 'Seattle'
   And Status   = 'X'
```

(You'll learn more about the Update statement in Chapter 7.)

Notice something important about the way this Update over a view works: Only those rows that meet all three conditions — CrdLimit >= 5000, ShipCity = 'Seattle', and Status = 'X' — will have their Status set to B. When the Update statement is processed, UDB/400 accesses only rows that satisfy the CustCrd view's selection criteria. To those rows, UDB/400 then applies the Update statement's selection criteria to determine which rows to update. Although you can't define constraints (as described in Chapter 4) for views, UDB/400 enforces all constraints defined on the table (or tables) upon which a view is defined whenever you try to insert, update, or delete rows in the view. As the example above demonstrates, you can think of a view as if it were a table that contained just those rows meeting the specified criteria. You can also use views in HLL programs, as you'll see in Chapter 10.

When the Create View statement shown above is executed, UDB/400 creates an externally described, unkeyed, logical file object with one member. The file object's member and record format have the same name as the view. (Chapter 1 describes logical files, file members, and record formats.)

Components of the Create View Statement

The Create View statement is one of the most complex DDL statements in SQL, and the best way to approach it is to look at one part at a time. After the Create View keywords, you provide the view name. A view must not have the same name as any base table, other view, index, or non-SQL file in the same collection.

The next part of the Create View statement is an optional list of column names in the view. If you don't specify a list of names (as in the example above), the view has the column names of the result table defined by the **subselect** specified after the As keyword. The subselect's result table determines which columns and rows from one or more underlying tables or views are encompassed by the view being defined.

Note

Keep in mind that a result table is an SQL concept, not necessarily a real table stored on disk or in memory.

In the example above, the subselect, which is

```
Select  *
  From  Customer
  Where CrdLimit >= 5000
```

defines a result table with all the columns from the Customer base table and only those rows that have a credit limit of at least 5000.

You may notice a similarity between the subselect shown above and the Select statements we looked at in Chapter 5. A subselect is a limited form of Select statement that can use the Select statement's From, Where, Group By, and Having clauses; however, you cannot use the Order By clause in a subselect. (A subselect is also part of a fullselect, something we discuss in detail in Chapter 8.)

A subselect always begins with the Select keyword. For the simplest subselect, you follow the Select keyword with a list of column names (or * to use an implicit list of all columns) and a From clause that specifies a base table or view.[1] The following Create View statement uses a subselect that defines a result table with all the rows from the Customer table defined in Figure 6.1 but only a subset of the columns:

```
Create View CustShip As
  Select  CustID,
          ShipLine1,
          ShipLine2,
          ShipCity,
          ShipState,
          ShipPsCd1,
          ShipPsCd1,
          ShipCntry
    From  Customer
```

1 You can also specify a non-SQL, externally described physical file in a view's subselect From clause. You can't specify a non-SQL logical file, however.

Figure 6.1
Customer Table

```
Create Table Customer
     ( CustID     Dec(    7, 0 ) Not Null,
       Name       Char(  30    ) Not Null,
       ShipLine1  Char( 100    ) Not Null,
       ShipLine2  Char( 100    ) Not Null,
       ShipCity   Char(  30    ) Not Null,
       ShipState  Char(   2    ) Not Null,
       ShipPsCd1  Char(  10    ) Not Null,
       ShipPsCd2  Char(  10    ) Not Null,
       ShipCntry  Char(  30    ) Not Null,
       PhnVoice   Char(  15    ) Not Null,
       PhnFax     Char(  15    ) Not Null,
       Status     Char(   1    ) Not Null
                                 With Default ' ',
       CrdLimit   Dec(    7, 0 ) With Default Null,
       EntDate    Date           Not Null,
Primary Key( CustID ) )
```

An SQL statement referencing the CustShip view can treat the view as if it were a table with just the columns listed and with all the rows in the Customer table.

The From clause can list a view as well as a table:

```
Create View CustCrdStl As
  Select  *
    From  CustCrd
    Where ShipCity = 'Seattle'
```

UDB/400 combines (AND's) the Where clauses for a view defined over another view. Given the previous definition of the CustCrd view, this definition of the CustCrdStl view includes only those rows from the Customer table for which CrdLimit = 5000 *and* ShipCity = 'Seattle'.

A From clause can also list multiple base tables and views. For example, the following statement defines a view that joins related rows in the Customer and Sale tables defined in Figures 6.2 and 6.3, respectively:

```
Create View CustSale As
  Select  Customer.CustID,
          Customer.Name,
          Sale.OrderID,
          Sale.SaleDate,
          Sale.SaleTot
    From  Customer Join Sale
          On Customer.CustID = Sale.CustID
```

Figure 6.2
Simple Customer Table

```
Create Table Customer
  ( CustID Dec(   7, 0 ) Not Null,
    Name   Char( 30    ) Not Null,
  Primary Key( CustID ) )
```

continued

Figure 6.2 ***Continued***

CustID	Name
10001	Ajax Plumbing
10003	Picante Software
10008	Bubba's Grill

Figure 6.3
Sale Table

```
Create Table Sale
  ( OrderID   Dec( 7, 0 ) Not Null,
    SaleDate  Date        Not Null,
    SaleTot   Dec( 7, 2 ) Not Null,
    CustID    Dec( 7, 0 ) Not Null,
  Primary Key( OrderID ),
  Constraint SaleCustFK Foreign Key
    References Customer( CustID )
    On Delete Restrict
    On Update Restrict )
```

OrderID	SaleDate	SaleTot	CustID
3678	2000-02-29	567.25	10003
3679	2000-03-06	1089.00	10001
3680	2000-03-06	376.50	10008
3681	2000-03-22	2012.90	10001
3682	2000-03-23	1233.00	10001
3683	2000-04-02	440.00	10003

Figure 6.4 shows the conceptual contents of the CustSale view. (Remember, views don't actually have data content.)

Figure 6.4
CustSale View

CustID	Name	OrderID	SaleDate	SaleTot
10001	Ajax Plumbing	3679	2000-03-06	1089.00
10001	Ajax Plumbing	3681	2000-03-22	2012.90
10001	Ajax Plumbing	3682	2000-03-23	1233.00
10003	Picante Software	3678	2000-02-29	567.25
10003	Picante Software	3683	2000-04-02	440.00
10008	Bubba's Grill	3680	2000-03-06	376.50

SQL/400 views can be created over a maximum of 32 base tables, including tables listed directly on the view's first From clause as well as tables upon which views listed in the From clause are based.

When you specify multiple tables and/or views in the From clause, conceptually UDB/400 produces an intermediate result table that has all combinations of all rows from all the listed tables and views.[2] (With outer and exception joins, which we cover in Chapter 8, there may be additional rows.) Each row has all the columns from all the tables as well. From this complete set of combinations, only those rows that satisfy the condition specified after the On keyword, as well as conditions specified in the Where and/or Having clauses (if any), are included in the subselect result table. And only those columns listed after the Select keyword are in the result table. In this example, only rows with matching CustID column values are in the result table. As a consequence, the result table contains one row for each sale (with a matching customer), and each row has both sale data and customer data. Because an explicit list of columns is specified following the Select keyword, the result table has only the five columns listed.

Notice how each subselect column name in this example is qualified with the table name from which the column is taken. For example, Customer.CustID specifies that this column in the result table is the CustID column from the Customer table. To qualify a column name, you code the table or view name followed by a period (.) before the column name. You always use a period (.) — never a slash (/) — to qualify column names, regardless of whether the system or SQL naming convention is in effect.

In this example, no explicit names are specified for the view's columns, so UDB/400 uses the same unqualified names as in the result table (i.e., CustID, Name, OrderID, SaleDate, and SaleTot). If you were subsequently to refer to the CustSale view's column names using qualification, you would use CustSale.CustID, CustSale.Name, and so on. If duplicate unqualified column names exist in the subselect result table (e.g., if the result table contained both Customer.CustID and Sale.CustID), you would have to use explicit and unique column names for the view's columns, as described later.

Recall from the previous chapter that a subselect can have a Group By clause to specify aggregation. The following view contains one row for each city in which there's at least one customer, and each row has the city name and average customer discount for customers in that city:

```
Create View CustDscAvg
     ( ShipCity,
       AvgDsc )
    As Select      ShipCity,
                   Avg( Discount )
         From      Customer
         Group By  ShipCity
```

This view might have rows that look like those in the following table:[3]

ShipCity	AvgDsc
Seattle	00.056
Eugene	00.009
Portland	00.012
Richmond	00.011
Loveland	00.003
Denver	00.024

2 UDB/400 usually takes a much more efficient approach to the actual implementation of a subselect that references multiple tables. What's described here is the logical definition of how a multitable subselect works.

3 Notice in this example how a view doesn't specify a particular order to the rows. Ordering of rows in SQL is always specified when the rows are retrieved (i.e., on a Select statement), never when a base table or view is defined.

With a view like this, it wouldn't make sense to let rows be inserted or updated through the view — if that were possible, which row(s) would UDB/400 change in the Customer base table, for instance, if you updated the AvgDsc value of the Eugene row in the CustDscAvg view?

There are a variety of cases in which a view is read-only:

- those in which the main (i.e., first) From clause specifies multiple tables and/or views or specifies another read-only view
- those in which the first Select (following the As keyword) specifies the Distinct keyword or a column function, such as Max(Discount)
- those in which a nested subselect specifies the same base table as the outer subselect
- those in which the outer subselect contains a Group By or Having clause
- those in which the first Select doesn't contain at least one column that is derived directly (i.e., without an expression) from a column of the underlying base table

You can't use a read-only view as the target of an SQL Insert, Update, or Delete statement.

The CustDscAvg example above also illustrates how to code view column names explicitly. The column list (if any) immediately follows the view name and is enclosed in parentheses, with commas used to separate each column's entry. The view column names correspond positionally to the columns in the subselect result table. In this example, the correspondence is

View column name	Result table column
ShipCity	ShipCity
AvgDsc	Avg(Discount)

As with the Create Table statement, you can optionally specify both a long column name and a system column name. You could code the previous example, with both types of names, as

```
Create View CustDscAvg
    ( CustShipCity         For ShipCity,
      CustAverageDiscount  For AvgDsc )
   As Select      ShipCity,
                  Avg( Discount )
        From      Customer
        Group By  ShipCity
```

You can't specify column data types, Not Null, or Default for view columns. The data type of a view column is determined by the data type of the result table column. As we discussed in Chapter 5, SQL/400 includes several functions (e.g., Decimal, SubStr) to convert from one column data type or length to another in a derived column.

With Check Option and With Local Check Option

The final options for a Create View statement are With Check Option and With Local Check Option. (You can also code With Cascaded Check Option, which is equivalent to With Check Option.) These options restrict row insert and update operations through an updatable view that selects a subset of rows.[4] For example, the following view definition

4 You can't specify either check option with a read-only view or a view that has nested subselects.

```
Create View CustCrd As
  Select  *
    From  Customer
    Where CrdLimit >= 5000
  With Check Option
```

will not allow an Insert or Update that would create a row with CrdLimit < 5000. This restriction prevents so-called "**phantom updates**" in which a row is inserted or updated through a view but can't subsequently be retrieved through the view. When a view specifies either With Check Option or With Local Check Option and another view is defined over the view with the check option, the check option restrictions also apply to the dependent view. For example, to insert a row into the following view

```
Create View CustCrdStl As
  Select  *
    From  CustCrd
    Where ShipCity = 'Seattle'
```

the row must have CrdLimit >= 5000, regardless of whether the CustCrdStl view definition specifies With Check Option or With Local Check Option (or neither check option).

If a view defined over another view specifies With Check Option, inserts and updates must satisfy all the lower-level views' search conditions (in addition to the search condition, if any, specified on the view being defined). If a view defined over another view specifies With Local Check Option, only the search conditions of the lower-level views that specify a check option must be met.

UDB/400 does some additional processing when you insert or update rows through a view that has a direct or indirect check option, so you should be careful about using such views for file updates when performance is critical. Prior to SQL/400 support for check constraints (covered in Chapter 4), views that had a With Check option provided one means to define data integrity rules. Check constraints are a much better approach, however, because they're enforced whether the base table is updated directly or through any view.

More View Examples

Let's look at some more examples of views. The first example uses some SQL syntax features covered in Chapter 5, such as Between and In. Notice how these predicates can improve the readability of search conditions.

```
Create View CustCrd As
  Select  *
    From  Customer
    Where ShipCity <> 'Richmond'
      And CrdLimit Between 1000 And 9999
      And Status   In ( 'A', 'B', 'C' )
```

You can reorder and rename columns, as in this example:

```
Create View CustShort
     ( CsStrt,
       CsCity,
       CsSt,
       CsZip,
       CsCrRt,
       CsAttn,
       CsCnry,
       CustID )
```

continued

continued...

```
    As Select ShipLine2,
              ShipCity,
              ShipState,
              ShipPsCd1,
              ShipPsCd2,
              ShipLine1,
              ShipCntry,
              CustID
         From Customer
```

The following example illustrates how you can derive columns in an SQL view using substring and concatenation operations.

```
Create View EmpNamPhn
     ( EmpID,
       PfxVoice,
       FullName )
    As Select EmpID,
              SubStr( PhnVoice, 5, 3 ),
              FstNam ConCat MdlInl ConCat LstNam
         From Employee
```

Recall from Chapter 5 that the SQL Strip scalar function provides a way to strip trailing blanks from fixed-length character columns. The above view can be reworked to produce a FullName column that strips both leading and trailing blanks and puts a single blank between each part of the name:

```
Create View EmpNamPhn
     ( EmpID,
       PfxVoice,
       FullName )
    As Select EmpID,
              SubStr( PhnVoice, 5, 3 ),
              Strip( FstNam )   ConCat ' ' ConCat
                Strip( MdlInl ) ConCat ' ' ConCat
                Strip( LstNam )
         From Employee
```

As a final example, consider the following view consisting of a table (defined in Figure 6.5) joined with itself:

```
Create View EmpMgr
     ( EmpID,
       LstNam,
       MgrEmpID,
       MgrLstNm )
    As Select  Emp.EmpID,
               Emp.LstNam,
               Emp.MgrEmpID,
               Mgr.LstNam
         From  Employee Emp Join
               Employee Mgr
           On Emp.MgrEmpID = Mgr.EmpID
```

Figure 6.5
Employee Table

```
Create Table Employee
     ( EmpID     Dec(   7, 0 ) Not Null,
       FstNam    Char( 20    ),
       MdlInl    Char(  1    ),
       LstNam    Char( 30    ) Not Null,
       MgrEmpID  Dec(   7, 0 ),
  Constraint EmpPK Primary Key( EmpID ) )
```

EmpID	FstNam	MdlInl	LstNam	MgrEmpID
104681	Barb	L	Gibbens	898613
227504	Greg	J	Zimmerman	668466
668466	Dave	R	Bernard	709453
898613	Trish	S	Faubion	668466
899001	Rick	D	Castor	898613

The From clause for the subselect in this view lists the Employee table twice. To have unambiguous references to the appropriate role of the table (that is, either the first role, which is as the whole set of employees, or the second role, which is the set from which matching manager rows are retrieved), each Employee table reference in the From clause is followed by a **correlation name** — Emp and Mgr, respectively. The unique correlation names are used as column qualifiers instead of the ambiguous table name. You can use correlation names in any subselect, not just ones that specify a join. For nested or other long, complex subselects, short correlation names can make the SQL code more readable.[5]

Retrieving Rows from a View with a Select Statement

As we mentioned, a Select statement can retrieve rows using views as well as base tables in the From clause. When you specify a view in a Select statement, UDB/400 merges the view specifications with the Select statement specifications to produce the result table. For example, consider the view defined by the following Create View statement:

```
Create View  CustStl
  As Select  *
       From  Customer
       Where ShipCity = 'Seattle'
```

The CustStl view uses a subselect to specify that the view contains only rows from the underlying Customer table that meet the specified condition: ShipCity = 'Seattle'. You can use this view in a Select statement that further restricts the returned rows to customers who get a discount:

```
Select  *
  From  CustStl
  Where Discount > 0
```

This Select statement's result table contains only rows from the Customer table for Seattle customers who get a discount. In general, when both the view and the Select statement contain Where clauses, SQL tests the conjunction (i.e., And) of the two search conditions.

5 However, you should not use cryptic one- or two-letter correlation names just to save a few keystrokes.

Coding Suggestions

- Use check constraints defined for base tables, rather than views that specify With Check Option, to enforce data integrity. You should use With Check Option and With Local Check Option only to prevent phantom updates through a view.

Chapter Summary

A view is an SQL object defined over one or more base tables or other views that provides an alternative way to access the data in the underlying base tables. You can use views to

- select a subset of the rows in a base table
- include only a subset of a base table's columns
- derive new view columns based on one or more underlying base table columns
- join related rows from multiple base tables into a single row in the view

A subselect is a limited form of Select statement that plays a central part in view definition. A subselect is a specification of a result table with the following structure:

```
Select      select-list
   From     table-list
 [ Where    search-condition     ]
 [ Group By grouping-column-list ]
 [ Having   search-condition     ]
```

(The brackets, or [ ], indicate clauses that are optional.)

The full power of the SQL subselect is available to define views. SQL view rows do not have any ordering.

You can change table data through a view only if the view is updatable (i.e., not read-only).

The With Check Option and With Local Check Option clauses prevent "phantom updates," in which a row is inserted or updated through a view but can't subsequently be retrieved through the view.

When you execute a Select statement on a view, UDB/400 combines (ANDs) the conditions specified on the view's Where clause and the conditions specified on the Select statement.

Key Terms

correlation name
phantom update
subselect
view

Exercises

1. Code the Create View statement for a view that contains a subset of the records in the Customer table defined in Figure 6.1. Selected rows should satisfy the following conditions:
   - Status must not be X.
   - Postal Code 1 (ShipPsCd1) must be 23225, 23227, or 23229, or the credit limit (CrdLimit) must be between 500 and 1000 (inclusive).
   - The view should have the same columns as the Customer table.

2. Code the Create View statement for a view called CustStatusCount that is based on the Customer table defined in Figure 6.1. There should be one row for each Status code that occurs in the table, containing the following columns:
   - Status
   - NumCustWthStatus (i.e., the number of Customer rows with that status)

   For example, if there are 1,234 Customer rows with status A, there will be a row in your view where Status = A and NumCustWthStatus will be 1234.

3. Explain why you think SQL/400 views that are based on more than one table are read-only.

Chapter 7

Insert, Update, and Delete Statements

Chapter Overview

In this chapter, we explain the three main SQL DML statements used to modify table contents: Insert, Update, and Delete. The Insert statement lets you add new rows to a table. Update lets you change the contents of a row or set of rows. Delete lets you remove rows from a table.

Using DML to Modify Table Data

SQL has three DML statements that can be used to change table data: Insert, Update, and Delete. All three statements can modify either a single row in a table or a set of rows in a table. None of the statements can modify more than one table in a single statement. All three statements let you use a Where clause to specify the set of rows to be inserted, updated, or deleted. The general form of the Where clause in these statements parallels the form in the Select statement described in Chapters 5 and 8.

You can specify an updatable view rather than a base table in an Insert, Update, or Delete statement. To be updatable, a view must be created over a single base table or updatable view, and the view's outer Select cannot use column functions, the Distinct, Group By, or Having clauses, or an inner subselect (e.g., in a Where clause) that specifies the same base table as the outer Select. An updatable view must also have at least one column that is derived directly (i.e., without an expression) from a column of the underlying base table.

The Insert Statement

To add a new row to a table, you use the **Insert** statement. For example, to add a new customer, you enter

```
Insert Into Customer
         ( CustID,
           Name,
           ShipCity,
           Discount )
  Values ( 678987,
           'Atlas Inc.',
           'Portland',
           Null )
```

A column list in parentheses follows the table name, and the Values clause specifies a list of new values, also in parentheses, for the columns that correspond positionally in the column list. You can omit the column list, in which case the implicit column list is all columns in the order they were defined by Create Table (or Create View) and Alter Table DDL statements. Omitting the column list is not generally a good practice, however, because it's error-prone and provides poor documentation.

You must insert a value for any column that specifies Not Null and that doesn't have an explicit default (e.g., the Default clause was not specified on the Create Table statement). A column's default value (or null, as explained in Chapter 3) is used for any base table column not specified on the Insert statement.

The example above illustrates the use of the Null keyword to set the Discount column to null. Of course, a column that is set to null must have been defined without the Not Null clause. You can use the Default keyword to insert a column's default value:

```
Insert Into Customer
          ( CustID,
            Name,
            ShipCity,
            Discount )
  Values  ( 678987,
            'Atlas Inc.',
            'Portland',
            Default )
```

A *multirow* Insert copies data from one table to another and implements the closest SQL equivalent to the relational assignment operation discussed in Chapter 18. For example, the following Insert copies all rows from an old version of a customer table to a new version that has an additional column, ShipState:

```
Insert Into Customer
       ( CustID,
         Name,
         ShipCity,
         Discount,
         ShipState )
  Select CustID,
         Name,
         ShipCity,
         Discount,
         ' '
    From CustOld
```

Initially, all rows in the new table have a blank ShipState column because the result table for the Select includes the ' ' literal as the final element in its select list.

Although the Insert statement can add rows to only a single table, the inserted rows can be constructed from more than one table. For example, the following Create Table and Insert statements make a temporary copy of combined customer and sale information:

```
Create Table TmpSale
  ( OrderID Decimal(  7, 0 ),
    TotAmt  Decimal( 11, 2 ),
    Name    Char(    30    ) )

Insert Into TmpSale
        ( OrderID,
          TotAmt,
          Name )
  Select  OrderID,
          TotAmt,
          Name
    From  Customer
            Join
          Sale
            On Customer.CustID = Sale.CustID
```

After the Insert statement is executed, changes to the data in the Customer or Sale table are not reflected in the TmpSale table. A multirow insert, unlike a view, copies the data from the tables referenced in the From clause.

As the previous two examples show, you can use a form of the Select statement within an Insert statement to specify the rows to be inserted. This nested Select statement can use all the clauses and operators (e.g., From, Where, Group By, Having, Order By, and Union) discussed in Chapters 5 and 8.

If the target is a view, only insert-capable columns can be assigned values. A view column is not insert-capable if it's a literal, an expression, or a scalar function. You also can't insert values into more than one column derived from the same base table column. When you use a view, any base table column not present as an updatable column in the view must have a default value, as discussed earlier, and the new row gets this default value for the column.

The Update Statement

You can update a specific row by using its primary key value in the Where clause of an **Update** statement and assigning new values to one or more columns. For example, the following Update statement changes the name and adds 2 percent to a customer's current discount:

```
Update  Customer
  Set   Name     = 'Wood Products',
        Discount = Discount + .02
  Where CustID = 905011
```

You can update a *set* of rows by using a search condition that specifies more than one row. An Update with no Where clause or with a Where clause that specifies a search condition is known as a **searched Update** because UDB/400 searches for the rows to be updated. (Using an embedded SQL cursor, there's also a positioned Update, in which you first retrieve the row you want to update and then specify Where Current Of *cursor-name* in an Update statement that updates the current row. Chapter 11 covers cursors and positioned Update statements.)

The following statement gives all Portland customers a 10 percent discount.

```
Update  Customer
  Set   Discount = .10
  Where ShipCity = 'Portland'
```

If you don't specify a Where clause, all rows in the specified table are updated.

You can set a null-capable column to null by using the Null keyword:

```
Update  Customer
  Set   Discount = Null
  Where ShipCity = 'Portland'
```

To set a column to its default value (if one is defined), you can use the Default keyword:

```
Update  Customer
  Set   Discount = Default
  Where ShipCity = 'Portland'
```

The right side of the Set clause can also be a **scalar subselect** — that is, a subselect that returns one column and no more than one row. The Update statement

```
Update Customer
  Set  CreditLimit =
       ( Select Avg( TotAmt ) * 1.10
           From Sale )
```

sets every customer's credit limit to the current average sale amount (of all sales) plus 10 percent. The subselect can contain references to columns in the target table (e.g., Customer), in which case all values used in the subselect are from the table *before* it is updated. If the subselect returns no row, the updated column is set to null. If the subselect returns more than one row, UDB/400 generates an exception.

Set Clause Variations

There are several alternative forms of the Set clause that you can use. In the first of these, you group column names and values into two lists, similar to the form used for an Insert statement:

```
Update   Customer
  Set (  CustID,
         Name,
         ShipCity,
         Discount ) =
       ( 905011,
         'Wood Products',
         'Roseburg',
         Discount = Discount + .02 )
 Where CustID = 905011
```

This form also allows a *single-row* subselect on the right-hand side:

```
Update   Customer
  Set (       CreditLimit,
              Discount ) =
  ( Select    CreditLimit,
              Discount
      From    CrdDiscLimits
      Where   Customer.CreditRating =
              CrdDiscLimits.CreditRating )
```

In this example, each Customer row has a CreditRating column, which is used as a "lookup" value in the CrdDiscLimits table. Based on each customer's credit rating, the respective credit limit and discount columns are set to values from the CrdDiscLimits table. When you use this form of Update, the subselect must have the same number of columns in the result table as exist in the Set clause column list. If the subselect returns no row, the updated columns are set to null. If the subselect returns more than one row, UDB/400 generates an exception.

You can use another form of the Set clause to assign values to *all* the columns in selected rows of a base table or view:

```
Update   Customer
  Set    Row = ( 905011,
                 'Wood Products',
                 'Roseburg',
                 Discount = Discount + .02 )
 Where CustID = 905011
```

With this form of Set, you use the Row keyword and a list of values that correspond positionally to the table (or view) columns in the order they were defined by Create Table (or Create View) and Alter Table DDL statements. This form isn't commonly used because in SQL it's most efficient to update only columns that have new values. Using explicit column names also is less error-prone.

To update multiple tables, you must use more than one DML statement. For example, to increase the hourly rate of both employees and contractors, you would use two statements:

```
Update Employee
  Set  HourlyRate = HourlyRate * 1.05

Update Contractor
  Set  HourlyRate = HourlyRate * 1.05
```

When you perform an update, you must take constraints (primary key, unique, foreign key, and check constraints) into consideration. For example, to change a customer's ID, you must be sure the CustID column value is changed in the Customer table's row as well as in all rows in tables that use CustID as a foreign key. If no foreign key constraints exist, you can just use multiple Update statements, such as

```
Update Customer
  Set   CustID = 123789
  Where CustID = 888402

Update Sale
  Set   CustID = 123789
  Where CustID = 888402
```

But if the Sale table has a foreign key constraint specified for the CustID column, both statements cause an error because either statement by itself would result in unmatched Sale rows.[1] UDB/400 doesn't support a Cascade option for the foreign key Update action (as it does for the Delete action), so you can't use that technique to automatically update the Sale table rows when a Customer row's CustID is updated. One solution is the UDB/400 trigger program facility, which can be used to implement an ad hoc "cascade" for primary key updates. Chapter 16 discusses trigger programs.

The Delete Statement

To remove a row from a table, you enter a **Delete** statement such as

```
Delete
  From  Customer
  Where CustID = 905011
```

You can delete a set of rows from a single table using a search condition that specifies more than one row. As with the Update statement, this type of Delete is known as a **searched Delete**:

```
Delete
  From  Customer
  Where ShipCity = 'Portland'
```

SQL also has a positioned Delete, which we discuss in Chapter 11.

You can clear all rows from a table — intentionally or accidentally — by entering a Delete statement with no Where clause:

```
Delete
  From Customer
```

Naturally, you may want to check interactive Delete statements carefully before you press the Enter key.[2] Note that after you clear all rows from a table, the table still exists; it's just an empty table. To clear and delete a table from the catalog, you use the Drop statement (covered in Chapter 3).

As we discussed for the Update statement, if you want to delete rows from multiple tables, you must execute multiple Delete statements. You can use a foreign key constraint with a Delete Cascade

1 Technically, the update to Sale rows might not fail if there were already a Customer row with CustID = 123789. But the Customer row would normally be updated first to ensure that the new CustID value isn't a duplicate of some existing Customer row's CustID.

Of course, one way to accomplish this sequence is to insert a new Customer row that's identical to the current Customer row except for a new CustID value, then update the CustID value for all the associated Sale rows, and then delete the old Customer row.

2 ISQL requires you to confirm an Update or Delete statement that has no Where clause.

rule to delete all dependent rows along with a parent row. Thus, given the Customer and Sale table definitions in Figures 7.1 and 7.2, the statement

```
Delete
  From  Customer
  Where CustID = 499320
```

deletes one Customer row and three Sale rows.

Figure 7.1

Sample Customer Base Table

```
Create Table Customer
     ( CustID    Dec(    7, 0 ) Not Null,
       Name      Char( 30     ) Not Null,
       ShipCity Char( 30     ),
       Discount Dec(    5, 3 ),
  Primary Key( CustID ) )
```

CustID	Name	ShipCity	Discount
133568	Smith Mfg.	Portland	.050
246900	Bolt Co.	Eugene	.020
275978	Ajax Inc.	Albany	<null>
499320	Adapto	Portland	.000
499921	Bell Bldg.	Eugene	.100
518980	Floradel	Seattle	.000
663456	Alpine Inc.	Seattle	.010
681065	Telez Co.	Albany	.000
687309	Nautilus	Portland	.050
781010	Udapto Mfg.	Seattle	.000
888402	Seaworthy	Albany	.010
890003	AA Products	Portland	.010
905011	Wood Bros.	Eugene	.010

Figure 7.2
Sample Sale Base Table

```
Create Table Sale
     ( OrderID  Dec(  7, 0 ) Not Null,
       CustID   Dec(  7, 0 ) Not Null,
       TotAmt   Dec( 11, 2 ) Not Null,
       SaleDate Date         Not Null,
       ShipDate Date,
  Constraint SalePK      Primary Key( OrderID ),
  Constraint SaleCustFK Foreign Key( CustID  )
    References Customer ( CustID )
    On Delete Cascade
    On Update Restrict )
```

OrderID	CustID	TotAmt	SaleDate	ShipDate
234112	499320	35.00	2000-05-01	2000-05-15
234113	888402	278.75	2000-05-01	2000-05-04
234114	499320	78.90	2000-05-03	<null>
234115	890003	1000.00	2000-05-04	2000-05-10
234116	246900	678.00	2000-05-04	2000-05-08
234117	133568	550.00	2000-05-05	2000-05-08
234118	905011	89.50	2000-05-05	2000-05-10
234119	499320	201.00	2000-05-05	<null>
234120	246900	399.70	2000-05-06	2000-05-08

Coding Suggestions

- Store most DML statements to perform production (dynamic) Insert, Update, and Delete statements in source members, and execute them using the RunSqlStm (Run SQL Statement) command.
- Use a source file with a meaningful source file name, such as SqlDmlSrc.
- Use the name (or abbreviation) of the SQL table or view you're updating as part of the source member name (e.g., DltOldCust).
- Enter a source member description that describes the action taken and includes the name of the table or view.
- Place comments at the beginning of your SQL source to describe the action taken.
- Use spaces, blank lines, and separator line comments to improve the readability of your source code.
- Align the beginning and continuation of each clause (e.g., the columns listed in an Update statement's Set clause).
- Align column names, expressions, compound search conditions, and so on in multiline statements for readability.
- Consider null-capable columns when specifying expressions, functions, and search conditions.
- Be sure that a subselect used on the right-hand side of the Set clause in an Update statement can never have more than one row.

- Use an explicit list of columns in the Insert statement to make clear which column each new value corresponds to.
- Be careful to include a Where clause in an Update or Delete statement unless you intend to update or delete all rows in the table.
- Whenever updating or inserting a row into a table, be certain to adhere to check constraints defined on the table.
- Be sure to consider the effect of primary key, unique, and foreign key constraints when updating a primary key, unique, or foreign key column or when deleting a row in a table referenced by a foreign key.

Chapter Summary

The Insert, Update, and Delete statements are the SQL DML statements used to manipulate table rows. With the Insert statement, you can insert a single row using the Values clause or insert multiple rows using a nested form of the Select statement.

The Update statement lets you change the contents of one or more columns by specifying new values in a Set clause. The right-hand side of a Set clause assignment can be any expression (including a scalar subselect) that is compatible with the data type of the column being updated. The Set clause also has several variations that use column lists and/or a list of expressions or a multi-column subselect. You can use a Where clause in an Update or a Delete statement to specify which subset of rows is changed or deleted. In both cases, if you omit the Where clause, all rows in the table are updated or deleted.

Key Terms

Delete statement
Insert statement
scalar subselect
searched Delete
searched Update
Update statement

Exercises

1. Show the Insert statements to add to the Customer table in Figure 7.1 two new customers with the following values:

Customer ID	Name	ShipCity	Discount
906785	Humble Bagel	Oakridge	0.010
907744	New Frontier Market	Pendleton	<null>

2. Show the Update statement to reduce all customers' discounts to half of their current rate.
3. Using the sample data in Figure 7.1, show the Update statement to change the name of the customer Alpine Inc. to Rocky Mountain Sports Inc.

   Hint: As a general solution, be sure you consider the unlikely — but possible — case in which two customers might have the same name.
4. Show the Delete statement to delete all customers with a null discount. Given the definition of the Sale table in Figure 7.2, what will happen to rows in the Sale table for the deleted customers?
5. Show the Update statement to assign the customer whose CustID is 257978 a discount that's equal to the average of all discounts for all customers. Use the table definition in Figure 7.1.

Chapter 8

Advanced DML Statement Features

Chapter Overview

In Chapters 5 and 7, we covered the basics of Data Manipulation Language (DML). This chapter continues that discussion with more advanced DML features. We start by describing SQL/400's support for casting between different data types. Then we explore a range of more complex queries, beginning with the use of subqueries in basic, In, Exists, and quantified predicates. We also look at how the Join and Union operators can combine rows from multiple tables and views. And you'll see how nested and common table expressions can be used to simplify queries and reduce the need for views or temporary tables. Last, we introduce a type of user-defined function, known as a sourced function, that lets you apply SQL's built-in functions to user-defined data types.

Casting Between Data Types

SQL treats every column and literal as a specific data type (e.g., Character). Whenever you compare two values, assign a value to a column, use a value in an expression, or pass an argument to a function or procedure, SQL makes sure that the value has an appropriate data type. For example, you can't directly concatenate a Decimal(5, 3) column with a character literal; SQL would prevent the following Update statement:

```
Select 'Discount is ' ConCat
       Discount
  From Customer
```

SQL does, however, provide **cast expressions** that can convert data from one type to another, as long as the conversion is reasonable. Two forms of casting expressions exist. The first uses the Cast keyword, as shown in the following example:

```
Select 'Discount is ' ConCat
       Cast( Discount As Char(7) )
  From Customer
```

Following the Cast keyword, you code, within parentheses, the value to be converted (e.g., the Discount column) and the data type to which the value is to be converted (e.g., Char(7)). Be sure the value to be cast is valid. For example, when you cast a character string to one of the numeric types, the character string must be a valid number. The following cast is valid:

```
Cast( '123' As Integer )
```

But this cast causes an error:

```
Cast( 'ABC' As Integer )
```

As an alternative to the Cast keyword, you can use the name of the target data type as a casting function in most situations. Here's another example of casting a Decimal(5, 3) column to a character string:

```
Select 'Discount is ' ConCat Char( Discount )
  From Customer
```

In this example, the Char function returns a character string with a maximum length two characters longer than the precision of the Discount column. One character is for a leading minus sign, and the other is for a decimal point.

SQL/400 allows only certain casts; Figure 8.1 shows a complete list of allowable casts between all built-in data types.

Figure 8.1

Allowable Casting Between Built-In Data Types

Source data type	SmallInt, Int, BigInt	Dec	Real, Double	Char, VarChar, Clob	Graphic, VarGraphic, DbClob	Date	Time	Timestamp	Blob	DataLink
SmallInt	Y	Y	Y	Y	N	N	N	N	N	N
Int	Y	Y	Y	Y	N	N	N	N	N	N
BigInt	Y	Y	Y	Y	N	N	N	N	N	N
Dec	Y	Y	Y	Y	N	N	N	N	N	N
Numeric	Y	Y	Y	Y	N	N	N	N	N	N
Real	Y	Y	Y	Y	N	N	N	N	N	N
Double, Float	Y	Y	Y	Y	N	N	N	N	N	N
Char	Y	Y	Y	Y	UCS-2 only	Y	Y	Y	Y	N
VarChar, Long VarChar	Y	Y	Y	Y	UCS-2 only	Y	Y	Y	Y	N
Clob	Y	Y	Y	Y	UCS-2 only	Y	Y	Y	Y	N
Graphic	Y	N	N	UCS-2 only	Y	N	N	N	Y	N
VarGraphic, Long VarGraphic	Y	N	N	UCS-2 only	Y	N	N	N	Y	N
DbClob	Y	N	N	UCS-2 only	Y	N	N	N	Y	N
Date	N	N	N	Y	N	Y	N	Y	N	N
Time	N	N	N	Y	N	N	Y	Y	N	N
Timestamp	N	N	N	Y	N	Y	Y	Y	N	N
Blob	N	N	N	N	N	N	N	N	Y	N
DataLink	N	N	N	N	N	N	N	N	N	Y

Note that you can always cast a value to its own data type (for example, to change the size of a Character or Decimal variable).

Distinct data types (also referred to as user-defined data types, or UDTs), which we discussed in Chapter 3, have their own set of casting rules. Recall that a distinct type is always based on one of the built-in data types. You can cast a distinct type to its based-on data type and vice versa. SQL/400 also supports a variety of data type *promotions*, as listed in Figure 8.2.

Figure 8.2
Promotable Built-In Data Types

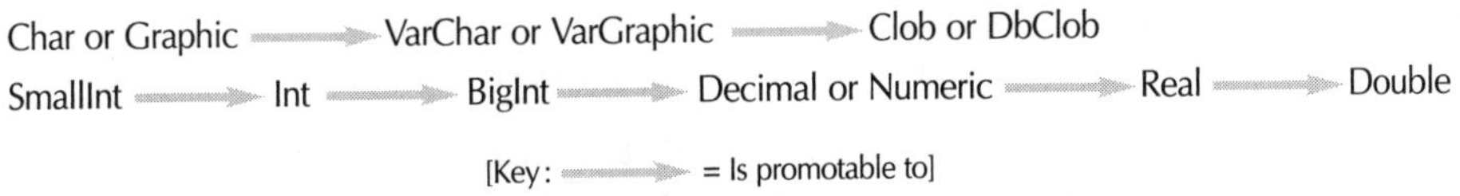

Char or Graphic → VarChar or VarGraphic → Clob or DbClob
SmallInt → Int → BigInt → Decimal or Numeric → Real → Double

[Key: → = Is promotable to]

For example, a SmallInt value can be promoted to the Integer, BigInt, Decimal, Numeric, Real, or Double data type. As a consequence, you can also cast a SmallInt value to a distinct type that's based on the Integer data type. In general, you can cast a built-in type to a distinct type based on a built-in data type to which the value you're casting can be promoted. You can also make the following casts of built-in data types:

Built-in data type	Can be cast to a distinct type with based-on type
Integer	SmallInt
Double	Real
VarChar	Char
VarGraphic	Graphic

Subqueries

In Chapters 5 and 6, we discussed several kinds of predicates and introduced the form of Select statement known as a subselect. Recall that a subselect begins with the Select keyword followed by a list of columns or expressions, a From clause, and optional Where, Group By, and Having clauses. A subselect doesn't allow an Order By clause (or a Union operator, which we cover later in this chapter). Here, we continue our discussion of predicates and subselects, explaining how a **subquery** can be used with a variety of predicates.

A subquery is a subselect that is part of a search condition (i.e., is used in a Where or Having clause). The following Select statement displays all customers who have an above-average discount:

```
Select  CustID,
        Name
  From  Customer
  Where Discount > ( Select Avg( Discount )
                       From Customer )
```

In this example, the subquery is

```
Select Avg( Discount )
  From Customer
```

This subquery defines a result table with a single row and one column, which contains the average discount for all customers. The search condition in the outer Select statement then compares each customer's discount to the average discount and includes in the Select statement's result table only those Customer rows with a Discount column value greater than the average.

You can also use subqueries in an Update, Delete, or Insert statement search condition. The following Update statement uses a subquery to select rows to be updated. The statement increases to 10 percent the discount of customers who currently get less than a 10 percent discount and who have placed orders with a grand-total amount greater than 1000:

```
Update  Customer
  Set   Discount = .10
  Where ( Discount < .10 Or Discount Is Null )
    And 1000 < ( Select  Sum( TotAmt )
                 From    Sale
                 Where Sale.CustID = Customer.CustID )
```

Note that if a subquery in an Update, Delete, or Insert statement's search condition refers to the same table that's being updated, the subquery is evaluated completely before any rows are updated.

Basic Predicate with Subquery

The search conditions in the previous two examples illustrate another form of the **basic predicate** (which we introduced in Chapter 5). This form uses a subselect to provide one of the values being compared. In general, a basic predicate can have the form

expression θ (*subselect*)

where *expression* is a column name, a literal, or some valid arithmetic, string, or other form of expression and θ is one of the logical comparison operators in Figure 8.3.

Figure 8.3

SQL Comparison Operators

Operator	Meaning
=	Equal
<>	Not equal
<	Less than
<=	Less than or equal
>	Greater than
>=	Greater than or equal

The subselect in a basic predicate must be **scalar** — that is, it must specify exactly one column and produce a result table with no more than one row. If the subquery returns no rows, it's treated as null and the basic predicate's value is unknown.

In Predicate with Subquery

You can also use a subquery in another form of the **In predicate** (introduced in Chapter 5) to define the set of values to be compared:

```
Select  CustID,
        Name
  From  Customer
  Where ShipCity In ( Select City
                        From  Warehouse )
```

In this example, the subquery produces a result table with at least one row for each city in which there's a warehouse. Rows from the Customer table are then selected only if their ShipCity column contains one of the cities in the subquery's result table. The Select statement's final result table contains only those customers who are in the same city as a warehouse. Note that an In predicate's subquery must specify a result table with just one column. You also can specify the Not keyword before the In predicate to negate the test.

Exists Predicate and Correlated Subquery

The **Exists predicate** is one form of SQL predicate that *requires* a subquery. The syntax is

```
Exists (subselect)
```

This predicate is true if the subselect's result table contains one or more rows; otherwise, the predicate is false. The value of an Exists predicate is never unknown (i.e., never null). The subselect's select list can specify any number of columns, but the column values are ignored, so generally you just use an asterisk (*) after the Select keyword. You can specify the Not keyword before the Exists predicate; in that case, the value of the negated predicate will be true only if the subselect's result table is empty.

The following predicate is true if and only if there is at least one customer in Seattle:

```
Exists ( Select  *
           From  Customer
           Where ShipCity = 'Seattle' )
```

This example may not appear very practical because it just tells us whether there are any customers in Seattle, which won't be very useful as part of a search condition.[1] Figure 8.4 shows a more useful example of the Exists predicate.

Figure 8.4

A Subselect Using a Not Exists Predicate

```
Select  Customer.CustID,
        Customer.Name
  From  Customer
  Where Not Exists
        ( Select  *
            From  Sale
            Where Sale.CustID = Customer.CustID )
```

The subselect used in Figure 8.4's search condition is known as a **correlated subquery** because the inner subselect (the one following Not Exists) refers to Customer.CustID, which is a reference to a column of a table specified in the outer subselect.[2] Thus, the evaluation of the inner subselect is correlated to the outer subselect's current row. Later in this chapter, you'll see how you can produce the same result table using an exception join.

A close look at this example can help clarify both correlated subqueries and the usefulness of the Exists predicate. The example's Exists predicate answers the question "Do any sales exist for this customer?" If the answer is No, the search condition (Not Exists...) is true and the customer is selected. This Exists predicate tests whether the customer has any sales by using a subquery that defines a result table containing all the Sale rows for the customer. If this set of rows isn't empty, the Exists predicate is true — the customer has one or more sales.

The result table with the customer's sales is defined by the subquery

```
Select  *
  From  Sale
  Where Sale.CustID = Customer.CustID
```

1 If we want an answer to how many customers are in Seattle, we can just use

```
Select  Count( * )
  From  Customer
  Where ShipCity = 'Seattle'
```

2 This type of reference is known as a *correlated reference*.

Because we're interested only in whether or not the result table contains any rows, we use * to specify an implicit list of columns rather than listing explicit column names. The search condition we use for this subselect is quite simple: A Sale row is included in the subselect's result table if its CustID column contains the same customer ID as the current Customer row being tested in the outer subselect. You can think of SQL executing the following algorithm for the complete Select statement:

```
For all Customer rows
    Set CurCustID = Customer.CustID
    Set TmpSaleResultTable to Empty (remove all rows)
    For all Sale rows
        If Sale.CustID = CurCustID
            Add Sale row to TmpSaleResultTable
        EndIf
    EndFor
    If TmpSaleResultTable is Empty
        Add Customer row to final result table
    EndIf
EndFor
```

Although SQL/400 doesn't necessarily use this algorithm to carry out the Select statement, the algorithm provides a logical way to understand a correlated subquery's result.

Quantified Predicate

The **quantified predicate** is another kind of SQL predicate that requires a subquery. The syntax is

expression θ *quantifier* (*subselect*)

The comparison operator can be any of those listed in Figure 8.3. The quantifier can be either of the keywords All or Any[3].

The following example selects Customer rows that have a discount greater than all the Portland customers:

```
Select   CurCust.CustID
  From   Customer CurCust
  Where  CurCust.Discount > All
         ( Select   CityCust.Discount
             From   Customer CityCust
             Where  CityCust.ShipCity = 'Portland'
               And  CityCust.Discount Is Not Null )
```

This example's > All quantified predicate is true if the subquery's result table is empty or if the current customer's discount is greater than all the values in the subquery's result table. The subselect used in a quantified predicate must have only one column, and the comparison test is applied to each value in the subselect's result table.

In general, a predicate with the All quantifier is

- true if the subselect's result table is empty or the comparison test is true for all values in the result table
- false if the comparison test is false for at least one value in the result table
- unknown if the comparison test doesn't evaluate to false for at least one value in the result table and the comparison test is unknown for at least one value in the result table

3 The Some keyword can be used as a synonym for Any.

A predicate with the Any quantifier is

- true if the comparison test is true for at least one value in the result table
- false if the subselect's result table is empty or the comparison test is false for all values in the result table
- unknown if the comparison test doesn't evaluate to true for at least one value in the result table and the comparison test is unknown for at least one value in the result table

When you code a quantified predicate, be careful not to confuse informal ways of expressing a condition in English with the specific meanings of the All and Any quantifiers. For example, you might hear someone ask for a list of "customers who have a bigger discount than any of the Portland customers." But if you use the following Select statement

```
Select  CurCust.CustID
  From  Customer CurCust
  Where CurCust.Discount > Any
        ( Select  CityCust.Discount
            From  Customer CityCust
            Where CityCust.ShipCity = 'Portland'
              And CityCust.Discount Is Not Null )
```

the retrieved list would include all customers who have a discount greater than the lowest discount of any Portland customer. This list obviously might include some customers in Portland (those who have a discount that isn't the lowest among Portland customers). Using the All quantifier (as in the previous example) retrieves customers who have a discount greater than the highest discount of any Portland customer — which, of course, excludes all Portland customers.[4]

Joins

A subselect's From clause can list up to 256 tables and views (128 before V4R5). (The subselect in an SQL view is limited to 32 tables.) If you list more than one table or view in the From clause (without a Join operator), the Select statement is executed as if you had specified a single table that has all the columns from the specified tables and all possible combinations of rows from the tables (i.e., the Cartesian product of the two tables). This potentially large intermediate table isn't always created when you execute a multitable Select statement, but that's the simplest way to think about what happens. For example, the two tables in Figures 8.5 and 8.6 can be used in the following Select statement:

```
Select *
  From Customer,
       Sale
```

4 A simpler approach to this Select statement would be to use the following basic predicate:

```
Select  CurCust.CustID
  From  Customer CurCust
  Where CurCust.Discount > ( Select  Max( CityCust.Discount )
                               From  Customer CityCust
                               Where CityCust.ShipCity = 'Portland' )
```

Figure 8.5

Sample Customer Table

```
Create Table Customer
     ( CustID   Dec(   7, 0 ) Not Null,
       Name     Char( 30    ) Not Null,
       ShipCity Char( 30    ),
       Discount Dec(   5, 3 ),
  Primary Key( CustID ) )
```

CustID	Name	ShipCity	Discount
133568	Smith Mfg.	Portland	.050
246900	Bolt Co.	Eugene	.020
275978	Ajax Inc.	Albany	<null>
499320	Adapto	Portland	.000
499921	Bell Bldg.	Eugene	.100
518980	Floradel	Seattle	.000
663456	Alpine Inc.	Seattle	.010
681065	Telez Co.	Albany	.000
687309	Nautilus	Portland	.050
781010	Udapto Mfg.	Seattle	.000
888402	Seaworthy	Albany	.010
890003	AA Products	Portland	.010
905011	Wood Bros.	Eugene	.010

Figure 8.6

Sample Sale Base Table

```
Create Table Sale
     ( OrderID  Dec(  7, 0 ) Not Null,
       CustID   Dec(  7, 0 ) Not Null,
       TotAmt   Dec( 11, 2 ) Not Null,
       SaleDate Date         Not Null,
       ShipDate Date,
  Constraint SalePK      Primary Key( OrderID ),
  Constraint SaleCustFK Foreign Key( CustID  )
    References Customer ( CustID )
    On Delete Cascade
    On Update Restrict )
```

OrderID	CustID	TotAmt	SaleDate	ShipDate
234112	499320	35.00	2000-05-01	2000-05-15
234113	888402	278.75	2000-05-01	2000-05-04
234114	499320	78.90	2000-05-03	<null>
234115	890003	1000.00	2000-05-04	2000-05-10
234116	246900	678.00	2000-05-04	2000-05-08
234117	133568	550.00	2000-05-05	2000-05-08
234118	905011	89.50	2000-05-05	2000-05-10
234119	499320	201.00	2000-05-05	<null>
234120	246900	399.70	2000-05-06	2000-05-08

The result (Figure 8.7) isn't very useful because some rows combine information from unrelated customers and sales.

Figure 8.7

Sample Retrieval Using Cross Product

```
<------  Customer table columns ------> <--------------- Sale table columns ----------->
CustID   Name          ShipCity Discount OrderID  CustID    TotAmt    SaleDate      ShipDate
133568   Smith Mfg.    Portland   .050   234112   499320     35.00    2000-05-01    2000-05-15
133568   Smith Mfg.    Portland   .050   234113   888402    278.75    2000-05-01    2000-05-04
133568   Smith Mfg.    Portland   .050   234114   499320     78.90    2000-05-03    <null>
133568   Smith Mfg.    Portland   .050   234115   890003  1,000.00    2000-05-04    2000-05-10
133568   Smith Mfg.    Portland   .050   234116   246900    678.00    2000-05-04    2000-05-08
133568   Smith Mfg.    Portland   .050   234117   133568    550.00    2000-05-05    2000-05-08
133568   Smith Mfg.    Portland   .050   234118   905011     89.50    2000-05-05    2000-05-10
133568   Smith Mfg.    Portland   .050   234119   499320    201.00    2000-05-05    <null>
133568   Smith Mfg.    Portland   .050   234120   246900    399.70    2000-05-06    2000-05-08
246900   Bolt Co.      Eugene     .020   234112   499320     35.00    2000-05-01    2000-05-15
246900   Bolt Co.      Eugene     .020   234113   888402    278.75    2000-05-01    2000-05-04
246900   Bolt Co.      Eugene     .020   234114   499320     78.90    2000-05-03    <null>
246900   Bolt Co.      Eugene     .020   234115   890003  1,000.00    2000-05-04    2000-05-10
246900   Bolt Co.      Eugene     .020   234116   246900    678.00    2000-05-04    2000-05-08
246900   Bolt Co.      Eugene     .020   234117   133568    550.00    2000-05-05    2000-05-08
246900   Bolt Co.      Eugene     .020   234118   905011     89.50    2000-05-05    2000-05-10
246900   Bolt Co.      Eugene     .020   234119   499320    201.00    2000-05-05    <null>
246900   Bolt Co.      Eugene     .020   234120   246900    399.70    2000-05-06    2000-05-08
275978   Ajax Inc.     Albany   <null>   234112   499320     35.00    2000-05-01    2000-05-15
275978   Ajax Inc.     Albany   <null>   234113   888402    278.75    2000-05-01    2000-05-04
275978   Ajax Inc.     Albany   <null>   234114   499320     78.90    2000-05-03    <null>
275978   Ajax Inc.     Albany   <null>   234115   890003  1,000.00    2000-05-04    2000-05-10
275978   Ajax Inc.     Albany   <null>   234116   246900    678.00    2000-05-04    2000-05-08
275978   Ajax Inc.     Albany   <null>   234117   133568    550.00    2000-05-05    2000-05-08
275978   Ajax Inc.     Albany   <null>   234118   905011     89.50    2000-05-05    2000-05-10
275978   Ajax Inc.     Albany   <null>   234119   499320    201.00    2000-05-05    <null>
275978   Ajax Inc.     Albany   <null>   234120   246900    399.70    2000-05-06    2000-05-08
499320   Adapto        Portland   .000   234112   499320     35.00    2000-05-01    2000-05-15
499320   Adapto        Portland   .000   234113   888402    278.75    2000-05-01    2000-05-04
```

omitted rows ...

```
890003   AA Products   Portland   .010   234119   499320    201.00    2000-05-05    <null>
890003   AA Products   Portland   .010   234120   246900    399.70    2000-05-06    2000-05-08
905011   Wood Bros.    Eugene     .010   234112   499320     35.00    2000-05-01    2000-05-15
905011   Wood Bros.    Eugene     .010   234113   888402    278.75    2000-05-01    2000-05-04
905011   Wood Bros.    Eugene     .010   234114   499320     78.90    2000-05-03    <null>
905011   Wood Bros.    Eugene     .010   234115   890003  1,000.00    2000-05-04    2000-05-10
905011   Wood Bros.    Eugene     .010   234116   246900    678.00    2000-05-04    2000-05-08
905011   Wood Bros.    Eugene     .010   234117   133568    550.00    2000-05-05    2000-05-08
905011   Wood Bros.    Eugene     .010   234118   905011     89.50    2000-05-05    2000-05-10
905011   Wood Bros.    Eugene     .010   234119   499320    201.00    2000-05-05    <null>
905011   Wood Bros.    Eugene     .010   234120   246900    399.70    2000-05-06    2000-05-08
```

But if you use a select list and use a Join operator in the From clause, you get a very useful table:

```
Select Sale.OrderID,
       Sale.CustID,
       Customer.Name
  From Customer
         Join
       Sale
         On Sale.CustID = Customer.CustID
```

The resulting table (Figure 8.8) provides a list with the customer ID and name for each sale.

Figure 8.8

Sample Retrieval Using Join

OrderID	CustID	Name
234112	499320	Adapto
234113	888402	Seaworthy
234114	499320	Adapto
234115	890003	AA Products
234116	246900	Bolt Co.
234117	133568	Smith Mfg.
234118	905011	Wood Bros.
234119	499320	Adapto
234120	246900	Bolt Co.

You can define this same result table without a Join operator by specifying a Where clause:

```
Select  Sale.OrderID,
        Sale.CustID,
        Customer.Name
  From  Customer, Sale
  Where Sale.CustID = Customer.CustID
```

Although this programming idiom was widely used before the introduction of the Join operator, the Join operator provides clearer documentation.

With either technique, the two-table operation in these examples is known as an **equijoin**, one of the most common and useful relational database operations. An equijoin selects only those rows from the Cartesian product in which columns from separate tables have identical values; in both examples, the equijoin selects columns in which the customer ID of the sale (Sale.CustID) matches the customer ID of the customer (Customer.CustID). In addition to the equijoin, SQL allows tables to be joined using other comparison operators, such as greater than or not equal. As this example illustrates, when a column with the same name exists in more than one table, you use a qualified column name of the form *table.column.*[5]

As we indicated in Chapter 6, you also can join a table to itself. That is, a table can assume several roles in the From clause. To keep clear which table role you mean when you specify a column name in any of the other clauses, you must add a unique correlation name for any table listed more than once in a From clause. For example, you could enter the following statement, referencing the Employee table defined in Figure 8.9, to produce the table shown in Figure 8.10, which includes both employees' names and their managers' names.

5 As the next example shows, the qualifier can be a correlation name rather than a table name. A period (.) is always used between the table or correlation name and the column name, regardless of whether you use the system or SQL naming convention.

```
Select Emp.EmpID,
       Emp.LstNam,
       Mgr.LstNam
  From Employee Emp
         Join
       Employee Mgr
         On Emp.MgrEmpID = Mgr.EmpID
```

Figure 8.9
Sample Employee Base Table

```
Create Table Employee
     ( EmpID    Dec(   7, 0 ) Not Null,
       FstNam   Char( 20    ),
       MdlInl   Char(  1    ),
       LstNam   Char( 30    ) Not Null,
       MgrEmpID Dec(   7, 0 ),
  Constraint EmpPK Primary Key( EmpID ) )
```

EmpID	FstNam	MdlInl	LstNam	MgrEmpID
104681	Barb	L	Gibbens	898613
227504	Greg	J	Zimmerman	668466
668466	Dave	R	Bernard	709453
898613	Trish	S	Faubion	668466
899001	Rick	D	Castor	898613

Figure 8.10
Sample Retrieval Using Join of a Table with Itself

```
Emp.EmpID   Emp.LstNam   Mgr.LstNam
104681      Gibbens      Faubion
227504      Zimmerman    Bernard
898613      Faubion      Bernard
899001      Castor       Faubion
```

In this example, the Employee table is used in two roles: once to provide the set of employees (correlation name Emp) and once to provide a lookup table to find the name for each MgrEmpID value (correlation name Mgr). Using a qualified column name such as Emp.LstNam makes it clear from which role of the Employee table the column value is drawn.

The types of joins we have examined thus far have been **inner joins** (i.e., where unmatched rows from the first table are dropped from the result). If you want to see information about all rows from the first table regardless of whether a match exists, you use a **left outer join**:

```
Select Customer.CustID,
       Customer.Name,
       Sale.SaleDate
  From Customer
         Left Outer Join
       Sale
         On Customer.CustID = Sale.CustID
```

Figure 8.11 shows the result of this Select statement.

Figure 8.11
Sample Retrieval Using Left Outer Join

CustID	Name	SaleDate
133568	Smith Mfg.	2000-05-05
246900	Bolt Co.	2000-05-04
246900	Bolt Co.	2000-05-06
275978	Ajax Inc.	<null>
499320	Adapto	2000-05-01
499320	Adapto	2000-05-03
499320	Adapto	2000-05-05
499921	Bell Bldg.	<null>
518980	Floradel	<null>
663456	Alpine Inc.	<null>
681065	Telez Co.	<null>
687309	Nautilus	<null>
781010	Udapto Mfg.	<null>
888402	Seaworthy	2000-05-01
890003	AA Products	2000-05-04
905011	Wood Bros.	2000-05-05

In a left outer join, one row exists in the result table for each pair of rows satisfying the On condition (just as with inner joins). In addition, the result table contains one row for each row in the first table that does not satisfy the On condition (i.e., has no matching row in the second table). All columns from the second table in these unmatched rows are null. Note that a result table column for a left outer join may be null even when the column in the underlying base table is not null-capable.

An **exception join** is the complement of an inner join in that it includes *only* unmatched rows. This example produces a result table that includes only unmatched Customer rows:

```
Select Customer.CustID,
       Customer.Name,
       Sale.SaleDate
  From Customer
         Exception Join
       Sale
         On Customer.CustID = Sale.CustID
```

Figure 8.12 shows this result table.

Figure 8.12
Sample Retrieval Using Exception Join

CustID	Name	SaleDate
275978	Ajax Inc.	<null>
499921	Bell Bldg.	<null>
518980	Floradel	<null>
663456	Alpine Inc.	<null>
681065	Telez Co.	<null>
687309	Nautilus	<null>
781010	Udapto Mfg.	<null>

Note that this subselect produces a result table with the same customers as the subselect of Figure 8.4.

Joining More Than Two Tables

Let's look at an example that joins more than two base tables. Figures 8.13–8.15 show the definitions and sample data for the three tables: Sale, SaleItem, and Part.

Figure 8.13
Sale Table Definition

```
Create Table Sale
  ( OrderID  Dec( 7, 0 ) Not Null,
    SaleDate Date        Not Null,
    SaleTot  Dec( 7, 2 ) Not Null,
    CustID   Dec( 7, 0 ) Not Null,
  Primary Key( OrderID ),
  Constraint SaleCustFK Foreign Key
    References Customer( CustID )
    On Delete Restrict
    On Update Restrict )
```

OrderID	SaleDate	SaleTot	CustID
3678	2000-02-29	567.25	10003
3679	2000-03-06	1089.00	10001
3680	2000-03-06	376.50	10008
3681	2000-03-22	2012.90	10001
3682	2000-03-23	1233.00	10001
3683	2000-04-02	440.00	10003

Figure 8.14
SaleItem Table Definition

```
Create Table SaleItem
  ( OrderID Dec( 7, 0 ) Not Null,
    PartID  Dec( 7, 0 ) Not Null,
    Qty     Dec( 7, 0 ) Not Null,
  Primary Key ( OrderID, PartID ),
  Constraint SaleItemSaleFK Foreign Key( OrderID )
    References Sale( OrderID )
    On Delete Cascade
    On Update Restrict,
  Constraint SaleItemPartFK Foreign Key( PartID )
    References Part( PartID )
    On Delete Restrict
    On Update Restrict )
```

OrderID	PartID	Qty
3678	2654	1
3679	3620	10
3679	4101	2
3680	4101	3
3681	2654	2
3682	2654	1
3682	4101	1
3683	3620	5

Figure 8.15

Part Table Definition

```
Create
 Table Part
  ( PartID    Dec(   7, 0 ) Not Null,
     PartDesc Char( 50    ) Not Null,
  Primary Key( PartID ) )
```

PartID	PartDesc
2654	Fax machine
3620	Stapler
4101	Desk

We can create a view (SaleItemPart) over these three base tables as shown in Figure 8.16.

Figure 8.16

SaleItemPart View Definition

```
Create View SaleItemPart
  ( OrderID,
    SaleDate,
    PartDesc,
    Qty       )
   As Select SaleItem.OrderID,
             Sale.SaleDate,
             Part.PartDesc,
             SaleItem.Qty
        From ( Sale
                Join
               SaleItem
                 On Sale.OrderID = SaleItem.OrderID )
                 Join
               Part
                 On SaleItem.PartID = Part.PartID
```

The resulting rows in the SaleItemPart view would appear as shown in Figure 8.17.

Figure 8.17

SaleItemPart View Rows

```
OrderID   SaleDate     PartDesc      Qty
  3678    2000-02-29   Fax machine     1
  3679    2000-03-06   Stapler        10
  3679    2000-03-06   Desk            2
  3680    2000-03-06   Desk            3
  3681    2000-03-22   Fax machine     2
  3682    2000-03-23   Fax machine     1
  3682    2000-03-23   Desk            1
  3683    2000-04-02   Stapler         5
```

Combining Subqueries and Joins

Joins can occur in subqueries as well as in an outer query. Here is a fairly complex but useful example. Suppose you want to perform the following retrieval:

> *Retrieve the name and city for each customer who has placed any order with a total amount greater than the average total amount of orders placed by customers in the same city.*

The following Select statement retrieves the desired list of customers:

```
Select  CurCust.Name,
        CurCust.ShipCity
  From  Customer CurCust
  Where Exists
      ( Select  *
          From  Sale BigSale
          Where BigSale.CustID = CurCust.CustID
            And BigSale.TotAmt >
              ( Select  Avg( AvgSale.TotAmt )
                  From  Customer AvgCust
                          Join
                        Sale     AvgSale
                          On AvgCust.CustID = AvgSale.CustID
                  Where AvgCust.ShipCity = CurCust.ShipCity ) )
```

A detailed look at how this Select statement is structured illustrates many of SQL's advanced retrieval capabilities.

The first From clause specifies that the result table rows come from the Customer table and that the correlation name CurCust is used elsewhere in the statement to qualify columns that come from this particular role of the Customer table.

The first Where clause uses the Exists predicate to see whether the customer has any orders that meet the specified criteria. The set of orders to be tested is specified by the first subquery (i.e., beginning with the second Select keyword). Remember, when you use a subquery, you can think of UDB/400 as executing the subquery for every row defined by the From clause in the outer Select statement. Thus, in this example, consider that for every row in Customer, the subquery is executed and then tested to see whether its result contains any rows.

The first subquery retrieves rows from the Sale table. Because the only test made on the result of this subquery is whether it contains any rows, the * is specified for the column list (Select *). The From clause specifies that the rows from this use of Sale are qualified by the correlation name BigSale. The only rows retrieved in this subquery are those that are for the current customer and that have a total sale amount greater than the average total amount of orders placed by customers in the same city as the current customer.

The Where clause specifies the conjunction of two predicates that must be true for a Sale row to be in the subquery's result. The first predicate is that a Sale row must have the same customer ID as the current Customer row's customer ID.

The second predicate is a basic predicate that uses another subquery. The total amount for each sale is compared to the average total amount of a set of sales. In this example, the greater than (>) test is used, and because both values in a basic predicate must be scalar, the set the subquery returns in this example must include no more than one value (i.e., one row with one column). By specifying only the Avg column function in the subquery's list of result columns, the subquery retrieves a single row with a single column that has the desired average value. This value is then compared to the column value BigSale.TotAmt.

The second subquery (i.e., the third Select statement) specifies the set of rows from which the average is calculated. The rows come from the equijoin of the Customer and Sale tables (AvgCust.CustID = AvgSale.CustID). But only those rows that have customers from the same city as the current customer are included in the average. To evaluate this condition, the city of each row in the innermost subquery (AvgCust.ShipCity) is compared to the city for the current customer in the main query (CurCust.ShipCity).

The SQL Union Operator

A join operation combines data from two or more tables by combining column values from related rows into a single row in the result table. Another way to combine data is with the **Union** operator. In the following example, the Union operator combines rows from the Customer and ArchivedCustomer tables, which have the same column definitions.

```
Select *
  From Customer
Union
Select *
  From ArchivedCustomer
```

This statement produces a result table consisting of all rows and all columns from the Customer table plus all rows and all columns from the ArchivedCustomer table. Duplicate rows — ones with identical values for all columns — in the result table are eliminated. If you want duplicate rows to be included, you specify Union All, as in this example:

```
Select *
  From Customer
Union All
Select *
  From ArchivedCustomer
```

You can specify a column list (rather than *) as well as any of the other allowable subselect clauses for each of the subselects specified in a Union operation. For example:

```
Select  Name, ShipCity
  From  Customer
  Where Discount < .03
Union
Select  Name, ShipCity
  From  ArchivedCustomer
  Where ShipCity = 'Portland'
```

When you use a Union operator to combine rows from two or more subselect result tables, the statement is called a **fullselect**. To specify the union of two subselects, the subselects' result tables must be **union-compatible**, which means they must have the same number of columns and each pair of corresponding columns (by position in the respective select lists) must have compatible column definitions. Figure 8.18 lists the compatible column types and the column type of the resulting column in the fullselect's result table.

Figure 8.18
Union-Compatible Column Types

If one column is the following type	The other column can be the following type	The data type of the column in the result table is
Char(x)	Char(y)	Char(z) where $z = \max(x, y)$
VarChar(x) or Long VarChar(x)	Char(y) or VarChar(y)	VarChar(z) where $z = \max(x, y)$
Bit data	Bit, mixed, or SBCS data	Bit data
Mixed data	Mixed or SBCS data	Mixed data
SBCS data	SBCS data	SBCS data
Graphic(x)	Graphic(y)	Graphic(z) where $z = \max(x, y)$
VarGraphic(x) or Long VarGraphic(x)	Graphic(y) or VarGraphic(y)	VarGraphic(z) where $z = \max(x, y)$
Blob(x)	Blob(y)	Blob(z) where $z = \max(x, y)$
Clob(x)	Clob(y)	Clob(z) where $z = \max(x, y)$
Clob(x)	DbClob(y)	DbClob(z) where $z = \max(x, y)$
DbClob(x)	DbClob(y)	DbClob(z) where $z = \max(x, y)$
Date	Date	Date
Time	Time	Time
Timestamp	Timestamp	Timestamp
Float (double) or Double	Any numeric type	Float (double)
Float (single) or Real	Float (single)	Float (single)
Float (single) or Real	Decimal, Numeric, Integer, or SmallInt	Float (double)
Decimal(w, x)	Decimal(y, z) or Numeric(y, z)	Decimal(p, s) where $p = \min(31, \max(x, z) + \max(w - x, y - z))$ and $s = \max(x, z)$
Decimal(w, x)	Integer	Decimal(p, x) where $p = \min(31, x + \max(w - x, 11))$
Decimal(w, x)	SmallInt	Decimal(p, x) where $p = \min(31, x + \max(w - x, 5))$
Numeric(w, x)	Numeric(y, z)	Numeric(p, s) where $p = \min(31, \max(x, z) + \max(w - x, y - z))$ and $s = \max(x, z)$
Numeric(w, x)	Integer	Numeric(p, x) where $p = \min(31, x + \max(w - x, 11))$
Numeric(w, x)	SmallInt	Numeric(p, x) where $p = \min(31, x + \max(w - x, 5))$
BigInt	BigInt	BigInt
BigInt	Integer	BigInt
BigInt	SmallInt	BigInt
Integer	Integer	Integer

continued

Figure 8.18 ***Continued***

If one column is the following type	The other column can be the following type	The data type of the column in the result table is
Integer	SmallInt	Integer
SmallInt	SmallInt	SmallInt
Nonzero scale binary	Nonzero scale binary	Nonzero scale binary (if either column is nonzero scale binary, both columns must be binary with the same scale)
Distinct type	Distinct type (must be the same distinct type)	The distinct type
DataLink(*x*)	DataLink(*y*)	DataLink(*z*) where *z* = max(*x*, *y*)

The other attributes of the fullselect's result table columns are determined as follows:

- If the two corresponding columns in the subselects' result tables have identical unqualified names, the fullselect's result table column has the same name; otherwise, the fullselect column is unnamed.
- If neither of the corresponding columns in the subselects' result tables allows nulls, the fullselect's result table column doesn't allow nulls; otherwise, the fullselect column allows nulls.

When a column in a fullselect has no name (or even if it does have a name), you can assign it a name by specifying the keyword As followed by the name in the first select list:

```
Select Name,
       Discount * 100 As DiscountPct
  From Customer
Union
Select Name,
       Discount * 100
  From ArchivedCustomer
```

This example specifies DiscountPct as the name of the calculated column.

A useful technique is to specify a different literal as a "tag" column for each subselect. This value in the fullselect's result table identifies which subselect supplied the row. The following Select statement retrieves the names (including people with the same name) of all employees and contractors, ordered by the person's name:

```
Select   'Employee' As Tag,
         FstNam,
         MdlInl,
         LstNam
  From   Employee
Union All
Select   'Contractor',
         FstNam,
         MdlInl,
         LstNam
  From   Contractor
Order By LstNam,
         FstNam,
         MdlInl
```

As the sample results in Figure 8.19 show, each row includes a tag value to indicate whether the person is an employee or a contractor.

Figure 8.19

Sample Retrieval Using the Union Operator

```
Tag          FstNam    MdlInl   LstNam
Employee     Dave        R      Bernard
Employee     Rick        D      Castor
Contractor   Bill        M      Dutcher
Employee     Trish       S      Faubion
Employee     Barb        L      Gibbens
Contractor   Cricket     S      Katz
Contractor   Tim         L      Murphy
Contractor   Richard     M      Rubin
Employee     Greg        J      Zimmerman
```

This example also shows how you code an Order By clause to sequence the rows in a complete Select statement.

Table Expressions

A **nested table expression** is a subselect specified in the From clause of another (outer) subselect. Here's an example:

```
Select ShipCity,
       MinDiscount,
       MaxDiscount
  From ( Select     ShipCity,
                    Min( Discount ) As MinDiscount,
                    Max( Discount ) As MaxDiscount
           From     Customer
           Group By ShipCity )
         As ShipCityMinMaxDisc
  Where MinDiscount < .02
    And MaxDiscount > .03
```

The nested table expression is

```
( Select      ShipCity,
              Min( Discount ) As MinDiscount,
              Max( Discount ) As MaxDiscount
    From      Customer
    Group By ShipCity )
```

This nested expression produces a result table with the name, minimum discount, and maximum discount of each city in the Customer table. From this result table, the outer Select includes only those rows where the minimum discount is less than .02 and the maximum is greater than .03. Figure 8.20 shows the result table for the entire query.

Figure 8.20

Result Table for a Query Using a Nested Table Expression

```
ShipCity    MinDiscount    MaxDiscount
Eugene      .010           .100
Portland    .000           .050
```

You can think of a nested table expression as somewhat like a temporary view, except no actual view is created for a nested table expression. (UDB/400 may create a temporary table, if necessary.) To use a nested table expression, you enclose the subselect in parentheses followed by the As keyword and a correlation name for the result table. As the example shows, you can also specify names for columns in the result table (e.g., MinDiscount). An alternate form of the nested table expression lets you specify column names in a list following the correlation name:

```
Select ShipCity,
       MinDiscount,
       MaxDiscount
  From ( Select      ShipCity,
                     Min( Discount ),
                     Max( Discount )
           From      Customer
           Group By ShipCity )
         As ShipCityMinMaxDisc ( ShipCity,
                                 MinDiscount,
                                 MaxDiscount )
  Where MinDiscount < .02
    And MaxDiscount > .03
```

In this example, you could produce the same query result table without a nested table expression by using a Having clause instead of a Where clause:

```
Select     ShipCity,
           Min( Discount ) As MinDiscount,
           Max( Discount ) As MaxDiscount
  From     Customer
  Group By ShipCity
  Having   Min( Discount ) < .02
     And   Max( Discount ) > .03
```

But there are some cases when a nested table is essential:

```
Select     MaxDiscount,
           Count( * ) As CityCnt
  From     ( Select ShipCity,
                    Max( Discount ) As MaxDiscount
               From Customer
               Group By ShipCity )
             As MaxDiscGrp
  Group By MaxDiscount
```

This query produces a result table (Figure 8.21) with rows consisting of maximum discounts found in each city with at least one customer and the number of cities having those maximums.

Figure 8.21

Result Table for a Query That Requires a Nested Table Expression

MaxDiscount	CityCnt
.010	2
.050	1
.100	1

This query couldn't be specified as a single Select statement without a view or a nested table expression because there are two levels of grouping (by city and maximum discount). When the database design doesn't require a permanent view, nested queries provide a good solution.

A **common table expression** is similar to a nested table expression but is specified using the With keyword and a subselect before the main Select keyword. The result table is then available in any clause, not just the From clause. In the following example

```
With DeptEmpCnt
             ( DeptId,
               EmpCnt )
  As ( Select  DeptId,
               Count( * )
         From  Employee
         Group By DeptId )
Select  DeptId,
        EmpCnt
  From  DeptEmpCnt
  Where EmpCnt > ( Select Avg( EmpCnt )
                     From DeptEmpCnt )
```

the common table expression specifies a result table with the correlation name DeptEmpCnt. This table has two columns: DeptId and EmpCnt, which are defined by a subselect using a form very much like the syntax of the Create View statement presented in Chapter 6. This common table expression can be referenced by its correlation name anywhere a table name is valid in the main Select statement; in this example, DeptEmpCnt is referenced in both the From and Where clauses.

Keep in mind that when your applications have many queries that reference the same result table, a view may simplify your Select statements. But when a view is infrequently used, common table expressions provide a helpful alternative. Note that common table expressions also provide the flexibility of host variables when coded in SQL statements embedded in an HLL program (topics we'll cover in Chapter 10).

An Introduction to User-Defined Functions: Sourced Functions

As we saw in Chapter 5, SQL provides a variety of built-in scalar and column functions. These functions accept and return values defined by the built-in data types, such as Character and Integer. To handle values defined with distinct types (i.e., UDTs), SQL lets you create **user-defined functions (UDFs)** that are based on built-in functions. This type of function is known as a **sourced function**. (SQL supports other types of user-defined functions as well; we'll cover these in Chapter 13.)

For example, consider the following DescriptionType distinct type definition and a (partial) Part table definition that uses that type:

```
Create Distinct Type DescriptionType
  As VarChar( 100 )

Create Table Part
  ( ...,
    Description DescriptionType Not Null,
    ... )
```

Although the Description column is based on a VarChar(100) type, SQL/400 doesn't let you use any built-in string functions, such as SubStr or ConCat, on this column.[6] But you can create a UDF to handle the DescriptionType distinct type:

6 The reason SQL/400 doesn't let built-in functions operate on columns defined with a distinct type is to prevent operations that aren't appropriate for the intended purpose of the distinct type. For example, it wouldn't make sense to permit the Log mathematical function on a distinct type intended to be used as a row identifier, even if the distinct type was based on a Decimal(7,0) type.

```
Create Function SubStr( DescriptionType, Int, Int )
  Returns VarChar( 100 )
    Specific DescriptSubStr
  Source SubStr( VarChar( 100 ), Int, Int )
```

You can then use this new function in a Select statement such as the following:

```
Select SubStr( Description, 1, 20 )
  From Part
```

For a sourced function, the Source clause of the Create Function statement must specify the name of an SQL built-in function (e.g., SubStr) or another UDF, followed by a parenthesized list of the existing function's parameter types (e.g., (VarChar(100), Int, Int)). Together, the function name and the parameter types define exactly which function SQL should invoke when you call the new sourced function. Because an SQL function is uniquely identified within a collection by its name and number and type of parameters, a UDF can have the same name as the function it's based on (as the one in this example does), as long as the parameter types are different. In fact, this is a common practice for sourced functions that merely make a built-in function available for a UDT.

In the example, Create Function SubStr is followed by a parenthesized list of data types — (DescriptionType, Int, Int) — for the sourced function's parameters. The sourced function must have the same number of parameters as the based-on function specified in the Source clause, and each sourced function parameter type must be castable to the corresponding parameter type in the Source clause.

The optional Specific clause provides a unique name (e.g., DescriptSubStr) to use when dropping this function.[7] When you use an existing function name for a new sourced function, we recommend you provide a meaningful specific name.

As you'll learn in Chapter 13, SQL/400 supports **external** and **SQL UDFs** as well as sourced functions. Sourced UDFs are based on other existing functions. A sourced UDF always specifies the Source clause in its Create Function statement. An external UDF is based on a user-written HLL program and never uses the Source clause in its Create Function statement. An SQL UDF uses the SQL Procedural Language (SPL) to implement the function and also doesn't use a Source clause.

You can use UDFs almost everywhere you can use a built-in function. However, you can't use UDFs in check constraints (covered in Chapter 4). And you can't use external or SQL UDFs in an Order By or Group By clause unless the SQL statement is read-only and is executed in an environment that allows temporary files for statement processing (e.g., when the CrtSql*Xxx* command's AlwCpyDta parameter is *Yes or *Optimize).

Coding Suggestions

- Use meaningful correlation names.
- Be sure that a subquery used in a basic predicate can never have more than one row in the result table.
- Be careful to use the proper Any or All keyword in quantified predicates.
- When a Union operator is used and two subselects have corresponding columns with different names, use the As clause in one or both of the subselects to give the columns the same name. This technique ensures that the column has a name in the fullselect's final result table.

7 For example, to delete the function in this example you would code

```
Drop Specific Function DescriptSubStr
```

- Consider using nested or common table expressions rather than a (permanent) view when the view would seldom be used.

Chapter Summary

A Cast expression lets you convert a value from one data type to another, compatible data type.

Subqueries are subselects that are part of a search condition. You can use subqueries in the following predicates:

- *basic predicate* — The subquery must specify a single column in the result table and return at most one row. This value is compared to an expression specified in the predicate.
- *In predicate* — The subquery must specify a single column. The result table is tested to see whether it contains the value of the expression specified in the predicate.
- *Exists predicate* — This predicate tests whether a subquery result table contains any rows.
- *quantified predicate* — This predicate compares an expression against all values in the subquery result table.

All predicates using a subquery can be preceded with Not to negate the predicate.

An SQL join combines related information from two or more tables or views. The join's On condition specifies a basic predicate that defines how rows are matched.

For an inner join, unmatched rows from the first table are not included in the result table. A left outer join produces at least one row for each row in the first table specified. For rows from that first table that have no matching row in the second table, result table columns from the second table are set null. An exception join includes only unmatched rows in the result table.

The hierarchy of subselect, fullselect, and Select statement can be summarized as follows:

- A subselect is a specification of a result table with the following structure:

  ```
  Select       select-list
     From      table-list
   [ Where     search-condition      ]
   [ Group By  grouping-column-list  ]
   [ Having    search-condition      ]
  ```

  The Where, Group By and Having clauses are optional. A subselect is part of a fullselect and can be used in the Create View statement (covered in the Chapter 6).
- A fullselect is a single subselect or two or more subselects connected by the Union or Union All operator. The Union operator combines rows from the intermediate result tables of two subselects to produce the result table for the fullselect. With Union All, duplicate rows are included in the result table; otherwise, duplicates are eliminated.

  A fullselect is part of a Select statement.
- A Select statement is a fullselect with an optional common table expression and an optional Order By clause. The Order By clause specifies the column(s) whose value(s) are used to sequence the rows in the result table.

  A Select statement can be used interactively to retrieve and display rows or — in a nested form — as part of an Insert statement (see Chapter 7). A Select statement can also be used as part of an embedded cursor definition, a topic we cover along with additional Select statement clauses in Chapter 11. The other optional clauses are the For Update Of, For Read Only, Optimize, and Isolation clauses.

Nested and common table expressions define temporary result tables that can be referenced in a Select. A table expression can be used instead of a permanent view when the view would not be used frequently.

The Create Function statement creates a user-defined function (UDF) that can be used in SQL statements. A sourced function is a UDF that is based on an existing built-in function or other UDF. Sourced functions are especially useful for extending SQL built-in functions to operate on values that are defined as a distinct type.

Key Terms

basic predicate
cast expression
common table expression
correlated subquery
equijoin
exception join
Exists predicate
external UDF
fullselect
In predicate
inner join
left outer join
nested table expression
quantified predicate
scalar subselect
sourced function
SQL UDF
subquery
Union operator
union-compatible
user-defined function (UDF)

Exercises

1. Suppose column ShipCity is defined as Char(7) in table ArchivedCustomer and all other columns of ArchivedCustomer agree in name, type, length, and scale with the definition in Figure 8.5 for the Customer table. Explain what happens when the following Insert statement is executed:

```
Insert Into ArchivedCustomer
  Select  *
    From  Customer
```

   Show a modified Insert statement that uses a Cast expression to avoid the problem.

2. Using the Customer table defined in Figure 8.5 and the following partial definition for a Warehouse table, show the Select statement to retrieve the list of cities in which there's either a customer or a warehouse (or both). Sequence the result table by city.

```
Create Table Warehouse
     ( WhseID   Dec(   7, 0 ) Not Null,
       City     Char( 30     ),
  Primary Key( WhseID ) )
```

3. Using the same tables you used for Exercise 2, show the Select statement to retrieve customers who are in a city without a warehouse.
4. Using the same tables you used for Exercise 2, show the Delete statement to delete customers who are in a city without a warehouse.
5. Show the Select statement to retrieve customers who have a discount identical to at least one customer in Portland. Will all customers in Portland necessarily be included in this retrieval? Why or why not?

6. Modify the Select statement you created for Exercise 5 to include the following additional criteria:
   - A Portland customer must have a discount identical to at least one *different* customer in Portland.
   - A customer with a null discount *is* included in the result table if and only if at least one different customer in Portland also has a null discount. (The "different customer" restriction is relevant only to customers in Portland.)

   Hint: This problem may be harder than it looks; consider a fullselect.
7. Show the Update statement necessary to change the Discount for the customer whose CustID is 133568 to the average of all other customer's discounts. Use a subquery in your solution that does not hard code the CustID 133568.

   Hint: Consider using a correlated subquery.
8. Change the definition of the SaleItemPart (join) view presented in Figure 8.16 so that
   a. only items that were ordered in quantities of two or more are included in the view's rows, and
   b. if an order doesn't include any items ordered in quantities of two or more, the order itself isn't in the view's rows, and
   c. if any part is not ordered in quantities of two or more, then no rows for that part should be included in the view's rows.

   Use the definitions in Figures 8.13, 8.14, and 8.15 for the Sale, SaleItem, and Part tables.

   Hint: The required modifications may be simpler than you first think.
9. Show the statement necessary to implement a Length sourced function that has a parameter defined as a LongDescription distinct type and which returns a LongDescription distinct type. Use the following definition of the LongDescription distinct type:

```
Create Distinct Type LongDescription
  As VarChar( 300 )
```

   Hint: Look at Figure 5.6 in Chapter 5.

Chapter 9

Database Security and the Grant and Revoke Statements

Chapter Overview

The AS/400's operating system, OS/400, provides a wide variety of security mechanisms to control access to the contents of a UDB/400 database. This chapter introduces the way OS/400 implements security and how you can set up user profiles and authorities to restrict the types of operations people can perform. You'll learn how to use the SQL Grant and Revoke statements, as well as OS/400 commands to specify appropriate access to database objects. In addition to user profiles, we also focus on collections, database tables and views, distinct types, stored procedures, user-defined functions, and SQL packages, which are the central SQL objects in database security.

Security Basics

As we discussed in Chapter 1, OS/400 is organized so that everything is an object, and SQL/400 uses these OS/400 objects for SQL-oriented database objects, as laid out in Figure 9.1.

Figure 9.1
SQL and OS/400 Object Types

SQL object	OS/400 object	Special value (used in OS/400 commands)
Alias	Distributed Data Management (DDM) file	*File
Authorization ID	User profile	*UsrPrf
Collection	Library	*Lib
Distinct type	SQL user-defined type	*SqlUdt
Index	Logical file	*File
Package	SQL package	*SqlPkg
Procedure	Program	*Pgm
Table	Physical file	*File
User-defined function	Program or service program	*Pgm *SrvPgm
View	Logical file	*File

In general, SQL/400 security builds directly on OS/400 security; however, some aspects of database security can be controlled *only* using OS/400's Control Language (CL). Accordingly, we discuss OS/400 objects and commands along with SQL/400 objects and statements. To start, we explain the basic foundations of OS/400 security and then look at how you control security using both OS/400 commands and SQL statements.

We start with the OS/400 **user profile** object which, as the name implies, represents a user of the AS/400. In SQL/400 terminology, **authorization ID** refers to a particular user profile that's checked for appropriate authority when an SQL statement is executed. A user profile has a name, password, and set of values that control various aspects of security and the OS/400 interactive and batch job environments. Typically, when a person who's not already authorized to use the AS/400 needs access to UDB/400 data, the organization's security officer or authorized representative uses the CrtUsrPrf command to create a user profile object for the person. (There is no SQL statement to create a user profile.) Each user profile is created with a unique password that the person uses to sign on to the AS/400. The security officer or someone in charge of the organization's applications then grants the user profile appropriate **authority** to various OS/400 objects so the person can work with application programs and data.

When someone signs on to the AS/400, he or she must supply a valid combination of user profile name and password.[1] After a person has signed on with a particular user profile, that user profile governs all access to other OS/400 objects, including libraries, database files, and programs. When a person submits a batch job, the job normally runs under the submitter's user profile, and that user profile also governs data access in the batch environment.[2] Because all SQL/400 objects are OS/400 objects, this same principle applies to SQL operations: User profiles govern all access.

In concept, OS/400 security is simple: When an operation is attempted, OS/400 checks to ensure that the job's user profile has adequate authority to perform the operation on the target object. For example, when someone tries to run a program to display employee data, OS/400 first checks that the user profile the person signed on with has authority to execute the program, and then OS/400 checks that the user profile has authority to read rows from the employee table.

In practice, OS/400 security can become quite complex because a user profile might obtain authority to an object in many different ways. In this chapter, we explore many details of OS/400 security as it relates to a variety of database objects, but keep in mind the following simple picture:

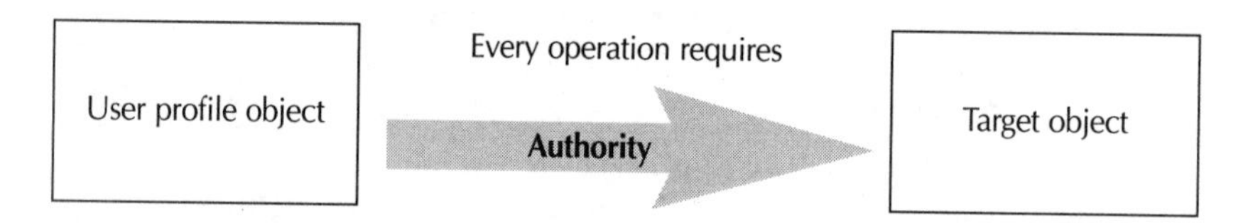

Every operation on the AS/400 (e.g., running a program or opening a table to read rows) requires appropriate authority to the target object. If you want a person to be able to perform a particular operation on an object, you must ensure that his or her user profile has the required authority. If you want to prevent a person from performing a particular operation on an object, you must ensure that his or her user profile does not have the required authority.

Object Ownership

User profiles play another essential role in OS/400. Every object is owned by a user profile.[3] Thus, it's important to plan which user profiles will own application objects.

1 A password is not required when the QSecurity system value is set to 10. Level 10, the lowest allowable value for QSecurity, essentially specifies that the AS/400 operates with no security. Levels 20 and higher require a user profile and password to sign on.

2 You can configure some batch jobs so they run under a different, prespecified user profile, in which case the prespecified user profile's authority governs the access allowed the batch job.

3 User profile objects themselves are normally owned by the user profile that created them. IBM-supplied user profiles, such as QPgmr, are normally owned by the IBM-supplied QSys user profile. The QSys user profile owns itself.

The owner of an object normally has all authorities to the object. For that reason, once you put application tables, views, programs, and so forth into production, you shouldn't leave the programmer who created them as the owner. Instead, there should be one or more special-purpose user profiles created to own production versions of application objects. In small organizations, a single user profile — e.g., PrfAppOwn (profile — application owner) — may suffice. For larger organizations, there may be several user profiles, each owning objects of a particular application (e.g., PrfSaleOwn, PrfEmpOwn). An application's collection and most of the tables, views, programs, and other objects in the collection can be owned by one of the special-purpose user profiles. (Later in the chapter we'll look at a special case: programs that adopt the authority of the user profile that owns the program.)

The ChgObjOwn (Change Object Owner) command can be used to transfer ownership from one user profile to another — for example, from a programmer's user profile to a special-purpose profile to own production objects. (Again, there's no SQL statement to transfer object ownership.) Another way to have production objects owned by a special-purpose profile — once development and testing of an application is complete — is to delete the test version of the objects and re-create them in a job that runs under the special-purpose user profile that should own production objects.

OS/400 Authorities

As we said, OS/400 governs operations based on the authorities a user profile has. There are two major categories of OS/400 authority:

- special authorities
- specific authorities

Special authorities are assigned to a user profile (e.g., by the security officer) using the SpcAut parameter of the CrtUsrPrf or ChgUsrPrf (Change User Profile) command. (There is no SQL statement to assign OS/400 special authorities.) Figure 9.2 lists the special authorities, which generally have a systemwide scope and aren't associated with individual objects.

Figure 9.2

OS/400 Special Authorities

Special authority	Special value (used in OS/400 commands)	Sample operations allowed
All object	*AllObj	• Access any object with all specific authorities listed in Figure 9.3
Audit	*Audit	• Change system auditing configuration
I/O system configuration	*IOSysCfg	• Change system I/O configuration
Job control	*JobCtl	• IPL the system • Manage subsystems and jobs • Manage queues, writers, and spooled files that are configured to allow operator control
Save system	*SavSys	• Save, restore, and free storage for all objects
Security administrator	*SecAdm	• Create, change, and delete user profiles
Service	*Service	• Start the system service tools • Debug programs with only *Use special authorities (see Figure 9.4A)
Spool control	*SplCtl	• Manage spooled files • Manage job queues

In general, no one on the system should have *AllObj or *SecAdm special authorities unless he or she is responsible for systemwide security. In typical installations, trained and trusted system operators are usually given *SavSys authority so they can do regular backups. The user profiles for most end users have none of these special authorities and so need specific object authorities to work with the database.

Specific authorities are assigned to one or more user profiles to use one or more objects.[4] Specific authorities are further subdivided into three groups: object authorities, data authorities, and field authorities, as shown in Figure 9.3. OS/400 also has several special values for specific authorities, as shown in Figures 9.4A and 9.4B.

Figure 9.3

OS/400 Specific Authorities

Type of authority	Special value (used in OS/400 commands)	Operations allowed
Object authorities		
Object operational	*ObjOpr	• Retrieve an object's description • Use an object as determined by the user's data and field authorities to the object
Object management	*ObjMgt	• Grant and revoke authorities for an object • Rename or move an object to another library (or SQL collection) • All *ObjAlter and *ObjRef operations
Object existence	*ObjExist	• Delete an object • Free an object's storage on a save operation • Transfer ownership of an object to another user profile
Object alter	*ObjAlter	• Add, clear, initialize, and reorganize member(s) of a database file (or SQL table or view — note that tables and views always have a single member) • Alter and add attributes of a database file (or SQL table or view), including adding and removing trigger programs on physical files (or SQL tables) • Change the attributes of an SQL package object
Object reference	*ObjRef	• Specify a physical file (or SQL table) as the parent file (or table) in a foreign key constraint
Authorization list management	*AutLMgt	• Add and remove user profiles and their authorities from an object's authorization list
Data authorities		
Read	*Read	• Read the contents of an object (e.g., read rows from a table)
Add	*Add	• Add entries to an object (e.g., insert new rows into a table)
Update	*Upd	• Update the entries in an object (e.g., update rows in a table)

continued

4 The terminology here can be somewhat confusing. "Specific authorities" include the subcategory "object authorities." Informally, "object authority" is often used synonymously with "specific authority." Where there's little chance for confusion, this book also uses "object authority" for "specific authority."

Figure 9.3 *Continued*

Type of authority	Special value (used in OS/400 commands)	Operations allowed
***Data authorities** continued...*		
Delete	*Dlt	• Delete entries from an object (e.g., delete rows from a table)
Execute	*Execute	• Run a program or service program or execute statements in an SQL package • Invoke an SQL stored procedure or user-defined function • For library (or collection) objects, locate objects in the library (or collection)
Field authorities		
Management	*Mgt	• Specify authority for a field (or column)
Alter	*Alter	• Change attributes for a field (or column)
Reference	*Ref	• Specify the field (or column) as part of the parent key in a foreign key constraint
Read	*Read	• Read the contents of a field (or column)
Add	*Add	• Add contents to a field (or column)
Update	*Update	• Update the contents of a field (or column)

Figure 9.4A

Special Values for Sets of Specific Authorities (Used by Most OS/400 Commands)

Special value	Equivalent specific authorities	Notes
*All	All object and data authorities listed in Figure 9.3	—
*Change	*ObjOpr and all data authorities	Lets a user have full read and update access to a database table or view, as well as execute a program
*Use	*ObjOpr, *Read, and *Execute authorities	Lets a user execute a program or have read access to a database table or view
*Exclude	—	Explicitly denies all access to the object

Figure 9.4B

Special Values for Sets of Specific Authorities (Used by WrkAut and ChgAut Commands)

Special value	Equivalent specific authorities	Notes
*RWX	*ObjOpr and all data authorities	Equivalent to *Change
*RW	*ObjOpr and all data authorities except *Execute	Read/write access
*RX	*ObjOpr, *Read, and *Execute authorities	Read/execute access
*R	*ObjOpr and *Read authorities	Read-only access
*WX	*ObjOpr and all data authorities except *Read	Write/execute access
*W	*ObjOpr, *Add, *Upd, and *Dlt authorities	Write-only access
*X	*ObjOpr and *Execute authorities	Execute-only access
*Exclude	—	Explicitly denies all access to the object

The special values in Figure 9.4A (e.g., *All) are typically used for most OS/400 commands; the special values in Figure 9.4B (e.g., *RW) provide Unix-like levels of access and are used with the WrkAut (Work with Authority) and ChgAut (Change Authority) commands, typically for nondatabase, integrated file system (IFS) files. (See Chapter 1 for an explanation of IFS files.) Note that the special values — other than *Exclude — are simply shorthand for various sets of values; they are *not* additional types of OS/400 specific authorities. The *Exclude special value is not really an OS/400 authority but rather a way to explicitly *deny* authority.

You can grant authority to any OS/400 object with the GrtObjAut command or by using the EdtObjAut command to edit a displayed list of user profiles and their authorities to an object. To enable a user named Betty L. Smith with the user profile SmithBL to display Customer rows, you could use a command such as

```
GrtObjAut Obj( AppDta/Customer )
          ObjType( *File )
          User( SmithBL )
          Aut( *Use )
```

If you wanted Betty to be able to read and add Customer rows but not delete or update them, you could use the following command:

```
GrtObjAut Obj( AppDta/Customer )
          ObjType( *File )
          User( SmithBL )
          Aut( *ObjOpr *Read *Add )
```

You can revoke authority with the RvkObjAut command or by using the EdtObjAut command. To revoke Betty's authority to add Customer rows, you could use a command such as

```
RvkObjAut Obj( AppDta/Customer )
          ObjType( *File )
          User( SmithBL )
          Aut( *Add )
```

This command leaves intact any other authorities that the SmithBL user profile has to the Customer file object.

To grant or revoke authority to an object, your user profile must satisfy one or more of the following conditions:

- own the object (typically as a result of creating it)
- be the system security officer (QSecOfr)
- have *AllObj special authority
- have *ObjMgt authority to the object

The *ObjMgt authority by itself lets you grant and revoke only those authorities your user profile has to the object, and *ObjMgt authority (again, by itself) doesn't let you grant another user profile *ObjMgt authority.

The GrtObjAut, RvkObjAut, and EdtObjAut commands can use the *All, *Change, *Use, and *Exclude special values. The WrkAut and ChgAut commands, which use an IFS path to specify an object, can use *RWX, *RW, *RX, *R, *WX, *W, *X, and *Exclude, as in the following example:

```
ChgAut Obj( '\QSys.Lib\AppDta.Lib\Customer.File' )
       User( SmithBL )
       DtaAut( *R )
```

Public Authority

So far, we've considered only individual user profiles. OS/400 has two features — public authority and group profiles (discussed later in this chapter) — that let you grant authority to more than one user profile at a time. Every object has **public authority**, which controls access by user profiles that aren't otherwise authorized to the object. An object's public authority can include any of the object authorities listed in Figures 9.3 and 9.4A, which you can grant and revoke using the *Public special value instead of a user profile name on the GrtObjAut and RvkObjAut commands. For example, to grant public authority to read data from the Customer file, you could use the following command:

```
GrtObjAut Obj( AppDta/Customer )
          ObjType( *File )
          User( *Public )
          Aut( *Use )
```

On the CrtLib (Create Library), CrtPf (Create Physical File), CrtLf (Create Logical File), CrtPgm (Create Program), CrtSrvPgm (Create Service Program), and some other Crt*Xxx* commands, you also can specify one of the special values listed in Figure 9.4A for the respective command's Aut parameter.[5] The following command creates the Customer file with public authority to read the file:

```
CrtPf File( AppDta/Customer )
      SrcFile( AppSrc/QDdsSrc )
      Aut( *Use )
```

Although it's common practice in many AS/400 installations to allow *Use public authority to most application objects, you should be sure you want everyone to be able to run a program or read data from a file before you grant *Use public authority. A more cautious approach is to specify *Exclude for library, program, and database file objects' public authority unless there's a clear reason for allowing some higher level of access to everyone.

Default Public Authority for New Objects Created with an OS/400 CrtXxx Command

When you create an object with a Crt*Xxx* command and you don't specify the Aut parameter, the default is Aut(*LibCrtAut), which means that the object's public authority is set from a value associated with the library (i.e., collection) in which the object is created. This value is specified on the CrtAut parameter of the CrtLib and ChgLib (Change Library) commands.[6] For example, if a library is created with CrtAut(*Change), new objects created with a Crt*Xxx* command in the library will have public authority *Change, unless you specify an Aut parameter value other than the default (*LibCrtAut) on the Crt*Xxx* command.

CrtAut(*SysVal) is the default parameter for the CrtLib command. (The next section discusses libraries created with an SQL Create Collection statement.) This default specifies that a new library's CrtAut value is taken from the QCrtAut system value. IBM ships OS/400 with QCrtAut set to *Change. As a result, if you use the default CrtAut parameter for CrtLib commands and use the default Aut parameter for other Crt*Xxx* commands, new objects will have *Change as their public authority. This is generally not a good practice because it allows too much access.

5 If you want some combination of authorities other than those provided by the special values listed in Figure 9.4A, you should specify *Exclude for the Aut parameter on the Crt*Xxx* commands and then use the GrtObjAut command to grant the appropriate specific authorities to *Public.

6 A new object's public authority is set when it's created. A subsequent change to the containing library's CrtAut value does not affect existing objects.

You can't avoid this potential security risk by simply changing the QSysVal system value to a more restrictive setting, such as *Exclude, because doing so can cause other problems. Unfortunately, IBM ships some OS/400 system libraries (e.g., QSys) with CrtAut(*SysVal), so changing QSysVal may affect objects created in these system libraries. For example, workstation devices created in QSys using a default Aut parameter might not be accessible by end users.

For most installations, application libraries and collections should be created with a CrtAut value of *Exclude or *Use. To simplify this practice, you can change the CrtLib command's default CrtAut parameter value to something other than *SysVal, as in the following example:

```
ChgCmdDft Cmd( CrtLib )
          NewDft( 'CrtAut(*Exclude)' )
```

This change will affect libraries subsequently created with the CrtLib command, but it will *not* affect libraries created with the Create Collection statement, which is covered below. You can use the ChgLib command to change the CrtAut attribute of existing libraries and collections.

Default Public Authority for New Objects Created with an SQL Create Statement

When you use an SQL Create statement to create a database object, the object's public authority is determined by the naming option in effect. Chapter 13 provides a complete discussion of the two SQL/400 naming options, which were introduced in Chapter 3: *system naming* and *SQL naming*. Here, we just describe how they affect public authority.

With system naming, public authority works similarly to the way it works with the OS/400 Crt*Xxx* commands. The Create Collection statement creates an OS/400 library with public authority set from the QCrtAut system value and with the library's CrtAut value set to *SysVal. All other Create statements create OS/400 objects with public authority determined by the containing collection's CrtAut value.

With SQL naming, the public is generally excluded from access when an object is created. The Create Collection statement creates an OS/400 library with *Exclude public authority and CrtAut also set to *Exclude. All other Create statements, except Create Function and Create Procedure, also create objects with *Exclude public authority, regardless of the collection's CrtAut value. When a Create Function or Create Procedure statement creates a new OS/400 program or service program, the object's public authority is determined by the collection's CrtAut value.

SQL/400 Privileges

In SQL terminology, a **privilege** is the authorization to use one of the following objects:

- table or view
- distinct type
- stored procedure or user-defined function
- SQL package

(We cover SQL packages in Chapter 12 and stored procedures in Chapter 13.) If you have the appropriate authority, you can grant and revoke privileges using the SQL Grant and Revoke statements. You grant privileges to an OS/400 user profile object (or Public), and then anyone who signs on to the AS/400 under that user profile has the corresponding authority you've granted.

Table privileges correspond to OS/400 authorities to the database physical file. Figure 9.5 lists the privileges you can grant to an SQL table and shows the corresponding authority that's granted to the physical file. The With Grant Option privilege is an optional clause on the SQL Grant statement, which we discuss later in this chapter.

Figure 9.5
SQL Table Privileges

SQL privilege	SQL statement privileges that are granted or revoked	Corresponding OS/400 authorities to physical file
All	All	*ObjAlter *ObjMgt *ObjOpr *ObjRef *Add *Dlt *Read *Upd
Alter	Alter Table Comment On Label On	*ObjAlter
Delete	Delete	*ObjOpr *Dlt
Index	Create Index	*ObjAlter
Insert	Insert	*ObjOpr *Add
References	Add a foreign key constraint that references this table as parent	*ObjRef
Select	Select Create View	*ObjOpr *Read
Update	Update	*ObjOpr *Upd
With Grant Option	Grant Revoke Alter Table Comment On Label On Create Index Add a foreign key constraint that references this table as parent	*ObjMgt

View privileges correspond to OS/400 authorities to database logical and physical files. Figure 9.6 lists the privileges you can grant to an SQL view and shows the corresponding authority that's granted to the database files.

Figure 9.6
SQL View Privileges

SQL privilege	SQL statement privileges that are granted or revoked	Valid for views	Corresponding OS/400 authorities to logical file	Corresponding OS/400 authorities to referenced physical or logical files
All	All	All views	*ObjAlter *ObjMgt *ObjOpr *ObjRef *Add *Dlt *Read *Upd	*Add *Dlt *Read *Upd
Alter	Comment On Label On	All views	*ObjAlter	None
Delete	Delete	If not read-only	*ObjOpr *Dlt	*Dlt
Insert	Insert	If view is not read-only and allows inserts	*ObjOpr *Add	*Add
References	—	Allowed, but not used for views	*ObjRef	None
Select	Select Create View	All views	*ObjOpr *Read	*Read
Update	Update	If not read-only	*ObjOpr *Upd	*Upd
With Grant Option	Grant Revoke Comment On Label On	All views	*ObjMgt	None

Distinct type privileges correspond to OS/400 authorities to an SQL user-defined type (*SqlUdt) object. Figure 9.7 lists the privileges you can grant to a distinct type and shows the corresponding authority that's granted to the SQL user-defined type. The Alter privilege lets you use the SQL Comment On statement, and the Usage privilege lets you use the distinct type in table definitions, stored procedures, functions, and Create Distinct Type statements.

Stored procedure and user-defined function[7] privileges correspond to OS/400 authorities to a program or service program object. Figure 9.8 lists the privileges you can grant to an SQL procedure or function and shows the corresponding authority that's granted to the program or service program. The Alter privilege lets you use the SQL Comment On statement, and the Execute privilege lets you invoke the procedure or function.

7 You can grant and revoke SQL privileges only to user-defined functions. Built-in functions are always accessible to any user.

Figure 9.7
SQL Distinct Type Privileges

SQL privilege	Corresponding OS/400 authorities to SQL user-defined type
All	*ObjAlter *ObjOpr *ObjMgt *Execute
Alter	*ObjAlter
Usage	*ObjOpr *Execute
With Grant Option	*ObjMgt

Figure 9.8
SQL Stored Procedure and User-Defined Function Privileges

SQL privilege	Corresponding OS/400 authorities to program or service program
All	*ObjAlter *ObjOpr *ObjMgt *Execute
Alter	*ObjAlter
Execute	*ObjOpr *Execute
With Grant Option	*ObjMgt

Package privileges correspond to OS/400 authorities to an SQL package (*SqlPkg) object. Figure 9.9 lists the privileges you can grant to an SQL package and shows the corresponding authority granted to the OS/400 object. The Alter privilege lets you use the SQL Comment On and Label On statements, and the Execute privilege lets you execute statements in the package.

Figure 9.9
SQL Package Privileges

SQL privilege	Corresponding OS/400 authorities to SQL package
All	*ObjAlter *ObjOpr *ObjMgt *Execute
Alter	*ObjAlter
Execute	*ObjOpr *Execute
With Grant Option	*ObjMgt

Accessing the Main Database Objects

Now that we've covered some of the foundations of OS/400 and SQL/400 security, we need to examine more closely how OS/400 authorities and the corresponding SQL privileges control user access to important database objects, including collections, tables, views, distinct types, stored procedures, functions, packages, programs, and service programs.

Collections

To access any object, a user profile must have *Execute authority to the collection (i.e., library) that contains the object. Without this authority, the user profile can't do *anything* with objects that exist in the collection. The actual operations allowed on an object are, of course, also limited by the user profile's authorities for the specific object. To create most types of objects, a user profile must have at least *Add authority to the collection that will contain the object. All of the SQL Create statements require both *Execute and *Add authority to the containing collection, and the Create Alias and Create Distinct Type statements also require *Read authority to the collection.

As we explained previously, the Create Collection statement creates a library with either *Exclude public authority (with SQL naming) or with the public authority specified by the QCrtAut system value (with system naming). Generally, you can increase security by specifying *Exclude for public authority to collections. That way, only explicitly authorized users can access objects in the library. Note that there isn't an SQL statement to explicitly specify privileges for a collection; instead, you must use OS/400 commands to grant and revoke OS/400 authorities to the corresponding library object.

If you want to enable a user to access one or more of the objects in a collection, you should normally grant the person's user profile *Use authority (which includes the *Execute and *Read authorities) to the collection. If any authorized application creates temporary or permanent objects in the collection, you should also grant the user profile *Add authority (which is *not* included in *Use authority) to the collection.

Tables and Views

Application programs can access the data in a table either directly by accessing the table or indirectly by opening a view defined over the table. To access data in a table, a user profile must have Select, Insert, Update, or Delete privileges to the table.

To access data in a table by way of a view, a user profile must have similar privileges (i.e., Select, Insert, Update, or Delete) to the view. Notice from Figure 9.6 how each view privilege corresponds to OS/400 authorities both to the view's logical file and to the physical file(s) for the based-on table(s). For example, to read and update rows through a view, the user profile must have *ObjOpr, *Read, and *Upd authorities to the logical file and *Read and *Upd authorities to the physical file.

This dual check on data rights provides the basis for a column-level approach to database access. With a view, you can limit access to a subset of rows and columns (as explained in Chapter 6). If you grant a user profile appropriate privileges to the view — but not to the underlying table — the user profile is limited to accessing only those columns and rows accessible through the view. (The lack of *ObjOpr authority to the table's physical file prevents opening the table directly.)

Distinct Types

To use a distinct type in a Create Table statement's column definition or in other SQL statements, a user profile must have the Usage privilege for the data type.

Stored Procedures, User-Defined Functions, and Packages

To invoke a stored procedure or user-defined function, or to execute statements in an SQL package, a user profile must have the Execute privilege for the procedure, function, or package. The Execute privilege corresponds to the *ObjOpr and *Execute OS/400 authorities to the corresponding program, service program, or SQL package object.

Programs and Service Programs

Most applications also include OS/400 programs and service programs that aren't SQL stored procedures or functions. These include programs and Integrated Language Environment (ILE) service programs called from application menus or other programs. To call a program or service program, the user profile requires *ObjOpr and *Execute OS/400 authorities to the object. These authorities must be granted or revoked with an OS/400 command; even though SQL stored procedures are OS/400 program objects and user-defined functions are OS/400 service programs, the SQL Grant and Revoke statements can reference only stored procedures and user-defined functions — not all programs and service programs.

As you'll see in the "Program Adopted Authority" section, programs and service programs — including SQL stored procedures and functions — can provide an important means of controlling database access, so you should be careful to grant authority to these executable objects only to those users who should be allowed to run them.

Column-Level Privileges

The authorities and privileges we've looked at thus far apply to the entire object. In the case of tables and views, this means that if you have the Update privilege to a table, for example, you can update any column in any row in the table. For tables and views, SQL/400 also supports a finer-grained control with column-level privileges. As of V4R5 of SQL/400, the only supported privileges are Update for tables and views and References for tables. These two column-level privileges correspond to the Update and Reference field-level authorities listed in Figure 9.3. Although OS/400 has other field-level authorities (e.g., Read), you can't yet control this with SQL/400 (or any other OS/400 interface).[8]

When a user profile has column-level Update privileges to a table or view, the user can modify only those specific columns for which he or she has privileges. In other words, having column-level Update privileges is more limited than having the Update privilege to the entire table or view. The only way to grant or revoke column-level privileges is with the SQL Grant and Revoke statements; there is no comparable OS/400 command. When a user profile has column-level References privileges to a table, the user can specify the listed columns as the part of a parent key in a foreign key constraint. (A column-level References privilege can be granted for a view, but it's not used because foreign key constraints must reference a table, not a view.)

The Grant and Revoke Statements

The SQL Grant statement grants privileges on database objects to user profiles (or the public). The owner of an object, or anyone who's been granted appropriate OS/400 authority, can grant privileges on the object. There are several variations of the Grant statement, depending on the type of object you're granting privileges to. In general, all variations have the form

8 Presumably the other field-level authorities were added with the intent to support them fully in future OS/400 releases.

```
Grant privilege(s)
  On   object(s)
  To   user-profile(s)
  [With Grant Option]
```

Figures 9.5 through 9.9 provide the valid privileges for each type of object. The general form of the Revoke statement is similar:

```
Revoke privilege(s)
  On    object(s)
  From user-profile(s)
```

Granting Table and View Privileges

Let's look first at granting and revoking table and view privileges. Suppose you've created a Customer table (and are the table's owner), and you want to grant the user profile SmithBL the ability to retrieve rows from this table. You could enter a statement such as

```
Grant Select
  On  Customer
  To  SmithBL
```

In a Grant statement, you list the privileges (or the All keyword), then the On keyword followed by one or more table and/or view names, and then the To keyword followed by one or more user profile names (or the Public keyword). Here's a more comprehensive example:

```
Grant Select,
      Insert
  On  Customer,
      CustCrd
  To  SmithBL,
      JonesRK
```

The All keyword can be used instead of a list of privileges, and the implicit list contains those privileges that you're authorized to grant and that are relevant to the type of SQL object (e.g., the Index privilege applies to base tables but not to views).[9]

The Public keyword is an alternative to a user profile name and, if used, refers to the privileges that are available to all user profiles who don't have any other explicit authority (i.e., granted to their user profile by name) to the table or view.

On the Grant statement, you can optionally specify With Grant Option following the list of user profiles. This clause permits the user profiles (or Public) listed on the Grant statement to themselves grant the same privileges on the listed tables and views, as well as to perform operations allowed with the Alter and References privileges:

```
Grant Select
  On  Customer
  To  SmithBL
  With Grant Option
```

For tables and views, you can grant column-level Update and References privileges by including a list of columns after the respective keyword. The following statement grants privileges to let the SmithBL user profile read all columns from the Customer table, but update only the CustStatus and CustCreditLimit columns:

9 Note that the Grant statement's All keyword does not have the same meaning as the OS/400 *All special value listed in Figure 9.4A.

```
Grant Select,
      Update( CustStatus,
              CustCreditLimit )
  On  Customer
  To  SmithBL
```

To limit which of a parent table's columns can be referenced in a foreign key constraint, you can use a Grant statement such as the following:

```
Grant References( CustID )
  On  Customer
  To  SmithBL
```

Several additional considerations apply when granting privileges to views. The Insert, Update, and Delete privileges can be granted only to views that allow those operations. A view can reference other views, as well as tables. The rightmost column in Figure 9.6 shows the OS/400 authorities that are granted to all the directly or indirectly referenced tables and views. Note, however, that the *Add, *Upd, and *Dlt authorities are granted only to objects that are not referenced by the view definition's Where clause (see Chapter 6 for a discussion of view definitions) — only the *Read authority is granted to objects referenced by the Where clause. Also, authorities are *not* granted to a referenced object if the object provides adequate public authority or if the user profile has adequate authority from an indirect source, such as by belonging to a group profile (discussed later). This means, for example, that if the physical file for a table referenced by a view already has *Use public authority, granting a user profile the Select privilege on the view will not grant explicit *Read authority to the referenced table's physical file.

Revoking Table and View Privileges

To revoke privileges, you use a Revoke statement that has a structure similar to the Grant statement:

```
Revoke Select,
       Insert
  On   Customer,
       CustCrd
  From SmithBL,
       JonesRK
```

When you revoke privileges to a table or view, the corresponding OS/400 authorities (as shown in Figures 9.5 and 9.6) are revoked from the underlying database file. However, when you revoke Select, Insert, Update, or Delete privileges, the *ObjOpr authority to the database file is not revoked unless the user no longer has any data authorities (i.e., *Read, *Add, *Upd, *Dlt) to the object. A Revoke statement does not revoke any privileges on tables and views referenced by a view because the user profile might be intended to have these authorities regardless of the authorities to the referencing view.

Granting a user profile the same privilege multiple times, whether done by the same user or different users, enables just one instance of the privilege. Thus, when you revoke a privilege, you remove the privilege completely, no matter how many times it has previously been granted.[10]

10 The SQL/400 Grant and Revoke statements do not work as specified in the ANSI standard — fortunately! According to the ANSI standard, each Grant statement creates one or more unique, unnamed privilege descriptors, which indicates that a specific grantor has granted a specific grantee a particular privilege. A Revoke statement can remove only those privilege descriptors that the authorization ID (i.e., user profile) for the Revoke statement originally granted or that were granted by an authorization ID to whom the With Grant Option was granted. To completely revoke a privilege, all privilege descriptors must be removed, which may require multiple Revoke statements by multiple users. The approach can get incredibly complex, which can result in improperly managed authorization. The OS/400 and SQL/400 approach is much simpler and just as effective.

If a user profile has previously been granted the With Grant Option privilege for an object, the user profile has the OS/400 *ObjMgt authority. The only way in SQL/400 to revoke the *ObjMgt authority is to use a Revoke All. . . statement. Of course, you can always use the RvkObjAut and EdtObjAut commands to manage OS/400 authorities directly.

Granting and Revoking Privileges on Other Database Objects

To grant and revoke privileges to a distinct type, you use statements such as the following:

```
Grant Usage
  On   Distinct Type Dollar
  To   SmithBL

Revoke Usage
  On    Distinct Type Dollar
  From SmithBL
```

Figure 9.7 lists the possible privileges that can be granted and revoked on a distinct data type.

The Grant and Revoke statements for stored procedures and user-defined functions can have several forms. You use one of the following keywords before the name of the object:

- Function
- Procedure
- Specific Function
- Specific Procedure

Following either the Function or Procedure keyword, you use the same object name that was specified after the Create Procedure or Create Function keywords when the object was created. This name can optionally be qualified by the collection that contains the function. The following example shows how you might grant the SmithBL user profile the privilege to invoke the EffectiveRate function.

```
Grant Execute
  On   Function EffectiveRate
  To   SmithBL
```

As we explained in Chapter 8, the same name can be used for different functions, as long as the functions have different numbers or types of parameters. If you have multiple functions with the same name, you can identify a particular function by specifying a list of the target function's parameter types following its name:

```
Grant Execute
  On   Function EffectiveRate ( Int, Int )
  To   SmithBL
```

A final way to identify a function is to use the Specific Function keywords and specify the function's *specific name*, as described in Chapter 8. This name is typically a unique name you specify on the Specific Name clause of the Create Function statement.

```
Grant Execute
  On   Specific Function EffectiveRate2
  To   SmithBL
```

Note that you never specify a list of parameter types after a function's specific name.

The Revoke statements for user-defined functions allow similar alternative ways to specify which function is the target. The Grant and Revoke statements for stored procedures are the same as for functions, except for the use of the Procedure keyword instead of Function.

An SQL package is an object that lets an application on one system execute SQL statements on another system. To grant privileges to a package, use a statement such as the following:

```
Grant Execute
  On  Package GetItem
  To  SmithBL
```

The package must be on the same system as the job in which the Grant statement is executed. The Revoke statement follows the same pattern.

Group Profiles

Group profiles are an OS/400 feature that provides a way to identify an individual user profile as a member of one or more groups. You can then grant authority to the group rather than to the individual user profiles. This approach can greatly simplify the administration of authority. SQL/400 itself has no explicit statements to create group profiles or to assign individual (i.e., non-group) user profiles to group profiles, but the Grant and Revoke statements can specify group profiles in the To and From clauses.

To establish a group, the security officer or someone with appropriate authority creates a user profile that serves as the group profile. This user profile should be created with no password (i.e., use the Password(*None) parameter on the CrtUsrPrf command) so no individual actually uses the profile to sign on.[11]

To assign an individual user profile to a group, you specify the group profile name for the GrpPrf or SupGrpPrf (supplemental group profiles) parameter on the CrtUsrPrf or ChgUsrPrf command for the individual user profile. A user profile implicitly becomes a group profile when it's referenced as a group profile for any other user profile.[12] A group profile cannot itself be a member of another group; that is, you cannot specify anything other than GrpPrf(*None) and SupGrpPrf(*None) — the defaults — for a group profile.

An individual user profile can be a member of up to 16 group profiles. The first group profile must be specified on the GrpPrf parameter, and up to 15 additional group profiles can be specified on the SupGrpPrf parameter.[13] The following command assigns Betty L. Smith to the GrpSales and GrpAccount group profiles:

```
ChgUsrPrf UsrPrf( SmithBL )
          GrpPrf( GrpSales )
          SupGrpPrf( GrpAccount )
```

When OS/400 checks for a user profile's authority to an object and the individual user profile has no explicit authority (including not having *Exclude authority) to the object, OS/400 then checks the user profile's group profile(s), if any, to see whether group profiles provide any authorities

11 This isn't a requirement of a group profile, but it's a good administrative practice not to use the same profile both for an individual and as a group profile.

12 A user profile is explicitly designated a group profile if you specify a value other than *None for the GID (group ID) parameter on the CrtUsrPrf or ChgUsrPrf command. Group ID numbers are used for accessing files in the hierarchical part of the AS/400 integrated file system, not UDB/400 files.

13 The significance of the group profile specified in the GrpPrf parameter is that the Owner, GrpAut, and GrpAutTyp attributes of the individual user profile (i.e., the one that belongs to the group profile) apply just to the group profile specified in the GrpPrf parameter, not to any group profile specified in the SupGrpPrf parameter.

to the object. If they do and the combination of authorities granted to the group profile(s) is adequate, OS/400 permits the operation.[14] If there are no group profiles or the group profile(s) provide no authorities to the object, OS/400 next checks the object's public authority.[15] If the group profile(s) have any authorities (including *Exclude) to the object but the combination of authorities isn't adequate for the operation, OS/400 skips the check for public authority and continues with the check for program adopted authority (discussed later).

There are a couple of important aspects to the way OS/400 checks authority. First, notice that the search for sufficient authorities stops with the individual user profile if the profile has any authority to the object. This means you can use the *Exclude authority or any other specific authority to "short circuit" the authority an individual user profile derives from its group profiles and public authority because OS/400 won't check either group profile authority or public authority if the individual user profile has any authority to the object. A similar principle applies for group profile authorities to an object — if there are any, OS/400 doesn't check the object's public authority.[16]

This approach means OS/400 does *not* add together the individual, group, and public authorities. Consider the following authorities:

- The SmithBL individual user profile has *ObjOpr authority to the Customer table.
- The GrpSales group profile has *Upd authority to the Customer table.
- The Customer table has *Read public authority.

Even if the GrpSales profile is a group profile for SmithBL, a job running under SmithBL would not be able to open the Customer table for read and update or any other operations. What's required is one of the following conditions:

- The SmithBL user profile has *ObjOpr, *Read, and *Upd authorities to the Customer table.
- The SmithBL user profile has no authorities (not even *Exclude) to the Customer table, and the GrpSales user profile has *ObjOpr, *Read, and *Upd authorities to the Customer table.
- Neither the SmithBL nor the GrpSales user profile has any authorities to the Customer table, and the Customer table has *ObjOpr, *Read, and *Upd public authorities.

14 If any group profile has the *AllObj special authority, this provides the group profile with adequate authority for any operation, regardless of the group profile's specific authorities to the object.

15 The actual steps OS/400 goes through to check for authority are more complex than this; however, this is the basic mechanism that lets you use group profiles or public authority to simplify granting authority. The *OS/400 Security — Reference* manual includes a complete flowchart for OS/400's authority search algorithm.

16 IBM originally introduced this approach as a tool for security management by exception. The idea was that you could grant more group or public authority than some individuals should have and use *Exclude or other limited authorities for just those individual profiles you wanted to restrict. Unfortunately, using this technique can be dangerous and difficult to manage because you can't easily see the net effect of changes to group or public authorities. No foolproof solution exists because granting an individual user profile more authorities than its group profiles could unintentionally leave authorities in place for an individual when you reduce a group's authorities. The dilemma results from the fact that you have to grant all the group profile's authorities plus any additional ones for an individual user profile because OS/400 doesn't add individual and group profile authorities together when determining authority to an object.

Our advice is to use group profiles as the primary way you grant authority, but don't assign any individual user profile to a group that has more authority than the individual profile should have. That way, you won't have to grant a more limited set of authorities to the individual profile to short circuit the authority the individual profile would get from the group profile. Instead, when an individual profile must have more authority than provided by any of the individual profile's group profiles, grant the necessary authority to the individual user profile directly.

OS/400 does add together the group profile authorities when an individual user profile has more than one group profile with some authority to the target object. But this combination of authorities applies only for the group profile step of the authority check.

As a performance tweak, you can use the ChgObjPgp command to set or change an object's **primary group**. The following command sets the Customer table's primary group profile to GrpSales:

```
ChgObjPgp Obj( AppDta/Customer )
          ObjType( *File )
          NewPgp( GrpSales )
```

This command doesn't change the GrpSales group profile's or any other profile's authority to the Customer file. All it does is store some information about the GrpSales profile's authority to the Customer file in the file object itself,[17] thus speeding up OS/400's authority checking in some cases. As a rule of thumb, you may get some improvement in performance if you set up group profiles so that individual user profiles that frequently access an object have as their first group profile (i.e., as specified on the CrtUsrPrf command's GrpPrf parameter) a group profile that's also been made the primary group for the frequently accessed object. Obviously, there may be objects that are frequently accessed by user profiles that belong to different groups, and only one of the group profiles can be designated as an object's primary group.

Authorization Lists

Group profiles provide a way to organize groups of individual user profiles so authorities can be granted to a single group profile and thus indirectly be made available for the individual user profiles that belong to the group. **Authorization lists** provide a somewhat comparable feature that lets you organize sets of objects for which identical authorities are granted. SQL/400 provides no statements to work with authorization lists, but you can use OS/400 authorization list commands to work with the OS/400 objects (e.g., database files) that are created by SQL statements.

An authorization list is an OS/400 object that represents a list of objects. If you associate other objects with an authorization list object, you indirectly grant authority to the objects associated with the authorization list when you grant public authority or authority for a user profile to the authorization list. To create an authorization list, you use a command such as the following:

```
CrtAutL AutL( SalesObj )
        Aut( *Exclude )
        Text( 'Sales objects' )
```

This command creates the SalesObj authorization list and does not provide any public authority to the authorization list or the objects subsequently associated with it. All authorization lists are created in the QSys library, so you cannot specify a qualified name on the AutL parameter of any command.

To take advantage of an authorization list, you associate two lists with the authorization list:

- a list of objects that are in the scope of the authorization list
- an implicit list of individual user profiles and/or group profiles that are authorized to the authorization list

You put an object under the scope of an authorization list by using a command such as the following:

17 This information is stored in the object header part of the object (as described in Chapter 1), not in the file's records.

```
GrtObjAut Obj( AppDta/Sale )
          ObjType( *File )
          AutL( SalesObj )
```

As an alternative, you can use the EdtObjAut command to edit a display of the authorities that exist for an object. This display contains an entry field for the object's associated authorization list (if any). An object can be associated with only one authorization list at a time, and you can't nest authorization lists (i.e., you can't specify ObjType(*AutL) along with the AutL parameter on the GrtObjAut command).

To grant a user profile authority to an authorization list, and hence to the associated objects, you can use a GrtObjAut command, such as the following:

```
GrtObjAut Obj( SalesObj )
          ObjType( *AutL )
          User( SmithBL )
          Aut( *Use )
```

OS/400 has an AddAutLE (Add Authorization List Entry) command to slightly simplify granting a user profile authority to an authorization list. The following example is equivalent to the GrtObjAut command above:[18]

```
AddAutLE AutL( SalesObj )
         User( SmithBL )
         Aut( *Use )
```

When you grant a user profile authority to an authorization list, you effectively provide the specified authorities to the user profile for all the objects associated with the authorization list.[19] Notice that each user profile has its own set of authorities, which are the same for all objects associated with the authorization list. You can specify any of the values in Figures 9.3 and 9.4A for the Aut parameter on a GrtObjAut or AddAutLE command. A user profile can be granted authority to more than one authorization list.

If an object is associated with an authorization list, OS/400 performs another round of authority checks when an operation is attempted. In simple terms, OS/400

1. checks the individual user profile's authority to the target object
2. checks the individual user profile's authority to the target object's associated authorization list object
3. checks the group profile (if any) authority to the target object or to the target object's associated authorization list object. If multiple group profiles exist, their authorities are added together for the test.

   Each group profile is first checked for authority to the target object. If the group has any authorities (including *Exclude) to the target object, the group contributes these authorities to the combined total for all groups. If the group has no authority to the target object, the system checks the group's authority to the target object's associated authorization list object

18 The AddAutLE command may confuse more than simplify the understanding of the relationship between user profiles and authorization lists, especially because the security manuals sometimes give the impression that adding an authorization list entry is somehow different from just granting a user profile authority to the authorization list. The GrtObjAut and AddAutLE commands with comparable parameter values achieve identical results.

19 For the User parameter, you can specify the *Public special value instead of a user profile name. Public authority to an authorization list provides public authority only to those objects associated with the list that have their public authority set to use the authorization list (i.e., the object has Public(*AutL) specified).

and, if any authorities exist, adds them to the combined total for all groups. (Note that each group contributes either its authorities to the object or its authorities to the authorization list, but not both.)

4. checks the public authority either for the target object or for the target object's associated authorization list object

At the completion of each of these steps, if OS/400 finds any authority to the target object, either directly or to its associated authorization list, OS/400 stops checking.

As step 4 implies, an object's public authority can also be controlled with an authorization list. To do this, you use the name of the authorization list as the value for the Aut parameter on the Crt*Xxx* command, as in the following command:

```
CrtPf File( AppDta/Sale )
      SrcFile( AppSrc/QDdsSrc )
      Aut( SalesObj )
```

After this command is executed, the public authority to the Sale file is defined by the SalesObj authorization list's public authority (which may be *Exclude or any of the authorities in Figures 9.3 and 9.4A).[20]

Authorization lists can reduce the number of specific authorities you have to grant to individual and group profiles. But because authorization lists add additional steps to OS/400 authority checking, they may adversely affect performance. As a rule of thumb, if you have several objects for which the same set of authorities is frequently granted, consider an authorization list. It's not uncommon to have sets of application programs and files for which *Use authority is frequently granted en masse (and public authority is *Exclude). Such sets are good candidates for authorization lists.

Program Adopted Authority

With all the different ways you can specify authority under OS/400, you might think every possible situation could be covered. In fact, there are many types of database-access rules that can't be directly specified with what we've looked at so far. The problem stems from the broad meaning of the four kinds of data authorities: *Read, *Add, *Upd, and *Dlt. If a user profile has *ObjOpr and *Upd authorities to a table (i.e., physical file), any type of update to any column in any row in any member is allowed. This level of access is not usually desirable. Instead, most applications are intended to let a user make only valid changes to some columns, often for only a subset of the rows in the table.

As described earlier, you can use views to limit access to a subset of a table's rows and columns. You can also use column-level Update privileges to control update capabilities on a column-by-column basis. These column-level approaches to access are somewhat limited, however. The biggest problem is that they provide no way to control the *values* that are put in columns that can be updated. Thus, a

20 In this example, when you specify Aut(SalesObj), the SalesObj authorization list must already exist. Specifying Aut(SalesObj) associates the Sale file with the SalesObj authorization list, so it's not necessary to execute a subsequent GrtObjAut command to make the association, as shown in the earlier example. As mentioned, the Aut parameter also sets the object's public authority to *AutL.

For an object created without an authorization list specified for the Aut parameter, you can use the GrtObjAut or EdtObjAut command to set the object's public authority to *AutL so OS/400 will check the public authority of the object's associated authority list. Before doing this, the object must first be associated with an authorization list (also using either a GrtObjAut or EdtObjAut command).

Note that OS/400 checks public authority by first looking at the object's public authority setting. If this is *AutL, OS/400 then looks at the associated authorization list object's public authority setting. Otherwise, OS/400 uses the target object's specific authorities for the public (if any). This either-or approach is different from the way OS/400 checks individual and group profile authorities. In both those cases, OS/400 first checks the user profile's authorities to the target object and then checks the user profile's authorities to the authorization list (if any).

payroll clerk authorized to update the salary column in employee rows can put in any value for the salary.[21] Another problem is that the available row selection criteria on view definitions can't express all application constraints.

Ultimately, you'll find you must use application program logic to control some access and to limit updates to valid values. OS/400 provides an excellent tool for this purpose: **program adopted authority**.

Normally when you create a program, any operations it performs (e.g., updating rows in a table) require the job's user profile to have adequate authority (either directly or via a group profile, public authority, or an authorization list). You can optionally, however, create a program that can perform any operation that the program's owner has authority to perform (in addition to operations the job's user profile has authority to perform). Service program and SQL package objects can also adopt authority, and because SQL stored procedures and user-defined functions are actually OS/400 programs and service programs, these SQL objects can also adopt authority.

Let's look at a simple example. Suppose there's a user profile (created expressly for this purpose) named PrfChgEmp (profile — change employee). This user profile is made the owner of the ChgEmpSal (change employee salary) program — we'll discuss how in a moment. The PrfChgEmp user profile is also granted *Change authority to the Employee table. Last, the ChgEmpSal program is designated as a program that adopts the authority of its owner when the program runs (again, we'll see how in a moment). With this arrangement, any user profile that has *Execute authority to the ChgEmpSal program can run it. And, while that user profile is running the ChgEmpSal program, the program can perform any retrieval or update operations on the Employee table, regardless of the authority of the user profile running the program.

What this setup lets you do is not grant individual user profiles full *Change authority to the Employee table. Instead, you can grant them *Use or no specific authority to the Employee table and *Execute authority to the ChgEmpSal program. Then the only way they can update the Employee table is through operations provided by the ChgEmpSal program — which, presumably, enforces the appropriate business rules for the application.[22]

The user profiles that own programs that adopt authority don't represent end users, programmers, or security personnel. These user profiles should be created with names that reflect their purpose and with Password(*None) specified so no one can sign on with the user profile.

Using a command such as the following makes a special-purpose user profile the owner of a program:

21 The values may be limited by check constraints specified for the column, but check constraints don't let you specify cross-row conditions or conditions based on which user is performing an update.

22 There's another approach — often called "menu-based security" or "menu access control" — that's used in many AS/400 organizations. This approach grants extensive private or public authority to tables and other objects and then tries to limit how the users can get at objects by confining them to selecting options from application menus. Typically, the user profile is also set up with LmtCpb(*Yes) to limit the user profile's capability to run commands from interactive jobs.

The theory is that the user will never be able to perform any operation except those made available from an application menu. This approach is ineffective and should never be used as a substitute for resource security (as we've been discussing in this chapter). There are many ways to circumvent application menus, and someone serious about breaching security will not be deterred by this approach. Furthermore, this approach leaves data exposed to improper access when PCs or Web browsers are connected to the AS/400 (because remote access doesn't flow through AS/400-based menu programs). Additional AS/400 security features not covered in this chapter might appear to provide adequate mechanisms to make menu-based security viable, but they don't. IBM's own security specialists, as well as the leading AS/400 security experts, agree that menu-based security by itself is not an adequate approach to database security.

```
ChgObjOwn Obj( AppExc/ChgEmpSal )
          ObjType( *Pgm )
          NewOwn( PrfChgEmp )
```

Then, the appropriate security person or application administrator changes the program so it adopts the authority of the program owner's user profile:

```
ChgPgm Pgm( AppExc/ChgEmpSal )
       UsrPrf( *Owner )
```

The PrfChgEmp special-purpose user profile can be granted authority, just like any other user profile:

```
GrtObjAut Obj( AppDta/Customer )
          ObjType( *File )
          User( PrfChgEmp )
          Aut( *Change )
```

or, in SQL:

```
Grant Select,
      Update,
      Delete,
      Insert
  On  AppDta.Customer
  To PrfChgEmp
```

With programs that adopt authority, you have available a method to control access in precisely the way applications require.

Programs that adopt authority normally propagate their authority to programs they call. OS/400 adds together all the adopted and propagated authority for programs in the job's program call stack[23] when authority is checked. You can create a program with the UseAdpAut(*No) parameter to prevent the program from inheriting any adopted authority from the program that calls it.[24]

A user profile created to own a program that adopts authority should own only one program or a few programs that are closely related to the same application operations. The user profile should have the *minimum* authorities needed to perform the operations it implements. Do not use a user profile that owns all database tables and views as the owner of programs that adopt authority. This practice provides too much authority for a job while the program is executing. Although a full discussion of security risks and program adopted authority is beyond the scope of this chapter, you want to be sure that if a user is able to circumvent constraints that are part of the program, the scope of the harm the user can do is as limited as possible.[25]

23 The job's call stack is essentially the list of programs that have been called but have not yet returned to the program that called them.

24 This isn't a particularly useful capability because the problem isn't inheriting too much adopted authority; rather, the problem is propagating authority unnecessarily. (See footnote 25.)

25 For example, let's say PgmA adopts authority and calls PgmB. If the person who calls PgmA can introduce a different version of PgmB (e.g., by changing the job's library list so OS/400 finds the program object named PgmB in a different library), then he or she can perform operations in the "impostor" PgmB (which he or she may have written for this purpose) using the authority adopted (and propagated) by PgmA. As this example points out, you must carefully control program calls from programs that adopt authority.

As a side note, at the operating-system level, you can specify on a program Call operation whether to propagate adopted authority. This option isn't available in any of the major AS/400 HLLs. It would be a highly valuable feature to be able to prevent a program that adopts authority from being able to propagate the authority to any nonsystem program it calls.

Database Security Principles and Guidelines

OS/400 security is an important and extensive topic. This section provides some principles and guidelines to help you lay a solid foundation for your UDB/400 database security. The annotated bibliography lists several references that provide more detailed discussions and advice.

General

- Security is a business function of protecting an organization's resources and operations; computer systems security should be designed within the context of the organization's overall security plan.
- Security rules cover different levels of threat — the more vital a security policy is to your organization's well-being, the more thoroughly you must enforce the policy.
- Assume that people who will intentionally try to breach your security understand the technical aspects of the AS/400 as well as you do. Don't rely on an attacker's ignorance of the AS/400 to protect your system. What they shouldn't know are the passwords.
- If the implementation of a security mechanism fails, the error should result in unintended restrictions on access rather than unintended additional access.

AS/400-Specific

- Set your AS/400's QSecurity system value to 30 or higher. This setting enforces password protection and resource-level security, as we've discussed in this chapter.

  Level 40 is recommended and provides all the security enforcement of level 30 plus additional checks to see that various features of the operating system aren't tampered with or used improperly to circumvent security.
- Assign a unique user profile and password to each individual who uses your system.
- Consider changing the CrtLib command's CrtAut parameter default to *Exclude.
- Carefully consider how much public authority (if any) each application file and program should have.
- Use group profiles to organize user profiles into groups that can be granted identical authority for many objects.
- Use authorization lists to organize sets of objects for which identical authorities are frequently granted.
- Be aware of how OS/400's authority search works and the way granting any authority to an individual user profile short circuits the search of group profile and public authorities. Avoid using this short-circuit technique unless it's necessary.
- Grant the minimum authority necessary for any operation. This principle applies for individual and group profiles, authorization lists entries, and adopted authority.
- Use program adopted authority to provide required authority under control of a program when you don't want to give the full capabilities of a specific authority (e.g., *Upd) to a user profile.
- For the user profile that owns a program that adopts authority, do not have a user profile that owns other application objects or that has more authority than the program needs for its operations.

- Have special-purpose user profiles (not programmer or end-user user profiles) own application objects.
- Be sure to consider remote PC and Web access to your AS/400 when setting up security and granting authorities.

Chapter Summary

OS/400 controls access to objects by checking the authority a user profile has to the target object. A user profile is an AS/400 object with a name, password, and other attributes. In general, each person that uses the AS/400 should have a unique user profile. Each OS/400 object is owned by a user profile, and an object's owner normally has all authorities to the object. SQL/400 uses OS/400 authority to control access to SQL objects, including collections, tables, views, distinct types, stored procedures, user-defined functions, and packages.

The two main categories of OS/400 authorities are special authorities and specific authorities. The *AllObj special authority provides all access to all objects on the AS/400 and is usually assigned only to user profiles for people responsible for systemwide security. The *SavSys special authority lets the user profile save and restore objects and is usually assigned to the user profiles for some members of the system operations staff.

Specific authorities are granted to a user profile or the public to provide various levels of access to a specific object. Specific authorities are subdivided into object authorities, data authorities, and field authorities. Object authorities control general use of the object, including basic access, changing object attributes, management operations (e.g., renaming), and existence. Data authorities control read, add, update, and delete operations on an object's contents, as well as the ability to find objects in a collection and to run a program. Field authorities control access to individual fields (or columns) in a database table or view. You can use the OS/400 GrtObjAut, RvkObjAut, and EdtObjAut commands to grant and revoke specific authorities to OS/400 objects. SQL privileges correspond to OS/400 specific authorities.

An object's public authority governs access to the object when an individual user profile has no specific authorities to the object and the individual user profile's group profiles (if any) also have no specific authorities to the object.

You can use the SQL Grant and Revoke statements to grant and revoke privileges to SQL objects, which results in the corresponding OS/400 authorities to the underlying OS/400 objects being granted or revoked. The Grant and Revoke statements also let you specify column-level privileges to update specific columns or to reference specific parent key columns in a foreign key constraint. You can also use views as a means of limiting access to selected columns and/or a subset of rows in a table.

To use an object in a collection, a user profile must have *Execute authority to the collection. To run a program or service program, a user profile must have *ObjOpr and *Execute authorities to the program. To access data in a database file, a user profile must have *ObjOpr authority and one or more of the *Read, *Add, *Upd, and *Dlt data authorities to the file. In SQL terms, the user profile must have the Select, Update, Delete, or Insert privilege on a table or view in order to access the table or view data. To use a distinct type requires the Usage privilege. To invoke a stored procedure or user-defined function or to execute statements in an SQL package, the user profile must have the Execute privilege on the object.

The Grant and Revoke Statements grant and revoke one or more privileges to one or more specified user profiles to perform certain operations on one or more database objects. You can use a With Grant Option clause on a Grant statement to let the specified user profile(s) also grant the same privileges to other user profiles.

Group profiles provide a way to simplify authority management by organizing individual user profiles into groups and granting authority to the group profiles. A user profile can have up to 16 group profiles. A group profile is just a user profile object referenced as the group profile by some individual (i.e., nongroup) user profile. When an individual user profile has no authority to an object, OS/400 checks the individual user profile's group profiles (if any) for sufficient authority. If the individual user profile has more than one group profile with any authority to the object, all of the group profiles' authorities are added together.

An authorization list object provides a way to organize objects for which the same set of OS/400 authorities is frequently granted. The GrtObjAut command (or the Aut parameter on a Crt*Xxx* command) associates an object with an authorization list. All authorities granted to a user profile for an authorization list then apply to all objects that are associated with the authorization list.

Program adopted authority provides a way to control access under program logic, for example, to allow only certain types of updates to a file. A program that has the UsrPrf(*Owner) attribute can perform any operation for which the user profile that owns the program has sufficient authority. A special-purpose user profile can be made the owner of a program that adopts authority and can be granted the required authorities to perform the program's functions. Subsequently, any user profile authorized to run the program can use it to perform the operations the program implements, regardless of the authority the job's user profile has for the target object.

Special-purpose user profiles should be created to own application objects. One or more of these special-purpose user profiles can own files and programs that don't adopt authority. Each program that adopts authority should be owned by a separate user profile that is not one of the user profiles that own other application objects. A user profile that owns a program that adopts authority should have no more than the necessary authorities to perform the operations the program implements.

Key Terms

authority
authorization ID
authorization list
data authority
field authority
group profile
object authority
primary group
privilege
program adopted authority
public authority
special authority
specific authority
user profile

Exercises

1. Explain why each person who uses the AS/400 should have their own user profile and password.
2. Discuss the reasons production application objects should not be owned by programmers' user profiles. Can you think of any problems this rule might cause?
3. List the SQL table privileges that must be granted to grant the OS/400 *ObjOpr, *ObjRef, *Read, and *Upd authorities to the underlying database file.
4. Code the Grant statement to allow the user profile HarrisAK to read rows from and insert rows into the Customer and Employee tables.
5. Assume that the Customer table has the following columns: CustID, CustName, and ShipAddress. Assume the CustShip view is defined as an updatable view over the Customer

table and the view includes only the CustID and ShipAddress columns. Also assume that the SmithBL user profile has no privileges to either object and that both objects have no public authority. Show the SQL statements necessary to allow the following capabilities:

- Anyone can read the information in the CustID and ShipAddress columns (but not the CustName column).
- In addition, SmithBL can update information in the ShipAddress column.

6. Considering the CustShip view and Customer table in Exercise 5 and the privileges you granted to the public and SmithBL, describe the necessary steps to let SmithBL also read all the Customer table data and add new Customer rows (but still not be able to update any information other than the ShipAddress column).

   Hint: This problem isn't as simple as it might appear. Consider carefully the OS/400 authorities that will be granted to the underlying logical and physical files. To answer this question, you can use OS/400 GrtObjAut and RvkObjAut commands, as well as SQL Grant and Revoke statements, if you want.

7. Why do you think IBM doesn't allow a group profile to be a member of another group? What would be the advantages for managing security if you could create nested group profiles? How does the current limitation affect your design for setting up security for an organization?
8. Show how you would authorize the JonesRK user profile to have *Use authority to the Employee and Training tables (i.e., physical files) with the following constraints:
   - JonesRK should have GrpEmp as a group profile.
   - Neither JonesRK nor GrpEmp should have specific authorities to the Employee or Training table.
   - The public should have *Exclude authority to the Employee and Training tables.
   - No programs that adopt authority are used.
   - The same authorities are always granted for the Employee and Training tables.

   To answer this question, you can use OS/400 commands, as well as SQL Grant and Revoke statements, if you want.
9. Assume the following conditions:
   - There's a Customer table that has no public authority.
   - The ChgCust program (which is not a stored procedure) provides the ability to read, update, and delete (but not insert) rows in the Customer table. This program is currently owned by the AppOwn profile that owns all application database files.
   - The SmithBL user profile currently has Select, Update, and Delete privileges to the Customer table and no authorities to the ChgCust program.
   - The security officer will create any new user profile you need.

   Show the necessary commands and/or SQL statements so the SmithBL user profile can read, update, and delete rows in the Customer table under control of the ChgCust program but no other way. Be sure your actions don't potentially give SmithBL more than the specified authority.
10. Show an alternative solution to Exercise 9 when ChgCust is a stored procedure.

Chapter 10

Static and Dynamic Embedded Statements

Chapter Overview

This chapter builds on Chapters 5, 7, and 8, which covered SQL Data Manipulation Language (DML), and shows how to embed SQL DML statements in a program written in an HLL, such as RPG IV or ILE COBOL/400. It covers how to use host variables in SQL statements, error handling, and how to create and execute entire SQL statements dynamically using the Execute Immediate, Prepare, and Execute statements.

Introduction to Embedded SQL

In Chapter 7, you learned how dynamic, ad hoc SQL (e.g., a statement entered in Operations Navigator or ISQL) could be used to update a set of rows. For example, the following statement sets all Portland customers' discount to 10 percent:

```
Update  Customer
  Set    Discount = .10
  Where ShipCity = 'Portland'
```

Interactive entry of an SQL statement is quite useful for ad hoc retrieval and updates. However, there are a number of reasons you might want to control the execution of SQL statements from within an HLL program rather than using the statements interactively:

- Unrestricted dynamic execution of Insert, Update, and Delete statements lets the user make *any* change to the data. This may not be something you want to allow.
- Ad hoc entry of statements can be error-prone. For example, if a user mistypes the greater than (>) symbol for the less than (<) symbol, an Update statement will change the wrong set of rows.
- Ad hoc entry of statements can be complex. For example, constructing the proper quantified predicates or subqueries may be difficult for end users not trained in SQL.
- SQL alone may not provide adequate computational or logic capabilities to perform a required operation. For example, an Update statement's Set clause can't conditionally retrieve a value from one of several tables (the Case structure doesn't allow a scalar subselect as a result). You can implement such operations with multiple SQL statements using program variables.
- SQL doesn't provide user interface (e.g., display file) programming capabilities. To present retrieved results or to prompt for input for updates in ways other than those provided by Operations Navigator and ISQL, you need HLL (or other utility) capabilities.

Fortunately, SQL statements can be **embedded** (i.e., coded) in HLL programs. And you can use program variables to receive retrieved values as well as to supply values used in a statement's search condition or as the input values for an Insert or Update statement. The following example shows how the Update statement above could be coded as an embedded statement, using two program variables:

```
Update  Customer
  Set   Discount = :NewDisc
  Where ShipCity = :SlcCusCity
```

Before this statement, the program would set the values of the NewDisc and SlcCusCity variables. If these two variables were set to .10 and Portland, respectively, the effect of this Update statement would be exactly the same as in the previous example. With the use of program variables in this SQL statement, an application can both simplify and control the update action. For example, the user could be presented with a simple interface into which he or she enters the discount amount and city. The program could even provide a list of cities from which the user selects. The program could also check the discount the user enters, making sure it's not negative and not over some maximum allowed discount.

To create an HLL program with embedded SQL, you code SQL statements along with HLL statements in a source member. You then execute an appropriate CL command to create a program object[1] from the source member. For example, to create an RPG IV program from a source member with embedded SQL, you use a CrtSqlRpgI (Create SQL ILE RPG Object) command, such as the following:

```
CrtSqlRpgI Obj( AppExc/UpdCust )
           SrcFile( AppSrc/QRpgleSrc )
           SrcMbr( UpdCust )
```

Although it takes only one CL command to create a program, the underlying process involves two major steps, as shown in Figure 10.1.

Figure 10.1
Creation Steps for HLL Program with Embedded SQL

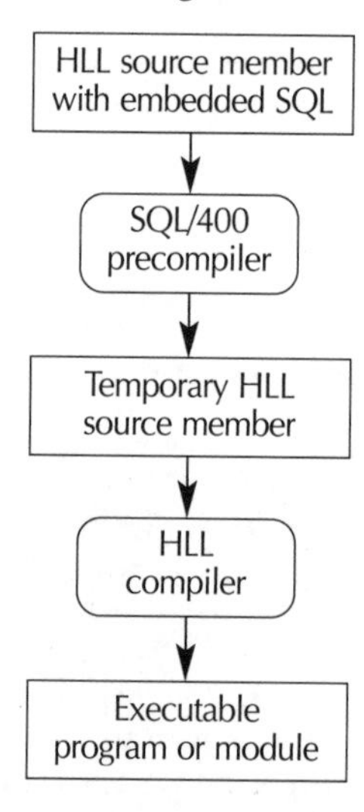

1 For RPG IV, ILE COBOL/400, and other Integrated Language Environment (ILE) languages, you can create an OS/400 module or service program object instead of a program object. If you create a module object, you can subsequently bind one or more modules to create a program or service program object. "The SQL/400 Translation Process" section in Chapter 12 discusses different aspects of program creation.

The first step is called **precompilation**; it translates the input source member with the embedded SQL statements into a temporary output source member with all the embedded SQL statements translated into HLL declarations and procedural statements. The second step is the normal HLL compilation process, which translates the temporary source member input into an executable program object. The details of the process are more complex than this overview, but we'll defer discussion of the details until Chapter 12.

The SQL precompiler requires some way to differentiate embedded SQL statements from HLL statements. For example, SQL, RPG IV, and ILE COBOL/400 all have a Delete statement; without some way to differentiate between an SQL Delete statement and an HLL Delete statement, the precompiler wouldn't know whether to translate the statement or pass it on (untranslated) as an HLL statement.

The solution is quite simple: You code a pair of **precompiler directives** around each embedded SQL statement. In RPG IV, you code all embedded SQL statements in the C-specs, which require a C in position 6. Before each SQL statement, you code /Exec SQL in positions 7–15. After each SQL statement, you code /End-Exec in positions 7–15. Any lines (other than blank lines and RPG IV comments) between the /Exec SQL and /End-Exec delimiters must have a plus sign (+) in position 7; this character marks an SQL continuation line.[2] Exactly one SQL statement must be coded between /Exec SQL and /End-Exec. Here's the previous example as it would be coded in RPG IV:

```
....1....+....2....+....3....+....4....+....
C/Exec SQL
C+ Update   Customer
C+    Set   Discount = :NewDisc
C+    Where ShipCity = :SlcCusCity
C/End-Exec
```

A similar approach is used in ILE COBOL/400. Most SQL statements, including all the DML statements, must be coded in the Procedure Division. All parts of an embedded SQL statement must be coded in positions 12–72.[3] Before each SQL statement, you code Exec SQL; after each SQL statement, you code End-Exec. End-Exec can optionally be followed by a period to end an ILE COBOL/400 sentence that includes the SQL statement. Here's the previous example as it would be coded in ILE COBOL/400:[4]

```
....1....+....2....+....3....+....4....+....
      Exec SQL
        Update  Customer
          Set   Discount = :NewDisc
          Where ShipCity = :SlcCusCity
      End-Exec
```

Between the Exec SQL and End-Exec delimiters, you can use blank lines or HLL comment lines. You can also code SQL comments by beginning a comment anywhere in a line with two dashes (--); the comment then includes the rest of the line. You can code SQL comments that span multiple lines by beginning them with /* and ending them with */. The following example shows blank lines, an RPG IV comment, and SQL single- and multiple-line comments as they're coded in RPG IV:

2 You can also begin an SQL statement in position 17 of the line containing the /Exec SQL directive. The examples in this book always begin the SQL statement on the line following the /Exec SQL directive.

3 The SQL/400 precompiler actually allows the Exec SQL and End-Exec directives to begin in position 8 of an ILE COBOL/400 source line.

4 This ILE COBOL/400 example shows the ruler to indicate where the statement is coded. Subsequent ILE COBOL/400 examples don't use a ruler because, other than being coded in positions 12–72, SQL statements embedded in ILE COBOL/400 have no positional requirements.

```
....1....+....2....+....3....+....4....+....5....+....6....+....7....
C/Exec SQL

 * Change the discount for all customers in a city

C+ Update  Customer
C+   Set   Discount = :NewDisc      -- New discount
C+   Where ShipCity = :SlcCusCity   -- Selected city

C+ /* This Update statement contains 2 host variables that
C+    must be set prior to its execution.                    */
C/End-Exec
```

In SQL, a program variable coded in an embedded SQL statement is called a **host variable**. You always put a colon (:) at the beginning of a host variable name within an SQL statement. You can see how this is done for the NewDisc and SlcCusCity host variables in the example above. Note that you do not use the : with the host variable when coding normal HLL statements. Here's how a sequence of two RPG IV Eval statements and the embedded Update statement would look:[5]

```
....1....+....2....+....3....+....4....+....5....+....6....+....7....
C                   Eval      NewDisc    = InpDisc
C                   Eval      SlcCusCity = InpCusCity
C/Exec SQL
C+                  Update  Customer
C+                    Set   Discount = :NewDisc
C+                    Where ShipCity = :SlcCusCity
C/End-Exec
```

In SQL/400, you don't need to do anything special to declare a host variable that's used in an SQL statement, although there are some restrictions as to the types of host variables that can be used. Host variables, however, should be declared before their first use in an SQL statement.[6]

In ILE COBOL/400, you code qualified host variable names within an SQL statement using an SQL-like syntax such as

```
CustomerRow.CustID
```

rather than the standard Cobol syntax of

```
CustID of CustomerRow
```

You can also use an RPG data structure name to qualify an RPG subfield used in an SQL statement, but doing so serves only a documentation purpose because the unqualified names of all RPG subfields must be unique within a source member.

Each HLL has its own variations on variable data types, and SQL has its set of column data types as well. Figures 10.2 and 10.3 show the correspondence between the SQL, RPG IV, and ILE COBOL/400 data types.

5 This example shows a recommended coding style for embedding SQL statements in an RPG IV program. The SQL statement is aligned with the RPG opcodes so that the code layout flows smoothly rather than jumping to the left for SQL statements. In this book, when SQL examples do not include RPG IV statements, they're shown left justified.

6 This is required in ILE COBOL/400 but not in RPG IV or RPG/400. It's good programming practice in all HLLs.
In ILE COBOL/400 (but not RPG IV or RPG/400), you can optionally code the SQL Begin Declare Section and End Declare Section statements in the Working-Storage and Linkage sections to identify host variables that will be used in SQL statements. You code normal ILE COBOL/400 variable declarations between the Begin Declare Section and End Declare Section statements. If you code Begin Declare Section and End Declare Section statements, only variables declared between the two statements can be used in SQL statements. You can have multiple SQL declare sections within a program.

Figure 10.2

SQL/400 Column Data Types and Corresponding RPG IV Host Variable Data Types

<table>
<tr><th>SQL/400</th><th>RPG IV Definition Specification (D-spec)</th></tr>
<tr><td colspan="2">Character</td></tr>
<tr><td>Char(nnnnn)</td><td><pre>....1....+....2....+....3....+....4....+....5
D   S   nnnnnA</pre></td></tr>
<tr><td>VarChar(nnnnn)</td><td><pre>....1....+....2....+....3....+....4....+....5
D   S   nnnnnA   Varying</pre></td></tr>
<tr><td>Graphic(nnnnn)</td><td><pre>....1....+....2....+....3....+....4....+....5
D   S   nnnnnG</pre></td></tr>
<tr><td>VarGraphic(nnnnn)</td><td><pre>....1....+....2....+....3....+....4....+....5
D   S   nnnnnG   Varying</pre></td></tr>
<tr><td colspan="2">Numeric</td></tr>
<tr><td>Dec(pp,ss)</td><td><pre>....1....+....2....+....3....+....4....+....5
D   S   ppPss</pre></td></tr>
<tr><td>Numeric(pp,ss)</td><td><pre>....1....+....2....+....3....+....4....+....5
D   S   ppSss</pre></td></tr>
<tr><td>SmallInt</td><td><pre>....1....+....2....+....3....+....4....+....5
D   S   5I 0</pre></td></tr>
<tr><td>Int</td><td><pre>....1....+....2....+....3....+....4....+....5
D   S   10I 0</pre></td></tr>
<tr><td>BigInt (V4R5 and later)</td><td><pre>....1....+....2....+....3....+....4....+....5
D   S   20I 0</pre></td></tr>
<tr><td>Real</td><td><pre>....1....+....2....+....3....+....4....+....5
D   S   4F</pre></td></tr>
<tr><td>Double</td><td><pre>....1....+....2....+....3....+....4....+....5
D   S   8F</pre></td></tr>
<tr><td>Float(precision)</td><td>Use the appropriate declaration for Real or Double (above).</td></tr>
<tr><td colspan="2">Date, Time, Timestamp</td></tr>
<tr><td>Date</td><td><pre>....1....+....2....+....3....+....4....+....5
D   S   D</pre></td></tr>
<tr><td>Time</td><td><pre>....1....+....2....+....3....+....4....+....5
D   S   T</pre></td></tr>
<tr><td>Timestamp</td><td><pre>....1....+....2....+....3....+....4....+....5
D   S   Z</pre></td></tr>
</table>

continued

Figure 10.2 *Continued*

SQL/400	RPG IV Definition Specification (D-spec)
Large objects	

Blob, Clob, DbClob, and Blob locators and files	Use `SqlType(type)` where `type` is:
	`Blob:len`
	`Clob:len`
	`DbClob:len`
	`Blob_Locator`
	`Blob_File`
	`Clob_File`
	`DbClob_File`

Datalinks	
DataLink	Use `DLXxxxx` function to return a string.

Figure 10.3
SQL/400 Column Data Types and Corresponding ILE COBOL/400 Host Variable Data Types

SQL/400	ILE COBOL/400
Character	
Char(*length*)	`Pic X(length)`

VarChar(*max-length*)	`01 host-variable-name.`
	`49 string-length Pic S9(4) Binary.`
	`49 string-identifier Pic X(max-length).`

Graphic(*length*)	`Pic G(length)`

VarGraphic(*max-length*)	`01 host-variable-name.`
	`49 string-length Pic S9(4) Binary.`
	`49 string-identifier Pic G(max-length).`

Numeric	
Dec(*precision, scale*)	`Pic S9(precision - scale)V9(scale) Packed-Decimal` Maximum precision is 31.
Numeric(*precision, scale*)	`Pic S9(precision - scale)V9(scale) Display` Maximum precision is 31.
SmallInt	`Pic S9(4) Binary`
Int	`Pic S9(9) Binary`
BigInt (V4R5 and later)	`Pic S9(18) Binary`
Real	`Comp-1`
Double	`Comp-2`
Float(*precision*)	No exact equivalent. Use `Comp-2`.

continued

Figure 10.3 *Continued*

SQL/400	ILE COBOL/400
Date, Time, Timestamp	
Date	`Format Date` or `Pic X(`*`length`*`)` where *`length`* is at least large enough to accommodate the date format used
Time	`Format Time` or `Pic X(8)`
Timestamp	`Format Timestamp` or `Pic X(26)`
Large objects	

Blob, Clob, DbClob, and Blob locators and files	Use `SqlType Is` where *`type`* is:
	`Blob:`*`len`*
	`Clob:`*`len`*
	`DbClob:`*`len`*
	`Blob_Locator`
	`Blob_File`
	`Clob_File`
	`DbClob_File`

Datalinks	
DataLink	Not supported

In general, when you use a host variable to receive a column value, compare a host variable to a column in a predicate, or use a host variable as a value assigned to a column in an Insert or Update statement, it's preferable to declare the host variable with a data type and size that matches the associated column's data type and size exactly. SQL/400 also allows host variables that are structures (e.g., RPG IV data structures, ILE COBOL/400 group items) as well as arrays of structures. Chapter 13 describes using host variable structures and arrays in detail.

Recall that SQL has support for null-capable columns and that you can use the Null keyword to set a column to null on an Insert or Update statement. SQL also has provisions for handling nulls with embedded statements that include host variables. Wherever you can specify a host variable, you can optionally code an **indicator variable** after the host variable. The following example shows the use of the NewDiscNul indicator variable in an Update statement:

```
....1....+....2....+....3....+....4....+....5....+....6....+....7....
C                   If        InpDiscNul = 'Y'
C                     Eval    NewDisc    = 0
C                     Eval    NewDiscNul = -1
C                   Else
C                     Eval    NewDisc    = InpDisc
C                     Eval    NewDiscNul = 0
C                   EndIf
C                   Eval      SlcCusCity = InpCusCity
C/Exec SQL
C+                  Update  Customer
C+                    Set   Discount = :NewDisc :NewDiscNul
C+                    Where ShipCity = :SlcCusCity
C/End-Exec
```

To understand the use of the NewDiscNul indicator variable, first notice how this example sets it. If the user input indicates that the discount should be set to null (i.e., InpDiscNul = 'Y'), the NewDisc host variable is set to 0[7] and the NewDiscNul indicator variable is set to –1. Otherwise, the NewDisc host variable is set to the user input (InpDisc) and the NewDiscNul indicator variable is set to 0. For an indicator variable, a negative number means null and a non-negative number (including zero) means not null.

Next, look at the Update statement's Set clause — the indicator variable is coded after the host variable.[8] When the indicator variable is negative, the value of the host variable is ignored and the result is the same as if the Set clause were

```
Set Discount = Null
```

If the indicator variable isn't negative, the result is the same as if the Set clause were

```
Set Discount = :NewDisc
```

An indicator variable must be a declared as a two-byte, binary integer. In RPG IV, the D-spec for NewDiscNul would be[9]

```
....1....+....2....+....3....+....4....+....
D NewDiscNul       S                 5I 0
```

In ILE COBOL/400, the declaration would be

```
01   NewDiscNul   Pic S9(4) Binary.
```

Indicator variables are also used for other purposes (e.g., to hold the length of a truncated string) in embedded SQL Select and Fetch statements, which we cover in this chapter and Chapter 11, respectively.

Embedded SQL Error Handling

When an embedded SQL statement is executed, UDB/400 sets several program variables to provide feedback about any exceptional conditions that may occur during execution. You should always check these variables to handle both anticipated conditions (e.g., no row found) and unexpected errors (e.g., invalid data).[10] The SQL-related program variables, known as the **SQL communication area (SQLCA)**, are automatically generated by the SQL precompiler for RPG IV programs. For ILE COBOL/400 programs, you should always code the following statement in the Working-Storage section to have the SQL precompiler generate the SQLCA group and elementary items:

```
Exec SQL
  Include SQLCA
End-Exec.
```

7 As the next paragraph explains, the NewDisc variable is ignored when the indicator variable is negative; however, it's good programming practice to set this variable to some known value in case it's used elsewhere in the program.

8 You can optionally code the Indicator keyword between the host variable and the indicator variable. This example's Set clause would look like `Set Discount = :NewDisc Indicator :NewDiscNul`

9 You can also declare an RPG IV indicator variable as `4B 0`.

10 SQL also has a Whenever statement that generates tests and GoTo statements based on the values of the SQLState and SQLWarn0 variables. You should never use Whenever, however, because it's error-prone (simply rearranging source code can inadvertently change the way exceptions are handled) and provides only a GoTo as a way to handle an exception.

In Chapter 13, we look more closely at the SQLCA, but for now we focus on the SQLState variable, which is a five-character return code set after the execution of an embedded SQL statement.[11] Note that the variable's RPG IV name is SQLStt, not SQLState; it is shortened to the six-character length imposed by RPG/400. The ILE COBOL/400 name is SQLState, the industry-standard SQL name.[12] In the explanations that follow, we use the longer names except when discussing RPG IV specifically.

The possible conditions that can result from executing an embedded SQL statement can be categorized as follows:

Condition	SQLState value
No warning or exception	`'00000'`
No row found	`'02000'`
Warning	`'01xxx'`
Error	`'yyxxx'`, where *yy* is not `00`, `01`, or `02`

You can use RPG IV code such as the following to cover all categories:

```
....1....+....2....+....3....+....4....+....5....+....6....+....7....
C/Exec SQL
C+                   Update  Customer
C+                     Set    Discount = :NewDisc
C+                     Where ShipCity = :SlcCusCity
C/End-Exec
C                    Select
C                      When     SQLStt = '00000'
C                        ExSr   ProcessRow
C                      When     SQLStt = '02000'
C                        ExSr   SQLNoRow
C                      When     %Subst( SQLStt : 1 : 2 ) = '01'
C                        ExSr   SQLWarning
C                      Other
C                        ExSr   SQLError
C                    EndSl
```

In ILE COBOL/400, you can use the following code:

```
Exec SQL
  Update  Customer
    Set    Discount = :NewDisc
    Where ShipCity = :SlcCusCity
End-Exec
Evaluate True
  When SQLState = "00000"
    Perform ProcessRow
  When SQLState = "02000"
    Perform SQLNoRow
  When SQLState( 1 : 2 ) = "01"
    Perform SQLWarning
  When Other
    Perform SQLError
End-Evaluate
```

11 SQL also provides the SQLCode variable, which is set after each SQL statement. You should use SQLState because it's now part of the SQL standard.

12 The C/C++ name is lowercase: **sqlstate**.

It might seem cumbersome to code these 10 lines of error-handling code after each embedded SQL statement, but you can place the code in a source member and use an RPG IV /Copy or ILE COBOL/400 Copy directive to have the compiler automatically copy the code into the source input during compilation.[13] In RPG IV, this more concise approach looks like this:

```
....1....+....2....+....3....+....4....+....5....+....6....+....7....
C/Exec SQL
C+                    Update  Customer
C+                      Set    Discount = :NewDisc
C+                      Where ShipCity = :SlcCusCity
C/End-Exec
C/Copy AppSrc/RpgCpySrc,SqlErrChk
```

Several common conditions can result from executing an embedded SQL statement. One of these, "No row found" (SQLState = '02000'), occurs when no rows satisfy the search condition of a Select, Update, or Delete statement or when a Fetch statement has already retrieved the last available row from an open cursor. Another case is a duplicate value for a primary or unique key on an Insert or Update operation, in which case SQLState is set to '42910'. The complete set of SQLState values is listed in an appendix of the *DB2 UDB for AS/400 SQL Programming* manual. To handle a specific exception, you can add a condition to the sample error-handling code shown above, or you can check for the condition in the routines you invoke to handle errors and warnings (e.g., in an RPG IV or ILE COBOL/400 subroutine, procedure, or called program).

Static Statements

Most of the DDL and DML statements we discussed in Chapters 3 through 9, including Select, Insert, Update, and Delete, can be embedded in an HLL program. When you code an SQL statement directly in the source code (as in the Update examples we've been looking at), the statement is known as a **static statement** — static because the structure of the statement doesn't change; only the values supplied by host variables used in the statement may change. DDL statements (e.g., Create Table) aren't typically coded in HLL application programs. It is valid to use them when appropriate, however, as shown by the following example, which creates and later deletes a temporary table:

```
....1....+....2....+....3....+....4....+....5....+....6....+....7....
C/Exec SQL
C+ Create Table TmpSale
C+     ( OrderID Decimal(  7, 0 ),
C+       TotAmt  Decimal( 11, 2 ),
C+       Name    Char(    30    ) )
C/End-Exec

C*     Use TmpSale as temporary table....

C/Exec SQL
C+ Drop Table TmpSale
C/End-Exec
```

13 As an alternative, you could use an SQL Include statement to include the error-checking code. In ILE COBOL/400, this could be coded as

```
Exec SQL
  Include SqlErrChk
End-Exec
```

The member specified on an SQL Include statement (e.g., SqlErrChk) must exist in the source file specified on the IncFile parameter of the CrtSql*Xxx* command used to create the program.

Static Select Into Statement

As embedded statements in HLL programs, DML statements are more common than DDL statements. One DML statement, the Select statement, has a special form when coded as a static statement. This form, known as the Select Into statement, retrieves a single row into host variables. For example, using the Customer base table defined in Figure 10.4, the following code segment shows how a specific customer could be retrieved:

```
....1....+....2....+....3....+....4....+....5....+....6....+....7....
D CustomerR       DS
D  CsCustID                     7P 0
D  CsName                      30A
D  CsShipCity                  30A
D  CsDiscount                   5P 3
D CsCityNull      S             5I 0
D CsDiscNull      S             5I 0

D SlcCustID       S                   Like( CsCustID )
      .
      .
      .
C* Get the selected customer ID from user input and place
C* the value in the SlcCustID variable.
      .
      .
      .
C/Exec SQL
C+                  Select  CustID,
C+                          Name,
C+                          ShipCity,
C+                          Discount
C+                    Into :CsCustID,
C+                         :CsName,
C+                         :CsShipCity :CsCityNull,
C+                         :CsDiscount :CsDiscNull
C+                    From  Customer
C+                    Where CustID = :SlcCustID
C/End-Exec
```

Figure 10.4

Sample Customer Base Table

```
Create Table Customer
     ( CustID   Dec(   7, 0  ) Not Null,
       Name     Char( 30     ) Not Null,
       ShipCity Char( 30     ),
       Discount Dec(   5, 3  ),
Primary Key( CustID ) )
```

In addition to the From, Where, Group By, Having, and Order By clauses, a Select Into statement has an Into clause that follows the list of columns in the result table. The Into clause must list one host variable (and optionally, an indicator variable) for each column in the select list.[14] When the Select Into statement is executed, the result table must have no more than one row. If exactly one row is retrieved, its column values are assigned to the corresponding host variables listed in the Into clause.

14 An appropriate host structure variable can be used instead of listing each variable individually, as discussed in Chapter 13.

If no row is retrieved, UDB/400 sets the SQLState variable to '02000'. If the result table contains two or more rows, UDB/400 sets SQLState to '21000' and the host variables' values are undefined.

A Select Into statement can't retrieve more than one row at a time for each execution of the statement because there's no straightforward way to provide the right amount of storage — such as an array with enough elements — to hold an indeterminate number of rows. The SQL cursor, which we look at in Chapter 11, provides a way to specify a set of rows and then retrieve them one at a time using a Fetch statement.

In the example above, if the row that's retrieved has a null ShipCity or Discount column, the respective null indicator (CsCityNull or CsDiscNull) is set to –1 (or –2, if the retrieved value is null because of a data mapping error). If a column is non-null (i.e., has a valid value), the corresponding indicator variable is set to 0 (unless the value is a truncated string, in which case the null indicator holds the original length of the string[15]). On a Select Into statement, you should always code an indicator variable for a null-capable column because if no indicator variable is specified and the column is null, an exception occurs and SQLState is set to '22002'.

In addition to retrieving a single row by supplying its primary key value (as in the example above), another standard use of the Select Into statement is to retrieve the count, average, and so on of a set of rows using a column function. The following statement retrieves the average discount for all customers into the AvgDisc host variable:

```
....1....+....2....+....3....+....4....+....5....+....6....+....7....
D AvgDisc           S                 5P 3
D AvgDiscNul        S                 5I 0

C/Exec SQL
C+                   Select  Avg( Discount )
C+                     Into :AvgDisc :AvgDiscNul
C+                     From   Customer
C/End-Exec
```

This Select Into statement retrieves one row with one column. An indicator variable (AvgDiscNul) is coded to handle the unlikely cases in which there are no customers or all customers have a null discount — in either case, the Avg column function returns null.

Other Static DML Statements

The Insert, searched Update, and searched Delete statements[16] are exactly the same in both static and dynamic SQL except for the use of host variables. We've already seen examples of the Update statement. A static Insert statement to add a new customer looks like the following:

```
....1....+....2....+....3....+....4....+....5....+....6....+....7....
D CustomerR        DS
D   CsCustID                          7P 0
D   CsName                           30A
D   CsShipCity                       30A
D   CsDiscount                        5P 3
D CsCityNull        S                 5I 0
D CsDiscNull        S                 5I 0
```

continued

15 Or, if the value is a time value with the seconds portion truncated, the indicator variable holds the seconds.

16 Recall that a searched Update or Delete is an Update or Delete statement with a Where clause that specifies a search condition.

```
....1....+....2....+....3....+....4....+....5....+....6....+....7....
C* Get the values for the customer from user input and
C* place in the host variables CsCustID, etc.
C* Also set the CsCityNull and CsDiscNull indicator
C* variables to 0 if a value is supplied for the column
C* or to -1 if the column should be set to null.
      .
      .
      .
C/Exec SQL
C+                Insert Into Customer
C+                        (  CustID,
C+                           Name,
C+                           ShipCity,
C+                           Discount )
C+                  Values ( :CsCustID,
C+                           :CsName,
C+                           :CsShipCity :CsCityNull,
C+                           :CsDiscount :CsDiscNull )
C/End-Exec
```

The main thing to be aware of when you use a static Insert statement is that you must set any indicator values to the proper setting, depending on whether the column should be set to a valid value (use 0 for the indicator variable) or set to null (use –1 for the indicator variable). When the indicator variable is negative, the associated host variable value is ignored. Note that an indicator variable isn't required and is useful only when you need to set a column to null. If no indicator variable is specified, the host variable value is always considered a valid value. You also can specify an appropriate host structure instead of a list of host variables, as well as an array of structures to insert a set of rows with one operation. We cover both techniques in Chapter 13.

You can use a static Delete statement to delete a single row or a set of rows from a table. The following example shows how to delete a row using the primary key value a user enters:

```
....1....+....2....+....3....+....4....+....5....+....6....+....7....
D SlcCustID       S              7P 0
      .
      .
      .
C* Get the selected customer ID from user input and place
C* the value in the SlcCustID variable.
      .
      .
      .
C/Exec SQL
C+                Delete
C+                  From  Customer
C+                  Where CustID = :SlcCustID
C/End-Exec
```

If no row exists with the specified customer ID, SQLState is set to '02000' (no row found).

Other SQL DML statements, such as Lock Table, Commit, and Rollback, can also be coded as static statements and have the form described in Chapter 13.

Dynamic Embedded Statements

As we've seen, static statements have a hard-coded structure, and host variables provide the ability to execute the same statement using different values in a search condition or as values assigned to a column on an Insert or Update statement. A static statement can't, however, change its structure from one execution to the next. For example, the same static Update statement can't use a particular search condition, such as ShipCity = :SlcShpCity, in one execution and a different search condition, such as Discount > :SlcDisc, in a subsequent execution. Of course, you can code two static Update statements and use HLL program logic to decide which one is to be executed on a particular iteration through the program. But **dynamic embedded SQL statements** provide even greater flexibility and let you construct entire SQL statements on the fly in an HLL program.

The simplest form of dynamic SQL uses HLL string operations to construct an SQL statement as a string in a host variable and then executes the string using the SQL Execute Immediate statement. Here's a (not very practical) example:

```
....1....+....2....+....3....+....4....+....5....+....6....+....7....
D SqlStmtStr      S              256A

C                   Eval      SqlStmtStr = 'Delete From Customer +
C                                          Where ShipCity Is Null'
C/Exec SQL
C+                  Execute Immediate :SqlStmtStr
C/End-Exec
```

The SqlStmtStr variable is assigned a string that's a complete SQL Delete statement. The host variable is then specified on an Execute Immediate statement that executes the string contained in the variable. If the string in SqlStmtStr doesn't contain a syntactically valid SQL statement, or if an exception occurs when the statement is executed, UDB/400 sets SQLState and other SQLCA variables.

A slightly more complex example shows how you can use dynamic SQL to add flexibility to embedded SQL. This example lets the user input any valid SQL search condition as a string that's stored in the InpSrchCnd host variable:

```
....1....+....2....+....3....+....4....+....5....+....6....+....7....
D SqlStmtStr      S              256A
D InpSrchCnd      S              256A

C* Get a search condition (as a string) from user input
C* and place the string in the InpSrchCnd variable.
     .
     .
     .
C                   Eval      SqlStmtStr =
C                               'Delete From Customer Where ' +
C                               InpSrchCnd
C/Exec SQL
C+                  Execute Immediate :SqlStmtStr
C/End-Exec
```

In this example, only the first part of the statement (i.e., Delete From Customer Where) is coded as a literal in the program. The user input is then concatenated to the literal to complete the statement. Thus, the user could enter "ShipCity Is Null", "Discount < .01", or any other valid search condition, and the Delete statement would delete the rows that satisfied the search condition.[17]

You can break dynamic execution of a statement into two steps, preparation and execution, as in the following example:

```
....1....+....2....+....3....+....4....+....5....+....6....+....7....
D SqlStmtStr      S              256A
D InpSrchCnd      S              256A

C* Get a search condition (as a string) from user input
C* and place the string in the InpSrchCnd variable.
      .
      .
      .
C                   Eval      SqlStmtStr =
C                               'Delete From Customer Where ' +
C                               InpSrchCnd
C/Exec SQL
C+                  Prepare DynSqlStmt
C+                    From :SqlStmtStr
C/End-Exec
C                   If        SqlStt = '00000'
C/Exec SQL
C+                    Execute DynSqlStmt
C/End-Exec
C                     If       ( SQLStt <> '00000')
C                       ExSr   SqlError
C                     EndIf
C                   Else
C                     ExSr     SqlError
C                   EndIf
```

Here, the HLL statements to create a string with an SQL statement are the same. But the string is first prepared for execution by the SQL Prepare statement. The Prepare statement has the syntax

```
Prepare statement-name From :host-variable
```

where *host-variable* is a string variable containing an SQL statement and *statement-name* is any name you choose; it doesn't have to be the name of a host variable (in fact, it generally shouldn't be the same name to avoid confusion).[18] The statement name serves to identify an internal SQL structure that has the translated form of the statement. Be sure to check for successful completion of a Prepare statement, as the example above does, before a subsequent Execute statement. After an SQL statement has been successfully prepared from a string, the statement can be executed by the Execute statement. Note how Execute specifies a statement name, whereas Execute Immediate specifies a host string variable — don't confuse the two forms.

17 You probably wouldn't create an application exactly like this because the potential for deleting the wrong rows would still be great. However, the example serves to show how SQL statements can be created with string operations.

As another way to understand how dynamic SQL can be used, consider that ISQL is essentially an application that gets user input in the form of complete SQL statements and stores the input in a string variable that is then used on an Execute Immediate statement. The actual internals of ISQL are slightly different, but the point is still valid, and you could write your own replacement for ISQL using dynamic SQL.

18 The Prepare statement also has an optional Into descriptor clause that places information about the statement in an SQL descriptor area (SQLDA). SQL descriptors are discussed briefly in Chapter 11.

Separate Prepare and Execute statements allow the relatively time-consuming process of translating an SQL statement from a string into an executable form to be done just once,[19] and then the statement can be executed more efficiently multiple times during the same program execution.

Figure 10.5 lists the statements that can be executed using either Execute Immediate or Prepare and Execute.

Figure 10.5
SQL/400 Statements That Can Be Executed Dynamically

Alter Table
Call
Comment On
Commit
Create Alias
Create Collection
Create Distinct Type
Create Function
Create Index
Create Procedure
Create Table
Create View
Delete
Drop
Free Locator
Grant
Insert
Label On
Lock Table
Rename
Revoke
Rollback
Set Path
Set Transaction
Update

Notice that you can't use either method to execute a Select statement; however, you can prepare a Select statement and use the prepared form in a cursor declaration, a technique discussed in Chapter 11.

When a statement is prepared for subsequent execution, you can use one or more question marks (?) as **parameter markers** in the statement to designate a place in the statement where a host variable (or a host variable and indicator variable) will supply a value when the prepared statement is executed. This approach makes it possible to prepare a statement and still change search condition values or values assigned to columns when the statement is executed, providing flexibility similar to that gained by using host variables in static statements.[20] The following example shows how a parameter

19 That is, once per program execution. The Prepare statement does not save a permanent copy of the executable form of the prepared statement after the program ends. The copy is also destroyed when a subsequent Prepare is executed for the same statement name or when a Commit or Rollback statement — without Hold — is executed or other actions (e.g., ending commitment control) cause a unit of work to be ended. We discuss Commit and Rollback in Chapter 13.

20 The difference, of course, is that static statements are hard coded in the source, whereas dynamic statements are constructed as string values during program execution.

marker can be placed in a statement string and how a host variable is subsequently specified to supply the value at the location of the parameter marker.

```
....1....+....2....+....3....+....4....+....5....+....6....+....7....
D SlcShpCity      S             30A
D SqlStmtStr      S            256A

C                   Eval      SqlStmtStr = 'Delete From Customer +
C                                          Where ShipCity = ?'
C/Exec SQL
C+                  Prepare DynSqlStmt
C+                    From :SqlStmtStr
C/End-Exec

C                   If        SqlStt = '00000'

C* Get the selected city from user input and place
C* the value in the SlcShpCity variable.
      .
      .
      .
C/Exec SQL
C+                    Execute DynSqlStmt
C+                      Using :SlcShpCity
C/End-Exec
C                     Select
C                      When    SqlStt = '00000'
 *                       Skip
C                      When    SqlStt = '02000'
C                        ExSr SqlNoRow
C                      When     %SubSt(SqlStt : 1 : 2) = '01'
C                        ExSr  SqlWarning
C                      Other
C                        ExSr  SqlError
C                     EndSl
C                   Else
C                     ExSr     SqlError
C                   EndIf
```

The Using clause of the Execute statement specifies one host variable for each ? in the statement string that was prepared.[21] The host variables in the Using clause correspond positionally to the parameter markers in the string. When the Execute statement is executed, the value of the first host variable is used in place of the first ?, and so on. An indicator variable can follow the host variable in the Using clause, but only one ? should be used in the statement string (i.e., don't include one ? for the host variable and another ? for the indicator variable). SQL/400 ignores the Using clause if the prepared statement has no parameter markers.

We wrap up this chapter by looking at a more complex, but more realistic, example. The following RPG IV code segment lets a user enter a search condition to select a category of customers to be updated (e.g., the customers in Portland). Then, for this category, the user can repeatedly enter a pair of old and new discount values. The resulting Update statement is executed once for each pair of old and new discount values and sets the discount for customers who meet the search condition and who have the specified old discount value.

21 Or a host structure can be used, as discussed in Chapter 13.

```
....1....+....2....+....3....+....4....+....5....+....6....+....7....
D OldDisc         S              5P 3
D NewDisc         S              5P 3
D SqlStmtStr      S            256A
D InpSrchCnd      S            256A

C* Get a search condition (as a string) from user input
C* and place the string in the InpSrchCnd variable.
      .
      .
      .
C                   Eval      SqlStmtStr = 'Update Customer +
C                                          Set Discount = ? +
C                                          Where Discount = ? And ('
C                   Eval      SqlStmtStr = %TrimR( SQLStmtStr ) +
C                                            InpSrchCnd + ')'
C/Exec SQL
C+                  Prepare DynSqlStmt
C+                    From :SqlStmtStr
C/End-Exec
C                   If        SqlStt = '00000' )
C                     ExSr    ExcSqlStmt
C                   Else
C                     ExSr    SqlError
C                   EndIf

C     ExcSqlStmt    BegSr

C* Repeat the following until done or error....
C*
C*      Get old and new discount values from user.
      .
      .
      .
C*
C                   Eval      NewDisc = InpNewDisc
C                   Eval      OldDisc = InpOldDisc
C/Exec SQL
C+                  Execute DynSqlStmt
C+                    Using :NewDisc,
C+                          :OldDisc
C/End-Exec
C                   Select
C                    When   SqlStt = '00000'
 *                    Skip
C                    When   SqlStt = '02000'
C                      ExSr SqlNoRow
C                    When    %SubSt(SqlStt : 1 : 2) = '01'
C                      ExSr  SqlWarning
C                    Other
C                      ExSr  SqlError
C                   EndSl
C* ...End of repeated loop
C                   EndSr
```

Coding Suggestions

- Always check SQLState after each executable SQL statement to check for exceptions. Use standard error-handling routines to handle exceptions.
- Follow the applicable SQL coding suggestions (e.g., alignment) listed in Chapters 3 through 8.
- In RPG programs, align SQL statements (other than Declare Cursor and Include, which aren't executable statements) with the opcode column.
- In general, declare host variables so that they have the same data type and size as any column with which they're used.
- Use an Include, /Copy, or Copy to include commonly used declarations, mnemonics, SQL source code, or HLL source code in programs. Remember that the Include statement and RPG /Copy compiler directive include a source member during precompilation; an ILE COBOL/400 Copy includes source during the compile phase.
- For a search condition that's used in multiple embedded SQL statements (within the same or multiple programs), consider creating a view and referencing that view in embedded SQL statements rather than repeating the search condition in multiple statements.
- As an alternative to using an explicit select list (i.e., a list of columns) that is used by multiple Select Into statements, consider creating a view with the subset of columns used in these Select Into statements. The Select Into statements can then use an implicit select list (i.e., one that specifies * to select all columns) while specifying the view in the From clause.
- For any SQL statement executed in more than one place in a program, place the statement in a subroutine, paragraph, or internal procedure and execute that routine rather than coding the statement multiple times in the program.
- For any SQL statement that's used in multiple programs, consider putting the statement in a source member by itself and using an Include statement to include it during the precompilation phase.
- Never use a Select Into statement with a search condition that might be satisfied by more than one row. In general, use Select Into only to retrieve individual rows by primary or unique key or to retrieve column functions (without a Group By clause).
- In a Select Into statement, always use an indicator variable for null-capable columns.
- Performance-related suggestions:
  - To get additional information about how UDB/400 performs embedded SQL operations, run the HLL program in debug mode by entering the StrDbg (Start Debug) AS/400 command. When a program with embedded SQL runs in debug mode, UDB/400 puts informational messages in the job log. The *DB2 UDB for AS/400 SQL Programming* manual provides a guide to these messages.
  - List only the columns you need to retrieve on a Select Into statement.
  - When a particular dynamic SQL statement will be executed only once in a program, use Execute Immediate. If a statement may be executed more than once, use Prepare and Execute statements.

Chapter Summary

Embedded SQL statements are SQL statements coded in HLL programs. You can code most DDL and DML statements as embedded statements. Each embedded statement is coded between an Exec SQL and an End-Exec precompiler directive. The SQL precompiler translates embedded SQL statements into HLL declarations and procedural code, which an HLL compiler then compiles.

You can use host variables in embedded SQL statements. A host variable can be used to supply a value in a search condition or expression in the select column list. A host variable can also receive data returned by a Select Into statement or can provide a value to be assigned to a column on an Update or Insert statement. Wherever you can use a host variable, you can follow it with an indicator variable, which is used to handle columns that are null (on the Select Into statement) or that should be set to null (on the Update and Insert statements).

This chapter covered two of three major categories of embedded SQL statements: static and dynamic statements (the third being cursors, discussed in Chapter 11). Static statements have a fixed structure and can use host variables to supply new column values and search condition values. The Select Into statement is the static form of the Select statement and can retrieve a single row's values into host variables. Static Select, Update, and Delete statements that specify a search condition on a table's primary or unique key provide direct access by key for input and update operations. The static Insert statement provides a way to add new rows to a base table.

Dynamic embedded statements are contained in a host string variable and are prepared and executed at runtime. The Execute Immediate statement prepares and executes an SQL statement all in one step. The Prepare statement prepares an SQL statement from a string for subsequent execution by an Execute statement. The question mark (?) can be used as a parameter marker in a string that's prepared as an SQL statement. When the statement is executed, host variables can be specified on the Execute statement to provide values that are substituted for the parameter markers.

After execution of every SQL statement, UDB/400 sets the SQLState (SQLStt in RPG IV) variable and (in some cases) other variables that are part of the SQL communication area (SQLCA). A program should always check SQLState after each SQL statement.

The Include statement lets you include a source member into the program during the precompile phase.

Embedded SQL combines HLL logic, procedural, and user-interface capabilities with SQL's data-access capabilities to provide better control, greater functionality, and a user interface that's designed specifically for the application.

Key Terms

dynamic embedded SQL statement
embedded SQL statement
host variable
indicator variable
parameter marker
precompilation
precompiler directive
SQL communication area (SQLCA)
static statement

Exercises

Note: In all the following exercises that require HLL or embedded SQL statements, use any suitable AS/400 HLL (e.g., RPG IV or ILE COBOL/400).

1. Describe two examples of application operations in which embedded SQL would be necessary to perform database updates that couldn't be done with interactive SQL.
2. Using the Customer table defined in Figure 10.4, show a static Update statement to change the discount to .05 for customer 707899. Use host variables instead of literals in the Update statement. Show the necessary HLL host variable declarations and the HLL statements to set the host variables before the Update statement and to detect and handle the following conditions after the Update statement:
   - No customer exists with a customer ID of 707899.
   - Some other error or warning occurred on the Update statement.
   - The update was completed successfully.

   (You can use ExSr, Perform, or Call statements to indicate what action is taken for each condition. It's not necessary to show the code for the actual routines that handle each condition.)
3. Modify the code you created for Exercise 2 to let the discount be set either to a valid value or to null. Show the required variable declarations as well as the essential program logic. Assume there are two variables set from the user interface:
   - InpDiscNul, which is Y if the discount should be set to null or N if the discount should be set to the value in the InpDisc variable
   - InpDisc, which contains the new discount value if InpDiscNul is N
4. Show the HLL variable declarations and Select Into statement to get the maximum discount of any customer into a host variable. Be sure to consider all possible contents of the Customer table (e.g., an empty table). (Use the table defined in Figure 10.4. You don't need to show error-handling code.)
5. Show the HLL variable declarations and Select Into statement to get the number of customers in a selected city into a host variable. Also use a host variable for the city. (Use the Customer table defined in Figure 10.4. You don't need to show error-handling code.)

   Are indicator variables required or useful for this statement? Explain why you would or would not use indicator variable(s) in either or both the Into and the Where clause.
6. Show the HLL code and static Delete statements to let an end user select which customers to delete based on the city the customer is in. Implement your solution so the end user can specify either a specific city name (as a string) or that rows with a null city should be deleted. (Use the Customer table defined in Figure 10.4. You don't need to show error-handling code.)

   Explain why a solution that uses static Delete statements requires two Delete statements.
7. Show two alternative solutions to Exercise 6 that use a single Execute statement to dynamically execute an appropriate Delete statement. For the first solution, use a parameter marker in the statement string (when a valid city is specified). For the second solution, do not use any parameter markers. What are the advantages and disadvantages of the two approaches? (Show error-handling code in your solutions.)

Chapter 11

SQL Cursors

Chapter Overview

This chapter adds SQL cursors to the arsenal of embedded SQL statements introduced in Chapter 10. Cursors provide row-at-a-time retrieval and update similar to built-in I/O statements in HLL programs. We cover the basics of SQL cursors, including the use of the Declare Cursor, Open Cursor, Close Cursor, and Fetch statements. We also examine the use of scrollable cursors, which provide added flexibility for positioning to a particular row. Last, we'll see how dynamic cursors let you delay specification of the cursor's Select statement until runtime.

Basic Elements of SQL Cursors

As we mentioned in Chapter 10, a static Select Into statement can retrieve no more than one row. SQL has another form of embedded statement — those that use **cursors** — to input rows from a result table containing more than one row. The main programming steps to use a cursor are

- declare the cursor
- open the cursor
- fetch (i.e., read) rows from the cursor
- (optionally) update or delete the most recently fetched row
- close the cursor

The Declare Cursor statement declares an SQL cursor. The Declare Cursor statement is a declaration, not an executable statement.[1] Only when an SQL Open statement is executed does the cursor get opened.

The Declare Cursor statement uses a nested SQL Select statement to specify the table(s) and/or view(s) that are accessed when the cursor is opened. The following example shows a very simple form of the Declare Cursor statement that provides access to all rows and columns of the Customer table, in order by customer ID:

```
Declare CustomerCursor Cursor
  For Select     *
        From     Customer
        Order By CustID
```

The cursor name (which you choose) follows the Declare keyword. Following the For keyword, you specify a Select statement, which can have all the clauses we discussed in Chapters 5 and 8 — From, Where, Group By, Having, and Order By — as well as the Union operator. (There are several other optional clauses, which we cover later.) Because it is defined with a Select statement, a cursor can specify row selection, derived columns, aggregation (e.g., the Sum column function), union, and other data manipulations. Notice that you specify the order in which rows are retrieved in the cursor

1 The SQL/400 precompiler converts all Declare Cursor statements to HLL comments. The precompiler uses the information you specify in the Declare Cursor statement to properly translate subsequent statements and to set up internal tables used by UDB/400 when the program is executed.

declaration — not in the base table or view definition. The following sequence of embedded statements provides a preview of how you use a cursor in an HLL program (for simplicity, this example omits error handling):

```
....1....+....2....+....3....+....4....+....5....+....6....+....
D CustomerR       DS
D   CsCustID                      7P 0
D   CsName                       30A
D   CsShipCity                   30A
D   CsDiscount                    5P 3
D CsCityNull      S               5I 0
D CsDiscNull      S               5I 0
      .
      .
      .
C/Exec SQL
C+ Declare CustomerCursor Cursor
C+   For Select    *
C+         From    Customer
C+         Order By CustID
C/End-Exec
C/Exec SQL
C+                   Open CustomerCursor
C/End-Exec
C* Repeat the following Fetch until no more rows or error....
C/Exec SQL
C+                   Fetch Next
C+                     From  CustomerCursor
C+                     Into :CsCustID,
C+                          :CsName,
C+                          :CsShipCity :CsCityNull,
C+                          :CsDiscount :CsDiscNull
C/End-Exec
C/Exec SQL
C+                   Close CustomerCursor
C/End-Exec
```

We cover more details of the Open, Fetch, and Close statements later. For now, notice how the Open makes the result table defined by the cursor's Select statement available and how the Fetch retrieves the next available row (if any) into host variables in much the same way the static Select Into statement does.

As the example above shows, the Declare Cursor statement (like all other embedded SQL statements) must be coded in the C-specs in RPG IV programs. In ILE COBOL/400 programs, a Declare Cursor statement must be coded in the Procedure Division. In all HLLs, the Declare Cursor statement must be coded before any embedded SQL statement that references the cursor. A good coding practice is to place cursor declarations at the beginning of the C-specs or Procedure Division.[2]

A cursor's Select statement can include host variable references, which provides the ability to determine the selection criteria for rows when the cursor is opened rather than when the program is created. You can also use host variables in expressions in the select list. These host variables are also evaluated only when the cursor is opened. The following example shows how to code a cursor so that the rows available through it are from a city that's specified when the program is run:

2 It's somewhat anomalous that the Declare Cursor statement, which is a declaration, must be coded in the procedural part of an HLL program. The coding practice recommended here follows the principle that all declarations should be made at the beginning of the source code that's within the same scope. Because SQL cursors are scoped to the whole program (rather than to a subroutine or internal procedure), the beginning of the program's main block of procedural code is the appropriate location.

```
....1....+....2....+....3....+....4....+....5....+....6....+....
D SlcShpCity      S                30A
C/Exec SQL
C+ Declare CustomerCursor Cursor
C+   For Select     *
C+          From     Customer
C+          Where    ShipCity = :SlcShpCity
C+          Order By CustID
C/End-Exec

C* Get the selected city from user input and place
C* the value in the SlcShpCity variable.
      .
      .
      .
C/Exec SQL
C+                     Open CustomerCursor
C/End-Exec
```

When the Open statement is executed, UDB/400 evaluates the SlcShpCity host variable and uses its value in the search condition of the cursor's Select statement. If SlcShpCity contains 'Portland' when the cursor is opened, subsequent Fetch operations retrieve only customers with a ShipCity value of Portland. Host variables used in a cursor declaration are evaluated only when the Open statement opens the cursor; changing the value of a host variable has no effect on the cursor until the cursor is closed and reopened. By closing and reopening a cursor, you can use the same cursor to retrieve different sets of rows (e.g., Portland customers, then Seattle customers) in the same program execution.

A cursor can be declared as either a read-only or an updatable cursor. If you add the For Read Only clause to the cursor's Select statement,[3] the cursor is read-only:

```
Declare CustomerCursor Cursor
  For Select  *
        From  Customer
        Where ShipCity = :SlcShpCity
  For Read Only
```

It's good practice to declare read-only cursors explicitly with the For Read Only clause because doing so provides better documentation and can sometimes improve performance.

A cursor that is declared with a single subselect (no Union operator) over a single base table or updatable view and that has a Select statement that satisfies the restrictions on updatable views (discussed in Chapter 6) can be used for Update and Delete, as well as Fetch, operations. To use a cursor for Update operations, you should add a For Update Of clause to the cursor's Select statement. Following the For Update Of keywords, you list one or more columns that will be referenced in a subsequent Update statement's Set clause.[4] Here's an example of a cursor that allows updates of a customer's city and discount:

3 For Fetch Only is synonymous with For Read Only. Technically, the For Read Only, For Update Of, Optimize For, and isolation level clauses are part of the Select statement. In practical terms, they're used almost exclusively in cursor declarations.

4 If you specify the For Update Of clause without any columns, all updatable columns in the cursor's base table or view are updatable. A column listed in the For Update Of clause does not have to be included in the select list. That is, you can update a column even if it's not in the result table defined by the cursor's Select statement.

If the cursor will be used for Delete operations but not for Update operations, you should not specify the For Update Of clause. As long as the cursor meets the requirements for an updatable cursor and the program contains a Delete statement that references the cursor, the cursor is opened as a delete-capable cursor. Specifying a For Update Of clause may cause poorer performance and causes a cursor open error if the user doesn't have Update privileges to the table.

```
Declare CustomerCursor Cursor
  For Select  *
        From  Customer
  For Update Of ShipCity,
                Discount
```

For an updatable cursor without a For Update Of clause, a subsequent Update statement can reference any updatable column (i.e., one not derived using an expression, constant, or function). Limiting the columns that can be updated through a cursor provides some protection against coding mistakes and can also improve performance.

If the cursor's Select statement includes an Order By clause and you want to use the cursor for updates, you must specify a For Update Of clause that doesn't include any of the columns listed in the Order By clause.[5] The following example adds a valid Order By clause to the example above:

```
Declare CustomerCursor Cursor
  For Select     *
        From     Customer
        Order By CustID
  For Update Of ShipCity,
                Discount
```

If you don't specify a For Read Only or a For Update Of clause and the cursor satisfies the restrictions on updatable cursors, the cursor is opened as an updatable cursor if the program contains an Update or Delete statement that references the cursor or contains an Execute or Execute Immediate statement.[6] It's much better, however, to explicitly code the For Read Only or For Update Of clause so you don't rely on the default open mode. This practice also avoids unintentionally changing the nature of a cursor when you revise the SQL statements in a program.

Specifying Insensitive in the cursor declaration guarantees that once the cursor is open, its result table remains unchanged until closed. UDB/400 insulates the result table by creating a temporary table with a copy of the result table data.

```
....1....+....2....+....3....+....4....+....5....+....6....+....
C/Exec SQL
C+   Declare CustomerCursor Insensitive Cursor
C+     For Select CustID,
C+                Name,
C+                Discount
C+          From Customer
C+          Order By CustID
C+     For Read Only
C/End-Exec
```

After this cursor is opened, insert, delete, and update operations to the underlying table (Customer) will *not* be reflected in the cursor's result table.[7] A cursor specified with Insensitive must be read-only, and therefore you can't specify the For Update Of clause. For documentation purposes, it's a good idea to code an explicit For Read Only clause when you specify the Insensitive keyword. Also, the CrtSql*Xxx* command used to create the program must specify AlwCpyDta(*Optimize) or AlwCpyDta(*Yes) to allow UDB/400 to copy the result table data.

5 This is an understandable requirement — you can't update one of the columns used to sequence the rows; otherwise, the row's relative position in the cursor might change.

6 However, the cursor is read-only if the program is created with the AlwBlk(*AllRead) parameter and does not contain an Update or Delete statement that references the cursor — regardless of whether the program contains an Execute or Execute Immediate statement.

7 As you'll see later in this chapter, specifying the Scroll keyword (without Dynamic) also produces a cursor that is insensitive to database changes.

When a commitment control environment is active (discussed in detail in Chapter 13), you generally should code a With Hold clause on cursor declarations so the cursor remains open when a Commit or Rollback statement that does not have a With Hold clause is executed. The With Hold clause follows the Cursor keyword, as shown here:

```
Declare CustomerCursor Cursor
  With Hold
  For  Select     *
         From     Customer
         Order By CustID
  For  Update Of ShipCity,
                 Discount
```

Opening and Closing the Cursor

The SQL Open statement has a simple syntax:

```
Open cursor-name
```

where *cursor-name* is the name specified on a Declare Cursor statement.[8] A cursor must be closed when the Open statement is executed. As we mentioned earlier, the cursor's Select statement — including any host variables — is evaluated when the Open statement is executed. If the Open is successful, the cursor is positioned before the first row in the result table. If the result table is empty, the cursor is effectively positioned after the last row. In this case, the first Fetch operation will fail with a "no row" condition (SQLState = '02000').

The SQL Close statement is equally simple:

```
Close cursor-name
```

A cursor must be open when the Close statement is executed.[9] In general, you should close a cursor as soon as you're done using it.

The Fetch Statement

The Fetch statement provides two capabilities: setting the position of the SQL cursor for subsequent input or update operations and reading one or more rows into host variables. There are several variations of the Fetch statement, providing forward and backward positioning and input operations. In this chapter, we look only at single-row input; in Chapter 13, we look at multiple-row input.

We've already seen an example of a simple Fetch statement that reads the next row in the result table defined by a cursor. The following example shows how this Fetch might be used in a loop to read the Customer table sequentially by customer ID and process all rows:

8 For cursors that use a dynamically prepared Select statement with parameter markers, the Open statement includes a Using clause to identify the values for the parameter markers. Dynamically prepared Select statements are discussed later in the chapter.

9 UDB/400 implicitly closes SQL cursors in several cases, including when a job, activation group, program, or module ends — depending on the CloSqlCsr parameter value of the CrtSql*Xxx* command used to create the program. A Commit or Rollback statement without a With Hold clause closes a cursor declared without a With Hold clause. A Disconnect statement also closes cursors associated with the connection to a remote database.

```
....1....+....2....+....3....+....4....+....5....+....6....+....
D CustomerR       DS
D  CsCustID                       7P 0
D  CsName                        30A
D  CsShipCity                    30A
D  CsDiscount                     5P 3
D CsCityNull      S               5I 0
D CsDiscNull      S               5I 0
      .
      .
      .
C/Exec SQL
C+ Declare CustomerCursor Cursor
C+    For Select     *
C+          From     Customer
C+          Order By CustID
C+    For Read Only
C/End-Exec
C/Exec SQL
C+                   Open CustomerCursor
C/End-Exec
C                    If        SQLStt <> '00000'
C                      ExSr    SQLError
C                      Return
C                    EndIf
C                    Eval      MoreRows = *On

C                    DoW       MoreRows = *On
C/Exec SQL
C+                     Fetch Next
C+                       From  CustomerCursor
C+                       Into :CsCustID,
C+                            :CsName,
C+                            :CsShipCity :CsCityNull,
C+                            :CsDiscount :CsDiscNull
C/End-Exec
C                      Select
C                       When   SQLStt = '00000'
C                         ExSr ProcessRow
C                       When   SQLStt = '02000'
C                         Eval MoreRows = *Off
C                       When   %Subst( SQLStt : 1 : 2 ) = '01'
C                         ExSr SQLWarning
C                       Other
C                         ExSr SQLError
C                         Eval MoreRows = *Off
C                      EndSl
C                    EndDo
C/Exec SQL
C+                   Close CustomerCursor
C/End-Exec
C                    If        SqlStt <> '00000'
C                      ExSr    SQLError
C                      Return
C                    EndIf
```

The basic algorithm for sequentially processing all rows of an SQL cursor is

```
Open cursor
If error
   Handle error
   Quit
EndIf
While more rows and no error
   Fetch next row
   If normal return condition
      Process current row
   Else If "no row" condition
      Do nothing (end loop)
   Else If other warning condition
      Handle warning (continue or end loop)
   Else
      Handle error (end loop)
   EndIf
EndWhile
Close cursor
If error
   Handle error
EndIf
```

Remember that an SQLState value of '02000' indicates that there are no more rows to be read.

Reading by Key Value

SQL/400 cursors don't provide an exact equivalent to HLL direct, keyed positioning and read operations, such as RPG IV's SetLL and Chain opcodes and ILE COBOL/400's Start and Read statements. As you saw earlier, a static Select Into statement can be used to read a single row based on a primary (or unique) key value, which provides comparable function to an HLL direct read by key value.

Another common sequence of HLL I/O operations is to position to the first record in a set of records with a common partial key value (e.g., the first order in the set of orders for a customer) and then read sequentially by full key through the set. In RPG IV or ILE COBOL/400, this task requires that the file be opened once and that repeated positioning and read operations be executed. In SQL, this type of task is normally implemented by repeated cursor open/close operations, with each cursor open selecting the desired subset, based on host variable values (e.g., the customer ID).[10] For example, the following cursor could be used to access, in order ID sequence, only those Sale table[11] rows for a particular customer:

```
Declare SaleForCustCursor Cursor
  For Select      *
        From      Sale
        Where     CustID = :SlcCustID
        Order By OrderID
  For Read Only
```

Before the cursor is opened, the appropriate customer ID must be assigned to the SlcCustID host variable.

10 When an SQL cursor is opened and closed multiple times in the same program execution, UDB/400 tries to avoid repeated internal file opens and closes. Thus, the performance of repeated cursor open and close statements may be much faster than repeated HLL open and close operations on a physical or logical file.

11 See Figure 8.6 (page 138) for the Sale table definition.

The Optimize Clause

You can use the Optimize clause to improve performance when you are processing only a small number of rows in the result table at a time. For example, consider an interactive application in which you want to present only 20 rows on the screen at a time. The following statement, which produces a cursor consisting of Portland customers, is optimized to retrieve the first 20 rows as quickly as possible.

```
Declare CustCsr Cursor
  For Select  *
        From  Customer
        Where ShipCity = 'Portland'
  For Read Only
  Optimize For 20 Rows
```

The Optimize clause can also specify the number of rows to optimize as a host variable, as in this example:

```
Declare CustCsr Cursor
  For Select  *
        From  Customer
        Where ShipCity = 'Portland'
  For Read Only
  Optimize For :ScrFld Rows
```

Scrollable Cursors

In addition to the Next keyword of the Fetch statement, you can specify any of the alternatives shown in Figure 11.1 if you add the Scroll or Dynamic Scroll option to the cursor declaration.

Figure 11.1

Fetch Statement Positioning Keywords

Keyword	Positions cursor
Next	On the next row after the current row
Prior	On the row before the current row
First	On the first row
Last	On the last row
Before	Before the first row
After	After the last row
Current	On the current row (no change in position)
Relative *n*	*n* < –1 Positions to *n*th row before current *n* = –1 Same as Prior keyword *n* = 0 Same as Current keyword *n* = 1 Same as Next keyword *n* > 1 Positions to *n*th row after current

The following example shows the required Declare Cursor and Fetch statements to read the row before the current row:

```
....1....+....2....+....3....+....4....+....5....+....6....+....
C/Exec SQL
C+ Declare CustomerCursor Scroll Cursor
C+   For Select    *
C+         From     Customer
C+         Order By CustID
C+   For Read Only
C/End-Exec
      .
      .
      .
C/Exec SQL
C+                      Fetch Prior
C+                        From  CustomerCursor
C+                        Into :CsCustID,
C+                             :CsName,
C+                             :CsShipCity :CsCityNull,
C+                             :CsDiscount :CsDiscNull
C/End-Exec
```

The Scroll and Dynamic Scroll options define a **scrollable cursor**, which is one that lets you use Fetch operations in addition to Fetch Next. The Scroll option (without the Dynamic keyword) implicitly defines the cursor as a read-only cursor, and because UDB/400 may make temporary copies of the result table's rows, changes to a row in the underlying table made by another job or another SQL statement in the same program may not be reflected immediately in the data retrieved by a Fetch. The Dynamic Scroll option can be used with an updatable cursor, and in most cases, a dynamic scrollable cursor does immediately reflect changes to a row made by another job or SQL statement.[12]

When you use Fetch without an Into clause, the operation positions the cursor but doesn't input anything. The Into clause cannot be used with the Before and After positioning keywords and is optional with all other positioning keywords. The purpose of the Before and After options is to reset the cursor position to the beginning or end of the result table:

```
....1....+....2....+....3....+....4....+....5....+....6....+....
C/Exec SQL
C+                      Fetch After
C+                        From CustomerCursor
C/End-Exec
```

This Fetch statement positions (without retrieving any data) the cursor at the end of the cursor's result table such that a subsequent Fetch Prior statement would retrieve the last row in the cursor's result table.

Positioned Update and Delete Statements

You can use a **positioned Update** or **positioned Delete** statement to update or delete the current row of an updatable cursor.[13] A successful Fetch must be executed before a positioned Update or Delete

12 The Dynamic keyword is ignored when UDB/400 produces a temporary table to implement the cursor or when the cursor's Select statement includes certain types of subqueries. The *DB2 UDB for AS/400 SQL Reference* manual's Declare Cursor documentation provides a complete list of the cases in which the Dynamic keyword is ignored.

13 In those cases in which the necessary cursor definition forces the cursor to be read-only, you can still update or delete a retrieved row by using a searched Update or Delete statement that specifies the retrieved row's primary key.

Note that you should not use a searched update with Where RRN(*table-name*) = :RowRRN to try to execute a direct retrieval or update by relative record number because this causes a sequential scan of the table to find the specified row. The performance would be extremely slow for large tables.

statement. Instead of a Where clause that specifies a search condition, positioned Update and Delete statements use a Where clause with the syntax

```
Where Current Of cursor-name
```

The following example shows a Declare Cursor, Fetch, and subsequent positioned Update statement:

```
....1....+....2....+....3....+....4....+....5....+....6....+....
C/Exec SQL
C+ Declare CustomerCursor Cursor
C+    For Select      CustID,
C+                    Name,
C+                    Discount
C+          From      Customer
C+          Order By  CustID
C+    For Update of   Discount
C/End-Exec
      .
      .
      .
C/Exec SQL
C+                    Fetch Next
C+                      From  CustomerCursor
C+                      Into :CsCustID,
C+                           :CsName,
C+                           :CsDiscount :CsDiscNull
C/End-Exec
      .
      .
      .
C/Exec SQL
C+                    Update Customer
C+                      Set  Discount = :NewDisc
C+                      Where Current of CustomerCursor
C/End-Exec
```

Other than the Where clause, the syntax of positioned Update and Delete statements is the same as for searched Update and Delete statements. You code the cursor name in the Where clause of a positioned Update or Delete statement, but you code the table or view name that's specified in the From clause of the cursor's Select statement after the Update or Delete From keywords. Any columns that are assigned values in the Set clause must either be listed in a For Update Of clause in the cursor's Select statement or be an updatable column included in the cursor's select list, if no For Update Of clause is specified.

A positioned Update doesn't change the cursor's position — the updated row remains the current row.[14] A positioned Delete changes the current position to before the row (if any) following the current row.

There is no cursor-related Insert statement; the static Insert covered in Chapter 10 provides the SQL mechanism to add new rows to a base table regardless of whether a cursor is also opened for the table.

14 If the cursor is declared with the Dynamic Scroll option and has an Order By clause, and an update by a different job (or through a different cursor in the same job) changes one of the current row's Order By column values such that the relative position of the current row changes within the result table, a subsequent attempt to use Fetch Current...will fail.

Dynamic Cursors

SQL lets you combine the capabilities of dynamic execution and a cursor by dynamically preparing the Select statement that's used for a cursor declaration. The following code shows a simplified example of the statements used for this type of dynamic cursor:

```
....1....+....2....+....3....+....4....+....5....+....6....+....
D CustomerR       DS
D   CsCustID                      7P 0
D   CsName                       30A
D   CsShipCity                   30A
D   CsDiscount                    5P 3
D CsCityNull      S               5I 0
D CsDiscNull      S               5I 0
D SqlStmtStr      S             256A
D InpSrchCnd      S             256A

C/Exec SQL
C+ Declare CustomerCursor Cursor
C+    For   DynSqlStmt
C/End-Exec
      .
      .
      .
C* Get a search condition (as a string) from user input
C* and place the string in the InpSrchCnd variable.
      .
      .
      .
C                   Eval      SqlStmtStr = 'Select * +
C                                           From Customer +
C                                           Where ' +
C                                           InpSrchCnd
C/Exec SQL
C+                  Prepare DynSqlStmt
C+                    From :SqlStmtStr
C/End-Exec
C/Exec SQL
C+                  Open CustomerCursor
C/End-Exec
C/Exec SQL
C+                  Fetch Next
C+                    From  CustomerCursor
C+                    Into :CsCustID,
C+                         :CsName,
C+                         :CsShipCity :CsCityNull,
C+                         :CsDiscount :CsDiscNull
C/End-Exec
```

The Declare Cursor statement's For clause specifies the DynSqlStmt statement name rather than a nested Select statement as we saw earlier in the chapter. The DynSqlStmt statement is prepared from a Select statement that's contained in the SqlStmtStr host variable. The statement must be successfully prepared before the Open statement opens the cursor. At the time the Open statement is executed, UDB/400 uses the Select statement that's been prepared to determine which rows are in the cursor's result table. You can use question marks (?) as parameter markers in the Select statement string and then specify a Using clause with corresponding host variables on the Open statement. The host variables' values are used in place of the parameter markers, as we saw in Chapter 10 with the dynamic execution of other DML statements using the Execute statement.[15]

Coding Suggestions

- For an explicit select list (i.e., a list of columns) used in multiple cursor definitions, consider creating a view that's referenced by the statements.
- In a Fetch statement, always use an indicator variable for a null-capable column.
- On cursor declarations:
  - For a read-only cursor, always specify the For Read Only clause.
  - For a cursor that will be referenced in an Update statement, always specify the For Update Of clause.
  - For a cursor that will be referenced in a Delete statement — but not an Update statement — don't specify either a For Read Only or a For Update Of clause.
  - In general, use the With Hold option on cursor declarations.
  - Specify the Insensitive keyword if you want the contents of your cursor to be unchanged after it is opened. This isn't necessary for a cursor in which the Scroll keyword has been specified (without the Dynamic keyword).
- Explicitly close any open cursor when it is no longer needed or an unrecoverable exception occurs. Be careful not to recursively execute SQL error handling when you're closing a cursor while still handling another SQL error.
- Performance-related suggestions:
  - List only the columns you need to retrieve in a cursor declaration.
  - Add the Optimize For *n* Rows clause to a cursor declaration when you know approximately how many rows you intend to fetch and when the number of rows is significantly fewer than the expected number of rows in the result table.
  - Don't use expressions in the Set clause of a positioned Update. (UDB/400 does an open for the first execution of a positioned Update when the Set clause has an expression.) Calculate the new column value in a host variable, and use just the host variable in the Set clause assignment.

15 SQL provides an even more flexible facility for dynamic cursor definitions. You can use the Describe statement to retrieve information about a prepared statement (e.g., the columns in a Select statement's result table). You can use a Describe Table statement to retrieve information about a table or view (e.g., a table's column definitions). The information retrieved by a Describe or Describe Table statement is stored in an SQL structure known as an SQL descriptor area (SQLDA). You can also place addresses of program variables (i.e., pointers) in an SQLDA and then use the descriptor name instead of a list of host variables on an Open, Fetch, or Execute statement.

The combination of these two uses of the SQLDA provides a way to construct and execute any DML statement without having to hard code any host variable names or parameter markers. Using descriptors is an advanced level of SQL programming and is more typically used in general-purpose utilities than in application programs. *DB2 UDB for AS/400 SQL Programming* (or *DB2 UDB for AS/400 SQL Programming with Host Languages* in V4R5) provides a more detailed explanation and examples of these techniques.

Chapter Summary

An SQL cursor provides a result table through which a program can perform input, update, and delete operations. A cursor uses a nested Select statement to define the result table. This Select statement can have a From, Where, Group By, Having, and Order By clause, as well as a Union operator. The Where and Having clauses can contain host variables that are evaluated when the cursor is opened. Thus, a cursor can be used to access different sets of rows depending on the value of host variables. A cursor can also have a For Read Only clause to specify that the cursor is read-only or a For Update Of clause to specify an updatable cursor. You can use the Insensitive keyword to define a read-only cursor whose result table won't be affected by database updates.

After a cursor is opened, the Fetch statement is used to retrieve one or more rows into host variables. The Fetch Next statement reads rows sequentially in the order (if any) specified on the Order By clause of the cursor's Select statement. A positioned Update or Delete statement can be used to update the column values in an updatable cursor's current row or to delete the current row.

A scrollable cursor is one defined with the Scroll option (for read-only access) or Dynamic Scroll option (which allows updates). A scrollable cursor allows other Fetch statement positioning options in addition to Next. With these positioning options, the cursor's current position can be moved forward or backward from the current position or set to the beginning or end of the result table.

Dynamic cursors let you use dynamically prepared Select statements with parameter markers. The name of this prepared Select statement is specified in the For clause of the Declare Cursor statement.

Key Terms

cursor
positioned Delete statement
positioned Update statement
scrollable cursor

Exercises

Note: In all the following exercises that require HLL or embedded SQL statements, use any suitable AS/400 HLL (e.g., RPG IV or ILE COBOL/400).

1. Show the HLL code and cursor-related statements (including cursor declaration, Open, Close, and Fetch statements) to sequentially read all customers with a non-null discount. For each row, execute a ListCust routine (e.g., an RPG IV subroutine or ILE COBOL/400 paragraph — you don't need to show the routine's code). Read the rows in order by city and, within city, by descending discount. Include the necessary option to make the cursor a read-only cursor. Include appropriate error-handling code. Use the Customer table defined by the following Create Table statement:

```
Create Table Customer
     ( CustID   Dec(   7, 0  ) Not Null,
       CustName Char( 30     ) Not Null,
       ShipCity Char( 30     ),
       Discount Dec(   5, 3  ),
Primary Key( CustID ) )
```

2. Revise your solution to Exercise 1 to use an updatable cursor and a positioned Update statement to insert one blank character at the beginning of each customer's name. *Tip: The RPG IV statement to append a blank to the beginning of a string in a character variable is*

```
....1....+....2....+....3....+....4....+....5....+....6....+....
C                    Eval      StrVar = ' ' + StrVar
```

3. Revise the cursor definition you produced in Exercise 1 to allow multiple passes through the result table without closing and reopening the cursor. Show the embedded SQL statement that would position you properly so that the loop you coded in Exercise 1 would always start out retrieving the first row in the cursor's result table.
4. Modify the code produced in Exercise 1 to first let an end user choose a search condition for the rows to use for the cursor's result table. This search condition should be used instead of the search condition you used to ensure that the discount column in each row is not null.

   Hint: Consider using a dynamic cursor.

Chapter 12

The Create SQL Program Commands

Chapter Overview

We now turn our attention to the task of creating an executable program from a source member containing embedded SQL. We discuss the commands used to compile embedded SQL, including the most important parameters used with those commands. Also, we describe the translation process that takes place to convert embedded SQL source into pure HLL source and this HLL source into a module, program, or service program object.

Creating SQL/400 Programs

Once you've entered your HLL and embedded SQL source code, you execute one of the commands listed in Figure 12.1 to create the program, module, or service program object from the source code.

Figure 12.1
CL Commands to Create Programs or ILE Modules and Service Programs

Command	Language
Non-ILE programs	
CrtSqlCbl	COBOL/400
CrtSqlFtn	FORTRAN
CrtSqlPlI	PL/I
CrtSqlRpg	RPG/400
ILE programs, modules, and service programs	
CrtSqlCI	ILE C/400
CrtSqlCppI	C++
CrtSqlCblI	ILE COBOL/400
CrtSqlRpgI	RPG IV

You can enter the CrtSql*Xxx* command from any display screen that lets you enter CL commands. Or, if you're using Programming Development Manager (discussed in Appendix C), you enter option 14 (Compile) or 15 (Create Module) beside the source member name to execute the CrtSql*Xxx* command. In either case, you can press the F4 key to prompt for the command's parameter values. These commands can also be used in CL programs.

The following example shows a typical command to create a program from RPG IV source containing embedded SQL:

```
CrtSqlRpgI Obj( AppExc/UpdCust )
           SrcFile( AppSrc/QRpgLeSrc )
           Option( *Sql )
           ObjType( *Pgm )
           IncFile( AppSrc/SqlIncSrc )
           Commit( *None )
```

In this example, the object to be created is a program named UpdCust, and it is created in library AppExc. The source for this program is in source file QRpgLeSrc in library AppSrc. The command specifies the SQL naming option (which we introduced in Chapter 3 and discuss further in Chapter 13). The source file for Include statement members (also discussed in Chapter 13) is SqlIncSrc in library AppSrc. No commitment control is in effect when this program is executed.

Figure 12.2 lists commonly used parameters and their default values for the CrtSql*Xxx*I commands that create ILE objects.

Figure 12.2

Commonly Used Command Parameters for CrtSQLXxxI Commands

Parameter	Purpose	Default (other values)
Obj	Name of program, module, or service program to be created	—
SrcFile	Source file that contains HLL and embedded SQL source	*Libl/QCSrc, *Libl/QCblLeSrc, or *Libl/QRpgLeSrc
SrcMbr	Source member that contains HLL and embedded SQL source	*Obj
ObjType	Type of object to create (program, module, or service program)	*Pgm (*Module, *SrvPgm)
Text	Description of the created object	*SrcMbrTxt
Option	Naming convention, object generation (and other options)	*Sys, *Gen (*Sql, *NoGen)
IncFile	Source file to use for embedded Include statements	*Libl/*SrcFile
Commit	Level of commitment control environment for program execution	*Chg (*None, *CS, *All, *RR, *UR, *RS, *NC)
Rdb	Database name for distributed program	*Local
DatFmt	Format used when accessing date result columns	*Job (*USA, *ISO, *EUR, *JIS, *MDY, *DMY, *YMD, *JUL)
DatSep	Separator used when accessing date result columns	*Job (*separator-character*)
TimFmt	Format used when accessing time result columns	*HMS (*USA, *ISO, *EUR, *JIS)
TimSep	Separator used when accessing time result columns	*Job (*Blank or *separator-character*)
AlwCpyDta	Specifies whether a copy of the data can be used in a Select statement	*Optimize (*Yes, *No)
CloSqlCsr	Specifies when SQL cursors are implicitly closed, prepared statements are implicitly discarded, and Lock Table locks are released	*EndActGrp (*EndMod)

continued

Figure 12.2 *Continued*

Parameter	Purpose	Default (other values)
AlwBlk	Allow blocking for read-only cursors	*AllRead (*Read, *None)
DftRdbCol	Default collection for unqualified names in static statements	*None (*collection-name*)
DynDftCol	Whether to use DftRdbCol for dynamic statements	*No (*Yes)
SqlPath	List of collections to search for unqualified data type, stored procedure, or function names	*Naming (*Libl or *list-of-collections*)
UsrPrf	User profile for static statements	*Naming (*User, *Owner)
DynUsrPrf	User profile for dynamic statements	*User (*Owner)
ToSrcFile	Source file to receive the precompiled output	QTemp/QSqlTemp or QTemp/QSqlTemp1

Online help provides a full description of all CrtSql*Xxx* command parameters. In this section, we discuss the more important parameters.

The CrtSql*Xxx*I commands' Obj parameter specifies the name of the object you're creating. Normally, you should provide a qualified name to ensure that the new object is placed in the correct library. The SrcFile and SrcMbr parameters identify the source file and member in which the object's source code is stored. By default, all the CrtSql*Xxx*I commands use the same source member name as the object name you specify in the Obj parameter.

The ObjType parameter indicates which type of AS/400 object you want to produce. In addition to the default of *Pgm, which means you want to produce a program object, you can create an ILE module (*Module) or service program (*SrvPgm). The Text parameter lets you specify up to 50 characters of descriptive text for the object you're creating.

The Option parameter lets you specify several precompiler options. In this example, we've specified that we want to use SQL naming. Another important option is *NoGen, which tells the SQL precompiler to stop processing after the precompile step. We'll discuss more about this option and its usefulness later in this chapter.

The IncFile parameter specifies the source file for included source members, as explained in Chapter 13.

The Commit parameter specifies whether commitment control is in effect when the program is run and which lock level (or isolation level) is used. Chapter 13 explains commitment control and isolation levels.

The Rdb (remote database) parameter is used in distributed database applications to permit you to access databases on other systems. We cover some additional details regarding distributed database in Chapter 16.

When you create a program that accesses tables or views with date or time columns, you should generally use the CrtSql*Xxx* command's DatFmt(*ISO) and TimFmt(*ISO) parameters or code a Set Option statement in your program to set these two options. (The DatSep and TimSep parameters let you specify date and time separator characters.) All SQL table and view columns with a Date or Time data type use the *ISO format. You can avoid the performance overhead of converting between different formats by also using *ISO for the format of date and time values that are returned to your program (e.g., by a Fetch statement) or which are passed by your program to UDB/400 (e.g., by an Insert statement). You *must* use *ISO date and time format when your program uses multiple-row Fetch or block Insert (as described in Chapter 13) or you may get hard-to-diagnose data errors.

The AlwCpyDta parameter specifies when the UDB/400 query optimizer can make a copy of data to improve retrieval performance. Consider the following query:

```
Select     *
  From     Customer
  Order By Name
```

If the Customer table is large, it may be faster for UDB/400 to copy and sort the Customer table rather than using an index over the Name column, if one exists.

Specifying AlwCpyDta(*Optimize) for a CrtSql*Xxx* command (the default) lets the query optimizer decide whether to create a copy of the data. When you specify AlwCpyDta(*Yes), the query optimizer uses a copy of the data only if it must do so in order to run the query. (Note the somewhat counterintuitive meaning of the *Yes special value.) Specifying AlwCpyDta(*No) prevents the query optimizer from making a copy of the data; if a query requires that a copy be made, an error occurs when the query is attempted.

The CloSqlCsr parameter controls when UDB/400 closes a cursor left open by the program. This parameter also controls when the system discards SQL prepared statements, releases locks placed by a Lock Table statement (discussed in Chapter 13), and frees other internal resources. Specifying the default, CloSqlCsr(*EndActGrp), causes these actions to be taken when the activation group is deleted; the *EndMod option does so when the module is exited.

The AlwBlk parameter controls record blocking. Specifying AlwBlk(*None) prevents blocking. The *Read option allows blocking for read-only cursors when Commit(*None) is also specified. The *AllRead option allows blocking for read-only cursors when Commit(*None) or Commit(*Chg) is also specified. In addition, this option causes SQL to open a cursor that isn't explicitly updatable as a read-only cursor, even when the program contains Execute or Execute Immediate statements.

Chapter 13 explains the use of the DftRdbCol, DynDftCol, SqlPath, UsrPrf, and DynUsrPrf parameters and their relationship to the recommended SQL naming option.

Specifying Additional HLL Program Creation Parameters

The CrtSql*Xxx* commands include some, but not all, of the parameters available with the various HLL compiler commands (e.g., CrtBndRpg to compile an RPG IV program). If you want to use one of the compiler command options that's not available on a CrtSql*Xxx* command, you can specify Option(*NoGen) on the CrtSql*Xxx* command to terminate the translation process when the precompile step is completed. The default location for the output of the precompiler is the QTemp/QSqlTemp source file (or QTemp/QSqlTemp1 for RPG IV) with the same member name as the object name specified in the CrtSql*Xxx* command's Obj parameter. You can change this to a permanent source physical file contained in a permanent library by specifying the name of the source file in the ToSrcFile parameter of the CrtSql*Xxx* command:

```
CrtSqlRpgI Obj( AppExc/UpdCust )
           SrcFile( AppSrc/QRpgLeSrc )
           Option( *Sql *NoGen )
           ObjType( *Pgm )
           IncFile( AppSrc/SqlIncSrc )
           Commit( *None )
           ToSrcFile( AppSrc/QSqlSrc )
           Text( 'Update Customer table data' )
```

This statement sends precompiler output to the UpdCust member in the AppSrc/QSqlSrc source file and terminates the translation process after the precompiler finishes.

Once you have created this output object, you can then execute any compiler command, specifying this source member as the input file and adding other compiler command parameters as needed. You should not edit this source member. If you do, any subsequent attempt to compile the modified source member will fail. Also, you should not attempt to copy and compile a copied version of this source member. [1]

Specifying SQL Character String Delimiters for Cobol Programs

If you're coding embedded SQL in a Cobol program, you can choose the character string delimiter by specifying either *QuoteSql or *ApostSql in the Option parameter. The default is Option(*QuoteSql), which specifies that the quotation marks character (") is used to delimit SQL character string constants.

The following example shows how to specify a character constant in a Cobol program when Option(*QuoteSql) is in effect:

```
Exec SQL
  Update  Customer
    Set   Name = "Ajax Inc."
    Where CustId = 34567
End-Exec.
```

If you want to use an apostrophe (') for SQL character string literals in a Cobol program, specify Option(*ApostSql) in the CrtSqlCbl or CrtSqlCblI command.

The SQL/400 Translation Process

In Chapter 10, we looked at a simplified view of the steps involved in creating a program object from a source member that contains embedded SQL. The process consists of two major steps: translating embedded SQL statements to HLL statements and creating a program from the combined original HLL and translated SQL statements. Figure 12.3 shows a more detailed picture of the complete **SQL/400 translation process** for RPG IV, ILE COBOL/400, and ILE C/400.

The **SQL/400 precompiler** initiates the overall process. A component of the precompiler performs the first step, in which embedded SQL statements are translated into HLL statements. For most embedded SQL statements, this precompiler component generates some or all of the following HLL statements:

- variable declarations for temporary work variables
- assignment operations (e.g., RPG IV Move) that copy programmer-defined host variable values to temporary precompiler-generated variables
- a Call statement that calls QSqRoute or another IBM-supplied program
- assignment operations (e.g., RPG IV Move) that copy some of the temporary variables' values back to the programmer-defined host variables

The precompiler writes the generated HLL code and the original, untranslated HLL statements to a member of a source file indicated in the ToSrcFile parameter of the CrtSql*Xxx*I command. In addition, the precompiler processes the embedded SQL statements to produce a set of internal structures

1 This restriction is built in to compiler commands to prevent inconsistencies between the source member's HLL code and the application plan information that the SQL precompiler generates.

Figure 12.3
Detailed SQL/400 Translation Process

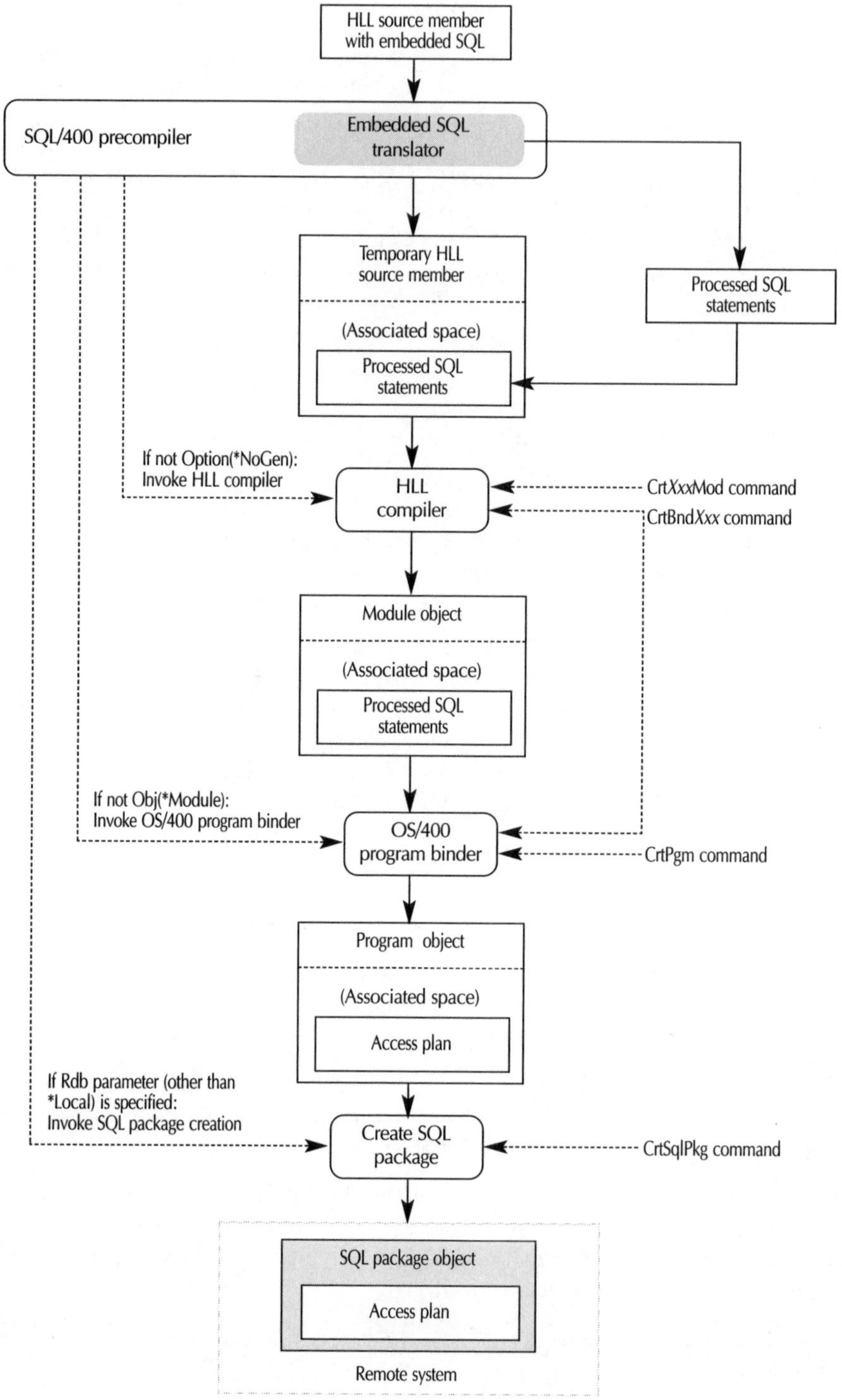

HLL source member with embedded SQL

SQL/400 precompiler

Embedded SQL translator

Temporary HLL source member

(Associated space)

Processed SQL statements

Processed SQL statements

If not Option(*NoGen): Invoke HLL compiler

HLL compiler

Crt*Xxx*Mod command

CrtBnd*Xxx* command

Module object

(Associated space)

Processed SQL statements

If not Obj(*Module): Invoke OS/400 program binder

OS/400 program binder

CrtPgm command

Program object

(Associated space)

Access plan

If Rdb parameter (other than *Local) is specified: Invoke SQL package creation

Create SQL package

CrtSqlPkg command

SQL package object

Access plan

Remote system

that will be used later in the translation process to create an **access plan**. An access plan is another set of internal tables and executable code used by UDB/400 when the QSqRoute or other program is called to perform an embedded SQL operation. The processed SQL statements are stored in the associated space of the temporary source member.[2]

After the initial translation of embedded SQL statements (unless you specified Option(*NoGen)), the precompiler invokes the appropriate HLL compiler, which reads the temporary source file member and produces a module object. If this step is successful, the compiler copies the processed SQL statements (which were built during the first step) from the temporary source file member's associated space to the associated space of the module object.

After a module is created, the precompiler invokes the OS/400 program binder (unless you specified Option(*Module)), which combines or links modules into a program object. The binder invokes a set of system routines that translate the processed SQL statements in the modules' associated spaces into the access plan, which is stored in the associated space of the program object. If ObjType(*Module) is specified on the CrtSql*Xxx*l command, the precompiler doesn't invoke the OS/400 program binder, and you must subsequently use a CrtPgm (Create Program) command to create a program from one or more module objects.[3]

UDB/400 supports distributed database access by programs with embedded SQL. A distributed database program is one that accesses data on a remote system. A distributed database program requires an **SQL package** object on the remote system. The package contains the access plan to perform the program's SQL operations on the remote system's tables, views, and other objects. As Figure 12.3 shows, a package is created from a program object. The SQL precompiler invokes this step automatically when you specify a relational database name on the Rdb parameter (other than *Local) on a CrtSql*Xxx*l command. Or you can use the CrtSqlPkg (Create SQL Package) command to create a package from a program object.

Coding Suggestions

- Specify Option(*Sql) to use the SQL naming convention. This renders the SQL portion of an embedded SQL program more portable.
- Be sure to specify Option(*ApostSql) if you want to use the apostrophe for the character string delimiter in a Cobol program with embedded SQL.
- Specify the Text option to associate up to 50 characters of descriptive text with your program.
- Performance-related suggestions:
  - Use AlwBlk(*AllRead) to allow record blocking for read-only cursors.
  - Unless your application requires maximum data currency for read-only cursors, use the default of AlwCpyDta(*Optimize).
- Use *ISO for the DatFmt and TimFmt parameters.

2 Recall from Chapter 1 that an OS/400 object has a header, a part that contains the main contents of the object, and an associated space that's used for miscellaneous data. In a database file object (which is the type of AS/400 object for tables and views), each member also has an associated space that can be used for miscellaneous data. The associated space is not where the member's records are stored, and the contents of the associated space are not accessible by I/O operations.

3 You can also create service program objects by specifying ObjType(*SrvPgm) on the CrtSql*Xxx*l commands. An ILE service program is somewhat like a dynamic link library (DLL) under Windows. If you create module objects with the CrtSql*Xxx*l command, you can subsequently bind them into a service program using the CrtSrvPgm command.

- If you want to use HLL compile options not available in the CrtSql*Xxx* commands, specify Option(*NoGen) and a permanent library and source file name in the ToSrcFile parameter. When the precompiler finishes, you can compile its output source with the HLL compiler, specifying the compile options you want.

Chapter Summary

Each language has its own CrtSql*Xxx* command for compiling embedded SQL into program — or module or service program — objects). Figure 12.2 lists the most commonly used parameters.

The SQL translation process (i.e., the process of producing an executable object, or module, from embedded source) consists of a precompile followed by a compile followed by a bind. The precompiler creates HLL source where non-SQL statements from the original source are copied unmodified and SQL statements are translated into calls to IBM system routines. The SQL statements are also translated into structures saved in the output source member's associated space.

The source output of the precompiler is then compiled with the HLL compiler to produce a module object. This module object is then bound into a program or service program. The SQL statement structures are carried forward in this process and in the final step (that produces the program or service program) are used to produce an access plan that is stored in the associated space of the program or service program object.

Key Terms

access plan
SQL/400 precompiler
SQL/400 translation process
SQL package

Exercises

1. Show the CrtSqlRpgI (or CrtSqlCblI) command to create program object AppExc/ListCust from source member ListCust in source file AppSrc/QRpgLeSrc (or AppSrc/QCblLeSrc). The program object should have the following attributes:
   - Use the SQL naming convention.
   - Use AppSrc/SqlIncSrc as the source file used for Include statements.
   - Use the commitment control environment with cursor stability (*CS) isolation level.
   - Implicitly close SQL cursors when the module ends.
   - Store the text 'Customer List' in the program object produced.
2. Show additional and modified parameters (if any) for Exercise 1 that will place the source output of the precompiler into source file SqlSrc in library AppSrc and that will ensure that the process stops once the precompiler finishes.
3. In Exercise 1, is it necessary to code additional parameters to ensure that the job's default date format and separators will be used? If so, show the additional parameters that must be coded.
4. What additional parameters would you add to Exercise 1 to get maximum data currency for read-only queries and allow all queries to be run? What are the tradeoffs you assume when you code the parameter this way? (That is, what might you be sacrificing in order to achieve maximum data currency?)

Chapter 13

Additional SQL/400 Programming Techniques

Chapter Overview

This chapter builds on previous chapters' introduction to SQL programming and shows you how to use a variety of SQL/400 and UDB/400 features. We cover the Include statement, the SQL communication area, host structures and arrays, object and row locks, transaction integrity and commitment control, stored procedures, user-defined functions, and SQL/400's two naming options. The topics covered in this chapter are important for real-world, production-level database applications.

The Include Statement

The **Include statement** lets you include SQL and HLL source statements from a source member other than the one you're coding. Suppose you have the following standard RPG IV error-checking code in a source member called SqlErrChk:

```
....1....+....2....+....3....+....4....+....5....+....6....+....
C                   Select
C                     When     SqlStt = '00000'
 *                      Skip
C                     When     SqlStt = '02000'
C                       ExSr   SqlNoRow
C                     When     %SubSt( SqlStt : 1 : 2 ) = '01'
C                       ExSr   SqlWarning
C                     Other
C                       ExSr   SqlError
C                   EndSl
```

You can specify that the SQL precompiler include this code after an SQL statement by using an Include statement:

```
....1....+....2....+....3....+....4....+....5....+....6....+....
C/Exec SQL
C+                  Update  Customer
C+                    Set   Discount = :NewDisc
C+                    Where ShipCity = :SlcCusCity
C/End-Exec
C/Exec SQL
C+ Include SqlErrChk
C/End-Exec
```

The source member name follows the Include keyword. The IncFile parameter on the CrtSqlRpgI (Create SQL ILE RPG Object) or other command used to create the program specifies the library and source file containing the member. (See Chapter 12 for a description of the CrtSql*Xxx* commands and the SQL/400 translation process.[1]) For any single HLL source member, all SQL Include statements refer to members in the same include source file; that is, there's no way to include members from two different source files when you compile an SQL program.

The SQL Communication Area

As we mentioned in Chapter 10, UDB/400 sets values in a set of variables known as the **SQL communication area (SQLCA)** to provide feedback to your HLL program after it executes an embedded SQL statement. In HLL programs, this area is stored in the SqlCa data structure. In RPG IV programs that contain embedded SQL, this data structure and its subfield declarations are automatically generated. Figure 13.1 shows the layout of the RPG IV SqlCa data structure.

Figure 13.1

RPG IV SqlCa Data Structure

```
....1....+....2....+....3....+....4....+....5
D*     SQL Communication Area
D SQLCA
D   SQLAID                     1      8A
D   SQLABC                     9     12B 0
D   SQLCOD                    13     16B 0
D   SQLERL                    17     18B 0
D   SQLERM                    19     88A
D   SQLERP                    89     96A
D   SQLERRD                   97    120B 0 DIM(6)
D   SQLERR                    97    120A
D     SQLER1                  97    100B 0
D     SQLER2                 101    104B 0
D     SQLER3                 105    108B 0
D     SQLER4                 109    112B 0
D     SQLER5                 113    116B 0
D     SQLER6                 117    120B 0
D   SQLWRN                   121    131A
D     SQLWN0                 121    121A
D     SQLWN1                 122    122A
D     SQLWN2                 123    123A
D     SQLWN3                 124    124A
D     SQLWN4                 125    125A
D     SQLWN5                 126    126A
D     SQLWN6                 127    127A
D     SQLWN7                 128    128A
D     SQLWN8                 129    129A
D     SQLWN9                 130    130A
D     SQLWNA                 131    131A
D   SQLSTT                   132    136A
```

In ILE COBOL/400 programs, you use an Include SqlCa statement in the Working-Storage section to generate the group and elementary items shown in Figure 13.2.

1 When the SQL precompiler processes source code, it does a limited amount of parsing of the HLL source to determine such things as the data types of host variables. But the precompiler doesn't process all language statements. In the case of RPG IV, it's important to know that the RPG IV conditional compilation directives (e.g., /If Defined) do *not* affect precompilation. One impact of this limitation is that you can't conditionally include source members during precompilation — a technique that would be useful if it were supported.

Figure 13.2

ILE COBOL/400 SqlCa Structure

```
01   SQLCA GLOBAL.
     05 SQLCAID      PIC  X(8).
     05 SQLCABC      PIC S9(9) BINARY.
     05 SQLCODE      PIC S9(9) BINARY.
     05 SQLERRM.
        49 SQLERRML PIC S9(4) BINARY.
        49 SQLERRMC PIC  X(70).
     05 SQLERRP      PIC  X(8).
     05 SQLERRD      OCCURS 6 TIMES
                     PIC S9(4) BINARY.
     05 SQLWARN.
        10 SQLWARN0 PIC X(1).
        10 SQLWARN1 PIC X(1).
        10 SQLWARN2 PIC X(1).
        10 SQLWARN3 PIC X(1).
        10 SQLWARN4 PIC X(1).
        10 SQLWARN5 PIC X(1).
        10 SQLWARN6 PIC X(1).
        10 SQLWARN7 PIC X(1).
        10 SQLWARN8 PIC X(1).
        10 SQLWARN9 PIC X(1).
        10 SQLWARN0 PIC X(1).
        10 SQLWARNA PIC X(1).
     05 SQLSTATE     PIC X(5).
```

Figure 13.3 provides a description of the contents of the SQL communication area.

Figure 13.3

SQL Communication Area Structure Contents

Variable	Data type	Purpose
SqlCaId	Char(8)	Structure identifying literal: "SQLCA"
SqlCaBc	Integer	Length of SqlCa
SqlCode	Integer	Return code: < 0 = Error 0 = Successful execution (SqlWarn indicators may have been set) > 0 = Successful execution with warning
SqlErrMl	SmallInt	Length of SqlErrMc
SqlErrMc	Char(70)	Message replacement text
SqlErrP	Char(8)	For statements other than Connect, identifies the product and module returning the information. The first three characters identify the product (QSQ for UDB/400). For a Connect statement, contains *pppvvrrm*, where *ppp* identifies the product, *vv* the version number, *rr* the release, and *m* the modification (e.g., QSQ04040 for UDB/400 V4R4M0).

continued

Figure 13.3 *Continued*

Variable	Data type	Purpose
SqlErrD	Array of Integer	SqlErrD(1) — Treated as Char(4); contains the last four characters of CPF or other escape message, if any.
		SqlErrD(2) — Treated as Char(4); contains the last four characters of CPD or other diagnostic message, if any.
		SqlErrD(3) — For Fetch, Insert, Update, or Delete, the number of rows retrieved or updated. For Prepare, the estimated number of rows affected. For Connect (with no argument specified), returns the status of the connection: 1 = Committable updates can be performed for the current unit of work. 2 = Committable updates cannot be performed.
		SqlErrD(4) — For Fetch, the length of the row retrieved. For Prepare, a relative number indicating estimated resources required for execution. For Call, the message key of the error that caused the procedure to fail (the message can be retrieved with the QMhRtvPm API). For a trigger error in an Update, Insert, or Delete statement, the message key of the error sent by the trigger program (the message can be retrieved with the QMhRtvPm API). For Connect, indicates whether the conversation is protected and whether committable updates can be performed: 1 = protected/committable 2 = unprotected/not committable 3 = protected/unknown 4 = unprotected/unknown 5 = local connection or application requester driver program, unknown if committable
		SqlErrD(5) — For multiple-row Fetch, contains 100 if last available row is fetched. For Delete, the number of rows affected by referential constraints. For Prepare, the number of parameter markers in the prepared statement. For Connect or Set Connection, contains –1 if connection is unconnected, 0 if connection is local, or 1 if connection is remote.
		SqlErrD(6) — When SqlCode is 0, contains SQL completion message identifier.
SqlWarn	Char(11)	Set of 11 warning indicators; each is blank, W, or N. (The following 11 items describe these warning indicators.)
SqlWarn0	Char(1)	Blank if all other SqlWarn*X* warning indicators are blank; W if any warning indicator contains W or N.
SqlWarn1	Char(1)	W if a string column was truncated when assigned to host variable; N if C program host variable was large enough for string but not for null terminator and *NoCNulRqd was specified for program.
SqlWarn2	Char(1)	W if null values were eliminated from a function
SqlWarn3	Char(1)	W if number of columns is larger than number of host variables
SqlWarn4	Char(1)	W if prepared Update or Delete statement doesn't include a Where clause
SqlWarn5	Char(1)	Reserved
SqlWarn6	Char(1)	W if date arithmetic results in end-of-month adjustment
SqlWarn7	Char(1)	Reserved

continued

Figure 13.3 *Continued*

Variable	Data type	Purpose
SqlWarn8	Char(1)	W if result of character conversion contains the substitution character.
SqlWarn9	Char(1)	Reserved
SqlWarnA	Char(1)	Reserved
SqlState	Char(5)	Return code; 00000 if no error or warning.

We've already looked at several of the variables in the SQLCA, including SqlState, SqlCode, and SqlWarn0. An appendix in *DB2 UDB for AS/400 SQL Programming* lists all SqlCode values and the corresponding SqlState values. As you can see, other variables provide additional information about both normal and exceptional conditions. The main purpose of these variables is to provide better diagnosis and reporting of exceptional conditions. You can also use variables such as SqlErrD(3) — which contains the number of rows Fetched, Inserted, Updated, or Deleted — to provide user feedback for normal operations.

Host Structures

SQL/400 provides an option to code an HLL structure variable, such as an RPG IV data structure or a Cobol group item, in many places that a list of individual (i.e., scalar) host variables is allowed. For example, you can use a **host structure variable** in the Into clause of a Select Into or Fetch statement or in the Values clause of an Insert statement. The SQL/400 precompiler generates the list of individual host variables from the variables declared as elements (e.g., RPG IV subfields, Cobol elementary items) of the structure. To specify corresponding indicator variables with a host structure, you must specify an *array* of indicator variables (*not* a structure).

As an example, consider a simplified Customer table defined as follows:

```
Create Table Customer
     ( CustID   Dec(   7, 0 ) Not Null,
       Name     Char( 30    ) Not Null,
       ShipCity Char( 30    ),
       Discount Dec(   5, 3 ),
  Primary Key( CustID ) )
```

The following sample code illustrates the use of the CustomerR host structure variable and the CustomerI host indicator array in a Select Into statement:

```
....1....+....2....+....3....+....4....+....5....+....6....+....
D CustomerR         DS
D  CsCustID                      7P 0
D  CsName                       30A
D  CsShipCity                   30A
D  CsDiscount                    5P 3
D CustomerI         S            5I 0 Dim( 4 )
      .
      .
      .
C/Exec SQL
C+                   Select  CustID,
C+                           Name,
C+                           ShipCity,
C+                           Discount
C+                     Into :CustomerR :CustomerI
C+                     From  Customer
C+                     Where CustID = :SlcCustID
C/End-Exec
```

The resulting Select Into statement is equivalent to

```
....1....+....2....+....3....+....4....+....5....+....6....+....
C/Exec SQL
C+                    Select  CustID,
C+                            Name,
C+                            ShipCity,
C+                            Discount
C+                      Into :CsCustID    :CustomerI( 1 ),
C+                           :CsName      :CustomerI( 2 ),
C+                           :CsShipCity :CustomerI( 3 ),
C+                           :CsDiscount :CustomerI( 4 )
C+                      From  Customer
C+                      Where CustID = :SlcCustID
C/End-Exec
```

The four individual host variables (e.g., :CsCustID) come from the subfields of the first host structure that follows the Into keyword, and the four individual indicator variables (e.g., :CustomerI(1)) come from the array elements of the indicator array.

You can make a significant improvement in the names used for indicator variables by having the indicator array overlay a set of individual indicator subfields in a data structure. The following code shows how to define this type of structure in RPG IV:

```
....1....+....2....+....3....+....4....+....5....+....6....+....
D CsColCnt          C                    Const( 4 )

D CsNullDs          DS
D  CsIDNull                       5I 0
D  CsNameNull                     5I 0
D  CsCityNull                     5I 0
D  CsDiscNull                     5I 0
D  CustomerI                      5I 0 Dim( CsColCnt )
D                                      Overlay( CsNullDs )
```

Notice how CustomerI still is declared as an array and is the variable you specify on SQL statements such as the previous example. (In this example, we've used the CsColCnt named constant to define the number of columns and thus the number of elements in the array.) But now the same storage occupied by the four array elements can be referenced by the meaningfully named subfields: CsIDNull, CsNameNull, CsCityNull, and CsDiscNull.

This feature is especially convenient when you use an RPG IV externally described data structure or a Cobol Copy directive to create the host structure.[2] The host structure and indicator array can be coded in a simpler and less error-prone way as follows:

2 There's no automatic way to generate a host structure for a list of indicator variables. A helpful programming practice is to create an SQL Include source member with the structure declarations for the indicator variables. With RPG IV, you can also use the /Copy compiler directive, which the SQL/400 precompiler processes. You can't use Cobol Copy source members for this purpose because the host indicator structure must be included during the precompile phase, and the Cobol Copy directive operates only during the compile phase.

```
....1....+....2....+....3....+....4....+....5....+....6....+....
D CsColCnt          C                   Const( 4 )

D CustomerR       E DS                  ExtName( Customer )
D                                       Prefix( Cs )
D CsNullDs          DS
D  CsIDNull                      5I 0
D  CsNameNull                    5I 0
D  CsCityNull                    5I 0
D  CsDiscNull                    5I 0
D  CustomerI                     5I 0 Dim( CsColCnt )
D                                       Overlay( CsNullDs )
      .
      .
      .
C/Exec SQL
C+                 Select  *
C+                   Into :CustomerR :CustomerI
C+                   From  Customer
C+                   Where CustID = :SlcCustID
C/End-Exec
```

Notice the use of the asterisk (*) to specify an implicit list of columns in the Select statement's result table. When an externally described host structure is used in the Into clause, both the result table's implicit column list and the Into clause's generated host variables include all columns in the table, in the same order. When you use an indicator array with this technique (as shown), it's essential that you have one null indicator subfield for each column in the table and that you correctly define the subfields so that they correspond positionally to their associated columns.

This example also uses the Prefix keyword on the CustomerR data structure definition. This RPG IV keyword adds Cs to the beginning of all the column names so that the resulting subfield names will be unique within the program.

To work with a subset of columns, you can simply create and use a view that includes the desired subset and has no Where clause (and thus includes all rows from the underlying table). The view name can be specified on the RPG IV externally described data structure, as well as on the Select statement.

In Cobol, the equivalent statements to define both the host structure for a list of host variables and a host array (and corresponding structure) for a list of indicator variables are

```
01  CustomerRow.
    Copy DDS-All-Formats of Customer With Alias.

01  CustomerNullDta.
    02 CustIDNull     Pic S9(4) Binary.
    02 NameNull       Pic S9(4) Binary.
    02 ShipCityNull   Pic S9(4) Binary.
    02 DiscountNull   Pic S9(4) Binary.
01  CustomerNullArray  Redefines CustomerNullDta.
    02 CustomerNullInd Pic S9(4) Binary
                       Occurs 4 Times.
      .
      .
      .
    Exec SQL
      Select  *
        Into :Customer :CustomerNullInd
        From  Customer
        Where CustID = :SlcCustID
    End-Exec
```

In Cobol, you can use the DDS-All-Formats or the DDS-All-Formats...With Alias form of the Copy directive; DDS-All-Formats generates the short column names, and DDS-All-Formats...With Alias generates the long column names. Note that for the host structure, you use the 05-level group item name (Customer) generated by the Copy directive, not the 01-level name (CustomerRow). Also, the Occurs value for the indicator array must be the number of elementary items in 01-level that the array overlays.

Host Structure Arrays

As a performance enhancement, SQL/400 also lets you retrieve multiple rows into a **host structure array** with a single Fetch operation, as well as add multiple rows to a base table by specifying a host structure array on an Insert statement. To declare a host structure array in RPG IV, you use a multiple-occurrence data structure (the Occurs keyword in positions 44–80). In Cobol, you use the Occurs clause on the declaration of the group item for the host structure.

A **multiple-row Fetch** uses a For *n* Rows clause, as in the following example:

```
....1....+....2....+....3....+....4....+....5....+....6....+....
 * Mnemonics
D True              C                   Const( '1' )
D False             C                   Const( '0' )
D SqlStateOk        C                   Const( '00000' )
D SqlStateNoRow     C                   Const( '02000' )
D SqlErr5LastRow    C                   Const( 100     )

 * Constants for number of columns and elements in array
D CsColCnt          C                   Const(  4 )
D CsAryElem         C                   Const( 10 )

D CustomerR       E DS                  ExtName( Customer )
D                                       Prefix( Cs )
D                                       Occurs( CsAryElem )

D CsNullDs          DS                  Occurs( CsAryElem )
D   CsIDNull                       5I 0
D   CsNameNull                     5I 0
D   CsCityNull                     5I 0
D   CsDiscNull                     5I 0

D CustomerI         DS                  Occurs( CsAryElem )
D                                       Based( CsNullDsAd )
D   CsNullAry                      5I 0 Dim( CsColCnt )

 * Initialize the basing pointer for the indicator array so
 * the indicator array overlays the indicator structure.
D CsNullDsAd        S               *   Inz( %Addr( CsNullDs ) )

D CsRowCnt          S              7P 0 Inz( CsAryElem )
D CsTopRow          S              7P 0
D CsCurRow          S              7P 0

D CsMoreRows        S              1A   Inz( False )
      .
      .
      .
C/Exec SQL
C+ Declare CustomerCursor Cursor
C+    For Select     *
C+          From     Customer
C+          Order By CustID
C/End-Exec

 * Open the cursor and (if successful) set CsMoreRows to True.
 * Then loop across the table, fetching and processing
 * blocks of rows -- for example, printing each row.
```

continued

continued...

```
C/Exec SQL
C+                    Open CustomerCursor
C/End-Exec
      .
      .
      .
C                    Eval      CsMoreRows = True
C                    DoW       CsMoreRows = True
C/Exec SQL
C+                     Fetch Next
C+                       From  CustomerCursor
C+                       For  :CsRowCnt Rows
C+                       Into :CustomerR :CustomerI
C/End-Exec
 *                     Save the number of rows retrieved
C                      Eval      CsTopRow = SqlErrD( 3 )
C
C                      Select
C                       When     SqlStt = SqlStateOk
C                         If     SqlErrD( 5 ) = SqlErr5LastRow
 *                         The last row is already in the array
C                          Eval CsMoreRows = False
C                         EndIf
C                         ExSr  ListCustRowAry
C                       When     SqlStt = SqlStateNoRow
C                         Eval  CsMoreRows = False
C                       Other
C                         ExSr  RptSqlErr
C                         Eval  CsMoreRows = False
C                      EndSl
C                    EndDo
      .
      .
      .
 * - - - - - - - - - - - - - - - - - - - - - - - - - - - - - - -
C      ListCustRowAryBegSr

C      1             Do        CsTopRow      CsCurRow
C      CsCurRow        Occur   CustomerR
C      CsCurRow        Occur   CustomerI
C      CsCurRow        Occur   CsNullDs

 *                     The ListCustRow subroutine can now
 *                     operate on the CustomerR and CustomerI
 *                     data structures for the current element.

C                      ExSr    ListCustRow
C                    EndDo
C                    EndSr
 * - - - - - - - - - - - - - - - - - - - - - - - - - - - - - - -
C      ListCustRow   BegSr

 *     As an example, set printer fields (e.g., CsPrtCustID).

C                    Eval      CsPrtCustID  = CsCustID
C                    Eval      CsPrtName    = CsName
C                    Eval      CsPrtShpCity = CsShipCity

 *                   Replace null with 0

C                    If        CsDiscNull >= 0
C                      Eval    CsPrtDiscount = CsDiscount
C                    Else
C                      Eval    CsPrtDiscount = 0
C                    EndIf

 *                   Write output to a spooled file....

C                    EndSr
```

As you can see, declaring an RPG IV multiple-occurrence data structure to hold multiple rows is quite straightforward — just add an Occurs keyword to the D-spec you use for a single row. In this example, the named constant CsAryElem specifies the number of occurrences (and, thus, the maximum number of rows that can be retrieved in one Fetch operation).

The CustomerI multiple-occurrence data structure shows the way you declare indicator variables — each occurrence of the multiple-occurrence data structure is an indicator array. To declare meaningful names for the null indicators is a bit trickier than for a single row. You can't use the Overlay technique (the SQL/400 precompiler doesn't allow it), so you have to use a *based* multiple-occurrence data structure (e.g., CustomerI). In RPG IV, the actual storage for a based data structure is at the virtual memory address contained in the *basing pointer* variable specified in the Based keyword. In this example, CsNullDsAd is the basing pointer for the CustomerI multiple-occurrence data structure. To make the CustomerI storage the same as the CsNullDs multiple-occurrence data structure's storage — and thus act as if the two were overlayed — you just use the RPG IV %Addr built-in function to initialize the CsNullDsAd basing pointer to the virtual memory address of the CsNullDs data structure. This technique may seem a bit complex, but it's actually very easy to use in a "cookbook" fashion if you just follow the pattern shown in this example.

In the Fetch statement, the For *n* Rows clause specifies the maximum number of rows to be fetched. As the example above shows, you can specify the number of elements in the host structure array (in this case, in the CsRowCnt host variable) to retrieve a full array's worth, if that many rows are available. After a multiple-row Fetch statement, the SqlErrCode(3) variable (part of the SqlCa, described earlier) has the number of rows returned. If no rows are returned because no more were available and if no other exception occurs, the SqlStt variable is set to 02000. If one or more rows are returned and the last available row was returned by the Fetch, the SqlErrD(5) variable is set to 100. Be sure to check SqlStt before doing any processing, and use SqlErrD(3) to determine how many elements in the array hold rows returned by the most recent Fetch. Once you've fetched a block of rows into an array, you can process them using standard RPG IV loop and multiple-occurrence data structure opcodes, as shown.

A successful multiple-row Fetch operates in two steps:

1. The cursor is positioned according to the positioning keyword (e.g., Next, Relative).
2. The row on which the cursor is positioned is fetched, and up to $n - 1$ (where n is the number specified on the For *n* Rows clause) additional rows are fetched as if a Fetch Next were specified.

The first row fetched is placed in the first element of the host structure array, the next row fetched into the second array element, and so on. Fetching stops when *n* rows have been fetched or there are no more available rows in the cursor. Fetching is always forward from the position set by the positioning keyword. If you wanted to fetch the previous three rows in one operation, you could use

```
C/Exec SQL
C+                   Fetch Relative -3
C+                     From  CustomerCursor
C+                     For   3 Rows
C+                     Into :CustomerR :CustomerI
C/End-Exec
```

You shouldn't use a Fetch Prior...For 3 Rows statement for this purpose because that would fetch the previous row, the current row, and the next row — not the previous row, the one before the previous row, and the one before that. In other words, Fetch Prior...For *n* Rows does *not* mean "fetch the previous *n* rows."

A **blocked Insert** lets you specify that multiple elements from a host array structure are inserted into a table. The following example shows how to use this form of Insert statement:

```
....1....+....2....+....3....+....4....+....5....+....6....+....
D CsColCnt          C                   Const(  4 )
D CsAryElem         C                   Const( 10 )

D CustomerR       E DS                  ExtName( Customer )
D                                       Prefix( Cs )
D                                       Occurs( CsAryElem )

D CsNullDs          DS                  Occurs( CsAryElem )
D  CsIDNull                      5I 0
D  CsNameNull                    5I 0
D  CsCityNull                    5I 0
D  CsDiscNull                    5I 0

D CustomerI         DS                  Occurs( CsAryElem )
D                                       Based( CsNullDsAd )
D  CsNullAry                     5I 0 Dim( CsColCnt )

 * Initialize the basing pointer for the indicator array so
 * the indicator array overlays the indicator structure.
D CsNullDsAd        S               *   Inz( %Addr( CsNullDs ) )

D CsRowCnt          S            7P 0
     .
     .
     .
C* Fill n rows of the CustomerR and CustomerI multiple-
C* occurrence data structures (you can use the CsNullDs
C* data structure to set the indicators). Then set CsRowCnt
C* to n (the number of occurrences you've filled with row
C* data).
     .
     .
     .
C/Exec SQL
C+                  Insert Into Customer
C+                    :CsRowCnt Rows
C+                    Values( :CustomerR :CustomerI )
C/End-Exec
```

The first through the *n*th elements of the host structure array, where *n* is the value of the Rows clause, are inserted into the table, just as if *n* Insert statements had been specified, one for each element of the host structure array. Notice that this example uses an implicit column list in the Insert statement. As we mentioned earlier, when an externally described host structure is used instead of a list of individual host variables, an implicit column list provides a perfectly corresponding list of columns.

Multiple-row Fetch statements and block Insert statements can provide significant performance improvement, especially for batch jobs that process large numbers of rows.

Object and Row Locks and the Lock Table Statement

The AS/400 lets multiple users access application objects simultaneously. To prevent one job's operations from interfering with another job's operations, OS/400 provides object- and row-locking facilities. When one job holds an object or row lock, it restricts what other jobs can do with the locked object or row. UDB/400 uses OS/400 object and row locking to avoid conflicting database updates from multiple jobs. For many situations, UDB/400's default locking is adequate; however, in some cases you may need to add explicit locks to your applications to prevent conflicts.

For example, if one user starts end-of-day batch transaction processing and another user, not knowing this, calls an interactive program to add a few last-minute transactions, unless your program is designed to handle this situation, transactions entered by the interactive job may be lost as they're added behind those already processed by the batch job. UDB/400's default object locking would let both jobs have update access to the table. However, you can use the SQL Lock Table statement or the OS/400 AlcObj (Allocate Object) command to let the batch job place a lock on the table so no other job can perform any updates until the lock is released. We'll take a look at some examples of the Lock Table statement after covering object locking basics.

Object Locks

When you allocate an object during a job, OS/400 places an **object lock** on the object. This lock serves two purposes: it guarantees to your job specific types of access to the object, and it prevents other jobs from having specific types of access to the object. The lock is released when a program executes an OS/400 DlcObj (Deallocate Object) command, when the routing step ends,[3] or when the object is deleted by the job holding the lock. We'll cover some additional cases later, when we discuss the SQL Lock Table statement.

The type of lock placed on an object governs the way the object is shared among different jobs. This mechanism lets the AS/400 give different users a high degree of concurrent access to programs, data, and other objects. While sharing is allowed, the object is protected against simultaneous uses that would conflict; for example, a job cannot delete a table if another job is currently reading it.

Object allocation differs from object authorization, which is used to protect the security of shared objects (see Chapter 9). Object authorization allows a user profile specific types of access to an object; this authority generally remains in effect even when no job is active (the exception is the authority that may be adopted while a program is executing).

Object allocation, on the other hand, is used to protect the integrity of shared objects while they're in use. Object allocation grants a specific type of lock to the routing step that requests the allocation; objects are allocated only by active jobs. The allocation remains in effect only while the routing step is active. Here are some of the things you can use an AlcObj command for:

- to prevent a program from being deleted while someone is executing it
- to permit only one job at a time to execute a program
- to obtain database table locks that aren't available with the SQL Lock Table statement
- to guarantee access to a group of required objects before using any one of them

In this section, we'll cover primarily those concepts related to locks for database tables and views.

Types of Object Locks

Suppose you've decided you need to explicitly allocate an object. In doing so, you guarantee your job a certain level of access to the object. You also lock, to some degree, other jobs out of the object — the degree depends on the kind of lock you obtain. You have five types of locks from which to choose:

3 A routing step is one part of an AS/400 job. Most jobs have a single routing step that starts when the job starts and ends when the job ends. For one-step jobs, it might be simpler to think of allocating an object to a job rather than to a routing step. Where this chapter uses the term "routing step," you can read "job" for most situations.

- *Exclusive (*Excl)* — Only the routing step holding the lock can use the object; routing steps in other jobs cannot access the object.
- *Exclusive-allow-read (*ExclRd)* — The routing step that holds the lock can read or update the object, while routing steps in other jobs can only read it.
- *Shared-for-update (*ShrUpd)* — The routing step that holds the lock, as well as routing steps in other jobs, can read or update the object.
- *Shared-no-update (*ShrNUp)* — The routing step that holds the lock is guaranteed only read access to the object;[4] routing steps in other jobs can only read the object.
- *Shared-for-read (*ShrRd)* — The routing step that holds the lock is guaranteed only read access to the object; routing steps in other jobs can read or update it.

The table in Figure 13.4 summarizes these locks.

Figure 13.4

Object Lock Types to Use for Required Access Control

	And you want to allow a routing step in another job the following access		
Your routing step needs this type of access	**No access**	**Read-only**	**Update**
None, but restrict other jobs	*Excl	*ShrNUp	(No lock)
Read-only	*Excl	*ShrNUp	*ShrRd
Update	*Excl	*ExclRd	*ShrUpd

You can use this table to quickly determine the type of lock to obtain in a given instance. Suppose you've decided to update a table, and while you're updating it, you want other jobs or routing steps to be able to read the table but not update it. In the left column of the table in Figure 13.4, find "Update." Then move across the Update row to the Read-only column for routing steps in other jobs. The type of lock you need in this instance is *ExclRd.

Although a lock gives the routing step that holds it a guarantee of access to an object and limits access by routing steps in other jobs, it does not limit subsequent access in the same routing step that holds the lock. For example, a program can execute an SQL Lock Table statement to obtain an *ExclRd lock on a table. A program in another job cannot open the locked table for updating. However, it's possible for the program holding the *ExclRd lock to call a program that updates the same table.[5]

When a routing step attempts to obtain a lock, it gets the lock unless a routing step in another job already holds a conflicting lock on the same object. OS/400 ensures proper sharing of an object by preventing conflicting locks. Figure 13.5 shows the types of locks that are allowed if a routing step in another job already holds a lock.

4 With this lock, the routing step may also be able to update the object, as long as no other job holds a conflicting lock. But this lock doesn't *guarantee* update access.

5 The point of object locking is to restrict *other* jobs, not the job holding the lock.

Figure 13.5
Allowable Object Lock Combinations

If a routing step already has this lock	A routing step in another job can obtain this lock				
	*Excl	*ExclRd	*ShrUpd	*ShrNUp	*ShrRd
*Excl	N	N	N	N	N
*ExclRd	N	N	N	N	Y
*ShrUpd	N	N	Y	N	Y
*ShrNUp	N	N	N	Y	Y
*ShrRd	N	Y	Y	Y	Y

At different times in its processing, a routing step can obtain multiple locks of the same or a different type on an object. The system keeps a count of each type of lock placed on the object. Eventually, each lock must be released individually, even if the locks are of the same type. Thus, if at two different points in a routing step a *ShrRd lock is placed on an object, at some point both *ShrRd locks must be released on that object to return the system lock count to zero. Not until the count returns to zero is the *ShrRd lock totally removed from the object.

A routing step can use a single AlcObj command to obtain a lock on more than one object. Therefore, a group of objects required to complete an operation can be allocated at one time. Often, a program requires several tables — some for read-only access, others for updating. By allocating the tables before calling the program, you can simplify error handling. If explicit allocation is not used, you must either open all tables before processing begins so you're assured of access to them all or you must use a restart procedure to continue at an interruption point (if one of the tables turns out to be unavailable).

The following statement shows an AlcObj command that allocates the following objects: a daily transaction input table that no other job will be allowed to update, a customer name table that will be read, a customer account table that will be updated, and an OS/400 data area with the last transaction number processed that will be updated and can be read by other jobs:[6]

```
AlcObj  Obj( ( DailyTran *File    *ShrNUp )
             ( CustName  *File    *ShrRd  )
             ( CustAct   *File    *ShrUpd )
             ( LstTrnNbr *DtaAra *ExclRd ) )
        Wait( 10 )
```

If any one of these locks cannot be obtained, none of the objects will have locks placed on them by this AlcObj command. This all-or-none approach makes it easy to allocate the set of objects you need before you start to use any of them.

An AlcObj command succeeds if all the requested locks can be obtained. If any of the locks cannot be granted, an escape message (CPF1002) is sent to the program executing the AlcObj command. If the command is in a CL program, you can monitor for the message using the MonMsg command. If an HLL program's operation (e.g., an SQL cursor open or Lock Table statement) cannot allocate an object, the HLL program's exception procedures must handle the problem.

6 For multimember database files (not SQL tables and views), you can optionally specify a member to lock. When no member is specified, the default is to lock the first member. Recall that database files for SQL tables and views always have a single member.

The Wait(10) parameter in the example above specifies that the AlcObj command can wait up to 10 seconds for the locks. Such a wait may be necessary if a routing step in another job has one or more of the objects allocated with a lock that conflicts with the requested lock. If such a conflict exists and the conflicting locks are released within 10 seconds, this routing step gets the locks it has requested unless a job with a higher dispatching priority also has requested locks on any of the objects.

A routing step also can release more than one lock with a single DlcObj command. When the objects in the example above are no longer needed, they can be deallocated with the following command:

```
DlcObj  Obj( ( DailyTran *File    *ShrNUp )
             ( CustName  *File    *ShrRd  )
             ( CustAct   *File    *ShrUpd )
             ( LstTrnNbr *DtaAra *ExclRd ) )
```

In general, for every AlcObj command in your job, there should be a corresponding DlcObj command with the same object list.[7] However, if the job (or routing step) ends when the objects are no longer needed, no DlcObj command is necessary, and all objects are deallocated automatically.

Within a routing step, you may need to change the type of lock you have on an object. You should first obtain the new lock and then release the old lock. This technique prevents a routing step in another job from obtaining a conflicting lock before you obtain the new lock. For example, if you want to use a table first for updating and then just to read, execute the following sequence of commands:

```
AlcObj  Obj( ( Customer *File *ShrUpd ) )
.
. Call a program that updates the file.
.
AlcObj  Obj( ( Customer *File *ShrRd  ) )
DlcObj  Obj( ( Customer *File *ShrUpd ) )
.
. Call a program that reads the file.
.
DlcObj  Obj( ( Customer *File *ShrRd ) )
```

Any time an SQL statement opens a table or view for access, the routing step obtains default locks determined by the type of open operation (input, output, input/output). When an open operation is executed on a table or view, a lock is placed on the table's physical file or the view's logical file, but the locking doesn't end there. For a table, a lock is also placed on the physical file member being opened, on any access path(s) used to access the opened member, and on the data of the opened member. For a view, a lock is placed on the logical file member being opened, and a lock is placed on the access path(s) used for the opened member and the data of all physical file members included in the scope of the view. If all this seems a bit complex, just remember that when you open a table or view, you lock the data that's accessed through a database file member and anything else that's necessary to protect the integrity of related database files and members.

The Lock Table Statement

SQL/400 uses OS/400 object locks as the basis for table locking. In many cases, the default locks may be adequate; however, when two AS/400 jobs access the same base table, there's a possibility that one

7 The use of DlcObj for an object that has not been allocated by an AlcObj is allowed, but it can be dangerous. Deallocating objects that you have not specifically allocated can release locks implicitly placed by your job and cause malfunctions.

job's row updates might conflict with the other job's retrieval or update. For example, if one job (JobA) executes the Select Into statement

```
Select  Avg( Discount )
  Into  :AvgDiscount
  From  Customer
```

while another job (JobB) is executing the statement

```
Update  Customer
  Set   Discount = .10
  Where ShipCity = 'Portland'
```

to update the Discount column, the first job may get an average based on the old Discount value for some Portland customers and the new Discount value for others. UDB/400 (and other database management systems) don't automatically do anything to prevent these two jobs from interleaving the retrieval and update of individual rows.

The SQL **Lock Table statement** provides an alternative to the AlcObj command to explicitly lock a base table to prevent conflicting access. The Lock Table statement can provide a shared lock to let other jobs read, but not modify, the table. For this example, you could execute the following statement to protect JobA's Select statement above from conflicting updates:

```
Lock Table Customer In Share Mode
```

The Share keyword causes an OS/400 *ShrNUp object lock to be placed on the physical file member for the table. A shared lock does *not* guarantee that the job holding the lock can update the table, which isn't necessary in this case because JobA just needs to block JobB from doing updates while JobA reads the table.

Looking at the problem from JobB's perspective, JobB may want not only to prevent other jobs from updating the table but also to be assured of the ability to perform the updates. This requires a more restrictive exclusive-allow-read lock:

```
Lock Table Customer In Exclusive Mode Allow Read
```

This type of lock prevents other jobs from performing conflicting updates and prevents them from getting an SQL shared lock as well. It places an OS/400 *ExclRd object lock on the physical file member for the table.

For the most restrictive lock, a Lock Table statement can specify an exclusive lock to prevent any type of access to the table by another job. The following statement places a *Excl object lock on the physical file member for the table and assures that no other access to the Customer table occurs while the job holds the lock:

```
Lock Table Customer In Exclusive Mode
```

The basic rules for the Lock Table statement's lock modes are:

- If a job holds a share table lock, other jobs can read, but not update, the table, and they can also obtain a share lock.
- If a job holds an exclusive-read table lock, other jobs can read the table but cannot use Lock Table to obtain a share, exclusive-read, or exclusive lock.
- If a job holds an exclusive table lock, other jobs can't access the table and can't obtain any type of lock.

Refer to Figure 13.5 for the complete lock compatibility rules for OS/400 locks. If a lock can't be placed because a different job already holds a conflicting lock, the Lock Table fails and the SqlState variable (described in Chapter 10 and the "SQL Communication Area" section, above) is set to 57033.

A lock placed by a Lock Table statement can be removed with an SQL Commit or Rollback statement that doesn't have the Hold keyword specified, as we discuss later. You can also use the DlcObj command to remove the lock. Table locks are also implicitly removed when the object is deleted, the routing step ends, the activation group ends, SQL closes its internal cursors for the table (see the description of the CloSqlCsr parameter in Chapter 12), or a remote connection is disconnected. In general, you should keep a table locked for the briefest time necessary because a table lock may block other jobs from executing their normal access to a table.

Row Locks

Locks placed on a table through the Lock Table statement, an AlcObj command, or implicitly by an SQL statement that accesses the table should not be confused with **row locks**. Table locks establish, for the entire table, allowable access methods by routing steps in different jobs. Row locks, on the other hand, restrict access to individual rows within a table. Without commitment control (discussed in the next section), a row lock is generally obtained at the beginning of an I/O operation for the row and is held until the I/O statement for the next row begins, at which time the first row lock is released. If you use commitment control, which allows processing a series of database rows as a single transaction, row locks are generally held from the I/O operation until the next commitment boundary (e.g., the next commit or rollback operation).

Without commitment control, an *update*-type row lock is held by a UDB/400 open data path (ODP), which is the control structure used to access database files. (We introduced ODPs in Chapter 1.) An update row lock is similar to the *ExclRd object lock in that it lets a locked row be read, but not updated or locked, through another ODP. If all ODPs for a table are in use under commitment control, the row lock is held by the commitment control environment. With commitment control, there are two types of row locks: *read*[8] and *update*. The type of lock obtained and the allowable operations by other jobs depend on the isolation level for the commitment control environment in effect (which is explained in a later section).

An important point to keep in mind is that row locks held by an ODP can conflict within the same routing step (unlike object locks). This conflict can occur if the same row is accessed for updating through separate ODPs — for example, by having opened two views at the same time that are over the same base table.

Transaction Integrity and the Commit and Rollback Statements

An important consideration when updating a UDB/400 database is maintaining consistent data when multiple rows are modified. Suppose you enter the following Update statement to increase the discount for all customers with a non-null discount:

```
Update  Customer
  Set   Discount = Discount + 0.001
  Where Discount Is Not Null
```

8 The SQL/400 manuals also refer to a *read* lock as a *share* lock in some places.

To execute this statement, UDB/400 retrieves, tests, and updates each row that satisfies the search condition. If the job in which this statement is being executed abruptly terminates (e.g., because of a power failure) after some — but not all — Customer rows have been processed, the Customer table could be in an inconsistent state. Some rows might have the increase, but others wouldn't. The Update statement couldn't just be re-entered either, because that might add an additional discount to the customers who were already updated in the previous, possibly incomplete statement execution.

UDB/400 provides a facility called **commitment control**, which lets you specify all-or-none execution of multirow transactions. With this feature active, all row changes made by an update that fails before completion (and being committed) will automatically be backed out by UDB/400 — even if the system is shut down by a power failure. Under commitment control, after a failed update, all rows in the table are reset to exactly their values before the update was started.[9] This same principle applies to multirow Delete and Insert statements as well.

To use commitment control, you first define a commitment environment by specifying either *Chg (change), *CS (cursor stability), *All (all), or *RR (repeatable read) for the Commit parameter on the StrSql (Start SQL), RunSqlStm (Run SQL Statement), or CrtSql*Xxx* command.[10] When the interactive, batch, or embedded SQL statements are executed, they operate under commitment control at the specified **isolation level** (which we explain in more detail below).

Another way to specify that embedded SQL statements in a program are run under commitment control is to code a statement such as

```
Set Option Commit = *CS
```

as the first SQL statement in a program. The Set Option statement acts as a precompiler directive to set isolation level, date and time formats, sort sequence, and other options that are available as parameters on the CrtSql*Xxx* commands. The allowable Set Option Commit values are *Chg, *CS, *All, *RR, and *None.

You can also use the SQL Set Transaction statement to establish (or end) a commitment environment and/or to change the isolation level at runtime. The statement has the syntax

```
Set Transaction Isolation Level isolation-level
```

where *isolation-level* is one of the following:

Isolation-level value	Equivalent Commit parameter value on a command
No Commit	*None
None	*None
NC	*None
Read Uncommitted, Read Write	*Chg
Chg	*Chg
UR	*Chg

continued

9 There's no magic to this UDB/400 capability. When a table is being updated under commitment control, UDB/400 simply stores in a journal receiver object (an OS/400 object designed for this purpose) a before image (copy) of each row just before the row is updated. If the whole update isn't completed normally, UDB/400 uses these before images to change each row back to its pre-update values.

10 The OS/400 StrCmtCtl (Start Commitment Control) and EndCmtCtl (End Commitment Control) commands provide another way to explicitly start and end commitment control. The StrCmtCtl command's LckLvl parameter allows the isolation levels *Chg, *CS, and *All (but not *RR).

continued...

Isolation-level value	Equivalent Commit parameter value on a command
Read Committed	*CS
CS	*CS
Repeatable Read	*All
All	*All
RS	*All
Serializable	*RR
RR	*RR

Note that there are several synonymous keywords (e.g., Repeatable Read, All, and RS) for each isolation level. If a program executes a Set Transaction Isolation Level None, it effectively ends commitment control.

Some other considerations apply for the Set Transaction Isolation Level statement. For trigger programs (which we discuss in Chapter 16):

- The Set Transaction Isolation Level statement can be used anywhere but should generally be executed at the beginning of the trigger program.
- The specified isolation level lasts only until the next Commit or Rollback statement or until the trigger program returns.

For nontrigger programs:

- The Set Transaction Isolation Level statement can be executed only at the beginning of a transaction.
- The specified isolation level lasts only until the end of the transaction (e.g., the next Commit or Rollback statement).

To dynamically change the isolation level on an individual statement, you can specify a With *isolation-level* clause on Select, Insert, Update, and Delete statements, as in the following example:

```
Update  Customer
  Set   Discount = Discount + 0.001
  Where Discount Is Not Null
  With  CS
```

For this clause, *isolation-level* is one of the values NC, UR, CS, RS, or RR, corresponding to the levels shown in the table above. The isolation level specified on an individual statement lasts just for the duration of the statement. This level is in effect regardless of any value specified on a command's Commit parameter, a Set Option Commit statement, or a Set Transaction Isolation Level statement.

You can also use an isolation clause on a Declare Cursor statement. In that case, the isolation level applies just to the table(s) accessed via the cursor and lasts while the table(s) are open.

Determining Which Commitment Control Environment Is Used

A job can actually have multiple commitment control environments, including

- one *job-level* commitment control environment
- one *activation-group–level* commitment control environment for each activation group

When an SQL program that was created with a CrtSql*Xxx* command that specified a Commit parameter other than *None (or a corresponding Set Option statement) begins, the system follows this sequence to determine which commitment control environment to use for statements in the program:

1. Use the activation-group–level environment — if the activation group of the program calling the SQL program is using an activation-group–level environment.
2. Use the job-level environment — if the activation group of the program calling the SQL program is using the job-level environment.
3. Use the job-level environment if one exists.
4. Start a new activation-group–level environment.

The program's Commit value is used to (re)set the isolation level. When the program returns, if there was a previous commitment environment, the isolation level is returned to the previous level.

The Commit and Rollback Statements

When a commitment environment is active, you follow individual update statements or groups of update statements with a Commit or Rollback statement.[11] Because UDB/400 automatically backs out partially completed updates when your job ends, you must explicitly indicate when all related updates are ready to be committed (i.e., made permanent). With the example shown earlier, the Commit statement would immediately follow the Update statement, as in the following sequence:

```
Update  Customer
  Set   Discount = Discount + 0.001
  Where Discount Is Not Null
Commit
```

If the Update statement is completed successfully, the changes to the Customer table are permanent as soon as the Commit statement is completed.[12]

Commitment control can be used to group multiple update statements into a single **transaction** (also called a **logical unit of work**). All the database changes for all the Update, Insert, and Delete statements in a transaction can then be guaranteed to execute "all-or-none" — that is, either all the changes will be made or none of them will be made. Consider a classic banking transaction in which an amount is transferred from a savings account to a checking account. This transaction requires at least two Update statements, and it's essential that both be completed or neither be completed. Using commitment control, the sequence of statements would be

```
Update  Saving
  Set   Balance = Balance - 100.00
  Where AcctID = 123987
Update  Checking
  Set   Balance = Balance + 100.00
  Where AcctID = 123987
Commit
```

11 You can use the optional Work keyword after Commit or Rollback (e.g., Commit Work or Rollback Work). The Work keyword has no effect on either statement.

12 Essentially, UDB/400 just adds an entry to the journal that says the updates for the rows whose before images were previously saved have now been completed and committed.

If you decide you want to back out updates that have not yet been committed, you can execute a Rollback statement, such as the following:

```
Rollback
```

Both Commit and Rollback statements are typically used in HLL programs rather than in interactive SQL interfaces such as ISQL. In particular, a Rollback statement is usually coded to back out uncommitted updates when an error is detected. Chapter 10 discussed basic SQL error handling; when you use commitment control, here's a sketch of how you'd code the logic for the banking example:

```
Update  Saving
  Set   Balance = Balance - 100.00
  Where AcctID = 123987
If Error
   Rollback
Else
  Update  Checking
    Set   Balance = Balance + 100.00
    Where AcctID = 123987
  If Error
     Rollback
  Else
     Commit
  EndIf
EndIf
```

The transaction is committed only if both parts of the funds transfer are completed successfully.

You can optionally specify the Hold keyword after Commit or Rollback, as in the following example:

```
Commit Hold
```

When you specify Hold, all prepared statements (discussed in Chapter 10) are kept. (Without Hold, they're discarded when you execute a Commit or Rollback statement.) Also, the Hold keyword avoids releasing a table lock (as discussed in a previous section). You can also add the Hold keyword to avoid closing embedded SQL cursors, as discussed in Chapter 11. But, in most situations, a better solution to keep cursors open is to code the With Hold option on the Declare Cursor statement itself.

Notice that there isn't a "begin transaction" SQL statement. UDB/400 always begins a transaction implicitly — either when you start a commitment control environment or when you end the previous transaction with a Commit or Rollback statement.

The main thing to consider with Commit and Rollback statements that are embedded in HLL programs is where in your program logic to place these statements and the impact of a commit or rollback on other resources, such as open cursors. In brief, you should try to code Commit and Rollback at the point(s) in your application where you have completed (successfully or not) all the SQL statements that are involved in a transaction. By checking for errors after each statement, you can quit performing further update operations when an unrecoverable error occurs. At that point, your program flow should return control to a higher-level statement (e.g., by returning from a subroutine or procedure call) where a Rollback can be executed. The main mistake to avoid is coding lots of Rollback statements at each point where an error might be detected. A program should have few Commit and Rollback statements, and these should be executed at the appropriate point where the overall transaction is started and ended.

Isolation Levels

To use commitment control effectively, you must consider which isolation level to use and how row locking operates under commitment control. Otherwise, you may experience problems with conflicting updates or conflicting row locks arising from concurrent access of the database by multiple jobs. The following discussion describes the general characteristics of each isolation level.

None

Commitment control is not in effect with this level, and there is minimal protection against conflicting updates. In an application running without commitment control, each individual row update is effectively committed when it is completed, and there is no transaction rollback or recovery support. A job running without commitment control can retrieve rows that have been changed — but not yet committed — by another job. These are so-called "dirty reads" because they may read data that is subsequently rolled back by the other job. This is generally not a recommended isolation level except for read-only applications when an adequate object lock (as described above) is held on a table to protect against conflicting updates by another job.

Read Uncommitted, Read Write

This is the lowest isolation level that provides commitment control's all-or-none transaction support, including commit/rollback operations and transaction recovery. This level still allows dirty reads, so you should use it only when the application won't malfunction if it reads changes that are subsequently rolled back or when the application obtains an appropriate object lock to avoid conflicts.

Read Committed

This isolation level prevents an application from reading uncommitted data and is the minimum level to use unless you also use object locking. Be careful, however, with applications that may re-retrieve rows (which weren't updated) within the same transaction. With the Read Committed isolation level, a job may get different results when it re-retrieves a row because it can see any *committed* changes (by another job) made to rows that aren't updated in the transaction.

Repeatable Read

An application running at this level is guaranteed to always see the same row contents for any row it retrieves more than once in the same transaction. It's possible, however, for a query result set (e.g., all the customers in Portland) to contain additional rows if the query is re-executed in the same transaction. With Repeatable Read, other jobs are allowed to insert new rows (so-called "phantoms") into the range of a query made by another job running at the Repeatable Read isolation level.

Serializable

This isolation level guarantees that concurrent transactions will produce results exactly the same as if each transaction were run by itself (i.e., as if all transactions were run serially, one after the other). Any query that's repeated within a transaction will always retrieve the same rows with the same contents. SQL/400 assures this outcome by placing an appropriate object lock on an accessed table as soon as any query references the table.[13] The object lock is released when the transaction is committed

13 The Serializable isolation level is available only through SQL and actually uses the same OS/400 commitment control level (*CS) as the Repeatable Read isolation level. It's the SQL/400 runtime that manages the object locks to provide the necessary isolation. The Serializable isolation level doesn't always need to place an object lock, however. For a transaction that just inserts individual rows by specifying column values, the row locking provided by the *CS commitment control level is adequate.

or rolled back. A *ShrNUp lock is placed on read-only tables, and an *ExclRd lock is placed on tables that are updated.

When you consider which isolation level to use, don't jump immediately to Serializable just because it offers the strongest guarantee that another job won't interfere with your application's transactions. The stronger isolation levels also increase the possibility of a different type of interference caused by conflicting row locks, which we look at in the next section. As a broad rule of thumb, most applications should use either the Read Committed or Repeatable Read isolation level, depending on whether or not they re-retrieve rows in the same transaction.

Row Locking with Commitment Control

To see more precisely how the various isolation levels work, we'll take a closer look at the duration of row locks and the compatibility of different kinds of concurrent I/O operations under commitment control. As we mentioned in the previous section, with the Serializable isolation level, an object lock may be placed on the entire table. All five isolation levels use row locks to provide different levels of isolation. Figure 13.6 shows when a row is locked and when the lock is released for each system-level I/O operation.

Figure 13.6
Row Lock Duration

		Time →				
System I/O operation	**Isolation level**	**This I/O**	**Release**	**Another read**	**Update or delete**	**Commit or Rollback**
Read-for-input	None or Read Uncommitted, Read Write	●				
	Read Committed	●———	———	———●		
		Or, if no subsequent read operation:				
		●———	———	———	———	———●
	Repeatable Read or Serializable	●———	———	———	———	———●
Read-for-update, then release	None or Read Uncommitted, Read Write	●———	———●			
	Read Committed	●———	———	———●		
		Or, if no subsequent read operation:				
		●———	———	———	———	———●
	Repeatable Read or Serializable	●———	———	———	———	———●
Read-for-update, then update or delete	None	●———	———	———	———●	
	Read Uncommitted, Read Write; Read Committed; Repeatable Read; or Serializable	●———	———	———	———	———●

continued

Figure 13.6 ***Continued***

System I/O operation	Isolation level	Time → This I/O	Another release	Update or read	Commit or delete	Rollback
Add	None	●				
	Read Uncommitted, Read Write; Read Committed; Repeatable Read; or Serializable	●	———	———	———	●
Delete	None	●				
	Read Uncommitted, Read Write; Read Committed; Repeatable Read; or Serializable	●	———	———	———	●

Keep in mind that an SQL set-at-a-time operation, such as a searched Update, may cause a sequence of system-level I/O operations. In the case of an SQL Update, for example, two system-level I/O operations — read-for-update and update — occur for each row that's updated.

As the last three rows of Figure 13.6 show, when commitment control is in effect, row locks on updated, added, and deleted rows are held until the next commitment boundary. In a non-commitment control environment, the row lock is released as soon as a row is updated, added, or deleted. The first two rows of the figure illustrate the different ways the four isolation levels — Read Uncommitted, Read Write; Read Committed; Repeatable Read; and Serializable — handle locks for rows that aren't updated.

Rows read for input are locked only when the Read Committed, Repeatable Read, or Serializable isolation level is used. The Repeatable Read and Serializable isolation levels — but not Read Committed — hold a row lock on all input-only rows until the next commitment boundary.

Without commitment control or with the Read Uncommitted, Read Write isolation level, rows fetched for update — but released[14] without being updated — are unlocked when the release occurs. With the Read Committed isolation level, however, the lock is retained until the next read to the table (or the next commitment boundary, if there's no subsequent read operation in the transaction). And with the Repeatable Read or Serializable isolation level, the lock is always retained until the next commitment boundary.

With no commitment control or with the Read Uncommitted, Read Write or the Read Committed isolation level, the lock on a row that has been read for update can be implicitly released by executing, before any update of the row, another read-for-update via the same ODP.

Figure 13.7 shows the allowable access of a row by a second job (Job B) when a job (Job A) has read the row either for input or for update and has not yet released the row lock (if any) by one of the actions listed in Figure 13.6.

14 This applies mainly to HLL I/O operations, such as the RPG IV Unlock opcode.

Figure 13.7
Allowable Row Access

Job A		*Allowed Type of Access by Job B*		
Isolation level	**Read row for**	**Non-commitment environment**	**Read Uncommitted, Read Write**	**Read Committed; Repeatable Read; or Serializable**
None	Input	Update	Update	Update
	Update	Input	Input	None
Read Uncommitted, Read Write	Input	Update	Update	Update
	Update	Input	Input	None
Read Committed; Repeatable Read; or Serializable	Input	Input	Input	Input
	Update	Input	Input	None

As you may have determined from the lock duration rules of Figure 13.6, the rules for a second job's access are the same for a non–commitment control environment and for the Read Uncommitted, Read Write isolation level of commitment control.[15] However, note that the row lock for an updated, added, or deleted row is held until a commit or rollback with the Read Uncommitted, Read Write isolation level. The Read Committed and Repeatable Read isolation levels, on the other hand, require a read-type row lock to perform a read-for-input. Two jobs can hold read-type row locks on the same row, but there can't be simultaneous read and update locks on a row.

Although it takes some planning to set up properly, commitment control offers substantial benefits in improved database integrity and recovery. Most production-level AS/400 applications should be designed to run under commitment control.

Stored Procedures

SQL provides the ability to call an executable procedure, known as a **stored procedure**. On the AS/400, a stored procedure is simply a program with or without embedded SQL statements. You can create the program for a stored procedure in two ways:

- by compiling RPG IV, ILE COBOL/400, or other AS/400 high-level language source code
- by using **SQL Procedural Language (SPL)**[16]

There is nothing special about an HLL program used as a stored procedure, and, as mentioned, the program itself doesn't even have to contain any SQL statements. If you use SPL to create a stored procedure, SQL/400 actually translates the SPL code into ILE C source code with embedded SQL and then creates a normal HLL program object from the ILE C source, as described in Chapter 12.

A stored procedure can be called by an embedded SQL Call statement, but this method is mainly useful for distributed processing — when the stored procedure exists on a different system. Otherwise, to call a program on the same system, an application can simply use the HLL's Call operation. Also, an SPL procedure can call another program only if the program is also a stored procedure. The

15 For simplicity, the figures and discussion refer to two different jobs, each with a job scope commitment control environment. The same principles apply to any two commitment control environments, whether they have job scope or activation group scope.

16 In the ANSI SQL standard, this capability is referred to as the Persistent Stored Modules (PSM) feature.

following RPG example calls the MyProcX procedure with three host variables, Arg1, Arg2, and Arg3, passed as arguments:

```
....1....+....2....+....3....+....4....
C/Exec SQL
C+ Call MyProcX ( :Arg1,
C+                :Arg2,
C+                :Arg3 )
C/End-Exec
```

Rather than embedded SQL Call statements, the most common scenario is for a client application (e.g., a Web or PC application) to use a Java Database Connectivity (JDBC) method or an Open Database Connectivity (ODBC) function to call a stored procedure. Because stored procedures can execute complex data access and business logic, they can benefit client applications in several ways: simplify coding the client application, increase performance, and improve security.

To use an HLL program as a stored procedure, you must execute a Create Procedure statement before any call to the procedure.[17] The Create Procedure statement stores a permanent definition of a stored procedure's interface and the location of its associated OS/400 program object in the SQL system catalog, and UDB/400 uses this information to properly handle subsequent calls. Here's an example for a procedure with three parameters:

```
Create Procedure MyProcX
  ( In     Parm1    Int,
    InOut Parm2    Char( 10 ),
    Out   RtmMsgId Char(  7 ) )
  Language RPGLE
  Specific MyProcXParam3
  Not Deterministic
  Reads SQL Data
  External Name MyPgmX
  Parameter Style General
```

The Create Procedure statement specifies the procedure's parameter types and whether they're used for input, output, or both (from the perspective of the called procedure). For the MyProcX procedure defined above, the corresponding RPG IV program's parameter list would look like this:

```
....1....+....2....+....3....+....4....+....5....+....6....+....
 * Parameters
 * - - - - - - - - - - - - - - - - - - - - - - - - - - - - - -
D Parm1              S             10I 0
D Parm2              S             10A
D RtnMsgId           S              7A
 .
 .
 .
 * Entry point
 * - - - - - - - - - - - - - - - - - - - - - - - - - - - - - -
C     *Entry        Plist
C                   Parm                    Parm1
C                   Parm                    Parm2
C                   Parm                    RtnMsgId
```

17 SQL/400 also has a Declare Procedure statement, but you should use the Create Procedure statement instead. The Declare Procedure Statement affects only the program that contains it, whereas the Create Procedure statement places an entry in the system catalog to be used by all programs and client applications that call the stored procedure.

The code in the RPG IV program should use Parm1 only as an input value. The program can also use Parm2 as an input value and can change the value of Parm2 and RtnMsgId. Otherwise, the program code can perform any valid RPG IV or embedded SQL operations.

A procedure can also return a read-only result set of rows by opening an SQL cursor in the program and leaving it open. The result set can be processed by JDBC methods or ODBC functions, topics beyond the scope of this book. If a procedure returns a result set, you must add a Create Procedure statement clause specifying how many result sets are returned, as in the following example:

```
Create Procedure MyProcY
  ( In  Parm1 Int )
  Result Set 1
  Language RPGLE
  Not Deterministic
  Modifies SQL Data
  External Name MyPgmY
  Parameter Style SQL
```

This example also illustrates the use of the Parameter Style SQL clause, which we describe in more detail later. The corresponding RPG IV parameter list would look like this:

```
....1....+....2....+....3....+....4....+....5....+....6....+....
 * Parameters
 * - - - - - - - - - - - - - - - - - - - - - - - - - - - - - -
D Parm1           S             10I 0

D Parm1NullInd    S              5I 0
D ParmSqlState    S              5A
D ParmProcName    S            517A    Varying
D ParmSpecName    S            128A    Varying
D ParmMsgText     S             70A    Varying
.
.
.
 * Entry point
 * - - - - - - - - - - - - - - - - - - - - - - - - - - - - - -
C     *Entry        Plist
C                   Parm                    Parm1
C                   Parm                    Parm1NullInd
C                   Parm                    ParmSqlState
C                   Parm                    ParmProcName
C                   Parm                    ParmSpecName
C                   Parm                    ParmMsgText
```

Both of these examples illustrate some of the other Create Procedure clauses, which we cover briefly here.

`Language` ***`language`***

Possible values for *language* are

- RPGLE, CobolLE, C, or another HLL name — for external HLL programs
- SQL — for SQL procedures that include a procedure body (i.e., written with SPL, as discussed below)

`Specific` ***`specific-name`***

This clause provides a unique name within the collection. If you have only one procedure with a particular procedure name, you can omit this clause or use the procedure name as the specific name. Specify a different name here if several procedures have the same name but a different number of parameters.

`[Not] Deterministic`

- Not Deterministic — for programs that may return different results for the same argument values. Use this if you're not sure (it's the default).
- Deterministic — for programs that always return the same results for the same argument values and that have no side effects (the client system may use a previously retrieved value and not actually call the program)

`Reads SQL Data, Modifies SQL Data, Contains SQL, No SQL`

- Reads SQL Data — The program may use SQL statements to read data. It can contain any SQL statement other than Delete, Insert, Update, Commit, Rollback, Set Transaction, any Create or Drop statement, Alter Table, Rename, Comment On, Label On, Grant, Revoke, Connect, Disconnect, Release, or Set Connection.
- Modifies SQL Data — The program may use SQL statements to read and/or modify data. It can contain any SQL statement other than Commit, Rollback, Set Transaction, Connect, Disconnect, Release, or Set Connection.
- Contains SQL — The program can contain SPL statements (e.g., Declare and Set), as well as Commit, Rollback, Set Transaction, Connect, Disconnect, Release, and Set Connection.
- No SQL — The program should not contain any SQL statement.

The following two clauses can be specified only for an external HLL program (not a procedure written with SPL):

`External Name` ***`HLL-program-name`***

Specify the external HLL program name. If no name is specified, the default is the procedure name. You can specify an unqualified or a qualified name; see the section "A Guide to SQL/400 Naming" later in this chapter to decide whether to use qualification.

`Parameter Style` ***`style`***

Possible values for *style* are

- General — Use this option for existing HLL programs (no extra parameters are passed). The following parameters are passed to the HLL program:
  - One parameter for each parameter specified in the procedure's parameter list
- SQL — Use this option for newly implemented HLL programs that are (mainly) intended to be called from SQL, JDBC, or ODBC.[18] The following parameters are passed to the HLL program:
  - One parameter for each parameter specified in the parameter list
  - One indicator variable (`InOut SmallInt`) for each parameter in the list. Set by SQL runtime for In and InOut parameters to <0 for null, ≥0 for non-null; can be reset by the program for Out and InOut parameters.

18 Another Parameter Style option is General With Nulls, which also includes parameters for null indicators. We recommend you use Parameter Style SQL instead because it provides a standard approach to returning an SqlState value to the caller.

- InOut Char(5) — SqlState. Passed in as 00000; should be set by the program if
  - Warning — Set to 01H*xx*, where *xx* is any two digits or uppercase letters
  - Error — Set to 38*yxx*, where *y* is an uppercase letter T–Z and *xx* is any two digits or uppercase letters
- In VarChar(517) — The fully qualified procedure name (e.g., APPDTA.MYPROCX)
- In VarChar(128) — The specific name of the procedure (e.g., MYPROCXPARAMS)
- InOut VarChar(70) — Initialized on input, can be set to message text by the program. If this parameter is set by the program, the SqlState parameter (above) should be set to indicate a warning or error (otherwise, the message text is ignored).

To remove a procedure definition from the SQL catalog, you execute a Drop Procedure statement:

```
Drop Procedure AppDta.MyProcX
```

If more than one procedure in the same collection has the same name, you can specify a list of parameter types along with the procedure name:

```
Drop Procedure
  AppDta.MyProcX( Int,
                  Char( 10 ),
                  Char(  7 ) )
```

Alternately, you can use the procedure's specific name:

```
Drop Specific Procedure AppDta.MyProcXParam3
```

You must drop a procedure before you can re-create it with a Create Procedure statement.

SQL Procedure Language

For portability to other databases in IBM's DB2 UDB family, or any other relational database management system (RDBMS) that supports the ANSI-standard SQL Procedural Language (SPL), you can implement a procedure with SPL. Figure 13.8 shows a simple stored procedure written with SPL (for simplicity, this example omits error handling and assumes the caller handles commitment control).

Figure 13.8

TransferPart Stored Procedure Implemented in SPL

```
Create Procedure
  TransferPart ( In  XfrPartId    Int,
                 In  XfrQtyRqs    Int,
                 In  FromWhsId    Int,
                 In  ToWhsId      Int,
                 Out XfrQtyActual Int )
  Language SQL

Begin
  -- Transfer up to XfrQtyRqs units of
  -- part XfrPartId from FromWhsId to
```

continued

Figure 13.8 *Continued*

```
    -- ToWhsId and return the actual units
    -- transferred in XfrQtyActual.

    Declare QtyToXfr Int;

    Set XfrQtyActual = 0;

    Select  Qty
      Into  QtyToXfr
      From  Inventory
      Where PartId = XfrPartId
        And WhsId  = FromWhsId;

    If QtyToXfr > XfrQtyRqs
      Then Set QtyToXfr = XfrQtyRqs;
    End If;

    Update  Inventory
      Set   Qty = Qty - QtyToXfr
      Where PartId = XfrPartId
        And WhsId  = FromWhsId;

    Update  Inventory
      Set   Qty = Qty + QtyToXfr
      Where PartId = XfrPartId
        And WhsId  = ToWhsId;

    Set XfrQtyActual = QtyToXfr;

  End -- TransferPart
```

The first part of the Create Procedure statement is similar to that for a stored procedure written with an HLL and specifies the parameter names, types, and usage. To use SPL for the implementation, you specify SQL as the language and include a procedure body within a pair of Begin/End delimiters. (If the procedure body consists of only one SQL statement, the delimiters aren't required.)

Within the procedure body, you can have comments, local variable declarations, assignment statements, SQL data manipulation statements, conditional tests, and a variety of other types of statements. SPL essentially provides a fairly complete programming language, although it doesn't include any user interface support. Keep in mind that you can use an SQL Call statement within a stored procedure to call other stored procedures, including ones written in either SPL or an AS/400 HLL. This capability lets you decompose a complex procedure into a hierarchy of simpler procedures.

When you execute a Create Procedure statement that includes SPL for the procedure body, UDB/400 uses the multistep process shown in Figure 13.9 to create an OS/400 program (*Pgm) object. The first step translates the SPL source into ILE C source code with embedded SQL statements. This source is then precompiled with the CrtSqlCI (Create SQL ILE C Object) command, which generates pure C code with the embedded SQL statements translated to function calls. Last, the CrtCMod (Create C Module) and CrtPgm (Create Program) commands compile the C source into a program object with *Caller as its activation group.

Figure 13.9
*Process to Create *Pgm Object from SPL Source*

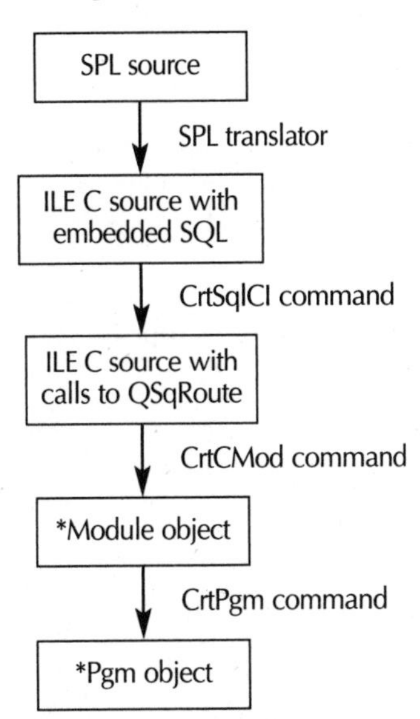

This multistep process using C as an intermediate language has a couple of implications. First, to create a stored procedure with SPL, you must purchase and install IBM's ILE C for AS/400 product, as well as the DB2 Query Manager and SQL Development Kit for AS/400 product, to provide the necessary C compiler and precompiler. Second, the generated C program has hidden parameters used by UDB/400 to make the stored procedure call. These extra parameters mean you can't call an SPL program with an HLL Call statement as you can with an HLL program used as a stored procedure.[19]

The approach IBM took of creating a program object from SPL has an important security-related benefit. You can use program adopted authority (as described in Chapter 9) with an SPL stored procedure just as with HLL stored procedures. This capability lets you handle a wide variety of security requirements that UDB/400's object and column-level security alone can't completely handle.

A Create Procedure statement with SPL also stores the procedure body's source in the SQL catalog (as long as it's less than 18 K). In any case, you should generally put the whole Create Procedure statement in a source member and use the RunSqlStm command to run the SQL statement from the source member. This approach lets you edit the source and re-create the procedure without having to retrieve source from the catalog.

SPL Language Features

The full SPL syntax and programming documentation is covered in the manuals *DB2 UDB for AS/400 SQL Reference* and *DB2 UDB for AS/400 SQL Programming*. To give you an idea of what's available, we'll briefly cover some of the most important features of the language.

19 Because of these extra program parameters, SPL can't currently be used to write database trigger programs, which are perhaps even more important than stored procedures for cross-system database portability. As of V4R5, IBM says it's aware of these issues and is considering them in its plans for future SQL/400 enhancements. For now, the best workaround is to write a short HLL program that has an embedded SQL Call to an SPL stored procedure. This HLL program can serve as the UDB/400 trigger program and pass the trigger buffer (or parts of it) to the SPL stored procedure.

All SPL statements end with a semicolon (;). You can code comments following a double dash (--) and running to the end of the line:

```
-- This is a comment
```

Declarations

As you can see in Figure 13.8, SPL supports parameter and local variable declarations. These declarations can use any of the column data types (e.g., Char, Int, Float) available in the Create Table statement. You can also declare a default, or initial, value:

```
Declare QtyToXfr Int Default 0;
```

Note that unlike all major HLLs, SPL doesn't support arrays.

Assignment

The SPL Set statement lets you assign an expression value to a local variable or to an Out or InOut parameter. SPL also lets you set a local variable or parameter to Null, as in the following statement:

```
Set XfrQtyActual = Null;
```

You can also test a local variable or parameter for Null:

```
If QtyToXfr Is Not Null Then ...
```

This feature simplifies dealing with null-capable columns because you don't have to provide a separate null indicator variable, as you do when using embedded SQL Select, Fetch, Update, and Insert statements in an HLL program.

SQL Data Definition and Manipulation Statements

In SPL, you can use SQL data definition and manipulation statements in a similar way to embedded SQL statements in an HLL program. In SPL, however, you don't need to use Exec SQL and End-Exec to delimit SQL statements, nor do you need to prefix a variable or parameter name with a colon (:), as you do with HLL host variables used in SQL statements.

Conditional Statements

SPL has both If and Case conditional statements. An If statement can have a series of tests, using ElseIf clauses, as well as a final Else clause:

```
If XfrPartId = 123 Then
  Set QtyToXfr = 1;
ElseIf XfrQtyRqs > 100 Then
  Set QtyToXfr = 100;
Else
  Set QtyToXfr = XfrQtyRqs;
End If;
```

The Case statement can be used in two ways. The first form branches based on the value of a scalar expression:

```
Case PartId
  When 123
    Set QtyToXfr = 1;
  When 234
    Set QtyToXfr = 10;
  Else
    Set QtyToXfr = XfrQtyRqs;
End Case;
```

The second form is precisely equivalent to a multiway If/ElseIf/Else:

```
Case
  When XfrPartId = 123 Then
    Set QtyToXfr = 1;
  When XfrQtyRqs > 100 Then
    Set QtyToXfr = 100;
  Else
    Set QtyToXfr = XfrQtyRqs;
End If;
```

Loop Control Structures

SPL has four loop structures:

- Loop — infinite loop (use the Leave statement to exit)
- While — test is at the beginning of the loop
- Repeat — test is at the end of the loop
- For — iterate over a set of rows

You can use the Loop, While, and Repeat structures the way you use comparable HLL loop structures to control program flow. The example in Figure 13.10 shows a simple While loop that conditionally allocates some of each warehouse's inventory. (For simplicity, this example assumes warehouse IDs run from 1 to 10.)

Figure 13.10

While Statement Example

```
TotalAlloc = 0;
CurWhsId   = 1;

While ( CurWhsId   <= 10       ) And
      ( TotalAlloc <  RqsAlloc ) Do

  Select  Qty Into CurQty
    From  Inventory
    Where PartId = CurPartId
      And WhsId  = CurWhsId;

  If SqlCode = 0 Then
    Case
      When CurQty > 2 * (RqsAlloc - TotalAlloc) Then
        Set CurAlloc = RqsAlloc - TotalAlloc;
      When CurQty > (RqsAlloc - TotalAlloc) Then
        Set CurAlloc = (RqsAlloc - TotalAlloc) / 2;
      When CurQty > 0 Then
        Set CurAlloc = 1;
      Else
        Set CurAlloc = 0;
    End Case;
  End If;

  If CurAlloc > 0 Then
    Update  Inventory
      Set   Qty = Qty - CurAlloc
      Where PartId = CurPartId
        And WhsId  = CurWhsId;
```

continued

Figure 13.10 *Continued*

```
      If SqlCode = 0 Then
        Set TotalAlloc = TotalAlloc + CurAlloc;
      End If;
    End If;

    Set CurWhsId = CurWhsId + 1;
  End While;
```

The Repeat loop is similar to the While loop, but the structure places the test at the end of the loop:

```
Repeat
  loop-body
Until condition
End Repeat;
```

The Loop structure generally begins with a label and is exited by a Leave statement, as in this example:

```
AllocLoop: Loop
  ...
  If SqlCode <> 0 Then
    Leave AllocLoop;
  End If;
  ...
End Loop AllocLoop;
```

You can also use a Leave statement to exit from the middle of a While or Repeat loop, as long as you code a label for the loop to be exited.

Just as in HLL programs, you can use any of the loop structures just covered to iterate over an open SQL cursor (which you've declared with a Declare Cursor statement earlier in the procedure), executing repeated Fetch statements. As a more convenient alternative, SPL also provides a special form of For loop to process a selected set of rows. Figure 13.11 shows an example of a For loop that implements the same operation as the While loop in Figure 13.10.

Figure 13.11

For Statement Example

```
TotalAlloc = 0;

For InvRow As InvCursor Cursor For
  Select  Qty
    From  Inventory
    Where PartId = CurPartId
Do
  Case
    When Qty > 2 * (RqsAlloc - TotalAlloc) Then
      Set CurAlloc = RqsAlloc - TotalAlloc;
    When Qty > (RqsAlloc - TotalAlloc) Then
      Set CurAlloc = (RqsAlloc - TotalAlloc) / 2;
    When Qty > 0 Then
      Set CurAlloc = 1;
    Else
      Set CurAlloc = 0;
  End Case;
```

continued

Figure 13.11 ***Continued***

```
    If CurAlloc > 0 Then
      Update   Inventory
        Set    Qty = Qty - CurAlloc
        Where Current Of InvCursor;
      If SqlCode = 0 Then
        Set TotalAlloc = TotalAlloc + CurAlloc;
      End If;
    End If;
  End For;
```

Notice how the first part of the For loop is a cursor specification. Within the loop body, you can refer to any column defined in the cursor's Select list (e.g., Qty) as a variable. The loop terminates when the last row in the cursor's result set has been processed. Note that the index variable (e.g., InvRow) in this form of the For loop is not used.

Note that in a For loop, the same identifier (e.g., Qty) might be used for an implicit variable defined by the cursor's Select column list as well as for a column in a subsequent Update statement. The SPL processor treats as a column name any unqualified identifier that names both a column and a variable. When this type of ambiguity arises, you can use a label for a loop or compound statement (discussed next) as a qualifier for a local variable within the scope of the loop or compound statement.

SPL also has a GoTo statement, but you should generally avoid goto's in your code. To branch out of a loop or to the next statement after the end of a compound statement, use the Leave statement.

Compound Statements

You can combine any series of SPL statements within a Begin/End block and treat the block as a single compound statement. As of V4R5, SQL/400 doesn't allow nested compound statements, however. Variables and condition handlers (discussed next) declared within a block are local to that block.

Optionally, you can follow the Begin keyword with the Atomic keyword to specify that if an error occurs during execution of any statement in the block, the effect of all prior statements in the block are rolled back. You must be at a commitment control boundary (e.g., by having just executed a Commit or Rollback operation) when you begin executing an atomic block. Because a stored procedure can be defined as a single block, you can create atomic stored procedures.

Conditions and Condition Handlers

To provide a mechanism for handling exceptional conditions, SPL lets you define conditions and condition handlers. A condition is just a name for a value of the SqlState variable that's set for every SQL operation. The following statement declares CursorNotOpenState as a condition name for the corresponding SqlState value:

```
Declare CursorNotOpenState
        Condition For '24501';
```

A condition handler specifies what to do when a condition occurs, as in the following example:

```
Declare Continue Handler For
  CursorNotOpenState
  Set RowCount = 0;
```

There are three main parts to a condition handler declaration. The first is a keyword: Continue, Exit, or Undo, that specifies what system-defined action to take when an exception occurs. The second part is a list of one or more conditions. Each condition must be one of the following:

- a previously declared condition name
- the keyword SqlState followed by an SQLState string value
- one of the keywords SqlException, SqlWarning, or Not Found

The final part is a simple SQL statement that specifies user-defined actions to take. Figure 13.12 summarizes the effect of various condition handler options.

Figure 13.12
Condition Handler Options

System-Defined Actions	
Continue	Perform user-defined actions and continue with the statement after the statement that raised the condition.
Exit	Perform user-defined actions and continue at the end of the compound statement that contained the statement that raised the condition.
Undo	First, rollback all changes made during execution of the compound statement that contained the statement that raised the condition. Then, perform user-defined actions and continue at the end of the compound statement that contained the statement that raised the condition.
Conditions	
Condition name	The handler is invoked when SqlState is set to the value specified in the condition declaration.
SqlState keyword followed by an SqlState string value	The handler is invoked when SqlState is set to the specified value.
SqlWarning	The handler is invoked when SqlState is set to 01*xxx*.
Not Found	The handler is invoked when SqlState is set to 02*xxx*.
SqlException	The handler is invoked when SqlState is set to a value other than 00*xxx*, 01*xxx*, or 02*xxx*.

Note that this version of SPL doesn't support compound SQL statements in condition handlers; however, you can use a one-pass loop as a workaround, as in the following example:

```
Declare Continue Handler For
  CursorNotOpenState
  CursorNotOpenStateLoop: Loop
    Set RowCount = 0;
    Set ErrMsg = 'Cursor not open';
    ...
    Leave CursorNotOpenStateLoop;
  End Loop CursorNotOpenStateLoop;
```

Signaling User-Defined Warnings and Exceptions

If you want to generate a user-defined condition to be handled by a program or procedure that calls a stored procedure, your stored procedure can execute a Signal statement, such as the following:

```
Signal SqlState '99U002'
  Set Message_Text = 'Failed transfer of part.';
```

You can specify either the SqlState keyword and value (as in this example) or a previously defined SQL condition name. You can also set the text for a message that will be placed in the SqlErrMc field of the SQL communication area.

To avoid using system-defined SqlState values to signal your own application-defined errors, use a digit from 7 through 9 or an uppercase character I through Z as the third character in your SqlState values. Recall that the first two characters of SqlState indicate the severity of the condition: 00 means no warning or error, 01 means a warning, 02 means no data, and other values mean error. When you execute a Signal, if the same compound statement also includes a handler for that condition, control transfers to the handler. Otherwise, control transfers to the caller of the procedure. If you execute a Signal statement within a handler, control also passes to the caller.

If you want to handle a condition and then return to the procedure's caller with the same condition, you can use a Resignal statement, such as the following, within a handler:

```
Resignal
```

Optionally, you can provide user-define message text by using a statement such as

```
Resignal
  Set Message_Text = 'Failed transfer of part.';
```

A Resignal statement can also specify SqlState or a condition (just as with the Signal statement), but if you want to specify your own SQL state, you should use a Signal statement.

Diagnostic Feedback

To get feedback in an SQL procedure, you can declare a variable for SqlState and/or SqlCode:

```
Declare SqlState Char( 5 );
Declare SqlCode  Integer;
```

When you declare either or both of these variables, the SQL/400 runtime sets them after every statement, except the following:

- an assignment that references the SqlState variable — for example, Set SaveSqlState = SqlState
- an assignment that references the SqlCode variable — for example, Set SaveSqlCode = SqlCode
- Get Diagnostics Exception 1 . . .

In general, you should save SqlState immediately after any statement so you can use it in subsequent statements to diagnose the errors.

SPL includes the Get Diagnostic statement to retrieve information after a statement is executed. For DML statements, the following example shows how to retrieve the number of rows affected:

```
Declare RowCnt Integer;
 .
 .
 .
Update  Customer
  Set   Discount = 0.0
  Where Status   = 'X';

Get Diagnostics RowCnt = Row_Count;
```

The Row_Count built-in special register provides the same value as the SqlErrD(3) field of the SQL communication area.

When a statement is completed with a warning or exception, you can get the message text (SqlErrMc) and message length (SqlErrMl) with another form of the Get Diagnostics statement:

```
Declare MsgText    Char(70);
Declare MsgTextLen Integer;
  .
  .
  .
Get Diagnostics Exception 1
 MsgText    = Message_Text,
 MsgTextLen = Message_Length;
```

In general, if you use this statement, it should be the first statement in a condition handler. Otherwise, if other SPL statements precede it, you won't get the message for the appropriate statement.

User-Defined Functions

In Chapter 8, we introduced **user-defined functions** (**UDFs**) and showed how to create a sourced function based on a built-in function. You can also create functions for which you code the full implementation. Like a stored procedure, a UDF can be implemented either with an HLL program (this is referred to as an **external function**) or by coding SPL (referred to as an **SQL function**). Many of the principles that apply to stored procedures also apply to scalar UDFs. For example, you can use the same SPL statements for either a procedure or a function. Here's an example of creating a simple SPL function:

```
Create Function Right
  ( Str        VarChar ( 2000 ),
    SubStrLen Int )
  Returns  VarChar ( 2000 )
  Language SQL
  Returns  Null On Null Input
Begin
  -- Return a string that contains the rightmost
  -- SubStrLen characters of the Str string.

  Declare StrLen    Int;
  Declare RtnStrLen Int;
  Declare RtnStrBgn Int;
  Declare RtnStr    VarChar ( 2000 );

  Set StrLen    = Length( Str );
  Set RtnStrLen = Min( StrLen, SubStrLen );
  Set RtnStrBgn = ( StrLen - RtnStrLen ) + 1;
  Set RtnStr    = SubStr( Str, RtnStrBgn, RtnStrLen );

  Return RtnStr;

End -- Right
```

All parameters for a function are input parameters, so you don't specify the In, Out, or InOut keyword for function parameters as you do for procedure parameters. The Right function has two parameters: the string and the length of the desired substring. A UDF always returns a single value, for which you specify the data type (e.g., VarChar(2000) in this example) on the Returns clause that follows the parameter list. The SPL Return *expression* statement exits the function and returns the function's value to its caller.

On the Create Function statement for an external or SQL function, you can use the following clauses, as explained for the Create Procedure statement:

- Language
- Specific

- [Not] Deterministic
- Reads SQL Data, Modifies SQL Data, Contains SQL, or No SQL
- External Name
- Parameter Style

You can't use a Result Sets clause because functions can't return result sets. Also, you can specify a procedure in an OS/400 service program, instead of a program, on the External Name clause, using the following form:

```
...
External Name 'APPDTA/APPFUNCS(RIGHT)'
```

Note a few particulars about this form of the External Name clause. You must enclose the name in apostrophes ('), and you must specify a library, service program, and procedure or function within the service program. In general, the library and program names, which are OS/400 object names, should be all upper case. The procedure or function name should match the case of the name that's exported from the service program; typically, this means all upper case in RPG IV and Cobol and mixed case in C. In a quoted external name, the library and service program names must be separated by a slash (/), regardless of the naming option (discussed later). The procedure or function name is enclosed in parentheses following the service program name.

One clause you can optionally specify for UDFs, but not for procedures, is Returns Null On Null Input. When this clause is specified, UDB/400 doesn't call the function if any of its arguments are null. Instead, UDB/400 just returns null. The default, or coding an explicit Called On Null Input clause, causes the function to be called even when one or more arguments are null. *DB2 UDB for AS/400 SQL Reference* describes additional Create Function clauses that exist primarily for compatibility with other products in the DB2 UDB family.

For an external function, the correspondence between the function definition's parameter list and the HLL program or service program procedure or function is slightly different than for a stored procedure, as explained above. When you specify Parameter Style SQL, you can implement the stored procedure with either an HLL program or an HLL procedure in a service program. In the program or procedure, you should declare one input parameter for each of the function's parameters, followed by an output parameter for the function's return value. Next, the HLL program or procedure should declare indicator parameters for the function's parameters followed by an additional indicator parameter for the function's return value. The HLL program or procedure should *not* change any of the input parameters or their respective indicator parameters and should always set the output parameter and its indicator parameter. Following the return value indicators are the additional parameters for SqlState, function name, specific name, and message text as described above for stored procedures.

When you specify Parameter Style General, you must use an HLL function coded as part of a service program. The HLL function's parameters and return value correspond one-to-one with the UDF's parameters and return value, and there are no indicator or other additional parameters.

Keep in mind that the same function name can be used for different functions, as long as the functions have different number and/or types of parameters. When you use the same function name for more than one function, it's a good idea to include the Specific clause to give each function a unique specific name.

A Guide to SQL/400 Naming

One of the challenges you'll encounter in using SQL to create and access database objects is how to use the myriad naming features available with SQL/400. Among the most important decisions you face are whether to explicitly qualify object names with the collection containing the object and whether to use system naming or SQL naming. We covered the basics in Chapter 3; in the following sections, we provide deeper explanations for the most important naming rules and lay out specific recommendations for all the major choices you'll face.

SQL/400 Object Names

SQL includes a variety of object types, and you'll recall that most of them are implemented as OS/400 object types. For example, an SQL table is an OS/400 physical file. Figure 13.13 lists SQL objects and the corresponding OS/400 or other types of system objects.

Figure 13.13
SQL and OS/400 Object Types

SQL object	OS/400 object	OS/400 special value
Alias	DDM file	*File
Authorization ID	User profile	*UsrPrf
Collection	Library	*Lib
Constraint	Access path	Internal object owned by physical file for the table
Database	System	Entry in AS/400 relational database directory
Server	System	Entry in AS/400 relational database directory
Distinct type	SQL user-defined type	*SqlUdt
Function	Program or service program	*Pgm *SrvPgm
Index	Logical file	*File
Package	SQL package	*SqlPkg
Procedure	Program	*Pgm
Table	Physical file	*File
View	Logical file	*File

Every SQL object has a name. For all objects except a constraint — which is always part of a table definition — you must assign a name when you create the object. You can optionally assign a name to a constraint as well. Names for many types of SQL objects can be longer than the 10-character limit for OS/400 object names, and these types of SQL objects actually have two names: an *SQL name* and a *system name*. You generally use the SQL name in SQL statements; the system name is the name of the corresponding OS/400 object, which you use with non-SQL interfaces, such as OS/400 commands.

When you execute one of the SQL Create statements to create an object with an SQL name of 10 characters or less, SQL/400 creates the system name as the SQL name. When you specify a longer SQL name, SQL/400 generates a system name using the first five characters of the SQL name and a five-digit sequence number. For example, for the SQL table name PartSupplier, SQL/400 would generate a physical file name such as PartS00001. Because you must use some non-SQL interfaces (e.g., OS/400 save and restore commands) to work with SQL objects, it helps to have more meaningful system names than those generated by SQL/400. Figure 13.14 shows the maximum length of SQL object names and, where applicable, how you can specify or rename the system name to a meaningful name.

Figure 13.14
SQL and System Names

SQL object	Maximum length of name	How to set the system name
Alias	128	Not applicable (the whole point of an SQL alias is to provide another name for an object, so just specify the desired type of name)
Authorization ID	10	CrtUsrPrf command (there is no SQL statement to create a user profile)
Collection	10	Always the same as the SQL name
Constraint	128	Not applicable (the OS/400 object isn't visible, and the OS/400 RmvPfCst command lets you specify the SQL name)
Database or Server	18	Not applicable (the name is an entry in the relational database directory)
Distinct type	128	Not possible (but SQL data types are used only in SQL statements)
Function or Procedure	128	Specify the system name on the Create Function or Create Procedure statement's Specific clause.
Index	128	Use SQL Rename Index statement with a System Name clause.
Package	10	Always the same as the SQL name
Table or View	128	Use SQL Rename Table statement with a System Name clause.

For example, to create a meaningful system name for a PartSupplier table, you could use an SQL Rename statement such as the following:

```
Rename Table PartSupplier
    To System Name PartSupplr
```

Our first recommendation makes it easier to work with SQL objects that have long names:

Create meaningful system names for SQL names longer than 10 characters.

To follow this standard, use the techniques listed in Figure 13.14. It's a good idea to create SQL objects by using the RunSqlStm command to run SQL scripts stored in a source member (or use a comparable approach with a software configuration management product). You can place both the Create and the Rename SQL statements in the same source member, so the process is simple and foolproof.

Qualified Names and Uniqueness

The following SQL objects can be referenced by either an *unqualified name* (e.g., Customer) or a *qualified name*, which includes the name of the collection containing the object (e.g., AppDta.Customer or AppDta/Customer):

- alias
- distinct type
- function
- index
- procedure
- table
- view

An alias, distinct type, index, table, or view is uniquely identified by its qualified name and its underlying OS/400 object type (i.e., *File or *SqlUdt). For any of these object types, you can have two objects of the same underlying type with identical names, as long as they're in different collections. Put another way, you can't have an alias, index, table, or view with the same name as another alias, index, table, or view in the same collection. Also, no two aliases, indexes, tables, or views in the same collection can have the same system name, even if their SQL names are different. You also can't have two distinct types with the same name in the same collection.

The uniqueness rules for function and procedure names are a little more complex. SQL lets you have more than one function with the same name in the same collection, as long as the functions have different *signatures* — a function's signature comprises its name and number and type of parameters. Similarly, no two procedures in the same collection can have the same name and number of parameters.

Each function and procedure in a collection must also have a unique *specific name*. You can use the Specific clause on the Create Function or Create Procedure statement (as described earlier in this chapter) to specify a specific name. If you don't specify a name, SQL/400 uses the function or procedure name, unless it's the same as the specific name of an existing function or procedure in the same collection, in which case SQL/400 generates a name. The only time you really need to specify a specific name is when you create a function or procedure implemented with SPL, in which case the specific name is used as the name of the generated OS/400 service program (for a function) or program (for a procedure). If a service program or program with the same name already exists in the collection, SQL/400 generates a unique OS/400 object name.

Another somewhat helpful use for specific names is when you have more than one function or procedure with the same name (and different signatures) in the same collection. By assigning a unique specific name, you can use a Drop Function or Drop Procedure statement that identifies the function or procedure by its specific name rather than the full signature.

Using Qualified or Unqualified Names

For those cases where you have the choice between using a qualified or an unqualified name, you need to weigh the benefits of each. A qualified name guarantees that SQL/400 places an object you're creating, or looks for an object you're referencing, in the collection you use to qualify the object name. Qualified names may be necessary in a few cases in which SQL/400's rules for implicit qualification can't produce the required results (for example, when you need to create a view in one collection over a table in another collection). Qualified names also avoid the potential for an unqualified name to be implicitly qualified in a way you weren't expecting — leading the wrong object to be accessed. Qualified names can be somewhat cumbersome to code, however, especially in complex data manipulation statements.

The most significant disadvantage of qualified names is that you must modify source code when you want to use the same SQL statement to reference an object in different collections. It's common practice to have test and development collections (with different names) on the same AS/400, in which case you have to modify any qualified names to move an SQL script or program from a test environment to the production environment. Many companies also need to deploy the same production code to multiple remote sites, and if these sites don't use the same collection names, you have similar issues as with production and test environments. The burden of modifying qualified names leads to our next recommendation:

Use unqualified SQL object names wherever possible.

Note that this recommendation is consistent with the longstanding practice in many AS/400 development organizations of using unqualified OS/400 object names in non-SQL, AS/400 applications.

Choosing the System or SQL Naming Option

Now we come to the most important naming decision you have to make: whether to use the **system naming** or the **SQL naming** option. You choose one or the other naming option when you create an SQL program, run an SQL script, or use the Interactive SQL (ISQL) utility. The naming option determines three important things:

- the syntax of qualified names
- the implicit qualifier for unqualified names
- the default user profile whose authorities are used for SQL statements in an HLL program (see Chapter 9 for more information about user profiles and authorities)

In very simplified terms, system naming works more like OS/400 naming, and SQL naming provides greater compatibility with other SQL platforms. Don't make the decision on which to use, however, until you understand more about the implications.

The syntactic differences are simple. With system naming, you use a slash (/) to separate a collection name and the object name it qualifies. With SQL naming, you use a period (.) as the separator. Here are two examples:

AppDta/Customer — system naming

AppDta.Customer — SQL naming

This syntax affects only SQL statements, not RPG, CL, or any other aspect of OS/400 applications. Because SQL naming follows the ANSI standard, it's the preferred syntax.

But the naming option also plays a crucial role in how SQL/400 determines implicit qualifiers, a more complex issue that you must evaluate carefully before deciding which naming option to use. Again, in simplified terms, here's how the two options stack up:

- Either option lets you specify a single default collection on the CrtSql*Xxx* or RunSqlStm command, and SQL/400 uses this default to qualify unqualified alias, index, table, or view names.
- Either option lets you specify a list of collections (the SQL path, discussed later) on the CrtSql*Xxx* or RunSqlStm command, and SQL/400 uses this list to search for distinct types, functions, and procedures that are referenced with an unqualified name.

- Only system naming provides the ability to search the job's library list for alias, index, table, or view names.

At first glance, it might seem the system naming option is preferable because only it supports the OS/400 library list. However, for many organizations, SQL naming — when used with the default collection and SQL path — provides adequate functionality. In addition, if you design your applications to work with SQL naming, they'll be more portable to other SQL platforms. Remember that the concept of a job's library list exists only on the AS/400, so relying on it ties your SQL code more closely to the AS/400. We'll cover more details of unqualified names shortly, but at this point here's our recommendation:

> *Unless you require searching the job's library list for aliases, tables, or views, use the SQL naming option for SQL programs and scripts.*

Note that we don't mention indexes in this recommendation because you never reference an SQL index directly except to create, rename, or drop it — operations that you can adequately manage by specifying a default collection or by qualifying the reference. The SQL path (which we discuss below) provides a facility that's equivalent to the library list for searching for distinct types, functions, and procedures, so these also aren't a deciding factor.

To specify SQL naming, use any of the following:

- the Option(*Sql) parameter on CrtSql*Xxx* commands to create SQL programs
- the Set Option Naming statement as the first SQL statement in an HLL program's source member (note that the Set Option statement is an SQL precompiler directive, not an executable statement)
- the Naming(*Sql) parameter on the RunSqlStm command to run an SQL script from a source member
- the Naming(*Sql) parameter on the StrSql command to start the Interactive SQL utility (but see the following comments)

If you adopt SQL naming as your general standard, you can still use system naming for specific SQL programs or to run specific scripts. As indicated in the list above, each CrtSql*Xxx* and RunSqlStm command specifies the naming option in effect for the command. Although you should consistently use one naming option, by deciding to use SQL naming, you're not putting yourself in a position in which the library list can never be used for any SQL application. And even with SQL naming as your standard for programs and scripts, you'll probably still prefer to use system naming for ISQL because ISQL doesn't support a default collection or SQL path, essentially requiring qualified names in interactive sessions that use SQL naming.

Specifying a Default Collection

The next two sections assume you're going to use SQL naming, and they explain how to specify the default collection and SQL path. If you don't specify a default collection or SQL path with SQL naming, SQL/400 uses either the current job's user profile or the user profile that owns the program containing the statement as the qualifier for unqualified statements. Neither of these is usually a good choice for a qualifier. (If you're porting an application from another SQL platform on which this is the only available choice for implicit SQL qualifiers, you can still create an SQL/400 collection that has the same name as a user profile and specify this collection as the default.)

SQL/400 lets you control the default collection used for static and dynamic SQL statements separately. To specify a default collection for static statements (which are always in a compiled HLL program), use the CrtSql*Xxx* command's DftRdbCol (default relational database collection) parameter. For example, you could specify DftRdbCol(AppDta) to have the AppDta collection be used for any unqualified alias, index, table, or view names in static SQL statements in the program.

You can also set the default collection by coding an SQL Set Option DftRdbCol statement at the beginning of an HLL program, but doing so hard codes the implicit qualifier in the source code. Note that the Set Option statement sets precompiler options and isn't an executable statement. (Later in this section, we show an effective technique for using the Set Option command.) In addition, you can use the QSqChgDc system API to change the default collection for dynamic embedded statements, but keep in mind that this API is an OS/400-specific feature and won't be available on other SQL platforms.

If you use Distributed Relational Database Architecture (DRDA) to execute static SQL statements on a remote system, you can specify a DftRdbCol value for an SQL package that you create with the CrtSqlPkg command. For a package, you can specify either a collection name (which can differ from the name you specified on the CrtSql*Xxx* command that created the local program) or *Pgm, which means to use the same default collection name specified when the program was created.

To specify a default collection for dynamic statements in a compiled HLL program, specify *Yes for the CrtSql*Xxx* command's DynDftCol (dynamic default collection) parameter. This value uses the collection specified in the DftRdbCol parameter to qualify unqualified alias, index, table, or view names in dynamic SQL statements in the program. The SQL Set Option DynDftCol statement also sets this precompiler option.

To specify the default collection for client applications that connect with JDBC, the Java client should set the first entry in the `libraries` property to the desired default before opening a connection. For ODBC clients, you must configure the ODBC datasource's Default Libraries value.

To specify a default collection for SQL scripts, use the RunSqlStm command's DftRdbCol parameter. Because all statements in a script are executed dynamically, this value applies to all unqualified alias, index, table, or view names in the script. The RunSqlStm command has no DynDftCol parameter.

From this information, we can distill out three recommendations:

> *Always specify a default collection on the DftRdbCol parameter for the CrtSqlXxx and RunSqlStm commands.*
>
> *On the CrtSqlPkg command, either accept the command default of DftRdbCol(*Pgm) or specify an explicit collection name — don't use DftRdbCol(*None).*
>
> *Always specify DynDftCol(*Yes) on the CrtSqlXxx commands (or set the corresponding JDBC property or ODBC configuration value).*

The StrSql command has no DftRdbCol parameter, so you can't specify a default collection to qualify alias, index, table, or view names when using interactive SQL with SQL naming. That's why we suggested earlier that you may want to use system naming (which uses the library list) when you run ISQL. Note that the StrSql command's LibOpt parameter does *not* provide for an implicit qualifier; it just controls which libraries are used in ISQL object list prompts.

Specifying the SQL Path

Although SQL naming provides only a single collection to be used as the implicit qualifier for alias, index, table, and view names, SQL provides a more flexible search list — known as the **SQL path** — for distinct types, functions, and procedures. With SQL naming, if you specify a default collection (e.g., with the DftRdbCol parameter), the default SQL path is

QSys, QSys2, *default-collection*

so you don't need to specify an explicit default path unless you want to search collections other than the default collection.

You can specify an SQL path in several ways:

For static statements:

- in the CrtSql*Xxx* commands' SqlPath parameter
- with the Set Option SqlPath precompiler directive at the beginning of an HLL program's source member

For dynamic statements (i.e., the runtime SQL path):

- with the SQL Set Path executable statement
- by setting the list of collections in the JDBC `libraries` property or configuring an ODBC data-source's Default Libraries value

The Set Path statement can be executed in an SQL script or interactively, as well as in an HLL program, so it provides the SQL path capability when you use the RunSqlStm and StrSql commands.

When an SQL program begins execution, the runtime SQL path has the same SQL path value as was in effect for static statements when the program was created. Note that executing a Set Path statement in an SQL program will *not* change the path used to resolve static procedure and function calls — these are resolved when the program is created. In an SQL program, the Set Path statement affects only dynamic statements — those prepared and executed with the Execute Immediate or Prepare and Execute statements. There's a slight wrinkle to embedded procedure calls, however, that may be useful for some situations. In an SQL program, the runtime — not static — SQL path is searched if you code a procedure call using a host variable to hold the procedure name, as in the following statement:

```
Call :MyProc ( :Arg1, :Arg2 )
```

If you need to have all your procedure calls resolved to collections that are determined at runtime, you could pass an argument containing the SQL path string to the HLL program, use this string in the Set Path statement, and make all your procedure calls using the technique above. As an example, you might use a CL "shell" program to retrieve the job's current library list, reformat it, and pass this list on a call to the SQL program, which would then use it to resolve procedure calls.

Although using the SQL path to control the search for functions and procedures may look similar to the way non-SQL applications use a job's library list to search for service programs and programs, keep in mind that for static SQL statements, the search occurs when the program is created — not when it's run. (In contrast, non-SQL references to unqualified OS/400 procedure names in service programs and to unqualified program names are generally resolved at runtime.) Also be aware that the rules for finding an SQL function or procedure are more complex than those OS/400 uses to find a service program or program object. The SQL process involves finding the function or procedure whose signature best matches the specific function or procedure call's list of arguments.

Also, when you create a function or procedure that uses an *unqualified* service program or program name, SQL/400 stores the collection name where the function or procedure is created as the qualifier for the program. At runtime, SQL/400 *always* uses the qualified name of the service program or program when you invoke a function or procedure created with SQL naming. If a function or procedure must reference a service program or program in a different collection, you must qualify the object name on the Create Function or Create Procedure statement.

Distilling out the essential guidelines for the SQL path leads to these recommendations:

When possible, create functions and procedures in the same collection as any external service program or program objects specified on the Create Function or Create Procedure statement. Otherwise, use a qualified OS/400 object name in the Create Function or Create Procedure statement's External Name clause.

Specify an SQL path (e.g., with the SqlPath parameter) when you need to search collections other than the default collection for static statements that reference distinct types, functions, or procedures. Remember that these names are resolved when the program is created, not when it's run.

If you need to change the search path at runtime, use the Set Path statement and use dynamic statements or a procedure call that uses a host variable to hold the procedure name.

Running SQL Programs Under the Correct User Profile

When an SQL program runs, it uses the authority of either the current user or the program owner to execute static and dynamic SQL statements in the program. (Chapter 9 explains the security implications of programs that adopt the owner's authority.) For nondistributed programs created with SQL naming, the default is to use the program owner's authority for static statements and use the current user's authority for dynamic statements. In some cases, this may be how you want a program to run, but the following practice will make certain every program runs with the intended authorities:

*Always specify explicit *User or *Owner values for the CrtSqlXxx commands' UsrPrf and DynUsrPrf parameters.*

As you might expect, specifying UsrPrf(*User) means the current user's authorities are used for static statements, and specifying DynUsrPrf(*User) means the current user's authorities are used for dynamic statements. You can specify *Owner instead of *User if you want either static or dynamic statements (or both) to run under the program owner's authorities. As an alternative, you can code Set Option UsrPrf and Set Option DynUsrPrf precompiler directives at the beginning of your SQL program source code.

For distributed SQL programs, the user profile for static statements is the same as for nondistributed programs. However, for dynamic statements, DynUsrPrf(*User) uses the authorities of the remote system's application server job's user profile. DynUsrPrf(*Owner) uses the authorities of the user profile that owns the SQL package on the remote system.

SQL statements executed interactively or with the RunSqlStm command always use the current user profile's authorities.

Using an SQL Options Source Member

To simplify adopting the recommended standards, you may want to consider using an SQL options source member that you include when you create an SQL program. To incorporate the above recommendations into an RPG IV program, create a member named SqlOptions in a separate source file (e.g., SqlSrc) for each environment. For example, if you have one test and one production environment, you might have two source files: TstSrc/SqlSrc and AppSrc/SqlSrc. Then put code such as the following in each source member:

```
C/Exec SQL
C+      Set Option
C+          Naming     = *Sql,
C+          DftRdbCol  = AppDta,
C+          DynDftCol  = *Yes,
C+          UsrPrf     = *User,
C+          DynUsrPrf  = *User
C/End-Exec
```

Each source member should have the appropriate value for the DftRdbCol option. For example, the above member (in the AppSrc/SqlSrc file) might be used to create production programs that use AppDta for the default collection. For the SqlOptions member in the TstSrc/SqlSrc file, you would code DftRdbCol = TstDta. The other options shown above can generally be the same for all environments. If you need to create programs that adopt the owner's authority, create another set of source members that specify *Owner instead of *User. You can also add other standard SQL options, such as the transaction isolation level, to the SqlOptions members.

Your RPG program should code the following statement at the beginning of the C-specs, before any other embedded SQL statements:

```
C/Exec SQL
C+      Include SqlOptions
C/End-Exec
```

To use the appropriate SqlOptions source member, you simply specify the IncFile parameter on your CrtSql*Xxx* command — for example, IncFile(AppSrc/SqlSrc). If the SqlOptions member is in the same source file as the program's main source, the CrtSql*Xxx* command default of IncFile(*SrcFile) is adequate.

Additional Considerations

As you can see, by using the right SQL/400 features, you can use SQL naming and retain a lot of flexibility. Keep in mind, however, that unless you use the QSqChgDc system API, you must re-create SQL programs to use a different default collection for static statements. To produce an SQL program for a remote site that uses a different default collection and that doesn't have the DB2 Query Manager and SQL Development Kit for AS/400 product, you must create the program on your production system. It's *not* necessary, however, to have the remote system's collection exist on the production system.

Another tool that can be used to resolve unqualified table and view references at runtime is the OS/400 OvrDbF (Override with Database File) command. SQL/400 uses the OvrDbF command's File, ToFile, and Mbr parameters just like "native" database access uses them.

To create a view in one collection when the view is based on tables or views in another collection, you can use unqualified names only for objects in one collection — objects in other collections must be qualified. This requirement is true whether you use system or SQL naming, and it applies to other Create statements (e.g., Create Index) that reference multiple objects.

As we mentioned earlier, the default collection doesn't affect non-SQL statements. In particular, the ILE RPG compiler uses the library list to resolve a file name specified on an externally described data structure (as was used in several of the examples in the "Host Structures" and "Host Structure Arrays" sections of this chapter) even if the file is an SQL table.

Chapter Summary

The Include statement lets you specify a source member to be incorporated into the source code that's processed during the SQL/400 precompilation step. Using Include members can improve application consistency and improve productivity by reusing common source code.

The SQL communication area provides a set of variables that provide completion and diagnostic feedback to your HLL program after you execute an SQL statement. The SqlState (SqlStt in RPG IV) variable is the most important element of the SQL communication area and indicates the completion status of the most recent statement.

SQL/400 has special extensions that let an HLL program read or insert a row using a host language structure that contains a field for each column. Additional extensions allow multiple rows to be read with a single Fetch statement or inserted with a single Insert statement. Both of these options also let you specify an array of null indicators. By using a few standard coding techniques, you can simplify the use of host structures and arrays. Multirow retrieval and inserts can yield a significant performance improvament for some applications.

OS/400 uses object and row locks to control the allocation of resources so that simultaneous object or row access by different jobs won't result in conflicting operations. OS/400 provides many automatic object and row locks, but you can also place additional locks explicitly. The AlcObj (Allocate Object) and DlcObj (Deallocate Object) OS/400 commands, as well as SQL's Lock Table statement, let you place and remove object locks. OS/400 has five types of object locks and prevents conflicting types of locks from being obtained by different jobs. UDB/400 places row locks automatically when you access a file for update or when commitment control is in effect. Transaction isolation levels (i.e., commitment control lock levels) let you specify that UDB/400 should place additional row locks beyond those normally placed without commitment control.

Commitment control provides an all-or-none facility for transactions that involve multiple database rows. Under commitment control, an application must execute a commit operation to make permanent those database changes performed since the last complete transaction. If the application or system fails before file changes are committed, the system subsequently backs out all uncommitted changes. An application can also explicitly execute a rollback operation to remove uncommitted changes. There are several transaction isolation levels, which provide different levels of isolation for transactions in different jobs. Each isolation level provides a unique combination of row lock types and duration, which results in varying degrees of protection from conflicting updates.

Stored procedures are a named chunk of code with optional parameters that can be called with an SQL Call statement, with JDBC methods, or with ODBC functions. A stored procedure can be implemented as an HLL program or using the SQL Procedural Language (SPL). An HLL program that implements a stored procedure can optionally included embedded SQL. A stored procedure can return one or more result sets to a JDBC or ODBC client. To define a stored procedure in a collection, you use the Create Procedure statement.

Nonsourced, user-defined functions (UDFs) are similar to stored procedures, except a UDF always returns a value. A UDF can be used most places a built-in scalar function can be used. You can implement a UDF with an HLL program or a procedure or function in a service program. You can also use SPL to implement a UDF. To define a UDF in a collection, you use the Create Function statement.

SQL/400 provides two naming options: system naming and SQL naming. The naming option determines the syntax for qualified names, the rules for implicit qualification of unqualified names, and the rules for which user profile a statement executes under. In general, we recommend SQL naming for greater consistency with the SQL standard and for increased application portability. Various command parameters and SQL options let you specify the default collection(s) for unqualified names used in static and dynamic statements. Additional parameters and options let you explicitly specify which user profile a statement executes under.

Key Terms

blocked Insert
commitment control
external function
host structure array
host structure variable
Include statement
isolation level
Lock Table statement
logical unit of work
multiple-row Fetch statement
object lock
row lock
SQL communication area (SQLCA)
SQL function
SQL naming
SQL path
SQL Procedural Language (SPL)
stored procedure
system naming
transaction
user-defined function (UDF)

Exercises

Note: In all the following exercises that require HLL or embedded SQL statements, use any suitable AS/400 HLL (e.g., RPG IV, Cobol).

1. Show the HLL code and static Insert statement to insert a single new row into the Customer table defined by the following statement, using an externally described host structure as well as an indicator array overlayed with a structure for indicator variables. (You don't need to show error-handling code.)

```
Create Table Customer
     ( CustID   Dec(   7, 0 ) Not Null,
       CustName Char( 30    ) Not Null,
       ShipCity Char( 30    ),
       Discount Dec(   5, 3 ),
  Primary Key( CustID ) )
```

2. Modify your solution to Exercise 1 to use a separate source member for the HLL declarations of the host indicator array. Use an Include statement to incorporate this code at the appropriate place in your sample program.
3. Show the HLL code and cursor-related statements (including cursor declaration, Open, Close, and Fetch statements) to sequentially read all employees from the following table:

```
Create Table Employee
     ( EmplID   Dec(   7, 0 ) Not Null,
       EmplName Char( 30    ) Not Null,
       DeptID   Dec(   7, 0 ) Not Null,
       HireDate Date          Not Null,
  Primary Key( EmplID ) )
```

   For each row, execute a ListEmpl routine (e.g., an RPG IV subroutine or Cobol paragraph — you don't need to show the routine's code). Read the rows in order by department ID and, within department ID, by descending employee ID. Use a multiple-row Fetch that reads 50 rows at a time. Include the necessary HLL loop structures to process all rows and terminate when there are no more rows or an unanticipated error occurs. Include appropriate error-handling code.

   Hint: You'll need nested loops.

4. Explain why the technique used for a multiple-row Fetch wouldn't be a complete solution to the problem of retrieving multiple rows for a static Select Into statement.
   Describe an approach that might make the Select Into more flexible for retrieving sets of rows. Would this have any advantages over a cursor?
   Describe how the static Update statement might be enhanced to support multiple-row updates. If this feature were available, would it make a multiple-row Select Into more useful?
5. Which type of object lock should you get if you want to be sure that a job can have update access to an object and that no other job can update the object?
6. List the types of object locks that another job can get if a job already holds a *ShrNUp lock on an object.
7. Explain why row locks are necessary. Would row locks ever be necessary if only one person used the AS/400 at a time? Why or why not?
8. Describe an example of a multiple-row transaction (other than the funds transfer example used in this chapter). Explain why commitment control is necessary with this type of transaction.
9. Describe a situation in which the Repeatable Read isolation level is necessary. Is there an alternative solution to the problem? If so, describe the advantages and disadvantages of each approach.
10. Code the Create Procedure statement and the HLL (e.g., RPG IV or ILE COBOL/400) implementation for a Calc stored procedure that has the following parameters:
    - Value1In — Integer input parameter
    - Value2In — Integer input parameter
    - ResultOut — Integer output parameter

    The Calc procedure should set ResultOut to
    - 0, if Value1In >= Value2In; or
    - Value2In – Value1In, if Value1In < Value2In

    Use Parameter Style SQL, and set an appropriate SqlState and error message text if either of the input values is null.
11. Code the Create Function statement for an SQL function (using SPL) that accepts a Date parameter value and returns the name of the day of the week (e.g., Sunday) for the input date.

    Hint: Use SQL's DayOfWeek built-in function in your implementation.
12. List the main advantages and disadvantages of the SQL naming option.
13. Show how to code a CrtSqlRpgI command for the ListCust program so that AppDta is used as the default collection for both static and dynamic statements and the current user profile is used as the user profile under which all static and dynamic statements are executed.

Chapter 14

Creating an RPG IV Program to Update the Customer Table

Chapter Overview

In this chapter, we present a working RPG IV program (UpdCust) to illustrate how the techniques you learned in Chapters 10, 11, and 13 are used in a more complete RPG IV example.

The UpdCust Program

We've covered most of the programming details related to embedded SQL; now let's put them together in a couple of sample programs that include the type of error handling a production application should use. In this chapter, we cover an RPG IV program called UpdCust. In Chapter 15, we describe an ILE COBOL/400 version of the UpdCust program.

UpdCust is a batch update program that uses rows in the CustUpd transaction table (Figure 14.1) to add, change, and delete rows in the Customer table (Figure 14.2).

Figure 14.1
CustUpd Table

```
Create Table CustUpd
  ( CustID                  Int        Not Null
                            Check ( CustID > 0 ),
    SeqNbr                  Int        Not Null
                            Check ( SeqNbr > 0 ),
    CustomerName For Name   Char( 30 ) Not Null,
    RowAction               Char(  1 ) Not Null,
  Primary Key ( CustID,
                SeqNbr ) )
```

Figure 14.2
Customer Table

```
Create Table Customer
  ( CustID                  Int        Not Null
                            Check ( CustID > 0 ),
    CustomerName For Name   Char( 30 ) Not Null,
  Primary Key ( CustID ) )
```

The sample tables include just a few columns so that we can concentrate on the embedded SQL programming techniques. The Customer table has a primary key (CustID) and one non-key column, CustomerName (the short form is Name). The CustUpd table has these two columns plus the SeqNbr column, used to sequence transactions within a particular customer ID, and the RowAction column, which contains a one-letter code for the action (or the status after an update is attempted). The basic requirements for a valid CustUpd row are that together the CustID and SeqNbr values are unique within the table and that:

- *To add a row:* RowAction is A, CustID must be a key value that's not already in the Customer table, and CustomerName can be anything (it should be a valid name, but it isn't checked).
- *To change a row:* RowAction is C, CustID must be a key value that exists in the Customer table, and CustomerName can be anything (it should be a valid name, but it isn't checked).
- *To delete a row:* RowAction is D, CustID must be a key value that exists in the Customer table, and CustomerName isn't used.

After the application attempts to perform a transaction, it replaces the RowAction column value with X if the transaction is successful or E if an error occurs. When the CustUpd table rows are fetched, rows with X or E in the RowAction column are skipped.

The application handles all types of SQL exceptions. If a "row not found" or "duplicate key" error occurs, it's treated as a transaction error; a message is displayed, and the CustUpd row is flagged with an E in the RowAction column. Other errors cause a message to be displayed, and the application terminates. Regardless of whether the application terminates normally or because of an unanticipated exception, it always explicitly closes any open SQL cursor because program termination may not automatically close cursors (whether it does so depends on the value of the CloSqlCsr parameter on the CrtSql*Xxx* command that created the program).

The application doesn't reflect all the considerations you might have to cover in a real application, but it does illustrate a full range of embedded SQL operations for the two most common types of table access: sequential access by key (for CustUpd) and direct access by key (for Customer). It also shows a production-level approach to error detection (although the error handling itself is less sophisticated than might be used in a production program).

Because SQL/400 is used to access the database, the RPG IV version of the application (Figure 14.3, page 284) and the ILE COBOL/400 version (Figure 15.3 in the next chapter) have almost identical I/O code. The coding for host variables and non-SQL procedural code is, of course, language dependent. In both versions, the Customer and CustUpd tables are accessed through updatable cursors declared with Declare Cursor statements. The CustomerTable cursor's For Update clause specifies that only the CustomerName column is updated. The CustUpdTable cursor specifies that only the RowAction column is updated.

For each table, an externally described host structure variable is declared to provide variables into which to fetch a row. The host structure variable for the Customer table is also used to insert a new row.

The RPG IV data structures are declared with the Prefix keyword so that their subfield names will be unique within the program. The subfield names for the two data structures are

```
CustomerR
        CsCustID
        CsName

CustUpdR
        UpCustID
        UpSeqNbr
        UpName
        UpRowAction
```

One coding technique to point out is the use of implicit column lists in the cursors' Select statements (i.e., the use of * instead of a list of columns) and in the Insert statement (i.e., no column names follow the table name). When individual host variables are used for a Select or Insert statement, we suggest you use explicit column names. That way, you know you have the right number and correspondence of host variables and columns, even if the table definition changes. But with externally described host structure variables, each time you compile the program, you get an exact match of the generated column list and the generated host variable list, so implicit column lists are simpler and less error-prone.

The sample program also illustrates how you handle update and delete operations somewhat differently with SQL than with HLL built-in I/O operations. The program shows two alternatives: a positioned Update using repeated opens and closes of a cursor and a searched Delete. In both cases, a primary key value is used to select the record to be updated or deleted.

The CustomerTable cursor isn't opened just once at the beginning of the program. Instead, when an update action is processed, the CsCustID host variable is set and the cursor is opened. If a row with the specified customer ID exists, the cursor's result table contains that row; otherwise, the cursor's result table is empty. A single Fetch Next operation retrieves the row to be updated (or, if no row exists, SqlStt is set to '02000'). If the row is Fetch'd successfully, a positioned Update statement changes the Name column. After the update action (whether successful or unsuccessful), the CustomerTable cursor is closed. Although this might seem like a slow approach to updating a single row, UDB/400 doesn't actually open and close the underlying table repeatedly. Instead, the first time the cursor is opened, UDB/400 opens the table, and subsequently UDB/400 just changes the rows that are made available through the cursor using the already open table.

The delete action uses an alternative approach: a searched Delete that specifies the primary key value of the row to be deleted. This same technique could have been used for the update action. Even though the Delete statement doesn't occur through a cursor, UDB/400 uses the same technique described for the Update statement — the table is opened only once and each delete operation requires only repositioning to the selected row.

Using a searched Update or Delete is a little simpler coding for an application such as this. However, if you already have an updatable cursor open to retrieve rows, a positioned Update to the current row may be equally simple and slightly faster (if you don't have to reposition the cursor).[1]

A standard approach is used for detecting and handling various conditions that can occur during execution of an SQL statement. After each statement, a Select or If statement checks the SqlStt variable for one of the following:

- successful completion of the operation
- an anticipated condition (such as duplicate key)
- an unanticipated error condition

The complete set of SqlStt values is documented in an appendix of *DB2 UDB for AS/400 SQL Programming*, but the two mnemonics declared in this program are the most common ones to anticipate.[2] If you want to handle any other SqlStt value explicitly, all you have to do is add another When condition to the appropriate Select statement.

The error routines demonstrate how you can provide precise information about the cause of an SQL error. The sample routines are just a starting point; you can provide much more information if

1 Another consideration is row locking (discussed in Chapter 13). You may want to minimize locks on rows that the user is browsing (and, thus, use a read-only cursor) until the user indicates he or she wants to perform an update. For an update, you can use a single-row, updatable cursor such as the one in the sample programs to re-retrieve the row with a lock. A subsequent positioned Update can then update the locked row.

2 For simplicity, this example doesn't use the SQL Include or RPG IV /Copy directive, nor does it call external programs or bound procedures. All these techniques are valuable for production applications. You can use an Include or /Copy member to hold constant declarations for the complete set of SqlStt values as well as any declarative or executable code that you need to use repeatedly. More sophisticated error handling can be put in a separate program or bound procedure and called with an RPG IV Call, CallP, or CallB statement. Using a called program or procedure simplifies application coding and standardizes the way applications handle errors. See Appendix E for RPG IV and other references that provide help with these techniques.

you want. You can also write error messages to a log table or send them to an OS/400 message queue so they're available for subsequent diagnosis. Thorough, informative handling of errors is a crucial part of production application development.

Figure 14.3

RPG IV UpdCust Program

```
 * - - - - - - - - - - - - - - - - - - - - - - - - - - - - - - -
 * Program name: UpdCust
 * Author:       Paul Conte.
 * Date-Written: 2000-02-21.
 * Purpose:      Update Customer table from CustUpd table rows.
 * - - - - - - - - - - - - - - - - - - - - - - - - - - - - - - -
 *


 * Externally described host structure variables

D CustomerR       E DS                  ExtName( Customer )
D                                       Prefix( Cs )

D CustUpdR        E DS                  ExtName( CustUpd )
D                                       Prefix( Up )

 * Mnemonics

D True              C                   Const( '1' )
D False             C                   Const( '0' )
D SqlSttOK          C                   Const( '00000' )
D SqlSttNoRow       C                   Const( '02000' )
D SqlSttDupKey      C                   Const( '23505' )
D CsTblName         C                   Const( 'Customer' )
D UpTblName         C                   Const( 'CustUpd' )
D AddAct            C                   Const( 'A' )
D ChangeAct         C                   Const( 'C' )
D DeleteAct         C                   Const( 'D' )
D ComplTAct         C                   Const( 'X' )
D ErrAct            C                   Const( 'E' )
D CloseLbl          C                   Const( 'Close'  )
D DeleteLbl         C                   Const( 'Delete' )
D OpenLbl           C                   Const( 'Open'   )
D FetchLbl          C                   Const( 'Fetch'  )
D UpdateLbl         C                   Const( 'Update' )
D InsertLbl         C                   Const( 'Insert' )
D InvActLbl         C                   Const( 'Invalid action' )
D NoKeyLbl          C                   Const( 'Key not found in table' )
D DupKeyLbl         C                   Const( 'Duplicate key in table' )

 * Program variables

D PgmErr            S              1A   Inz( '0' )
D CsOpen            S              1A   Inz( '0' )
D UpOpen            S              1A   Inz( '0' )
D UpMoreRows        S              1A   Inz( '0' )
D TblName           S             10A
D SqlStmt           S             10A
D ErrText           S             50A
D Msg               S             51A

 * - - - - - - - - - - - - - - - - - - - - - - - - - - - - - -
```

continued

Figure 14.3 *Continued*

```
 * Table cursor definitions

C/Exec SQL
C+
C+ Declare CustomerTable Cursor
C+   With Hold
C+   For  Select          *
C+          From          Customer
C+          Where         CustID = :CsCustID
C+          For Update of CustomerName
C/End-Exec


C/Exec SQL
C+
C+ Declare CustUpdTable Cursor
C+   With Hold
C+   For  Select          *
C+          From          CustUpd
C+          Order by      CustID,
C+                        SeqNbr
C+          For Update of RowAction
C/End-Exec


 * - - - - - - - - - - - - - - - - - - - - - - - - - - - - - -
 *    Main block
C                   ExSr      OpnTables

C                   DoW       ( UpMoreRows = True ) And ( PgmErr = False )
C                     ExSr    PrcNxtCust
C                   EndDo

C                   ExSr      ClsTables

C                   ExSr      ExitPgm

 * - - - - - - - - - - - - - - - - - - - - - - - - - - - - - -
C     OpnTables     BegSr

 * Don't open the CustomerTable cursor here, since it will
 * be opened and closed for each update.

C                   ExSr      OpnCustUpd

C                   EndSr
 * - - - - - - - - - - - - - - - - - - - - - - - - - - - - - -
C     OpnCust       BegSr

C/Exec SQL
C+                  Open CustomerTable
C/End-Exec
C                   If        SqlStt = SqlSttOK
C                     Eval    CsOpen = True
C                   Else
C                     Eval    CsOpen  = False
C                     Eval    SqlStmt = OpenLbl
C                     ExSr    CsSqlErr
C                   EndIf

C                   EndSr
 * - - - - - - - - - - - - - - - - - - - - - - - - - - - - - -
```

continued

Figure 14.3 *Continued*

```
C     OpnCustUpd    BegSr

C/Exec SQL
C+                  Open CustUpdTable
C/End-Exec
C                   If        SqlStt = SqlSttOK
C                     Eval    UpOpen     = True
C                     Eval    UpMoreRows = True
C                   Else
C                     Eval    UpOpen     = False
C                     Eval    UpMoreRows = False
C                     Eval    SqlStmt    = OpenLbl
C                     ExSr    UpSqlErr
C                   EndIf

C                   EndSr
 * - - - - - - - - - - - - - - - - - - - - - - - - - - - - - - -
C     ClsTables     BegSr

 * Close table(s) that are currently open.

C                   If        CsOpen = True
C                     ExSr    ClsCust
C                   EndIf

C                   If        UpOpen = True
C                     ExSr    ClsCustUpd
C                   EndIf

C                   EndSr
 * - - - - - - - - - - - - - - - - - - - - - - - - - - - - - - -
C     ClsCust       BegSr

 * Set the Customer table state to "closed" in all cases, so the
 * error handling for an error on the close doesn't attempt
 * another close.

C                   Eval      CsOpen = False
C/Exec SQL
C+                  Close CustomerTable
C/End-Exec
C                   If        SqlStt <> SqlSttOK
C                     Eval    SqlStmt = CloseLbl
C                     ExSr    CsSqlErr
C                   EndIf

C                   EndSr
 * - - - - - - - - - - - - - - - - - - - - - - - - - - - - - - -
C     ClsCustUpd    BegSr

 * Set the CustUpd table state to "closed" in all cases, so the
 * error handling for an error on the close doesn't attempt
 * another close.

C                   Eval      UpOpen     = False
C                   Eval      UpMoreRows = False
C/Exec SQL
C+                  Close CustUpdTable
C/End-Exec
C                   If        SqlStt <> SqlSttOK
C                     Eval    SqlStmt = CloseLbl
C                     ExSr    UpSqlErr
C                   EndIf

C                   EndSr
 * - - - - - - - - - - - - - - - - - - - - - - - - - - - - - - -
```

continued

Figure 14.3 *Continued*

```
C     PrcNxtCust    BegSr

 * Read a CustUpd row, and dispatch on its action code.
 *
 * Each action-handling routine attempts to perform the action
 * and then changes the action code to indicate either
 * successful completion or an error. The modified CustUpd
 * row is then rewritten.

C/Exec SQL
C+                  Fetch Next
C+                    From  CustUpdTable
C+                    Into :CustUpdR
C/End-Exec
C                   Select
C                    When     SqlStt = SqlSttOK
C                      ExSr   DoTransact
C                      If     PgmErr = False
C                        ExSr UpdCustUpd
C                      EndIf
C                    When     SqlStt = SqlSttNoRow
C                      Eval   UpMoreRows = False
C                    Other
C                      Eval   SqlStmt = FetchLbl
C                      ExSr   UpSqlErr
C                   EndSl

C                   EndSr
 * - - - - - - - - - - - - - - - - - - - - - - - - - - - - - - -
C     DoTransact    BegSr

C                   Select
C                     When    UpRowAction = AddAct
C                       ExSr  AddCust
C                     When    UpRowAction = ChangeAct
C                       ExSr  ChangeCust
C                     When    UpRowAction = DeleteAct
C                       ExSr  DeleteCust
C                     When    UpRowAction = CompltAct
 *                      Skip
C                     When    UpRowAction = ErrAct
 *                      Skip
C                     Other
C                       Eval  ErrText = InvActLbl
C                       ExSr  ActionErr
C                   EndSl

C                   EndSr
 * - - - - - - - - - - - - - - - - - - - - - - - - - - - - - - -
```

continued

Figure 14.3 *Continued*

```
C     AddCust        BegSr

C                    Eval      CsCustID = UpCustID
C                    Eval      CsName   = UpName
C/Exec SQL
C+                   Insert Into Customer
C+                     Values(  :CustomerR )
C/End-Exec
C                    Select
C                      When     SqlStt = SqlSttOK
C                        Eval  UpRowAction = CompltAct
C                      When     SqlStt = SqlSttDupKey
C                        Eval  ErrText = DupKeyLbl
C                        ExSr  ActionErr
C                        Eval  UpRowAction = ErrAct
C                      Other
C                        Eval  SqlStmt = InsertLbl
C                        ExSr  CsSqlErr
C                    EndSl

C                    EndSr
 * - - - - - - - - - - - - - - - - - - - - - - - - - - - - - -
C     ChangeCust     BegSr

 * Attempt to fetch the specified Customer row, change its
 * data (i.e., name), and update the row.
 *
 * It would be as fast or faster to use a searched Update
 * (instead of a Fetch and positioned Update), similar to the
 * way the DeleteCust subroutine (below) is implemented.
 * This example uses a positioned Update to demonstrate the
 * technique.

C                    Eval      CsCustID = UpCustID

C                    ExSr      OpnCust

C                    If        CsOpen = True
C/Exec SQL
C+                     Fetch Next
C+                       From  CustomerTable
C+                       Into :CustomerR
C/End-Exec
C                      Select
C                       When   SqlStt = SqlSttOK
C                         ExSr UpdateCust
C                       When   SqlStt = SqlSttNoRow
C                         Eval ErrText = NoKeyLbl
C                         ExSr ActionErr
C                         Eval UpRowAction = ErrAct
C                       Other
C                         Eval SqlStmt = FetchLbl
C                         ExSr CsSqlErr
C                      EndSl

C                      ExSr    ClsCust
C                    EndIf

C                    EndSr
 * - - - - - - - - - - - - - - - - - - - - - - - - - - - - - -
```

continued

Figure 14.3 *Continued*

```
C     UpdateCust    BegSr

 * Note that a No Row Found condition indicates an unexpected
 * error because the row was just fetched with the same key.

C/Exec SQL
C+                  Update  Customer
C+                    Set   CustomerName = :UpName
C+                    Where Current of CustomerTable
C/End-Exec
C                   If        SqlStt = SqlSttOK
C                     Eval    UpRowAction = CompltAct
C                   Else
C                     Eval    SqlStmt = UpdateLbl
C                     ExSr    CsSqlErr
C                   EndIf

C                   EndSr
 * - - - - - - - - - - - - - - - - - - - - - - - - - - - - - -
C     DeleteCust    BegSr

 * Use a positioned Delete.

C/Exec SQL
C+                  Delete From Customer
C+                    Where     CustID = :UpCustID
C+
C/End-Exec
C                   Select
C                     When    SqlStt = SqlSttOK
C                       Eval  UpRowAction = CompltAct
C                     When    SqlStt = SqlSttNoRow
C                       Eval  ErrText = NoKeyLbl
C                       ExSr  ActionErr
C                       Eval  UpRowAction = ErrAct
C                     Other
C                       Eval  SqlStmt = DeleteLbl
C                       ExSr  CsSqlErr
C                   EndSl

C                   EndSr
 * - - - - - - - - - - - - - - - - - - - - - - - - - - - - - -
C     UpdCustUpd    BegSr

C/Exec SQL
C+                  Update  CustUpd
C+                    Set   RowAction = :UpRowAction
C+                    Where Current of CustUpdTable
C/End-Exec
C                   If        SqlStt <> SqlSttOK
C                     Eval    SqlStmt = UpdateLbl
C                     ExSr    UpSqlErr
C                   EndIf

C                   EndSr
 * - - - - - - - - - - - - - - - - - - - - - - - - - - - - - -
```

continued

Figure 14.3 *Continued*

```
C     CsSqlErr      BegSr

C                   Eval      TblName = CsTblName
C                   ExSr      SqlErrRtn

C                   EndSr
 * - - - - - - - - - - - - - - - - - - - - - - - - - - - - - - - -
C     UpSqlErr      BegSr

C                   Eval      TblName = UpTblName
C                   ExSr      SqlErrRtn

C                   EndSr
 * - - - - - - - - - - - - - - - - - - - - - - - - - - - - - - - -
C     SqlErrRtn     BegSr

 * Handle an unexpected SQL error.
 * Emit an error message, close tables, and exit.

 * Globals used as input parameters: TblName
 *                                   SqlStt
 *                                   SqlStmt
 *
 * Globals used as work variables:   Msg
 *

C                   Eval      Msg = 'SQL error '
C                                 + SqlStt
C                                 + ' on '
C                                 + %TrimR( SqlStmt )
C                                 + ' for '
C                                 + %TrimR( TblName )
C                                 + ' table.'
C     Msg           Dsply (E)

C                   Eval      PgmErr = True

C                   EndSr
 * - - - - - - - - - - - - - - - - - - - - - - - - - - - - - - - -
C     ActionErr     BegSr

 * Globals used as input parameters: UpCustID
 *                                   UpRowAction
 *                                   ErrText
 *
 * Globals used as work variables:   Msg

C                   Eval      Msg = 'Error for customer '
C                                 + %Trim( %EditC( CsCustID : '3' ) )
C                                 + ' on "'
C                                 + UpRowAction
C                                 + '" action.'
C     Msg           Dsply (E)

C                   Eval      Msg = %TrimR( ErrText ) + '.'
C     Msg           Dsply (E)

C                   EndSr
 * - - - - - - - - - - - - - - - - - - - - - - - - - - - - - - - -
```

continued

Figure 14.3 *Continued*

```
C     *Pssr          BegSr

 * Globals used as work variables: Msg

C                    Eval      Msg = 'Unexpected program error.'
C     Msg            Dsply (E)

 * To avoid recursive call to *Pssr, don't attempt to close cursors.

C                    ExSr      ExitPgm

C                    EndSr
 * - - - - - - - - - - - - - - - - - - - - - - - - - - - - - - - - -
C     ExitPgm        BegSr

C                    Eval      *InLR = *On
C                    Return

C                    EndSr
 * - - - - - - - - - - - - - - - - - - - - - - - - - - - - - - - - -
```

Coding Suggestions

- When using an implicit column list in a cursor's Select statement or in a Select Into statement, use an RPG IV externally described data structure for the host variable to hold the contents of retrieved results.
- Use named constants (such as SqlSttOK in the UpdCust program shown in Figure 14.3) to assign meaningful names to the various SqlStt values used. Use an Include or /Copy member to hold constant declarations for the complete set of SqlStt values as well as any declarative or executable code that you need to use repeatedly.
- Create standard SQL (and other) error-handling routines that can be invoked after executing an embedded SQL statement. These can be callable as external programs or included in the source via the RPG IV /Copy directive or the SQL Include statement. As an alternative, consider placing these routines into service programs to ease maintenance and common access.

Exercises

1. Show the cursor declaration changes necessary to exclude previously processed rows (whether successful or not) from the CustUpdTable cursor.
2. Show the embedded SQL statement that would have applied all of the RowAction = 'A' transactions in a single statement. What would be the drawback to this single-statement approach?

Chapter 15

Creating a Cobol Program to Update the Customer Table

Chapter Overview

In the last chapter, we presented a working RPG IV program (UpdCust) to illustrate how the techniques you learned in Chapters 10, 11, and 13 are used in a more complete example. This chapter shows how the same thing can be accomplished in an ILE COBOL/400 program.

The UpdCust Program

The sample application is a batch update program that uses rows in the CustUpd transaction table (Figure 15.1) to add, change, and delete rows in the Customer table (Figure 15.2).

Figure 15.1
CustUpd Table

```
Create Table CustUpd
  ( CustID                   Int         Not Null
                             Check ( CustID > 0 ),
    SeqNbr                   Int         Not Null
                             Check ( SeqNbr > 0 ),
    CustomerName For Name    Char( 30 ) Not Null,
    RowAction                Char(  1 ) Not Null,
  Primary Key ( CustID,
                SeqNbr ) )
```

Figure 15.2
Customer Table

```
Create Table Customer
  ( CustID                   Int         Not Null
                             Check ( CustID > 0 ),
    CustomerName For Name    Char( 30 ) Not Null,
  Primary Key ( CustID ) )
```

The sample tables include just a few columns so that we can concentrate on the embedded SQL programming techniques. The Customer table has a unique key (CustID) and one non-key column, CustomerName (the short form is Name). The CustUpd table has these two columns plus the SeqNbr column, used to sequence transactions within a particular customer ID, and the RowAction column, which contains a one-letter code for the action (or the status after an update is attempted). The basic requirements for a valid CustUpd row are that together the CustID and SeqNbr values are unique within the table and that:

- *To add a row:* RowAction is A, CustID must be a key value that's not already in the Customer table, and CustomerName can be anything (it should be a valid name, but it isn't checked).

- *To change a row:* RowAction is C, CustID must be a key value that exists in the Customer table, and CustomerName can be anything (it should be a valid name, but it isn't checked).
- *To delete a row:* RowAction is D, CustID must be a key value that exists in the Customer table, and CustomerName isn't used.

After the application attempts to perform a transaction, it replaces the RowAction column value with X if the transaction is successful or E if an error occurs. When the CustUpd table is read, rows with X or E in the RowAction column are skipped.

The application handles all types of SQL exceptions. When a "row not found" or "duplicate key" error occurs, it's treated as a transaction error; a message is displayed, and the CustUpd row is flagged with an E in the RowAction column. Other errors cause a message to be displayed, and the application terminates. Regardless of whether the application terminates normally or because of an unanticipated exception, it always explicitly closes any open SQL cursor because program termination may not automatically close cursors (whether it does so depends on the value of the CloSqlCsr parameter on the CrtSql*Xxx* command that created the program).

The application doesn't reflect all the considerations you might have to cover in a real application, but it does illustrate a full range of embedded SQL operations for the two most common types of table access: sequential access by key (for CustUpd) and direct access by key (for Customer). It also shows a production-level approach to error detection (although the error handling itself is less sophisticated than might be used in a production program).

Because SQL/400 is used to access the database, the RPG IV version (Figure 14.3 in the previous chapter) and the ILE COBOL/400 version (Figure 15.3, page 296) have almost identical I/O code. The coding for host variables and non-SQL procedural code is, of course, language-dependent. The Customer and CustUpd tables are accessed through updatable cursors declared with Declare Cursor statements. The CustomerTable cursor's For Update clause specifies that only the CustomerName column is updated. The CustUpdTable cursor specifies that only the RowAction column is updated.

For each table, an externally described host structure variable is declared to provide variables into which to fetch a row. The host structure variable for the Customer table is also used to insert a new row.

The ILE COBOL/400 program uses Copy-DDS-All-Formats...With Alias directives to generate two group items. Each generated group item has the same name as a table (e.g., Customer and CustUpd). Because the With Alias option is specified on the Copy directives, the elementary items in each group have long column names, as follows:

```
Customer
        CustID
        CustomerName

CustUpd
        CustID
        SeqNbr
        CustomerName
        RowAction
```

One coding technique to point out is the use of implicit column lists in the cursors' Select statements (i.e., the use of an asterisk, or *, instead of a list of columns) and in the Insert statement (i.e., no column names follow the table name). When individual host variables are used for a Select or Insert statement, we suggest you use explicit column names. That way, you know you have the right number and correspondence of host variables and columns, even if the table definition changes. But with externally described host structure variables, each time you compile the program, you get an exact match of the generated column list and the generated host variable list, so implicit column lists are simpler and less error-prone.

The sample program also illustrates how you handle update and delete operations somewhat differently with SQL than with HLL built-in I/O operations. The two SQL examples show two alternatives: a positioned Update using repeated opens and closes of a cursor and a searched Delete. In both cases, a primary key value is used to select the record to be updated or deleted.

The CustomerTable cursor isn't opened just once at the beginning of the program. Instead, when an update action is processed, the CustID of Customer host variable is set and the cursor is opened. If a row with the specified customer ID exists, the cursor's result table contains that row; otherwise, the cursor's result table is empty. A single Fetch Next operation retrieves the row to be updated (or, if no row exists, SqlState is set to "02000"). If the row is Fetch'd successfully, a positioned Update statement changes the CustomerName column. After the update action (whether successful or unsuccessful), the CustomerTable cursor is closed. Although this might seem like a slow approach to updating a single row, UDB/400 doesn't actually open and close the underlying table repeatedly. Instead, the first time the cursor is opened, UDB/400 opens the table, and subsequently UDB/400 just changes the rows that are made available through the cursor using the already open table.

The delete action uses an alternative approach: a searched Delete that specifies the primary key value of the row to be deleted. This same technique could have been used for the update action. Even though the Delete statement doesn't occur through a cursor, UDB/400 uses the same technique described for the Update statement — the table is opened only once and each delete operation requires only repositioning to the selected row.

Using a searched Update or Delete is a little simpler coding for an application such as this. However, if you already have an updatable cursor open to retrieve rows, a positioned Update to the current row may be equally simple and slightly faster (if you don't have to reposition the cursor).[1]

A standard approach is used for detecting and handling various conditions that can occur during execution of an SQL statement. After each statement, an Evaluate or If statement checks the SqlState variable for one of the following:

- successful completion of the operation
- an anticipated condition (such as duplicate key)
- an unanticipated error condition

The complete set of SqlState values is documented in an appendix of *DB2 UDB for AS/400 SQL Programming*, but the two mnemonics declared in the UpdCust program are the most common ones to anticipate.[2] If you want to handle any other SqlState value explicitly, all you have to do is add another When condition to the appropriate Evaluate statement.

The error routines demonstrate how you can provide precise information about the cause of an SQL error.[3] The sample routines are just a starting point; you can provide much more information if

1 Another consideration is row locking (discussed in Chapter 13). You may want to minimize locks on rows that the user is browsing (and, thus, use a read-only cursor) until the user indicates he or she wants to perform an update. For an update, you can use a single-row, updatable cursor such as the one in the sample programs to re-retrieve the row with a lock. A subsequent positioned Update can then update the locked row.

2 For simplicity, this example doesn't use the SQL Include or Cobol Copy directive, nor does it call external programs or bound procedures. All these techniques are valuable for production applications. You can use an Include or Copy member to hold constant declarations for the complete set of SqlState values.

3 The error routines are implemented as ILE COBOL/400 nested programs. These are an ANSI-standard Cobol feature that was introduced in V3R1 ILE COBOL/400.

you want. You can also write error messages to a log table or send them to an OS/400 message queue so they're available for subsequent diagnosis. Thorough, informative handling of errors is a crucial part of production application development.

Figure 15.3

ILE COBOL/400 UpdCust Program

```
 Id Division.

   Program-Id.   UpdCust.
   Author.       Paul Conte.
   Date-Written. 05/12/00.
*  Purpose:      Update Customer table from CustUpd table rows.

* - - - - - - - - - - - - - - - - - - - - - - - - - - - - - - -
* - - - - - - - - - - - - - - - - - - - - - - - - - - - - - - -
 Data Division.
 Working-Storage Section.

     Exec SQL
       Include SQLCA
     End-Exec.

* Externally described host structure variables

 01  CustomerRow.
     Copy DDS-All-Formats of Customer
       With Alias.

 01  CustUpdRow.
     Copy DDS-All-Formats of CustUpd
       With Alias.


 01  DataTypes            Global.
     02 AS400NameType     Pic X(10).
     02 BooleanType       Pic 1.
     02 SqlStmtType       Pic X(10).
     02 SqlStateType      Like SqlState.
     02 TextType          Pic X(50).

 01  Mnemonics.
     02 SqlStateOK        Like SqlStateType   Value "00000".
     02 SqlStateNoRowFnd  Like SqlStateType   Value "02000".
     02 SqlStateDupKey    Like SqlStateType   Value "23505".

     02 CustomerTableName Like AS400NameType Value "Customer".
     02 CustUpdTableName  Like AS400NameType Value "CustUpd".

     02 SqlErrPgm         Like AS400NameType  Value "SQLERR".
     02 ActionErrPgm      Like AS400NameType  Value "ACTIONERR".

     02 AddAction         Like RowAction of CustUpd
                                              Value "A".
     02 ChangeAction      Like AddAction      Value "C".
     02 CompletedAction   Like AddAction      Value "X".
     02 DeleteAction      Like AddAction      Value "D".
     02 ErrorAction       Like AddAction      Value "E".
```

continued

Figure 15.3 ***Continued***

```
       02 CloseLabel        Like SqlStmtType    Value "Close".
       02 DeleteLabel       Like SqlStmtType    Value "Delete".
       02 OpenLabel         Like SqlStmtType    Value "Open".
       02 FetchLabel        Like SqlStmtType    Value "Fetch".
       02 UpdateLabel       Like SqlStmtType    Value "Update".
       02 InsertLabel       Like SqlStmtType    Value "Insert".

       02 InvActionLabel    Like TextType
                            Value "Invalid action".
       02 NoKeyLabel        Like TextType
                            Value "Key not found in table".
       02 DupeKeyLabel      Like TextType
                            Value "Duplicate key in table".

   01  ProgramErrorState        Like BooleanType Value B"0".
       88 NoProgramError                         Value B"0".
       88 ProgramError                           Value B"1".

   01  CustomerOpenState        Like BooleanType Value B"0".
       88 CustomerNotOpen                        Value B"0".
       88 CustomerOpen                           Value B"1".

   01  CustUpdOpenState         Like BooleanType Value B"0".
       88 CustUpdNotOpen                         Value B"0".
       88 CustUpdOpen                            Value B"1".

   01  CustUpdNoMoreRowsState Like BooleanType Value B"1".
       88 CustUpdMoreRows                        Value B"0".
       88 CustUpdNoMoreRows                      Value B"1".

  * - - - - - - - - - - - - - - - - - - - - - - - - - - - - - - -
  * - - - - - - - - - - - - - - - - - - - - - - - - - - - - - - -
   Procedure Division.

  * Table cursor definitions

       Exec SQL

         Declare CustomerTable  Cursor
           With Hold
           For  Select          *
                  From          Customer
                  Where         CustID = :Customer.CustID
                  For Update of CustomerName
       End-Exec.


       Exec SQL

         Declare CustUpdTable Cursor
           With Hold
           For  Select          *
                  From          CustUpd
                  Order by      CustID,
                                SeqNbr
                  For Update of RowAction
       End-Exec.

  * - - - - - - - - - - - - - - - - - - - - - - - - - - - - - - -
```

continued

Figure 15.3 *Continued*

```
 MainBlock.

     Perform OpenTables.

     Perform ProcessNextCustomer
       Until CustUpdNoMoreRows Or ProgramError.

     Perform CloseTables.

     GoBack.
* - - - - - - - - - - - - - - - - - - - - - - - - - - - - - - -
 OpenTables.

* Don't open the CustomerTable cursor here, because it will
* be opened and closed for each update.

     Perform OpenCustUpdTable.

* - - - - - - - - - - - - - - - - - - - - - - - - - - - - - - -
 OpenCustomerTable.

     Exec SQL
       Open CustomerTable
     End-Exec.

     If SqlState = SqlStateOK
        Set CustomerOpen to True
     Else
        Set CustomerNotOpen to True

        Call SqlErrPgm Using by Content
             OpenLabel
             CustomerTableName
             SqlState
             ProgramErrorState
     End-If.
* - - - - - - - - - - - - - - - - - - - - - - - - - - - - - - -
 OpenCustUpdTable.

     Exec SQL
       Open CustUpdTable
     End-Exec.

     If SqlState = SqlStateOK
        Set CustUpdOpen     to True
        Set CustUpdMoreRows to True
     Else
        Set CustUpdNotOpen    to True
        Set CustUpdNoMoreRows to True

        Call SqlErrPgm Using by Content
             OpenLabel
             CustUpdTableName
             SqlState
             ProgramErrorState
     End-If.
* - - - - - - - - - - - - - - - - - - - - - - - - - - - - - - -
```

continued

Figure 15.3 ***Continued***

```
 CloseTables.

* Close table(s) that are currently open.

     If CustomerOpen
       Perform CloseCustomerTable
     End-If.

     If CustUpdOpen
       Perform CloseCustUpdTable
     End-If.

* - - - - - - - - - - - - - - - - - - - - - - - - - - - - - - -
 CloseCustomerTable.

* Set the Customer table state to "closed" in all cases, so the
* error handling for an error on the close doesn't attempt
* another close.

     Set CustomerNotOpen to True.

     Exec SQL
       Close CustomerTable
     End-Exec.

     If SqlState Not = SqlStateOK
        Call SqlErrPgm Using by Content
             CloseLabel
             CustomerTableName
             SqlState
             ProgramErrorState
     End-If.

* - - - - - - - - - - - - - - - - - - - - - - - - - - - - - - -
 CloseCustUpdTable.

* Set the CustUpd table state to "closed" in all cases, so the
* error handling for an error on the close doesn't attempt
* another close.

     Set CustUpdNotOpen    to True.
     Set CustUpdNoMoreRows to True.

     Exec SQL
       Close CustUpdTable
     End-Exec.

     If SqlState Not = SqlStateOK
        Call SqlErrPgm Using by Content
             CloseLabel
             CustUpdTableName
             SqlState
             ProgramErrorState
     End-If.

* - - - - - - - - - - - - - - - - - - - - - - - - - - - - - - -
 ProcessNextCustomer.

* Read a CustUpd row, and dispatch on its action code.
```

continued

Figure 15.3 *Continued*

```
*
* Each action-handling routine attempts to perform the action
* and then changes the action code to indicate either
* successful completion or an error. The modified CustUpd
* row is then rewritten.

     Exec SQL
       Fetch Next
         From  CustUpdTable
         Into :CustUpd
     End-Exec.

     Evaluate True
         When SqlState = SqlStateOK
                Perform DoTransactionForCurCustomer
                If NoProgramError
                   Perform UpdateCustUpd
                End-If
         When SqlState = SqlStateNoRowFnd
                Set CustUpdNoMoreRows to True
         When Other
                Call SqlErrPgm Using by Content
                     FetchLabel
                     CustUpdTableName
                     SqlState
                     ProgramErrorState
     End-Evaluate.
* - - - - - - - - - - - - - - - - - - - - - - - - - - - - - - -
 DoTransactionForCurCustomer.

     Evaluate RowAction of CustUpd
         When AddAction        Perform AddCustomer
         When ChangeAction     Perform ChangeCustomer
         When DeleteAction     Perform DeleteCustomer
         When CompletedAction Continue
         When ErrorAction      Continue
         When Other Call ActionErrPgm Using by Content
                         InvActionLabel
                         RowAction of CustUpd
                         CustID    of CustUpd
     End-Evaluate.
* - - - - - - - - - - - - - - - - - - - - - - - - - - - - - - -
 AddCustomer.

     Move CustId of CustUpd to
          CustId of Customer.

     Move CustomerName of CustUpd to
          CustomerName of Customer.

     Exec SQL
       Insert Into Customer
         Values(  :Customer )
     End-Exec.
```

continued

Figure 15.3 *Continued*

```
     Evaluate True
         When SqlState = SqlStateOK
                Move CompletedAction to RowAction of CustUpd
         When SqlState = SqlStateDupKey
                Perform DupeKeyErr
         When Other
                Call SqlErrPgm Using by Content
                     InsertLabel
                     CustomerTableName
                     SqlState
                     ProgramErrorState
     End-Evaluate.

* - - - - - - - - - - - - - - - - - - - - - - - - - - - - - -
 ChangeCustomer.

* Attempt to fetch the specified Customer row, change its
* data (i.e., name), and update the row.
*
* It would be as fast or faster to use a searched Update
* (instead of a Fetch and positioned Update), similar to the
* way the DeleteCustomer paragraph (below) is implemented.
* This example uses a positioned Update to demonstrate the
* technique.

     Move CustId of CustUpd to
          CustId of Customer.

     Perform OpenCustomerTable.

     If CustomerOpen

        Exec SQL
          Fetch Next
            From  CustomerTable
            Into :Customer
        End-Exec

        Evaluate True
          When SqlState = SqlStateOK
                 Move CustomerName of CustUpd to
                      CustomerName of Customer

                 Perform UpdateCustomer
          When SqlState = SqlStateNoRowFnd
                 Perform NoKeyErr
          When Other
                 Call SqlErrPgm Using by Content
                      FetchLabel
                      CustomerTableName
                      SqlState
                      ProgramErrorState
       End-Evaluate

        Perform CloseCustomerTable
     End-If.
* - - - - - - - - - - - - - - - - - - - - - - - - - - - - - -
```

continued

Figure 15.3 *Continued*

```
 UpdateCustomer.

* Note that a No Row Found condition indicates an unexpected
* error because the row was just read with the same key.

     Exec SQL
       Update  Customer
         Set   CustomerName = :Customer.CustomerName
         Where Current of CustomerTable
     End-Exec.

     If SqlState = SqlStateOK
        Move CompletedAction to RowAction of CustUpd
     Else
        Call SqlErrPgm Using by Content
             UpdateLabel
             CustomerTableName
             SqlState
             ProgramErrorState
     End-If.
* - - - - - - - - - - - - - - - - - - - - - - - - - - - - - -
 DeleteCustomer.

* Use a positioned Delete.

     Exec SQL
       Delete From Customer
         Where     CustID = :CustUpd.CustID
     End-Exec.

     Evaluate True
         When SqlState = SqlStateOK
                Move CompletedAction to RowAction of CustUpd
         When SqlState = SqlStateNoRowFnd
                Perform NoKeyErr
         When Other
                Call SqlErrPgm Using by Content
                     DeleteLabel
                     CustomerTableName
                     SqlState
                     ProgramErrorState
     End-Evaluate.
* - - - - - - - - - - - - - - - - - - - - - - - - - - - - - -
 UpdateCustUpd.

     Exec SQL
       Update  CustUpd
         Set   RowAction = :CustUpd.RowAction
         Where Current of CustUpdTable
     End-Exec.

     If SqlState Not = SqlStateOK
        Call SqlErrPgm Using by Content
             UpdateLabel
             CustUpdTableName
             SqlState
             ProgramErrorState
     End-If.

* - - - - - - - - - - - - - - - - - - - - - - - - - - - - - -
```

continued

Figure 15.3 *Continued*

```
 DupeKeyErr.

     Call ActionErrPgm Using by Content
          DupeKeyLabel
          RowAction of CustUpd
          CustID    of CustUpd.

     Move ErrorAction to RowAction of CustUpd.

* - - - - - - - - - - - - - - - - - - - - - - - - - - - - - -
* - - - - - - - - - - - - - - - - - - - - - - - - - - - - - -
 NoKeyErr.

     Call ActionErrPgm Using by Content
          NoKeyLabel
          RowAction of CustUpd
          CustID    of CustUpd.

     Move ErrorAction to RowAction of CustUpd.

* - - - - - - - - - - - - - - - - - - - - - - - - - - - - - -
* - - - - - - - - - - - - - - - - - - - - - - - - - - - - - -

 Id Division.

   Program-Id. SqlErr.
*  Purpose:    Handle an unexpected SQL error.
*              Emit an error message, close tables,
*              and set ProgramErrorState to True.

*------------------------------------------------------------
 Data Division.
 Working-Storage Section.


 Linkage Section.

 01  SqlStmt              Like SqlStmtType.
 01  TableName            Like AS400NameType.
 01  SqlState             Like SqlStateType.
 01  ProgramErrorState Like BooleanType.
     88 ProgramError      Value B"1".

 Procedure Division Using SqlStmt
                          TableName
                          SqlState
                          ProgramErrorState.

 MainBlock.

     Display "SQL error " SqlState
             " on "       SqlStmt
             " for "      TableName  " table.".

     Set ProgramError to True.

     GoBack.

 End Program SqlErr.
* - - - - - - - - - - - - - - - - - - - - - - - - - - - - - -
```

continued

Figure 15.3 ***Continued***

```
* - - - - - - - - - - - - - - - - - - - - - - - - - - - - - -

 Id Division.

   Program-Id. ActionErr.
*  Purpose:    Handle an action error.
*              Emit an error message.

*-----------------------------------------------------------------
 Data Division.

 Linkage Section.

 Ø1  ErrorText   Like TextType.
 Ø1  Action      Pic X(1).
 Ø1  CustID      Pic S9(9) Binary.

 Procedure Division Using ErrorText
                          Action
                          CustID.

 MainBlock.

     Display "Error for customer " CustID
             " on '"               Action
             "' action: '"         ErrorText "'.".

     GoBack.

 End Program ActionErr.

* - - - - - - - - - - - - - - - - - - - - - - - - - - - - - -
* - - - - - - - - - - - - - - - - - - - - - - - - - - - - - -

 End Program UpdCust.
```

Coding Suggestions

- When using an implicit column list in a cursor's Select statement or in a Select Into statement, use the ILE COBOL/400 format-2 Copy directive to include an externally described data structure for the host variable to hold the contents of retrieved results.
- Use an 01-level Mnemonics group item as shown in this chapter's CustUpd program to create meaningful names for the discrete values used for SqlState and other coded values used in the program. Use an Include or Copy member to hold constant declarations for the complete set of SqlState values as well as any declarative or executable code that you need to use repeatedly.

- Create standard SQL (and other) error-handling routines that can be invoked after executing an embedded SQL statement. These can be callable as external programs or included in the source via the ILE COBOL/400 Copy directive or the SQL Include statement. As an alternative, consider placing these routines into service programs to ease maintenance and common access.

Exercises

1. Show the cursor declaration changes necessary to exclude previously processed rows (whether successful or not) from the CustUpdTable cursor.
2. Show the embedded SQL statement that would have applied all of the RowAction = 'A' transactions in a single statement. What would be the drawback to this single-statement approach?

Chapter 16

Additional Database Topics

Chapter Overview

In this chapter, we cover some additional database programming topics that a professional SQL/400 developer ultimately must master. We begin with a discussion of file overrides. In particular, we explain the way overrides can be used in an SQL environment. Database triggers are introduced, including a sample RPG IV trigger program. A technique for soft coding the trigger buffer in RPG IV is explained. We discuss the interaction and ramifications of using triggers and constraints together. And we touch briefly on distributed database support as well as DRDA, ODBC, JDBC, and Net.Data.

File Overrides

On the AS/400, a **file override** provides a way to redirect file access or to specify a runtime change to one or more file-access properties. You specify a file override by executing an OvrDbF (Override with Database File) CL command. File overrides are commonly used with applications that use built-in HLL I/O statements to access physical and logical files; however, you can also use file overrides with applications that use SQL to access tables and views. In this section, we focus on file overrides as they apply to SQL/400 access.

One of the common uses of the OvrDbF command is to redirect an unqualified table name from its default collection (or library) to a different one. Recall from Chapter 13 the role of the system or SQL naming option and various CrtSql*Xxx* command parameters (e.g., DftRdbCol) in determining which collection(s) are searched for unqualified table and view names. With the OvrDbF command, you can explicitly direct the system to resolve a name to a particular collection:

```
OvrDbF  File( Customer )
        ToFile( AppDta/CustName )

Call    Pgm( ListCust )
```

When this OvrDbF command is executed before the ListCust program is called, UDB/400 opens the AppDta/CustName table when the ListCust program accesses the Customer table.

As this example shows, an important use of overrides is to let a single program work with a variety of tables, views, and file members. The File parameter specifies the system name (i.e., the short name, as explained in Chapter 3) of the table or view within the program, and the ToFile parameter specifies the OS/400 file to be opened. (Recall that SQL tables and views are implemented as OS/400 database files.) You can also use an OvrDbF command to specify that a specific file member be opened:

```
OvrDbF  File( Customer )
        ToFile( AppDta/CustName )
        Mbr( OldCust )

Call    Pgm( ListCust )
```

Redirecting to a specific member is generally useful only when working with non-SQL files because SQL tables and views have only a single member. By default, UDB/400 opens the first (and possibly only) member when no Mbr parameter is specified.

A table override also lets you temporarily change some of a table's attributes when the table is opened. UDB/400 recognizes the following OvrDbF parameters for SQL/400 access:

- File — table or view system name to be overridden
- ToFile — OS/400 file to open
- Mbr — file member to open
- InhWrt — inhibit insert, update, and delete operations
- SeqOnly — process rows sequentially
- NbrRcds — number of records transferred as a unit from disk to memory
- WaitRcd — seconds to wait for a row lock
- OvrScope — scope of the override
- Secure — prevent merged overrides

For example, the following command specifies that UDB/400 should ignore row insert, update, and delete operations to the Customer table after it is opened.

```
OvrDbF  File( Customer )
        ToFile( AppTst/Customer )
        InhWrt( *Yes )
```

The InhWrt(*Yes) attribute lets you run a program that makes changes to the Customer table without the changes actually occurring.[1] Appendix B lists all the OvrDbF command's parameters; in this section, we look more closely at a few of these.

The OvrDbF command causes only temporary effects. The attributes on a table override apply only for table access in the job in which the override is executed; other jobs running concurrently are not affected by a different job's overrides. All the overrides still in effect when a job ends are deleted when the job ends (they may be deleted sooner).

Although you can use an OvrDbF command interactively, for most production applications OvrDbF commands are usually coded in CL programs[2] before calling an HLL application program that opens the table specified in the File parameter (as in the example above). An OvrDbF command applies only to tables opened after the command is executed; tables already opened are not affected, even if a table name is the same as the one specified on the OvrDbF command's File parameter.

The SeqOnly parameter specifies that multiple records (rows) should be transferred as a block into the program's internal buffer storage for a cursor opened for sequential, read-only processing. This parameter can also specify blocking for multirow Insert operations. Blocking can improve performance for some high-volume sequential-processing applications. The following example specifies a block size of 100 records for the Customer table when the table is opened for sequential input or output:

```
OvrDbF  File( Customer )
        SeqOnly( *Yes 100 )
```

1 With InhWrt(*Yes), UDB/400 lets your program execute any insert, update, and delete operations to the table, but UDB/400 just throws the changes in the "bit bucket," letting you test a program without changing the target table. We don't advise using InhWrt(*Yes) as a means to run tests on production tables. The danger is that you may omit the InhWrt parameter on the OvrDbF command or the attribute may be changed by another level of override. Notice how this example specifies the AppTst (test) library as the library containing the table that's opened. You can also use the job's library list to control which version — test or production — of a table is opened by a program when *Libl is specified for the table's library.

2 CL, which stands for Control Language, comprises the command interface to OS/400. CL commands can be compiled into programs. A common use of CL programs is to perform preliminary setup (such as executing override commands) and then call an HLL application.

If you specify SeqOnly(*Yes) without an explicit block size, UDB/400 calculates a block size.

The NbrRcds parameter specifies the blocking size for an earlier stage of the I/O process — when data is actually transferred from auxiliary storage (disk) to memory. In general, you should let the system determine this block size; however, for some high-volume sequential processes, you may be able to improve performance by experimenting with different NbrRcds values.[3]

The WaitRcd parameter specifies the maximum number of seconds that UDB/400 waits to obtain a row lock (as discussed in Chapter 13) before returning an error. The default for SQL tables and views is 60 seconds. You can also specify *Immed for no wait or *NoMax for an unlimited wait.

Override Scope

When you execute an OvrDbF command, you can specify one of the following values for the OvrScope parameter to indicate the **override scope**:

- *CallLvl
- *ActGrpDfn (the default scope)
- *Job

A *CallLvl (call level) scope means that the override is in effect for any tables or views subsequently opened by the same program or any program at a higher call level.[4] OS/400 deletes a call-level override when the program that executed it returns to its caller or when you execute an appropriate DltOvr command to explicitly delete the override. To illustrate, the following diagram shows the call-level scope of the Customer table override.

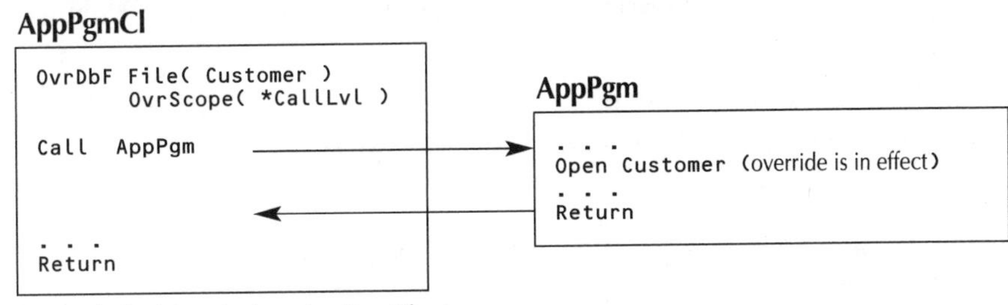

Override is deleted when AppPgmCl returns

You can see from this diagram why you normally execute an OvrDbF command in a CL program and then call an HLL application program that opens the table that you've overridden. Don't make the mistake of having the HLL program call a CL program to execute the override before you open a table in your HLL program, as in the diagram on the next page:

3 The NbrRcds parameter is ignored for SQL access in V4R3 and earlier releases. A program temporary fix (PTF) must be installed for V4R4 to recognize NbrRcds for SQL access.

4 The first program in a job's invocation stack has call level 1, the next program in the stack has call level 2, and so on. Thus, if a job's current program stack starts with PgmA, which calls PgmB, which calls PgmC, the three programs' call levels would be 1, 2, and 3, respectively.

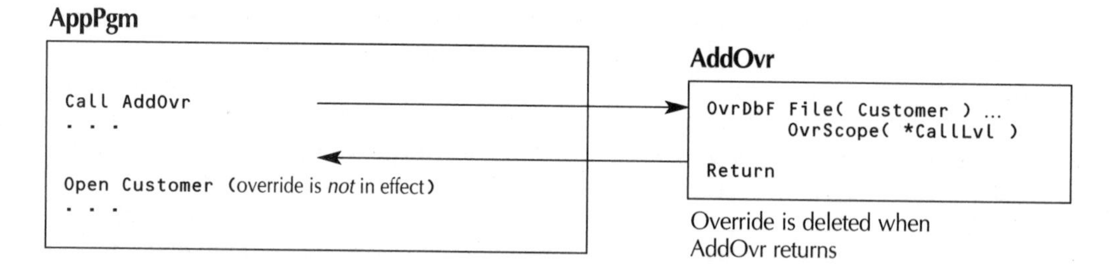

This approach won't do any good with call-level scope because the override established by the AddOvr CL program is deleted when AddOvr returns to the application program.[5]

The OvrScope parameter's default *ActGrpDfn (activation group definition) option determines the override scope based on the type of Integrated Language Environment (ILE) activation group.[6] If you execute an OvrDbF command with OvrScope(*ActGrpDfn) while in the job's default activation group, the effect is the same as with OvrScope(*CallLvl). If you execute the OvrDbF command while in a nondefault activation group, the override is in effect for any tables subsequently opened by any program in the same activation group. OS/400 deletes the override when the activation group ends or when you execute an appropriate DltOvr command to delete the override explicitly.

The OvrScope parameter's *Job option specifies that the override is in effect for any tables subsequently opened by any program in the same job. OS/400 deletes the override when the job ends or when you execute an appropriate DltOvr command to delete the override explicitly.

Merging Overrides

For each table name specified on the OvrDbF command's File parameter, OS/400 limits the overrides to the following:

- one override per table at each call level in the job
- one override per table for each nondefault activation group in the job
- one job scope override per table

This means multiple overrides may apply when a table is opened. If that's the case, OS/400 merges the overrides for the table as follows:

1. call-level overrides starting at the current call level and working back to the lowest call level in the same activation group
2. activation-group–level overrides
3. call-level overrides for all call levels below the lowest call level in the activation group (from highest to lowest)
4. job-level overrides

5 To override a file from within an HLL program, you can call the IBM-supplied QCmdExc program and pass it a string containing an OvrDbF command. OS/400 treats the QCmdExc program as a special case and leaves a call-level scoped override in effect until the program that called QCmdExc returns. The effect is the same as if the program that called QCmdExc executed the OvrDbF command directly.

6 An activation group is an ILE substructure of a job. All jobs have a default activation group. You can also create programs to run in other, named activation groups (nondefault activation groups). One purpose of activation groups is to insulate file opens in an application running in its own activation group from file opens in a different application running in a different activation group. When you specify OvrScope(*ActGrpDfn), the attributes on overrides in a nondefault activation group won't affect opens in a different activation group.

As each additional override is processed, any parameter values specified on the override's OvrDbF command replace the corresponding parameter values (if any) specified on previously merged overrides.

You can specify the Secure(*Yes) parameter on an OvrDbF command to stop OS/400 from merging further overrides after processing the override on which Secure(*Yes) is specified. This guarantees that the parameters you specify on the OvrDbF command won't be replaced by some previously entered OvrDbF command.

As OS/400 checks for the next override to merge, it looks for the most recent name specified on the ToFile parameter, if any. To see how this can affect which overrides are merged, consider an application program that opens the Customer table. OS/400 begins by looking for an override that was specified with File(Customer). If OS/400 finds an override added with the following command

```
OvrDbF  File( Customer )
        ToFile( CustName ) ...
```

then from that point on in the merging process described above, OS/400 checks for overrides for the CustName file — that is, ones that were specified with an OvrDbF File(CustName)... command, not ones specified with File(Customer).

In most cases, applications require nothing more complicated than a single override scoped to the call level or activation group. If you get into more complex situations, be sure you carefully analyze the way overrides are merged.

Deleting and Displaying Overrides

The DltOvr command deletes overrides. The following command deletes the override for the Customer table:

```
DltOvr  File( Customer )
```

Instead of a specific table name, you can specify *All to delete all file overrides. The DltOvr command has an optional Lvl parameter that parallels the OvrDbF command's OvrScope parameter. As it is for the OvrDbF command, the default value for this parameter is *ActGrpDfn, which limits the deleted overrides to those scoped to the current call level or to the current activation group (as explained for OvrScope(*ActGrpDfn)). The other values are an asterisk, or * (overrides are scoped to the current call level) and *Job (job scope overrides).

The DspOvr command displays the overrides currently in effect. You can view overrides individually as well as see the net effect of OS/400's merging of multiple overrides. For more information about file overrides, see the *Data Management* (V4R4 and earlier) or *File Management* (V4R5) manual.

Introduction to Database Triggers

A **trigger**, in general database terms, is a condition that causes some procedure to be executed. On the AS/400, a **trigger program** is a program that UDB/400 calls when an application program tries to insert, update, or delete a database record. You write and compile a trigger program just as you do any other HLL program and then use the AddPfTrg (Add Physical File Trigger) command to associate the trigger program with a table.

UDB/400 supports six trigger conditions for a table:

- before insert
- before update
- before delete
- after insert
- after update
- after delete

The AddPfTrg command associates a trigger program with one or more of these conditions for a physical file. When a trigger condition is true (i.e., right before or right after an insert, update, or delete event), UDB/400 automatically calls the trigger program you specify for the associated file and condition.

The advantage of trigger programs is that you can be sure the actions of the trigger program occur regardless of which application or system utility tries to change the table. You can use trigger programs to block table inserts, updates, and deletes that don't meet specified conditions, to propagate table updates to other tables, or to log changes to specific columns. Also, for row inserts and updates, a trigger program can change the row being inserted or updated. Thus, trigger programs provide an important tool to extend UDB/400 capabilities for enforcing database integrity and providing other database functions.

Implementing triggers is a two-step process: You code the trigger program and then associate it with one or more trigger conditions for a table. (The same trigger program can be used for multiple conditions or even for multiple tables.) Because the second step is simpler, we cover that first.

Suppose you've written a trigger program named CustChk to make additional integrity checks before permitting a row insert or update and you want to associate the trigger program with the Customer table. The following commands make the proper association:

```
AddPfTrg  File( AppDta/Customer )
          TrgTime( *Before )
          TrgEvent( *Insert )
          Pgm( AppExc/CustChk )
          RplTrg( *Yes )

AddPfTrg  File( AppDta/Customer )
          TrgTime( *Before )
          TrgEvent( *Update )
          Pgm( AppExc/CustChk )
          RplTrg( *Yes )
```

You can specify either *Before or *After for the TrgTime parameter. A trigger program that's called before file changes occur can perform actions before UDB/400 checks other constraints, such as foreign key constraints. Because a trigger program can itself perform file I/O, a before trigger program can take necessary actions to ensure that the constraints are satisfied. When you specify TrgTime(*After), UDB/400 calls the trigger program after the file is updated.[7]

The choices for the TrgEvent parameter are *Insert, *Update, and *Delete. You can specify any one of the six combinations of TrgTime and TrgEvent values on an AddPfTrg command. To associate the same program with multiple conditions, you use several AddPfTrg commands, as in the example above.

The RplTrg parameter determines whether the trigger program replaces an existing trigger program for the same file and condition. If you specify *No for this parameter, the AddPfTrg command fails if the specified condition already has an associated trigger program. Each of the six possible trigger conditions for a file can have only one trigger program.

An optional TrgUpdCnd parameter lets you specify *Change so that UDB/400 calls a trigger program for an update event only if the update is changing the contents of the row. Or, you can specify *Always (the default) to have UDB/400 call a trigger program for an update event whether or not the row is changed.

7 Recall from Chapter 4 that specifying On Delete No Action or On Update No Action for a foreign key constraint causes UDB/400 to check the constraint after any after-event trigger program has been called. Later in this section, we look at the details of how UDB/400 sequences database actions, including calling trigger programs and checking constraints.

Another optional parameter is AlwRepChg (Allow repeated change). Specifying AlwRepChg(*Yes) for a before-insert or before-update trigger lets the trigger program change the affected row by modifying the trigger buffer's after image (discussed later in this section) before the insert or update. Also, the AlwRepChg parameter determines whether an after-insert or after-update trigger program can directly update (i.e., by an SQL Update statement) the row that the application program is inserting or updating. With AlwRepChg(*No), which is the default, the trigger program can't perform I/O to the same row; with AlwRepChg(*Yes), it can.[8]

A trigger program must exist when you execute the AddPfTrg command, as well as when UDB/400 attempts to call it for subsequent file operations.[9] However, after associating a trigger program with a table, you can delete and re-create the program without having to re-execute the AddPfTrg command. You can use the RmvPfTrg (Remove Physical File Trigger) command to remove a trigger program for one or more trigger conditions. The following example shows how to remove the before-insert trigger program for the Customer table:

```
RmvPfTrg  File( AppDta/Customer )
          TrgTime( *Before )
          TrgEvent( *Insert )
```

The RmvPfTrg command's TrgTime and TrgEvent parameters allow the same values as the parameters for the AddPfTrg command, as well as *All for all times and/or events. Trigger programs can't be added or removed while a table is open.

UDB/400 also imposes two trigger program restrictions on a table with a foreign key constraint:

- A table with an On Delete Cascade foreign key rule can't have a before- or after-delete trigger program.
- A table with an On Delete Set Null or On Delete Set Default foreign key rule can't have a before- or after-update trigger program.

These restrictions prevent a cascaded delete or indirect update to a dependent table from firing a trigger program for that table. These restrictions are necessary because UDB/400 implements delete rule actions at a lower operating-system level than it does triggers, so a cascaded delete or indirect update can't fire a trigger program under the current UDB/400 architecture.

Coding a Trigger Program

You can code a trigger program in RPG IV, ILE COBOL/400, or another AS/400 HLL. The only requirement for a trigger program is that it have two parameters that conform to the IBM-defined interface for UDB/400 trigger programs. These two parameters provide the trigger buffer and the trigger buffer length. When UDB/400 calls a trigger program, it fills the trigger buffer with the before and/or after image of the affected row, along with some control information. UDB/400 also places the length of this buffer in the trigger buffer length parameter. The trigger program can use these parameters to inspect and — if AlwRepChg(*Yes) is specified for the trigger program — change the row's contents.

8 In most cases, it's preferable to update the trigger buffer with a before-event trigger program (rather than use an Update statement in an after-event trigger program) if you want to change the row that caused the trigger to be invoked.

9 If you omit the library or specify *Libl for the library on the Pgm parameter, the library list is searched for the program at the time the AddPfTrg command is executed. The name of the library in which the program is found is stored in the OS/400 file object's description so that subsequent calls to the trigger program are explicitly qualified. If you move a trigger program from one library to another, you must execute the AddPfTrg command to replace the trigger program with the program in the new library.

Figure 16.1 shows the layout of the trigger buffer.

Figure 16.1
Trigger Buffer Layout

Field	Description	Codes	Type	Length	Starting position
TbFile	File (table) name	—	Char	10	1
TbLib	Library (collection) name	—	Char	10	11
TbMbr	Member name	—	Char	10	21
TbTrgEvt	Trigger event	'1' = Insert '2' = Delete '3' = Update	Char	1	31
TbTrgTime	Trigger time	'1' = After '2' = Before	Char	1	32
TbCmtLvl	Commit lock level	'0' = *None '1' = *Chg '2' = *CS '3' = *All (or Repeatable Read)	Char	1	33
—	Reserved	—	Char	3	34
TbCcsId	Coded Character Set Identifier (CCSID)	—	Binary	4	37
TbRrn	Relative record number	—	Binary	4	41
	Reserved	—	Char	4	45
TbBfrOfs	Before row image offset	—	Binary	4	49
TbBfrLen	Before row image length	—	Binary	4	53
TbBfrNulOf	Before null column map offset	—	Binary	4	57
TbBfrNulLn	Before null column map length	—	Binary	4	61
TbAftOfs	After row image offset	—	Binary	4	65
TbAftLen	After row image length	—	Binary	4	69
TbAftNulOf	After null column map offset	—	Binary	4	73
TbAftNulLn	After null column map length	—	Binary	4	77
—	Reserved	—	Char	16	81
TbBfrRcd	Before row image (update and delete events)	—	Char	Varies (physical file record length)	Varies (TbBfrOfs)
TbBfrNul	Before null column map (update and delete events)	'0' = Not null '1' = Null	Char	Varies (equal to number of columns in the table)	Varies (TbBfrNulOf)

continued

Figure 16.1 ***Continued***

Field	Description	Codes	Type	Length	Starting position
TbAftRcd	After row image (insert and update events)	—	Char	Varies (physical file record length)	Varies (TbAftOfs)
TbAftNul	After null column map (insert and update events)	'0' = Not null '1' = Null	Char	Varies (equal to number of columns in the table)	Varies (TbAftNulOf)

The buffer starts with fixed-length fields that name and describe the table (i.e., physical file) and the trigger condition (event and time). The buffer ends with four variable-length fields that contain the before and after images of the row and null column maps for the images. Each null column map is a series of one-character flags that indicate whether the corresponding column (in the before or after image) is null ('1') or not null ('0').

Because different tables can have different numbers of columns and column sizes and, thus, the before and after image fields in the trigger buffer can vary in length, the starting positions of the images and the null column maps can vary as well.[10] The fixed part of the trigger buffer provides eight fields that contain the offsets and lengths of the four variable fields. An offset is the number of bytes from the start of the trigger buffer to the first byte of the field. Figure 16.2 depicts the trigger buffer layout and the relationship of the offset and length fields that describe the variable part of the buffer.

Figure 16.2
Depiction of Trigger Buffer Layout

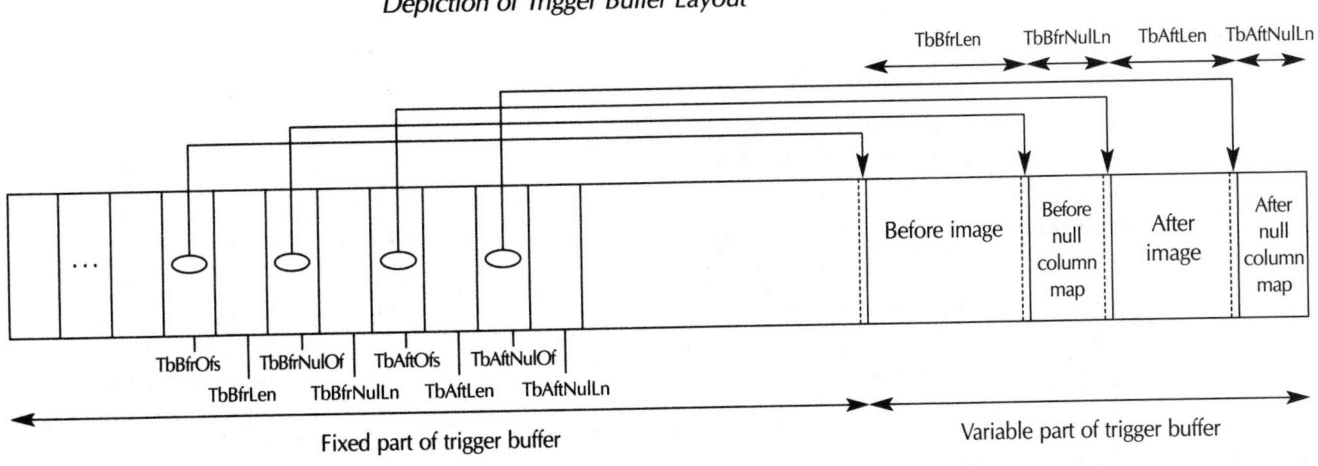

10 One implication is that when adding, deleting, or changing columns in a table definition, you must be sure to keep any trigger programs associated with the table up-to-date. In particular, the layout of the trigger buffer parameter must accurately reflect the OS/400 physical record format for the table. You can use RPG externally described data structures or ILE COBOL/400 Copy-DDS-. . . compiler directives to help keep your trigger programs synchronized with your tables. Later in the chapter, we look at a technique for soft coding the trigger buffer's before and after image layouts.

For a simplified Customer table, such as the one defined in Figure 16.3, the starting positions and lengths are as follows:

Field	Starting position	Length
Before image	97	38
Before null column map	135	3
After image	138	38
After null column map	176	3

Figure 16.3
Customer Table

```
Create Table Customer
  ( CustID        Dec(   7, 0 ) Not Null,
    Name          Char( 30    ) Not Null,
    CrdLimit      Dec(   7, 0 ) Not Null,
  Primary Key ( CustID ) )
```

Using this information, we can code the definition of the trigger buffer parameter. Figure 16.4 shows a simple RPG IV trigger program (CustChk) that prevents setting a customer's credit limit to a negative value.

Figure 16.4
RPG IV Trigger Program CustChk

```
....1....+....2....+....3....+....4....+....5....+....6....+....7....
 * CustChk --      Sample trigger program to check for non-negative
 *                 values in the CrdLimit field in the Customer table.

 * Requirements: This trigger program must be associated only with
 * before-insert and before-update conditions. If associated with
 * other conditions (e.g., a delete event), errors may occur.

 * Data structure for trigger buffer parameter, including:
 *   The trigger buffer header fields (bytes 1-96)
 *   Before image fields     (prefix Bf)
 *   Before null column map (prefix Bn)
 *   After  image fields     (prefix Af)
 *   After  null column map (prefix An)

D TrgBuf            DS
D  TrgBufHdr                    96A
D  BfCustID                      7P 0
D  BfName                       30A
D  BfCrdLimit                    7P 0
D  BnCustID                      1A
D  BnName                        1A
D  BnCrdLimit                    1A
D  AfCustID                      7P 0
D  AfName                       30A
D  AfCrdLimit                    7P 0
D  AnCustID                      1A
D  AnName                        1A
D  AnCrdLimit                    1A
```

continued

Figure 16.4 *Continued*

```
....1....+....2....+....3....+....4....+....5....+....6....+....7....
 * Trigger buffer length parameter

D TrgBufLen       S                 9B 0

 * Constant

D CrdLmtMsg       C                      Const( 'CRDLMTMSG' )


 * - - - - - - - - - - - - - - - - - - - - - - - - - - - - - -
 * Main block

C     *Entry        PList
C                   Parm                    TrgBuf
C                   Parm                    TrgBufLen

 * Check after image value; valid only for insert and update events.

C                   If        AfCrdLimit < 0
C                     ExSr    CrdLmtErr
C                   EndIf

C                   Return

 * - - - - - - - - - - - - - - - - - - - - - - - - - - - - - -
 * Credit limit error

C     CrdLmtErr     BegSr

 * Call program to send escape message to caller of this trigger
 * program.

C                   Call (E)  CrdLmtMsg
C                     Parm                  AfCrdLimit

C                   EndSr
```

In this example, the only trigger buffer fields defined are the before and after image fields and null column maps. (The AfCrdLimit field is the only essential field; the others are coded to illustrate the trigger buffer layout.) This trigger program should be associated with the before-insert and before-update conditions. Figure 16.5 shows the comparable ILE COBOL/400 program.

Figure 16.5

ILE COBOL/400 Trigger Program CustChk

```
...1....+....2....+....3....+....4....+....5....+....6....+....7....
 Id division.

   Program-Id.    CustChk.
   Author.        Paul Conte.
   Date-Written.  05/01/2000.
*  Purpose:       Sample trigger program to check for non-negative
*                 values in the CrdLimit field in the Customer file.

*  Requirements: This trigger program must be associated only with
*  before-insert and before-update conditions. If associated with
*  other conditions (e.g., a delete event), errors may occur.
* - - - - - - - - - - - - - - - - - - - - - - - - - - - - - -
```

continued

Figure 16.5 *Continued*

```
...1....+....2....+....3....+....4....+....5....+....6....+....7....
 Data division.

 Working-Storage section.

 01  Mnemonics.
     02 CrdLmtMsgPgm      Pic  X(10)  Value "CRDLMTMSG".

 Linkage section.

 01  TriggerBuffer.
     02 Header            Pic  X(96).
     02 BeforeImage.
        03 CustId         Pic S9(7) Packed-Decimal.
        03 Name           Pic  X(30).
        03 CrdLimit       Pic S9(7) Packed-Decimal.
     02 BeforeNullFieldMap.
        03 CustId         Pic 1.
        03 Name           Pic 1.
        03 CrdLimit       Pic 1.
     02 AfterImage.
        03 CustId         Pic S9(7) Packed-Decimal.
        03 Name           Pic  X(30).
        03 CrdLimit       Pic S9(7) Packed-Decimal.
     02 AfterNullFieldMap.
        03 CustId         Pic 1.
        03 Name           Pic 1.
        03 CrdLimit       Pic 1.

 01  TriggerBufferLength Pic S9(9) Binary.


* - - - - - - - - - - - - - - - - - - - - - - - - - - - - - -
* - - - - - - - - - - - - - - - - - - - - - - - - - - - - - -
 Procedure division Using TriggerBuffer
                          TriggerBufferLength.

 MainBlock.

* Check after image value; valid only for insert and
* update events.

     If CrdLimit of AfterImage < 0
        Perform CrdLimitErr
     End-If.

     GoBack.
* - - - - - - - - - - - - - - - - - - - - - - - - - - - - - -
 CrdLimitErr.

* Call program to send escape message to caller of this
* trigger program.

     Call CrdLmtMsgPgm Using by Content
          CrdLimit of AfterImage.

 End program CustChk.
```

Both examples of the CustChk trigger program test the after image's credit limit column and, if it's less than zero, call the CrdLmtMsg CL program shown in Figure 16.6.[11]

Figure 16.6

CrdLmtMsg CL Program

```
/* CrdLmtMsg -- Send escape message to caller of CustChk trigger program */

Pgm Parm( &CrdLmt )

Dcl &CrdLmt     *Dec  ( 7 0 )    /* Input parameter                      */
Dcl &CrdLmtChr  *Char   8        /* Credit limit in character format     */
Dcl &MsgDta     *Char 256        /* Message data for escape message      */
Dcl &Blank      *Char   1       VALUE( ' ' )    /* Mnemonic              */

/* Convert credit limit to character, leave room for minus sign.         */
/* If error occurs, just use blank for the value in the message.         */

ChgVar     &CrdLmtChr  &CrdLmt
           MonMsg ( CPF9999 ) Exec( Do )
                  ChgVar &CrdLmtChr &Blank
           EndDo

ChgVar     &MsgDta ( 'Invalid credit limit value: ' *Cat &CrdLmtChr )


SndPgmMsg MsgId( CPF9898 )                                               +
           MsgF( QCpfMsg )                                               +
           ToPgmQ( *Prv ( CustChk ) )                                    +
           MsgDta( &MsgDta )                                             +
           MsgType( *Escape )

           MonMsg MsgId( CPF0000 MCH0000 ) /* Ignore error               */

Return
EndPgm
```

The CrdLmtMsg program sends an escape message to the program that called trigger program CustChk. UDB/400 handles this message and returns an error to the application program that attempted the I/O operation. In RPG IV, you can test for an error with the %Error built-in function. Also, the RPG IV file status value (which you can retrieve using the %Status built-in function) is set to '1023' for before-event trigger programs and to '1024' for after-event trigger programs. In ILE COBOL/400, the file status is set to "9T". In SQL/400, the SqlState variable is set to '38501'. Your application program should be designed to handle errors signaled by a trigger program just like other I/O errors.

11 The CrdLmtMsg program is intentionally shown as a single-purpose program to simplify this example. For a production application, you should use a more general-purpose approach. You can either use a CL program with appropriate parameters or call the OS/400 system API QMHSNDPM to send program messages.

Any messages sent by the trigger program normally appear in the job's message queue and can be received by the application program using the RcvMsg command or the QMHRCVPM system API. Sending messages from trigger programs involves a number of issues beyond the scope of this book; for details, see the IBM publication *DB2/400 Advanced Database Functions.*

Soft Coding the Trigger Buffer[12]

The example above provides an introduction to how a trigger program works, but in production applications, you can benefit from a somewhat more advanced set of programming techniques. The basic idea in the example we look at next is that the trigger buffer is soft coded so that changes to the physical file's record can be incorporated by simply recompiling the trigger program. This example also shows how RPG IV /Copy source members let you reuse standard source code for parts of your trigger programs.[13]

The sample trigger program uses three /Copy source members. The DtaType member (Figure 16.7) declares a set of RPG IV variables of various data types. These are used as the basis for other declarations in the program. The TrgDcl member (Figure 16.8) declares an RPG IV data structure for the trigger buffer parameter along with several other variables used with this technique. The TrgEntry member (Figure 16.9) declares the trigger program's parameter list and includes some initial setup code.

Figure 16.7

RPG IV /Copy Source Member DtaType

```
....1....+....2....+....3....+....4....+....5....+....6....+....7....
 * DTATYPE -- Standard data type definitions
 *
 * Note that the Based keyword is just a technique to
 * avoid any storage being allocated for the variables
 * because they're never referenced during execution.

D NulTypePtr      S               *

D TypeBin2        S              4B 0 Based( NulTypePtr )
D TypeBin4        S              9B 0 Based( NulTypePtr )
D TypeChr         S              1A   Based( NulTypePtr )
D TypeIdx         S              7P 0 Based( NulTypePtr )
D TypeLgl         S              1A   Based( NulTypePtr )
D TypeSysNam      S             10A   Based( NulTypePtr )
D TypePtr         S               *   Based( NulTypePtr )
D TypeQlfNam      S             20A   Based( NulTypePtr )
D TypeTxt         S             50A   Based( NulTypePtr )
```

12 The technique shown in this section was originally suggested by Julian Monypenny and published in "Before Pulling the Trigger in RPG IV," *NEWS/400*, April 1996. The material here is derived from that article and is used with permission.

13 Although space limitations prevent showing an ILE COBOL/400 program that uses the same techniques, ILE COBOL/400 has all the necessary language elements: the Copy compiler directive, pointers, and based variables. The implementation in ILE COBOL/400 corresponds closely to the example shown here.

Figure 16.8

RPG IV /Copy Source Member TrgDcl

```
....1....+....2....+....3....+....4....+....5....+....6....+....7....
 * TrgDcl -- Trigger program standard declarations
 *
 * Requires copy modules: DtaType

D TbBufDs         DS
D  TbFile                             Like( TypeSysNam )
D  TbLib                              Like( TypeSysNam )
D  TbMbr                              Like( TypeSysNam )
D  TbTrgEvt                           Like( TypeChr )
D  TbTrgTime                          Like( TypeChr )
D  TbCmtLvl                           Like( TypeChr )
D  TbReserve1                   3A
D  TbCcsId                            Like( TypeBin4 )
D  TbRrn                              Like( TypeBin4 )
D  TbReserve2                   4A
D  TbBfrOfs                           Like( TypeBin4 )
D  TbBfrLen                           Like( TypeBin4 )
D  TbBfrNulOf                         Like( TypeBin4 )
D  TbBfrNulLn                         Like( TypeBin4 )
D  TbAftOfs                           Like( TypeBin4 )
D  TbAftLen                           Like( TypeBin4 )
D  TbAftNulOf                         Like( TypeBin4 )
D  TbAftNulLn                         Like( TypeBin4 )

D* -- End of TbBufDs --

D TbBufLen        S                   Like( TypeBin4 )

D TbBfrPtr        S                   Like( TypePtr )
D TbAftPtr        S                   Like( TypePtr )

D TbEvtIns        C                   Const( '1' )
D TbEvtDlt        C                   Const( '2' )
D TbEvtUpd        C                   Const( '3' )
D TbTimeBfr       C                   Const( '2' )
D TbTimeAft       C                   Const( '1' )
```

Figure 16.9

RPG IV /Copy Source Member TrgEntry

```
....1....+....2....+....3....+....4....+....5....+....6....+....7....
 * TrgEntry -- Trigger program standard entry and setup code
 *
 * Requires copy module: TrgDcl
 *
 * Side effects:
 *   Sets TbBfrPtr   Pointer to before image in trigger buffer
 *   Sets TbAftPtr   Pointer to after  image in trigger buffer

 * - - - - - - - - - - - - - - - - - - - - - - - - - - - - - -
C     *Entry        PList
C                   Parm                    TbBufDs
C                   Parm                    TbBufLen

C                   Eval      TbBfrPtr = %Addr( TbBufDs ) + TbBfrOfs
C                   Eval      TbAftPtr = %Addr( TbBufDs ) + TbAftOfs
```

The CustLog trigger program (Figure 16.10) uses three /Copy directives to incorporate the standard code into the program. CustLog is a simple program that checks to see whether the value of the customer credit limit has been changed and, if it has, calls another program (not shown) to write the change to a log file.

Figure 16.10

RPG IV Trigger Program CustLog

```
....1....+....2....+....3....+....4....+....5....+....6....+....7....
 * CustLog --     Sample trigger program to log changes to
 *                CrdLimit column in the Customer table.

 * Standard data types and trigger program declarations

 /Copy DtaType
 /Copy TrgDcl

 * Data structures to provide templates for before and after images

D BfCustomer    E DS                    ExtName( Customer )
D                                       Prefix ( Bf )
D                                       Based( TbBfrPtr )

D AfCustomer    E DS                    ExtName( Customer )
D                                       Prefix ( Af )
D                                       Based( TbAftPtr )

 * Mnemonics and constants

D CrdLimit0       S                     Like( BfCrdLimit )
D                                       Inz( 0 )

D LogCrdChg       C                     Const( 'LOGCRDCHG' )


 * - - - - - - - - - - - - - - - - - - - - - - - - - - - - - -
 * Entry point and setup code

 /Copy TrgEntry

 * Dispatch on event (insert, update, or delete).

C                   Select
C                     When    TbTrgEvt = TbEvtIns
C                       ExSr  InsRcdEvt

C                     When    TbTrgEvt = TbEvtUpd
C                       ExSr  UpdRcdEvt

C                     When    TbTrgEvt = TbEvtDlt
C                       ExSr  DltRcdEvt
C                   EndSl

C                   Return

 * - - - - - - - - - - - - - - - - - - - - - - - - - - - - - -
```

continued

Figure 16.10 *Continued*

```
....1....+....2....+....3....+....4....+....5....+....6....+....7....
C     InsRcdEvt     BegSr

 * Log first credit limit assigned to new customer.
 * Use after image (new record) for customer ID and
 * zero for "before" credit limit.

C                   Call (E)  LogCrdChg
C                     Parm                  AfCustId
C                     Parm                  CrdLimit0
C                     Parm                  AfCrdLimit

C                   EndSr

 * - - - - - - - - - - - - - - - - - - - - - - - - - - - - - -
C     UpdRcdEvt     BegSr

 * Log changed credit limit for customer.
 * Use before image (old record) for customer ID.

C                   If        AfCrdLimit <> BfCrdLimit
C                    Call (E) LogCrdChg
C                      Parm                 BfCustId
C                      Parm                 BfCrdLimit
C                      Parm                 AfCrdLimit
C                   EndIf

C                   EndSr

 * - - - - - - - - - - - - - - - - - - - - - - - - - - - - - -
C     DltRcdEvt     BegSr

 * Log last credit limit assigned to customer being deleted.
 * Use before image (old record) for customer ID and
 * zero for "after" credit limit.

C                   Call (E)  LogCrdChg
C                     Parm                  BfCustId
C                     Parm                  BfCrdLimit
C                     Parm                  CrdLimit0

C                   EndSr
```

The CustLog trigger program declares two externally defined record structures (BfCustomer and AfCustomer). Notice that the Prefix keyword is used on the declarations to provide a unique two-character prefix for every field name (e.g., Bf for the before image fields and Af for the after image fields). The trigger program picks up the layouts for the trigger buffer's before and after images from these declarations. For any table's trigger program, you must code similar declarations that refer to the table with which the trigger program is associated.

Both declarations use the Based keyword, which specifies that a declaration is a template for storage that begins at the address contained in the pointer variable coded as the Based keyword argument. As a result, the compiler won't allocate storage for the BfCustomer data structure but instead treats whatever storage starts at the address in TbBfrPtr as if it were the data structure. Obviously, this requires the program to place an appropriate address in the TbBfrPtr variable before referencing any of the data structure's subfields. The same considerations apply to the AfCustomer data structure and the TbAftPtr variable. In a moment, we look at how these two pointer variables are set.

Following the data structure declarations, two /Copy directives incorporate the DtaType and TrgDcl source members. The declarations in the TrgDcl member (Figure 16.8) include the TbBufDs data structure, which has subfields for the fixed portions of the trigger buffer. This declaration corresponds to the layout described in Figure 16.1. Two crucial subfields of the TbBufDs data structure are TbBfrOfs and TbAftOfs, which are used in the calculation of the address of the before and after images described shortly. The subfield declarations use RPG IV's Like keyword to specify each subfield's data type using one of the standard data types declared in the DtaType source member (Figure 16.7).

The rest of the declarations in TrgDcl include the trigger buffer length parameter (TbBufLen), the two pointers discussed earlier, and constants for the codes UDB/400 uses for the trigger event and time fields in the trigger buffer.

Looking back at Figure 16.10, the next /Copy directive incorporates the code from the TrgEntry source member (Figure 16.9). This code declares the program's entry point with the two parameters — TbBufDs and TbBufLen — required by UDB/400. The copied code sets the two pointers. The TbBfrPtr pointer variable is set to the address of the first byte in the before image part of the trigger buffer parameter. This is done by adding the offset to the before image (TbBfrOfs) to the address of the buffer itself (using the %Addr built-in function to obtain the trigger buffer address). A similar calculation is done to set the TbAftPtr pointer variable. After these two pointers are set, subsequent statements in the trigger program can refer to the subfields of the BfCustomer and AfCustomer data structures and the references will be to the appropriate fields in the trigger buffer.

The statements in the CustLog program's UpdRcdEvt subroutine illustrate this technique. If the after image credit limit isn't the same as the before image credit limit, the before image customer ID and the before and after image credit limit values are passed to the LogCrdChg program (not shown) to log the change.

With the techniques illustrated in this trigger program, when columns are added, deleted, or changed in the table, you need only recompile the trigger program to synchronize its declarations with the new row definition. This approach substantially reduces maintenance effort and the possibility of errors when you make these kinds of changes to your table.

Considerations for Using Trigger Programs

You should create trigger programs that perform their own I/O so they execute within the same ILE activation group and use the same commitment control environment as the application program.[14] With this approach, the application program executes all commit and rollback operations, and any I/O that the trigger program performs is included in the transaction managed by the application program.

Keep in mind that any I/O performed by a trigger program may in turn cause another trigger program to be called. You should carefully design your trigger programs so they don't result in infinite recursive calls of the same trigger program. Also be sure to properly handle all errors that might occur when a trigger program performs its own I/O.

In addition, you should be aware of the performance implications of trigger programs. Each call to a trigger program adds some overhead, of course. If you run trigger programs in the caller's activation group and don't deactivate them (e.g., if you leave the RPG IV LR indicator off when you return from a trigger program), the call overhead isn't large compared to the time the system takes for a database I/O operation. The biggest impact comes because UDB/400 doesn't use record blocking

14 For ILE HLLs (RPG IV, ILE COBOL/400, and ILE C), specify ActGrp(*Caller) when you create the program.

when you insert rows into a table with an insert-event trigger. This restriction is enforced so that the trigger program is called for each table insert, not just when the database tries to write a block of rows to the table. For batch jobs that sequentially insert large numbers of rows, unblocked access may be significantly slower than blocked access. You may want to consider locking a table and removing its insert-event trigger program(s) before executing a long-running batch job. After the batch job is completed, the trigger program(s) can be added to the table again and the table unlocked. Of course, you must be very careful that any program that runs while trigger programs are not in effect performs all the integrity checks or other operations that the trigger program(s) normally carry out. Because this technique complicates your application design, you should consider using it only when performance is critical.

Interaction of Triggers with Constraints

Because a trigger program can change the contents of a row before the row is inserted or updated, you must understand how UDB/400 times constraint enforcement to prevent a trigger program from making a change that would circumvent a constraint. (Chapter 4 explains primary key, unique, foreign key, and check constraints.) Also, any trigger program that takes actions based on a successfully completed database operation must be executed at the right time in the sequence of steps UDB/400 takes for each I/O.

The timing of UDB/400's I/O operation steps depends on whether the table is being accessed under OS/400 commitment control. We strongly recommend you use commitment control for all applications that update tables. Commitment control provides important all-or-none transaction integrity as well as automated recovery, as described in Chapter 13. Commitment control also provides stronger row-locking protocols than database access not under commitment control. The following discussion provides the essential timing information for accessing tables under commitment control.

Interaction of Insert Triggers with Constraints

The following steps describe the sequence of events when doing an insert to a table with an insert trigger and constraints defined for the table:

1. Call the before-insert trigger program.
2. Insert the new row, and perform checks (e.g., member full) other than constraints.
3. Call the after-insert trigger program.
4. Check all this table's foreign key constraints (i.e., for each foreign key constraint, make sure there's a matching value for the new row's foreign key in the parent table or that one or more of the foreign key column(s) is null).
5. Check the primary key, unique, and check constraints.

If the before-insert trigger program sends an escape message, the process stops. Likewise, if an error occurs during step 2, the process stops. If the after-insert trigger program sends an escape message or any constraint is violated, the inserted row is rolled back (i.e., removed from the table) using the active commitment control environment, and the process stops.

Notice several important implications of this sequence:

- The before-insert trigger program can change the new row's column values before any constraints are checked. This lets the trigger program fix invalid data and also assures that any changes are still subject to constraint enforcement.

- Either a before-insert or an after-insert trigger program can insert a parent table row, if necessary, to satisfy a foreign key constraint.
- Neither a before-insert nor an after-insert trigger program can be certain the row will be permanently inserted. A constraint violation or an application rollback operation (even after a successful insert) may block or roll back the insert. For this reason, it's generally a good idea for trigger programs that perform I/O to run in the same commitment control environment as the application. That way, the application's subsequent commit or rollback operation covers any I/O done by the trigger program as well.

Note

If you delve a little deeper into the internal workings of UDB/400, you find that UDB/400 actually checks primary key and unique constraints in two stages. Database index maintenance is performed right before the row is inserted into the table (i.e., after step 2). If the primary key or unique index has a duplicate key error, this exception is deferred and the duplicate key rechecked in the constraint validation on the last step (step 5). Despite this nuance, the steps as we've listed them above provide an accurate picture of the *effective* sequence of events. As far as your application is concerned, a primary key or unique constraint violation occurs only if the constraint fails in the final step. UDB/400 uses this two-stage approach for update operations as well.

Interaction of Update Triggers with Constraints

Here is the sequence of events when updating a single row in a table with an update trigger and constraints defined for the table:

1. Call the before-update trigger program.
2. Check foreign key constraints for all dependent tables that specify On Update Restrict (i.e., make sure that a change to a column in this row doesn't leave any "orphan" rows in a dependent table).
3. Update the row, and perform checks (e.g., invalid decimal data) other than constraints.
4. Call the after-update trigger program.
5. Check foreign key constraints for all dependent tables that specify On Update No Action.
6. Check all this table's foreign key constraints.
7. Check the primary key, unique, and check constraints.

Looking at this sequence, you can see one of the differences between the On Update Restrict and On Update No Action rules for a foreign key constraint. There's a subtle, but important, implication of the different times these constraints are checked. At present, UDB/400 doesn't support an On Update Cascade foreign key option for updates as it does for deletes. However, you can implement your own with an after-update trigger, as long as the foreign key specifies On Update No Action. For example, to change all the dependent rows' foreign key values when you change a parent row's primary key, you can have the after-update trigger perform updates to the dependent table. By the time step 5 checks the dependent table for unmatched rows, all the dependent rows will match the updated parent row.

Notice that you can't implement this approach using a before-update trigger program. Assume a before-update trigger program tries to change the dependent rows' foreign key values to the parent row's *new* primary key value. The parent row is not yet changed, and the dependent row updates are blocked because their new foreign key values don't match any parent row. As a consequence, because you must use an after-update trigger program to implement a cascading update, you also must use On Update No Action to defer the foreign key constraint check until the after-update program is completed.

An SQL Update statement can specify that multiple rows be updated in one statement execution. When you execute an Update statement without commitment control active, UDB/400 evaluates all constraints completely as each row is updated. When you execute an Update statement under commitment control, however, UDB/400 defers all primary key and unique constraint checking until *all* rows have been updated. UDB/400 also defers foreign key constraints, except those that specify a Restrict rule. Thus, for a multirow Update statement under commitment control, the process occurs in two stages. First, for each row to be updated, the following steps are performed:

1. Call the before-update trigger program.
2. Check foreign key constraints for all dependent tables that specify On Update Restrict.
3. Update the row, and perform checks (e.g., invalid decimal data) other than constraints.
4. Call the after-update trigger program.
5. Check check constraints.

Once this part of the process is completed, the following steps are performed for each updated row:

1. Check foreign key constraints for all dependent tables that specify On Update No Action.
2. Check all this table's foreign key constraints.
3. Check the primary key and unique constraints.

Although it would be unusual, an application could perform an SQL statement to update a set of rows' primary key column, as in the following example:

```
Update Customer
  Set  CustID = CustID + 1
```

This statement might succeed if the Customer table were the parent in a foreign key constraint that specified On Update No Action. However, it would almost certainly fail if the foreign key constraint specified On Update Restrict. To succeed with No Action specified, all dependent rows require a matching parent row at the end of the Update statement. In the case of Restrict, the requirement is that no individual Customer row update can leave any unmatched dependent rows — something that would require a very precise ordering of the Customer row updates to succeed.

Interaction of Delete Triggers with Constraints

This is the sequence of events when deleting a row from a table with a delete trigger and constraints defined for the table:

1. Call the before-delete trigger.
2. Check foreign key constraints for all dependent tables that specify On Delete Restrict constraints for this table (i.e., make sure that deleting a row in this table doesn't leave any "orphan" row in a dependent table).
3. Delete the row, and perform checks other than constraints.
4. Call the after-delete trigger.

5. Perform cascaded row deletions for all dependent tables that specify On Delete Cascade constraints for this table.
6. Update rows for all dependent tables that specify On Delete Set Null or On Delete Set Default constraints for this table.
7. Check the foreign key constraints for all dependent tables that specify On Delete No Action constraints for this table.

You can see that the sequence of steps for a delete operation is an expanded version of the steps for an update. The main additions are steps to handle the additional options (Cascade, Set Null, and Set Default) for the On Delete foreign key rule. Delete operations, of course, can never violate a primary key, unique, or check constraint, so these aren't part of the process.

When an On Delete Cascade constraint is processed (step 5), it's possible that a dependent table is the parent table in another table's On Delete Restrict foreign key constraint. Consider the example in Figure 16.11, in which table T1 is the parent of Table T2 in an On Delete Cascade constraint, and table T2 is the parent of table T3 in an On Delete Restrict constraint.

Figure 16.11
Three Tables with Related Delete Rule Actions

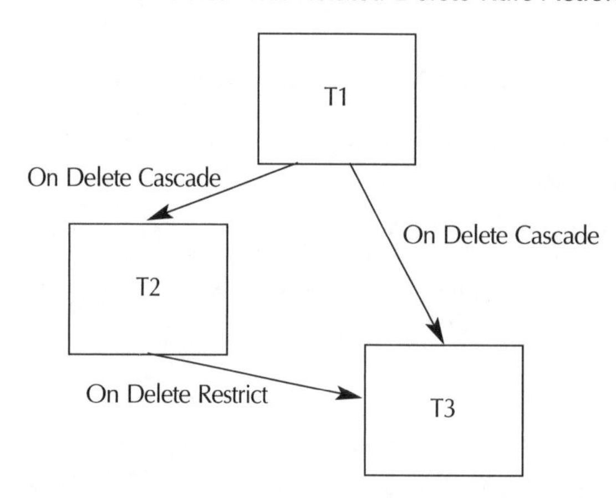

From step 2, above, you can see that an application cannot directly perform a delete operation on T2 if doing so would leave any orphan rows in T3. UDB/400 also prevents the completion of any delete operation to T1 if a resulting cascaded delete operation to T2 would leave orphan rows in T3. However, it's possible that T1 may also be the parent of table T3 in an On Delete Cascade constraint. That is, T3 would have two foreign key constraints: an On Delete Cascade constraint with T1 as the parent and an On Delete Restrict constraint with T2 as the parent. In this case, UDB/400 completes all the cascaded deletions in T2 and T3 before evaluating the T3 table's On Delete Restrict constraint with T2 as the parent. Similar logic governs On Delete Set Default and On Delete Set Null constraints.

In general, a delete operation is allowed as long as the final state of the database satisfies all foreign key constraints. There's one important exception: Any On Delete Restrict constraint for the main table (the one that the application is directly deleting rows from) is enforced immediately, one row at a time. Checking for an On Delete Restrict constraint is deferred until the end of the operation only when the constraint applies to cascaded deletions.

Distributed Database and DRDA

Distributed Relational Database Architecture (**DRDA**) is IBM's standard for interoperation among the DB2 UDB family of database management systems (DBMSs), including DB2 UDB for AS/400 and DB2 UDB on the mainframes, OS/2, Windows 2000 Server, and AIX. In addition to IBM's relational DBMS, many other vendors' relational DBMS products also use DRDA. To use DRDA from the AS/400, you must use SQL/400 because SQL is the common DRDA database access language.

An essential step in using DRDA is to identify remote databases to the system on which the application program runs. On the AS/400, you do this with an AddRdbDirE (Add Relational Database Directory Entry) command that adds an entry in the local system's relational database directory. The following example adds an entry for the EugBrnch database:

```
AddRdbDirE  RDB( EugBrnch )
            RmtLocName( EugBrnch )
            Text( 'Eugene branch office' )
```

Entries in the relational database directory identify the communications link and other optional attributes of the remote database.[15]

Within an application program, executing a statement on a remote system is simply a matter of executing a successful SQL Connect statement to connect to that system before executing the SQL statement (we'll look at an example shortly).

DRDA supports commitment control transactions that span operations on remote systems. Two levels of this support are available with UDB/400. DRDA-1 (remote unit of work support) lets a single transaction be on any one system, local or remote. You specify parameter RdbCnnMth(*RUW) on the CrtSql*Xxx* command to have the application program establish this type of remote connection when an SQL Connect statement is executed.

DRDA-2 (distributed unit of work support) lets a single transaction perform table updates on multiple systems, including the local system and/or remote systems. You specify RdbCnnMth(*DUW) on the CrtSql*Xxx* command to have the application program establish this type of remote connection when an SQL Connect statement is executed.

You should create SQL/400 application programs with the appropriate RdbCnnMth value for the types of transactions the program performs. The manual *DB2/400 Advanced Database Functions* provides additional information and examples of AS/400 applications that uses DRDA.

Accessing Remote Objects with SQL

Normally, all SQL statements in an AS/400 HLL program operate on base tables, views, and other SQL objects that are on the same system as the program that is executing. To operate on objects on a different system, you can use UDB/400's distributed database support by first establishing a connection to that system using a Connect statement[16] that names the database server (i.e., the remote database):

```
Connect To EugBrnch
```

Any statements executed after this sample connection is established operate on objects on the EugBrnch database.

15 In some cases, you may also need to use the AddRdbDirE command's Dev, Mode, and RmtNetID parameters to fully specify the appropriate connection to the remote system.

16 You can also have a program automatically establish a connection when it starts execution.

The Connect statement allows an optional user profile and password to be specified:

```
Connect To EugBrnch  User :UserName  Using :UserPassWd
```

To end a connection, you can execute either a Disconnect statement or a Release statement followed by a Commit or Rollback statement. The Disconnect statement is used when commitment control is not in effect for transactions involving the remote system. On the Disconnect statement, you can specify a currently connected system, the Current keyword to disconnect from the currently active connection, or the All keyword to disconnect from all connections. The following example disconnects the current connection:

```
Disconnect Current
```

When commitment control is in effect, a connection can't be ended until any pending database updates on the remote system are either committed or rolled back. Thus, you use a Release statement to indicate that the connection is no longer needed (except to complete the current transaction) and should be ended on the next Commit or Rollback operation or other implicit end to the current unit of work. The Release statement has the same options as the Disconnect statement; the following example shows how you would release all connections:

```
Release All
```

To switch among connections when several connections have been established, you use the Set Connection statement, specifying the name of the connection you want to make current. As with the other connection-related SQL statements, you can use a host variable for the database name:

```
Set Connection :CurDtaBase
```

To switch from a remote database to the local database, you use a Set Connection statement with the local database name.

To obtain information about the current connection, you can execute a Connect statement with no keywords or other arguments; the information is returned in the SQL communication area, or SQLCA (see Figure 13.3, page 231).

The following statements show how you could use UDB/400's distributed database capability to delete a customer row that's stored in the Customer table on an AS/400 identified as the EugBrnch database (we've omitted error handling for the Delete and Disconnect statements to simplify the example):

```
....1....+....2....+....3....+....4....+....5....+....6....
C/Exec SQL
C+                   Connect To EugBrnch
C/End-Exec
C                    If        SQLStt = '00000'
C                      ExSr    ExcSqlDlt
C                      ExSr    DiscnctEug
C                    Else
C                      ExSr    SqlError
C                    EndIf

C     ExcSqlDlt      BegSr
C/Exec SQL
C+                   Delete
C+                     From  Customer
C+                     Where CustID = :SlcCustID
C/End-Exec
C                    EndSr
```

continued

continued...

```
C       DiscnctEug      BegSr
C/Exec SQL
C+                      Disconnect EugBrnch
C/End-Exec
C                       EndSr
```

Note how this example checks for a successful connection before executing the Delete statement. Also note that this example is not using commitment control.

ODBC

Open Database Connectivity (**ODBC**) is a standard developed primarily by Microsoft for access to relational databases from Windows-based applications. The ODBC architecture is based on SQL but uses function calls rather than embedded SQL statements. Figure 16.12 (page 332) shows the main components of a Windows application that accesses a UDB/400 file using ODBC.

The ODBC driver manager is supplied by Microsoft and is a Windows dynamic link library (DLL) that contains functions that the application calls to connect to a database. Microsoft also supplies a program that lets you configure the ODBC driver manager and add one or more ODBC driver entries to the list of databases that the driver manager makes available.

The target DBMS vendor[17] supplies an ODBC driver (which is also a Windows DLL) that implements functions the ODBC driver manager calls to carry out the application's requests. For example, IBM provides an ODBC driver for UDB/400 as part of the Client Access family of products.

When an application uses ODBC, the first step is to call a function of the driver manager to connect to a specified database. The driver manager uses a list of available databases, each with a unique name. The application can supply one of these names for the connection, or the driver manager can display a list of available DBMSs and let the end user select one at runtime. After a connection is established, the application calls driver manager functions to perform SQL Insert, Update, and Delete operations, as well as to open cursors and perform Fetch operations. ODBC also supports dynamic SQL statements, calls to stored procedures, and other database functions.

The advantage of using ODBC is that an application can be written with calls to standard ODBC functions and then used with a variety of DBMSs, just by configuring the ODBC driver manager and selecting an available DBMS for the connection.

A number of Windows-based applications (e.g., Excel, Word) provide built-in support for ODBC. With such applications, the end user can request a connection to an available DBMS and the application treats the DBMS in a manner similar to the way it treats a local relational database, such as Microsoft's Access product. This facility lets the user perform application operations such as loading a Microsoft Excel spreadsheet from a table or running a Microsoft Word document mail merge with data from a table. The data can come from any available ODBC connection.

The *Microsoft ODBC 3.0 Software Development Kit and Programmer's Reference* provides comprehensive information about the standard ODBC functions. IBM's *AS/400 Client Access Express for Windows ODBC User's Guide* provides additional information about ODBC and IBM's ODBC driver for Windows.

17 And possibly other vendors.

Figure 16.12
Structure of an Application That Uses ODBC to Access a UDB/400 File

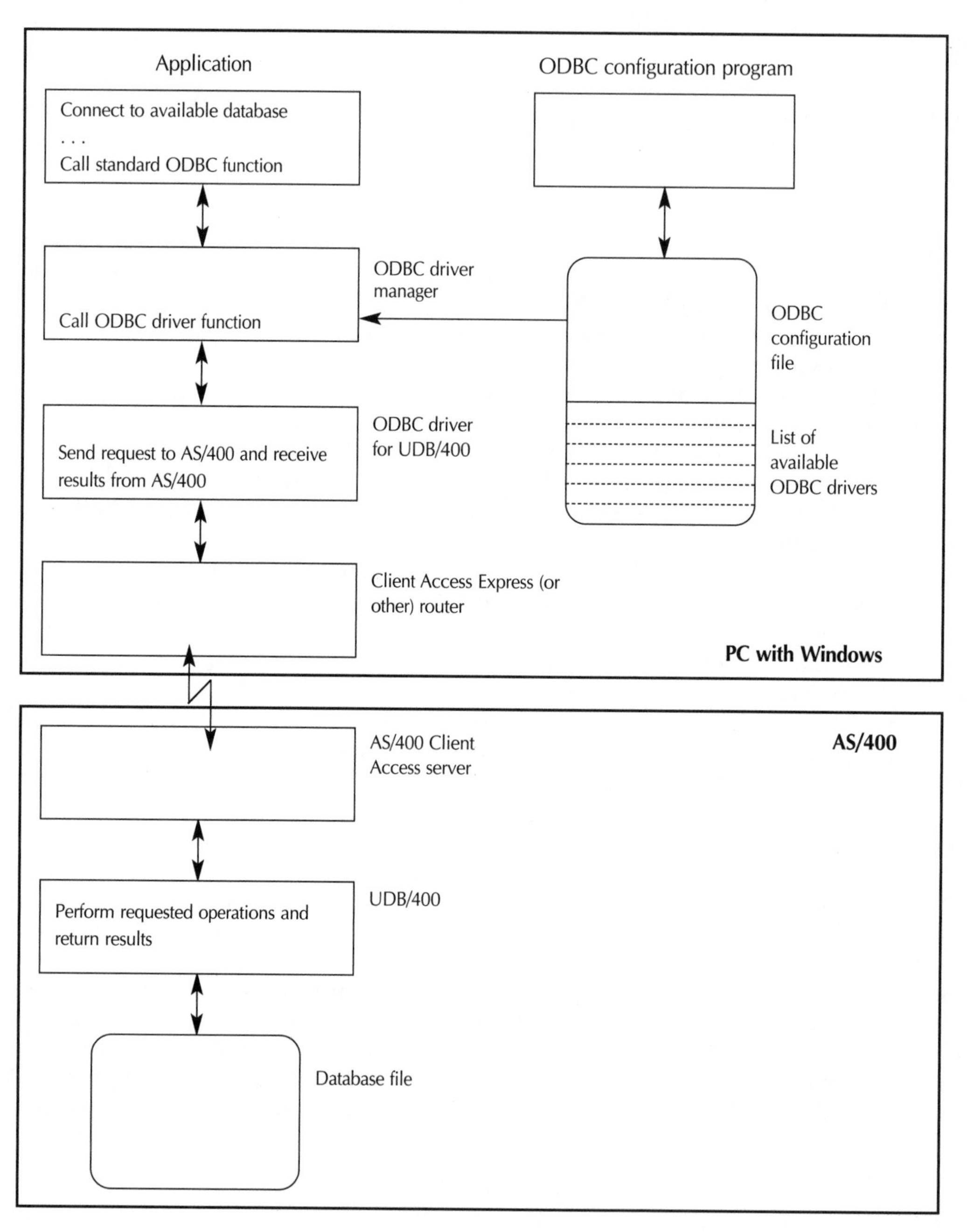

JDBC

Java Database Connectivity (**JDBC**), like ODBC, is a software standard that lets you access a relational database using SQL. JDBC (as its name implies) gives you SQL access in a Java software environment. Also, as with ODBC, database vendors supply a software component, known as a JDBC driver, to be "snapped in" to the infrastructure to let the SQL code access the vendors' products. Figure 16.13 depicts the client portion of this architecture. With JDBC, remote systems connect to a server using the TCP/IP communications protocol, and the server provides software to translate JDBC method calls to database requests.

Figure 16.13
JDBC Architecture

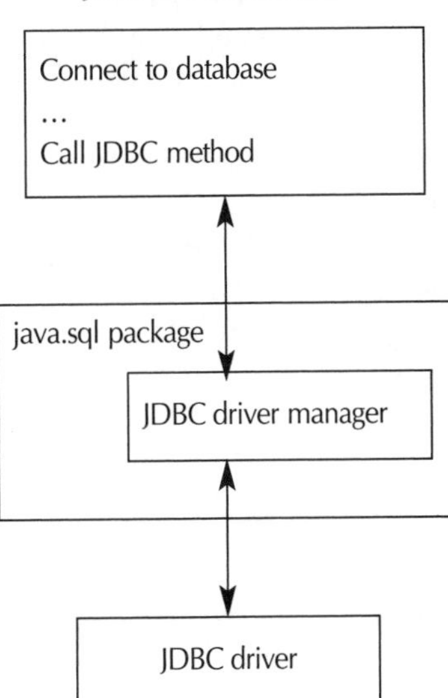

Notice the similarity between Figures 16.13 and 16.12. The architecture shown in Figure 16.13 indicates that the JDBC methods you call are contained in the java.sql package's classes.[18] The java.sql package contains classes for database connectivity, data manipulation, calling stored procedures, and so on. A class for the JDBC driver manager is also included in the java.sql package and serves as an interface to the different database-vendor–supplied JDBC drivers. This is analogous to ODBC's driver manager and database-specific driver architecture.

JDBC also has a JDBC–ODBC bridge that lets you develop JDBC applications and use an ODBC driver for the actual connection to a database. This support provides an alternative connection mechanism when a database-specific JDBC driver is unavailable.

UDB/400 has two JDBC drivers. One comes with OS/400 as part of the AS/400 Development Kit for Java and is used by Java applications running on the AS/400. The other is part of the AS/400 Toolbox for Java product, which comes with OS/400. The Toolbox driver is used for applications running on a remote client system.

18 In Java terminology, a package is a collection of related classes. Classes are definitions of data and methods (i.e., executable functions) that are used to declare Java objects.

For more information about using JDBC with UDB/400, see the "Java" topic in IBM's AS/400 Information Center Web site at *http://publib.boulder.ibm.com/pubs/html/as400/infocenter.html*.

Net.Data

With IBM's **Net.Data** product, you can create dynamic Web pages using data from UDB/400 and other database management systems. Net.Data is a macro processor that executes as an HTTP (Web) server Common Gateway Interface (CGI) program on the AS/400 (or other Web server machine). You can write Net.Data application programs, called macros, that Net.Data interprets to create dynamic Web pages with customized content based on input from the user and the current state of your database. Typically, Hypertext Markup Language (HTML) is used to describe the Web page layout, and SQL is used to retrieve the data that's displayed on the Web page.

A request, in the form of a Universal Resource Locator (URL) flows from a browser (e.g., Netscape Navigator, Microsoft Internet Explorer) to the HTTP server on the AS/400. Net.Data requests are forwarded to the IBM-supplied UDBWWW program, which implements the Net.Data macro processor. This program locates and interprets the specified macro source code and builds a Web page that merges UDB/400 data into the HTML that's included in the macro. Net.Data passes the constructed Web page to the HTTP server on the AS/400, which in turn transmits the page over the network for display at the browser.

For more information about Net.Data, see the *Net.Data Administration and Programming Guide for OS/400* and *Net.Data Reference* manuals.

Coding Suggestions

- When necessary, use file overrides to redirect a query to a different table or view rather than using explicit qualifiers in the SQL statements.
- Avoid using the InhWrt parameter of the OvrDbF command when testing programs on production data. Use test data instead.
- In general, trigger programs should not deactivate themselves. In RPG IV, this means the trigger program should return without setting on LR. ILE COBOL/400 programs should end with the GoBack instruction and should run in the *Caller activation group.
- Consider specifying SeqOnly(*Yes *n*) on an OvrDbF command to specify a blocking factor to use for large sequential table operations.
- Use the trigger buffer soft-coding technique described in this chapter to reduce future program maintenance when table columns are added, modified, or deleted.

Chapter Summary

File overrides, specified with the OvrDbF (Override with Database File) command, can be used to change processing defaults before opening a database table or view. With SQL/400 access, overrides can be used for

- redirection to a specific table or view or to a specific database file member (ToFile and Mbr parameters)
- preventing table data from being modified (InhWrt parameter)

- blocking (SeqOnly parameter)
- specifying how long to wait for a row lock (WaitRcd parameter)

A trigger program is a program that UDB/400 calls when an application program tries to insert, update, or delete a database record. You write and compile a trigger program just as you do any other HLL program and then use the AddPfTrg (Add Physical File Trigger) command to associate the trigger program with a table.

UDB/400 supports six trigger conditions for a table:

- before insert
- before update
- before delete
- after insert
- after update
- after delete

The two steps for implementing a trigger program are coding it and then associating it with one or more tables using the AddPfTrg command. A trigger can disallow the database action (insert, update, or delete). For insert and update, a trigger can modify the inserted or updated row.

A trigger program receives a trigger buffer and the length of the trigger buffer as its two parameters. The trigger buffer contains the before and after row image, null column maps for the before and after images, and other information about the trigger event.

UDB/400 has a defined sequence for checking database constraints and calling trigger programs. Be sure you consider this sequence when using these two UDB/400 features.

UDB/400 supports Distributed Relational Database Architecture (DRDA) for SQL access to data on a system other than the system on which an application runs. To support DRDA, each AS/400 has a relational database directory that associates a database name with a communications link to another system. An application program can use an embedded SQL Connect statement to connect to a remote database; subsequent SQL statements in the program are then executed on the remote system. DRDA supports commitment control for transactions that involve database operations on one or more remote systems.

Open Database Connectivity (ODBC) is a Microsoft standard for accessing a relational database from a Windows application. An application makes calls to standard ODBC functions, which are then routed to the target database system by an ODBC driver. IBM and other vendors supply ODBC drivers for UDB/400.

Java Database Connectivity (JDBC) is a standard for accessing a relational database from a Java application. The architecture of JDBC is similar to ODBC's. The AS/400 provides two JDBC drivers for UDB/400 access: the "native" driver for Java applications running on the AS/400 and the Toolbox driver for remote applications.

Net.Data is a macro-based Web development tool that can be used to combine HTML to define a displayable Web page with SQL to populate some or all of the data-related information in the Web page.

Key Terms

Distributed Relational Database Architecture (DRDA)
file override
Java Database Connectivity (JDBC)
Net.Data
Open Database Connectivity (ODBC)
override scope
trigger
trigger program

Exercises

1. Describe two practical uses of file overrides besides directing UDB/400 to open a specific table.
2. Describe two uses of a trigger program.
3. Suppose a table is defined with the following column:

   ```
   LastUpd        TimeStamp, ...
   ```

   The LastUpd column should be updated with the current timestamp whenever the row is updated. Discuss the relative advantages of updating this column using application program logic versus using a before-update trigger.
4. Show the AS/400 commands needed to establish the following trigger programs for the AppDta/Employee table:
   - Before inserts and updates: AppExc/ChkEmpl
   - After inserts, updates, and deletes: AppExc/LogEmpl
5. Describe the purpose of DRDA.
6. Many vendors (including IBM) supply custom application programming interfaces (APIs) that let you access their relational databases from a PC application. Explain the advantages of using ODBC or JDBC rather than using custom vendor-supplied APIs.
7. Describe a situation in which you might use Net.Data on the AS/400.

Chapter 17

Introduction to Data Modeling and Database Design

Chapter Overview

This chapter introduces logical data modeling and physical database design, two important stages of a development project that should precede the coding and creation of database tables. We look at why these steps are necessary and what they produce. We also discuss how relational concepts are related to data modeling and database design. When you finish this chapter, you'll have a better understanding of the importance of the topics covered in the next four chapters as well as of how data modeling and database design fit into the responsibilities of a professional application developer.

The Importance of Modeling and Design

It may seem obvious, but it's worth stating anyway: Before you use SQL/400, or any other facility for creating database tables, you should know exactly *what* kinds of tables you need to create. Consider how pointless it would be to create a Customer table before you knew what information about its customers a company needs to have — some companies might need to know their customers' occupations, while others might not care what their customers do for a living. The general requirement for database tables, of course, is to store data that the business (or other kind of organization) needs so the data can be used effectively. And figuring out exactly what those needs are and how best to implement a database that meets the requirements clearly should happen *before* coding starts.

Figuring out and documenting business requirements — including both data and processes that use data — are tasks often collectively referred to as "modeling" because the result of the effort is a model (in words and diagrams) of the way the business works and the information it uses. The part of this effort that concentrates on the organization's data requirements is called **logical data modeling** (or **data modeling**, for short).[1] Once you have a **data model** for an organization, you have a specification of what data needs to be stored and at least some of the ways in which the data is used. For example, the data model for a particular company might specify that the company needs to keep track of customers, including their names, shipping and billing addresses, voice and fax telephone numbers, and credit ratings. This data model might also document that the company needs complete customer lists, in order by the customers' names. From this model (or specification), you can then decide which data should be stored in database tables and which data should be stored in other ways — for instance, as paper documents in filing cabinets or on microfilm. It's important to realize that a data model might ultimately be implemented without *any* database tables at all. A data model says *what* the organization needs, not *how* a system will be implemented to address those needs.

1 Modeling, or some parts of it, are also referred to by the following, overlapping terms: business requirements assessment, analysis, systems analysis, and design. The term "logical data modeling" is widely used and clearly states what this part of application development produces: a logical model of the organization's data. The terminology isn't all that crucial — as long as the job gets done.

A system to provide for storing, updating, and retrieving the information specified in a particular data model might be implemented in any number of ways. For example, all customer records might be stored in a single database table, or customer records might be grouped by different countries, with customers from each country being stored in a separate table. The task of deciding how to implement a system for a particular data model is called **physical database design** (or **database design**, for short).[2] The result of a successful database design is a specification for the tables, columns, and other related items to be created on a specific computer system, such as the AS/400. The final development step (i.e., the actual **implementation**) is the almost "cookbook" coding and creation of the tables and related items according to the database design specification. Of course, the design stage of a development project may also specify that certain parts of the data model are to be implemented with facilities other than database tables, and the implementation stage may involve steps other than coding and creating database tables. For example, the design specification may state that some data is to be kept only on paper forms in file cabinets; the implementation would then involve laying out and printing the forms.

The successive stages of modeling, design, and implementation appear so rational that it would be easy to assume that these three stages are universally followed in *all* application development. Unfortunately, it's common practice among AS/400 development groups to spend a small amount of time jotting down a few notes from discussions with users and then jump straight into SQL and RPG or Cobol coding. Because of the widespread disparity between an apparently rational approach to application development and the actual practice among many application developers, it's worth examining why data modeling and database design are often neglected.

There are two probable reasons for this neglect:

- Many developers don't know how to go about data modeling and/or database design.
- In the minds of many developers, overly formal modeling and design methods take more time than they're worth.

The first barrier is easy to understand. Think about how hard it is to do something — even if you think it would be useful — if no one has ever shown you how to do it. Let's say you want to eat a low-fat, low-sodium diet because you've read that it's healthier. If you don't have any simple, tasty recipes to start with, you may balk at even trying to change your diet, or you may get discouraged and quit after a couple of bland meals. On the other hand, if an experienced cook offers some guidance or you find a good source of recipes, you're more likely to attempt — and succeed at — changing the way you eat.

Some developers find themselves in the position of the person who wants to change diets but has no cookbook. They've received training only in how to write SQL, RPG, or Cobol code, not in how to model data or design databases. An even larger group of developers has had some training in designing *programs* but no comparable training in designing an integrated *database.* A person in either category may avoid data modeling and/or database design because he or she isn't sure how to go about it. This is the barrier that the introductory material presented in the rest of this part of the book is designed to remove.

2 The term "database design" is often used as an abbreviated way to refer to both the logical data modeling and the physical database design processes. In this book, we generally refer to the two processes by the distinct terms "data modeling" and "database design."

The second barrier to more widespread use of data modeling and database design in "real-world" application development is the perceived lack of value for the amount of time that it takes.[3] This perception probably stems from a certain all-or-none approach to the modeling and design tasks — that is, people may think design and modeling have to be done with a lot of formality (and overhead) or not at all. While rigorous, labor-intensive approaches that record every minute detail of a data model or database design might be useful in an organization with a hundred or more developers, for many small organizations, a simpler, less formal approach can work much better. Smaller organizations (especially the one- or two-person shops) may find that a few simple word-processing documents, some hand-drawn diagrams, and a few spreadsheets or database tables to track tabular design information (e.g., a list of tables and their contents) are adequate. Such a "low-tech" solution can result in significantly less overhead and still produce the benefits of going through the modeling and design stages before coding.

One key to successful application development — including database programming and design — is to adapt your approaches to the specific goal and environment in which you work. As you study the rest of this chapter and the other chapters in Part III, remember two points:

- The principles are what is most important.
- Each situation calls for applying the principles in ways that improve the quality of the resulting application database and don't add extreme amounts of effort to development projects.

Logical Data Modeling

We've already mentioned how logical data modeling produces a specification of what the organization needs. Now let's briefly consider some general aspects of data modeling.

First, what does a data model document? Among other things, it specifies the following items of interest to the organization:

- objects (e.g., customers, employees)
- events (e.g., placing an order, approving a loan)
- relationships among objects and events (e.g., a customer places an order, a loan officer approves a loan)
- details about objects, events, and relationships (e.g., customers' names, dates orders were placed)
- business rules or policies (e.g., a borrower must have an adjusted gross income of at least half his or her total outstanding debt)

Your first reaction might be to say, "That's a *lot* of information to put into a data model," and to understand why people often skip the modeling process. Here are a couple of thoughts to counterbalance that reaction. First, many of an organization's rules are already documented in policy manuals, operating guides, or other documents. These documents can be referenced in a data model without re-documenting every detail. Second, if you are going to need a column or a table to track some piece of information, you'll be a lot better off if you clearly identify this requirement *before* you start

3 We've noticed that programmers who are insecure about their own lack of training or experience often claim that some well-proven design or programming practice isn't "practical" in the "real world." This claim has been made about structured programming, relational database, object-oriented programming, and a host of other practices that the highest-paid programmers in the industry use regularly. One has to wonder which group of programmers best reflects the "real world" of application development.

coding SQL. Ignoring the modeling and design stages of a project doesn't make the need to fully understand the system go away; it just postpones that step and usually makes it more difficult to implement a correct and efficient system.

By now, we hope you have a good picture of why you (or someone in the development group) should tackle the job of creating a data model before starting an implementation. The natural question then is, when do we know we're *done* with the data model? The answer is, you know you're done with data modeling when you have one or more documents (and possibly diagrams) that provide a statement of the organization's data and how it's used. This statement should be

- clear
- comprehensible
- comprehensive
- correct
- consistent

A specification is *clear* and *comprehensible* if all the people who need to agree on what it says can readily understand it and understand it in essentially the same way. A *comprehensive* model is one that covers all the relevant aspects of the data that the organization needs; nothing is omitted. A *correct* specification provides an accurate representation of the organization's information. A *consistent* model has no ambiguous or contradictory specifications.

If you've created a clear and comprehensible data model, the end users — the people in the organization who actually use the data — can tell whether the model is also comprehensive and correct. Likewise, the people who have to do the physical database design (and that might be you) should be able to judge whether the data model is comprehensive and consistent.

In effect, a data model serves as a contract between the end users and the designers. As with any contract, both parties should have no question about its meaning. The data model, as a contract, specifies the *minimum* requirements for the database design. With that perspective, it's apparent that the person(s) producing the data model can't take for granted that the person(s) doing the database design will put anything in the final design unless the data model clearly calls for it.

Physical Database Design

With a good idea of what the organization needs to keep track of and how that data is used, a developer's next step is to decide how best to implement a system to support the organization's requirements. Suppose the business has customers; is it obvious that a Customer database table is required? What if the business builds custom yachts and has only three or four customers a year? Maybe a filing cabinet and file folders are adequate, and no database is necessary. Or what if the business has fairly independent divisions in different regions of the country? Should there be a single Customer table at the home office, or should there be separate tables in each regional office? Questions such as these are answered in the database design stage, which follows the data modeling stage. The results of the data modeling efforts may answer some of these questions fairly well, but many others require closer consideration of the volume of data, types of data access, and the available hardware, software, and personnel.

Physical database design is the process that weighs the alternative implementation possibilities and carefully lays out exactly how tables and other elements of the system will be set up. For the database implementation, the most important tangible result of the design is a set of table layouts, including detailed column specifications. As you'll learn in the next four chapters, other important elements of the database design are specific end-user views of the data and various integrity constraints that must be enforced. The database design details how these will be implemented with a particular database system, such as UDB/400.

You might wonder why an intermediate step between data modeling and coding SQL is necessary. At some point, you must consider alternative implementation approaches and document which ones you chose and why. A design document often includes information about such things as anticipated volumes and access paths as well as the rationale for choosing a particular implementation. You don't normally find this important information in either the data model or the source code used to create database tables.

Earlier, we stressed that good modeling and design don't necessarily have to be overly formal. Keep this point in mind when considering how you might approach these tasks in a practical way. Nothing says that you can't combine a word-processing document with actual SQL to produce a design specification. After all, SQL can be a fairly readable way to present a table layout. With this approach, an associated word-processing document can include the other relevant information about the design so the parts that can't be expressed in SQL are still well documented. On the other hand, large organizations will probably find it more productive to use a computer-based database design tool that lets a team of developers work jointly on a design and have a shared set of machine-readable tables and diagrams on an AS/400 or LAN. Some of these tools can even generate SQL source code from a completed design so that part of the implementation step is automated. Whichever way the design is actually created, it should be specific enough so that a well-trained programmer can almost mechanically code and create the necessary database tables and other associated application components.

To wrap up this introduction to data modeling and database design, let's look at how a system appears from several different perspectives. Figure 17.1 (next page) shows three perspectives on a system.[4] At the top of the figure are various narrow and specialized end-user perspectives of the system. Note that any individual user "sees" only part of the overall data and its organization. Individual users also may have specialized ways of referring to various parts of the data. The middle layer shows the ideal, unified perspective of the data. At this level, the data and its organization are still understood in conceptual terms, but data that appears in multiple end-user perspectives (the top layer) is merged so there's not unnecessary redundancy in the middle layer's representation. The middle layer provides an integrated perspective and is what is documented in the data model. The bottom layer consists of tables and other application objects that are part of an actual implementation of the concepts in the middle layer. This layer is what's specified as a result of the database design process.

Clearly, what matters to the organization is that the system deliver the functionality represented in the top layer — the layer that most closely represents the organization's day-to-day requirements. But meeting that objective requires that all three layers be consistent with one another; that is, the middle layer must faithfully represent the top layer (in an integrated structure), and the bottom layer must fully implement the middle layer. This point brings us again to the importance of data modeling and database design as essential parts of application development — these two processes are how you get an implementation that effectively supports the end users as they carry out the organization's work.

4 This diagram is loosely based on the American National Standards Institute's "three-schema" architecture for database management systems.

Figure 17.1
Three Perspectives on a Database Management System (DBMS)

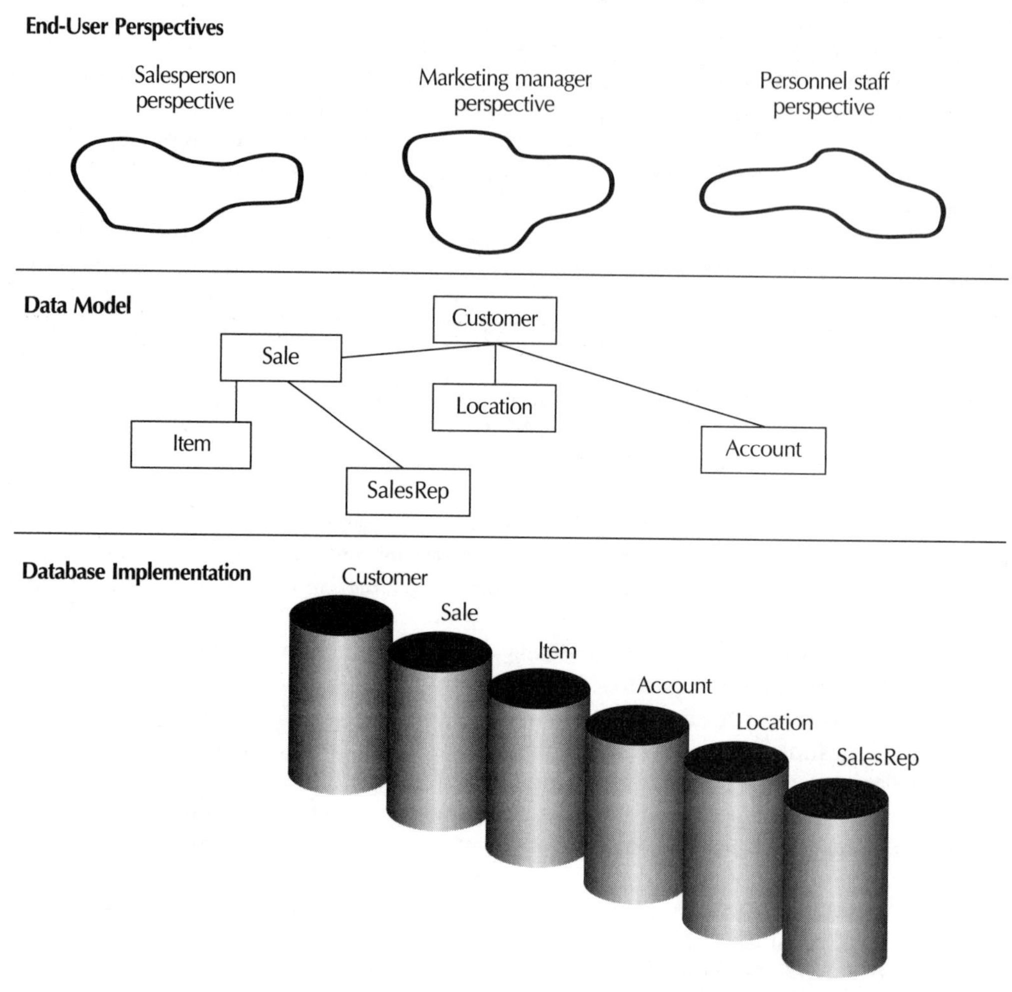

Relational Concepts As the Foundation

We've covered the purpose of data modeling and database design, as well as what these two processes produce in the way of specifications. Before we move on to subsequent chapters and a more detailed discussion of how these two tasks are done, you should understand the basis for the data modeling and database design methods presented in this book. In most good development methods, the specific techniques are based on a general framework. For data modeling and database design, a widely used foundation is the **relational model**.[5] Chapter 18 describes the relational model in detail and how

5 It may help to clarify the way the term "model" is used. When we speak of the relational model, we're speaking of a general conceptual model that isn't specific to a particular business or application. For example, the relational model incorporates the idea that a relation *(continued)*

it arose out of work with computer file and database systems. In this section, we briefly discuss why the relational model is so suitable for data modeling and database design techniques.

The relational model has three main advantages:

- There's a wide body of mathematical research that's been done on the relational model. (It helps to know that this isn't just an idea some programmer cooked up in a Jolt-induced trance one weekend.)
- Despite the relational model's substantial mathematical underpinnings, many of its most useful concepts have intuitive, informal representations. For example, a relation can be represented informally as a table. Both end users and developers with no training in the formal mathematics of the relational model can develop a precise model using these informal representations. Because clear communication between the end user and the person working to produce a data model is essential, this strength of the relational model is very valuable. It's especially nice that this intuitive side of the relational model doesn't compromise the formal side at all. In fact, as further developments have occurred on the research side, many of the results have found their way into the intuitive notations.
- Relational database management systems (DBMSs) are the most widely used type of business-oriented DBMSs today. Thus, a data model based on the relational model is the best starting point for developing a database design that targets a relational DBMS. If the data model is cast in terms of tables, primary keys, and other relational concepts, there's little problem translating these concepts into similar implementation objects for a relational DBMS. For example, UDB/400 table objects are equivalent to the relational model's tables (and vice versa) and can have primary keys. Using modeling, design, and implementation methods all based on the same conceptual model avoids some difficult problems that arise when different stages of development use fundamentally different conceptual models.

These advantages of the relational model have led to its widespread adoption as the basis for many modeling and design methods.

Chapter Summary

Before implementing database tables, the developer needs to know what the tables should contain and how they're related. This information is developed by two processes, logical data modeling and physical database design, that should occur before implementation.

Logical data modeling analyzes the organization's data requirements to develop a data model that's clear, comprehensible, comprehensive, correct, and consistent. This model integrates all the individual end-user perspectives. The data model documents objects, events, relationships, details about these items, and business rules and policy. The data model is a specification that says *what*

(5) (informally, a table) is used to represent some type of entity, such as a customer. But the relational model doesn't say anything specific about customers, employees, or other particular entities.

When we talk about creating a data model before the design and implementation stages of a development project, however, we are referring to a particular model. For example, if we produce a data model for Ajax Plumbing, Inc., that data model will have some representation (e.g., a relation or table) of customers, employees, and other types of entities in which the company is interested.

Note that there are other conceptual models (which we touch on in the next chapter), including hierarchical and object-oriented. And, of course, there's an unlimited number of possible particular models besides Ajax Plumbing, Inc., including Picante Software, Inc., IBM, and the Eugene Department of Parks and Recreation. Like many words, "model" has several uses, so don't be tripped up by the two common ways this term is used in the context of database programming and design.

information and capabilities the final database implementation must have, but the model doesn't state *how* the capabilities will be implemented.

Physical database design evaluates the anticipated volume of data, types of access, and available hardware, software, and personnel to decide the most effective way to implement the capabilities specified in the data model. The result of the database design is a specification for the database tables, columns, and other related items. The design specification is used as the basis for coding SQL and creating the actual tables.

Any system can be viewed from several perspectives: end-user, integrated conceptual model, and the actual implementation. One goal of data modeling and database design is consistency among all three perspectives. Data modeling assesses the end-user perspectives to produce an integrated perspective in the data model, and database design works with the data model and physical constraints to produce a specification for the implementation.

The formal, mathematical relational model underlies both the data modeling and database design techniques presented in this book and relational DBMSs, such as UDB/400. The relational model is a good basis for all of these because it has an intuitive representation that's effective for communicating with end users as well as a solid research foundation. When you as a developer use methods based on the relational model, the development process flows more smoothly from data modeling to database design to implementation.

Key Terms

data model
implementation
logical data modeling (data modeling)
physical database design (database design)
relational model

Exercises

1. Briefly explain the purpose of logical data modeling.
2. List at least five types of information that might be included in a logical data model. Can you think of any types of information — not mentioned in this chapter — that might be useful in a data model?
3. Briefly explain the purpose of physical database design.
4. Do you think it would be possible to combine logical data modeling and physical database design into a single stage of a development project? Explain the advantages and disadvantages of combining the two steps. If you think the steps might be combined, under what circumstances would it be appropriate to do so?
5. Give an example of two different end-user perspectives in a toy manufacturing business. Do the two perspectives involve any of the same data?
6. Briefly explain the advantages there might be to merging multiple end-user perspectives when you produce the data model. Can you think of any difficulties in merging end-user perspectives? *Hint: Consider the cases in which two or more perspectives use the same data but in different ways.*

Chapter 18

The Relational Database Model

Chapter Overview

This chapter covers the relational database model, the formal basis both for relational database management systems (DBMSs), such as UDB/400, and for popular database design methods, such as entity-relationship diagramming. As background, we look at the purpose and advantage of a DBMS over a conventional computer file system. Understanding the role of a DBMS makes clearer the importance of the relational database model to database programming. Knowledge of the relational model and its three main parts — data structure, integrity, and data manipulation — also provides the foundation for the design techniques discussed in the next chapter. Each of these areas is covered in a somewhat "formal" manner, but this chapter isn't filled with complex mathematics. Take the time to study the material in this chapter carefully because it will give you an invaluable basis for understanding UDB/400 and other relational DBMSs, as well as various approaches to database design.

Background: Database Management Systems

Although the relational database model underlies both the architecture of relational database management systems and popular database design methods, its origin was in the research community that was studying how computer systems could better handle application data. Thus, it's appropriate to start with a discussion of the whole problem of computerized data storage and manipulation.

According to some estimates, more than 80 percent of a typical business application is taken up with code related to file access (including file definition, record selection, and I/O) and the editing of input data for valid values.[1] Less than 20 percent of program code is concerned with calculations and transformations of data after the data is read as input and before it is written as output. The large proportion of code required just to get valid data for a computation and then to store the results is an expensive part of traditional application development, but when the same file-access and editing code is repeated in different programs — as it often is — both coding errors and software maintenance costs increase, too. Taken together, the large proportion of code not directly related to the main business function of an application system and the repetition of this code throughout the system have historically been obstacles to higher productivity in application development.

This problem led computer systems designers around the late 1960s to look for ways to reduce the 80 percent chunk of non–problem-oriented application code by having the system software automatically handle many record-specification, file-access, and field-editing functions, thus freeing application programmers to concentrate on the computations and data manipulation.[2] This effort led to what we now call **database management systems (DBMSs)**. In the decades since their first appearance, DBMSs have had a dramatic impact on data processing. As a result, more and more applications are being built on top of DBMSs instead of on more primitive conventional file systems. This requires, of

1 This proportion is reported for applications developed with an HLL and a traditional file system, not with an application generator or a DBMS.

2 With the introduction of graphical user interfaces (GUIs), programmers sometimes have to spend considerable time coding the user interface — making it even more valuable for a DBMS to simplify I/O and other programming tasks.

course, that applications be designed with the use of DBMS facilities in mind — a subject we cover later in this chapter.

Conventional File System vs. DBMS

Conventional file systems provide a relatively primitive set of facilities to store and retrieve data. A conventional file is either a sequence of bytes (a **stream-oriented file**) or a sequence of records (a **record-oriented file**). In conventional file systems, a record is just some chunk of bytes, either fixed or variable in length.[3] A conventional file system usually takes care of low-level device (e.g., disk) operations so the programmer can use HLL I/O statements (e.g., read, write) without being concerned with device-level programming. But conventional files systems don't usually do much more than that. In each program, the programmer has to code the layout of the data (i.e., field starting positions, lengths, and data types), as well as handle record sequencing and other file-related tasks. Although using RPG and Cobol Copy facilities (or a similar feature in other HLLs) can reduce some of the repetitive coding, it remains the programmer's responsibility to define a file and its contents within each program. Even more costly than the original coding of definitions is the effort required to change the source code in all programs that use a file if any change is made to its physical storage (i.e., adding a field, changing a field's length, or splitting files). Source code changes may be necessary even if a program doesn't use any of the modified items; for example, a change in one field's length may change the starting position of another field that the program uses.

A DBMS, on the other hand, attempts to free programs from physical data dependence and reduce the amount of code that must be repeated in multiple programs. Central to this goal is the ability to define to the DBMS some construct that represents an application **entity type** about which you want to store **properties**. In different types of DBMSs, entity types are represented by different constructs, among them record types, segments, relations, and tables.[4] In UDB/400, an SQL table represents an entity type. Figure 18.1 lists some of the terminology you're likely to encounter in various contexts.

Figure 18.1

Comparative Terminology Used in Different Contexts

Relational model	Table-oriented DBMS	Conventional file systems	Conceptually represents
Relation	Table	File	Entity type
Tuple	Row	Record	Entity instance
Attribute	Column	Field	Property
Domain	Column type	Data type	Allowable values and meaning
Element	Column value	Field value	Property value

What these various constructs have in common is that they represent a set of distinguishable objects of some sort, whether the objects are concrete (e.g., customers) or abstract (e.g., AS/400 jobs). This is true of conventional file systems as well — as far as it goes. What's important about DBMSs is that you include as part of a table or file definition (or other construct) some representation of the

3 Conventional files typically don't have record format definitions, members, or access paths as UDB/400 files do.

4 The closest representation of an entity type in a conventional file system is a file, but, as you'll see, a conventional file system doesn't know anything about what the file represents.

entity type's properties. Properties are usually represented by fields or columns. For example, if we defined a Customer entity type (e.g., as a table) in a DBMS, we would also define Customer ID, Name, Address, and other properties (e.g., as columns).[5] Conceptually, a property is simply some piece of information about an entity type.

So far, it may appear that a DBMS offers no earth-shattering improvement over the records and fields of an ordinary file. But for a conventional (nondatabase) file, every program must contain the layout of fields in a record, while a DBMS provides a **data definition language** (**DDL**) that's used to define constructs for both entity types and properties (including, for example, a table's columns) in a **system catalog** (also known as a **system dictionary**). UDB/400 has two alternative DDLs: Data Description Specifications (DDS, discussed briefly in Chapter 1) and SQL. UDB/400 also has two ways that it implements a system dictionary: the record format definition plus other information that's stored as part of OS/400 file objects, and a set of system files and SQL views that provide an SQL database catalog. As you learned in Chapter 1, once you create a UDB/400 table or file, every program that references the table automatically has access to the table's definition. Thus, a DBMS lets a program reference a property by name (e.g., Customer.Name) without a programmer-coded specification (in the program) of how the actual column-level data is physically stored.[6] Defining entity types and their properties *in the DBMS* is just the first step toward representing more of the logical structure and meaning of application data in a central place.

With most DBMSs, the way a property (column or field) is stored can be changed and programs that use the property continue to execute properly with no revisions. For example, you can change the length or relative location of a column in a UDB/400 table, and, at most, you need only to recompile programs that use the table for them to work properly with the changed definition.[7] Removing the physical storage aspects of a property from a program's code removes a significant amount of work, especially in system maintenance; it also removes a significant source of errors.

Besides requiring specification of the record layout in every program, a conventional file system also requires that every file-update program include code to check for legitimate values in the fields before a record is written. This validation is typically implemented by a series of conditional tests (e.g., If Age > 21 . . . , If ActTyp = 'A' or 'B' or 'C' . . .) on values entered on a display for interactive updating or on values in a transaction record read by a batch program. Not only is this code sometimes repeated (possibly with slight variations) in many programs, but also, when validity tests are directed at input values (i.e., before any program calculations or transformations) rather than at a record's output values at the time of a file update, it's still possible, due to a program error, to write a record containing invalid data to the file. Thus, most field-editing code in a conventional file system is both cumbersome to maintain and not wholly effective at guaranteeing the integrity of the data.

A DBMS can address this problem by providing DDL features you can use to specify **integrity constraints** in the system dictionary. The integrity constraints that can be specified vary among different DBMSs. At a minimum, they usually include range checks (e.g., "between 1 and 50") or allowable values (e.g., "equal to A or B or C").[8] More complex constraints may be specifiable as well.

5 The closest representation of a property in a conventional file system is a field, but see the previous footnote.

6 Of course, the degree to which UDB/400 and other current DBMSs achieve physical data independence, or any of the other concepts mentioned, varies greatly.

7 In some cases, AS/400 programs that use SQL/400 don't even need to be recompiled.

8 If you're familiar with the AS/400 DDS for defining database files, note that the COMP, RANGE, and VALUES DDS keywords, which you can specify for field definitions, do *not* apply to the database integrity. These attributes are used only when a *display file* defines an input-capable field based on a database file field with one of the keywords.

Examples include relationships between properties for the same entity type (e.g., an employee's hire date must be greater than his or her birth date) or inter-record relationships (a customer ID value in an order entity must exist as a customer ID value in exactly one customer entity). The DBMS, which handles all database updating, generally checks these constraints when database rows or records are inserted, updated, or deleted. If a constraint is not met, the DBMS blocks the operation and signals an error. Specifying integrity in a central dictionary helps immensely in speeding implementation and in achieving improved quality of the organization's data.

Historically, efficient DBMS support for built-in integrity has been difficult to achieve. Recent developments in hardware power and more efficient DBMS software implementations have prompted a trend toward improved DBMS capabilities for ensuring data integrity. This is an area in which you can expect significant change over the next few years.

At a level above the field level, a conventional file system leaves it to each program to implement relationships between entity types. For example, every program that deals with customers or orders (or both) must be aware of the relationship between these two entity types. Thus, a customer file-maintenance program must have code to ensure that a customer record isn't deleted if order records still exist for that customer. Likewise, a program that needs an order header record, a customer information record, and a set of order detail records must know which files to access and how to retrieve the related records. Applications implemented over conventional file systems typically use one of two methods to relate records: they use fields to store the relative record numbers (RRNs) of related records (in the same file or in different files), or they use matching values in common fields to associate records (e.g., having an order ID field in both the order header record and the order detail record). Whichever method is used in a conventional file system, the access strategy required to retrieve related records is reimplemented in every program that uses or affects a relationship between records.

But in many DBMSs, relationships can be defined in the dictionary using the DDL. Thus, an order header entity type might be defined as the parent of an order detail entity type, which is the dependent. Ideally, the implementation details of this relationship are hidden from application programs. A program doesn't know whether RRN pointers or indexes are being used; for that matter, a program doesn't know whether one, two, or more tables or files are used to store the data. The DBMS provides logical I/O operations such as "get first dependent," "get next sibling," "update current," and "get all records with specific property." In summary, a DBMS lets you define — *independently* from individual programs — entity types, properties, integrity constraints, and relationships. The DBMS can then enforce constraints and provide data-access methods that hide the physical storage details.

DDL capabilities are only part of the story: A DBMS also provides a **data manipulation language (DML)** to retrieve and update the data. The DML may be provided through extensions to HLL I/O facilities (as is the case with UDB/400 and the built-in I/O operations of AS/400 HLLs) or through a distinct language, such as SQL/400. The DML typically provides a superset of the conventional HLL I/O operations: read, write (or insert), delete, and update. DML operations may operate on one or more records at a time, depending on the DBMS system. An important distinction between a DBMS DML and conventional file I/O operations is the way in which the target of the action is specified. In a conventional file system, the I/O operation must target a specific record in the file using either an explicit RRN (or relative byte position in a stream file), an explicit key value, or a read next operation that implicitly targets a record based on the RRN or key of the previous record. Many DBMSs, on the other hand, support access by column or field contents regardless of whether the column or field is a key (e.g., get next course with course status = "Open"). And, based on relationships in the dictionary, a DBMS can retrieve related rows or records without explicit targeting (e.g., get first student for this course, or get first joined student and course). The power, consistency, and ease of use of a particular

DBMS's DML helps determine how useful it will be in complex application systems. If the DML is well implemented in the DBMS, it can significantly reduce the number of source code statements necessary to implement application functions.

Database Models

DBMSs vary in how much they provide the application developer. The best are powerful, highly dynamic, and easy to use; most important, they succeed in substantially reducing the proportion of non–problem-oriented code. DBMSs also vary in how they support the definition of entity types, properties, integrity constraints, and relationships between entity types and the types of manipulations that can be performed on the data. Most commercial DBMSs have been based on one of four major database models: **hierarchic**, **network** (also known as **CODASYL**), **inverted list**, and relational.[9] Both the hierarchic and network models are based on explicit *physical* links (e.g., RRNs) between records of the same type (siblings) or between records of different types (where one is the parent and one is the dependent). The major difference between the two is that the hierarchic model allows a dependent to have only one parent, just as in any familiar form of hierarchy (e.g., an organization chart), while the network model lets a record type be the dependent of any number of parent record types (e.g., in the case in which a course record type can be the dependent of both an instructor record type and a student record type).

Both the hierarchic and the network DBMS approaches have fallen into disfavor because they, like conventional file systems, require a knowledge of how the entity types are physically structured — that is, which entity types have explicit links to each other. These explicit links not only require that the programmer write procedural code to navigate the database along the link pathways, but they also make the database structure cumbersome to change: New or modified link types are not always easy to incorporate once the database has gone into production.

A third alternative, the inverted list model, is really little more than a conventional file system with enhanced file index facilities to aid in record retrieval. Records in different files are implicitly related by the values in key fields (rather than by pointers), but retrieval is still done by single-record read and write operations. As such, the inverted list is of interest not so much because of its particular approach but rather because a DBMS based on the inverted list model can be extended naturally to a relational DBMS by adding integrity rules and relational operators.[10]

The foundation of most commercial DBMSs today is the **relational database model**, which was first introduced in the paper "A Relational Model of Data for Large Shared Data Banks," published by Edgar Codd in June 1970. Since the publication of this paper, the relational model has been developed extensively, and products such as IBM's UDB/400, Oracle Corporation's Oracle, and Microsoft's SQL Server provide many of the capabilities covered in the previous section.

Relational Model: Data Structure

The relational database model has three main parts: data structure, integrity, and data manipulation. The data structure portion defines the form for representing data. Most basic to this form is the concept of a **relation**. Figure 18.2 shows an informal picture of a relation, which looks like what is commonly called a table. That is, a relation can be thought of as having columns that lay out properties (**attributes** in relational nomenclature) and rows (**tuples** in relational nomenclature) that hold

9 In recent years, a fifth model, **object-oriented**, has become more widespread. However, DBMSs based on the relational model are still the most widely used.

10 This approach, in fact, is how IBM's original S/38 file system evolved to the current UDB/400 relational DBMS.

specific instances of the entity type represented by the relation. This informal table representation is convenient for most purposes and is used in most parts of this book.

Figure 18.2
Components of a Relation

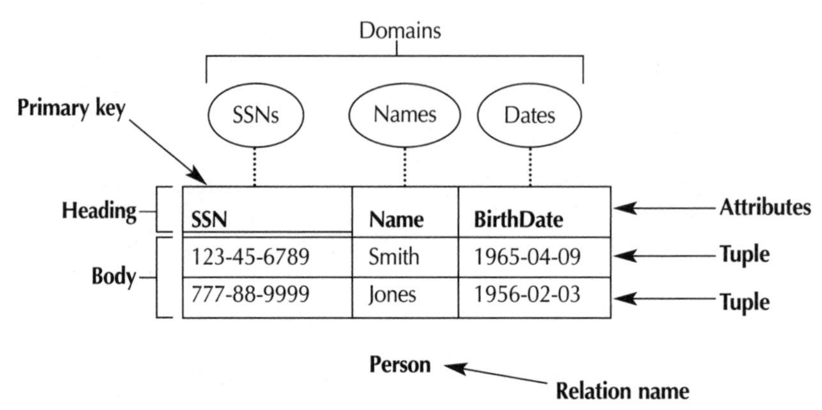

But to be more precise for the moment, a relation has two parts: the **relation heading** and the **relation body**. The heading is a set of attribute-and-domain pairs. For the Person relation represented informally by the table in Figure 18.2, the heading is the set of pairs {<SSN:SSNs>, <Name:Names>, <BirthDate:Dates>}. Because a set has no specific ordering of its elements, we also could have said that the heading is the set of attributes {<BirthDate:Dates>, <SSN:SSNs>, <Name:Names>}.[11] The number of attribute-and-domain pairs in a relation is known as its **degree**; for example, the relation in Figure 18.2 is a degree 3 relation.

The body of the relation is a set of tuples (each tuple is represented as a row in Figure 18.2). Each tuple in the Person relation represents information about a single person; that is, each tuple represents an **instance** of the Person entity type. Formally, each tuple is a set of attribute-and-value pairs. The tuple in the Person relation identified by SSN value 123-45-6789 is actually the following set of pairs: {<SSN:123-45-6789>, <Name:Smith>, <BirthDate:1965-04-09>}. Or, again, because sets are not ordered, we could have said the tuple is the following set of pairs: {<Name:Smith>, <SSN:123-45-6789>, <BirthDate:1965-04-09>}. Because the values in a tuple are not ordered, a value is always paired with the appropriate attribute that serves as a label; thus, you can keep track of the meaning of all the values in all the tuples in a relation. The number of tuples in a relation is known as its **cardinality**. For example, the relation in Figure 18.2 has a cardinality of 2.

At this point, you may wonder why something so simple as the row-column structure of a table must become as complex as a "set of attribute-and-value pairs." Because an unordered, labeled representation of data is used, the relational model can reference all values *by name* rather than by some physical mechanism, such as the position of the column in a table. This distinction is not a minor one — it's one of the breakthroughs in modeling data that the relational approach brought about. Nevertheless, in practical use of the relational model, it's perfectly adequate to use a table-like notation or other simplifications. It's important, however, not to make invalid inferences from the informal representation of a relation as a table. For example, although a table is depicted with a particular ordering of rows, relations do *not* have any particular ordering of tuples.

11 Notice how this differs from the way we usually think of a table, where a column's relative position is important.

If tuples have no ordering — and thus can't be identified by row number, how can you refer to a particular tuple? Every tuple in a relation can be referenced by specifying values for **primary key** attributes. For example, in Figure 18.2, a tuple can be referenced by specifying its SSN attribute value (SSN is thus a primary key attribute for the Person relation). This, of course, requires that a unique combination of attribute values exist for each tuple in a relation. This requirement is one of the integrity concepts we cover later.

Referencing attributes by name and referencing tuples by primary key values provide a data model that has no physical storage concepts associated with the data organization. The same statement cannot be made about the hierarchic, network, or inverted list DBMS approach. Thus, the relational database model is the only one that achieves complete **physical data independence**. Consider this: As long as the relational DBMS takes care of finding the right data when your program provides entity and attribute names along with primary key values, your program doesn't have to know *anything* about how the data is stored. The data could even be rearranged between program executions and it wouldn't matter (as long as the DBMS kept track of the data's physical location).[12]

Another fundamental part of data representation in the relational model is the concept of **domain**. Simply put, a domain combines two pieces of information: the set (possibly infinite) of allowable values and the semantics (or meaning) of the values.[13] A domain is not part of a relation, and it stores no particular values. Instead, a domain defines a pool of values that an attribute can have. Every attribute is specified as being "over" a domain. Two or more attributes can be over the same domain. Figure 18.3 shows some simplified examples of domains and attributes defined over those domains.

These examples point out some interesting and important facets of domains. First, as we just mentioned, domains define allowable values; thus, the attribute EmpSalary can never be negative because it is defined over the domain Salary, which has no negative values. Second, a domain often specifies the units of measure. Attributes defined over domains with similar units of measure can be compared or added, but attributes defined over domains with dissimilar units of measure cannot be compared or added meaningfully. Thus, a statement such as "If HairColor = EmpSalary" is not allowed. This type of mismatched comparison may seem obvious, but domains help clarify in a data model and to the DBMS more subtle distinctions. For example, in most HLLs a field used to store the number of children in a household (ChildCnt) will be an integer, as will the field to store the number of cars owned by a household (CarCnt). If you were to code an assignment such as "ItemCnt = ChildCnt + CarCnt" in RPG or Cobol, the compiler wouldn't report an error. However, it's most likely that this statement is the result of bad coding, not a medieval social philosophy in which children and cars are both merely possessions, and it should be prevented. In the relational database model, these two attributes could not be added because they are from different domains.[14]

What if you really did want to add such dissimilar units? In that case, you might use a mapping function — for example a function, UnitCvt, that is defined to map (i.e., convert) any integer value to a unitless value.[15] The required statement then becomes "ItemCnt = UnitCvt(ChildCnt) +

12 Note that, internally, a relational DBMS generally uses RRNs or other physical references to keep track of data. These physical references may or may not be accessible to application programs — for example, in UDB/400, HLL built-in I/O statements (e.g. Read) *can* use RRNs. The important thing for a relational DBMS is that it must at least allow applications to access data without physical references.

13 The concept of a database domain is generally equivalent to the formal programming language concept of *data type*. As of V4R4, UDB/400 doesn't currently support the explicit domain that we're discussing here.

14 Not many commercial relational DBMSs provide this level of support for domains, however.

15 In SQL, the Cast function lets you change the data type of a column or expression.

Figure 18.3
Sample Domains and Attributes

Domain:	Color Values {Red, Orange, Yellow, Green, Blue, Indigo, Violet, ...}	**Domain:**	Weight Range [0:100,000,000] Units Pounds
Attributes:	ProductColor HairColor	**Attributes:**	ShippingWeight EmpWeight
Domain:	Salary Range [0:100,000,000] Units Dollars/year	**Domain:**	Children Range Integers ≥ 0 Units People
Attributes:	EmpSalary ContractorSalary	**Attribute:**	ChildCnt
Domain:	Wages Range [0:1,000] Units Dollars/hour	**Domain:**	Cars Range Integers ≥ 0 Units Cars
Attributes:	EmpWages ContractorWages	**Attribute:**	CarCnt
		Domain:	Units Range Integers Units (none)
		Attribute:	ItemCnt

UnitCvt(CarCnt)." A more common example of a required mapping would be from annual salary values to hourly wages or vice versa. In this case, the numerator (e.g., dollars) for both units of measure is identical, but the denominators (year and hour) are different. This similarity (exacerbated by ambiguous field names) is precisely the cause of a typical HLL programming error in adding fields such as EmpSalary and EmpWages without converting either. The concept of domains allows system detection of invalid or questionable comparisons or computations.

Another point to be made about a relation is that a *database* relation (unlike the more general mathematical notion of relation) cannot have *sets* as values for an attribute.[16] Every attribute value in a tuple must be a single element drawn from the underlying domain.[17] Figure 18.4 shows the distinction between a mathematical relation (shown in table format) and a database relation.

Note that restructuring a mathematical relation that has sets of values into a database relation is a mechanical operation of adding additional tuples that repeat values for some attributes.

16 Actually, this restriction is part of the original relational model, but a variation known as the non-first normal form (NFNF) relational model *does* allow sets as attribute values. The reason for this restriction was that it greatly simplified the mathematical definitions of the relational operators. The NFNF model is also a step toward the object-oriented database model, which allows arbitrarily complex data attribute values.

17 And, of course, the domain's values themselves must not be sets.

Figure 18.4
Mathematical vs. Database Relations

Parent	Children
Smith	Bubba
Jones	Billy Susie Fred
Harris	Janice Tommy

Mathematical Relation

Parent	Children
Smith	Bubba
Jones	Billy
Jones	Susie
Jones	Fred
Harris	Janice
Harris	Tommy

Database Relation

Normal Forms

Consideration of repeating values introduces another facet of the relational database model: **normal forms.** By definition, a database relation is in what is called **first normal form** (1NF), which simply means that there are no sets as attribute values. Because a relation is in 1NF, all the referencing and manipulative operations of the relational model can be performed on it. However, a 1NF relation may not always be the ideal form for representing data. A relation in 1NF may appear to represent information redundantly. And, if a database file or table is subsequently implemented that corresponds directly to the relation, actual redundant data may be updated inconsistently.

Figure 18.5A shows a 1NF relation with apparent redundant storage of WarehouseAddress. Figure 18.5B shows the 1NF relation split into two relations that eliminate the WarehouseAddress redundancy.

Figure 18.5A
First Normal Form (1NF) Inventory Relation

ItemID	WarehouseID	Qty	WarehouseAddress
167	1	10	1511 Central Ave.
167	2	20	6803 Alder St.
448	1	26	1511 Central Ave.
302	2	18	6803 Alder St.

Inventory

Figure 18.5B

Inventory Relation Split into Two Relations to Eliminate Redundancy

ItemID	WarehouseID	Qty
167	1	10
167	2	20
448	1	26
302	2	18

Inventory

WarehouseID	WarehouseAddress
1	1511 Central Ave.
2	6803 Alder St.

Warehouse

The process of splitting relations with redundant representation of information into two or more relations without the redundancy is a process often called **normalization**. There are five main normal forms (1NF through 5NF) for relations. Each normal form addresses the potential for a particular type of redundancy.

In a moment, we take a closer look at the various normal forms, but it's important to be clear about the meaning of redundancy. First, any nontrivial set of relations will have some values repeated more than once in the database. For example, in the relations in Figure 18.5B, the warehouse IDs that appear in the Inventory relation all appear in the Warehouse relation as well. This is one of the central features of the relational model — tuples are related by values, not pointers or other physical means. So the three instances of warehouse ID 1 and warehouse ID 2 don't represent the type of redundancy with which we're concerned.

The redundancy we want to avoid is repeated representation of the same fact.[18] For example, in Figure 18.5A, the fact that warehouse 1 is located at 1511 Central Ave. is repeated in two tuples. If we actually created a database file with this structure, we'd have to ensure that any change to the warehouse address was made consistently to *all* records that stored the address.

Now, let's look at an example that's not so obvious. Suppose we have a relation for the items that are included in customers' orders:

OrderID	ItemID	Qty	Price
9877	73	2	50.00
9878	52	1	10.00
9878	73	5	50.00
9879	73	1	50.00

This relation appears to redundantly represent the fact that the item ID determines the price. In many business systems, this might be true. But what if the price were negotiated on each order? Then it would be possible for the relation to have (at some point in time) the following contents:

18 Formally, the concept of facts is known as *functional dependence.* In a nutshell, if a relation has two attributes A and B, B is functionally dependent on A if-and-only-if whenever two tuples in the relation have the same value for A, they necessarily have the same value for B.

OrderID	ItemID	Qty	Price
9877	73	2	50.00
9878	52	1	10.00
9878	73	5	45.00
9879	73	1	50.00

For the business model that this relation represents, no fact redundancy exists. This example brings us to a crucial point in understanding normal forms: If you want to *unambiguously* represent various facts in a (logical) database model that uses relations, you *must* structure the relations so they have no redundant representation of facts. The obvious consequence is that there's no mechanical method of normalizing relations. You first must know which facts you want to represent, and then you define the relations accordingly.

Despite these principles, some textbook and other presentations of normal forms convey the misconception that normalization is a process you apply when you *implement files.* Although informally you might consider some of the ideas related to nonredundant representation of facts when you implement files, normal forms are specifically a *design* concept. Chapter 19 takes up this issue more fully.

The misunderstanding probably stems from the conventional approach (which we more or less follow here) to introducing the normal forms and the examples that have obvious redundant representation of facts. Keep in mind as we go through the following examples, however, that each relation with apparent redundancy might, in some specific situations, be free of redundancy.

With that cautionary note, let's look at the main normal forms. To review, first normal form (1NF) requires that each attribute value be **atomic**; that is, it must not be a set (or other composite structure). The database relation in Figure 18.4 and the relation in Figure 18.5A illustrate first normal form.

Second normal form (2NF), which is illustrated by the two relations in Figure 18.5B, requires that the relation be in (at least) first normal form and that each non-key attribute depend on the *entire* primary key. The primary key for the Inventory relation includes both the ItemID and WarehouseID (neither alone is unique). Because we assume that a warehouse's address depends only on the WarehouseID attribute, the relation in Figure 18.5A violates the 2NF requirement. Looking at the problem from the other direction, if we assumed incorrectly that Figure 18.5A was already in 2NF, we'd think that, for some reason, the WarehouseAddress values could be determined only by knowing both the ItemID and the WarehouseID.

Third normal form (3NF) requires that the relation be in (at least) second normal form and that each non-key attribute depend *only* on the primary key. In the following relation, each tuple represents a customer order:

OrderID	OrderCustID	CustCity	Amt
601	123	Portland	2,000
602	789	Eugene	50
603	123	Portland	500
604	198	Portland	1,000

If we assume that a customer's city depends only on the customer's ID, the proper 3NF structure is

CustID	City
123	Portland
198	Portland
789	Eugene

OrderID	OrderCustID	Amt
601	123	2,000
602	789	50
603	123	500
604	198	1,000

Fourth normal form (4NF) requires that the relation be in (at least) third normal form and that there be no more than one **multivalued fact** in the relation. A multivalued fact is one in which several values for an attribute might be determined by one value for another attribute (e.g., the children of an employee or the courses taken by an employee). The following relation represents two multivalued facts:

EmployeeID	Child	Course
576	Bonnie	Math 101
576	Janice	Psych 203
576	Sam	?
601	Abigail	Art 101

Look at the problem in this relation — when an employee has an unequal number of children and courses, what value should be used as a placeholder? You can't use null (discussed in the next section) because all three attributes are necessary in the primary key, and primary key attributes can't have null. The solution is to use two relations:

EmployeeID	Child
576	Bonnie
576	Janice
576	Sam
601	Abigail

EmployeeID	Course
576	Math 101
576	Psych 203
601	Art 101

So far, the rules for normal forms are pretty intuitive, which should be no surprise because the intent is to make clear the facts represented by a relation. The final normal form is a bit more involved to explain but also has an intuitive rule: A table in **fifth normal form** (**5NF**) cannot be split into two or more tables without loss of information. Suppose we know the following rule about sales agents, products, and companies:

If a sales agent sells a certain product and he (or she) represents a company that makes the product, then he (or she) sells that product for that company.

We might try to represent this with the following relation:

Agent	Company	Product
Boyd	Ford	Car
Boyd	Ford	Truck
Boyd	GM	Car
Boyd	GM	Truck
Harper	GM	Car

But we observe that, by definition, this relation isn't in fifth normal form. It can be split into the following three relations with no loss of information because we know (with the previously stated rule) exactly what agents sell from the contents in these three relations:

Agent	Company
Boyd	Ford
Boyd	GM
Harper	GM

Agent	Product
Boyd	Car
Boyd	Truck
Harper	Car

Company	Product
Ford	Car
Ford	Truck
GM	Car
GM	Truck

But even if we *can* split the original table, why would we *want* to? To answer that question, consider how we'd store the (new) fact that Harper sells Ford trucks. In the three-relation representation, the answer is simple: insert a <Harper, Ford> tuple into the Agent-Company relation and a <Harper, Truck> tuple into the Agent-Product relation. However, in the single-relation representation, we'd have to add the following tuples:

<Harper, Ford, Truck>

<Harper, Ford, Car>

<Harper, GM, Truck>

What's going on here is that the single relation redundantly stores some of the more elementary facts (which products an agent sells) to satisfy the rule stated earlier. By splitting the relation, as long as we also state the rule about which companies' products an agent sells, we don't redundantly represent the elementary facts. It's important to note, however, that *without* the rule, we *would* need a relation like the Agent-Company-Product one to know which companies' products an agent sells. Although fifth normal form may be a bit difficult to grasp at first, it illustrates the real purpose of normal forms: establishing a clear meaning for what a set of relations represents.

In summary, the data structures of the relational model provide data independence (a separation of the conceptual and physical aspects), and when viewed — as they normally are — as tables, relations are easy to understand and work with. Relations also put a firm theoretical footing under any DBMS based on them. This combination of the conceptual simplicity and formal definition of relations forms the foundation for the next two parts of the model: data integrity and data manipulation.

Data Integrity

While the data structure portion of the relational database model defines the form for representing data, the data integrity portion of the model defines mechanisms for ensuring that the stored data is valid. This requires, at a minimum, that the attribute values each be valid, that the set of values in a tuple be unique, and that relations known to be interrelated have consistent values within the tuples.

In discussing the concept of domains in the previous section, we essentially covered the first form of data integrity, known as **attribute integrity** — that values for attributes come only from their respective underlying domains. A widely accepted variation of the relational model also permits an attribute to contain a marker, referred to as **null**, that indicates a missing or unknown value.[19] Note that null is not a value per se — it's merely a placeholder.

The domain concept covers the common HLL implementation technique of checking a value to see that it's within an allowable range or that it's one of a list of allowable values; it also extends the concept to the meaning of the values (e.g., whether units are children or cars). What it does not address is a large group of validity constraints that involve other attribute values in the same tuple (e.g., QtyShip ≤ QtyOrdered) or other tuples (e.g., Sum(LoanAmt) ≤ 10000). These more comprehensive aspects of attribute integrity are included as part of extensions to the relational database model that have been developed since its inception.

The second form of integrity essential to the relational database model is **entity integrity**. This is a fairly straightforward concept — every tuple in a relation represents an entity (i.e., an instance of an entity type) that must exist in the real world; therefore, every tuple must be uniquely identifiable.[20] It follows that there can be no completely duplicate tuples (all attribute values identical) in a relation; otherwise, the unique existence of entities is not represented in the database. From this property of uniqueness is derived the principle that there exists in every relation some set of attributes (possibly all the relation's attributes) whose values are never duplicated entirely in any two tuples in the relation. If you don't include any superfluous attributes (i.e., ones not needed to guarantee uniqueness) in the set of attributes, the set of attributes can serve as the relation's primary key. (More than one possible set of attributes may meet the criteria for a primary key; each of these is referred to as a **candidate key**, and one is picked arbitrarily as the primary key.[21])

The primary key is a minimal set of attributes whose values are unique for all tuples in a relation. Because of this, the primary key forms the only means of addressing a specific tuple in the relational database model. A consequence of the requirement for unique primary key values is that none of the values in a tuple's primary key attributes can be null (i.e., missing or unknown). None of the primary key attributes can be null because otherwise this tuple's primary key value couldn't be guaranteed to be unequal to some other tuple's primary key value.[22] Thus, if SSN is the attribute serving as the primary key in the Person relation and there exists a tuple with SSN = 123-45-6789, another tuple could not have SSN = null because you couldn't tell whether the actual SSN value is equal to123-45-6789. If

19 But some well-respected researchers believe the idea of null is a bad one and suggest default values instead. The C.J. Date book mentioned in the annotated bibliography provides a detailed discussion on the differing points of view.

20 Note that the "real world" includes both concrete and abstract entities.

21 Formally, there's actually no absolute requirement that you pick any specific candidate key as the primary key because all that's really necessary for entity integrity is that all tuples are unique. But, by convention, we usually select one candidate key to serve as the primary key for each relation.

22 In the relational model, null isn't a value in the attribute's domain; null is essentially a placeholder that means "the value of this attribute is unknown — *and it might be any value in the domain.*" Because the actual attribute value, if it were known, could be any domain value, there's no way to know that the value isn't also present in the same primary key attribute of some other tuple.

you can't tell whether the two values are equal, you can't guarantee uniqueness. A similar argument holds for primary keys made up of more than one attribute (i.e., **composite primary keys**), which need all attribute values to guarantee uniqueness and hence cannot have null for any of the attributes in the primary key.

The third, and final, form of integrity fundamental to the relational database model is **referential integrity**. Simply put, referential integrity requires that tuples that exist in separate relations, but that are interrelated, be unambiguously interrelated by corresponding attribute values. Let's look at the warehouse example again to understand referential integrity. In Figure 18.5B, two relations are used so that a warehouse address can be stored nonredundantly. The WarehouseID is stored as an attribute in both relations, so the WarehouseID value can be used in an Inventory tuple to reference (i.e., look up) the appropriate Warehouse tuple via the Warehouse relation's WarehouseID primary key. Thus, the tuples in the two relations are interrelated, based on matching values in the WarehouseID attributes in the two relations.

As we pointed out earlier, the WarehouseID attribute in the Warehouse relation serves as a primary key and can never be null. The WarehouseID attribute in the Inventory relation is referred to as a **foreign key** (it addresses "foreign" tuples that are usually outside the same relation). A foreign key value can be all null. That means that its related tuple is unknown. A foreign key value also can match exactly a primary key value in a related tuple. But a foreign key value cannot have some attribute values present (i.e., at least one attribute value is not null) and not match the primary key value of an existing tuple in the related relation. This requirement says nothing more than that if the foreign key points to a related tuple, the tuple must be there. A consequence of this rule is that composite foreign key values cannot be *partially* null because, by the entity integrity rule, no primary key attribute value can ever be null.

Together, the three integrity rules — attribute, entity, and referential — allow specification of important constraints that a relational DBMS can enforce automatically whenever a database update occurs. These rules protect not only the specific values in attributes, but also the identity and interrelationships of tuples. A DBMS that provides this level of integrity support lifts a large coding load off application programmers.

Data Manipulation

As we stated earlier, data representation and integrity do not make a complete model. There must be some means of manipulating the data as well. The relational database model defines data manipulations as the relational assignment operation and eight algebraic operations. The assignment operation simply allows the value of some arbitrary expression of relational algebra to be assigned to another relational variable. For example, the expression

```
RelationC ←—— RelationA JOIN RelationB
```

lets the relational variable RelationC take on the value (set of tuples) resulting from the JOIN operation performed over tuples in the RelationA and RelationB relations. This is analogous to arithmetic assignment in HLL computations.

The eight relational algebraic operations include four standard set operations and four operations specific to database relations.[23] The four relational algebraic operations found in conventional

23 In addition to these eight fundamental operations, various other operations have been proposed for relational algebra. Among these are *extend,* which adds a new, derived attribute to a relation, and *summarize,* which essentially creates a new relation by subtotaling groups of tuples (rows) in an existing relation. Rather than go into various extensions to the formal relational algebra, we refer you to the additional relational operations available with SQL, as discussed in Part I.

set theory (and the syntax of the corresponding operators used in expressions in the examples in this chapter) are

- **union** (rel_1 UNION rel_2)
- **intersection** (rel_1 INTERSECT rel_2)
- **difference** (rel_1 MINUS rel_2)
- **product** (rel_1 TIMES rel_2)

Figures 18.6A through 18.6D show Venn diagrams of these operations.

Figure 18.6A *Union*

Figure 18.6B *Intersection*

Figure 18.6C *Difference*

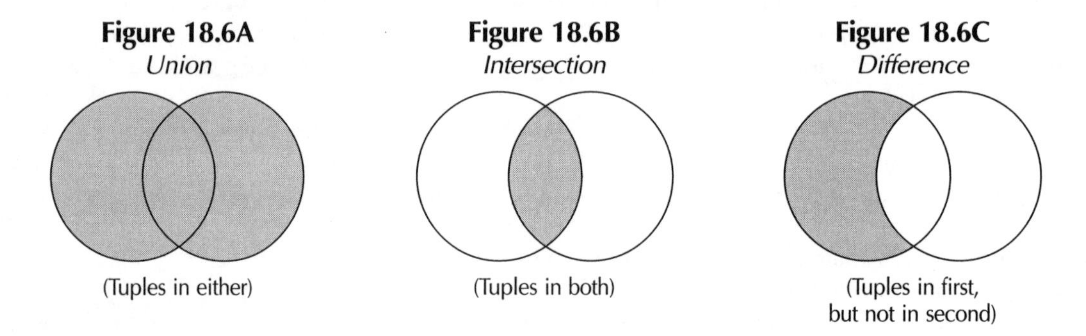

(Tuples in either) (Tuples in both) (Tuples in first, but not in second)

Figure 18.6D *Product*

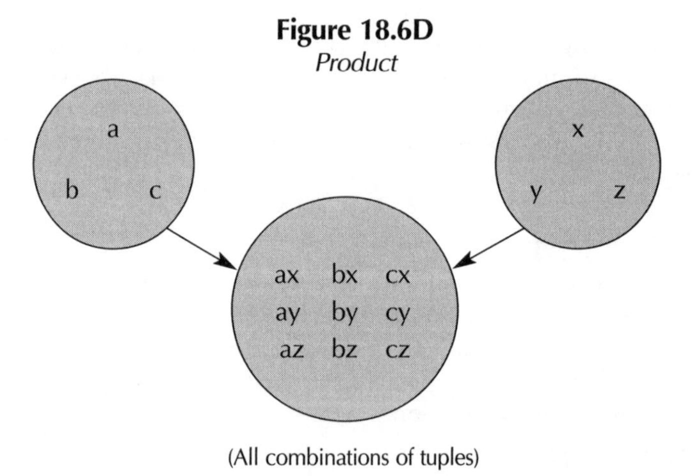

(All combinations of tuples)

The results of these four operations performed on the sample relations in Figure 18.7A are shown in Figures 18.7B through 18.7F.

Figure 18.7A
Three Relations Used As Operands

SSN	Name
123-45-6789	Smith
601-11-9999	Wilson

RelA

SSN	Name
145-67-8888	Jones
601-11-9999	Wilson

RelB

Course	Instructor
Math 101	Aldridge
Psych 203	Ulrich

RelC

Figure 18.7B
RelA UNION RelB

SSN	Name
123-45-6789	Smith
601-11-9999	Wilson
145-67-8888	Jones

(Duplicate tuples are dropped)

Figure 18.7C
RelA INTERSECT RelB

SSN	Name
601-11-9999	Wilson

Figure 18.7D
RelA MINUS RelB

SSN	Name
123-45-6789	Smith

Figure 18.7E
RelB MINUS RelA

SSN	Name
145-67-8888	Jones

(Difference is not commutative)

Figure 18.7F
RelA TIMES RelC

SSN	Name	Course	Instructor
123-45-6789	Smith	Math 101	Aldridge
123-45-6789	Smith	Psych 203	Ulrich
601-11-9999	Wilson	Math 101	Aldridge
601-11-9999	Wilson	Psych 203	Ulrich

Note that union, intersection, and difference require the two relations to have the same attributes (i.e., they must be **union-compatible**). The product operation can work on dissimilar relations; if one relation has *m* attributes and the other has *n* attributes, the result is a relation with $m + n$ attributes. Also, union, intersection, and product are **commutative** operations — the order of operands does not matter (e.g., A UNION B is equal to B UNION A). The difference operation is not commutative, as Figures 18.7D and 18.7E show.

The four special relational algebraic operations (and the syntax of the corresponding operators used in expressions in the examples in this chapter) are

- **projection** (PROJECT rel_1 [*attribute-list*])
- **selection** (SELECT rel_1 WHERE *predicate*)
- **division** (rel_1 DIVIDEBY rel_2)
- **join** (rel_1 JOIN rel_2 WHERE *predicate*)

Examples of these operations performed on the sample relations in Figure 18.8A are shown in Figures 18.8B through 18.8G.

Figure 18.8A
Sample Relations

CustID	City	Status	Credit
123	Portland	00	1,000
456	Portland	20	500
789	Eugene	10	10,000
304	Portland	00	2,000

Customer

OrderID	OrderCustID	Amt
601	123	2,000
602	789	50
603	123	500
604	198	1,000

Order

Company	Vehicle
Ford	Car
Ford	Truck
GM	Car
Nissan	Truck

AutoCompany

Vehicle
Car

CarsOnly

Vehicle
Car
Truck

CarsAndTrucks

Figure 18.8B
PROJECT Customer [CustID, City]

CustID	City
123	Portland
456	Portland
789	Eugene
304	Portland

Figure 18.8C
PROJECT Customer [City, Status]

City	Status
Portland	00
Portland	20
Eugene	10

Figure 18.8D
SELECT Customer WHERE City = "Portland"

CustID	City	Status	Credit
123	Portland	00	1,000
456	Portland	20	500
304	Portland	00	2,000

Figure 18.8E
AutoCompany DIVIDEBY CarsOnly

Company
Ford
GM

Figure 18.8F
AutoCompany DIVIDEBY CarsAndTrucks

Company
Ford

Figure 18.8G
Customer JOIN Order WHERE CustID = OrderCustID

CustID	City	Status	Credit	OrderID	OrderCustID	Amt
123	Portland	00	1,000	601	123	2,000
123	Portland	00	1,000	603	123	500
789	Eugene	10	10,000	602	789	50

Projection (Figures 18.8B and 18.8C) eliminates some attributes (columns) from a relation; any resulting duplicate tuples are then eliminated. Selection (Figure 18.8D) eliminates entire tuples (rows) if they don't satisfy a condition. Note that if you specify "WHERE CustID = 123," a specific tuple can be selected by its unique primary key value. The division operation (Figures 18.8E and 18.8F) results in tuples where all values of an attribute in the first relation match all values (in a different attribute) in the second relation.

The final special relational algebraic operation is join. Join is not a primitive operation (i.e., all join operations are equivalent to the product of two relations from which some tuples are then selected); however, its usefulness in interrelating two relations is so great that it's treated as one of the essential set of eight operations. Figure 18.8G provides an example of an **equijoin** in which the two relations (Customer and Order) are interrelated by equal values in the CustID and OrderCustID attributes. Conditions other than equality can be used to join tuples in two relations; for example, values of two attributes can be tested for greater than or unequal. In general, the test used can be any scalar comparison (=, >, <, <>, ≤, ≥). This comparison operator is often referred to by the Greek symbol for theta (θ), and thus the generic version of the operation is often called a **theta-join**.

The result of an equijoin always has two attributes with identical values in every tuple (in Figure 18.8G, these attributes are CustID and OrderCustID). If one of these redundant attributes is dropped from the resulting relation, the equijoin is said to be a **natural join**. The natural join is the join most commonly meant when you see a nonspecific reference to a database join.

Other variants of join are possible. Figure 18.8G shows an **inner join** — one in which unmatched tuples are dropped. If instead of dropping unmatched tuples, you include them and put null in the attributes of the missing tuple, you have an **outer join**. If only the first relation's (the one on the left of the JOIN operator) unmatched tuples are paired with nulls, the result is a **left outer join**; a mirror-image **right outer join** is also possible. A **full outer join** extends unmatched tuples from both relations with nulls.

This group of eight relational algebraic operations has the property of **algebraic closure**, which means that the result of any of the eight operations is a relation. Thus, the operations can be combined into complex, parenthesized expressions similar to the way ordinary arithmetic expressions can be built up. For example,

```
(RelationA UNION RelationB) TIMES RelationC
```

is a valid relational algebraic expression. Because the operands and results in relational algebra are relations, not simple values or single tuples (i.e., rows or records), the manipulations provide a very powerful base for database operations, as well as a means of expressing subsets in complex integrity constraints. To relate this concept to a conventional file system, think of how much you could accomplish with operations that are expressed in algebraic form but that treat entire files (or record subsets) as the operands.

The eight relational algebraic operations provide a standard by which to measure any DBMS that claims to support relational data manipulations. Although a particular DBMS may use a different syntax than is used here, it must provide equivalent power in manipulating relations without iteration (looping) or recursion.[24] The relational database model is unique among the various database models in that it provides for manipulations of entire sets of tuples. The following expression provides an example of using a set-at-a-time manipulation:

```
Update all Customers where AmtDue > 600, setting Status to "H"
```

Set-at-a-time operations provide a more powerful way to manipulate data than is possible with the record-at-a-time operations available with conventional file-system I/O or with other types of DBMSs. (Keep in mind that a set of tuples can contain a single tuple and, thus, that set-at-a-time operations provide both higher-level manipulations and record-at-a-time operations.)

Expressions in relational algebra are used not only to retrieve data or create new relations but also to define a scope for record-at-a-time retrieval and update. The result of a relational algebraic expression can be treated as a **view relation**[25] (rather than a **base relation** — one in which the data is actually stored). Figure 18.9 depicts (in table format) a view relation and the base relation over which it's defined.

Figure 18.9

View Relation and Its Base Relation

View Relation

CustomerHighDebt

CustID	AmtDue	InterestRate	Status
663309	1250.00	0.12	B
802145	630.00	0.55	A
264502	800.00	0.10	B

SELECT Customer WHERE AmtDue > 600.00

CustID	AmtDue	InterestRate	Status
123886	500.00	0.07	A
663309	1250.00	0.12	B
802145	630.00	0.55	A
264502	800.00	0.10	B

Customer

Base Relation

24 In fact, the most widely used relational DML is SQL, and it's based on *relational calculus,* another way of expressing relational operations that's equivalent to the relational algebra. In our experience, relational algebra is more intuitive than relational calculus for most people, so this introduction of the relational model uses that approach.

25 A view is technically a named, derived (or virtual) relation. There are also unnamed, derived relations and several other formal categories of relations. In this book, we keep things simple by using "view relations" somewhat loosely to cover various categories of relations other than base relations.

Also, recall from Chapter 1 that UDB/400 logical files are based on the concept of views in that they don't contain actual data but provide a way to access data in underlying physical files (which are like base relations). Logical files support record selection, field projection, join, derived fields, and a few other relational-like operations.

Changes to a tuple in a view are treated as changes to the underlying tuple in the base relation. Thus the statement

```
Update all [tuples in] CustomerHighDebt, setting Status to "H"
```

is equivalent to the statement

```
Update all Customers where AmtDue > 600, setting Status to "H"
```

because the CustomerHighDebt view defines a subset[26] of the Customer relation for purposes of set-at-a-time operations and the attribute update operation (setting Status to "H") is applied to all tuples in the base relation (Customer) that satisfy the view's predicate.

Those attributes in a view relation that are also in the base relation are known as **direct attributes**. Views can also have **virtual** (or **derived**) **attributes**, which are calculated from attribute values in the base relation. Figure 18.10 shows a simple example of a view that has one direct and one virtual attribute.

Figure 18.10

View Relation with a Virtual Field

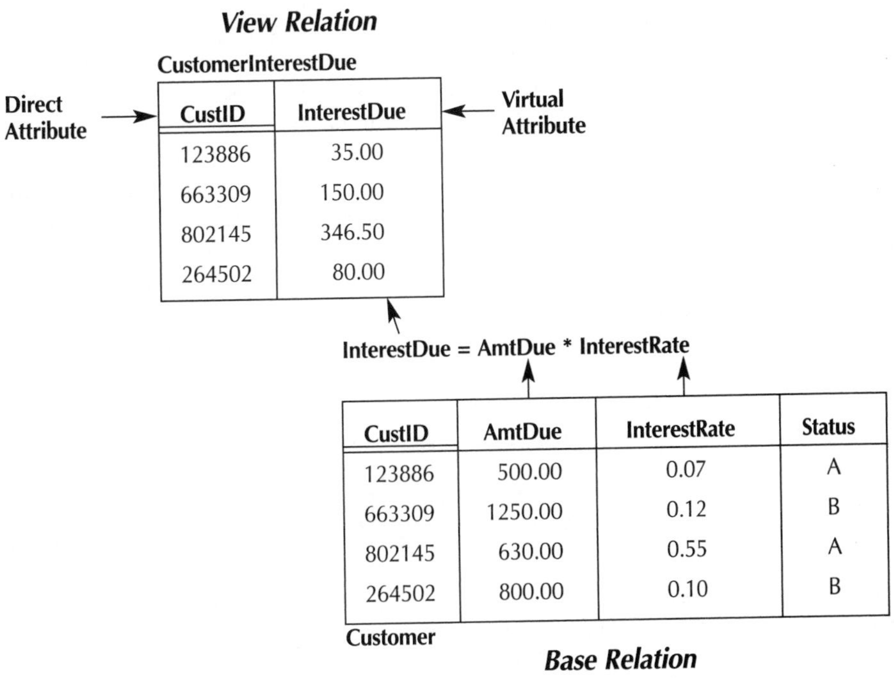

View Relation

CustomerInterestDue

Direct Attribute → CustID; Virtual Attribute → InterestDue

CustID	InterestDue
123886	35.00
663309	150.00
802145	346.50
264502	80.00

InterestDue = AmtDue * InterestRate

CustID	AmtDue	InterestRate	Status
123886	500.00	0.07	A
663309	1250.00	0.12	B
802145	630.00	0.55	A
264502	800.00	0.10	B

Customer

Base Relation

Chapter 6 covers SQL views and describes more ways to derive the contents of a view, as well as additional operations that use views.

Another important use of the relational algebra is to define complex integrity rules. For example, we could specify

```
For all Customers where AmtDue > 600, Status = "H"
```

26 Possibly empty or containing all tuples.

to require that the DBMS reject any update to the database that would violate this rule. We can use a full range of aggregation functions (e.g., SUM, AVERAGE) to specify many other integrity rules. For example, in a financial system, we might express a borrower's maximum permissible outstanding debt as

```
For each BorrowerID X in Borrowers,
(SUM(AmtDue) in Loans where Loans.BorrowerID = X) < 1,000,000
```

This type of rigorous specification is useful for both database modeling and specifying integrity rules in a DBMS so the DBMS can enforce the rule across all applications.

Taken together, the data structure, data integrity, and data manipulation components of the relational database model provide the foundation for both DBMS facilities and database design methods. If you've already studied the other parts of this book, you no doubt recognize many of the relational concepts in SQL/400 tables. Even more immediately, the next two chapters use relational concepts as part of a practical approach to database design.

Chapter Summary

Database management systems arose out of the need to reduce the amount of coding necessary to retrieve and update application data, as well as the desire to provide systemwide enforcement of integrity rules. DBMSs provide a data definition language to define tables, files, and so on in a system catalog so their definitions and integrity constraints don't have to be repeated in the source code for multiple applications. DBMSs also provide a data manipulation language to retrieve and update data. Typically, the DML is more powerful than HLL I/O operations for conventional file systems.

Of the four major models for DBMSs — hierarchic, network, inverted list, and relational — the relational database model has become the most widely accepted due both to the strong theoretical foundation that supports the relational model and its being the only model with physical data independence — that is, the relational model has no reference to physical storage characteristics such as pointers (links) or relative record numbers.

The relational database model has three major parts: data structure, data integrity, and data manipulation. Relations (often represented as tables) represent entity types. Each tuple in a relation (or row in a table) represents one instance of the relation's entity type. An attribute (or column in a table) represents some entity property. There is no particular ordering to the attributes or tuples. Each attribute is known by its name and is defined over a domain, which specifies the allowable values for the attribute. Each tuple is identified by a primary key value. The primary key is a minimal set of attributes that have unique values for all tuples. Tuples in one relation can be associated with tuples in another relation by foreign key values. A foreign key is a set of attributes in the referencing relation that correspond to the primary key attributes in the referenced relation.

Relations that satisfy the requirements for normal forms (1NF through 5NF) represent certain facts unambiguously and nonredundantly. The five major normal forms have the following requirements:

- 1NF — Attribute values are not sets.
- 2NF — Each non-key attribute is dependent on the entire primary key.
- 3NF — Each non-key attribute is dependent on nothing but the primary key.
- 4NF — No more than one multivalued fact exists in a relation.
- 5NF — No further splitting of a relation is possible without information loss.

The relational model includes several important integrity constraints. Attribute integrity states that all values for an attribute must come from the underlying domain (or, in some cases an attribute may be null, meaning that the value is missing or unknown). Entity integrity states that there must be no duplicate tuples in a relation. As a consequence, every relation must have some minimal set of attributes that can serve as a primary key. If the relation has more than one such set of attributes, the alternatives are known as candidate keys, and one is picked arbitrarily as the primary key. To guarantee entity integrity, no primary attribute can be null. Referential integrity states that all foreign key values must either be null or match some existing tuple's primary key.

The relational model's DML is the relational algebra (or equivalent) that includes the assignment operator plus eight set-oriented operations: union, intersection, difference, product, projection, selection, division, and join. These operations are useful not just to manipulate data in a relational DBMS but also to create expressions for defining the scope of data retrieval or update operations or to specify complex integrity constraints. A relational algebra expression can be used to define a view relation over a base relation (one that actually contains data). A view relation provides a way to access a derived set of tuples and attributes. Updates to a view relation affect the data in the underlying base relation.

The relational database model not only provides the foundation for UDB/400 and other relational DBMSs, but it also is the basis for popular database design methods.

Key Terms

algebraic closure
atomic
attribute
attribute integrity
base relation
candidate key
cardinality
commutative
composite primary key
data definition language (DDL)
data manipulation language (DML)
database management system (DBMS)
degree
derived attribute
difference
direct attribute
division
domain
entity integrity
entity type
equijoin
fifth normal form (5NF)
first normal form (1NF)
foreign key
fourth normal form (4NF)
full outer join
hierarchic data model
inner join
instance
integrity constraint
intersection
inverted list data model
join
left outer join
multivalued fact
natural join
network (CODASYL) data model
normal form
normalization
null
outer join
physical data independence
primary key
product
projection
property
record-oriented file
referential integrity
relation
relation body
relation heading
relational database model
right outer join
second normal form (2NF)

continued

continued...

selection
stream-oriented file
system catalog
system dictionary
theta-join
third normal form (3NF)
tuple
union
union-compatible
view relation
virtual attribute

Exercises

1. What advantages does a DBMS provide over a conventional file system? Are there any disadvantages?
2. Provide three specific examples of each of the following:
   - entity type
   - property
   - integrity constraint
3. What is the purpose of the system catalog?
4. List three useful kinds of data retrieval that the ideal DBMS might provide in addition to reading a single record by key or by RRN. What (if anything) would be required so you could use these features from RPG IV or ILE COBOL/400?
5. What problems might occur by storing one record's RRN in another record (as a link)?
6. What are the advantages and disadvantages of using attribute values as the only means to access data (as happens in the relational database model)? What might be done to alleviate some of the disadvantages?
7. Explain the difference between a database relation and a database table. What advantage is there to the use of the table representation?
8. Explain the difference between an entity type and an instance of an entity. How is each represented in the relational database model?
9. Explain the difference between a relation's degree and its cardinality.
10. What purpose does the domain concept serve in the relational database model?
11. The null placeholder can be used instead of a domain value in an attribute when the actual value is unknown or missing. Describe an alternative scheme that doesn't use nulls. Be sure to consider the following issues:
    - calculating sums, averages, and so on over attributes with numeric domains
    - domains that include *all* values of a particular type (e.g., numbers)
12. Give an example of a foreign key that references the same relation that contains the foreign key.
13. Use table-like notation to show a relation (with data) that's in first normal form but not in second normal form. Along with your table, explain (in a few words) what the facts are that the table is representing redundantly. Show how to correct the problem by restructuring the relation.
14. Repeat Exercise 13 for a relation that's in second normal form, but not in third normal form.
15. Can you think of other types of redundancy that should be avoided that aren't covered by the normal forms?

    Hint: Reread the section on views.

16. Give the result of the following expressions, using the relations shown below:
    - RelA UNION RelC
    - RelA INTERSECT RelC
    - RelA MINUS RelC
    - RelA TIMES RelB

RelA

SSN	Name
123-45-6789	Smith
601-11-9999	Wilson

RelB

Course	Instructor
English 201	Murphy
Biology 302	Dutcher

RelC

SSN	Name
123-45-6789	Smith
805-11-3445	Waldo
776-55-2323	Zephyr

17. Give the result of dividing the relation shown in Figure 18.7F by the RelC relation shown in Figure 18.7A.
18. Using the relations in Figure 18.8A, give the result of
    - PROJECT Customer [City, Credit]
    - SELECT Customer WHERE Credit > 600
19. Describe how the concept of a view relation might be helpful in
    - a database design method in which you model a company's data and how it's used
    - a DBMS facility that HLL programs can use

Chapter 19

Logical Data Modeling

Chapter Overview

As you learned in the previous two chapters, logical data modeling and physical database design are essential parts of business application development. The data modeling and database design processes produce a blueprint for implementation, whether the implementation uses a traditional language such as RPG IV or ILE COBOL/400 and a conventional file system, an application generator for a relational DBMS, or an object-oriented language and an object-oriented database. This chapter begins our coverage of the data modeling process by presenting a step-by-step process you can use to produce a good data model.

Introduction

There are many approaches to data modeling, including variations based on the popular relational database model presented in Chapter 18. The relational model uses relations to represent things of interest, with relation attributes representing the particular properties of whatever the relation represents. As an example, a Part relation that represents parts used in a manufacturing business might include attributes for the part's identifying number, description, and cost. In this chapter, we use the table representation of relations because tables are familiar objects to end users and the terminology of tables and columns is usually easier for end users to work with. Chapter 18 explained the finer distinctions between relations and their representation as tables; as long as you understand these differences, you'll have no problems using relations and tables as more or less interchangeable data modeling concepts.

Relational concepts fit many business applications well and have proven useful in years of business application development — not only are the underlying mathematical foundations quite powerful and well defined, but both developers and end users seem comfortable with the concept of a table as an abstraction for things with which businesses typically deal. The 11-step process we lay out in this chapter uses relational database concepts as a foundation, but many of the steps can be adapted to other methods, such as the increasingly popular object-oriented analysis and design.

Remember from Chapter 17 that implementing a database consists of three distinct stages: logical data modeling, physical database design, and database table or file implementation. Logical data modeling produces a description from the perspective of the business; physical database design produces a description from the perspective of the hardware and system software. Implementation converts the physical database specification to the proper source code and commands to create tables or files, programs, and other parts of an application. Conceptually, logical data modeling precedes physical database design, which precedes implementation. In practice, of course, there's often a lot of parallel activity.

Data modeling goes hand-in-glove with process modeling,[1] and the two occur together as a development project proceeds. Process modeling covers such aspects as how orders are entered and fulfilled and how customer credit limits are calculated. Obviously, the description of a process requires

1 Process modeling is sometimes referred to as "systems analysis" or by various other terms.

referring to the data model to identify where some of the values used in calculations come from and where user input and the results of calculations are stored. The data model may also refer to process definitions for actions that are triggered when some change occurs in the database (Chapter 16 discusses UDB/400 trigger programs). This book doesn't cover process modeling steps, but one commonly used method you might investigate is data flow diagrams (DFDs). DFDs dovetail nicely with relational data modeling methods. The annotated bibliography in Appendix E suggests several books on DFDs and other process modeling topics you may want to consult. A process model is the basis for a process design (often referred to as a system design), which in turn is the basis for implementing programs and accompanying manual procedures. Just as logical data modeling and process modeling occur together, so too do the two types of design (database and process) and implementation (tables or files and programs). Keep this in mind as you learn the following data modeling steps — they describe only part of what you must do when you tackle a complete development project.

The following sections present a series of 11 steps to produce a data model. Logically, they flow sequentially; however, in practice you skip around as you gather knowledge about the system you're developing. Much of the information is developed from interviewing end users or reading procedure manuals, forms, and other sources that explain how the business works. Thus, when you're talking to an end user or reading a procedure manual, you may learn things that are covered in several of the steps discussed below. For example, in a single conversation, you might learn about the existence of some **entity types**, about some of the entities' properties, including identifying properties (primary keys), and about relationships among the entity types. Rather than having a series of narrowly focused conversations — the first to discover the entity types, the next to discover entity properties, and so on — you try to learn as much as you can about all these dimensions when you discuss the system with an end user. Your first conversation may provide enough information to let you develop a broad overview of the most important entity types and their interrelationships, with details being filled in through further conversations and reading documents. As with all parts of data modeling and database design, be adaptable and fit the following steps to the nature of the project and organization.

Step 1. Establish a Naming Standard and a Data Dictionary

Before you embark on a major data modeling project, you should get two things in order: your naming conventions and how you'll store the information you gather. Many business applications involve hundreds of names, and keeping them straight is half the battle in data modeling. Establish abbreviation and naming standards for data model and process objects such as tables, columns, relationships, domains, and programs. The sections "Guidelines for SQL/400 Names" in Chapter 3 and "A Guide to SQL/400 Naming" in Chapter 13 explain the principles of a good naming system. Most important, names should be consistent and should express clearly what an item represents or stores.

Following your naming standard, create one table for valid abbreviations that can be used to form names and another table for valid names. In other words, before you start generating a bunch of names, know how you will form them and be ready to record them. You may need to record a lot of information about names — for example, short, standard, and long variations, synonyms, preferred usage, and a description.

Once you've established naming standards and have a place to track the names you use, you're ready to create a **data dictionary**.[2] A data dictionary isn't one thing; it's lots of things: all the

2 There are lots of alternative names for what we refer to as the "data dictionary," including "model portfolio" and "repository." There's no widely accepted standard for what you call the totality of all the computer files, file folders, and other containers of specification information, so call it whatever you prefer — just be sure you have some place to keep all the information you'll be recording.

containers you use to hold everything you record during the modeling process. These containers may be word-processing documents, database files, CASE[3] design tool project folders, or any other useful way to keep track of what you learn. In a typical project, you might have some word-processing documents that contain descriptions of business rules or processes, an AS/400 database table that contains table and column names and brief descriptions, and some entity relationship diagrams produced using a CASE product. Together, all these records of your data model make up the data dictionary.

It's a good idea to set up your naming standards and tables before you create too many other computer-based data dictionary objects (e.g., documents and files) because as the data model progresses, you'll find it's important for your dictionary objects as well as your business objects to follow a rational naming standard. And be sure you've got a place to record *all* aspects of the data model. You don't necessarily need expensive, sophisticated CASE tools to produce an effective data dictionary, but do have some place to store information so you can retrieve and distribute up-to-date information about the current version of the data model. For many purposes, word-processing documents will suffice.

Step 2. Record End Users' Views and Identify Entity Types

Think about who in the business best knows what needs to be implemented. Usually that's the end users — the people who carry out or manage the day-to-day operations of the organization. You might also need to work with top-level administrators, especially if the system is ultimately to implement major new ways of doing business. As you talk to end users, also collect manuals, documents, sample computer report listings, sample screen shots, and anything else that will help document the data the organization uses. Take care to make clear, written notes when you talk with an end user. Record a precise description of the various objects, events, relationships, and processes that individual users or departments are concerned with. Keep your notes and the materials you collect well organized.[4]

As you learned in the previous chapter, in relational terms an object (e.g., a customer) and an event (e.g., placing an order) are two types of entities (things about which you want to record facts) and can be represented as base tables. Complex objects and events may be represented by a group of tables, so there's not necessarily only one table per object. In relational terms, a view or view table is the perspective that a user has on objects and events. For example, an order entry clerk's view of an order might include information about several distinct entities, such as a customer, the order itself, and the individual items ordered. Views are defined in terms of relational operations, such as join, over base tables. The difference between base and view tables is that base tables represent the essential, nonredundant facts about entities, and view tables represent a way of looking at these facts.

Because you're working at this stage with end-user perspectives, you won't be able to determine in every case whether something the user thinks of as an object or event should be represented as a base table or as a view over one or more base tables. Simply record the user perspective using base tables for objects and events, doing whatever structuring is obvious or required by the following steps in this chapter. For example, if the user describes an order, you can initially represent that as an Order base table that references the Customer table. When you identify the order's properties (in Step 3), you

3 CASE stands for Computer Aided Software Engineering but has become an almost generic name for various kinds of application design and generator tools.

4 Do not return to your office after a conversation with an end user and throw the material in a pile on your desk. This may sound like obvious advice, but keeping project material well organized is crucial to successful data modeling.

can split out a new table, OrderItem, to represent the multiple items that might be ordered on a single order. At this stage, don't become too concerned with the relational purity of what you record; we get to normalization and other refinements later.

When you discover an entity type, be sure to enter it in your data dictionary. Here are some of the things you should record about an entity type:

- the official name for the entity type, as used in the rest of the data model (e.g., Employee)
- synonyms — other names for the entity type that end users use or that appear on such things as forms and screens (e.g., Worker)
- a short textual description (e.g., "Someone working for the organization under an Employment Contract or recognized as an employee for purposes of tax reporting")
- approximate or estimated yearly volumes (e.g., "Approximately 50 new employees are hired each year; approximately 40 employees leave employment")

This information can go into word-processing documents, spreadsheets, or database tables that you set up for the purpose or into some CASE product's files.

As you identify entity types, also identify **entity type hierarchies**. For example, if some parts are produced on-site and others are purchased, both are **subtypes** of the Part entity type. As another example, Manager and Nonmanager are subtypes of the Employee entity type. A subtype has all the properties and integrity rules of its supertype. For example, the Manager and Nonmanager subtypes have all the properties (e.g., employee ID, name, department) of their Employee supertype.

Step 3. Determine the Most Important Entity Properties

In relational terms, an object's or event's properties are represented as attributes of a relation. As you learn about properties, determine which ones are single-valued (e.g., a person's birth date) and which are multivalued (e.g., a person's children). Multivalued properties are generally represented as a separate table in a normalized relational data model.

Also identify which properties are time dependent. For example, if you need to know a part's cost on different dates, then cost is a **time-dependent property**. Also identify for each attribute whether there is a default value that should be used if no explicit value is supplied when a new instance is added.

As you learn about various properties that are important to the organization, list them in the data dictionary with at least the following information:

- the official name for the property, as used in the rest of the data model (e.g., AnnualSalary)
- synonyms — other names for the property that end users use or that appear on such things as forms and screens (e.g., Salary)
- a short textual description (e.g., "The annual gross pay before taxes for an Employee")
- the source in the business process (e.g., "Defined in employee's Employment Contract")
- the domain that defines the allowable values for the property — discussed in Step 7 (e.g., Salary > 0)
- whether a value for the property is required or optional
- the default value (if any) to be used when a new instance of the entity type is added and no explicit value is supplied for the property

- whether the property is part of a primary key, candidate key, or foreign key — discussed in Steps 4, 5, and 6
- whether the property is a *direct* or a *derived* property. Direct properties cannot be derived from other properties. For example, an employee's name is a direct property. An employee's number of months in service is a derived property because it can be calculated from the starting and ending dates in the employee's employment history. An employee's annual salary might be direct, or it might be derived — for example, if there's also a monthly salary property from which the annual salary can be computed.

At this stage of the data model, don't worry about all the details of each property.[5] Mainly, get some basic information into a list (which might be in a computer file, a word-processing document, or a CASE tool). As you go through the following steps, you'll learn more about the properties and the overall organization of the data model.

Step 4. Determine the Primary Key for Each Entity Type

In a proper data model, you must be able to identify each instance of an entity type (e.g., a particular Customer) by the values of one or more of its properties. In your data model, when you represent an entity type as a table, you specify the table's primary key, which is a column or group of columns that uniquely identify each row in the table (e.g., a CustomerID column). There may be several ways to identify rows uniquely, and any column or group of columns that could serve as a table's primary key is known as a **candidate key**. You should select one candidate key to serve as the table's primary key.[6] As you identify the candidate and primary keys, add them to the documentation for the respective entity type.

Each primary and candidate key must meet the following criteria:

- Candidate key values must be unique for each row in the table.
- Candidate key values must never be missing or incomplete for a row.
- Each candidate key must use no columns other than those necessary to identify a row uniquely.

A primary key should also meet the following criteria:

- It should be meaningless (other than as an identifier).
- A row's primary key value should never change.
- There should be no practical limit to the number of primary key values available.
- Only one primary key should be specified for each table.

5 Some items that you at first consider properties might later turn out to be entity types. For example, a product's color might first be mentioned by a salesperson as a simple (atomic) type of value (e.g., red, green, blue). But someone in manufacturing might view color as an entity type, with its own properties, including chemical components or suppliers. With a data modeling technique based on the relational model, this kind of adjustment is straightforward; those tables that had Color as a column now would have ColorID as a foreign key referencing the primary key of the Color table.

6 You should use the same primary key for all subtypes of an entity type. For example, if the primary key of the Employee entity type is EmployeeID, then EmployeeID should be the primary key for the Manager and NonManager subtypes as well.

Often, the best choice for a table's primary key is a large, meaningless, arbitrarily assigned, positive integer. This type of primary key may be something like an invoice number that's already part of the user's way of doing business, or you may have to introduce a new column as a **surrogate key**, when no naturally occurring columns meet the primary key criteria. Surrogate keys avoid problems that can sometimes occur with natural identifiers. For instance, a social security number, which might seem like a good candidate key for employees, in practice may change, may be missing, or may violate other rules for primary keys. A better choice might be an arbitrary employee ID that's assigned when a person is hired. To let users work with natural identifiers, you can include in the data model a table that maps surrogate keys to natural identifiers (when the natural identifier's value exists).

Because of their simplicity, primary keys consisting of just one column are preferable to keys with more than one column. However, there are two cases in which a composite primary key (i.e., a key consisting of more than one column) works satisfactorily in place of a single-column primary key. First, the primary key for a table that represents a many-to-many relationship (covered in Step 5) can be the combination of the foreign keys that designate the related tables. A foreign key is one or more columns whose values for a particular row match the primary key value of some other row (in the same or a different table). For example, an Order table might have a CustomerID column as a foreign key. Each order's CustomerID column would (normally) contain the value of some Customer row's primary key, thus identifying the customer who placed the order. As long as the foreign keys in a table representing a many-to-many relationship are defined as never being null,[7] the combination of them will have the same desirable qualities as a single-column surrogate key. For example, in a PartSupplier table that represents the relationship between suppliers and parts, the primary key might be a combination of the PartID and the SupplierID foreign key columns.

A composite primary key also works satisfactorily for tables whose sole purpose is to define multi-valued properties. For such tables, a sequence number that is unique within the same parent primary key value can be combined with the foreign key designating the parent. For example, an OrderItem table can have the combination of OrderID and SeqNbr columns as its primary key, where OrderID is a foreign key designating the OrderID of the parent Order table and SeqNbr is the line sequence number within an order.

Step 5. Determine the Relationships Between Entity Types

The entity types you discover don't exist in isolation — they're interrelated. When you identify a **relationship**, document it, including giving it a name. You can record relationships in textual or table form or use an entity relationship diagram (ERD). Chapter 20 provides a detailed explanation of ERD notation and advice on when its use is most appropriate. In addition, for each relationship, you should determine its **cardinality**. There are three major categories of cardinality:

- one-to-one (e.g., each company-owned car may have a single designated parking space, and each parking space may have a single authorized company car assigned to it)
- one-to-many (e.g., one customer may have many orders, but each order has only one customer)
- many-to-many (e.g., many suppliers may supply a part, and a supplier may supply many parts)

In the relational model, you can represent a simple one-to-one or one-to-many relationship with a foreign key. You should represent a many-to-many relationship in a new table reflecting two (or more)

7 Chapter 18 discusses the concept of a null placeholder instead of a column value.

one-to-many relationships. For example, you can represent a many-to-many relationship between parts and suppliers with a PartSupplier table. The Part and Supplier tables would then both have a one-to-many relationship with the PartSupplier table.

It helps to identify more specifically what a relationship's cardinality is. In general, after splitting your many-to-many relationships into one-to-many relationships, you need to determine

- for all "one" sides of the relationships, whether the "one" means "zero-or-one" or "exactly one," and
- for all "many" sides of the relationships, whether the "many" means "zero-or-more" or "one-or-more"

If there are more specific cardinality rules (e.g., "there must be exactly five players on each team"), record these, too. The most important reason to determine precise cardinality rules is so you know whether one side of a relationship is optional or required and so you know the maximum number (if any) of associated instances. (You wouldn't want to implement a basketball database that let a user put six people on the court.)

As you identify relationships, also determine the **degree** of the relationship — that is, how many entity types the relationship involves. Most relationships will be binary (between two entity types). Others may be nonbinary (involving three or more entities). For example, a relationship for which suppliers supply particular parts for specific projects is a three-way relationship. A nonbinary relationship should also be represented as a new table, with one foreign key referencing each table that represents one of the entity types involved in the relationship.

Step 6. Determine the Foreign Key Rules for Each Relationship

For each relationship you include in the data model, one table must include a foreign key that designates the rows in the table for the target (referenced or parent) entity type that are associated with rows in the table for the designating (referencing or dependent) entity type. For example, an Order table might include a CustomerID column as a foreign key to designate the row in the Customer table that is associated with a particular order. For each relationship, you should identify which column(s) in the designating table make up the foreign key.

Also specify the nature of the relationship by specifying the **delete-update-insert rules** for the primary and foreign keys in each relationship.[8] This task involves two parts. First, determine the action to take if a primary key value in the target table is deleted or updated, potentially leaving orphan rows in the designating table that no longer reference an existing row in the target table. For example, you need to specify what should or should not happen when a row is deleted from the Customer table and there are rows in the Order table that reference the deleted Customer row (i.e., how should the system handle an attempt to delete a customer who has outstanding orders). In this case, you can take several possible actions:

- Reject the delete or update (signal an error).
- Handle it with a custom procedure.
- Cascade the delete or update to all the related dependent tables.
- Set the related dependent foreign key column(s) to null or a default value (if allowed).

8 These rules define the specific way that referential integrity will be enforced.

The end user's description of how the business operates is the basis for making this decision.

Next, determine the action to take if an insertion or update in the designating table creates an unmatched, non-null foreign key value in the designating table. For example, you need to specify what should or should not happen when a row is inserted into the Order table and there is no row in the Customer table that matches the customer ID in the new Order row (i.e., an attempt to insert an order with no matching customer). You can specify any of the following rules:

- Reject the insert or update (signal an error).
- Handle it with a custom procedure.
- Create a default parent row in the target table, and give it the same primary key value as the new foreign key value.
- Reset the new or changed foreign key to null or to a default value (if allowed).

Note how the various rules can reflect different approaches to the structure of the organization's data and the way the organization operates. The delete-update-insert rules can be documented with the other information for the table that contains the foreign key to which the rules apply.

Step 7. Determine Additional Integrity Constraints

In Steps 4 and 6, you determined two important business rules: primary and foreign key integrity constraints. By describing the rules that the subsequent design and implementation must follow to ensure that the database always has valid primary and foreign key values, you can avoid ambiguous or incomplete identification of the entities your database stores and the interrelationships among those entities.

You should also identify several other categories of integrity constraints, including domains, **predicates**, and **transition constraints**. Business rules must be accurate and complete if you don't want the database to become a "garbage dump." Because end users often jumble their descriptions and even provide conflicting or incomplete rules, you must discuss and record the rules carefully — it's your neck out there when invalid or inconsistent data appears in the system. In this section, we look at some of the types of rules to record, starting with the simplest.

First, determine the domain of each property. A domain defines two aspects of a column: its allowable values and the allowable operations on the column. By explicitly defining domains, you establish guidelines for ensuring that your implementation won't let invalid values be put into a column and won't improperly use the column in an operation. For example, with clear definitions of the domains of HourlyWage and MonthlySalary, you can ensure that neither column ever contains negative values and that HourlyWage is not added to MonthlySalary without conversion.

You normally don't explicitly define the entire set of allowable operations on a domain because such a definition would require you to consider a very large number of cross-domain operations. Instead, define domains so their allowable values and meaning are clear, and the allowable operations can be inferred from the partial definition. Start by recording a concise, clear, verbal description of each domain, including its allowable values and constraints on operations. Once you have domains defined, you can add the appropriate domain name to each property definition.

Several characteristics of a domain can help further establish its meaning. You should express the domain's basic type (e.g., integer, string, date) in user-oriented terms, not computer-storage–oriented terms. For example, use "integer" or "decimal fraction with precision of 0.01" instead of "packed decimal." You can further restrict a domain's set of allowable values using various forms of set notation. For example, for integers you can use a range (e.g., Cost > 0); for enumerations, you can use a full or partial member list (e.g., DayOfTheWeek is {Sunday...Saturday}). For more complicated sets, it's best to use general set builder notation using logical predicates or use precise verbal set specifications.

When defining domains, you may encounter the need for a set that has values of a certain basic type plus one or more distinct values not of the same basic type. For example, to specify the beginning and ending dates for time-dependent data, you may want to use a domain that includes valid dates, plus distinct values for "open begin date" and "open end date" so you can store open-ended intervals. When you implement a column based on a domain with distinguished values such as these, you generally need to use two particular values (e.g., 0001-01-01 and 9999-12-31). But in the data model, the domain specification should identify the logical meaning of these distinguished values, not the specific implementation constants.

As you identify the domain for each property, you should also document whether either or both of the following possibilities are valid:

- The value of the property may be *unknown* for some rows.
- The value of the property may be *not-applicable* for some rows.

If it's valid for a row to exist with a particular column's value unknown (i.e., the column doesn't contain a valid value), the column is said to allow nulls. Remember that null is a placeholder (not a value from the domain) that means "unknown, but may exist." For example, null might be used to represent an unknown customer phone number. Null does not mean 0, blank, or not-applicable.

Not-applicable means that no meaningful value exists for a column. For example, a Part table might have a Color column, so a part that has no color could contain a not-applicable placeholder in its Color column. It's important to specify in the data model whether a column can contain null or not-applicable so the implementation can support these cases (or enforce that a valid value is always present, if null and not-applicable are not allowed). The way these two placeholders are implemented depends on the DBMS or file system used for the implementation. For example, UDB/400 supports columns that allow nulls, but there's no direct support for a not-applicable placeholder. An application implemented in UDB/400 might use null for both cases, or it might use special values to represent either or both cases.

Columns that allow a not-applicable placeholder are directly related to entity type hierarchies. You can always eliminate the need for a not-applicable placeholder in a column by splitting a table into separate tables representing the subtypes and omitting from the subtype tables columns where all rows would have not-applicable placeholders. For example, a Part table could be split into ColorPart and NoColorPart tables, representing subtypes of the Part entity type. The ColorPart table would have a Color column, but the NoColorPart would not. Whether to use subtypes or allow a not-applicable placeholder is a judgment call; pick the representation that's easier to work with. Use subtypes when there is a clear separation of the distinct subtypes in the business or end-user perspective. For example, you might use subtypes to distinguish between a part produced on-site and an equivalent purchased part, whereas you might simply specify that a column allows the not-applicable placeholder to distinguish a part that doesn't have a color from others that do.

Units of measure or rate (e.g., kilograms or dollars per month) provide another way to clarify a domain's meaning. Also keep in mind that, just as you can define a hierarchy of entity types, you can define domains as a hierarchy. For example, Date is a very general domain. FirstOfMonth is a domain that is a subset of the Date domain, restricted to just those dates where the DayOfTheMonth is 1.

After defining domains to limit the allowable values for each column, you can represent other business rules by specifying row predicates to limit the combination of values present in any row in a table. A row predicate is a constraint that can be evaluated with just the values from a single row in a single table. For example, if an EmploymentHistory table has HireDate and TerminationDate columns; you might define a row predicate as

```
TerminationDate is null OR HireDate <= TerminationDate
```

Multirow and **multitable predicates** are even broader forms of integrity constraint. You can define these constraints using the general notation of **assertions** and **triggered procedures**. Assertions are logical expressions that must be true for a valid database. For example, your data model might state that in any fiscal year, an employee's incentive bonuses cannot exceed his or her total salary. Triggered procedures are actions that occur when a specified condition exists. For example, your model might state that whenever a customer places an order for more than $100,000, a notice must be sent to the sales manager. You can use pseudo-SQL[9] or simply precise narrative descriptions of multirow and multitable constraints. If you're familiar with any of the mathematical notations for formal logic, they can be useful in some cases. However, because many end users (and other developers) may not be familiar with this type of notation, you may find that a less rigorous, but more widely understood, way of expressing constraints is the best technique.

You're also likely to encounter business rules that impose transition constraints on the data model. Transition constraints limit changes to the data. For example, the business rules may restrict a change to a customer's credit limit to either lowering the limit or increasing the limit a maximum of 100 percent in any one month. Assertions and triggered procedures provide good general mechanisms for specifying transition constraints.

Step 8. Determine Security Rules

Security rules are just a special case of integrity constraints that are dependent on the identity of the user. You can use the same notation for security rules that you use for other business rules. As you determine security rules, identify the following classes of constraints:

- *Value-independent* rules, which are restrictions on tables, views, and columns based solely on the type of data, not on particular values. For example, certain users may not be able to access customer data at all.
- *Value-dependent* rules, which are based on specific values. For example, a user may be authorized to see the Salary column in the Employee table only for rows with Salary < 50,000.
- *Statistical* rules, which limit the types of inferences that can be made about values in the database using statistical functions such as Sum and Count. For example, users who are not authorized to individual employee salaries may also be restricted from running salary totals on subsets of employees, because by getting totals for two subsets they might be able to calculate a specific employee's salary.
- *Context-dependent* rules, which are defined in terms of functions or system values, such as time of day. For example, users can be limited to updating the Employee rows of only the employees they supervise.

9 The term "pseudo-SQL" just means an SQL-like expression that doesn't have to conform strictly to any SQL standard or product's syntax.

Step 9. Integrate Multiple Users' Views into an Overall Schema

After you determine the objects, events, relationships, properties, and integrity constraints for each user view, you should combine them into a single, consistent, nonredundant logical data model. The users' views are sometimes referred to as **subschemas** (or **external schemas**) and the integrated model as the **schema** (or **conceptual schema**). Integrating multiple views involves

- identifying columns that are the same in multiple views
- resolving domain and other integrity and security conflicts between multiple definitions of the columns and tables
- synthesizing the schema's base tables from the multiple subschema tables and views

In practice, this integration process occurs as you record users' views. By working on the integrated schema, you uncover conflicts or ambiguities in users' views that you can (hopefully) resolve as you work with the end users.

The integration process demands a good naming convention and an effective data dictionary. Users often have many different synonyms for the same entity or property, and you'll want a single official name to use in all your table and integrity definitions. A synonym table in the data dictionary lets you relate end-user terminology to official names. The data dictionary should also let you record the original source(s) of an integrity constraint.

As an example of the type of synthesis that occurs during this step, you might find that one user perspective has a Customer table (representing a person who buys goods) and another user perspective has a Client table (representing a person who pays for services). If both tables represent a person who pays for goods and/or services, is billed, is sent marketing material, and so on, it's probably a good idea to have a single Customer or Client table (but not both) in the integrated data model. If there's a substantial amount of information that does not overlap for each role (customer or client) a person might play, it may be a good idea to define a Customer table with CustomerOfService and CustomerOfProducts subtypes of Customer. If two or more tables have the same primary key and/or many of the same columns, the tables should probably be combined.

Another common situation in merging users' views is discovering that from one user's perspective a piece of information is a property represented as a column and in another user's perspective this same information is represented as a table with columns for more information about the item. Earlier, we discussed how a product's color might be viewed in different ways by a salesperson and someone in the manufacturing division. In cases such as this, the more extensive perspective (i.e., representing the item with a table) belongs in the integrated data model.

As you integrate tables, you also must adjust foreign keys and tables that represent relationships accordingly. In addition, you may find (and need to revise the data model to document) that a column documented as a direct column in one user's view can actually be derived from columns that are documented in a different user's view. Another potential adjustment will be in the definition of underlying domains when two columns in different users' views are identified as representing the same property, but the different users' views perhaps document different ranges of values in the columns' respective domains. Similarly, whether a column can be null may need to be changed when column definitions are merged from different views.

A note on the integration step: In many cases, your data modeling work will be for only part of the organization's overall information requirements. If a complete or partial data model already exists, any new modeling will need to be integrated with the existing data model, which may necessitate adjustments to the existing data model.

Step 10. Eliminate Redundancy in Schema Base Tables

This step is just a check on the result of the integration of multiple users' views. Make certain that the schema base tables do not contain redundant facts.[10] For example, a PartSupplier table shouldn't normally include a SupplierAddress column because each supplier's address is likely to appear in many rows in the table. In most cases, the SupplierAddress column would be part of a Supplier table, with one row per supplier.

One approach to eliminating redundancy is to check each table to see that it doesn't violate any of the rules of normalization. The "Normal Forms" section in Chapter 18 explains the most important normal forms for relations and how each represents a way to avoid ambiguous representation of entity types and properties. Use that section as a guide to review your table definitions at this stage of the data modeling process. Your logical data model should be completely normalized (i.e., satisfy fifth normal form). This is the best way to communicate the business model accurately using tables as your notational tool. When you do the physical implementation design, you may choose to design files that don't correspond exactly to your data model's tables. Such controlled redundancy is perfectly acceptable but is part of the implementation design, not part of the logical data model.[11]

Another way to eliminate redundancy is to check all columns to see whether they can be derived from other columns. If a column can be derived, it should not be in a base table, but rather in a view (see Step 11). For example, an order's TotalAmount usually can be derived from the set of associated OrderItem rows; thus, TotalAmount is a column that belongs in a view, not in a base table.

Step 11. Determine Subschema Views

Once you have an integrated schema, you should review the original users' views (subschemas) and determine how each is derived from the schema's base tables. This step produces a revised set of users' views defined over the schema's base tables. You may need to express the following types of derivation through the views:

- restriction (subsetting) of rows
- projection (elimination) of columns
- combination of rows (joins or unions) from more than one table
- derivation of virtual columns that are a function of columns in underlying base tables (e.g., OrderItemTotal = ItemUnitPrice * ItemQuantity)
- ordering (sorting) of rows in a view

You can use expressions in relational algebra, as described in Chapter 18, or use a pseudo-SQL notation to describe views.

When you've successfully completed this step, the end users should all be able to validate that the data model reflects the type of information, its structure, and the necessary integrity constraints to

10 Of course, much of the elimination of redundancy happens while you're working with the users' views, before final integration. As with most of the steps described in this chapter, the order presented here isn't meant to be a rigid guideline.

11 This is a frequently misunderstood point in data modeling. *Normal forms have nothing to do with physical database design.* Normal forms are a relational data modeling convention for representing a data model as tables that reflect functional dependencies (i.e., "facts").

support the organization's activities. When the end users first described their own requirements, these elements were modeled in isolation (i.e., without regard to other end users); at this stage of the data modeling process, an end user should be able to see how his or her data fits into the larger picture.

After making one iteration through these 11 design steps, you may need to repeat some of them several times to get the data model right. As the organization's business model changes, you'll also have to revise the logical data model. But using this set of steps, you'll have a framework for analyzing and recording both the original data model and subsequent revisions.

This chapter has only touched the surface of the 11 data modeling steps. The annotated bibliography in Appendix E suggests several excellent books for learning more about this approach. Keep in mind that data modeling isn't an exact science, and you must adapt a variety of methods and documentation techniques to produce a useful data model. In the next chapter, we look at entity relationship diagrams, which are one technique you'll find helpful in documenting a data model. Then, once you have a good data model, you have a solid basis for designing the database implementation. Chapter 21 takes you forward from the data model through physical database design.

Chapter Summary

Logical data modeling is an essential part of application development. A data model provides a description, from the business perspective, of an organization's information requirements. The data model provides the basis for subsequent physical database design, which in turn is the blueprint for implementing database tables or files and related items.

The following 11 steps are a guideline for developing a data model based on the relational database model described in Chapter 18:

Step 1 Establish a naming standard and a data dictionary
Step 2 Record end-users' views and identify entity types
Step 3 Determine the most important entity properties
Step 4 Determine the primary key for each entity type
Step 5 Determine the relationships between entity types
Step 6 Determine the foreign key rules for each relationship
Step 7 Determine additional integrity constraints
Step 8 Determine security rules
Step 9 Integrate multiple users' views into an overall schema
Step 10 Eliminate redundancy in schema base tables
Step 11 Determine subschema views

To complete a data model, you normally work on several steps at the same time, and you may need to repeat some steps to refine the model. A process model is also developed in parallel with the data model. The process model references the data model and vice versa.

Data modeling involves talking to end users and researching manuals, forms, and other documents that the organization uses. This information is first collected from the individual user or department perspective and then integrated into a unified, organization-wide data model. During the integration, conflicts, redundancy, and ambiguity need to be resolved. The completed logical data model should describe entity types, properties, relationships, and integrity constraints upon which all the individual user perspectives can be based.

The data model is stored in a data dictionary, which is a collection of documents, tables or files, diagrams, and so on that contain all the descriptions that are part of the model. As with most application development processes, data modeling techniques must be adapted to the nature of the project and available resources.

Key Terms

assertion
candidate key
cardinality
conceptual schema
data dictionary
degree
delete-update-insert rules
entity subtype
entity type
entity type hierarchy
external schema
multirow predicate
multitable predicate
predicate
relationship
schema
subschema
subtype
surrogate key
time-dependent property
transition constraint
triggered procedure

Exercises

1. Briefly describe and provide examples of five types of information that would be included in a logical data model.
2. For each item you described for Exercise 1, suggest one or more ways you could store the information in a data dictionary.
3. Give an example of how some part of the process model for an order entry system might need to refer to information in the data model.
4. Give an example of how some part of the data model might need to refer to information in the process model for an order entry system.
5. List five ways (or sources of information) to gather the information needed to develop a data model for an organization.
6. Why do you think a primary key value should be unchanging? *(Hint: Consider relationships.)*
7. Give an example of when you might specify that the "cascade" foreign key rule should apply when a row is deleted. (Describe two entity types and the nature of their relationship that makes the "cascade" rule appropriate.)
8. Specify four examples of multirow or multitable integrity rules. Try to make your descriptions as clear and precise as possible.
9. Provide two examples of cases in which two (or more) end users' views (subschemas) might have conflicts when you try to merge them into an integrated data model (i.e., in the schema).

Chapter 20

Entity Relationship Diagramming

Chapter Overview

This chapter describes entity relationship diagrams (ERDs), which provide a way to represent parts of the logical data model in diagram form. You learn a standard set of symbols and other forms of notation that can be used in hand-drawn diagrams or with various computer-based diagramming tools. The chapter also provides guidance on when to use ERDs in your data model.

Introduction

In Chapter 19, we established a series of steps that occur during the data modeling stage of a development project. Many of these steps require some form of documentation to specify the data that the organization requires and how it's structured. Often, this documentation will be reviewed by the person creating the data model, the end user, and the person responsible for the physical database design. We noted in Chapter 17 that the data model must be clear and comprehensible. **Entity relationship diagrams (ERDs)** are a data modeling technique that can improve the clarity and comprehensibility of a data model.

ERDs describe data with pictures. For simple systems and high-level views of complex systems, an ERD's boxes, lines, and other symbols can be easier to understand than a textual description, which is what makes them a valuable data modeling tool for business systems. ERDs aren't suited for every data modeling task, however, and it's just as important to know when not to use ERDs as it is to know how to use them. We'll come back to that point at the end of the chapter.

There are many flavors of ERD notation and lots of religious wars about methodologies, most of which you can safely ignore, as this chapter does. The techniques we describe here are representative of a widely used ERD notation.

You can draw ERDs either by hand or using a variety of PC-based software tools. Usually, ER diagramming tools are part of a larger software package that may include other diagramming tools (e.g., for data flow diagrams), as well as dictionary facilities to store detailed definitions of various other elements of a complete data model. At the end of this chapter, we look at some of the advantages of both hand-drawn and tool-drawn ERDs, but first, let's get more familiar with how you construct ERDs.

Basic ERD Concepts and Symbols

In ERDs, boxes represent entities,[1] and lines connecting boxes represent relationships between entities — hence the name "entity relationship." An **entity** is some object, event, or association of interest in the data model. A **relationship** represents some dependency between two or more entities. The nature of relationships in an ERD tells us a lot about the structure of an organization's data.

1 More properly, boxes represent entity types. For simplicity, in this chapter we follow the common ERD terminology and use "entity" as shorthand for "entity type," except where the longer term is important for clarity.

The following diagram shows a simple ERD with Customer and Order entities and a Places relationship between them.

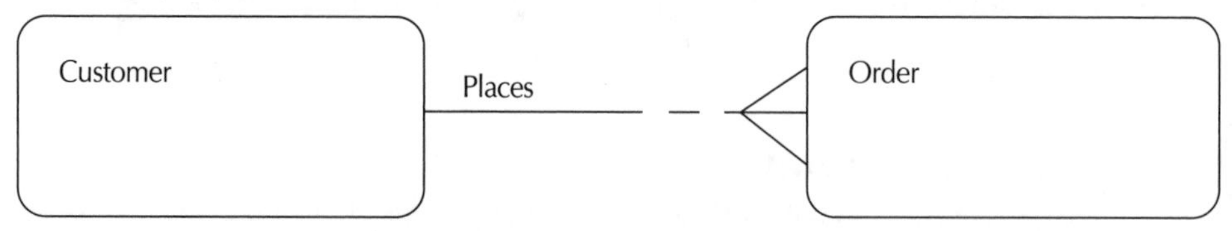

This ERD is a clear, quickly digested depiction of an important aspect of a business: The system under consideration deals with customers and orders. This ERD's clarity and simplicity illustrate why ERDs are a popular technique that business analysts use to describe a business model (or at least some part of its data) to end users.

The line representing the relationship in the diagram above indicates two other important aspects of the business model: Each order is placed by one customer, and a customer may place zero, one, or multiple orders.

The unbroken, single portion of the line attached to the Customer box specifies that each order has exactly one customer associated with it. The broken, crowsfoot portion of the line attached to the Order box specifies that each customer can have zero, one, or more associated orders. The following diagram shows an easy way to remember what the crowsfoot means and on which end of the line you should place it. As you can see, the crowsfoot is shorthand for showing multiple boxes.

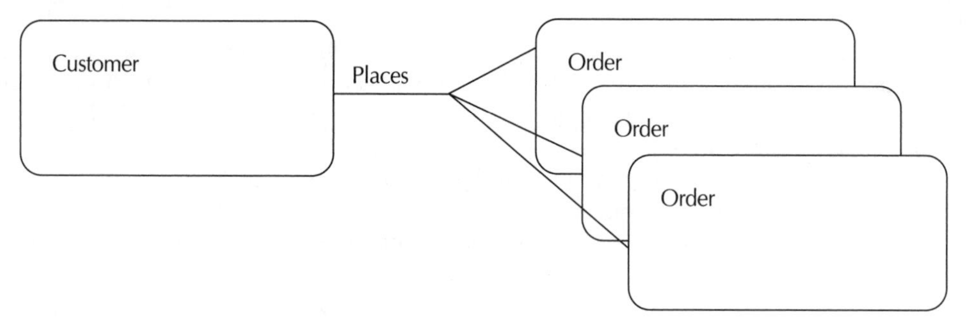

A break at one end of a relationship line means the entity is optional (there can be zero or more), whereas a solid line on an end means it is required (there must be one or more). You can combine broken- or solid-line endings with single-line or crowsfoot endings to depict four possibilities on each end of a relationship, as shown here:

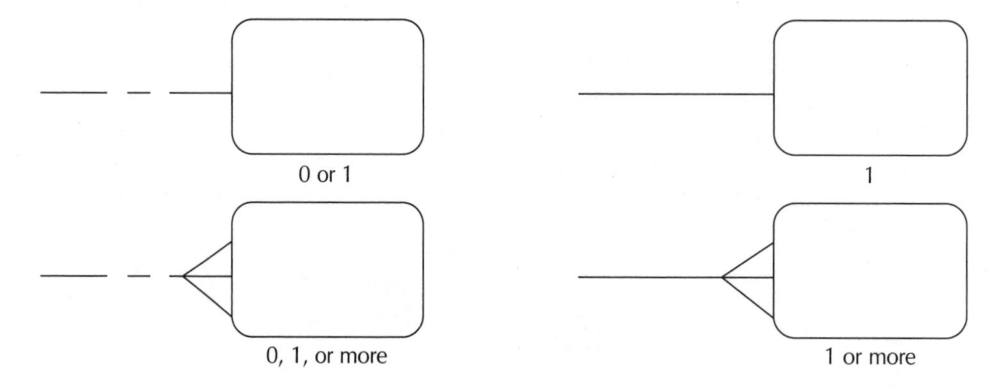

If you encounter a business situation that doesn't fit within these four possibilities, you can add your own annotation for the cardinality of the relationship (i.e., how many instances of one entity can be associated with an instance of the other entity). The following example shows one way to specify that an instance of a Team on court (e.g., a basketball team) must have exactly five instances of Player. The solid line ending next to Player states that Player is required, and the 5 above the crowsfoot specifies the number of Players that a Team on court must have.

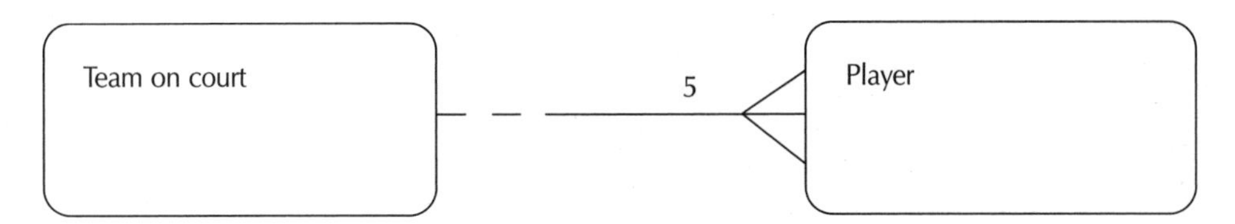

You can also specify a range for the cardinality of a relationship, using an annotation such as the following:

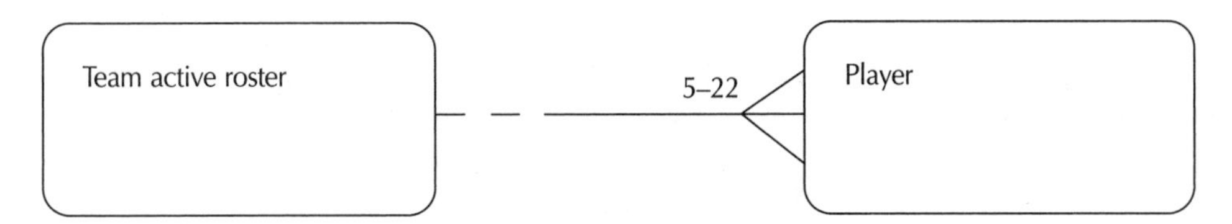

The 5–22 above the crowsfoot here specifies that a team has at least five but no more than 22 players on the Team active roster.

One final addition completes the basic ERD notation. The line representing the relationship between two entities is often labeled at both ends so it's easier to talk about the relationship from the perspective of either entity. The following example adds "Shows" to the Order end of the relationship.

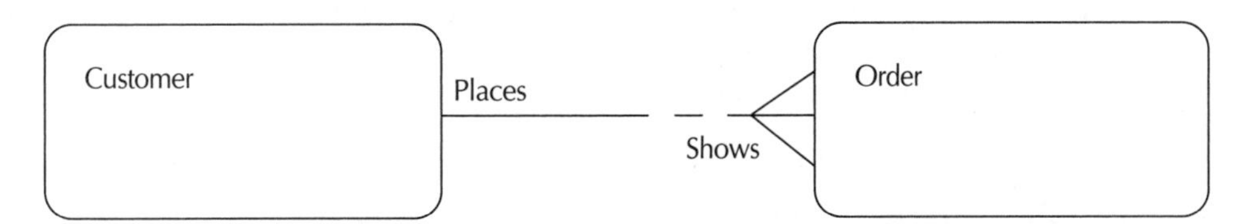

The entity and relationship labels, together with the way the relationship line is drawn, provide the pieces for verbal descriptions of the data model — for example, "Each customer places zero, one, or more orders, and each order shows exactly one customer."

The two relationship labels are alternatives for stating the same thing — there's still only one relationship — and the second label is optional. Don't clutter your diagrams with second labels that are merely passive voice constructions (e.g., "is placed by") for the relationship. While you're working on early versions of ERDs, you often don't need to label a relationship line at all, if the relationship is obvious. For example, in the Customer-Order diagram, it's pretty obvious that customers place orders. In your final diagrams, however, it's a good idea to label all relationship lines, even if a relationship is obvious.

Adding Properties to ERDs

A **property** is some identifying or descriptive piece of information for an entity.[2] For example, a Customer entity would likely have a Name property, and an Order entity would likely have an OrderDate property. You can list property names either inside an entity's box, as in the following entity box

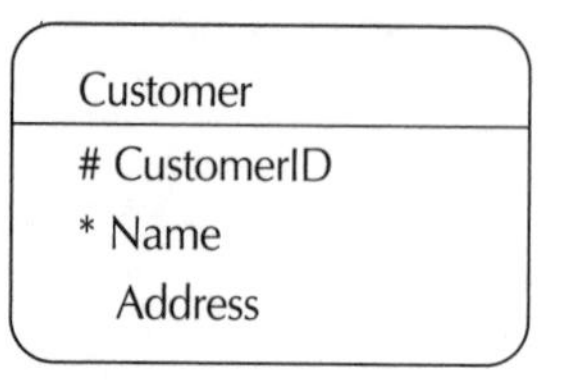

or in an attached list, as in

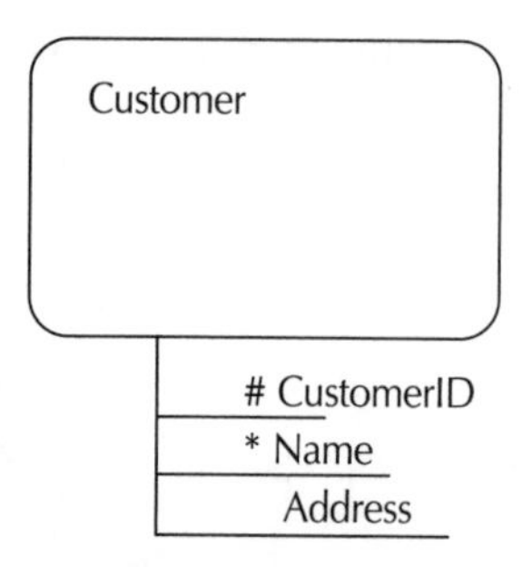

You place a number sign (#) before properties that uniquely identify an entity (in relational terminology, the attributes that constitute the primary key). You place an asterisk (*) before properties that must have a value (and that are not part of the entity's identifier). Any remaining properties you list are for optional values (in relational terminology, the attribute can be null).

A relationship between two entities implies that one of them has one or more properties that contain identifier values from the other entity (in relational terminology, the foreign key). The following ERD shows that you can think of the box for the Order entity as implicitly specifying a CustomerID property that associates each order with a specific customer:

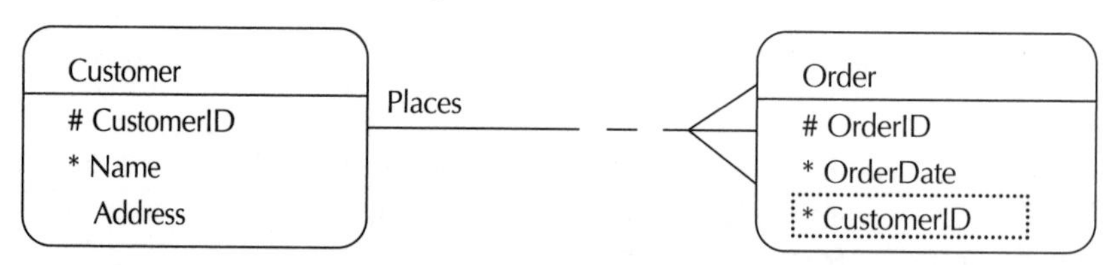

These properties don't need to be shown on an ERD because the relationship line tells us most of what we need to know about the logical relationship between the two entities and the required foreign key property. If a foreign key property is shown explicitly on an ERD, you may want to add some notation to indicate for which relationship it serves as a foreign key and with which property in the target entity it's paired, as in the following example.

2 For ERDs, the term "attribute" is frequently used instead of the term "property." We use "property" to avoid confusion with the specific meaning of attribute in the relational model discussed in Chapter 18. In actual practice, you can use the terms interchangeably.

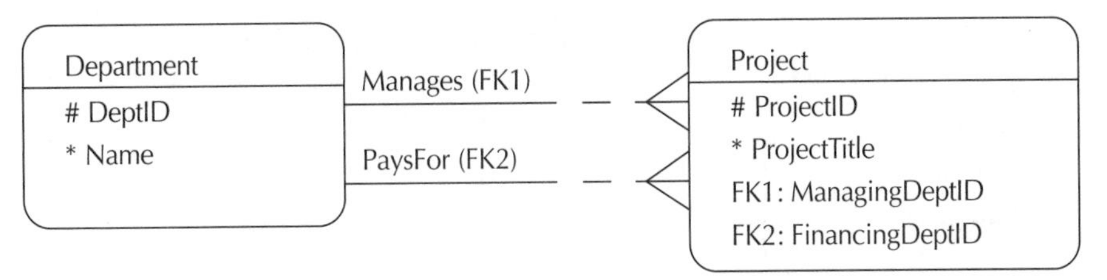

Here, there are two relationships between the Department and Project entities. The Manages relationship represents which department is responsible for managing specific projects. The PaysFor relationship represents which department is responsible for funding specific projects. This ERD tells us that a project's managing and funding departments may be different. The FK1 and FK2 annotations specify which Project property is used as the foreign key for each of the respective relationships. Although the property names make this fairly obvious, the FK1 and FK2 annotations remove any doubt.

In practice, you may find that listing all an entity's properties clutters your ERD and diminishes the value of presenting the data model pictorially. Nothing says you must use only ERDs to describe your entire data model. (In fact, it's unlikely you will.) It's often easier to record and discuss entity properties with end users using a table-formatted list rather than working with all the properties on ERDs. Some computer-based analysis and design tool products let you display properties either way, which is especially helpful if the tool lets you mark a subset of an entity's properties for display on ERDs, helping keep the ERD readable. With hand-drawn ERDs, you should choose the level of detail to put on a diagram depending on how you're using the diagram and at what stage of data model development you are. Final drawings typically have more detail than early, working drafts.

You may also want to specify the details of foreign key rules (e.g., update and delete restrictions) separately from the ERD, using pseudo-SQL or some other specification language, as discussed in Chapter 19.

Multivalued Properties

A property may be single-valued or multivalued. For example, a customer would typically have a single name but might have several phone numbers. There are two ways to represent multivalued properties on ERDs.[3] You can simply list a multivalued property under an entity and describe the property as permitting a set of values by enclosing the property name in braces ({}), as is done for the PhoneNbr property in the following example.

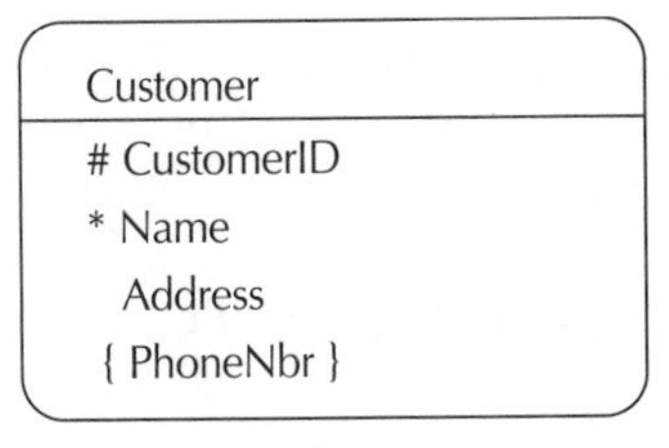

The other way is to show the multivalued property as another entity and associate it with the main entity in a many-to-one relation, as in the following example. (The vertical bar across the relationship

3 We learned in Chapter 18 that the basic relational model requires single-valued attributes, so it may at first seem like "relational heresy" to discuss ways to represent multivalued properties, but read on.

line indicates that the CustomerID property is part of the CustomerPhoneNumber entity's primary key; we explain this notation later.)

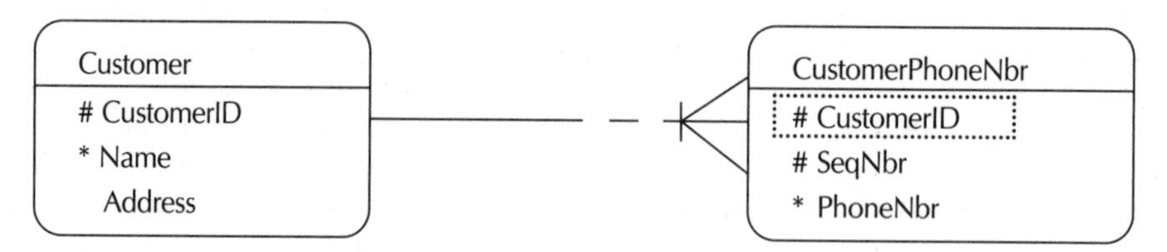

The latter method of specifying multivalued properties illustrates that, in ERDs, an entity can represent some "real" thing, such as a customer, or it can be a design artifact that represents a more abstract notion, such as the multivalued nature of a customer's telephone numbers.

Both techniques for showing multivalued properties can express the same underlying structure of the data. Although the basic, first normal form (1NF) of the relational model forbids using multivalued attributes, there's really no reason not to use the {} notation on ERDs during your data modeling stage — if doing so makes your model's diagrams easier for the end user to understand. You can rest easy knowing you're on firm theoretical ground, too. There's an extension to the basic relational model, known as non-first normal form (NFNF), that deals with nonatomic attributes, including multivalued attributes. When you start to develop your physical database design, you want to show multivalued properties as separate tables, but remember the guideline we discussed in Chapter 17: Adapt various techniques to the situation at hand, and don't get hung up on dogma during the data modeling stage.

Representing Associations

You can also use an entity to represent an association between other entities. Take the case of describing a many-to-many association between suppliers and parts. You can show the many-to-many aspect of the association as follows:

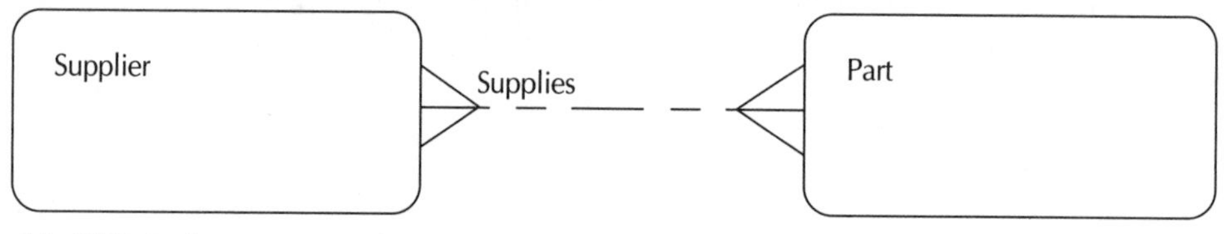

The way this ERD is drawn, a supplier may supply no parts or one or more parts, and a part may have no supplier or one or more suppliers. There's no place on this diagram, however, to place the price that a specific supplier charges for a particular part. The next example splits the many-to-many relationship into two one-to-many relationships and adds a new SupplierOfPart entity to represent the association. This new entity provides a place to list the Price property. This type of entity is sometimes called an **intersection entity**.

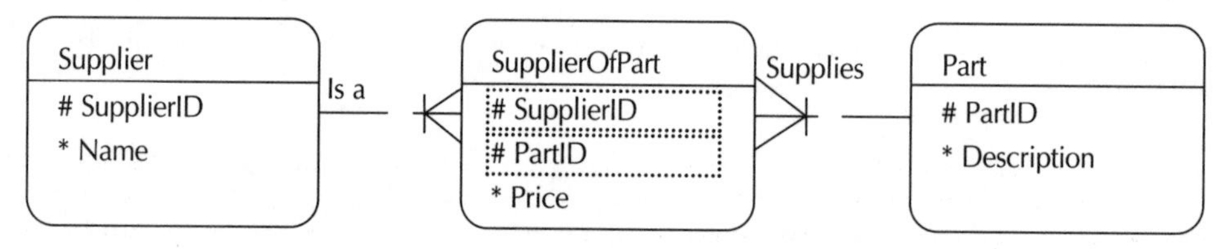

In this example, the SupplierOfPart entity's identifier consists of properties that contain ID values that match associated ID values of Supplier and Part instances. Remember that these two SupplierOfPart properties don't have to be listed explicitly because such foreign key properties are implied by the two relationships. However, you do need to specify that these implicit properties are part of the SupplierOfPart entity's identifier. In ERDs, you can explicitly represent the fact that one entity's identifier includes all its foreign key properties corresponding to the identifier properties of a parent entity by putting a bar across the dependent entity's end of the relationship line. The two bars across the relationship lines close to the crowsfeet connected to the SupplierOfPart entity mean that the identifier for SupplierOfPart contains all the foreign key properties that reference the identifier properties of the Supplier and Part entities.

The following example shows another case in which the bar notation is helpful:

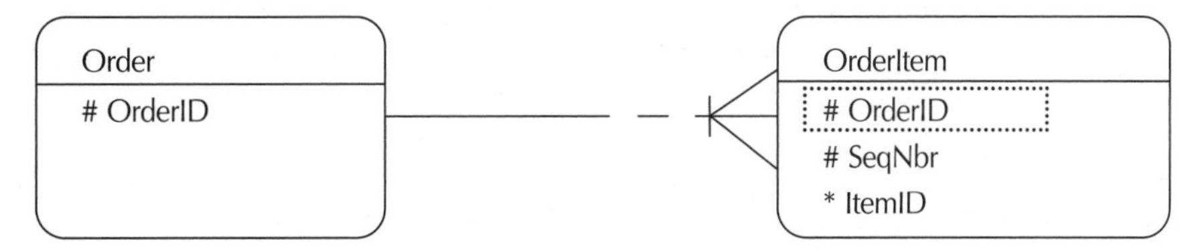

The OrderItem entity, which has a many-to-one relationship with the Order entity, uses an identifier comprising an order ID property and a sequence number unique within each order ID value. The only OrderItem identifier property that needs to be shown explicitly is SeqNbr.[4]

The formal meaning of the vertical bar is that the entity it's next to is a **weak entity** — one for which an instance cannot exist unless a corresponding entity on the other end of the relationship exists. For example, an instance of an OrderItem can't exist without a corresponding instance of an Order. An entity type that is not a weak entity is known as a **regular entity**.

Exclusive Relationships

There are lots of either-or situations in business, and ERDs provide a notation that helps identify them. The next ERD depicts the business situation in which an account is associated with either a person or a company, but not both:

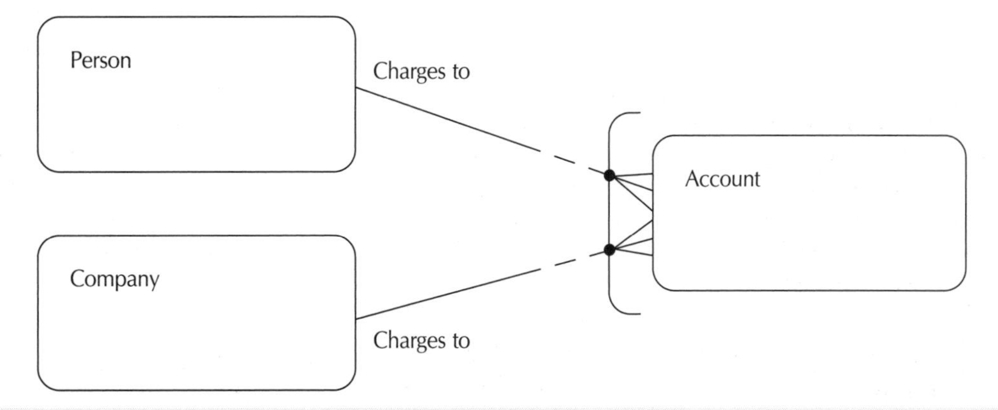

4 The examples in this chapter follow a naming convention wherein a property whose name ends with "ID" has values that are unique across all instances of an entity and a property named SeqNbr has unique values only within those instances that share a common value(s) for the other properties that compose the entity's complete identifier. For example, order ID values are unique across all orders, but an order item's sequence number is unique within a particular order.

The **exclusive relationship** arc with connector dots (•) specifies that an instance of the entity having multiple relationship lines connected by the arc can participate in one and only one of the alternative relationships. For example, account number 123 might be associated with person Jones, and account 456 might be associated with company Ajax, Inc., but no account could be charged to by more than one person, more than one company, or both a person and a company.

Entity Subtypes

When you encounter two potential entity types that seem very similar but not quite the same, you can use ERD **entity subtype** boxes to represent them. The following example shows a Vehicle entity that has Car and Truck subtypes.

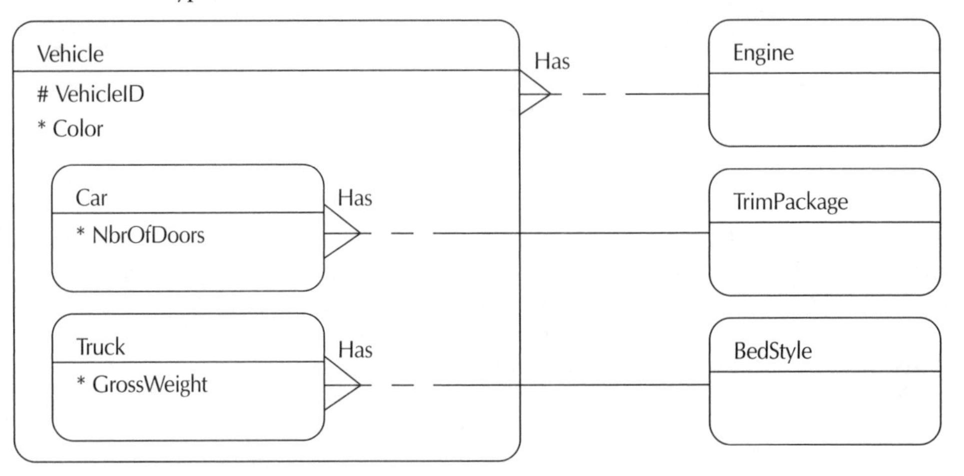

This diagram tells us that all cars are vehicles and all trucks are vehicles, and cars and trucks share some common properties of vehicles, such as color. Subtyping vehicles lets you show that there are properties of cars that don't apply to trucks, and vice versa. You can also show relationships between other entities and a Vehicle, Car, or Truck entity depending on how the organization's data is structured.

An implicit way to represent a subtype is to use a single entity with a "type" property and specify optional properties for properties that don't apply to all instances of the type. The following ERD shows how the Vehicle entity might be represented.

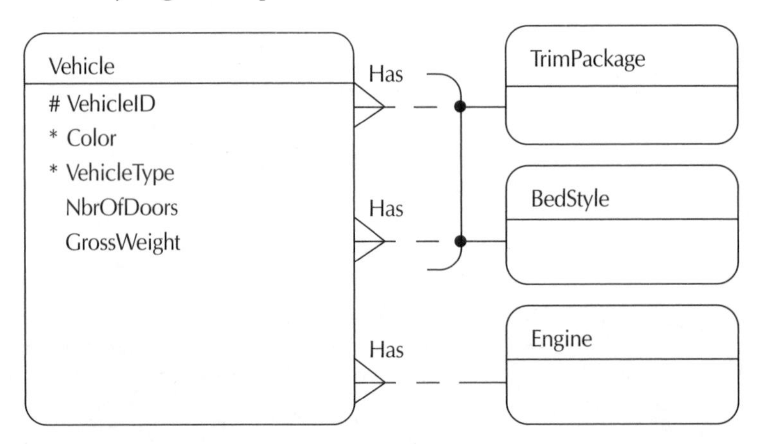

The two Has relationships that were connected in the previous example to Car and Truck, respectively, are now shown as exclusive relationships. The explicit depiction of subtypes gives a more precise view on the ERD of the underlying data model, but the simpler style of representing a subtype with a "type" property may be more appropriate for high-level diagrams on which it's not essential to show the subtype details. Note that although these alternative ERDs, in isolation, don't have identical semantics, they are consistent, and each ERD would be just part of a complete data model. Additional rules in the model specification would clarify details so that the same data model would be represented no matter which ERD was used.

When to Use ERDs

The ERD notation introduced in this chapter provides a simple but relatively powerful language for describing many important aspects of a business model. The following ERD provides one final, somewhat more complex, example of how you can represent a lot of information in a clear, concise manner using ERDs.

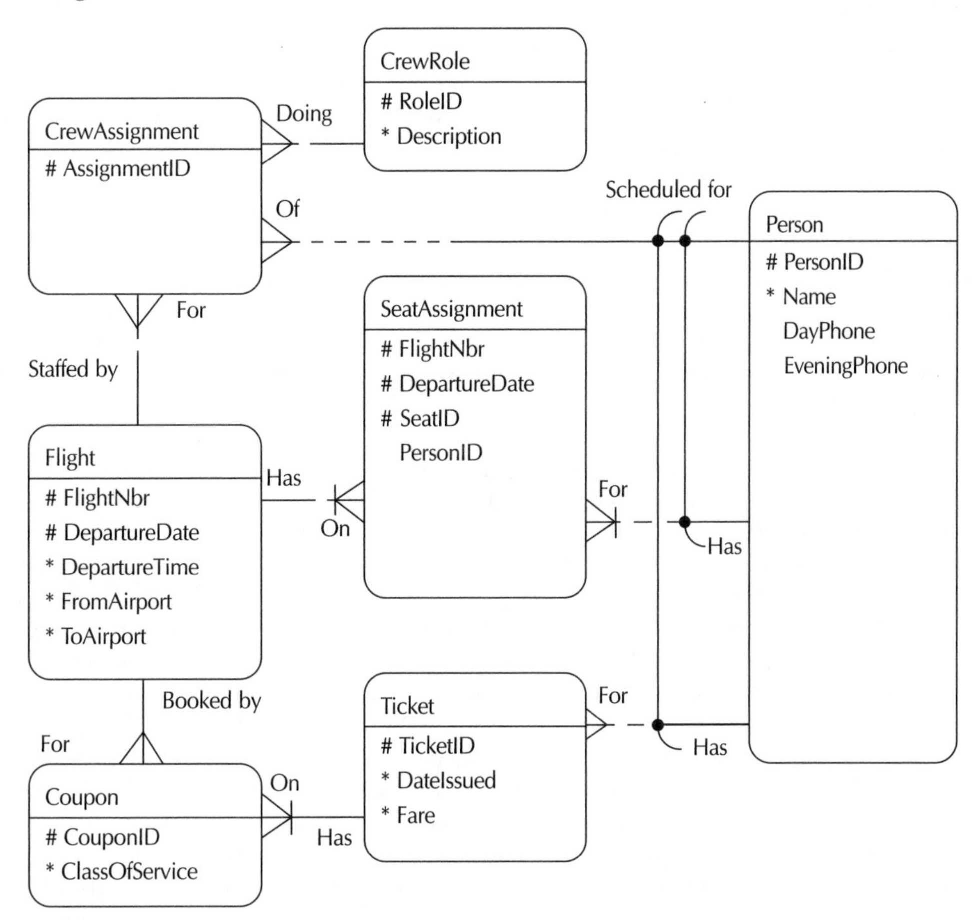

Here are a few of the things we know about this part of the business, just by looking at the ERD:

- A person either
  - *may* be scheduled for *one or more* crew assignments, or
  - *may* have *one or more* seat assignments
- A person either
  - *may* be scheduled for *one or more* crew assignments, or
  - *may* have *one or more* seat tickets
- A ticket *must* be for *exactly one* person
- A ticket *must* have *one or more* coupons
- A crew assignment *must* be of *exactly one* person
- A crew assignment *must* be for *exactly one* flight
- A crew assignment *must* do *exactly one* crew role

As you can see, this is an effective method for getting a high-level view of the entities and their interrelationships that are important to an organization.

Additional forms of notation are used in some versions of ERDs. You can explore these using the books listed in the annotated bibliography. Keep in mind, however, that ERDs are simply one of many possible ways to express the structure and rules of your data model. The ERD notation is well suited for simple systems, parts of complex systems, or high-level views of the most important entities and relationships of interest to a business.

On the other hand, ERDs may not be the best choice for expressing model details, such as the enumeration of all entities' properties, for a complex system. For a system of significant size, ERDs that include all entities, relationships, and properties become very difficult to read.[5] Further, ERDs may provide no way to express some business rules. For example, there's no standard ERD notation to represent a regulation that a construction company must use local subcontractors for projects funded by local government. Yet you can easily state and understand this business model rule in natural language, pseudo-SQL, or some other textual form. Researchers have expended a great deal of effort to add expressive capability to ERDs, but while these efforts may have academic value, practical applications for many of them are limited.

ERDs are almost always accompanied by textual and table-oriented specifications. Chapter 19 listed a number of important things to specify in a complete data model, including details about the entity types and their properties, integrity rules, and individual user's views. Some of this information can also be shown on an ERD, where adding the information enhances comprehensibility.

Remember two basic aspects of ERDs, however, before you go overboard learning dozens of arcane symbols in some extended ERD notation. First, ERD notations are based on formal logic and consequently do not add expressive power but offer an alternative means of expression. Second, ERDs are preferable as a means of expression when they are easier to understand than the alternatives, such as table- or text-oriented representations. In other words, ERDs are neither the only tool you need nor always the best. Yet when used for the right purpose, ERDs make a useful addition to your collection of analysis and design techniques. The best approach in most practical data modeling tasks is to use a mixture of ERDs, other diagrams, text, and tables to create the specification.

5 A complex ERD may look more like the circuit diagram for a computer chip — hardly a good way to create a comprehensible data model.

Chapter Summary

Entity relationship diagrams (ERDs) represent entities, relationships, and their properties in pictorial form. Boxes represent entities, lines represent relationships, and properties are listed in the boxes with annotation to show required and optional values and identifier properties and referencing properties.

ERD notation can show alternative types of relationships, including one-to-one, one-to-many, or many-to-many relationships. ERDs also show whether one or more related instances are optional or required. In addition, you can represent exclusive relationships (where only one or the other relationship exists for a particular instance) and entity subtypes (where an entity type that's a subtype of another entity type has all the properties and relationships of the other entity type).

ERDs are a good technique for showing high-level views of a data model or for small data models or parts of a larger data model. For complex data models, ERDs that include all details of the model can be difficult to read. In general, ERDs are only part of the complete data model and are accompanied by text and table-format specifications.

Key Terms

entity
entity relationship diagram (ERD)
entity subtype
exclusive relationship
intersection entity
property
regular entity
relationship
weak entity

Exercises

1. Explain the advantages and disadvantages of ERDs.
2. Show an example of the ERD notation for the following:
   - employee and department entity types
   - employee properties: employee ID, name, office phone
   - a "works in" relationship between the employee and department entity types
   - a "manager" subtype of the employee entity type
   - a "manages" relationship between the manager and employee entity types
3. Draw the ERD for the agent, company, and product entity types and their inter-relationships based on the example presented in the discussion of fifth normal form in Chapter 18 (beginning on page 356). Are there any parts of the data model for this example that you can't represent on the ERD? If so, how could you include the necessary information in your data model?
4. What are the advantages and disadvantages of representing a many-to-many relationship with or without a separate box (for the intersection entity)? Consider the alternatives from the perspective of both the end user and the person who's responsible for the physical database design.

Chapter 21

Physical Database Design

Chapter Overview

Physical database design provides the bridge between logical data modeling and implementation. This stage of an application development project determines how available hardware and system software resources will be used to implement an efficient set of tables, views, and other application components that provide the capabilities specified in the data model. This chapter provides a series of steps you can follow to produce a database design from a logical data model that's developed using the methods described in Chapters 19 and 20.

Introduction

As you learned in Chapter 19, logical data modeling analyzes an organization's information requirements to produce a data model that specifies entity types, properties of entities, relationships among entity types, and integrity rules. These elements are represented as base and view tables, columns, foreign keys, domains, and other design objects based on the relational model. The data model provides a description of both individual end-user or department views and an integrated set of tables and integrity rules. Both levels of description are from the business perspective and don't state particular implementation techniques.

If there were a DBMS that provided direct support for every concept we used in the data model (e.g., domains, multitable predicates) and the hardware and DBMS had infinite storage capacity and infinite speed, we could just use the data model as our finished database design — we wouldn't need to go through a distinct **physical database design** stage as part of our development process. In reality, current DBMSs (including UDB/400) lack built-in features for some of the things found in a typical data model, and the performance of current hardware and software is still such that we must consider capacity and performance when deciding how to implement some parts of the data model.

The limitations of facilities available for implementing a data model lead to the two major challenges of database design:

- How should we implement a data model concept for which the DBMS provides no direct support? For example, how should we enforce domain integrity with UDB/400, which has limited support for domains?
- How should we implement a data model concept that may be a performance bottleneck if implemented in the most direct manner? For example, an end-user view that includes selected rows and presents them in a particular sequence can be specified directly in an SQL/400 view definition. However, for a large table, if we don't do any performance-related design, scanning the entire underlying table to select and sort rows for the view may require an unacceptably long time. During database design, we can look at implementation options, such as creating an SQL index, to speed row selection and ordering.

Of course, some concepts in a data model may have a direct and efficient implementation. For example, an entity type represented as a base table in the data model can be implemented as an

SQL/400 table. These easy parts of database design nevertheless need to be documented explicitly in the final design document.

Database design is based on four major elements:

- the *logical data model* (and parts of the process model), which define what the implementation must do
- the expected *volumes* and *pattern of access* (e.g., numbers of customers and orders and frequency of retrieval and update of an order once it has been entered)
- the system software *functional characteristics* (e.g., whether the DBMS retrieval language supports date arithmetic)
- the hardware and system software *performance characteristics* (e.g., the relative cost of row retrieval by key versus sequentially)

Database design cannot be done properly without a complete logical data model, an estimate of the access patterns, and an understanding of the hardware and system software characteristics. For example, deciding how to enforce domain integrity requires knowing exactly what the DBMS provides in the way of domain support and other facilities. Consider columns that must contain only dates within a specified range. The implementation is different with a DBMS (such as UDB/400) that provides a built-in date data type than with a DBMS that provides no date data type. Likewise, because UDB/400 doesn't provide domains as a way to limit the values placed in a column, you must decide on some other mechanism, such as a check constraint, to enforce the constraint.

As an example of a performance-related design decision, determining which indexes to create requires estimating table sizes, the frequency of retrievals that might use the index, and the number of updates that might cause changes to the index.

Some design decisions have both a functional and a performance-related purpose. For example, to decide whether to include a redundant derived column in a table, you must know (or estimate) answers to the following questions:

- How frequently will the derived column be retrieved?
- Will it ever be retrieved using an end-user tool instead of an application program?
- Is it possible — and if so, how complex is it — to derive the column using an end-user tool?
- How frequently will the underlying source columns be updated?
- Will the underlying columns ever be updated using an end-user tool? If so, is it possible to calculate a new derived value automatically when such updates occur?
- How quickly can the system calculate the derived column during retrieval?

Specific database design decisions require a thorough understanding of the performance and complexity trade-offs. Separating logical data modeling and physical database design into two distinct stages is the best approach. You can concentrate on the conceptual aspects of the system during the data modeling stage. Then, as you work on the database design, you can focus on the numerous platform-specific details and design an efficient implementation without clouding your understanding of what the system needs to deliver.

Although physical database design tasks may proceed in parallel with logical data modeling tasks, conceptually the physical database design follows the logical data model — you must determine *what* you want to do before you decide *how* to do it. Here's a guideline to help keep the two processes distinct: Once you have a data model, you should be able to make all database design decisions based on the functionality and performance of the DBMS (and other system software) and the estimated pattern of data access. If you find yourself asking such conceptual questions as "What if there might be a nonstandard price of an item when it's sold?" you've got to go back to the data model and get the answer firmly established before you decide on an implementation — physical database design is not the time to address these types of questions.

The following sections lay out 10 steps you can follow to produce a database design. As with logical data modeling, you should establish naming standards and set up a data dictionary to hold your design specifications. Like the data dictionary used for the data model, the data dictionary used for database design is a set of containers, including documents, database tables, spreadsheets, and possibly CASE tool repositories. We won't repeat all the advice from Chapter 19 about keeping the elements of your design specification well-organized and about adapting the techniques presented here to fit a particular organization and project. Be sure to review that material as you consider how to tackle a database design assignment.

Also note that many of the database design steps relate directly to implementation specifics that are covered in other chapters. The following steps refer you to the appropriate chapters for additional details related to the design issue.

Step 1. Specify an SQL Table for Each Entity Type

This first step is simple when you've used a data modeling technique based on the relational model and you intend to implement your applications with a relational DBMS such as UDB/400. Each entity type is represented in the data model as a base table with columns representing the entity's properties. The first cut at your design should be a direct one-to-one mapping to SQL/400 tables and columns.[1] Other data model elements may not be as easy to handle. The following table summarizes the most common SQL/400 implementation objects or techniques for various data model elements. We cover these in more detail in the rest of this chapter.

Model elements	SQL/400 implementation objects
Entity type	Table
Property	Column
Domain	Column data type; check constraint
Primary key	Primary key
Candidate key	Unique index or unique constraint
One-to-many relationship (as foreign key)	Foreign key
Many-to-many relationship (as table)	Table with two or more foreign keys
Multirow predicates	Check constraint
Multitable predicates	Trigger program
Security rules	Table and view privileges; views with selected rows and/or columns; stored procedures
End-user view (subschema)	View

1 Recall that with UDB/400, an SQL/400 table is an OS/400 physical file object, an SQL/400 column is a field in a file, and an SQL/400 view is a logical file object. This chapter uses the SQL terminology for the implementation objects, but the principles also apply to physical and logical files created with Data Description Specifications (DDS).

For an SQL/400 table, you should record the following design information:

- full table name (maximum of 128 characters)
- system table name (specify if the full table name is longer than 10 characters; maximum of 10 characters)
- the name of the entity type in the related data model
- descriptive text for the table
- collection (OS/400 library) that will contain the table
- OS/400 user profile that will own the table
- initial and incremental storage limits

For each column, record the following design information:

- name of column
- table name that contains the column
- descriptive text for column (up to 2,000 characters for SQL/400 column comments)
- reference to the name of a standard column data type[2]
- default column heading(s) (up to three lines of 20 characters for SQL/400 column labels)
- domain name (the domain definition itself should specify the column or column data type, length and decimal positions, and allowable values)
- whether the null placeholder is allowed
- value used for not-applicable (if allowed)
- values used for special cases (e.g., open end date), if any
- default value, if any
- default display and print formats (e.g., for telephone numbers)

Later steps in this chapter suggest other information to add to the lists above. Most of the items listed are self-explanatory; however, a few require further discussion. Each OS/400 object must be contained in an OS/400 library (recall that an SQL/400 collection is an OS/400 library) and must have one user profile as its owner. Chapter 1 explains the OS/400 object-based architecture and the role of libraries and user profiles; Chapter 9 goes into more detail about OS/400 security, including object ownership and object authority.

AS/400 installations use various approaches to organizing objects into libraries. For database objects, there are several considerations. Often, organizations group objects into multiple libraries. This approach helps manage objects, but be aware of the following aspects of multiple libraries:

- Backup and recovery is much simpler if all SQL/400 views that reference a table are in the same collection as the table.
- An OS/400 job's library list can have a maximum of 25 user library entries. You don't want so many libraries that you can't include all the ones you need at a particular time in the library list.

2 If you use standard data type names, you can simply record "from referenced data type" for other column attributes in this list (e.g., data type) that can be derived from the referenced data type.

Some installations also use libraries to group different types of OS/400 objects. For example, they put executable programs (including SQL stored procedures) in one library and database tables and views in another. In general, you should keep all database tables and views related to an application in one library. If you have many different applications, you probably want to keep multiple, related applications in a single library to avoid an excessive number of libraries.

For object ownership, a common practice at many AS/400 installations is to have a single user profile (e.g., AppOwner) that owns all database objects. Specific authority to access these objects is then granted to other user profiles, which are the user profiles that end users specify when they sign on to the AS/400. For large installations, there may be several user profiles whose purpose is to own application objects; for example, the PayrollOwn user profile may own the payroll application objects, and the SalesOwn user profile may own the order-entry and marketing application objects.

Chapter 3 explains an approach to defining standard column definitions for use in creating tables. Step 3 in this chapter discusses approaches to designing the implementation for domains, which aren't directly supported in UDB/400. Using one or more of these techniques can reduce the need to specify some of the column-level items. For example, by using a set of standard column definitions, you don't need to specify explicitly in your database design the data type, length, or decimal positions for a column.

The implementation of special values or placeholders for a column requires careful consideration during design. One question is whether to specify an explicit default value to be used when a new row is added and no value is supplied for the column. The default value might also be used as the basis for the initial value put in an input field on a data-entry display. Chapter 3 discusses how SQL/400 handles explicit and system-defined defaults; in general, SQL/400 uses blank for character columns and zero for numeric columns. If some other value is appropriate, specify that value. In particular, you may want to use a value that represents unknown, not-applicable, or a special case such as "open end date."

Another fairly straightforward kind of value to consider is what we called a "distinguished value" in Chapter 19, Step 7. Recall the example of an ending date column for which we need some value that represents that the ending date is open-ended. For these cases, you generally can pick a valid value that represents the special case; for example, you might use 9999-12-31 for "open end date."

Two more difficult exceptional cases are not-applicable and unknown. The first arises when a column might not always have a sensible value — for example, the Color column of a part that has no particular color. The second case is different in that a value for the column might make sense; we just don't know what the value is at some particular time. With SQL/400, you have two choices for either or both of these situations: use the null placeholder, or use some designated value to represent the condition(s).

Chapter 3 explains how SQL/400 supports null-capable columns, and Chapter 5 describes some special considerations with SQL/400 data manipulations. For example, when you add together several columns, the result will be null if any column is null. Although null-capable columns have the advantage of being a system-supported way of identifying that a column contains no valid value, the use of nulls isn't problem-free. You should never allow null with primary key columns and rarely (if ever) with candidate key and foreign key columns.

Instead of null, you can designate a value that represents not-applicable and/or unknown. For example, for a column that contains the date an employee received his or her undergraduate degree, you might use 0000-01-01 for not-applicable (if he or she doesn't have a degree) and 0001-01-02 for unknown (if he or she has a degree but you don't know the date it was received). You need to consider a column's default value (if any) in conjunction with the way you represent not-applicable and unknown. In this case, you might specify the value for unknown (0001-01-02) as the default value.

When you design the implementation of views and processes that have computations involving numeric or date columns, be sure to consider the values used for default, not-applicable, and unknown. For example, to calculate the average age of employees, you must be sure to handle values that have the format of dates but aren't really valid birth date values — if the column for an employee's birth date can be 0001-01-02 to represent unknown, any summary routine should exclude employee rows with this value. If you allow null for a column, be sure to consider the SQL/400 and high-level language handling of null-capable columns.

Step 2. Specify Primary, Candidate, and Foreign Key Implementation

A primary key is one or more columns that provide a means of uniquely identifying rows. Candidate keys are other column(s) that are also unique for each row. A foreign key is one or more columns in a dependent table that reference the primary key in some (usually different) parent table. Each of these types of keys requires some implementation technique to enforce the corresponding integrity constraints. The SQL Create Table statement provides the Constraint clause to specify primary, unique, and foreign keys.[3]

The SQL/400 Create Table statement supports some, but not all, of the possible actions for foreign key rules. For example, Create Table supports a delete rule of "cascade" for the case when a row is deleted from a parent table. But Create Table supports only the "reject" rule when a row is inserted into the dependent table and the row's foreign key doesn't match an existing primary key in the parent table. For foreign key rules not available with the Create Table statement, you can use one of three techniques:

- attempt to prevent integrity violations by manual procedures
- create a **trigger program** for the parent and/or dependent table
- create a **table-access routine** in a stored procedure, and use that exclusively to perform table updates

You might specify in your design that one or more of these methods are to be used in the implementation. Obviously, depending on users to follow manual procedures isn't a foolproof way to enforce integrity. But don't immediately reject this alternative. Although using programmatic means to enforce integrity is generally recommended, there may be cases in which the implementation and performance costs of a programmatic approach are high and the consequences of an orphan row aren't great. If you do use manual methods, consider writing a batch program that can be used periodically to scan the entire table(s) to check for integrity violations.

Trigger programs are HLL programs that UDB/400 calls when a table update is attempted. You write the trigger program in an HLL, such as RPG IV, and associate it with the appropriate database table. When an update to the table is attempted, UDB/400 calls your program and passes it the before and after images of the updated row. Your program can analyze the pending table update and reject or accept it, as well as perform other actions. Chapter 16 explains more about writing and using trigger programs.

The final alternative is to write callable stored procedures (using either an HLL or the SQL stored procedure language) that perform database updates. Such stored procedures can check the validity of an update before performing it and return an error condition (e.g., no parent row with

3 For existing tables (or physical files created with DDS), you can use the SQL Alter Table statement to add a constraint.

matching primary key for foreign key) to the program that calls the stored procedure. This technique is similar to the use of triggers but offers more flexibility because the called stored procedure can have any interface (i.e., the set of parameters) required to provide enough information to determine the validity of the table update. Trigger programs essentially get nothing more than the name of the table and the before and after row images. On the other hand, custom stored procedures aren't called when a utility program is used to update the table,[4] but trigger programs are.

Step 3. Specify Domain Implementation

Unfortunately, UDB/400 (like many other relational DBMSs) provides only partial support for domains. You can specify a column's data type, length, and (if numeric) decimal positions. You can also specify whether the column allows null and define a check constraint that limits values that can be stored in the column (e.g., only values greater than or equal to zero). You can't define domain objects nor specify a domain name in a column definition. You can create user-defined data types that are based on a built-in type; however, a user-defined type doesn't include any restrictions on allowable values or other characteristics (e.g., units of measure) that might be part of a domain.

Because there's no SQL/400 support for domains, you should still follow the column definition principles discussed in Chapter 3 when you use SQL/400 to create tables — the general principle is to use a standard set of named data types to define columns. You must do this more or less manually in SQL/400 or create a program that lets you use macros[5] for column definitions. Such a program would take as input an SQL/400 statement such as

```
Create Table AppDta.Customer
   ( CustID @IDType,
     Name   @NameType, ... )
```

and produce as output an SQL/400 statement such as

```
Create Table AppDta.Customer
   ( CustID Int       Not Null,
     Name   Char(50)  Not Null, ... )
```

The macro-processing program would look for strings that begin with the at sign (@) and replace them with the corresponding text. In the example above, the macro named @IDType would be replaced with the text "Int Not Null."

Providing the basic definitions of columns is only the beginning of designing domain support. The more challenging part is determining how to enforce restrictions on values and operations with other columns. For those cases in which a check constraint isn't adequate, trigger programs and table-access routines provide two alternatives. One consideration with either technique is how to avoid unacceptable impact on performance. For example, suppose you have a table defined with 50 columns. If you check every column for every table update operation, you may add significant processing time to table updates.

Two programming techniques can help reduce the cost of checking domain integrity. First, you can design methods to temporarily disable column-level checks. Then, when a batch program or other program that updates lots of rows is run, you can (hopefully) rely on the program to check the

4 For this method to be effective, all application programs must call the table-access stored procedure to perform a table update. Any application that does table updates directly (e.g., with an SQL Update statement) will circumvent the integrity checks.

5 In simple terms, a source code macro is an identifier that's replaced with some substitution text by a program that processes the source code. Many HLLs, including C and C++, support macro definition and substitution. ILE COBOL/400 has a very primitive Replace compiler directive that is somewhat like a macro facility. RPG IV has nothing comparable.

columns affected by its computations before performing a table update. Of course, there's some risk in this approach — the program must implement the necessary checks properly. But it's often better than avoiding trigger programs or table-access stored procedures altogether because of performance concerns.

As an alternative, you can use a programming technique that compares the before and after row images and checks only those columns whose values differ. This approach assumes that the before image values for unchanged columns are valid, which is a relatively safe assumption if this method has been used for all previous table updates.

In the database design specification, for each domain in the data model, you should list how it should be implemented (e.g., by column check constraint, table-access stored procedure, manually observed SQL/400 column-definition standards, or a trigger program).

Step 4. Specify Implementation of Other Integrity Rules

You can implement row predicates using SQL/400 check constraints; however, there's no direct way to specify a multirow or multitable predicate.[6] Essentially, your alternatives for complex constraints are, again, trigger programs and table-access routines.

One other option, of course, is to code the integrity constraints piecemeal in all the programs that might update a table. Historically, this has been by far the most prevalent approach among AS/400 developers. The problem is that this approach is error-prone and hard to manage because rule enforcement is fragmented and often duplicated across many different programs. Even if you decide not to use check constraints, trigger programs, or table-access routines in your database design, at least specify one callable program (or a small group of programs) that will implement all the integrity checking for a table. Then specify that applications must call the appropriate validation routines before updating a table.

Step 5. Specify View Implementation

Once you have the initial database design for the integrated data model's base tables, it's time to specify how the database will provide for the necessary end users' views. Recall that end users may need to see only selected rows or columns from data that is stored in base tables. Users also may need to see data from several tables combined in a view (e.g., a CustomerOrder view may combine data from Customer, Order, OrderItem, and Part tables).

Before we look at ways to implement views that are different from base tables, we need to consider those views that correspond exactly to a single base table. Take the case of a Customer table in the data model, which will be implemented as an SQL/400 table. If the model also specifies that some user or application needs all the rows and columns from this table, we can just specify that the table will implement the logical view. This solution works fine and is the most common way AS/400 organizations implement access to table data.

There's an alternative approach, however, that may provide an implementation that can better handle subsequent changes to the base table definition. The technique is to create a "master" SQL/400 view over each table. The master view should select all rows and columns of the base table so that it is equivalent, for retrieval and update purposes, to the base table. The advantage to this

6 The SQL/400 Create View statement, discussed in Chapter 6, supports an optional With Check Option clause that also can be used somewhat like a row predicate; however, the option is enforced only when the view itself is used to access the data.

technique is that when you must change the table definition (e.g., to add a new column or change a column's definition), the view can provide a layer that insulates programs and utilities from the base table changes. For example, if a new column is added to the table, the master view can select only the original columns, excluding the new column. No immediate changes are necessary for applications that use the master view.[7] Obviously, the new column will have to be included in at least one existing or new view if the column is to be used by some application. And eventually, you need to create a new master view that incorporates all columns, including the newly added one. But the original master view buys time for you to revise applications to incorporate the table change.

For end users' views in the data model that aren't equivalent to a single base table, you have several design choices:

- an SQL/400 view
- table-access stored procedures
- an embedded SQL/400 cursor
- interactive SQL/400 Select statements and other data retrieval tools

An SQL/400 view provides a way to select, transform, or combine data from one or more underlying tables. Chapter 6 describes the capabilities of SQL/400 views. In general, SQL views provide a good way to implement end users' views, as long as the required capabilities are supported.

In earlier steps, we saw how stored procedures can be used to implement integrity constraints. For this purpose, these stored procedures are called to perform table updates. You can also use stored procedures to read one or more tables and derive the type of data required in an end-user view. This technique is particularly useful when the capabilities of an SQL/400 view aren't adequate.

As part of a table-access stored procedure, or for use directly by an application, an embedded SQL/400 cursor provides another way to select, transform, and combine data. A few functional differences exist between cursors and views, the main one being that views are persistent UDB/400 objects, whereas an open SQL/400 cursor exists only during the job that uses it. A cursor also lets a program specify the order in which rows are returned, whereas a view does not. In general, if a view provides the functionality you need to implement an end-user view, it's the simplest alternative. In some cases, however, an SQL/400 cursor may avoid the need for UDB/400 to maintain an access path and, thus, may be a desirable performance trade-off.

A final alternative for implementing end users' views is the use of interactive tools, such as the Interactive SQL (ISQL) component of IBM's DB2 Query Manager and SQL Development Kit for AS/400 product. This tool, as well as a number of PC-based data retrieval tools, can provide methods of access that satisfy the requirements of some end users' views.

After selecting the appropriate design to provide the information specified in an end-user view, you should specify exactly how the view is implemented. This specification might take the form of the necessary definitions for an SQL/400 Create View statement. Don't just stop at the general specification "use a view." Provide the full description so there's no ambiguity when the person responsible for implementation does his or her job. Note that Steps 8, 9, and 10 may revise some table designs, so you need to revisit this step when you make changes that affect the specification of a view or other implementation method for an end-user view.

7 Part I, which covers SQL/400 tables, views, and indexes, provides more details about the steps necessary to create various objects discussed in this section.

Step 6. Specify Security Implementation

Once you have the initial design for the implementation of base tables and end users' views, you have the objects necessary to design the implementation of security. This database design step specifies how read and update access will be controlled for SQL/400 tables and views, as well as for related objects such as programs that implement file-access routines.

On the AS/400, the first step is to specify public and private (i.e., individual user profile) authority for table and program objects. You can use the SQL/400 Grant statement or the GrtObjAut (Grant Object Authority) OS/400 command to grant authorities. Chapter 9 discusses UDB/400 security in detail. In general, you should grant only the resource-level authorities that you intend to be used in an unrestricted manner. For example, grant update rights to a table only if you intend the user profile to have the authority to update the table in any way — potentially changing any column in any row.

SQL/400 also allows column-level security for Update statements, providing a finer-grained level of security than table-level security. SQL/400 views can implement access that's restricted to selected rows or a subset of columns. This technique is especially useful for restricted read-only access. Trigger programs can provide some additional options for implementing specific update constraints based on the user profile.

For more context-sensitive control of database access, you can use stored procedures — either general-purpose table-access routines or more specialized, task-specific routines. These routines can use program adopted authority (discussed in Chapter 9) to provide controlled access beyond what a user profile normally has. For example, users who don't have general update authority to a table can still perform certain types of changes if they're authorized to use a stored procedure that adopts update authority to the table while the stored procedure is in use.

A final technique to consider in the database design is the implementation of an audit trail for some or all of the database access. OS/400 journaling (discussed briefly in Chapter 3) or trigger programs provide two system-supported ways to record who accesses various data and what changes they make.

Step 7. Specify Additional Indexes for Performance

Now we come to several performance-related database design steps. Before diving into the specific techniques, you should keep in mind a couple of general principles. First, there's only one way to know for certain the performance consequences of a particular implementation technique: Measure the results. Although we look at some rules of thumb for alternative designs, any production-level approach to performance must include some means of measurement. OS/400 has several built-in performance measurements, and IBM provides the Performance Management/400e product to examine performance in more detail. Be sure to use these or similar tools to assess performance-related design decisions.

Another important principle is to avoid unnecessary effort trying to improve performance when there's no performance problem to begin with.[8] For example, if a table is accessed only once a month in a night-shift batch job and the batch job can be completed in the allotted shift, it's probably not worth worrying about ways to improve the table design to reduce the time required for the batch job. Of course, if the situation changes and the job no longer finishes in its shift or there's some other

8 This point may sound obvious, but programmers sometimes expend time fine-tuning their code or database implementation when the improvement will have a negligible effect.

significant reason to improve its performance, it may be worthwhile to work on the table design or program to improve performance.

Finally, keep in mind that performance is only one part of the overall cost equation. Consider that if it costs $10,000 in programmer time to improve a program's performance by 10 percent and it costs $9,000 for a CPU upgrade that improves the system's overall performance by 10 percent, it's better to tackle the performance problem by buying hardware than by working on the implementation.

With these general principles in mind, let's look at **indexes**, one of the most common options for improving UDB/400 performance. An index usually provides an efficient way to access a specific row by key value or to process some or all of a table in a particular sequence. You can create an index by using the SQL/400 Create Index statement.[9] Your database design will already include at least one index for each primary key and potentially others for candidate and foreign keys. In most cases, the need to access individual rows using the value of one or more columns will correspond to a primary or other candidate key; thus, you won't need many additional indexes for this purpose.

Instead, the two most common reasons to consider additional indexes are for retrieving groups of rows in a particular sequence and as an efficient way to select a subset of rows. For large tables, indexes can speed these two types of retrieval. Indexes, however, add overhead to update operations because the system must keep index entries up-to-date when it adds, deletes, or changes rows in a table with one or more indexes.

There are no hard-and-fast rules about which indexes to include in a database design. As a rule of thumb, you usually won't encounter serious update performance problems with five or fewer indexes over a table, but more than 20 indexes (and often even fewer) can cause unacceptably slow update performance. Within the range of six to 20 indexes, each index should be scrutinized carefully to ensure it provides sufficient improvement in retrieval performance to warrant the additional update overhead.

One good candidate for an index is a column that's used frequently in an SQL/400 view that defines a join. If sets of joined rows are retrieved based on the one table's primary key, an index over the related column(s) in the other table may significantly improve performance.

For selection purposes, an index provides the greatest performance improvement when the table contains a lot of rows and the selection criteria selects a small percentage. For small tables, or once the number of selected rows reaches about 20 percent of the file, an index offers little, if any, performance improvement.

One type of index to avoid (unless it has a high payoff for retrieval) is an index over a frequently updated column. This type of index requires frequent updating and adds to the overhead of table updates.

When designing multiple indexes over the same table, consider UDB/400's ability to share indexes (access paths), as explained in Chapter 3. If possible, design multicolumn indexes so the major key columns are also the key columns for indexes with fewer key columns. For example, suppose you need to define an index to enforce uniqueness for a candidate key consisting of EmployeeID and ProjectID on a table that stores employee assignments to projects. To guarantee uniqueness, it doesn't matter whether the major key column in the index is EmployeeID or ProjectID. But if you also have a view that has a single-column key consisting of ProjectID (and you don't have a view keyed on

9 You can also use DDS to create a logical file with a keyed access path. The UDB/400 query optimizer will use logical files, as well as SQL/400 indexes, to improve query performance.

EmployeeID), it may be better to define the composite key with ProjectID as the major key column. If you do that, UDB/400 can share the same index for both purposes.[10]

Permanent indexes aren't the only way to design row selection and sequencing using UDB/400. If no appropriate index exists when you use an SQL/400 view or embedded SQL/400 cursor, UDB/400 handles the request by creating a temporary index, sequentially scanning the table, or a variety of other on-the-fly methods. If these methods provide satisfactory retrieval performance, the update overhead of a permanent index may not be worth incurring.

Although your database design should plan the initial indexes, you also need to measure performance continually and consider adding or dropping indexes as conditions change or you get better production statistics. Designing the right indexes is part science, part black magic, and a lot of trial and error.

Step 8. Introduce Controlled Redundancy

In the logical data model, we avoided redundantly representing facts. We used a set of guidelines, normal forms, to ensure that the tables in our data model unambiguously conveyed the structure of the organization's data. It's not uncommon for normal form tables to give a fragmented appearance to the structure of the organization's data, breaking up tables with lots of columns and not in a fully normalized form into numerous, fully normalized tables. This is the best way to approach the data model, but it may need some restructuring when the actual SQL/400 table design occurs.

The reason some restructuring may be necessary is twofold: It may be cumbersome (or impossible) for certain DBMSs or utility programs to combine related data, and it may create an unacceptable performance impact to join related rows that frequently are retrieved together. Fortunately, UDB/400 provides good support for combining related rows with SQL/400 join views, so, in most cases, performance is the only issue.

For large, frequently accessed tables, performance must be considered because it takes more time and system resources to return a joined row than to return a single row that has the combined information. As a result, you may decide to duplicate in related rows some columns that could be retrieved by a join. Consider the case of a Customer table and an Order table that has a foreign key referencing the Customer table. In the data model, the normal form base tables for these two entity types would typically have the customer's name and phone number as columns in the Customer table. A view table that joined the Customer and Order base tables would provide a way for an end user to see the customer name and phone number for an order. If Order table rows will be retrieved frequently and the end user needs the customer name and phone number, you may decide to design the tables so the customer name and phone number are redundantly stored in the Order table, avoiding the need to join to the Customer table for this end-user view.

Controlled redundancy is a trade-off. As general principles:

- Controlled redundancy usually makes retrieval faster and simpler.
- Controlled redundancy usually makes updates slower and more complex.

You can see from the previous example how controlled redundancy can reduce table I/O (thus improving speed) and potentially simplify working with the related data. You can understand why controlled redundancy often complicates table updates by considering what's necessary to update a customer's phone number. In addition to changing one Customer row, you must update all the Order

10 Also consider using DDS-defined logical files with rebuild or delayed access path maintenance for non-unique keyed access paths. These types of access path maintenance reduce the overhead for table updates.

rows for the customer if they also have the customer phone number in them. As with many performance-related design issues, the best solution depends on the estimated or measured access pattern. If you expect or observe all the following:

- very frequent retrieval of orders requiring customer name and phone number
- unacceptably slow retrieval using a join
- unacceptable cost to upgrade hardware to meet response time criteria
- infrequent updates to customer name and phone numbers
- acceptable cost to modify Customer table update programs to handle redundant data in Order table

then a database design with this type of redundancy would be appropriate. If the first two items aren't both true, there's not likely to be justification for redundant storage of the customer name and phone number. If the first two items are true, but not all of the other items are, you must balance the various costs to decide on the best design.

Other types of controlled redundancy include storing derived columns, such as the total amount of an order, to avoid recalculating the value on each retrieval. As with the previous example, this type of redundancy complicates updates to values used in the computation of the derived column. You must consider the same kinds of trade-offs to determine the optimal design.

Another type of controlled redundancy is replicated data. Snapshot copies of all or part of a table can be created periodically to provide read-only access for data analysis and other purposes. The data may be combined or partially transformed to make it easier to work with, and it may be copied to other systems, such as PCs, so additional tools (e.g., spreadsheet software) can use it. Because snapshot copies are intended as a view of the organization's data at some moment in time, the snapshot data usually doesn't have to be updated, except when the next snapshot is produced. Thus, this type of redundancy doesn't particularly complicate table updates; the only trade-off is that the data may be somewhat out-of-date.

One technique to improve consistency for redundant data is to use trigger programs to propagate changes. For example, a trigger program could be associated with the Customer table in our previous example so that when a Customer row's customer name or phone number is changed, the trigger program updates the corresponding rows in the Order table. Using a trigger program guarantees that all changes to the redundantly stored columns will be propagated, no matter which HLL program or utility updates the Customer table.

Step 9. Merge Base Tables

Another performance-related design alternative is to merge two or more base tables from the data model into a single SQL/400 table in the implementation. This technique is motivated by similar concern for the speed of data retrieval. Consider the case in which a customer might have multiple phone numbers, so your data model has a CustomerPhone table (as well as a Customer table) containing one row for each phone number. Implementing these two data model tables as two tables works fine but requires retrieving one or more joined rows to get a customer's phone number(s). An alternative database design could specify three phone columns (Phone1, Phone2, Phone3) in the Customer table and eliminate the separate table for telephone numbers (or use it for customers with more than three phone numbers).

Repeating columns complicate updates because you must find an open "bucket" to store a new phone number, and you may (or may not) want to shift down values when a phone number (other than the last) is deleted. In some cases, you also must decide whether to limit the number of values to the number of "buckets" in the row or use some (more complex) technique to handle the occasional overflow situation.

Although retrieval from a merged table may be faster than retrieving multiple rows from multiple tables, the use of repeating columns can also complicate some types of retrieval. For example, calculating a sum or average of numeric values stored in repeated columns requires summing both across the columns and across the rows, and some method of excluding unused "buckets" must be part of the process. For an HLL program or stored procedure, this isn't particularly difficult, but using interactive SQL/400 or other query tools may pose problems. Be sure you consider how all retrieval and update access of repeating columns will be handled before using a merged table in your database design.

Another case in which base tables may be combined is for entity subtypes. For example, if the data model has an Employee entity type and two subtypes, Manager and NonManager, you can implement these as three tables, all with a primary key column of EmployeeID. Each employee will have one Employee table row and either a Manager row or a NonManager row. Retrieving the complete information for an employee requires retrieving two rows. Some updates may also require changing or inserting two rows. You can always combine subtypes and their supertype by designing a table that has all the columns that would be defined for all the separate tables. You then need to specify in your database design how you'll represent the not-applicable placeholder for all the columns that would otherwise be defined for the subtype tables. For example, if Manager rows have a YearSalary column and NonManager rows have an HourlyWage column, in a combined table there must be some way to represent not-applicable in the HourlyWage column for Manager rows and in the YearSalary column for NonManager rows. In this case, you may simply specify that zero is used because zero would never (presumably) be a valid YearSalary or HourlyWage value. When you combine subtypes into one table, you also need a column to identify which type a particular row is. For example, our combined Employee table might have an EmplType column to hold this information.

We said in Chapter 19's discussion of data modeling that you can choose (based on how the organization views the entity types) whether to represent subtypes as separate tables or as columns that allow the not-applicable placeholder. In the database design stage, the decision has more to do with trade-offs among storage efficiency, retrieval and update performance, and implementation complexity. A combined SQL/400 table wastes storage for the unused columns, although in many cases the amount of storage isn't a big issue. As we mentioned, a combined table reduces retrieval and update I/O; it also generally simplifies retrieval and updates. For these reasons, it's fairly common to use a single, combined table for all the subtypes of an entity type.

Step 10. Adjust the Database Design to Anticipate Changes

Organizations and their information requirements change over time. You should anticipate changes in your database design and avoid rigid designs that will be expensive to modify. For example, we saw that one technique for merging tables was to use repeating columns. If, in the case of multiple phone numbers, you assume that the organization will never need to store more than three phone numbers for each customer, you might design your database (and the applications that use it) to depend on there being exactly three buckets for phone numbers in the Customer table. A better approach would be either not to merge the tables or to specify that the Customer table will have MaxCustPhone buckets for phone numbers. In other words, use a symbolic value for the limit. The actual value for

MaxCustPhone might be 3, 2, or 10, but all other items in the database design (e.g., table-access stored procedures) would be designed with the flexibility to handle different values for MaxCustPhone.

Another tactic that can help protect against major disruption caused by changes in the data model is to use trigger programs, table-access stored procedures, or other similar techniques when you incorporate into your database design some technique that isn't a direct implementation of the data model. We've already explored how you can use trigger programs to maintain consistency when data is stored redundantly. You can also use stored procedures to isolate performance-related techniques, such as repeating columns, to a stored procedure that's called by all programs that need access to the data. This way, if you change the number of buckets or add the ability to handle overflow values, the programs calling the stored procedure usually won't have to be changed. Only the stored procedure will need to change to handle the modified table structure.

As part of your database design, you may want to document the dependencies among various implementation elements. For example, views are dependent on the underlying tables, and columns are dependent on domains. This information can be presented so that you or another person can see the impact of a change to a table, a domain, or some other element. This type of **impact analysis** is important both during initial design work and for future revisions to the design. If you use database tables or CASE tools to keep track of design information, you may be able to produce the necessary "where referenced" lists automatically. After you create SQL/400 tables, views, and stored procedures, some of this type of information is available from the system catalog tables or by using OS/400 commands (e.g., DspDbR, or Display Database Relations).

As with logical data modeling, physical database design is an iterative process. After you make the first pass at your design, you'll probably have to revisit some of the steps. Remember that it's important to produce good documentation for both the specific implementation objects in your database design and the reason for any non-obvious design decision. Also try to keep your database design as simple and direct an implementation as possible of the data model as long as estimated or measured performance is acceptable. Avoid complex or tricky solutions because they increase the likelihood of errors and usually increase the cost of adapting to changing requirements. Once you have a well-laid-out database design, you have a good blueprint for the implementation.

Chapter Summary

Physical database design is the application development stage that produces a specification for the subsequent implementation. Database design uses the logical data model (produced in an earlier stage of the development project) and estimates of data volume and access patterns and frequency to plan an efficient database implementation that satisfies the requirements presented in the data model. The database design takes into account the functional capabilities of the DBMS and other system software, as well as the hardware and software performance characteristics, to decide among alternative implementations for each element of the data model.

The major steps in database design are

Step 1 Specify a table for each entity type

Step 2 Specify primary, candidate, and foreign key implementation

Step 3 Specify domain implementation

Step 4 Specify implementation of other integrity rules

Step 5 Specify view implementation

Step 6 Specify security implementation

Step 7 Specify additional indexes for performance

Step 8 Introduce controlled redundancy

Step 9 Merge base tables

Step 10 Adjust the database design to anticipate changes

In some cases, UDB/400 provides a direct way to implement an element of the data model. For example, SQL/400 supports tables to implement data model entity types. In other cases, you must design your own mechanism to implement some part of the data model. For example, UDB/400 doesn't offer much support for domains, so you must find alternatives (e.g., check constraints and trigger programs) to provide the required capability.

During the design, you should keep an eye out for potential performance problems, keeping in mind that in many cases the only way to evaluate the significance of performance differences between alternative implementation techniques is to measure them. Use techniques that complicate the database design (e.g., repeating columns) only when there's a clear basis for expecting significant and necessary performance improvement.

Throughout the database design process, try to anticipate change and incorporate designs that provide flexibility to handle changes to the data model. At the end of the process, you should have a full specification that describes exactly how the database tables, views, indexes, and related items will be created. The actual coding and creation of tables and other objects follows the completion of the database design stage.

Key Terms

impact analysis
index
physical database design
table-access routine
trigger program

Exercises

1. List the essential information you need to have as the basis for a good physical database design.
2. Briefly describe and provide examples of five types of information that would be included in a database design (i.e., in the specification).
3. For each item you described for Exercise 2, suggest one or more ways you could store the information in a data dictionary.
4. From the following list, identify which data model items you think would be relatively easy to design an implementation for:
   - entity type
   - property
   - domain
   - primary key
   - candidate key
   - one-to-many relationship
   - many-to-many relationship

- multirow and multitable predicates
- security rules
- end users' views (subschema)

5. For the items you listed in Exercise 4, briefly describe how you would design their respective implementations.
6. List all the data model items (from the list in Exercise 4) for which a trigger program might be used in the implementation.
7. Explain the disadvantages of coding some or all of the validity checks for column values directly in each application that updates a table. Explain the advantages (if any) of this method.
8. Compare the advantages and disadvantages of trigger programs and table-access stored procedures. Can you think of any programming techniques that could be used to increase the flexibility of trigger programs?
9. Describe a case (other than the examples in the text) in which you might want to use controlled redundancy in the database design.
10. Describe a case (other than the examples in the text) in which you might want to use merged tables in the database design.

Appendix A

SQL/400 Statement Syntax

This appendix contains a list of SQL/400 statements and their syntax. We show the most important syntax elements and a recommended style. For example, we don't show the fact that you can specify the Primary Key keyword within a column definition because we highly recommend specifying primary key constraints separately at the end of the column definitions. A complete syntax can be found in the manual *DB2 UDB for AS/400 SQL Reference.*

How to Read the Syntax Diagrams

In the syntax notation that follows, SQL keywords begin with uppercase characters (e.g., Table) and must be spelled as shown. However, because SQL is a case-insensitive language, you can use any case style you prefer when specifying keywords.[1] Optional syntactical elements appear within square brackets ([]). An ellipsis (...) indicates repeating elements. Replaceable elements appear in italics.

For example, in the statement

```
Declare statement-name1 [ , statement-name2, ... ] Statement
```

Declare and Statement are required keywords. The replaceable element *statement-name1* is required and must be replaced with a statement name. The replaceable element *statement-name2* (and its associated preceding comma), as well as any subsequent statement name, is optional.

In some cases, a replaceable element is further defined syntactically:

Somestatement:

```
Somestatement replaceable-element
```

replaceable-element:

```
Foo ( replaceable-element2, ... )
```

When you have a choice of syntactical elements, the options are listed separated by a vertical bar (|). The vertical bar signifies an exclusive set of choices in that you must choose exactly one of the listed elements. In addition, braces ({}) are used when necessary to delineate syntactical elements. In the following example,

```
Foo { Keyword1 | Keyword2 } Keyword3
```

the syntax consists of the keyword Foo followed by either Keyword1 or Keyword2, followed by Keyword3. The braces have been used here to show that Keyword3 is a standalone required syntactical element.

When you have a choice of optional elements and one of the elements is the default, the default will be underlined:

```
Foo [ Keyword1 | Keyword2 ]
```

In this example, Keyword1 is the default.

1 For improved readability, we recommend the use of mixed-case names as illustrated throughout this book.

Common Syntactical Elements

What follows is a list of syntactical elements that are used in multiple syntax diagrams. In the syntax diagrams, these common elements appear in small capital letters (e.g., *DATA-TYPE*). Note that some common syntactical elements rely on others. For example, the *COLUMN-DEFINITION* common syntactical element uses the *DATA-TYPE* common syntactical element.

CHECK-CONSTRAINT:

```
[ Constraint constraint-name ] Check ( check-condition )
```

COLUMN-DEFINITION:

```
column-name [ For [ Column ] system-column-name ] DATA-TYPE
```

COMMON-TABLE-EXPRESSION:

```
table-name [ ( column-name, ... ) ]
  As ( SUBSELECT )
```

CORRELATION-CLAUSE:

```
[ As ] correlation-name [ ( column-name [ , ... ] ) ]
```

DATA-TYPE:

```
{   Int
  | SmallInt
  | Dec [ ( scale [ , precision ] ) ]
  | Numeric [ ( scale [ , precision ] ) ]
  | Float
  | Double
  | BLOB [ maximum-size [ , [ { K | M } ] ] ]
  | Char [ ( length ) ]
  | VarChar [ ( maximum-size ) ] [ Allocate ( allocation-size ) ]
  | CLOB [ maximum-size [ , [ { K | M } ] ] ]
  | Graphic [ ( length ) ] [ CCSID ccsid ]
  | VarGraphic ( maximum-length ) [ CCSID ccsid ]
  | DBCLOB [ maximum-size [, [ { K | M } ] ] [ CCSID ccsid ] ]
  | Date
  | Time
  | Timestamp
  | Datalink [ ( maximum-length ) ] [ Allocate allocation-length ]
  | distinct-type    }
```

DEFAULT-CLAUSE:

```
[ With ] Default [ constant | Null | User | Current_Date | Current_Time
                 | Current_Timestamp ]
```

FROM-CLAUSE:

```
From { table-reference, ... }
```

table-reference:

```
single-table | nested-table-expression | joined-table
```

single-table:

```
table-or-view-name [ CORRELATION-CLAUSE ]
```

nested-table-expression:

```
( SUBSELECT ) CORRELATION-CLAUSE
```

joined-table:

```
{ table-reference | ( joined-table ) }
  [ Inner | Left Outer | Exception ] Join
  On join-condition
```

join-condition:

```
expression { = | <> | > | >= | < | <= } | ( join-condition )
[ { And join-condition } ... ]
```

FULLSELECT:

```
{ SUBSELECT | ( FULLSELECT ) }
  [ Union | Union All { SUBSELECT | ( FULLSELECT ) } ]
```

GROUP-BY-CLAUSE:

```
Group By { grouping-expression, ... }
```

HAVING-CLAUSE:

```
Having search-condition
```

ISOLATION-CLAUSE:

```
With [ NC | UR | CS [ Keep Locks ] | RS | RR ]
```

ORDER-BY-CLAUSE:

```
Order By { { select-list-column-name   |
             select-list-column-number | expression } [ Asc | Desc ] }
           [ , ... ]
```

PRIMARY-KEY-CONSTRAINT:

```
Primary Key ( column-name [ , ... ] )
```

REFERENTIAL-CONSTRAINT:

```
[ Constraint constraint-name ] Foreign Key ( column-name [ , ... ] )
   References table-name [ ( column-name, [ , ... ] ) ]
     On Delete { No Action | Restrict | Cascade | Set Null | Set Default }
     On Update { No Action | Restrict }
```

SEARCH-CONDITION:

```
[ Not ] { predicate | search-condition }
 [ { And | Or } [ Not ] { predicate | ( search-condition ) } ]
```

predicate:

```
basic-predicate  | quantified-predicate | between-predicate |
exists-predicate | in-predicate         | like-predicate    |
null-predicate
```

basic-predicate:

```
expression { = | <> | < | > | <= | >= } { expression | ( SUBSELECT ) }
```

quantified-predicate:

```
expression { = | <> | < | > | <= | >= } { Some | All } ( SUBSELECT ) }
```

between-predicate:

```
expression [ Not ] Between expression And expression
```

exists-predicate:

```
Exists ( SUBSELECT )
```

in-predicate:

```
expression [ Not ] In ( SUBSELECT )
```

like-predicate:

```
expression [ Not ] Like { User | Current Server | host-variable |
                          string-constant }
  [ Escape { host-variable | string-constant } ]
```

null-predicate:

```
expression Is [ Not ] Null
expression [ Not ] In ( { host-variable | constant | SPECIAL-REGISTER }, ... )
```

SELECT-CLAUSE:

```
Select [ All | Distinct ]
  {* | table-name.* | view-name.* | correlation-name.*
     | { expression [ As ] { column-name }, ... } }
```

SELECT-STATEMENT:

```
[ With { COMMON-TABLE-EXPRESSION }, ... ]
  FULLSELECT
  [ ORDER-BY-CLAUSE ]
  [ update-clause | read-only-clause | optimize-clause | ISOLATION-CLAUSE ]
```

update-clause:

```
For Update of { column-name } [ , ... ]
```

read-only-clause:

```
For [ Read | Fetch ] Only
```

optimize-clause:

```
Optimize for { integer | All } { Rows | Row }
```

SPECIAL-REGISTER:

```
Current Date   | Current Path | Current Function Path |
Current Server | Current Time
```

SUBSELECT:

```
SELECT-CLAUSE
  FROM-CLAUSE [ WHERE-CLAUSE GROUP-BY-CLAUSE HAVING-CLAUSE ]
```

UNIQUE-CONSTRAINT:

```
[ Constraint constraint-name ] Unique ( column-name [ , ... ] )
```

WHERE-CLAUSE:

```
Where search-condition
```

Statement Syntax Diagrams

Alter Table

Alters the description of a table.

```
Alter Table table-name { column-addition | column-change |
                         column-drop     | constraint-addition |
                         constraint-drop }, ...
```

column-addition:

```
Add [ Column ] COLUMN-DEFINITION
```

column-change:

```
Alter [ Column ] column-name {   Set { Data Type DATA-TYPE | DEFAULT-CLAUSE | Not Null }
                               | Drop { Default | Not Null }   }
```

column-drop:

```
Drop [ Column ] column-name
```

constraint-addition:

```
Add { UNIQUE-CONSTRAINT      | PRIMARY-KEY-CONSTRAINT |
      REFERENTIAL-CONSTRAINT | CHECK-CONSTRAINT }
```

constraint-drop:

```
Drop Primary Key [ constraint-name ]
Drop [ Foreign Key | Unique | Check | Constraint ] constraint-name
```

Call

Calls a procedure.

```
Call { procedure-name | host-variable }
```

Close

Closes a cursor.

```
Close cursor-name
```

Comment On

Replaces or adds a comment to the description of an alias, column, function, index, package, parameter, procedure, table, type, or view.

```
Comment On { comment-identifier Is string-constant | multiple-columns
           | multiple-parameters }
```

comment-identifier:

```
{  Alias alias-name
 | Column table-or-view-name.column-name
 | [ Distinct ] Type type-name
 | Function function-name [ ( type-definition, ... ) ]
 | Index index-name
 | Package package-name
 | Parameter function-or-procedure-name.parameter-name
 | Procedure procedure-name [ ( type-definition, ... ) ]
 | Specific { Function | Procedure } specific-name
 | Table table-or-view-name  }
```

multiple-columns:

```
Column table-or-view-name ( column-name Is { string-constant } [ , ... ] )
```

multiple-parameters:

```
Parameter { specific-identifier | non-specific-identifier }
  { parameter-name Is string-constant } [ , ... ]
```

specific-identifier:

```
Specific { Function | Procedure } specific-name
```

non-specific-identifier:

```
{ Function | Procedure } function-or-procedure-name
   [ ( { DATA-TYPE } [ , ... ] ) ]
```

Commit

Ends a unit of work and commits the database changes made by that unit of work.

```
Commit [ Hold ]
```

Connect

Connects to a remote database server.

```
Connect { to-clause | RESET }
```

to-clause:

```
To { remote-database-server-name | host-variable }
```

Create Alias

Creates an alias (or synonym) for a table or view name.

```
Create Alias alias-name
  For table-or-view-name [ ( member-name ) ]
```

Create Collection

Creates a collection.

```
Create Collection collection-name [ In Asp asp-number ]
```

Create Distinct Type

Creates a distinct (or user-defined) type.

```
Create [ Distinct ] Type distinct-type-name
  As DATA-TYPE [ With Comparisons ]
```

Create Function (External Scalar)

Creates an external scalar user-defined function.

```
Create Function function-name [ ( { parameter-name DATA-TYPE }, ... ) ]
  Returns DATA-TYPE
  [ Language { C | C++ | CL | COBOL | COBOLLE | RPG | RPGLE | SQL } ]
  [ Specific specific-name ]
  [ [ Not ] Deterministic | [ Is ] Deterministic ]
  [ Contains SQL | No SQL | Reads SQL Data | Modifies SQL Data ]
  [ Fenced | Not Fenced ]
  [ Called on Null Input | Returns Null on Null Input ]
  [ External Action | No External Action ]
  [ No Scratchpad | Scratchpad [ scratchpad-size ] ]
  [ No Final Call | Final Call ]
  [ Disallow Parallel | Allow Parallel ]
  [ No DBInfo | DBInfo ]
  [ Static Dispatch ]
  [ external-function-body | SQL-procedure-language-body ]
```

external-function-body:

```
   [ External | External Name external-program-name ]
      [ [ Parameter Style ] SQL | DB2SQL | General | General With Nulls ]
```

Create Function (Sourced)

Creates a sourced user-defined function (i.e., based on another function).

```
Create Function function-name [ ( { parameter-name DATA-TYPE }, ... ) ]
  Returns DATA-TYPE
  Source { function-name | Specific specific-function-name |
           function-name ( { DATA-TYPE } [ , ... ] ) }
```

Create Index

Creates an index on a table.

```
Create [ Unique [ Where Not Null ] | Encoded Vector ] Index index-name
  On table-name ( { column-name [ Asc | Desc ] } [ , ... ] )
  [ With distinct-value-count [ Distinct ] Values ]
```

Create Procedure

Creates an external procedure or a procedure written in the SQL Procedure Language (SPL).

```
Create Procedure procedure-name
  [ ( { In | Out | InOut } { [ parameter-name ] DATA-TYPE } [ , ... ] ) ]
  [ [ Dynamic ] Result { Set | Sets } result-set-count ]
  [ Language { C | C++ | CL | COBOL | COBOLLE | RPG | RPGLE | SQL } ]
  [ Specific specific-name ]
  [ Not Deterministic | Deterministic ]
  [ Contains SQL | No SQL | Reads SQL Data | Modifies SQL Data ]
  [ Fenced | Not Fenced ]
  [ Called on Null Input ]
  { SQL-procedure-language-body | external-procedure-body }
```

external-procedure-body:

```
   [ External | External Name external-program-name ]
      [ Parameter Style ] { SQL | General | General With Nulls }
```

Create Schema

Creates a collection and a set of SQL objects within the collection.

```
Create Schema² { collection-name | Authorization authorization-name }
  [ In ASP asp-number ]
  { [ comment-on-statement ] [ create-alias-statement ]
    [ create-distinct-type-statement ] [ create-index-statement ]
    [ create-table-statement ] [ create-view-statement ]
    [ grant-table-privileges-statement ]
    [ grant-distinct-type-privileges-statement ]
    [ label-on-statement ] } [ ... ]
```

Create Table

Creates a table.

```
Create Table table-name ( { COLUMN-DEFINITION } [ , ... ] )
  { [ , PRIMARY-KEY-CONSTRAINT ] | [ , UNIQUE-CONSTRAINT ] |
    [ , REFERENTIAL-CONSTRAINT ] | [ , CHECK-CONSTRAINT ] } [ ... ]
```

Create View

Creates a view of one or more tables or views.

```
Create View view-name
  [ ( { column-name [ For system-column-name ] }, ... ) ]
  As [ With { COMMON-TABLE-EXPRESSION }, ... ]
  SUBSELECT
```

Declare Cursor

Defines an SQL cursor.

```
Declare Cursor cursor-name
  [ Insensitive ] [ { Dynamic Scroll | Scroll } ]
  Cursor [ With Hold ]
  For { SELECT-STATEMENT | prepared-select-statement-name }
```

Declare Procedure

Defines an external stored procedure.

```
Declare procedure-name Procedure
  ( { In | Out | InOut } [ parameter-name ] DATA-TYPE )
  [ [ Dynamic ] Result { Set | Sets } result-set-count ]
  [ Language { C | C++ | CL | COBOL | COBOLLE | RPG | RPGLE | SQL } ]
  [ Specific specific-name ]
  [ [ Not ] Deterministic | [ Is ] Deterministic ]
  [ Contains SQL | No SQL | Reads SQL Data | Modifies SQL Data ]
  [ Fenced | Not Fenced ]
  external-procedure-body
```

external-procedure-body:

```
    External Name external-program-name
      Parameter Style { SQL | General | General With Nulls }
```

2 The syntax for all of these statements is specified elsewhere in this appendix.

Declare Statement

Lists names that are used in your program to identify prepared SQL statements.

```
Declare { statement-name } [ , ... ] Statement
```

Declare Variable

Declares a subtype or Coded Character Set Identifier (CCSID) other than the default for a host variable.

```
Declare { host-variable } [ , ... ] Variable
  [ For SBCS Data | For Mixed Data | CCSID ccsid | For Bit Data |
    Date          | Time           | Timestamp ]
```

Delete

Deletes rows from a table or view.

```
searched-delete | positioned-delete
```

searched-delete:

```
Delete From table-or-view-name CORRELATION-CLAUSE
  [ Where SEARCH-CONDITION ] [ ISOLATION-CLAUSE ]
```

positioned-delete:

```
Delete From table-or-view-name [ CORRELATION-CLAUSE ]
  Where Current Of cursor-name
```

Describe

Describes the result columns of a prepared statement.

```
Describe statement-name Into sqlda-name
  [ Using { Names | System Names | Labels | Any | Both | All } ]
```

Describe Table

Obtains information about a table or view.

```
Describe Table host-variable Into sqlda-name
```

Disconnect

Ends one or more connections.

```
Disconnect { remote-database-name | host-variable | Current | All }
```

Drop

Deletes an SQL object.

```
Drop {    Alias alias-name
        | Collection collection-name
        | Distinct Type type-name
        | Function user-defined-function-name [ ( { DATA-TYPE } [ , ... ] ) ]
        | Index index-name
        | Package package-name
        | Procedure procedure-name [ ( { DATA-TYPE } [ , ... ] ) ]
        | Specific { Function | Procedure } specific-name
        | Table table-name
        | View view-name    }
```

Execute

Executes a prepared statement.

```
Execute prepared-statement-name
  [ Using { host-variable } [ , ... ] | Descriptor sqlda-name ]
```

Execute Immediate

Prepares and executes an executable form of an SQL statement from a character string form of the statement.

```
Execute Immediate { host-variable | string-expression }
```

Fetch

Positions a cursor on a row of a result table. Can return zero, one, or multiple rows and assigns the values of the returned rows to host variables.

```
Fetch [ Next | Prior | First | Last | Before | After | Current |
        Relative { host-variable | integer } ]
  { single-fetch | multiple-row-fetch }
```

single-fetch:

```
Into { { host-variable } [ , ... ] | Descriptor sqlda-name }
```

multiple-row-fetch:

```
For { host-variable | integer } Rows
  { Into host-structure-array |
    Using Descriptor sqlda-name Into row-storage-area }
```

Grant (Distinct Type Privileges)

Grants privileges to a distinct (or user-defined) type.

```
Grant { All | Alter | Usage | Alter, Usage }
  On Distinct Type { type-name } [ , ... ]
  To { { authorization-name } [ , ... ] | Public } [ With Grant Option ]
```

Grant (Function or Procedure Privileges)

Grants privileges to one or more functions or procedures.

```
Grant { All | Alter | Execute | Alter, Execute }
  On { Function function-name [ ( { DATA-TYPE } [ , ... ] ) ]   |
       Procedure procedure-name [ ( { DATA-TYPE } [ , ... ] ) ] |
       Specific { Function | Procedure } specific-name }
  To { { authorization-name } [ , ... ] | Public } [ With Grant Option ]
```

Grant (Package Privileges)

Grants privileges to an SQL package.

```
Grant { All | Alter | Execute | Alter, Execute }
  On Package { package-name } [ , ... ]
  To { { authorization-name } [ , ... ] | Public } [ With Grant Option ]
```

Grant (Table Privileges)

Grants privileges to one or more tables or views.

```
Grant { All | { table-privilege } [ , ... ] }
  On Table { table-or-view-name }  [ , ... ]
  To { { authorization-name } [ , ... ] | Public } [ With Grant Option ]
```

table-privilege:

```
Alter | Delete | Index | Insert                          |
References [ { column-name } [ , ... ] ]                |
Select | Update [ { column-name } [ , ... ] ]
```

Include

Inserts declarations or statements into a source program.

```
Include { SQLCA | SQLDA | member-name }
```

Insert

Inserts rows into a table or view.

```
Insert Into table-or-view-name [ ( { column-name } [ , ... ] ) ]
  { Values ( { inserted-value } [ , ... ] ) [ ISOLATION-CLAUSE ] |
           insert-multiple-rows [ ISOLATION-CLAUSE ]               |
           SELECT-STATEMENT }
```

inserted-value:

```
constant | host-variable | SPECIAL-REGISTER | Null | Default
```

insert-multiple-rows:

```
{ number-of-rows | host-variable } Rows Values ( host-structure-array )
```

Label On

Adds or replaces labels in the catalog descriptions of tables, views, packages, or columns.

```
Label On
{   Alias alias-name Is string-constant
  | table-or-view-name ( { column-name [ Text ] Is string-constant } [ , ... ] )
  | Package package-name Is string-constant
  | Table table-or-view-name Is string-constant   }
```

Lock Table

Either prevents concurrent application processes from changing a table or prevents concurrent application processes from using a table.

```
Lock Table table-name
  In { Share Mode | Exclusive Mode Allow Read | Exclusive Mode }
```

Open

Open a cursor.

```
Open cursor-name [ { Using { host-variable } [ , ... ] |
                   Using Descriptor sqlda-name } ]
```

Prepare

Creates an executable form of an SQL statement from a character-string form of the statement.

```
Prepare statement-name
  [ Into sqlda-name
    [ Using { Names | System Names | Labels | Any | Both | All } ] ]
  From { string-expression | host-variable }
```

Release

Places one or more connections in the release-pending state.

```
Release { database-name | host-variable | Current | All }
```

Rename

Renames a table, view, or index.

```
Rename { Table table-or-view-name | Index index-name }
  To { sql-name | System Name system-name }
```

Revoke (Distinct Type Privileges)

Revokes privileges to a user-defined type.

```
Revoke { All | Alter | Usage | Alter, Usage }
  On Distinct Type { type-name } [ , ... ]
  From { { authorization-name } [ , ... ] | Public }
```

Revoke (Function or Procedure Privileges)

Revokes privileges to a function or procedure.

```
Revoke { All | Alter | Execute | Alter, Execute }
  On { Function function-name [ ( { DATA-TYPE } [ , ... ] ) ]   |
       Procedure procedure-name [ ( { DATA-TYPE } [ , ... ] ) ] |
       Specific { Function | Procedure } specific-name }
  From  { { authorization-name } [ , ... ] | Public }
```

Revoke (Package Privileges)

Revokes privileges to a package.

```
Revoke { All | Alter | Execute | Alter, Execute }
  On Package { package-name } [ , ... ]
  From { { authorization-name } [ , ... ] | Public }
```

Revoke (Table Privileges)

Revokes privileges to one or more tables or views.

```
Revoke { All | { table-privilege } [ , ... ] }
  On Table { table-or-view-name } [ , ... ]
  From { { authorization-name } [ , ... ] | Public }
```

table-privilege:

```
Alter | Delete | Index | Insert                   |
References [ { column-name } [ , ... ] ]          |
Select | Update [ { column-name } [ , ... ] ]
```

Rollback

Ends the unit of work in which it is executed and starts a new unit of work.

```
Rollback [ Hold ]
```

Select Into

Produces a result table consisting of at most one row and assigns the values in that row to host variables.

```
SELECT-CLAUSE Into { host-variable } [ , ... ]
   FROM-CLAUSE
      [ WHERE-CLAUSE ] [ GROUP-BY-CLAUSE ] [ HAVING-CLAUSE ]
      [ ORDER-BY-CLAUSE ] [ ISOLATION-CLAUSE ]
```

Set Connection

Establishes one of the current connections as current.

```
Set Connection { database-name | host-variable }
```

Set Option

Establishes the processing options to be used for SQL statements.

```
Set Option { option } [ , ... ]
```

option:

```
{ AlwBlk        = { *Read | *None | *AllRead } }                     |
{ AlwCpyDta     = { *Yes | *No  | *Optimize } }                      |
{ CloSqlCsr     = { *EndActGrp | *EndMod | *EndPgm | *EndJob } }     |
{ CNulRqd       = { *Yes | *No } }                                   |
{ Commit        = { *Chg | *None | *CS | *All | *RR } }              |
{ DatFmt        = { *Job | *ISO | *Eur | *USA | *JIS |
                    *MDY | *DMY | *YMD | *JUL } }                    |
{ DatSep        = { *Job | *Slash | '/' | *Comma | ',' |
                    *Dash | '-' | *Blank | ' ' } }                   |
{ DecPtn        = { *Period | *Comma | *Sysval | *Job } }            |
{ DftRdbCol     = { *None | collection-name } }                      |
{ DynDftRdbCol  = { *Yes | *No } }                                   |
{ DynUsrPrf     = { *Owner | *User } }                               |
{ LangID        = { *Job | *JobRun | language-ID } }                 |
{ Naming        = { *Sys | *Sql } }                                  |
{ OptLOB        = { *Yes | *No } }                                   |
{ RdbCnnMth     = { *DUW | *RUW } }                                  |
{ SqlPath       = { *LIBL | path-string-constant } }                 |
{ SrtSeq        = { *Job | *Hex | *JobRun |
                    *LangIDUnq | *LangIDShr |
                    *LIBL/srtseq-table-name |
                    *CurLib/srtseq-table-name |
                    library-name/srtseq-table-name } }               |
{ TimFmt        = { *HMS | *ISO | *EUR | *JIS } }                    |
{ TimSep        = { *Job | *Colon | ':' | *Period |
                    '.' | *Comma | ',' | *Blank | ' ' } }            |
{ UsrPrf        = { *Owner | *User | *Naming } }
```

Set Path

Changes the value of the Current Path special register.

```
Set Path = { *LIBL | { path-description }, [ , ... ] }
```

path-description:

```
{ collection-name | System Path | User |
  Current Path | host-variable | string-constant }
```

Set Result Sets

Identifies one or more result sets that can be returned from a procedure.

```
Set Result Sets { array-result-set | cursor-result-set } [ , ... ]
```

array-result-set:

```
Array host-structure-array For host-variable Rows
```

cursor-result-set:

```
Cursor cursor-name
```

Set Transaction

Sets isolation level for the current unit of work.

```
Set Transaction Isolation Level
  { No Commit | Read Uncommitted | Read Committed |
    Repeatable Read | Serializable }
```

Set (Variable)

Produces a result table consisting of at most one row and assigns the values in that row to host variables.

```
Set host-variable = { expression | Null | ( scalar-SUBSELECT³ ) }
```

Update

Updates the values of specified columns in rows of a table or view.

```
{ searched-update | positioned-update }
```

searched-update:

```
Update table-or-view-name [ CORRELATION-CLAUSE ]
  Set { column-assignment | row-assignment }
  [ Where SEARCH-CONDITION ] [ ISOLATION-CLAUSE ]
```

column-assignment:

```
{ column-name = { expression | Null | Default ( scalar-SUBSELECT ) } }
  [ , ... ]
```

row-assignment:

```
Row = { { expression | Null | Default } [ , ... ] | row-SUBSELECT }
```

positioned-update:

```
Update table-or-view-name [ CORRELATION-CLAUSE ]
  Set assignment-clause
  Where Current Of cursor-name
```

Values Into

```
Values { expression | Null | ( scalar-SUBSELECT ) } [ , ... ]
  Into { host-variable } [ , ... ]
```

Whenever

Specifies the action to be taken when a specified exception condition occurs.

```
Whenever { Not Found | SqlError | SqlWarning }
  { Continue | Go To host-label }
```

3 Recall from Chapter 8 that a scalar subselect is a subselect that returns one column and at most one row.

Appendix B

CL Command Descriptions for SQL and Related Objects

Commands

ADDHDBDLFM	(Add Host Database to DataLink File Manager)
ADDPFTRG	(Add Physical File Trigger)
ADDPFXDLFM	(Add Prefix to DataLink File Manager)
ADDRDBDIRE	(Add Relational Database Directory Entry)
CRTSRCPF	(Create Source Physical File)
CRTSQLCBLI	(Create SQL ILE Cobol Object)
CRTSQLCI	(Create SQL ILE C Object)
CRTSQLPKG	(Create SQL Package)
CRTSQLRPGI	(Create SQL ILE RPG Object)
DLTSQLPKG	(Delete SQL Package)
DSPCPCST	(Display Check Pending Constraint)
EDTCPCST	(Edit Check Pending Constraint)
INZDLFM	(Initialize DataLink File Manager)
MOVOBJ	(Move Object)
OVRDBF	(Override with Database File)
PRTSQLINF	(Print SQL Information)
RGZPFM	(Reorganize Physical File Member)
RMVPFTRG	(Remove Physical File Trigger)
RMVRDBDIRE	(Remove Relational Database Directory Entry)

Command Descriptions

The command summaries that follow provide abbreviated descriptions that list the command parameters followed by their allowable values but provide no detailed explanation. You can get additional information about any command by requesting prompting for it (using the F4 key) and pressing the Help (or F1) key. SQL/400-related commands (e.g., StrSql, RunSqlStm, CrtSql*Xxx*) are documented in *DB2 UDB for AS/400 SQL Programming*. The summaries that follow are adapted from the command help text.

Predefined parameter values start with an asterisk, or * (e.g., *File). Other parameter values are user defined (e.g., *SQL-package-name*), and you supply an appropriate value; these appear in italics. Default parameter values are underlined in the descriptions.

ADDHDBDLFM (Add Host Database to DataLink File Manager) Command

Either the HOSTDB parameter or the two parameters SRCFILE and SRCMBR must be specified.

Required Parameters

HOSTDB . . . . .Host database name to be registered.

host-DB-name — Relational DataLink File Manager (DLFM) that will be connecting to the local DLFM for link and unlink requests of DataLinks.

SRCFILE . . . . .Name of source file containing DataLink database information.

source-file-name — Name and library of a source file that will be used to provide host database information to be registered. Can be qualified with *LIBL, *CURLIB, or a library name.

SRCMBR . . . . .Source member within the source file used for identifying DataLink database information.

source-file-mbr-name — Name of the source member that contains the host database information to be registered.

Optional Parameters

HOSTDBLIB . . . . .Libraries that may contain database files with DataLinks.

host-lib-name — Name of one or more libraries in the host database that may contain database files with DataLinks.

HOSTDBINST . . . . .Database instance to be registered.

QSYS — One or more libraries in the host database that may contain database files with DataLinks. Currently, QSYS is the only valid instance value that can be used.

ADDPFTRG (Add Physical File Trigger) Command

Required Parameters

FILE . . . . .File name.

physical-file-name — Physical file to add trigger to. Name can be qualified with *LIBL, *CURLIB, or a library name.

TRGTIME . . . . .Trigger time.

*BEFORE — Call trigger before the file operation occurs.

*AFTER — Call trigger after the file operation occurs.

TRGEVENT . . . . .Trigger event.

*INSERT — Call trigger for insert operation.

*DELETE — Call trigger for delete operation.

*UPDATE — Call trigger for update operation.

PGM . . . . .Trigger program name.

program-name — Program to call for trigger. Name can be qualified with *LIBL, *CURLIB, or a library name.

Optional Parameters

RPLTRG . . . . .Replace trigger.
- *NO — Trigger doesn't replace any existing trigger for same event and time.
- *YES — Trigger replaces any existing trigger for same event and time.

TRGUPDCND . . . . .Conditions under which an update event calls the trigger program associated with the update event.
- *ALWAYS — An update event always calls a trigger program.
- *CHANGE — An update event calls a trigger program only when a value is changed.

ALWREPCHG . . . . .Allow repeated change.
- *NO — Do not allow changes to record being updated.
- *YES — Allow changes to record being updated.

ADDPFXDLFM (Add Prefix to DataLink File Manager) Command

Either PREFIX or the two parameters SRCFILE and SRCMBR are required.

Required Parameters

PREFIX . . . . .Prefix to be added.
- *prefix* — One or more prefixes to be registered with the DataLink File Manager. Up to 300 prefixes can be specified.

SRCFILE . . . . .Source file containing prefixes to be registered.
- *source-file-name* — Name and library of a source file that will be used to provide the prefixes to be registered. Name can be qualified with *LIBL, *CURLIB, or a library name.

SRCMBR . . . . .Source member containing prefix to be registered information.
- *source-mbr-name* — Name of the source member that contains the prefixes to be registered.

ADDRDBDIRE (Add Relational Database Directory Entry) Command

Required Parameter

RDB . . . . .Relational database.
- *relational-database-name* — Name of the entry to add to the relational database directory.
- RMTLOCNAME — Remote location name.
- *LOCAL — The relational database is located on the local system.
- *ARDPGM — The relational database is located by using the application requester driver program specified on the ARDPGM parameter.
- *remote-location-name* — Remote location name of the remote system.

Optional Parameters

PORT . . . . .Port number or service name.
- DRDA — The DRDA well-known port of 446 will be used.
- *port-number* — A port number (ranging from 1 to 65535).
- *service-name* — Specify a maximum of 14 characters for the service name.

DEV . . . . .APPC device description.

appc-device-name — Name of the Advanced Program-to-Program Communications (APPC) device description on the local system that is used with this relational database entry.

LCLLOCNAME . . . . .Local location.

*LOC — If APPC is being used, the system determines which local location name is used. If Advanced Peer-to-Peer Networking (APPN) is being used, the system uses the default local location defined in the network attributes.

*NETATR — The LCLLOCNAME value specified in the system network attributes is used.

local-location-name — A maximum of eight characters for the local location name.

RMTNETID . . . . .Remote network identifier.

*LOC — If APPC is being used, the system determines which remote network identifier is used. If APPN is used, the system uses the local network identifier defined in this system's network attributes for the remote network identifier.

*NONE — No remote network identifier is used.

remote-network-identifier — A maximum of eight characters for the remote network identifier.

MODE . . . . .SNA mode.

*NETATR — The mode in the network attributes is used.

mode-name — A maximum of eight characters for the mode name.

TNSPGM . . . . .Transaction program to use.

*DRDA — The Distributed Relational Database Architecture (DRDA) transaction program name, X'07F6C4C2', is used.

transaction-program-name — Transaction program name, specified in one of the following formats:

- A four-byte hexadecimal name, which is entered by enclosing the eight hexadecimal digits in apostrophes (') with a prefix of X. For example, X'07F6C4C2' is a four-byte hex name.
- An eight-byte character name.

ARDPGM . . . . .Application requester driver.

*DRDA — The DRDA application requester is used.

program-name — Name of the application requester driver program to be called to process the SQL requests. The name can be qualified with *LIBL, *CURLIB, or a library name.

CRTSRCPF (Create Source Physical File) Command

Required Parameter

FILE . . . . .File name to be created.

Optional Parameters

RCDLEN . . . . .Length (in bytes) of the records being stored in the source file.

MBR .... .Member name.

SYSTEM .... .Specifies local system or remote system.

EXPDATE .... .Expiration date.

MAXMBRS .... .Maximum number of members.

ACCPTH .... .Type of access path.

ACCPTHSIZ .... .Maximum size of access paths.

MAINT .... .Type of access path maintenance.

RECOVER .... .Recovery of the file is done if a system failure occurs.

FRCACCPTH .... .Access path changes are forced to auxiliary storage.

SIZE .... .Number of records in each member of the file.

ALLOCATE .... .Storage space is allocated for the initial number of records.

CONTIG .... .Records in each source file member are stored contiguously.

FRCRATIO .... .Number of changed records processed before being forced to storage.

IGCDTA .... .File contains double-byte character set (DBCS) data.

WAITFILE .... .Number of seconds the program waits for the file resources.

WAITRCD .... .Number of seconds the program waits for a record lock.

CCSID .... .Coded Character Set Identifier (CCSID) used to describe character data.

SHARE .... .Share open data path.

DLTPCT .... .Maximum percentage of deleted records that any member in the physical file can have.

ALWUPD .... .Records can be updated in the physical file.

ALWDLT .... .Records can be deleted from the physical file.

AUT .... .Authority given to users who do not have specific authority to the source file.

TEXT .... .Descriptive text.

CRTSQL*XXX*I (Create SQL ILE *XXX* Object) Command

The following parameters apply to the CRTSQLCBLI (Create SQL ILE Cobol Object), CRTSQLCI (Create SQL ILE C Object), and CRTSQLRPGI (Create SQL ILE RPG Object) commands as noted.

Required Parameter

OBJ .... .Program object to create.

object-name — Name to assign to this program. The name can be qualified with a library name of *LIBL, *CURLIB, or a library name.

Optional Parameters (CRTSQLCBLI, CRTSQLCI, CRTSQLRPGI)

SRCFILE . . . . .Source file name.

QCBLLESRC, QCSRC, or QRPGLESRC — If the source file name is not specified, the IBM-supplied source file QCBLLESRC contains the Cobol source; QCSRC contains the C source, or QRPGLESRC contains the RPG source.

source-file-name — Name of the source file that contains the Cobol source. The name can be qualified with a library name of *LIBL, *CURLIB, or a library name.

SRCMBR . . . . .Source member.

*OBJ — The source is in the member of the source file that has the same name as that specified on the OBJ parameter.

source-file-member-name — Name of the member that contains the source.

COMMIT . . . . .Level of commitment control.

*CHG or *UR — The objects referred to in SQL Alter, Call, Comment On, Create, Drop, Grant, Label On, Rename, and Revoke statements and the rows updated, deleted, and inserted are locked until the end of the unit of work (transaction). Uncommitted changes in other jobs can be seen.

*CS — The objects referred to in SQL Alter, Call, Comment On, Create, Drop, Grant, Label On, Rename, and Revoke statements and the rows updated, deleted, and inserted are locked until the end of the unit of work (transaction). A row that is selected but not updated is locked until the next row is selected. Uncommitted changes in other jobs cannot be seen.

*NONE or *NC — Commitment control is not used. Uncommitted changes in other jobs can be seen. If the SQL Drop Collection statement is included in the program, *NONE or *NC must be used.

*RR — The objects referred to in SQL Alter, Call, Comment On, Create, Drop, Grant, Label On, Rename, and Revoke statements and the rows selected, updated, deleted, and inserted are locked until the end of the unit of work (transaction). Uncommitted changes in other jobs cannot be seen.

RDB . . . . .Relational database.

*LOCAL — The program is created as a distributed SQL program. The SQL statements will access the local database. An SQL package object is not created as part of the precompile process.

*NONE — An SQL package object is not created.

relational-database-name — Name of the relational database where the new SQL package object is to be created.

OBJTYPE . . . . .Compile type.

*PGM — A program object is created.

*MODULE — A module object is created.

*SRVPGM — A service program object is created.

OUTPUT . . . . .Listing output.

*NONE — The precompiler listing is not generated.
*PRINT — The precompiler listing is generated.

TEXT . . . . .Descriptive text.

OPTION . . . . .Precompiler options.

*XREF — The precompiler cross-references items in the program to the statement numbers in the program that refer to those items.
*NOXREF — The precompiler does not cross-reference names.
*GEN — The precompiler creates the object that is specified by the OBJTYPE parameter.
*NOGEN — The precompiler does not create the object that is specified by the OBJTYPE parameter.
*COMMA — The value used as the decimal point in numeric literals is a comma (,).
*JOB — The value used as the decimal point for numeric constants used in SQL statements is a period (.).
*PERIOD — The value used as the decimal point for numeric constants used in SQL statements is a period (.).
*SYSVAL — The value used as the decimal point in numeric literals is from the QDECFMT system value.
*NOSECLVL — Second-level text descriptions are not added to the listing.
*SECLVL — Second-level text with replacement data is added for all messages on the listing.
*NOEVENTF — The compiler will not produce an event file for use by CoOperative Development Environment/400 (CODE/400).
*EVENTF — The compiler produces an event file for use by CoOperative Development Environment/400 (CODE/400).
*SYS — The system naming convention is used.
*SQL — The SQL naming convention is used.
*OPTLOB — The first FETCH for a cursor determines how the cursor will be used for large objects (LOBs) on all subsequent FETCHes.
*NOOPTLOB — There is no restriction on whether a column is retrieved into a LOB locator or into a LOB host variable. This option can cause performance to degrade.

For CRTSQLCBLI Only

*QUOTESQL — The character used as the string delimiter in the SQL statements is the double quotation mark (").
*APOSTSQL — The character used as the string delimiter in the SQL statements is the apostrophe (').
*QUOTE — The character used for nonnumeric literals and Boolean literals in the Cobol statements is the double quotation mark (").
*APOST — The character used for nonnumeric literals and Boolean literals in the Cobol statements is the apostrophe (').

For CRTSQLCI Only

*NOCNULRCD — For output character and graphic host variables, the NUL-terminator is not returned when the host variable is exactly the same length as the data. Input character and graphic host variables do not require a NUL-terminator.

*CNULRCD — Output character and graphic host variables always contain the NUL-terminator. If there is not enough space for the NUL-terminator, the data is truncated and the NUL-terminator is added.

For CRTSQLRPGI Only

NOSEQSRC — The source file member created by the precompiler has the same sequence numbers as the original source read by the precompiler.

SEQSRC — The source file member created by the precompiler contains sequence numbers starting at 000001 and incremented by 000001.

NOCVTDT — Date, time, and timestamp data types that are retrieved from externally described database files are to be processed using the native RPG date, time, and timestamp data types.

CVTDT — Date, time and timestamp data types that are retrieved from externally described database files are to be processed as fixed-length character fields.

TGTRLS . . . . .Target release.

*CURRENT — The object is to be used on the release of the operating system currently running on the user's system.

*PRV — The object is to be used on the previous release with modification level 0 of the operating system.

release-level — The release in the format V*x*R*x*M*x*. The object can be used on a system with the specified release or with any subsequent release of the operating system installed.

INCFILE . . . . .Include file.

*SRCFILE — The qualified source file you specify on the SRCFILE parameter contains the source file members specified on any SQL INCLUDE statements.

source-file-name — Specify the name of the source file that contains the source file members specified on any SQL INCLUDE statements. The name can be qualified with *LIBL, *CURLIB, or a library name.

ALWCPYDTA . . . . .Allow copy data.

*OPTIMIZE — The system determines whether to use the data retrieved directly from the database or to use a copy of the data. The decision is based on which method provides the best performance.

*YES — A copy of the data is used only when necessary.

*NO — A copy of the data is not used.

CLOSQLCSR . . . . .Close SQL cursor.

*ENDACTGRP — SQL cursors are closed and SQL prepared statements are implicitly discarded, and Lock Table locks are released when the activation group ends.

*ENDMOD — SQL cursors are closed and SQL prepared statements are implicitly discarded when the module is exited.

ALWBLK . . . . .Allow blocking.

*ALLREAD — Rows are blocked for read-only cursors if *NONE or *CHG is specified on the Commitment control prompt (COMMIT parameter).

*NONE — Rows are not blocked for retrieval of data for cursors.

*READ — Records are blocked for read-only retrieval of data for cursors when:

- *NONE is specified on the Commitment control prompt (COMMIT parameter), which indicates that commitment control is not in effect.
- The cursor is declared with a For Read Only clause, or there are no dynamic statements that could run a positioned Update or Delete statement for the cursor.

DLYPRP . . . . .Delay prepare.

*NO — Dynamic statement validation is not delayed.

*YES — Dynamic statement validation is delayed until the dynamic statement is used in an Open, Execute, or Describe SQL statement.

GENLVL . . . . .Severity level.

10 — Create option fails at level 10.

severity-level — Create option fails at level *severity-level*.

DATFMT . . . . .Date format.

*JOB — The date format specified for the job at precompile time or when a new interactive SQL session is created is used.

*USA — The United States date format *mm/dd/yyyy* is used.

*ISO — The International Standards Organization (ISO) date format *yyyy-mm-dd* is used.

*EUR — The European date format *dd.mm.yyyy* is used.

*JIS — The Japanese Industrial Standard date format *yyyy-mm-dd* is used.

*MDY — The date format *mm/dd/yy* is used.

*DMY — The date format *dd/mm/yy* is used.

*YMD — The date format *yy/mm/dd* is used.

*JUL — The Julian date format *yy/ddd* is used.

DATSEP . . . . .Date separator character.

*JOB — The date separator specified for the job at precompile time, when a new interactive SQL session is created, or when the RUNSQLSTM (Run SQL Statement) command is run is used.

*BLANK — A blank character is used.

'/', '.', '-', ',', or ' ' — The indicated character is used.

TIMFMT . . . . .Time format.

- *HMS — The *hh:mm:ss* format is used.
- *USA — The United States time format *hh:mmxx* (where *xx* is AM or PM) is used.
- *ISO — The ISO time format *hh.mm.ss* is used.
- *EUR — The European time format *hh.mm.ss* is used.
- *JIS — The Japanese Industrial Standard time format *hh:mm:ss* is used.

TIMSEP . . . . .Time separator.

- *JOB — The time separator specified for the job at precompile time, when a new interactive SQL session is created, or when RUNSQLSTM is run is used.
- *BLANK — A blank time separator is used.
- ':', '.', ',', or ' ' — The indicated time separator is used.

REPLACE . . . . .Replace object.

- *YES — A new SQL module, program, service program, or package is created.
- *NO — A new SQL module, program, service program, or package is not created if an SQL object of the same name and type already exists in the specified library.

RDBCNNMTH . . . . .Remote database connection method.

- *DUW — Connect (Type 2) semantics are used to support distributed unit of work. Consecutive Connect statements to additional relational databases do not result in disconnection of previous connections.
- *RUW — Connect (Type 1) semantics are used to support remote unit of work. Consecutive Connect statements result in the previous connection being disconnected before a new connection is established.

DFTRDBCOL . . . . .Default collection.

- *NONE — The naming convention specified on the Precompiler options prompt (OPTION parameter) is used in determining the collection for unqualified table, view, index, and SQL package names.
- *collection-name* — Name of the collection identifier to be used instead of the naming convention specified on the Precompiler options prompt (OPTION parameter) for unqualified table, view, index, and SQL package names.

DYNDFTCOL . . . . .Dynamic default collection.

- *NO — Do not use the value specified on the DFTRDBCOL parameter for unqualified names of tables, views, indexes, and SQL packages for dynamic SQL statements.
- *YES — The collection name specified on the DFTRDBCOL parameter will be used for the unqualified names of the tables, views, indexes, and SQL packages in dynamic SQL statements.

SQLPKG . . . . .SQL package.

*OBJ — The collection name specified on the DFTRDBCOL parameter will be used for the unqualified names of the tables, views, indexes, and SQL packages in dynamic SQL statements.

package-name — Name of the SQL package. If the remote system is not an AS/400, no more than eight characters can be specified. The name can be qualified with *OBJLIB (use the same library as was specified in the OBJ parameter) or a library name.

SQLPATH . . . . .SQL path for finding unqualified procedures, functions, and user-defined types.

*NAMING — For system naming, the path used is *LIBL, the current library list at runtime. For SQL naming, the path used is QSYS, QSYS2, *userid*, where *userid* is the value of the USER special register.

*LIBL — The path used is the library list at runtime.

collection-name — A list of one or more (up to 43) collection names to be used for the path.

SAAFLAG . . . . .IBM SQL flagging.

*NOFLAG — No checks are made to see whether SQL statements conform to IBM SQL syntax.

*FLAG — Checks are made to see whether SQL statements conform to IBM SQL syntax.

FLAGSTD . . . . .American National Standards Institute (ANSI) flagging.

*NONE — No checks are made to see whether SQL statements conform to ANSI standards.

*ANS — Checks are made to see whether SQL statements conform to ANSI standards.

PRTFILE . . . . .Print file for precompiler output.

QSYSPRT — If a file name is not specified, the precompiler file is directed to the IBM-supplied printer file, QSYSPRT.

print-file-name — Name of the printer device file to which the precompiler output is directed. The name can be qualified with *LIBL, *CURLIB, or a library name.

DBGVIEW . . . . .Debugging view.

*NONE — A debugging view is not generated.

*SOURCE — The SQL precompiler will provide the source views for the root and, if necessary, SQL Include statements. A view is be provided that contains the statements generated by the precompiler.

USRPRF . . . . .User profile associated with native code and static SQL in the generated object.

*NAMING — The user profile is determined by the naming convention. If the naming convention is SQL, USRPRF(*OWNER) is used. If the naming convention is *SYS, USRPRF(*USER) is used.

*USER — The profile of the user running the program or SQL package is used.

*OWNER — The user profiles of both the owner and the user are used when the program or SQL package is run.

DYNUSRPRF . . . . .User profile used for dynamic SQL in generated object.

*USER — Local dynamic SQL statements are run under the profile of the program's user. Distributed dynamic SQL statements are run under the profile of the application server job.

*OWNER — Local dynamic SQL statements are run under the profile of the program's owner. Distributed dynamic SQL statements are run under the profile of the SQL package's owner.

SRTSEQ . . . . .Sort sequence.

*JOB — The SRTSEQ value for the job is used.

*JOBRUN — The SRTSEQ value for the job is retrieved when the program is run. For distributed applications, SRTSEQ(*JOBRUN) is valid only when LANGID(*JOBRUN) is also specified.

*LANGIDSHR — The shared-weight sort table for the language specified on the LANGID parameter is used.

*HEX — A sort sequence table is not used, and the hex values of the characters are used to determine the sort sequence.

table-name — Name of the sort sequence table to be used with this program. The name can be qualified with *LIBL, *CURLIB, or a library name.

LANGID . . . . .Language ID.

*JOB — The LANGID value for the job is retrieved during the precompile.

*JOBRUN — The LANGID value for the job is retrieved when the program is run. For distributed applications, LANGID(*JOBRUN) is valid only when SRTSEQ(*JOBRUN) is also specified.

language-id — Language identifier to be used by the program.

TOSRCFILE . . . . .To source file (precompiler source output).

QSQLTEMP or QSQLTEMP1 — For CRTSQLCBLI and CRTSQLCI, the source file QSQLTEMP is used. For CRTSQLRPGI, the source file QSQLTEMP1 is used.

source-file-name — Name of the source file to contain the output source member. The name can be qualified with *LIBL, *CURLIB, or a library name.

CRTSQLCI-Only Optional Parameter

MARGINS . . . . .Source margins.

*SRCFILE — The file member margin values specified by the user on the SRCMBR parameter are used. The margin values default to 1 and 80.

left right — Explicit left and right margins. Values must be between 1 and 80.

CRTSQLPKG (Create SQL Package) Command

Required Parameters

PGM . . . . .Name of program for SQL package.

program-name — Name and library of the program for which the SQL package is being created.

Optional Parameters

RDB .... .Relational database.

- *PGM — Use the name specified for the RDB parameter in the CRTSQL*XXX* command that created the program specified in the PGM parameter of this command.
- *relational-database-name* — Relational database name.

USER .... .Associated user when executing package on the remote system.

- *CURRENT — User associated with the current job is used.
- *user-name* — Name being used for the package when executed on the remote system.

PASSWORD .... .RDB user password.

- * — No password is sent.
- *password* — Password of the user name specified on the USER parameter.

DFTRDBCOL .... .Default collection.

- *PGM — Use the collection specified for the DFTRDBCOL parameter of the CRTSQL*XXX* command used to create the program specified in this command's PGM parameter.
- *NONE — Use the default collection specified on the OPTIONS parameter of the CRTSQL*XXX* command used to create the program specified in this command's PGM parameter.
- *collection-name* — Name of the collection to use for unqualified table, view, index, and SQL package names.

OBJTYPE .... .Object type.

- *PGM — The object specified in the PGM parameter is a program.
- *SRVPGM — The object specified in the PGM parameter is a service program.

MODULE .... .List of modules from the program or service program specified in the PGM parameter to use in the SQL package.

- *ALL — Use all the modules from the program or service program specified in the PGM parameter.
- *module-names* — Names of modules to use from the program or service program specified in the PGM parameter.

TEXT .... .Up to 50 characters of text description.

- *PGMTXT — Use the description from the program or service program specified in the PGM parameter.
- *BLANK — No text is specified.
- *description* — Up to 50 characters of text description for the package being created.

GENLVL .... .Severity level tolerance.

- 10 — Package creation fails if an exception occurs with severity greater than 10.
- *severity-level* — Package creation fails if an exception occurs with severity greater than the specified value. Valid values are 0 to 40.

REPLACE . . . . .Replace an existing package with the same name.
- *YES — Replace an existing package with the same name.
- *NO — Do not replace an existing package with the same name.

PRTFILE . . . . .Printer file for error listing.
- QSYSPRT — Use QSYSPRT printer file for the error listing.
- *printer-file-name* — Name and library of the printer file to use for the error listing. Can be qualified with *LIBL, *CURLIB, or a library name.

DLTSQLPKG (Delete SQL Package) Command

Required Parameter

SQLPKG . . . . .SQL package.
- *SQL-package-name* — Name of the SQL package to be deleted. This name can be qualified with *LIBL, *CURLIB, *USRLIBL, *ALL, *ALLUS, or a library name.
- *generic-SQL-package-name* — Generic name of the SQL package to be deleted. A generic name is a character string of one or more characters followed by an asterisk (*). This name can be qualified with *LIBL, *CURLIB, *USRLIBL, *ALL, *ALLUS, or a library name.

DSPCPCST (Display Check Pending Constraint) Command

Required Parameters

FILE . . . . .The dependent file on which the referential constraint is defined for a referential constraint, or the file for a check constraint.
- *file-name* — Name of the table or physical file. This name can be qualified with *LIBL, *CURLIB, or the library name.

CST . . . . .Constraint name.
- *constraint-name* — Name of the constraint that is defined for the file.

OUTPUT . . . . .Format of command output.
- * — Output requested by an interactive job is shown on the display.
- *PRINT — The output is printed with the job's spooled output.

EDTCPCST (Edit Check Pending Constraint) Command

This command has no parameters.

INZDLFM (Initialize DataLink File Manager) Command

Optional Parameter

CLEARDB . . . . .Clear existing database.
- *LNKSTS — The database files containing the link status of DataLinks will be cleared. Database files containing registered prefixes and host database names will not be cleared.
- *ALL — All database files used by the DLFM will be cleared.

MOVOBJ (Move Object) Command

Required Parameters

OBJ . . . . .Object being moved to another library.

object-name	Name of the object that is moved. Object name can be qualified with *LIBL, *CURLIB, or a library name.

OBJTYPE . . . . .Type of the object being moved to another library.

object-type	Any valid OS/400 object type (e.g., *FILE, *PGM).

TOLIB . . . . .Library to which the object is being moved.

*CURLIB	Object is moved to the current library.
library-name	Library to which the object is moved.

OVRDBF (Override with Database File) Command

Required Parameter

FILE . . . . .File name.

file-name	File used by the program to which the override command is applied. File name can be qualified with *LIBL, *CURLIB, or a library name.

Optional Parameters

TOFILE . . . . .File used instead of the file specified in the FILE parameter.

*FILE	Use file named in FILE parameter.
database-file-name	File used instead of the file specified in the FILE parameter. File name can be qualified with *LIBL, *CURLIB, or a library name.

MBR . . . . .Member to open.

*FIRST	First member in the database file is used.
*LAST	Last member of the specified physical file is used.
*ALL	All members in the file are processed sequentially.
member-name	The member name to open.

POSITION . . . . .Starting position for retrieving records from the database file.

*NONE	No special positioning is specified.
*START	Starting position is the first record in the file.
*END	Starting position is the last record in the file.
*RRN *relative-record-number*	Relative record number of first record to retrieve.
key-relop nbr-of-fields rcdfmt 'key-value'	The *key-relop* value is one of the following:

*KEYB (key-before)	Record that precedes the record identified by the remaining search values.
*KEYBE (key-before or equal)	Record identified by the search values, or the record before the specified key value, is the first record retrieved.

*KEY (key-equal) — Record identified by the search values is the first record retrieved.

*KEYAE (key-after or equal) — Record identified by the search values, or the record after the specified key value, is the first record retrieved.

*KEYA (key-after) — Record that follows the record identified by the remaining search values.

The *nbr-of-fields* value is the number of key fields to use in the search.

The *rcdfmt* value is the name of the record format in the database file that contains the key value specified.

The '*key-value*' value is a quoted string or hexadecimal value.

RCDFMTLCK . . . . .Lock state of the named record format while it is used by the program.

record-format-name lock-type
: The *lock-type* value is one of the following:

*SHRRD	Shared read.
*SHRNUP	Shared read, no update.
*SHRUPD	Shared update.
*EXCLRD	Exclusive allow read.
*EXCL	Exclusive no read.

FRCRATIO . . . . .Number of insert, delete, or update operations that can occur on records before they are forced into storage.

<u>*NONE</u>
: There is no force write ratio; the system determines when the records are written to auxiliary storage.

number-of-records-before-force
: Number of inserted, updated, or deleted records processed before being explicitly forced to auxiliary storage.

FMTSLR . . . . .Record format selector.

program-name
: Name of the format selector program called when a record is inserted into a member having more than one format. Program name can be qualified by <u>*LIBL</u>, *CURLIBL, or a library name.

WAITFILE . . . . .Seconds the program waits for file resources and session resources to be allocated when the file is opened.

<u>*IMMED</u>
: The program does not wait; when the file is opened, an immediate allocation of the file resources is required.

*CLS
: The job default wait time is used.

number-of-seconds
: Number of seconds the program waits for the file resources to be allocated to the job. Valid values range from 1 to 32,767 seconds.

WAITRCD . . . . .Seconds the program waits for a lock for a record to be updated or deleted, or for a record read in the commitment control environment.

<u>60</u>
: The program waits 60 seconds.

*IMMED
: The program does not wait; when a record is locked, an immediate allocation of the record is required.

*NOMAX — The system maximum is used.
number-of-seconds — Number of seconds the program waits for the record to be allocated. Valid values range from 1 to 32,767 seconds.

NBRRCDS . . . . .Number of records moved as a unit from auxiliary storage to main storage.
number-of-records — Number of records to move at a time.

EOFDLY . . . . .Number of seconds to delay when end-of-file is reached before trying to retrieve additional records.
*NONE — Normal end-of-file processing is done.
number-of-seconds — Number of seconds the program waits between each attempt to get a record when an end-of-file condition occurs.

LVLCHK . . . . .Record format level identifiers in the program are checked against those in the device file when the file is opened.
*NO — The level identifiers are not checked.

EXPCHK . . . . .Expiration date of the named member is checked.
*YES — Expiration date of the physical file member is checked.
*NO — Expiration date is not checked.

INHWRT . . . . .Whether the processed records are written, deleted, or changed in the database file.
*YES — Records are prevented from being written into the database.
*NO — Processed records are written into the database.

SECURE . . . . .File is safe from previously executed file override commands.
<u>*NO</u> — File is not protected from the effects of other file overrides.
*YES — File is protected from the effects of any file override commands.

OVRSCOPE . . . . .The extent of influence (scope) of the override.
<u>*ACTGRPDFN</u> — Scope of the override is determined by the activation group of the program that called the OVRDBF command processing program.
*CALLLVL — Scope of the override is determined by the current call level.
*JOB — Scope of the override is the job in which the override occurs.

SHARE . . . . .Share open data path.
<u>*NO</u> — The open data path is not shared with other programs in the routing step. When a program opens a file with this attribute, a new open data path to the file is created and activated.
*YES — The open data path is shared with other programs in the routing step that also specify SHARE(*YES).

OPNSCOPE . . . . .Extent of influence (scope) of the open operation.
<u>*ACTGRPDFN</u> — Scope of the open operation is determined by the activation group of the program that called the OVRDBF command processing program.
*JOB — Scope of the open operation is the job in which the open operation occurs.

SEQONLY . . . . .Files whose records are processed in sequential order only.

- *NO — Database file is not restricted to sequential-only processing.
- *YES — Database file uses sequential-only processing. The system calculates the block size.
- *YES *number-of-records* — Database file uses sequential-only processing. Each block contains the number of records specified.

PRTSQLINF (Print SQL Information) Command

Required Parameter

OBJ . . . . .Program or SQL package.

- *object-name* — Name of the program or SQL package for which you want information printed. This name can be qualified with *LIBL, *CURLIB, or a library name.

Optional Parameters

OBJTYPE . . . . .Object type.

- *PGM — The object is a program.
- *SQLPKG — The object is an SQL package.
- *SRVPGM — The object is a service program.

RGZPFM (Reorganize Physical File Member) Command

Required Parameter

FILE . . . . .File name.

- *file-name* — File that contains the member to be reorganized. File name can be qualified with *LIBL, *CURLIB, or a library name.

Optional Parameters

MBR . . . . .Member name.

- *FIRST — First member in the database file is reorganized.
- *LAST — Last member of the specified physical file is reorganized.
- *member-name* — File member to be reorganized.

SRCOPT . . . . .For source files, whether reorganization places new numbers in the sequence number field, places zeros in the date field, or changes both fields.

- *SAME — Values do not change.
- *SEQNBR — Records have a new sequence number placed into the SRCSEQ (source sequence number) field.
- *DATE — Records have a zero date (000000) placed in the SRCDAT (source date) field.

SRCSEQ . . . . .For source files, sequence number given to the first record in the source file member and the increment value that is used to renumber all other records in the member.

Element 1 — Starting Value

1.00	First source record has a sequence number of 0001.00.
starting-value	Sequence number of the first record in the member.

Element 2 — Increment Value

1.00	Source records are renumbered in the member with whole number increments of 1.
increment-value	Increment value for renumbering all source records following the first record.

KEYFILE . . . . .Arrival sequence changed to match keyed sequence.

*NONE	Member is not reorganized.
*FILE	Sequence of the records changed to match keyed sequence.
logical-file-name member-name	Name of the logical file and member whose sequence is used to reorganize the physical file member. Logical file name can be qualified by *LIBL, *CURLIB, or a library name.

RCDFMT . . . . .Record format name if the physical file member is reorganized in the sequence of a multiple-format logical file.

*ONLY	Logical file specified by the KEYFILE parameter has only one record format.
record-format-name	Record format in the multiple-format logical file that is used to reorganize the physical file member.

RMVPFTRG (Remove Physical File Trigger) Command

Required Parameter

FILE . . . . .File name.

physical-file-name	Physical file to remove trigger from. Name can be qualified with *LIBL, *CURLIB, or a library name.

Optional Parameters

TRGTIME . . . . .Trigger time.

*ALL	Remove triggers for both before and after events.
*BEFORE	Remove triggers for before file operation events.
*AFTER	Remove triggers for after file operation events.

TRGEVENT . . . . .Trigger event.

*ALL	Remove triggers for insert, delete, and update events.
*INSERT	Removes trigger for insert events.
*DELETE	Remove triggers for delete events.
*UPDATE	Remove triggers for update events.

RMVRDBDIRE (Remove Relational Database Directory Entry) Command

Required Parameter

RDB . . . . .Relational database.

*ALLRMT	All remote entries in the relational database directory are removed.
*ALL	All entries in the relational database directory are removed.
relational-database-name	Name of the relational database entry to be removed.
generic-relational-database-name	Generic name of the relational database entries to be removed. A generic name is a character string that contains one or more characters followed by an asterisk (*).

Appendix C

Using Programming Development Manager (PDM)[1]

Introduction

PDM is an AS/400 programming environment that provides access to OS/400 and HLL compiler functions through a standard list interface. PDM is not a part of the OS/400 operating system. Rather, it's a component of IBM's Application Development ToolSet/400 (ADTS/400) product, which also includes Source Entry Utility (SEU), Screen Design Aid (SDA), Report Layout Utility (RLU), and Interactive Source Debugger (ISDB). Most AS/400s used for application development have ADTS/400 installed.

PDM is not an end-user tool. The functions that PDM provides are specifically designed for AS/400 programmers and system administrators. PDM includes functions to copy files, move objects from one library to another, edit (using SEU) and compile database files and HLL programs, display the contents of a library, and perform many other typical application development tasks. Most AS/400 programmers work from PDM as they develop and test application files and programs.

As described in Chapter 1, OS/400 is an object-based architecture. Among the object types are libraries, programs, and files, which play an important role in PDM. OS/400 objects have other attributes in addition to an object type, including a subtype. For example, recall that database files include data files (subtype PF-DTA and LF-DTA) and source files (subtype PF-SRC). Also recall that database files have members, and that source file members are where you store DDS, SQL, and HLL source code. Each source file member also has an attribute that identifies the type of source it contains. For example, a PF source member type indicates the member contains DDS statements for a physical file, whereas RPGLE indicates a member contains RPG IV source code.

PDM as a Navigational Tool

PDM provides access to three levels of the OS/400 object-based architecture: the library level, the object level, and the member level. With PDM you can navigate the various levels of OS/400 and move from one level to the next. For example, you can start at the library level, then select a library and drop down to the object level. From the object level, you can either go back up to the library level or select a database file and drop down to the member level.

You can start a PDM session from several AS/400 menus (e.g., use GO PROGRAM to display the Programming menu) or with one of the following commands:

- StrPdm (Start PDM)
- WrkLibPdm(Work with Libraries Using PDM)
- WrkObjPdm (Work with Objects Using PDM)
- WrkMbrPdm (Work with Members Using PDM)

The StrPdm command displays the PDM main menu shown in Figure C.1. Selecting option 1 (Work with libraries) is comparable to the WrkLibPdm command. Option 2 (Work with objects) is

1 This appendix is based on "Appendix B: Programming Development Manager (PDM)" in *Control Language Programming for the AS/400*, by Bryan Meyers and Dan Riehl, copyright 1993 by 29th Street Press. The material is used with the authors' permission.

comparable to the WrkObjPdm command. And option 3 (Work with members) is comparable to the WrkMbrPdm command. Option 9 (Work with user-defined options) lets you set various PDM options that are described in the *Programming Development Manager (PDM)* manual.

Figure C.1
PDM Main Menu

```
                 AS/400 Programming Development Manager (PDM)

 Select one of the following:

      1. Work with libraries
      2. Work with objects
      3. Work with members

      9. Work with user-defined options






 Selection or command
 ===> ____________________________________________________________

 F3=Exit       F4=Prompt       F9=Retrieve        F10=Command entry
 F12=Cancel    F18=Change defaults
```

Working with Libraries Using PDM

When you select option 1 from the PDM main menu, you're presented with the display shown in Figure C.2, on which you specify the libraries you want to work with. In this example, the entry app* specifies that all libraries whose names begin with APP should be included in the PDM list that's displayed next.

Figure C.2
Library Selection Display

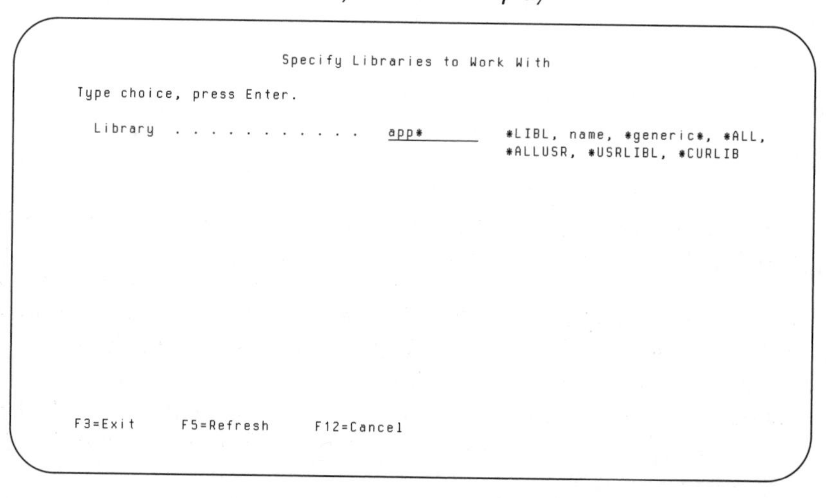

You can enter a single library name, a generic name (as in this example), or one of the following special values:

- *All (all libraries)
- *Libl (all libraries in the job's library list)
- *AllUsr (all user — i.e., non-IBM — libraries on the system)
- *UsrLibl (all libraries in the user part of the job's library list)
- *CurLib (the current library)

You can also use the * character as a wildcard in other parts of the library name. For example, *dta specifies all libraries with names that end in DTA.

If you need more information about this or any other PDM prompt, you can position the cursor on an input field and press the Help or F1 key to display an explanation of the allowable choices.

After you specify the libraries you want to work with, PDM shows the Work with Libraries Using PDM display in Figure C.3. As an alternative to the PDM menu, you can get to the same display by entering the following command:

```
WrkLibPdm Lib( app* )
```

Figure C.3

Work with Libraries Using PDM Display

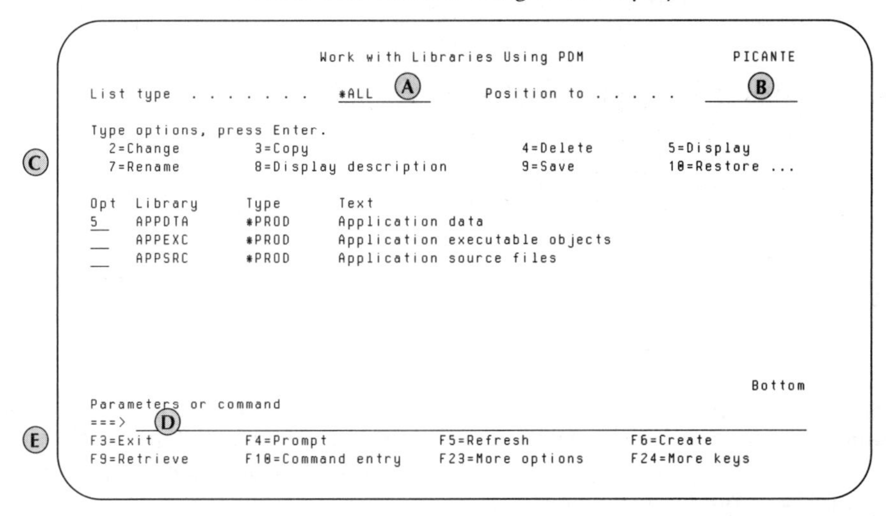

The Work with Libraries Using PDM display lists all the libraries you selected. For each selected library there's an option field, followed by the library name, type (production or test), and descriptive text. This display also has several input fields that control what's displayed and provides options for the listed libraries. To change the list of displayed libraries, you can enter *All, *Libl, *AllUsr, or *UsrLibl in the List type field (A). The Position to input field (B) lets you position the list starting at a specified library. This is useful when the list contains many libraries.

The list of options (C) indicates values that can be entered in the Opt field to the left of each listed library. For example, to display the contents of the AppDta library, you enter 5 in the Opt field next to that library and then press the Enter key.

There are more options available than PDM shows on a single display, so you can press the F23 (More options) key to toggle the display between sets of options. The valid options for the Work with Libraries Using PDM display are shown in Figure C.4. You can enter any valid option in the Opt field regardless of whether it's currently shown in the list of options.

Figure C.4
Work with Libraries Using PDM Options

Option	Operation	CL command used
2	Change the type and text of a library	ChgLib
3	Copy the contents of one library to another	CpyLib
5	Display a list of objects in a library	DspLib
7	Rename a library	RnmObj
8	Display a library's description	DspObjD
9	Save a library and its contents	SavLib
10	Restore a library and its contents	RstLib
12	Show the Work with Objects Using PDM display	WrkObjPdm
13	Change the descriptive text of a library	ChgObjD
20	Move a library to a different location in the job's library list	(built-in PDM function, when *Libl list is selected)
21	Move another library before this library in the job's library list	(built-in PDM function, when *Libl list is selected)
22	Move another library after this library in the job's library list	(built-in PDM function, when *Libl list is selected)
23	Remove a library from the job's library list	(built-in PDM function, when *Libl list is selected)

As you can see from Figure C.4, there's a corresponding CL command for most PDM options. The PDM environment provides a list-oriented front end for many CL commands. Options 20 through 23 let you reorder the job's library list, if the current display has selected *Libl libraries. These four options don't perform any operations on the libraries themselves.

This display also includes a command line (D), which can be used to enter any AS/400 command. The F4 (Prompt) key is available for commands entered on this line. You can also retrieve previously entered commands by pressing the F9 (Retrieve) key.

The command line also serves another function within PDM. When an option is entered next to an entry in the list, the command line can be used to enter command parameters. When you enter command parameters on the command line, PDM uses them with the CL command associated with the option, as listed in Figure C.4. For example, when you enter option 5 (Display), you can also enter Output(*Print) on the command line. PDM uses this parameter when it executes the DspLib command for the library entry. If you specify options for more than one list entry, any parameters you specify on the command line should be valid for all the options.

A partial list of valid function keys is shown at the bottom of the Work with Libraries Using PDM display (E). You can press F24 to toggle this list to show other keys. Figure C.5 lists all the function keys that are valid on PDM displays. You can use any valid function key regardless of whether it's currently shown in the list of keys.

Figure C.5

PDM Function Keys

Function key	Function	What the function does
F1	Help	Provides additional information. Place the cursor on a field and press F1.
F3	Exit	Exits from PDM
F4	Prompt	Prompts for a command associated with an option or entered on command line
F5	Refresh	Refreshes the list
F6	Create	Prompts for appropriate Crt*Xxx* command
F9	Retrieve	Retrieves previous command entered on command line
F10	Command Entry	Displays the Command Entry display
F11	Toggle displayed list fields	Toggles between different formats for what's shown in the library, object, or member lists
F12	Cancel	Cancels options or returns to previous display
F13	Repeat	Repeats option at position of cursor for all entries following the entry where cursor is positioned
F14	Display object sizes, or display member last-change dates	For WrkObjPdm, displays each object's size For WrkMbrPdm, displays the date each member was last changed
F15	Order member list by last-change date	For WrkMbrPdm, orders the member list based on the date each member was last changed
F16	User options	Shows display for changing PDM options
F17	Subset	Shows display to select a subset of list entries
F18	Change defaults	Shows display to change PDM defaults
F21	Print the list	Prints entries of the current list
F23	More options	Toggles display to show additional option values
F24	More keys	Toggles display to show additional function keys

Working with Objects Using PDM

When you select option 2 from the PDM main menu, PDM shows the display in Figure C.6, on which you specify which objects you want to include in the list. In this example, all objects in the AppDta library are specified. You can restrict the objects by entering a specific, generic, or wildcard object name; an object type; and a specific or generic object attribute (subtype). For example, if you want to work only with objects whose name starts with the letter L, you can enter L* in the Name field; or, if you want to work only with file objects, you can enter *File into the Type field.

As an alternative to the PDM menu option 2, you can enter a WrkObjPdm command with parameters that correspond to the fields shown in Figure C.6.

Figure C.6
PDM Object Selection Display

```
                     Specify Objects to Work With

 Type choices, press Enter.

   Library . . . . . . . . . .   appdta        *CURLIB, name

   Object:
     Name . . . . . . . . . . .  *ALL          *ALL, name, *generic*
     Type . . . . . . . . . . .  *ALL          *ALL, *type
     Attribute  . . . . . . . .  *ALL          *ALL, attribute, *generic*,
                                               *BLANK

 F3=Exit      F5=Refresh      F12=Cancel
```

The Work with Objects Using PDM display (Figure C.7) shows a list of all selected objects.

Figure C.7
Work with Objects Using PDM Display

```
                       Work with Objects Using PDM                    PICANTE

 Library . . . . .   APPDTA (A)       Position to . . . . . . . .    (B)
                                      Position to type  . . . . .

 Type options, press Enter.
   2=Change         3=Copy          4=Delete        5=Display        7=Rename
   8=Display description            9=Save         10=Restore       11=Move ...

 Opt  Object        Type        Attribute    Text
 __   QSQJRN0001    *JRNRCV                  COLLECTION - created by SQL
 __   QSQJRN        *JRN                     COLLECTION - created by SQL
 __   AUTOLOAN      *FILE       PF-DTA       Auto loans
 __   BUILDING      *FILE       PF-DTA       Buildings
 __   CONTRACTOR    *FILE       PF-DTA       Contractors
 __   COURSE        *FILE       PF-DTA       Courses
 __   CUSTOMER      *FILE       PF-DTA       Customers
 __   EMPLOYEE      *FILE       PF-DTA       Employees
                                                                       More...
 Parameters or command
 ===>
 F3=Exit          F4=Prompt            F5=Refresh           F6=Create
 F9=Retrieve      F10=Command entry    F23=More options     F24=More keys
```

The display works much like the Work with Libraries Using PDM display, except that it lists objects within one or more libraries, and the options correspond to functions for objects rather than functions for libraries. This display also has fields to control what's displayed and various operations. You can enter a library name (A) to work with the objects in a different library. You can also position the display to a specified object and object type (B).

The options available on the Work with Objects Using PDM screen are listed in Figure C.8. Some options are valid only for specific object types. For example, Option 16 (Run) is valid for *Pgm objects, but not for *File objects.

Figure C.8
Work with Objects Using PDM Options

Option	Operation	CL command used
2	Change object attributes	Chg*Xxx* (depending on object type)
3	Create duplicate object	CrtDupObj
4	Delete object	Dlt*Xxx* (depending on object type)
5	Display information about an object	Dsp*Xxx* (depending on object type)
7	Rename an object	RnmObj
8	Display an object's description	DspObjD
9	Save an object	SavObj or SavSavfDta
10	Restore an object	RstObj
11	Move an object from one library to another	MovObj
12	For files, show the Work with Members Using PDM display. For other object types, show the appropriate "Work with ..." display	WrkMbrPdm or Wrk*Xxx* (depending on object type)
13	Change the descriptive text of an object	ChgObjD
15	Copy data from one file to another	CpyF or CpySrcf
16	Run an object	Call (programs), ChgDta (for DFU applications), or RunQry (for query definitions)
18	Change database file data	UpdDta or StrDfu
25	Find a specified string in a physical file	(built-in PDM function)
26	Create program	CrtPgm
27	Create service program	CrtSrvPgm
34	Run debugger	StrIsdb
54	Compare physical file members	CmpPfM

Working with Members Using PDM

The lowest level in the object hierarchy that PDM provides access to is file members. Programmers frequently use this level of PDM because it lets you edit source and submit DDS and HLL program compiles. PDM provides three ways to display the Work with Members Using PDM display:

- From the PDM main menu, select option 3 – Work with members
- From the Work with Objects Using PDM display, enter option 12 next to a file object
- Enter the WrkMbrPdm command

Figure C.9 shows the member selection display on which you specify a file name as well as the specific, generic, or wildcard member name and member type.

Figure C.9
Member Selection Display

```
                        Specify Members to Work With

 Type choices, press Enter.

   File . . . . . . . . . .   LFSRC        Name, F4 for list

     Library . . . . . . . .   APPSRC      *LIBL, *CURLIB, name

   Member:
     Name . . . . . . . . .   *ALL         *ALL, name, *generic*
     Type . . . . . . . . .   *ALL         *ALL, type, *generic*, *BLANK


 F3=Exit      F4=Prompt      F5=Refresh      F12=Cancel
```

The Work with Members Using PDM display (Figure C.10) shows a list of all specified members. You can change the file whose members are displayed (A) and position to a specified member (B).

Figure C.10
Work with Members Using PDM Display

```
                        Work with Members Using PDM                  PICANTE

 File . . . . . .   LFSRC  (A)                                          (B)
   Library . . . .    APPSRC            Position to . . . . .

 Type options, press Enter.
  2=Edit          3=Copy  4=Delete 5=Display        6=Print      7=Rename
  8=Display description  9=Save  13=Change text  14=Compile  15=Create module...

 Opt  Member       Type        Text
 __   CUSTCTYCRD   LF          Customers by city and credit limit
 __   CUSTHICRD    LF          Customers with high credit limit
 __   CUSTNAME     LF          Customers by name
 14   CUSTSALE     LF          Customer and sales info by customer ID
 __   CUSTSEATLE   LF          Customers in Seattle
 __   CUSTSHPADR   LF          Customers shipping address fields
 __   LOANCUST01   LF          Auto and mortgage loans by customer ID
 __   SALE95DATE   LF          1995 sales by date
                                                                     More...
 Parameters or command
 ===>
 F3=Exit          F4=Prompt              F5=Refresh            F6=Create
 F9=Retrieve      F10=Command entry      F23=More options      F24=More keys
```

The list of members lets you change the member type and descriptive text. The rest of the Work with Members Using PDM display is similar to the other PDM "work with" displays. The function keys are the same as with the other PDM displays, but the options are different.

The member options have slightly different meanings, depending on the member type. Some options (e.g., option 2 – edit with SEU) are valid only with source file members. Figure C.11 lists the valid options for members.

Figure C.11
Work with Members Using PDM Options

Option	Operation	CL command used
2	Edit a source file member with SEU	StrSeu Option(2)
3	Copy a member	CpyF or CpySrcf
4	Remove member	RmvM
5	Display data in a physical file member	DspPfM
6	Print a source file member	StrSeu Option(6)
7	Rename a member	RnmM
8	Display a member's description	(built-in PDM function)
9	Save the file containing a member	SavObj
13	Change the descriptive text of a member	ChgPfM or ChgLfM
14	Compile a source file member to produce an object	Crt*Xxx* (depending on member type)
15	Compile an HLL source file member to produce an ILE module object	Crt*Xxx* (depending on member type)
16	Run the procedure contained in a source file member	StrRexPrc (for REXX procedures), StrBasPrc (for Basic), or StrS36Prc (for S/36 OCL)
17	Change the DDS source for a display file using SDA	StrSda
18	Change database file data	UpdDta
19	Change the DDS source for a printer file using RLU	StrRlu
25	Find a specified string in a member	(built-in PDM function)
54	Compare physical file members	CmpPfM
55	Merge source file members	MrgSrc

As mentioned earlier, you can press the F4 key to prompt for a command associated with a PDM option. Figure C.12 shows an example of the CrtLf command prompt displayed when you use option 14 for an LF type source file member (see Figure C.10). You can use the prompt to change command defaults or to supply additional parameter values. On a CL prompt display, you can press F11 to toggle between the prompt format shown in Figure C.12 and the keyword format shown in Figure C.13. The keyword format can be helpful if you're using CL examples in this book that list commands with the parameter keywords.

Figure C.12
Prompted CrtLf Command

```
                        Create Logical File (CRTLF)

 Type choices, press Enter.

 File . . . . . . . . . . . . . . > CUSTSALE      Name
   Library  . . . . . . . . . . . >   APPSRC      Name, *CURLIB
 Source file  . . . . . . . . . . > LFSRC         Name
   Library  . . . . . . . . . . . >   APPSRC      Name, *LIBL, *CURLIB
 Source member  . . . . . . . . . > CUSTSALE      Name, *FILE
 Generation severity level  . . .   20            0-30
 Flagging severity level  . . . .   0             0-30
 File type  . . . . . . . . . . .   *DATA         *DATA, *SRC
 Member, if desired . . . . . . .   *FILE         Name, *FILE, *NONE
 Physical file data members:        _
   Physical file  . . . . . . . .   *ALL          Name, *ALL
     Library  . . . . . . . . . .                 Name, *CURRENT
   Members  . . . . . . . . . . .                 Name, *NONE
                 + for more values
                 + for more values _
                                                                  More...
 F3=Exit   F4=Prompt   F5=Refresh   F10=Additional parameters   F12=Cancel
 F13=How to use this display        F24=More keys
```

Figure C.13
Prompted CrtLf Command with Parameter Keywords

```
                        Create Logical File (CRTLF)

 Type choices, press Enter.

 File . . . . . . . . . . . . . . FILE        > CUSTSALE
   Library  . . . . . . . . . . .             >   APPSRC
 Source file  . . . . . . . . . . SRCFILE     > LFSRC
   Library  . . . . . . . . . . .             >   APPSRC
 Source member  . . . . . . . . . SRCMBR      > CUSTSALE
 Generation severity level  . . . GENLVL        20
 Flagging severity level  . . . . FLAG          0
 File type  . . . . . . . . . . . FILETYPE      *DATA
 Member, if desired . . . . . . . MBR           *FILE
 Physical file data members:      DTAMBRS       _
   Physical file  . . . . . . . .               *ALL
     Library  . . . . . . . . . .
   Members  . . . . . . . . . . .
                          + for more values
                          + for more values _
                                                                  More...
 F3=Exit   F4=Prompt   F5=Refresh   F10=Additional parameters   F12=Cancel
 F13=How to use this display        F24=More keys
```

Changing PDM Defaults and Options

When you start PDM with a command (e.g., StrPdm or WrkMbrPdm), PDM uses various defaults that affect the way PDM performs certain functions. For example, one PDM default is the library into which file and program objects are created when you compile a source file member. By pressing the F18 function key, each PDM user can customize the PDM defaults for his or her sessions. Online help and the *Programming Development Manager (PDM)* manual provide a complete description of the PDM defaults and the valid settings.

In addition to the IBM-supplied options available for each PDM "work with" display, you can create your own user-defined PDM options. These user-defined options allow you to specify a new option value and an associated command that PDM executes when you enter the option. PDM lets you code substitution values for each element of a list entry (e.g., the library, file, and member names for an entry on the Work with Members Using PDM display), so commands can take their parameter values from the entry. The *Programming Development Manager (PDM)* manual provides a complete description of PDM user-defined options.

Appendix D

Using Source Entry Utility (SEU)[1]

Introduction

SEU is a full-screen, source code editor for the AS/400. SEU is not a part of the OS/400 operating system. Rather, it's a component of IBM's Application Development ToolSet/400 (ADTS/400) product, which also includes Programming Development Manager (PDM), Screen Design Aid (SDA), Report Layout Utility (RLU), and Interactive Source Debugger (ISDB). Most AS/400s used for application development have ADTS/400 installed. SEU is not an end-user tool and it's specifically designed for AS/400 programmers to enter and modify DDS, HLL, SQL, and other source code. Among SEU's features are built-in statement prompting and syntax checking for many languages, including DDS, RPG IV, ILE COBOL/400, and embedded SQL statements.

Running SEU

You can run SEU in several ways:

- Enter StrSeu on any command line
- Enter option 2 (Edit) or 5 (Display) for a member on the Work with Members Using PDM display (described in Appendix C)
- From within SDA, edit DDS comment lines

The following command runs SEU and edits the CustSale member of the AppSrc/LfSrc source file. Figure D.1 shows the SEU Edit display that's presented when you enter this command.

```
StrSeu SrcFile( appsrc/lfsrc )
       SrcMbr( custsale )
```

Four main sections comprise the SEU Edit display. At the top (A) is the SEU command line where you can enter various editing commands (e.g., FIND). This command line is different from the standard AS/400 command line shown on other displays; it's provided solely as a means to enter SEU commands. On the left (B) SEU displays the source sequence numbers. This area is also where you enter SEU line commands (typing over the sequence numbers), such as D to delete a line. The main area of the Edit display shows the source statements (C), which you can type over to change or insert new source. A partial list of valid function keys is shown at the bottom of the Edit display (D). You can press F24 to toggle this list to show other keys. Figure D.2 lists all the function keys that are valid on the Edit display. You can use any valid function key regardless of whether it's currently shown in the list of keys. (Function keys are discussed in more detail later.)

1 This appendix is based on "Appendix C: Source Entry Utility (SEU)" in *Control Language Programming for the AS/400*, by Bryan Meyers and Dan Riehl, copyright 1993 by 29th Street Press. The material is used with the authors' permission.

Figure D.1
SEU Edit Display

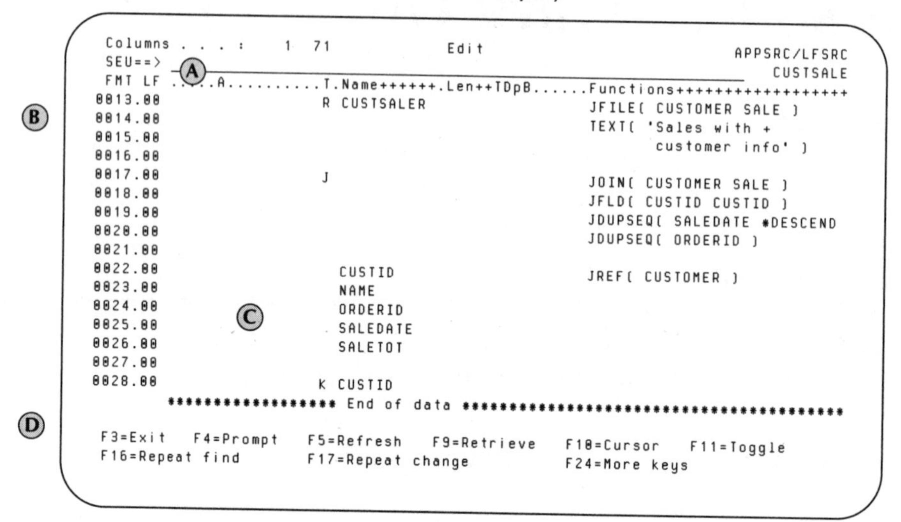

Figure D.2
SEU Edit Display Function Keys

Function key	Function	What the function does
F1	Help	Provides additional information. Place the cursor on a field and press F1.
F3	Exit	Exits from SEU
F4	Prompt	Prompts for a statement based on the type of source
F5	Refresh	Refreshes the Edit display, undoing any changes since the Enter key was last pressed
F6	Move the split line	When working with split screen, repositions the split line to the line containing the cursor
F9	Retrieve	Retrieves previous SEU command entered on command line
F10	Cursor	Moves the cursor from the editing area to the SEU command line and vice versa
F11	Toggle, or Previous record	When not prompting, toggles display between leftmost and rightmost parts of source lines When prompting, prompts for previous source line
F13	Change session defaults	Shows display to change session defaults
F14	Find/Change options	Shows display to search for strings and optionally replace matches with a new string
F15	Browse/Copy options	Shows display to browse other source members or spool files and optionally copy source to the member being edited
F16	Repeat find	Repeats the last FIND operation

continued

Figure D.2 *Continued*

Function key	Function	What the function does
F17	Repeat change	Repeats the last CHANGE operation
F18	DBCS conversion	Displays converted DBCS (double-byte character set) characters
F19	Left	Shifts the editing area so it displays information to the left of what's currently displayed
F20	Right	Shifts the editing area so it displays information to the right of what's currently displayed
F21	System command	Displays a command line for entering CL commands
F23	Select prompt	Shows the Select Prompt display, from which you can select source language prompts
F24	More keys	Toggles display to show additional function keys

The Source Sequence Number Area

In the source sequence number area, SEU displays each line's sequence number (stored as part of the records in a source file member) using the format of 9999.99. Although SEU doesn't allow you to directly change the sequence number of an existing line, you can type SEU line commands over the sequence number that's displayed. You use line commands for inserting, deleting, moving, and copying lines. You can also use line commands to position the display so a specified source line appears as the first line in the typing area.

Before getting into a full discussion of SEU line commands, let's look at a simple example of moving a source line within the member (Figure D.3).

Figure D.3
M (Move) and A (After) Line Commands

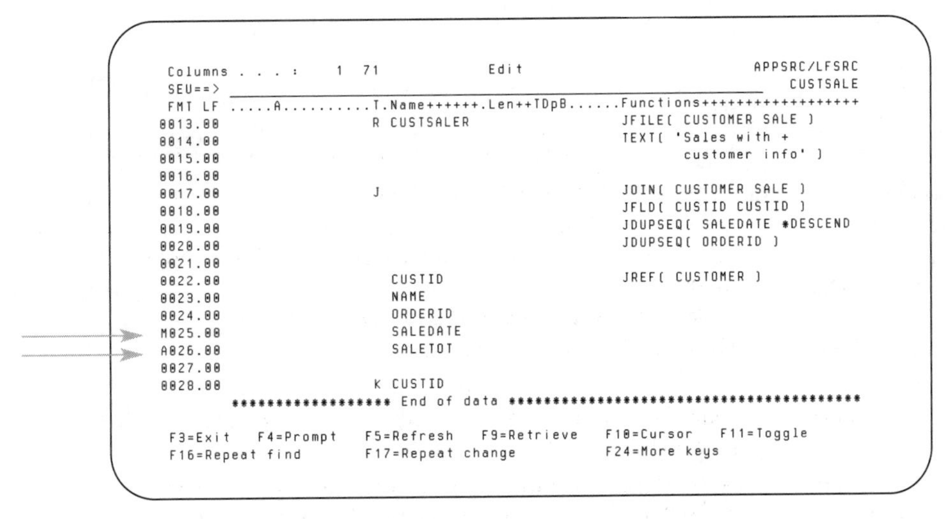

```
Columns . . . :    1  71           Edit                        APPSRC/LFSRC
SEU==> ____________________________________________________        CUSTSALE
FMT LF .....A..........T.Name++++++.Len++TDpB......Functions++++++++++++++++++
0013.00                R CUSTSALER                 JFILE( CUSTOMER SALE )
0014.00                                            TEXT( 'Sales with +
0015.00                                                   customer info' )
0016.00
0017.00                J                           JOIN( CUSTOMER SALE )
0018.00                                            JFLD( CUSTID CUSTID )
0019.00                                            JDUPSEQ( SALEDATE *DESCEND
0020.00                                            JDUPSEQ( ORDERID )
0021.00
0022.00                  CUSTID                    JREF( CUSTOMER )
0023.00                  NAME
0024.00                  ORDERID
M025.00                  SALEDATE
A026.00                  SALETOT
0027.00
0028.00                K CUSTID
       ****************** End of data ****************************************

 F3=Exit   F4=Prompt   F5=Refresh   F9=Retrieve   F10=Cursor   F11=Toggle
 F16=Repeat find       F17=Repeat change          F24=More keys
```

To move the source line that appears at line 0025.00 in Figure D.3 to the position immediately following line 0026.00, we enter the M (Move) line command on line 0025.00, place the A (After) line command on line 0026.00, and then press the Enter key. The combination of these two line commands tells SEU to move line 0025.00 after line 0026.00. After the move operation, there is no line 0025.00 and the moved line has the line number 0026.01 (see Figure D.4). You also can move lines to appear before a line, by specifying B instead of A for the target location.

Figure D.4

Result of the Move/After Operation

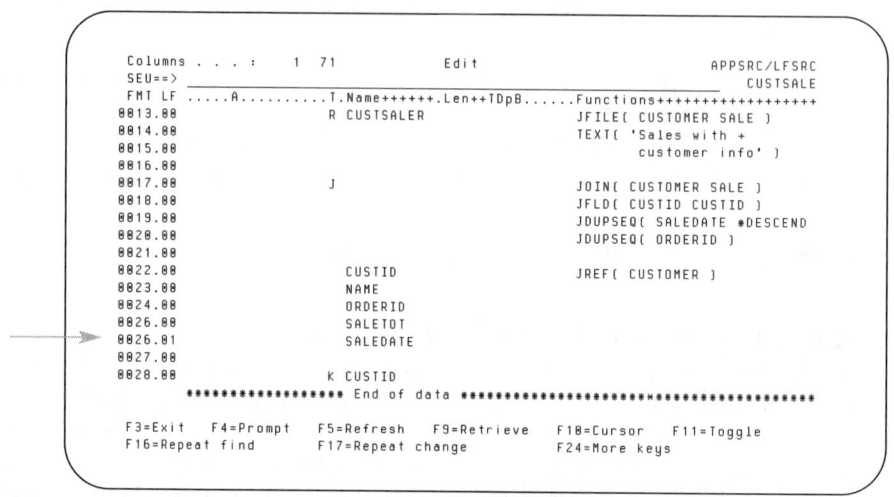

Other commonly used line commands are C (Copy) to copy a line to another location while retaining it at the original location and D (Delete) to delete a line from the source member. You can also use the X (eXclude) line command to "hide" lines from the editing area. Excluded lines remain in the file, but aren't displayed. This feature can be helpful if you need to work on sections of code that aren't adjacent and you want the sections' lines to appear together in the editing area.

In the previous example, we moved one source line to another position. You can also move several lines together in one operation; this is called a block operation. Consider the example shown in Figure D.5. Here we want to move the source lines 0023.00 through 0024.00 after line 0026.02. We place the MM block move command on the first and last lines to be moved and place the A (After) command on line 0026.02. When you press the Enter key, SEU moves all the lines between (and including) the two lines containing MM.

As an alternative to the block operation using MM, you can use the SEU line command M*n*, where *n* is the number of lines you want to move. In this example, we could have specified M2 on line 0023.00 to move the two lines.

Other common block commands are CC (Copy) to copy a block of source lines to another location while retaining them at the original location, DD (Delete) to delete a block of lines, and XX (eXclude) to exclude a block of lines.

Figure D.5
Sample Block Operation

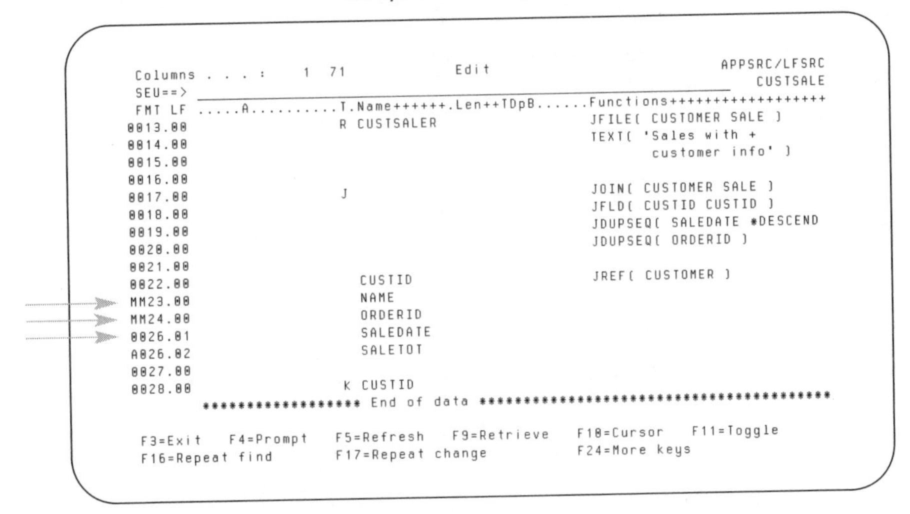

Line Commands for Positioning Within a Source Member

When SEU first displays a member, the first record is shown at the top of the editing area. You can use the RollUp/RollDown (or PageUp/PageDown) keys to scroll forward and backward through the file. You can also use line commands to change positions in the member. SEU has commands for both absolute and relative positioning.

To use absolute positioning, type a sequence number over an existing sequence number, and press the Enter key. This brings the line that has the sequence number you entered to the top of the typing area.

To specify relative positioning, overtype a sequence number with a plus sign (+) or a minus sign (–) followed by the number of source lines to be scrolled forward (+) or backward (–). For example, if you wanted to move the sixth record that's displayed to the top of the display, you would enter +5. If you wanted to then move back to the original position, you would use the command –5.

Inserting New Lines

The I (Insert) line command is used to add new source statements to an existing member. To insert a line after an existing line, enter the I command on the existing line and press Enter. SEU inserts a new, empty line, and you can enter the new source statement on this line. After you've entered the new source statement, you can press Enter and SEU inserts another empty line following the one you just added. You can continue adding new source in this fashion until you press Enter without typing anything on one of the new lines.

You can enter the I*n* command to have SEU insert *n* empty lines at once. For example, entering I5 inserts 5 new lines. After the empty lines are inserted, you can type new source into them.

Find/Change Options

As mentioned, SEU supports the function keys listed in Figure D.2. For several of these function keys, SEU shows additional displays.

The F14 key shows the Find/Change Options display (Figure D.6). On this display, you can specify a string for SEU to locate in the source member and, optionally, a replacement string for any matches. In the example in Figure D.6, SALETOT is the search string, and SALETOTAL is the replacement string.

Figure D.6
Find/Change Options Display

```
                         Find/Change Options

Type choices, press Enter.

  Find . . . . . . . . . . . . .   SALETOT
  Change . . . . . . . . . . . .   SALETOTAL
  From column number . . . . . .   1          1-80
  To column number . . . . . . .   80         1-80 or blank
  Occurrences to process . . . .   1          1=Next, 2=All
                                              3=Previous
  Records to search . . . . . . .  1          1=All, 2=Excluded
                                              3=Non-excluded
  Kind of match . . . . . . . . .  2          1=Same case
                                              2=Ignore case
  Allow data shift . . . . . . .   N          Y=Yes, N=No

  Search for date . . . . . . . .  96/07/06   YY/MM/DD or YYMMDD
    Compare . . . . . . . . . . .  _          1=Less than
                                              2=Equal to
                                              3=Greater than

F3=Exit   F5=Refresh            F12=Cancel   F13=Change session defaults
F15=Browse/Copy options         F16=Find     F17=Change
```

When you're browsing a spool file that contains a compiler listing, you can use the *ERR special value in the Find field to match error messages in the listing.

The From column number and To column number option fields let you specify the range of columns to search. This option is useful with DDS, RPG/400, and RPG IV, which have fixed-columnar syntax.

The Occurrences to process option lets you specify whether you want to process the next occurrence where the search string is found in the member, the previous occurrence, or all occurrences in the member.

The Records to search option lets you specify whether excluded records are to be included within the scope of the search. Excluded records are those that have been "hidden" from the display with the X line command.

The Kind of match option lets you specify whether the search is case sensitive. For example, if the search string is specified as SALETOT and you want to match SaleTot and saletot, you must specify 2 for this option to ignore case when matching strings.

When you specify a replacement string that's not the same length as the search string, the Allow data shift option determines whether the data on a line is shifted when a match is found. For example, if you're searching for the string SALETOT, which is seven characters long, and you want to replace it with the string SALETOTAL, which is nine characters long, you'll shift source to the right of the match by two characters after the replacement is performed. When you specify N for this option, SEU blank-pads a replacement string that's shorter than the search string and (if possible) overwrites adjacent blanks for a search string that's shorter than the replacement string.

The last options on this display are Search for date and Compare. These options let you find source member records that were modified before, on, or after a specified date. If you enter a value for the Compare option, SEU performs a search for records that meet the date search criteria.

Once you've entered values for the search string and other options, you press the F16 (Find) or F17 (Change) function key to start the search.

While the Find/Change Options display provides a helpful guide for new SEU users, many experienced AS/400 programmers perform searches directly from the SEU Edit display using the FIND and CHANGE commands on the SEU command line (covered later in this appendix).

Browse/Copy Options

The F15 key shows the Browse/Copy Options display (Figure D.7). On this display, you can select another source member or a spool file to view on the bottom of a split-screen display, such as that shown in Figure D.8. In this example, the Customer member of the AppSrc/PfSrc source file is displayed for browsing below the CustSale member that's being edited.

Figure D.7
Browse/Copy Options Display

```
                        Browse/Copy Options

Type choices, press Enter.

  Selection . . . . . . . . . . .   1              1=Member
                                                   2=Spool file
                                                   3=Output queue
  Copy all records  . . . . . . .   N              Y=Yes, N=No
  Browse/copy member  . . . . . .   CUSTOMER       Name, F4 for list
    File  . . . . . . . . . . . .     PFSRC        Name, F4 for list
      Library . . . . . . . . . .       APPSRC     Name, *CURLIB, *LIBL

  Browse/copy spool file  . . . .   CUSTSALE       Name, F4 for list
    Job . . . . . . . . . . . . .     CUSTSALE     Name
      User  . . . . . . . . . . .       QPGMR      Name, F4 for list
      Job number  . . . . . . . .       *LAST      Number, *LAST
    Spool number  . . . . . . . .     *LAST        Number, *LAST, *ONLY

  Display output queue  . . . . .   QPRINT         Name, *ALL
    Library . . . . . . . . . . .     *LIBL        Name, *CURLIB, *LIBL

F3=Exit        F4=Prompt        F5=Refresh        F12=Cancel
F13=Change session defaults     F14=Find/Change options
```

Figure D.8
Browsing a Second File with Split-Screen Display

```
Columns . . . :   1  71           Edit                         APPSRC/LFSRC
SEU==>                                                              CUSTSALE
FMT LF .....A..........T.Name++++++.Len++TDpB......Functions++++++++++++++++++
0013.00                R CUSTSALER                   JFILE( CUSTOMER SALE )
0014.00                                              TEXT( 'Sales with +
0015.00                                                       customer info' )
0016.00
0017.00                J                             JOIN( CUSTOMER SALE )
0018.00                                              JFLD( CUSTID CUSTID )
0019.00                                              JDUPSEQ( SALEDATE *DESCEND
Columns . . . :   1  71           Browse                       APPSRC/PFSRC
SEU==>                                                              CUSTOMER
0014.00
0015.00                R CUSTOMERR                   TEXT( 'Customers' )
0016.00       *        ==================================================
0017.00                  CUSTID          7P 0        TEXT( 'Customer ID' )
0018.00
0019.00                                              COLHDG( 'Cust.'
0020.00                                                      'ID' )

F3=Exit   F4=Prompt   F5=Refresh   F9=Retrieve   F11=Toggle   F12=Cancel
F16=Repeat find       F17=Repeat change          F24=More keys
```

The Browse section of the display does not allow any editing; however, you can copy source lines from a source member in this part of the display. To copy lines, enter C, CC, or C*n* line commands in the source sequence area of the browsed member and A or B line commands in the source sequence area of the member being edited.

The Browse/Copy Options display's Selection option (see Figure D.7) lets you select a source member, spooled output file, or output queue to browse. The value for this option determines which of the other options are applicable. You specify appropriate values for either the Browse/copy member, the Browse/copy spool file, or the Display output queue sets of options. For several of these options (e.g., Browse/copy member), you can place the cursor in the field and press the F4 key to display an appropriate selection list (e.g., of available members). This is handy when you don't know the exact name of a member or a spool file that you want to browse.

When you browse a source member or spool file, the result is a split-screen display, as in Figure D.8. When you display an output queue, no split screen is provided; you simply go to the DspOutQ (Display Output Queue) command display.

Also, if you enter 1 (Member) for the Selection option and Y for the Copy all records option, SEU places CC line commands on the first and last lines in the browsed member. You can then enter an A (after) or B (before) line command in the member being edited to tell SEU where to copy the records to.

Saving Your Work

When you've completed editing a source member, you can press the F3 (Exit) key to exit from the current editing session. SEU then shows the Exit display (Figure D.9). On this display, you specify how to end the editing session.

To save editing changes, you enter a Y (the default) in the Change/create member option. If you specify N, the work performed in your editing session is discarded. When you edit a source member with SEU, you're not working directly on the member itself; you're working on a temporary copy created by SEU when you begin editing a member. When you save your changes (i.e., by specifying Y for the Change/create member option), SEU copies the temporary member to the member specified in

Figure D.9
SEU Exit Display

```
                                 Exit

 Type choices, press Enter.

   Change/create member . . . . . . .   Y            Y=Yes, N=No
     Member . . . . . . . . . . . . .   CUSTSALE     Name, F4 for list
     File . . . . . . . . . . . . . .   LFSRC        Name, F4 for list
       Library . . . . . . . . . . .      APPSRC     Name
     Text . . . . . . . . . . . . . .   Customer and sales info by customer ID

     Resequence member . . . . . . . .  Y            Y=Yes, N=No
       Start . . . . . . . . . . . . .  0001.00      0000.01-9999.99
       Increment . . . . . . . . . . .  01.00        00.01-99.99

   Print member . . . . . . . . . . . . N            Y=Yes, N=No

   Return to editing . . . . . . . . .  N            Y=Yes, N=No

   Go to member list . . . . . . . . .  N            Y=Yes, N=No

 F3=Exit   F4=Prompt   F5=Refresh   F12=Cancel
```

the next three options (Member, File, Library). If you don't save your work, SEU discards the temporary copy.

For the Member, File, and Library options, you specify where SEU should store the member. By default, these options show the member you specified when you started the editing session. You can change these to save the (revised) temporary copy to a different member — in which case, the original member is *not* changed.

The Text option lets you specify the descriptive text for the saved source member. If you're not saving the member, the Text option is ignored.

The Resequence member options let you specify that SEU should assign new sequence numbers to the source member's lines. If you're not saving the member, this option is ignored.

The Print member option lets you print the contents of the member.

The Return to editing option lets you return to the editing session, with or without saving the previous changes. If syntax errors have been detected by SEU and not resolved in your editing session, SEU places Y in this option; otherwise, the option defaults to N.

The Go to member list option shows the Work with Members Using SEU list display, from which you can select another source member to edit.

The SEU Command Line

Most functions that you can perform from the Find/Change Options, Browse/Copy Options, and Exit displays can also be performed from the SEU command line.[2] As an example of an SEU command, Figure D.10 shows the FIND SALETOT command, which searches the source member for the first occurrence of the string SALETOT. If the string is found, the line containing it is displayed in the editing area. The FIND command invokes the same SEU search that you can specify on the Find/Change Options display.

2 Note that CL commands cannot be entered on the SEU command line. Use the F21 key to display a CL command line. Also, the commands you use on the SEU command line are not the same as SEU's line commands, discussed earlier.

Figure D.10
Using the SEU Command Line

```
 Columns . . . :    1  71              Edit                         APPSRC/LFSRC
 SEU==> FIND SALETOT                                                     CUSTSALE
 FMT LF .....A..........T.Name++++++.Len++TDpB......Functions++++++++++++++++++
0013.00                R CUSTSALER                  JFILE( CUSTOMER SALE )
0014.00                                             TEXT( 'Sales with +
0015.00                                                    customer info' )
0016.00
0017.00                J                            JOIN( CUSTOMER SALE )
0018.00                                             JFLD( CUSTID CUSTID )
0019.00                                             JDUPSEQ( SALEDATE *DESCEND
0020.00                                             JDUPSEQ( ORDERID )
0021.00
0022.00                  CUSTID                     JREF( CUSTOMER )
0023.00                  NAME
0024.00                  ORDERID
0025.00                  SALEDATE
0026.00                  SALETOT
0027.00
0028.00                K CUSTID
       ****************** End of data ****************************************

 F3=Exit   F4=Prompt   F5=Refresh   F9=Retrieve   F10=Cursor   F11=Toggle
 F16=Repeat find       F17=Repeat change          F24=More keys
```

The FIND command (or the abbreviation: F) has the basic form

```
FIND search-string
```

You can specify *ERR as the search string to find syntax errors in a compile listing spool file. If the search string includes blanks, you must enclose the search string in apostrophes ('), as in the following example:

```
FIND 'Customer name'
```

Figure D.11 shows an example of entering the SEU CHANGE command on the SEU command line; Figure D.12 shows the result of the command. Notice how SEU marks line 0026.00 as CHANGED after the operation.

The CHANGE (or C) command has the basic form:

```
CHANGE search-string  replacement-string
```

As with the FIND command, apostrophes must be used to delimit search or replacement strings with embedded blanks. For both the FIND and CHANGE commands, you can specify various options following the string(s). In this example the ALL option specifies that all matches are to be replaced by this operation. To see an explanation of the options, type FIND or CHANGE on the command line and press the F1 key.

You can use the TOP (or T) command to position the source member to the first line. The BOTTOM (or BOT or B) command positions the source member so the last line is displayed at the bottom of the editing area.

You can use the SAVE command to save changes you've made to the current source member. The SAVE command performs the same function as saving your work from the SEU Exit display but does not end the editing session. To save the member, simply type the command SAVE on the SEU command line. If you want to save the current source member to a different source member, specify the command as

```
SAVE library-name/file-name  member-name
```

Figure D.11
Using an SEU CHANGE command

```
Columns . . . :    1  71              Edit                       APPSRC/LFSRC
SEU==> CHANGE SALETOT SALETOTAL ALL                                  CUSTSALE
FMT LF .....A..........T.Name++++++.Len++TDpB......Functions++++++++++++++++++
0013.00                R CUSTSALER                 JFILE( CUSTOMER SALE )
0014.00                                            TEXT( 'Sales with +
0015.00                                                   customer info' )
0016.00
0017.00                J                           JOIN( CUSTOMER SALE )
0018.00                                            JFLD( CUSTID CUSTID )
0019.00                                            JDUPSEQ( SALEDATE *DESCEND
0020.00                                            JDUPSEQ( ORDERID )
0021.00
0022.00                  CUSTID                    JREF( CUSTOMER )
0023.00                  NAME
0024.00                  ORDERID
0025.00                  SALEDATE
0026.00                  SALETOT
0027.00
0028.00                K CUSTID
        ****************** End of data ****************************************

 F3=Exit   F4=Prompt   F5=Refresh   F9=Retrieve   F10=Cursor   F11=Toggle
 F16=Repeat find       F17=Repeat change          F24=More keys
```

Figure D.12
Result of the SEU CHANGE command

```
Columns . . . :    1  71              Edit                       APPSRC/LFSRC
SEU==>                                                               CUSTSALE
FMT LF .....A..........T.Name++++++.Len++TDpB......Functions++++++++++++++++++
0013.00                R CUSTSALER                 JFILE( CUSTOMER SALE )
0014.00                                            TEXT( 'Sales with +
0015.00                                                   customer info' )
0016.00
0017.00                J                           JOIN( CUSTOMER SALE )
0018.00                                            JFLD( CUSTID CUSTID )
0019.00                                            JDUPSEQ( SALEDATE *DESCEND
0020.00                                            JDUPSEQ( ORDERID )
0021.00
0022.00                  CUSTID                    JREF( CUSTOMER )
0023.00                  NAME
0024.00                  ORDERID
0025.00                  SALEDATE
CHANGED                  SALETOTAL
0027.00
0028.00                K CUSTID
        ****************** End of data ****************************************

 F3=Exit   F4=Prompt   F5=Refresh   F9=Retrieve   F10=Cursor   F11=Toggle
 F16=Repeat find       F17=Repeat change          F24=More keys
String SALETOT changed 1 times.
```

If you're saving the member to a different member of the same source file, you can simply use the command

`SAVE` *`member-name`*

The FILE command is similar to the SAVE command except the FILE command ends the current editing session.

You can use the CANCEL (or CAN) command to exit from SEU without saving your work. You also can use the CANCEL command on the bottom portion of a split-screen display to remove the split screen.

You can use the SET (or S) command to set SEU edit session defaults. The SET CAPS ON command converts all input to upper case; the SET CAPS OFF command lets you enter uppercase and lowercase source.

The SET ROLL command sets the number of lines to scroll forward or backward for RollUp/RollDown (or PageUp/PageDown) keys. The alternatives are

`SET ROLL FULL` — a full screen of lines
`SET ROLL HALF` — half the lines that fit on a screen
`SET ROLL CSR` — position the line with the cursor at the top or bottom of display
`SET ROLL` *nn* — *nn* lines

SEU Session Defaults

You can customize various SEU editing defaults (e.g., mixed-case/uppercase entry) by pressing F13 (Change session defaults) from the SEU Edit display. Online help and the *Source Entry Utility* manual provide complete information about changing your session defaults. Most session defaults can be saved and remain in effect for subsequent editing sessions.

Appendix E

Annotated Bibliography

Recommended books are grouped by topics. Within each topic, they're listed alphabetically by title.

AS/400 Architecture, OS/400, and Related Topics

Control Language Programming for the AS/400, Second Edition. Meyers, Bryan, and Dan Riehl. 29th Street Press, 1997.

A comprehensive textbook, with exercises, for learning CL. (An instructor's guide is also available.)

Implementing AS/400 Security, Fourth Edition. Madden, Wayne, and Carol Woodbury. NEWS/400 Books, 2000.

An excellent practitioner's handbook for setting up AS/400 security.

Inside the AS/400, Second Edition. Soltis, Frank G. 29th Street Press, 1996.

Soltis was the chief architect of the AS/400, and his book is interesting, clear, and authoritative in its explanation of the hardware and software architecture of the AS/400.

Mastering the AS/400, Third Edition. Fottral, Jerry. 29th Street Press, 2000.

This hands-on introductory textbook emphasizes mastery of the AS/400 system/user interface, member-object-library relationship, use of CL commands, basic database concepts, and program development utilities.

RPG IV

ILE by Example. Cravitz, Mike. NEWS/400 Books, 2000.

This book teaches the AS/400's Integrated Language Environment (ILE) using working examples that illustrate key ILE concepts, including service programs, subprocedures, and activation groups.

Programming in RPG IV, Second Edition. Meyers, Bryan, and Judy Yaeger. 29th Street Press, 2000.

An excellent and widely used RPG IV textbook. (An instructor's guide is also available.)

RPG IV Jump Start, Third Edition. Meyers, Bryan. NEWS/400 Books, 2000.

A concise guide to RPG IV for programmers who already know RPG/400. This book provides a quick way to make the transition to RPG IV.

Database Books

CASE*Method Entity Relationship Modelling. Barker, Richard. Addison-Wesley Publishing Co., 1990.

Barker provides an excellent book on business data modeling. The emphasis is on entity relationship diagrams (ERDs), which can be useful for recording or presenting parts of the data model. Chapter 20 in *SQL/400 Developer's Guide* is based on the ERD notation described in Barker's book.

A Complete Guide to DB2 Universal Database. Chamberlin, Don. Morgan Kaufmann Publishers, 1998.

This book provides a fairly complete description of what's available in DB2 UDB. It covers the subject from an overall point of view and makes no attempt to describe aspects that are unique to the various IBM DB2 UDB platforms.

Database Design and Programming for DB2/400. Conte, Paul. 29th Street Press, 1996.

This textbook provides a complete guide to database design and programming on the AS/400, covering physical and logical file DDS, SQL/400, and RPG IV and COBOL/400 database programming.

Handbook of Relational Database Design. Fleming, Candace C., and Barbara von Halle. Addison-Wesley Publishing Co., 1988.

These two "designing women" have written the best step-by-step guide to practical database design. Much of Chapters 19 and 21 in *SQL/400 Developer's Guide* is based on the process described in the *Handbook*. The authors understand both the formal foundations of the relational model and the practical aspects of business database design. This book is an absolute "must have" for anyone serious about database design.

An Introduction to Database Systems, Seventh Edition. Date, C. J. Addison-Wesley Publishing Co., 1999.

This book is another "must have" for the professional database designer. Date provides a highly readable, comprehensive, technically accurate explanation of the relational database model, as well as other important database topics. Chapters 9, 10, and 11 provide a very good explanation of normal forms.

Microsoft ODBC 3.0 Software Development Kit and Programmer's Reference. Microsoft Press, 1997.

This is an essential book for using the ODBC interface from a Windows application. It's comprehensive and well written, with lots of short examples.

Object Lifecycles: Modeling the World in States. Shlaer, Sally, and Stephen J. Mellor. Yourdon Press, 1992.

This is a good book for anyone worried that "relational" is passé and who wants to be "OO courant." It provides a good introduction to object-oriented database design, which, by the way, is not completely antithetical to relational design — the two approaches are compatible, and you can effectively use techniques from both.

General Design and Programming Books

Code Complete: A Practical Handbook of Software Construction. Steve McConnell. Microsoft Press, 1993.

This is our top recommendation for improving your programming skills. The author captures many essential principles and programming practices that separate the "amateur" from the "professional" programmer. The list of books and other references in Chapter 33 ("Where to Go for More Information") is excellent. This is a "must read" for any serious programmer.

Object-Oriented Analysis and Design with Applications. Booch, Grady. Addison-Wesley Publishing Co., 1994.

This is a clear introduction to OO design. Although some people try to position "relational" and "OO" as competing methodologies, they're actually quite complementary. In our experience, many OO design concepts work well when interviewing end users; however, relational (table-oriented) concepts work better for designing physical implementations, especially with most currently available DBMSs.

Object-oriented Software Construction, Second Edition. Meyer, Bertrand. Prentice-Hall, 2000.

This is an excellent book that explains OO language and programming principles using the language Eiffel. Although there are commercial Eiffel compilers available, not many AS/400 programmers will use Eiffel; for most AS/400 programmers, the main value of the language is that it lets Meyers show real programming examples for each of the OO facilities he discusses, and it provides a basis for his discussions on various language design trade-offs. Meyer has an excellent command of language principles, both in theory and in practice.

The Practical Guide to Structured Systems Design. Page-Jones, Meilir. Yourdon, Inc., 1980.

Of several books produced by Ed Yourdon and his colleagues, this one is the clearest on structured analysis and design. The data flow diagram (DFD) notation is quite handy for sketching the process part of a logical system model and dovetails nicely with relational data modeling techniques. Although structured analysis and design have given way to "OO" analysis and design, DFDs remain valuable and are an important diagramming component of many CASE tools.

IBM Manuals

The following publications are available from IBM. Many of the annotations are drawn from IBM descriptions of the manuals. The titles appear alphabetically, followed by their IBM publication number (where available) and release level. Documents for which no publication number is given are generally V4R4 and V4R5 online publications for which no publication number is available. Many of the references listed here can be found under the Database and File Systems topic in the AS/400 Information Center.

To view AS/400 manuals and other documentation online, see IBM's AS/400 Online Library (*http://publib.boulder.ibm.com/html/as400/onlinelib.htm*), IBM's AS/400 Information Center (*http://www.as400.ibm.com/infocenter*), or *NEWS/400*'s Index400 facility (*http://www.as400network.com/index400*).

AS/400 Client Access Express for Windows ODBC User's Guide. (V4R5)

This document describes how to install, configure, and use the Client Access Express for Windows ODBC driver. Included are chapters on performance, examples, and configuring specific applications to run with the Client Access Express ODBC driver.

AS/400 Glossary. (V4R5)

This manual provides definitions for many technical terms used on the AS/400, including for OS/400 and some IBM licensed programs. The Glossary is available in the AS/400 Information Center, at *http://publib.boulder.ibm.com/pubs/html/as400/v4r5/ic2924/info/index.htm.*

AS/400 ILE Concepts. SC41-5606 (V4R5)

This guide explains concepts and terminology pertaining to the Integrated Language Environment (ILE) architecture of the OS/400 licensed program. Topics covered include creating modules, binding, running programs, debugging programs, and handling exceptions.

AS/400 International Application Development. SC41-5603 (V4R2)

This guide provides information required to understand and use the national language support function on the AS/400. The book prepares the AS/400 user for planning, installing, configuring, and using AS/400 national language and multilingual support. It also explains the database management of multilingual data and application considerations for a multilingual system.

AS/400 National Language Support. SC41-5101 (V4R2)

This guide describes national language support concepts, using national language support functions in a multilingual environment, and how IBM licensed programs are affected by national language support functions in a multilingual environment.

AS/400 Tips and Tools for Securing Your AS/400. SC41-5300 (V4R5)

This guide explains how to use the AS/400 security functions and several IBM-supplied tools to improve AS/400 security.

Data Management. (V4R4)

This guide, available in the V4R4 AS/400 Information Center, provides information about using database and device files in application programs. The information is not as specific to database files as that contained in *DB2 UDB for AS/400 Database Programming*.

DB2/400 Advanced Database Functions. SG24-4249 (V4R2)

This redbook provides suggestions, guidelines, and practical examples for using AS/400 database features such as triggers, referential integrity, DRDA, two-phase commit, and stored procedures. The book provides examples developed in several programming languages (RPG, Cobol, C), using native and SQL data-access interfaces.

DB2 for AS/400 SQL Call Level Interface (ODBC). (V4R5)

This book describes how to use the X/Open SQL Call Level Interface to access SQL functions directly through procedure calls to a service program provided by UDB/400.

DB2 Multisystem for AS/400. (V4R5)

This guide provides information about fundamental DB2 Multisystem concepts, including distributed relational database tables, node groups, and partitioning, and discusses creating and using database tables that are partitioned across multiple systems.

DB2 UDB for AS/400 Database Performance and Query Optimization. (V4R5)

This manual contains database performance and query optimization information that was previously provided in *DB2 UDB for AS/400 SQL Programming*.

DB2 UDB for AS/400 Database Programming. (V4R5)

This guide provides a detailed description of the AS/400 database organization, including information about how to create, describe, and update database files on the system.

DB2 UDB for AS/400 Query Management Programming. (V4R5)

This book describes how to define an SQL query definition and define a report form definition using OS/400 query management. It also explains the relationship between OS/400 query management and the Query/400 licensed program.

DB2 UDB for AS/400 SQL Programming. (V4R4)

This manual, available in the AS/400 Information Center, gives an overview of how to design, write, run, and test SQL/400 statements and provides examples of how to write SQL/400 statements in Cobol, RPG, and C programs on the AS/400. In V4R5, this manual's content is provided in *DB2 UDB for AS/400 Database Performance and Query Optimization, DB2 UDB for AS/400 SQL Programming Concepts*, and *DB2 UDB for AS/400 SQL Programming with Host Languages.*

DB2 UDB for AS/400 SQL Programming Concepts. (V4R5)

This manual explains basic SQL programming concepts, including how to use SQL/400, how to access data in a database, and how to prepare, run, and test applications that contain SQL statements.

DB2 UDB for AS/400 SQL Programming with Host Languages. (V4R5)

This manual contains SQL programming information for host languages that was previously provided in *DB2 UDB for AS/400 SQL Programming.*

DB2 UDB for AS/400 SQL Reference. SC41-5612 (V4R5)

The reference for Structured Query Language (SQL) on the AS/400.

DDS Reference. (V4R5)

The Data Description Specifications reference. It covers DDS for physical and logical database files, as well as display, printer, and intersystem communications function (ICF) device files.

Distributed Data Management. (V4R5)

This guide provides information about remote file processing. It describes how to define a remote file to OS/400 Distributed Data Management (DDM), how to create a DDM file, what file utilities are supported through DDM, and the requirements of OS/400 DDM as related to other systems.

Distributed Database Programming. (V4R5)

This guide provides information about preparing and managing an AS/400 system in a distributed relational database using the Distributed Relational Database Architecture (DRDA). It describes planning, setting up, programming, administering, and operating a distributed relational database on more than one AS/400.

File Management. (V4R5)

This Information Center document describes the file management (formerly data management) portion of OS/400, which gives applications access to input and output file data that is external to the application.

ILE C for AS/400 Language Reference. SC09-2711 (V4R4)

The C reference for the AS/400.

ILE C for AS/400 Programmer's Guide. SC09-2712 (V4R4)

Provides information about developing applications using the ILE C/400 language. It includes information about creating, running, and debugging programs and covers programming considerations for interlanguage program and procedure calls, locales, exception handling, and database, externally described, and device files. Some performance tips are also described.

ILE C for AS/400 Reference Summary. SX09-1316 (V4R2)

Provides quick-reference information about ILE C/400 command syntax, elements of C, C library functions, and ILE C/400 machine interface (MI) library extensions.

ILE COBOL/400 Reference. SC09-2539 (V4R4)

The Cobol reference for the AS/400. This manual covers the ILE version of COBOL/400.

ILE COBOL for AS/400 Programmer's Guide. SC09-2540 (V4R4)

Provides information about how to write, compile, bind, run, debug, and maintain ILE COBOL/400 programs on the AS/400. It provides programming information about how to call other ILE COBOL/400 and non-ILE COBOL/400 programs, share data with other programs, use pointers, and handle exceptions. It also describes how to perform I/O operations on externally attached devices, database files, display files, and ICF files.

ILE RPG for AS/400 Programmer's Guide. SC09-2507 (V4R4)

This guide provides information about the ILE RPG/400 (RPG IV) programming language. It includes information about creating and running programs, with considerations for procedure calls and interlanguage programming. The guide also covers debugging and exception handling and explains how to use AS/400 files and devices in RPG IV programs. Appendixes include information about migration to RPG IV from (non-ILE) RPG/400 and sample compiler listings. The manual is intended for people with a basic understanding of data-processing concepts and of the RPG language.

ILE RPG for AS/400 Reference. SC09-2508 (V4R5)

The RPG IV reference. This manual describes, position by position and keyword by keyword, the valid entries for all RPG IV specifications and provides a detailed description of all the operation codes and built-in functions. This manual also contains information about the RPG IV logic cycle, arrays and tables, editing functions, and indicators.

Integrated File System Introduction. (V4R5)

This document provides an overview of the AS/400 integrated file system (IFS), including concepts, terminology, interfaces, and programming techniques.

Net.Data Administration and Programming Guide for OS/400. (V3R7)

This manual covers administration and programming concepts for Net.Data. Topics include configuration, security, performance, the Net.Data macro language, and database access.

Net.Data Reference.

This book explains the syntax and use of Net.Data language constructs, variables, and functions.

OS/400 Backup and Recovery. SC41-5304 (V4R5)

This manual provides general information about AS/400 recovery and availability options.

OS/400 CL Programming. SC41-5721 (V4R5)

This guide provides a wide-ranging discussion of AS/400 programming topics, including a general discussion of objects and libraries, Control Language (CL) programming, controlling flow and communicating between programs, working with objects in CL programs, and creating CL programs. Other topics include predefined and impromptu messages and handling, defining and creating user-defined commands and menus, and application testing, including debug mode, breakpoints, traces, and display functions.

OS/400 CL Reference. SC41-5722 (V4R4)

This manual provides detailed information about AS/400 CL and the OS/400-related commands. All non-OS/400 CL commands associated with other IBM AS/400 software products, including all the various languages and utilities, are described in the manuals for those products. For V4R5 CL reference information, see the Control Language (CL) topic in the AS/400 Information Center.

OS/400 Security — Reference. SC41-5302 (V4R5)

This manual covers system security concepts, planning for security, and setting up security on the system. It also provides information about protecting the system and data from being used by people who lack proper authorization, protecting data from intentional or unintentional damage or destruction, keeping security up-to-date, and setting up security on the system. For additional OS/400 security information, see the "Basic System Security and Planning" topic in the AS/400 Information Center.

OS/400 Work Management. SC41-5306 (V4R4)

This guide provides information about how to create and change an AS/400 work management environment. It also includes a description of tuning the system, collecting performance data, including information about record formats and contents of the data being collected, working with system values to control or change the overall operation of the system, and gathering data to determine who is using the system and what resources are being used.

Programming Development Manager (PDM). SC09-1771 (V3R1)

The PDM reference and user's guide.

Query/400 Use. (V4R5)

This guide gives the end user or programmer information about using AS/400 Query to get data from any database file. It describes how to start Query and how to define and run queries to create reports containing the selected data.

Query Manager Use. (V4R5)

This guide describes the SQL/400 Query Manager and how to use its different options.

Source Entry Utility. SC09-2605 (V4R2)

The SEU reference and user's guide.

Glossary

For additional definitions, see IBM's *AS/400 Glossary* in the AS/400 Information Center.

access path — The order in which records are organized for processing by a program: either arrival-sequence or keyed-sequence.

access plan — A UDB data structure used to store information about how one or more SQL statements will be processed.

algebraic closure — In the relational database model, the property of relational algebra such that the result of any operation is a relation.

alias — An alternate name for a table or view.

arrival-sequence access path — The ordering of records by their relative record numbers.

AS/400 — IBM's midrange business computer system.

assertion — In a data model, a rule that must be satisfied by the data and/or operations on the data.

atomic — Indivisible. This term may apply to attributes in the relational database model, to SQL/400 functions, or to transactions running under commitment control.

attribute — In the relational database model, a named property of the entity represented by a relation.

attribute integrity — In the relational database model, the rule that values for attributes come only from their respective domains.

authority — The right or capability to do something. On the AS/400 there are system-defined public and private authorities that govern a user profile's access to an object.

authorization ID — A system identifier that designates a user or group of users. An authorization ID is a user profile name on the AS/400.

authorization list — An OS/400 object (type *Autl) that controls access to one or more other objects.

base relation — A relation that represents an entity. Contrast with **view relation**.

base table — In SQL, a table that contains data. In SQL/400, a base table is a physical file. Contrast with **view**.

basic predicate — An SQL predicate that tests a simple condition, such as equality.

Between predicate — An SQL predicate that tests for membership in an inclusive range of values.

binary — In UDB/400, a numeric data type that stores numbers using a representation of the number in base 2.

binary radix tree (b-tree) index — An indexing technique used by the AS/400 and other platforms. This type of index is a multilevel structure that lets a large number of key values be stored efficiently while minimizing access times.

blocked Insert In SQL/400, an Insert statement that inserts multiple rows in a single operation.

candidate key In the relational database model, a minimal set of attributes that are non-null and always contain a unique value for each tuple in the relation. If there are multiple candidate keys, one is selected to serve as the relation's primary key.

cardinality The number of tuples in a relation. Also, in entity relationship diagrams, the number of instances of one entity that can be associated with an instance of another entity.

case expression An expression selecting a value based on the evaluation of one or more conditions.

cast expression An expression that applies a temporary change to the data type of another expression.

catalog In general, the system information that describes database objects. In SQL, the tables that contain descriptions of the database objects (e.g., tables, views, indexes, and packages).

check constraint A rule that specifies the values allowed in one or more columns of every row of a table.

Coded Character Set Identifier (CCSID) A 10-digit identifier specifying an encoding scheme for storing character data on a computer system.

collection In SQL, a container for database objects, such as tables and views. In SQL/400, a collection is an OS/400 library object.

column In SQL, the element of a table or view that represents some property of an entity. In SQL/400, a column is a field in a database file.

column definition The definition of a column specified in a Create Table, Create View, or Alter Table SQL statement.

column function In SQL, a function that calculates a value from a set of rows. Contrast with **scalar function**.

commitment control An OS/400 facility that allows all-or-none execution of a transaction.

common table expression A result table defined within a Select statement producing a result table that can be referenced only within the defining Select statement.

commutative The mathematical property that the order of operands is insignificant (e.g., A+B = B+A).

composite primary key A primary key that's composed of more than one field or attribute.

conceptual schema See **schema**.

constraint A restriction or limitation specified in a data model or specified for an SQL table or database file.

constraint state The current relationship of a table relative to one of its constraints (e.g., defined and disabled).

correlated subquery — In SQL, a subquery that references a table or view named in an outer subselect.

correlation name — In SQL, an identifier that designates a table, a view, or an individual row of a table or view within a single SQL statement.

cursor — In SQL, a named structure that's used to access rows individually within an HLL program.

data authority — In OS/400, one of the following specific authorities: *Read, *Add, *Upd, *Dlt, *Execute.

Data Definition Language (DDL) — In SQL, the set of statements that are used to create new database objects (e.g., Create Table).

Data Description Specifications (DDS) — An AS/400 language for defining database and device files.

data dictionary — In a logical data model or physical database design, the containers used to hold everything recorded during the modeling process. These may include word-processing documents, database files, CASE design tool project folders, or other types of containers.

data file — An AS/400 physical file — other than a source file — containing application data.

Data Manipulation Language (DML) — In SQL, the set of statements that are used to manipulate the contents of database objects (e.g., Update).

data model — An abstract representation of the content and structure of the information of interest to an organization.

data modeling — See **logical data modeling**.

data type — In general terms, a definition of a set of allowable values and operations. In SQL, the attribute of a column that determines how values are stored (e.g., character or packed decimal) and the allowable operations.

database — A set of computer files for storing information that's used by a business or other organization. With respect to SQL/400, all the database objects on one AS/400 constitute a single database.

database design — See **physical database design**.

database file — In OS/400, a physical or logical file object (type *File).

database management system (DBMS) — The software to create files and retrieve and update file contents.

datalink — An SQL/400 data type that encapsulates a logical reference (or a pointer) to a file stored outside the database.

date — A UDB/400 field and column data type that stores values for calendar dates.

date duration — In SQL, a value for an interval of time (e.g., a number of days).

DB2 Query Manager and SQL Development Kit for AS/400	The IBM product that contains SQL/400.
DB2 Universal Database for AS/400 (UDB/400)	The name of the AS/400's integrated, relational DBMS.
DBMS	See **database management system**.
DDL	See **Data Definition Language**.
DDS	See **Data Description Specifications**.
degree	In the relational database model, the number of attributes of a relation. In entity relationship diagramming, the number of relations participating in a relationship.
Delete statement	An SQL statement to remove one or more rows from a table.
delete-update-insert rules	For foreign key integrity or referential constraint specifications, the actions to take when a delete, update, or insert operation would leave an orphan row in the dependent file.
dependent table	The table in a referential constraint that contains the foreign key.
derived attribute	See **virtual attribute**.
difference	A relational algebra operation that returns a relation with all tuples in the first relation but not in the second.
direct access method	A file access method that allows reading records in an arbitrary order by key value or relative record number. Contrast with **sequential access method**.
direct attribute	In the relational database model, an attribute that's not derived; that is, one that represents an intrinsic property of an entity.
distinct type	An SQL user-defined data type. In SQL/400, a distinct type is a user-defined type that shares its internal representation with a built-in data type (its source type) but is considered a separate and incompatible type for most operations.
Distributed Relational Database Architecture (DRDA)	An IBM-standard and UDB/400 facility that lets an application on one system use SQL to perform operations on database files stored on remote systems, as if the remote files were local.
division	A relational algebra operation that takes two relations and returns a relation consisting of all values of one set of attributes in the first relation, for those tuples that match on the remaining attributes (in the first relation) all tuples in the second relation.
DML	See **Data Manipulation Language**.
domain	The allowable values that a column can assume and the allowable operations on the column.
double-byte character set (DBCS)	Any of the encoding schemes available on the AS/400 that requires two bytes (16 bits) to represent a single character.

double-precision floating-point number A 64-bit approximate representation of a real number with an approximate range of $2.2250738585072014 \times 10^{-308}$ to $1.7976931348623158 \times 10^{308}$.

DRDA See **Distributed Relational Database Architecture**.

dynamic embedded SQL statement Dynamic SQL statements embedded within a high-level language (HLL) program.

dynamic execution In SQL, the execution of a dynamic statement. Contrast with **static execution**.

dynamic statement An SQL statement that's prepared and executed when the program is run.

EBCDIC See **Extended Binary-Coded Decimal Interchange Code**.

embedded SQL Executable SQL statements contained within the source of an HLL program.

embedded SQL statement An SQL statement coded in an HLL program.

embedded statement See **embedded SQL statement**.

Encoded Vector Index (EVI) An indexing technique in which a list of key values and associated statistics is kept in a structure called a symbol table as well as a second structure, called a vector, that is used to build bit maps.

entity In data modeling, one instance of an entity type.

entity integrity In the relational database model, the rule that each tuple in a relation must be unique.

entity relationship diagram (ERD) A graphical diagram using a notation that represents entity types as boxes and relationships between entity types as lines.

entity subtype An entity type that has all the properties — and possibly more — of another entity type. All entities that are instances of the entity subtype are also instances of the other entity type (the entity supertype).

entity type A representation of a set of objects, events, or associations of interest in a data model. The entity type defines properties of all instances of the type.

entity type hierarchy A set of entity types arranged in a subtype/supertype hierarchy.

equijoin A join that selects rows based on equal values in specified columns of the joined tables.

ERD See **entity relationship diagram**.

exception join A join in which only unmatched rows in the primary (left-side) joined table are included in the result and are paired with null or default values.

exclusive relationship In entity relationship diagramming, a set of relationships for which each instance can participate in exactly one of the possible relationships.

Exists predicate An SQL predicate that tests for a nonempty result set for a subquery.

Extended Binary-Coded Decimal Interchange Code (EBCDIC) — The eight-bit per character encoding used for most UDB/400 character data.

external function — See **external UDF**.

external schema — See **subschema**.

external UDF — A user-defined function based on an HLL program.

externally described file — An OS/400 file that's created from DDS or SQL and which has field-level definitions for the file's records. Contrast with **program-described file**.

field — The smallest named unit of data in a database. A named group of bytes used to store a value in a record.

field authority — The authority (e.g., management, alter, reference, read, add, update) that an authorization ID — or user — has to a particular field (or column) within a table or view.

fifth normal form (5NF) — In the relational database model, the normal form of relations such that no further decomposition is possible without loss of information.

file description — The description of a file's layout, access path, and other information that OS/400 stores in the file object's header.

file override — A native AS/400 technique used to assign temporary runtime changes to the attributes of a file being referenced (e.g., redirecting to a different file).

first normal form (1NF) — In the relational database model, the normal form of relations such that each attribute value is atomic (i.e., not a set).

floating point — A method of encoding real numbers within the limits of finite precision available on computers.

foreign key — A set of columns that reference the primary key of a table. Used to associate rows in a dependent table with rows in a (not necessarily distinct) parent table.

foreign key constraint — In SQL/400 and UDB/400, a constraint that requires a set of non-null columns in a dependent table to have a matching value in the primary or unique key of a column in the parent table.

fourth normal form (4NF) — In the relational database model, the normal form of relations such that no more than one multivalued fact exists in a relation.

full outer join — A join in which unmatched rows in both joined tables are included in the result and are paired with null or default values.

fullselect — A form of SQL Select that is a subselect, or the union of multiple subselects.

group profile — An AS/400 user profile that's referenced as a group profile by some (nongroup) user profile.

grouping column — A column used in an SQL subselect to group rows into subsets for the purpose of selection and aggregation.

hierarchic data model — A data model that represents the structure of information in a hierarchy, with parent/child relationships among nodes in the hierarchy.

high-level language (HLL) — A general-purpose programming language, such as RPG IV or ILE COBOL/400.

HLL — See **high-level language**.

host structure array — In SQL/400, a program variable declared as an array of structures. This type of variable can be used in multiple-row Fetch or blocked Insert operations.

host structure variable — In SQL/400, a program variable declared as a structure (e.g., an RPG data structure or an ILE COBOL/400 group item).

host variable — In SQL/400, an HLL program variable used in an embedded SQL statement.

IFS — See **integrated file system**.

impact analysis — The analysis of what other changes will be required when a file definition or program change is made.

implementation — The actual coding and other tasks required to create a working application.

In predicate — An SQL predicate that tests for membership in a set of values.

Include statement — An SQL statement used to insert declarations and other types of source statements into an HLL program with embedded SQL.

index — In UDB/400, an internal structure that contains key values for records and their corresponding relative record numbers. In SQL, an object used to enforce unique keys and to provide an internal index to aid performance.

indicator variable — In SQL, a host variable that contains a Boolean value indicating whether a column or expression is null.

inner join — A join in which unmatched rows in both joined tables are not included in the result.

Insert statement — An SQL statement to add one or more new rows to a table.

instance — In the relational database model, one occurrence of an entity type. Represented by a tuple in a relation or a row in a table.

integrated file system (IFS) — A Unix-like directory structure and set of interfaces that's part of OS/400. The /QSYS.LIB subdirectory under the root directory of IFS contains UDB/400 files.

integrity constraint — See **constraint**.

Interactive SQL (ISQL) — An IBM interactive tool for entering SQL statements. A component of the DB2 Query Manager and SQL Development Kit for AS/400 product.

intersection entity — In entity relationship diagramming, an entity that represents an association among two or more entities.

intersection — A relational algebra operation that returns a relation with all tuples that occur in both the first relation and the second.

inverted list data model — A data model that resembles a conventional file system with enhanced file index facilities to aid in record retrieval.

isolation level — A value that defines the commitment control environment currently in effect.

ISQL — See **Interactive SQL**.

Java Database Connectivity (JDBC) — A software standard that lets a Java application access a relational database using SQL.

JDBC — See **Java Database Connectivity**.

join — A relational algebra operation that returns a relation that is the subset of the product of two relations, such that each row of the result satisfies a specified condition. The term "join" is frequently used to mean **equijoin**.

key field — In UDB/400, a field used to identify or arrange the records in a file member.

keyed-sequence access path — The ordering of records by values in their key fields.

labeled duration — In SQL, a number and keyword (e.g., 2 Days) that represents a duration of years, months, days, hours, minutes, seconds, or microseconds.

left outer join — A join in which unmatched rows in the primary (left hand) joined table are included in the result and are paired with null or default values.

library — An OS/400 object (type *LIB) that contains other OS/400 objects.

Like predicate — A predicate that searches for strings having a specified pattern.

Lock Table statement — A statement that restricts concurrent access to a table.

logical data modeling — The process of analyzing and specifying the information required by an organization.

logical file — A UDB/400 file that provides an alternative means of accessing data in one or more underlying physical files. Contrast with **physical file**.

logical unit of work — A set of database actions (i.e., inserts, updates, and deletes) performed in a commitment control environment that forms a committable resource performed on an all-or-none basis.

member — The component of a physical or logical file that contains records.

multiple-row Fetch statement — An SQL/400 Fetch statement that retrieves multiple rows on each execution. The component of a physical or logical file that contains records.

multirow predicate — A predicate that requires values from multiple rows in a table to evaluate.

multitable predicate A predicate that requires values from rows in multiple tables to evaluate.

multivalued fact In the relational database model, a dependency in which a value for one attribute may determine several values for another attribute (e.g., an employee ID may determine multiple courses taken by the employee).

naming convention The rules for qualifying names, as well as the rules for determining the collection used with unqualified names.

natural join An equijoin in which one of the two matching columns (or sets of columns) is not included in the result.

nested table expression A result table defined within a subselect producing a result table that can be referenced only within the defining subselect.

Net.Data An IBM AS/400 macro-based software product used for creating dynamic Web pages based on UDB/400 and other database data.

network (CODASYL) data model A form of data model that uses nodes and explicit links to represent information. Unlike in the hierarchical data model, a node may have more than one "parent."

normal form A form of relations that satisfies certain criteria related to the elimination of redundant representation of facts.

normalization A process to make sure the relations or tables in a data model conform to a particular normal form.

null In the relational database model, a placeholder that signifies a missing or unknown value.

Null predicate A predicate testing for the presence or absence of a null value.

null-capable column A column that can contain a null value.

object On the AS/400, a named storage space that consists of a set of characteristics that describe the object and, in some cases, data.

object authority A specific authority (e.g., *ObjMgt) that controls how a user profile can operate on an entire object.

object lock An AS/400 resource allocation mechanism that guarantees certain types of access by the process placing the lock and prevents certain types of access by other processes.

ODBC See **Open Database Connectivity**.

ODP See **open data path**.

open data path (ODP) An OS/400 control block created when a file is opened and used to provide access to the file's data.

Open Database Connectivity (ODBC) A Microsoft-developed standard for database access. Primarily used for access from Windows-based applications.

Operations Navigator IBM's graphical operational interface to the AS/400, which includes a comprehensive set of SQL and database functions.

OS/400
The AS/400 operating system.

outer join
A join in which unmatched rows in one or both of the joined tables are included in the result and are paired with null or default values. See **full outer join**, **left outer join**, and **right outer join**.

override scope
For an OvrDbF (Override with Database File) command, the scope within which file opens and other overrides are affected by this command.

package
See **SQL package**.

packed decimal
In UDB/400, a numeric data type that stores numbers using a representation of the number with one digit per half-byte.

parameter marker
In SQL, a question mark character (?) used to mark the location of a parameter in a string that's dynamically prepared for subsequent execution.

parent table
The table containing a primary or unique key referenced by a foreign key in the dependent table.

PDM
See **Programming Development Manager**.

phantom update
A row that is inserted or updated through a view but can't subsequently be retrieved through that view.

physical data independence
The DBMS architecture concept that users are not affected when the *physical* structure of stored data is changed, as long as the *logical* structure remains the same.

physical database design
The process of designing the files and other application objects needed to implement a particular logical data model.

physical file
A UDB/400 file that contains data. Contrast with **logical file**.

positioned Delete statement
In SQL, a Delete statement with a Where Current Of clause. Used to delete a row that has been Fetch'd through a cursor. Contrast with **searched Delete statement**.

positioned Update statement
In SQL, an Update statement with a Where Current Of clause. Used to update a row that has been Fetch'd through a cursor. Contrast with **searched Update statement**.

precision
In SQL, an attribute of a data type that describes the total number of digits that can be represented.

precompilation
A source translation process that occurs before the compilation step.

precompiler directive
A source language statement that causes some action during precompilation.

predicate
A logical expression that has a true or false value. In SQL, an expression that has a value of true, false, or unknown.

primary key
In the relational database model, the candidate key used to identify rows in the table. In UDB/400, the key identified on a physical file's primary key constraint.

primary key constraint In SQL/400 and UDB/400, a constraint that requires a set of columns to have unique, non-null values.

privilege In SQL, a capability given to a user by a Grant statement. In SQL/400, privileges correspond to OS/400 specific authorities.

product A relational algebra operation that returns a relation consisting of all possible combinations of two tuples, one from each of two specified relations.

program adopted authority The authority of the owner of a program, service program, or SQL package given to a user who is executing the object.

program-described file A file created without DDS or SQL and for which the fields in the records are described only in programs that process the file. Contrast with **externally described file**.

Programming Development Manager (PDM) An IBM programming utility that provides a list-oriented interface for working with libraries, objects, and file members. A component of the ADTS/400 product.

projection A relational algebra operation that returns a relation with all remaining (sub)tuples in a relation after specified attributes have been dropped.

property In a data model, some characteristic of an entity.

public authority The authority governing access by a user profile that has no private authority to an object.

qualified name In OS/400, the combination of a library name and an object name.

quantified predicate An SQL predicate that tests a basic predicate against all rows in a result table.

record A named collection of fields stored or accessed together.

record format A named part of an OS/400 file that identifies records with a specific layout.

record-oriented file A file organized as sequence of records. Contrast with **stream-oriented file**.

record-structured file A file in the QSYS.LIB file system whose data is organized into collections of records, which in turn are an ordered set of fields.

referential integrity In the relational database model, the requirement that tuples that exist in separate relations, but that are interrelated, be unambiguously interrelated by corresponding attribute values.

regular entity In entity relationship diagramming, an entity type that is not a weak entity. Contrast with **weak entity**.

relation In the relational database model, a relation heading and body. Informally, a relation can be thought of as a table.

relation body In the relational database model, a relation's set of tuples.

relation heading In the relational database model, the set of attribute-and-domain pairs.

relational database model A general model for representing information as a set of relations.

relational model See **relational database model**.

relationship — Some form of association or interdependence between two or more entity types.

relative record number (RRN) — The number representing a row's physical location in a table, relative to the first location.

result table — In SQL, the conceptual table defined by a fullselect.

right outer join — A join in which unmatched rows in the secondary (right hand) joined table are included in the result and are paired with null or default values.

row — In SQL, a row consists of a sequence of column values. In SQL/400, a row corresponds to a database record.

row lock — A UDB/400 allocation mechanism that prevents certain types of conflicting row access.

RRN — See **relative record number**.

scalar function — In SQL, a function that calculates a value from an expression that involves no more than one row. Contrast with **column function**.

scalar subselect — A subselect returning a single value or null — that is, a subselect whose result table will always consist of at most a single row and whose select list contains a single expression.

scale — In SQL, an attribute of a data type that describes the total number of digits available to represent the fractional part of a number.

schema — In a logical data model, the part of the model that represents the overall, integrated description of the data.

scrollable cursor — An SQL cursor declared with the Scroll keyword to allow nonsequential Fetch operations.

search condition — In SQL, one or more predicates that specify the criteria for selecting rows from a table.

searched Delete — In SQL, a Delete statement with an optional Where clause that specifies a search condition. Contrast with **positioned Delete statement**.

searched Update — In SQL, an Update statement with an optional Where clause that specifies a search condition. Contrast with **positioned Update statement**.

second normal form (2NF) — In the relational database model, the normal form of relations such that each non-key attribute is dependent on the entire primary key.

Select statement — An interactive SQL statement to retrieve rows from one or more tables or views. Also, a fullselect and an optional Order By, For Update Of, For Read Only, or Optimize For clause.

selection — A relational algebra operation that returns a relation with all tuples in a relation that satisfy a specified condition.

sequential access method — A file access method that allows reading records in their physical order in a file member. Contrast with **direct access method**.

set-at-a-time operation — In SQL, the capability of a Select, Insert, Update, or Delete statement to operate on a set of rows in one operation.

SEU — See **Source Entry Utility**.

single-byte character set (SBCS) — Any of the encoding schemes available on the AS/400 that requires one byte (eight bits) to represent a single character.

single-precision floating-point number — A 32-bit approximate representation of a real number with an approximate range of $1.17549436 \times 10^{-38}$ to $3.40282356 \times 10^{38}$.

Source Entry Utility (SEU) — An IBM full-screen source code editor for the AS/400. A component of the ADTS/400 product.

source file — A physical file that contains source records.

sourced UDF — A user-defined function that is based on another built-in or user-defined function.

special authority — An OS/400 authority (e.g., *SavSys) associated with a user profile and providing various access and system management capabilities.

specific authority — An OS/400 authority (e.g., *Read) granted to a user profile to allow a specific type of access to an object.

SQL — See **Structured Query Language**.

SQL catalog — See **catalog**.

SQL communication area (SQLCA) — A program record structure that's updated after every SQL operation.

SQL Development Kit — See **DB2 Query Manager and SQL Development Kit for AS/400**.

SQL function — A user-defined function based on a program coded in the SQL Procedural Language (SPL).

SQL index — See **index**.

SQL naming option — An industry-standard naming convention that uses a period (.) qualifier.

SQL package — An AS/400 object, used primarily for distributed database processing, containing the control structures used to run SQL statements on an application server.

SQL path — An ordered list of collections used for resolving unqualified distinct type, function, and procedure references.

SQL Procedural Language (SPL) — An SQL-based programming language that can be used to create programs that form the basis for stored procedures or user-defined functions.

SQL special register — One of the system-defined storage areas (e.g., Current Date) that contain information that can be used in SQL statements.

SQL UDF — See **user-defined function**.

SQL/400 precompiler — The UDB/400 software that receives control before the compiler phase of the SQL/400 translation process. The precompiler produces the temporary HLL source member as well as processed SQL statements stored in the source member's associated space.

SQL/400 translation process	The process the AS/400 uses in translating an HLL with embedded SQL into an executable object.
SQLCA	See **SQL communication area**.
standard data type	A set of locally defined data types applied in a consistent manner to column or field definitions.
static execution	In SQL, the execution of a static statement. Contrast with **dynamic execution**.
static statement	An embedded SQL statement that's prepared during program creation and executed when the program is run.
stored procedure	In SQL, a procedure that can be called with a Call statement. In SQL/400, a stored procedure is a program object.
stream file	A file organized into a sequence, or stream, of bytes for which the operating system is unaware of any record level of organization.
stream-oriented file	A file organized as a sequence of bytes. Contrast with **record-oriented file**.
Structured Query Language (SQL)	An industry-standard language for defining and manipulating relational database objects.
subquery	A subselect that's part of a predicate.
subschema	In a logical data model, the part of the model that represents specific end-user views.
subselect	An SQL expression that begins with the Select keyword and that defines a result table. A subselect is a component of a fullselect.
subtype	See **entity subtype**.
surrogate key	A column used as a primary key and that contains a meaningless, system-assigned number.
system catalog	See **catalog**.
system dictionary	See **catalog**.
system name	The one- to 10-character name of an object as it is known in the native AS/400 interface.
system naming option	A naming convention that uses the slash (/) qualifier.
table	A database object with rows and columns. A table may be a base table or a view table; however, "table" by itself is frequently used to mean base table.
table-access routine	A stored procedure providing the sole user interface to a table. Often used to enforce constraints not available through the normal SQL DDL constructs.
theta-join	A general term for any join that uses any operator (represented by the Greek symbol θ) to compare values in joined rows.
third normal form (3NF)	In the relational database model, the normal form of relations such that each non-key attribute is dependent on nothing but the primary key.

three-valued logic	In SQL, computational logic that uses the three values true, false, and unknown.
time	A UDB/400 field and column data type that stores values for time.
time-dependent property	In a data model, a property (e.g., a product's price) whose values must be stored for different date or time intervals.
timestamp	A UDB/400 field and column data type that stores values for system timestamps (e.g., a combination of date and time).
transaction	A group of individual changes to objects on the system that should appear as a single atomic change to the user.
transition constraint	In a data model, a rule governing changes to values.
trigger	In general database terms, a condition that causes some procedure to be executed.
trigger program	An HLL program associated with a trigger condition for a physical file.
triggered procedure	In general database terms, a procedure executed for some trigger.
tuple	In the relational database model, a set of attribute-and-value pairs. A tuple corresponds to a row in a table representation of a relation.
UDB/400	See **DB2 Universal Database for AS/400**.
union	A relational algebra operation that returns a relation with all tuples that occur in either the first relation or the second.
Union operator	An operator used in a fullselect that produces the set theoretic union of two subselect result tables.
union-compatible	In the relational database model, the property of two relations that have the same attributes. In SQL, two tables that have the same number of columns and for which corresponding columns have compatible data types.
unique constraint	In SQL/400 and UDB/400, a constraint that requires a set of columns to have unique values. Null values are allowed.
Universal Multiple-Octet Coded Character Set 2 (UCS-2)	A double-byte encoding scheme used in Java as well as other programming environments.
Update statement	An SQL statement to update one or more rows in a table.
user profile	An OS/400 object (type *UsrPrf) that represents a system user, and which is the basis for controlling access to system objects and functions.
user-defined function (UDF)	An SQL function created and used locally (i.e., not one of the SQL vendor-provided SQL functions).
user-defined type (UDT)	See **distinct type**.
view	In SQL, a table-like object that provides an alternative means of accessing data in one or more underlying base tables. In SQL/400, a view is a logical file. Contrast with **base table**.

view relation
In the relational database model, a named, derived relation that represents an alternative way to view the contents of one or more base relations. Contrast with **base relation**.

virtual attribute
In the relational database model, a view relation's attribute that's derived by some expression from one or more attributes in a base relation.

weak entity
In entity relationship diagrams, an entity for which an instance cannot exist unless a corresponding entity on the other end of a relationship exists. Contrast with **regular entity**.

zoned decimal
In UDB/400, a numeric data type that stores numbers using a representation of the number with one byte per digit.

Index

E

J

K

L

M

N

O

P

Q

R

T

U

V

Newest Books in the 29th Street Press® Library

JAVA AND THE AS/400, SECOND EDITION
Practical Examples for the iSeries and AS/400
By Daniel Darnell

The fully updated second edition of this respected Java guide helps you understand how Java works on the AS/400 and iSeries. Not just another Java tutorial, this detailed book takes you through everything you need to know about how Java is implemented on these systems and guides you through several small application examples to teach the techniques and technologies available today for AS/400 development in Java. Broadened to include coverage of the Java integration features in RPG and the fundamental aspects of Web applications, this edition is a must for all AS/400 Java developers. 347 pages.

PROGRAMMING IN RPG IV, THIRD EDITION
By Bryan Meyers and Judy Yaeger

The latest edition of this highly acclaimed textbook covers RPG IV as it exists in Version 5, a release that brings dramatic change to this popular programming language. The new free-format calculation specification, the latest built-in functions, and more are all covered in this fully updated text. Focusing on real-world problems and down-to-earth solutions, this textbook provides everything you need to know to write a well-designed RPG IV program. Topics covered include the development of RPG; top-down, structured design; RPG IV specifications, operations, and built-in functions; file definition, access, and manipulation; interactive applications; in-depth data definition (including RPG IV data types, tables, and arrays); and modular programming concepts. An instructor's kit is available. 458 pages.

ISERIES AND AS/400 VISUALAGE FOR JAVA
A Step-by-Step Guide to Building Java Graphical Business Applications
By Jerry Ropelato

There's a lot to learn about IBM's VisualAge for Java (VAJ) integrated development environment, but few of the learning tools out there are created with an iSeries-AS/400 audience in mind. In this book, author Jerry Ropelato remedies that problem by teaching VAJ from the perspective of an AS/400 developer. Designed as a step-by-step guide, the book is packed with chapter projects that put the concepts to work using practical examples. By the time you've completed the last chapter project, you'll have the tools and understanding you need to develop professional, high-quality Java applications for the AS/400. 516 pages.

GETTING STARTED WITH WEBSPHERE
The How-to Guide for Setting Up iSeries Web Application Servers
By Brian W. Kelly

This book is designed to be your practical companion for getting WebSphere Application Server up and running in an iSeries environment. The step-by-step approach and iSeries point of view — along with numerous hints and tips from one who's "been there" — will help ensure a smooth and successful installation. The book addresses all aspects of an iSeries WebSphere installation, including prerequisites, installation of WebSphere Application Server and its Administrative Console, and HTTP server configuration for use with WebSphere. 182 pages.

RPG IV JUMP START, FOURTH EDITION
Your Guide to the New RPG
By Bryan Meyers

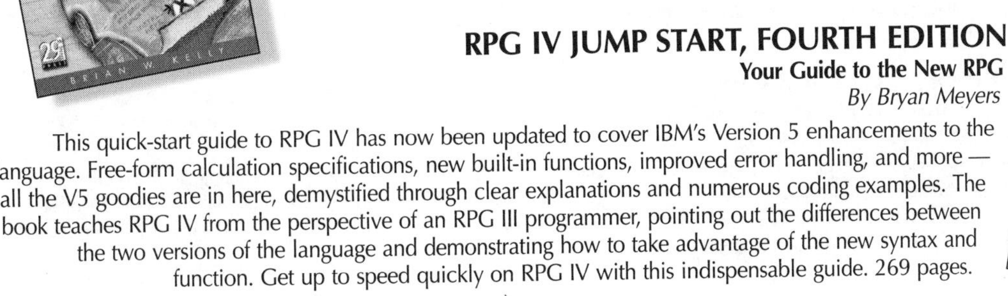

This quick-start guide to RPG IV has now been updated to cover IBM's Version 5 enhancements to the language. Free-form calculation specifications, new built-in functions, improved error handling, and more — all the V5 goodies are in here, demystified through clear explanations and numerous coding examples. The book teaches RPG IV from the perspective of an RPG III programmer, pointing out the differences between the two versions of the language and demonstrating how to take advantage of the new syntax and function. Get up to speed quickly on RPG IV with this indispensable guide. 269 pages.

FORTRESS ROCHESTER

The Inside Story of the IBM iSeries

By Frank G. Soltis

Go behind the scenes and get the inside story on the design and development of IBM's eServer iSeries. Dr. Frank Soltis, IBM chief scientist for the iSeries, examines the five sacred architectural principles of the system, hardware technologies, system structure, enabling technologies, and e-business. Special chapters cover iSeries security, Java, Domino, and Linux. 400 pages.

STARTER KIT FOR THE IBM ISERIES AND AS/400

By Gary Guthrie and Wayne Madden

Starter Kit for the IBM iSeries and AS/400 provides essential information to help you understand the basic concepts and nuances of iSeries and AS/400 systems. The book is arranged in logical order from basic system setup information through important areas you need to know about to operate, program, and manage your system. Comprehensive sections cover system setup, operations, file basics, basic CL programming, TCP/IP, and Operations Navigator. Whether you're a programmer, a system administrator, or an operator, this book will help you develop a basic working knowledge of many key concepts and functions and apply what you've learned to make your iSeries or AS/400 environment more secure, productive, and manageable. An accompanying CD contains all the utilities and sample code presented in the book. 578 pages.

IMPLEMENTING AS/400 SECURITY, FOURTH EDITION

By Carol Woodbury and Wayne Madden

For years, AS/400 professionals have depended on earlier editions of *Implementing AS/400 Security* to learn and implement essential AS/400 security concepts. This latest edition not only brings together in one place the fundamental AS/400 security tools and experience-based recommendations you need but also includes specifics on the security enhancements available in OS/400 V4R5. In addition, you'll find expanded coverage of network, communications, and Internet security — including thwarting hacker activities — as well as updated chapters covering security system values, user profiles, object authorization, database security, output-queue and spooled-file security, auditing, contingency planning, and more. 454 pages.

ILE BY EXAMPLE

A Hands-on Guide to the AS/400's Integrated Language Environment

By Mike Cravitz

Learn the fundamentals of the AS/400's Integrated Language Environment (ILE) by following working examples that illustrate the ins and outs of this powerful programming model. Major topics include ILE program structure, bind by copy, ILE RPG subprocedures, service programs, activation groups, ILE condition handling and cancel handling, and more. A CD contains all sample programs discussed in the book, as well as a sample ILE condition handler to address record locks and ILE RPG software to synchronize system clocks using the Internet SNTP protocol. 165 pages.

SQL/400 DEVELOPER'S GUIDE

By Paul Conte and Mike Cravitz

SQL/400 Developer's Guide provides start-to-finish coverage of SQL/400, IBM's strategic language for the AS/400's integrated database. This textbook covers database and SQL fundamentals, SQL/400 Data Definition Language (DDL) and Data Manipulation Language (DML), and database modeling and design. Throughout the book, coding suggestions reinforce the topics covered and provide practical advice on how to produce robust, well-functioning code. Hands-on exercises reinforce comprehension of the concepts covered. 508 pages.

MASTERING THE AS/400, THIRD EDITION

A Practical, Hands-On Guide

By Jerry Fottral

The latest edition of this best-selling introduction to AS/400 concepts and facilities takes a utilitarian approach that stresses student participation. The book emphasizes mastery of system/user interface, member-object-library relationship, use of CL commands, basic database concepts, and program development utilities. The text prepares students to move directly into programming languages, database management, and system operations courses. Each lesson includes a lab that focuses on the essential topics presented in the lesson. 553 pages.

DOMINO R5 AND THE AS/400

By Justine Middleton, Wilfried Blankertz, Rosana Choruzy, Linda Defreyne, Dwight Egerton, Joanne Mindzora, Stephen Ryan, Juan van der Breggen, Felix Zalcmann, and Michelle Zolkos

Domino R5 and the AS/400 provides comprehensive installation and setup instructions for those installing Domino R5 "from scratch," upgrading from a previous version, or migrating from a platform other than the AS/400. In addition, you get detailed explanations of SMTP in Domino for AS/400, dial-up connectivity, directory synchronization, Advanced Services for Domino for AS/400, and Domino administration strategies, including backup strategies. 512 pages.

E-BUSINESS

Thriving in the Electronic Marketplace

By Nahid Jilovec

E-Business: Thriving in the Electronic Marketplace identifies key issues organizations face when they implement e-business projects and answers fundamental questions about entering and navigating the changing world of e-business. A concise guide to moving your business into the exciting world of collaborative e-business, the book introduces the four e-business models that drive today's economy and gives a clear summary of e-business technologies. It focuses on practical business-to-business applications. 172 pages.

INTRODUCTION TO AS/400 SYSTEM OPERATIONS, SECOND EDITION

By Heidi Rothenbuehler and Patrice Gapen

Here's the second edition of the textbook that covers what you need to know to become a successful AS/400 system operator or administrator. *Introduction to AS/400 System Operations, Second Edition* teaches you the basics of system operations so that you can manage printed reports, perform regularly scheduled procedures, and resolve end-user problems. New material covers the Integrated File System (IFS), AS/400 InfoSeeker, Operations Navigator, and much more. 182 pages.

CREATING CL COMMANDS BY EXAMPLE

By Lynn Nelson

Learn from an expert how to create CL commands that have the same functionality and power as the IBM commands you use every day. You'll see how to create commands with all the function found in IBM's commands, including parameter editing, function keys, F4 prompt for values, expanding lists of values, and conditional prompting. Whether you're in operations or programming, *Creating CL Commands by Example* can help you tap the tremendous power and flexibility of CL commands to automate tasks and enhance applications. 134 pages.

IMPLEMENTING WINDOWS NT ON THE AS/400

Installing, Configuring, and Troubleshooting

By Nick Harris, Phil Ainsworth, Steve Fullerton, and Antoine Sammut

Implementing Windows NT on the AS/400: Installing, Configuring, and Troubleshooting provides everything you need to know about using NT on your AS/400, including how to install NT Server 4.0 on the Integrated Netfinity Server, synchronize user profiles and passwords between the AS/400 and NT, administer NT disk storage and service packs from the AS/400, back up NT data from the AS/400, manage NT servers on remote AS/400s, and run Windows-based personal productivity applications on the AS/400. 393 pages.

DOMINO AND THE AS/400

Installation and Configuration

By Wilfried Blankertz, Rosana Choruzy, Joanne Mindzora, and Michelle Zolkos

Domino and the AS/400: Installation and Configuration gives you everything you need to implement Lotus Domino 4.6 on the AS/400, guiding you step by step through installation, configuration, customization, and administration. Here you get an introduction to Domino for AS/400 and full instructions for developing a backup and recovery plan for saving and restoring Domino data on the AS/400. 311 pages.

ESSENTIALS OF SUBFILE PROGRAMMING AND ADVANCED TOPICS IN RPG IV

By Phil Levinson

This textbook provides a solid background in AS/400 subfile programming in the newest version of the RPG language: RPG IV. Subfiles are the AS/400 tool that lets you display lists of data on the screen for user interaction. You learn to design and program subfiles via step-by-step instructions and real-world programming exercises that build from chapter to chapter. A section on the Integrated Language Environment (ILE), introduced concurrently with RPG IV, presents tools and techniques that support effective modular programming. An instructor's kit is available. 293 pages.

DDS KEYWORD REFERENCE

By James Coolbaugh

Reach for the *DDS Keyword Reference* when you need quick, at-your-fingertips information about DDS keywords for physical files, logical files, display files, printer files, and ICF files. In this no-nonsense volume, author Jim Coolbaugh gives you all the keywords you'll need, listed alphabetically in five sections. He explains each keyword, providing syntax rules and examples for coding the keyword. *DDS Keyword Reference* is a friendly and manageable alternative to IBM's bulky DDS reference manual. 212 pages.

SQL/400 BY EXAMPLE

By James Coolbaugh

Designed to help you make the most of SQL/400, *SQL/400 by Example* includes everything from SQL syntax and rules to the specifics of embedding SQL within an RPG program. For novice SQL users, this book features plenty of introductory-level text and examples, including all the features and terminology of SQL/400. For experienced AS/400 programmers, *SQL/400 by Example* offers a number of specific examples that will help you increase your understanding of SQL concepts and improve your programming skills. 204 pages.

OPNQRYF BY EXAMPLE

By Mike Dawson and Mike Manto

The OPNQRYF (Open Query File) command is the single most dynamic and versatile command on the AS/400. Drawing from real-life, real-job experiences, the authors explain the basics and the intricacies of OPNQRYF with lots of examples to make you productive quickly. An appendix provides the UPDQRYF (Update Query File) command — a powerful addition to AS/400 and System/38 file-update capabilities. CD included. 216 pages.

DDS PROGRAMMING FOR DISPLAY AND PRINTER FILES, SECOND EDITION

By James Coolbaugh

DDS Programming for Display and Printer Files, Second Edition helps you master DDS and — as a result — improve the quality of your display presentations and your printed jobs. The second edition offers a thorough, straightforward explanation of how to use DDS to program display files and printer files. It includes extensive DDS programming examples for CL and RPG that you can put to use immediately because a companion CD includes all the DDS, RPG, and CL source code presented in the book. 429 pages.

THE AS/400 EXPERT: READY-TO-RUN RPG/400 TECHNIQUES

By Julian Monypenny and Roger Pence

Ready-to-Run RPG/400 Techniques provides a variety of RPG templates, subroutines, and copy modules, sprinkled with fundamental advice, to help you write robust and effective RPG/400 programs. Highlights include string-handling routines, numeric editing routines, date routines, error-handling modules, and tips for using OS/400 APIs with RPG/400. The tested and ready-to-run code building blocks — provided on an accompanying CD — easily snap into existing RPG code and integrate well with new RPG/400 projects. 203 pages.

TCP/IP AND THE AS/400

By Michael Ryan

Transmission Control Protocol/Internet Protocol (TCP/IP) has become a major protocol in the AS/400 world because of TCP/IP's ubiquity and predominance in the networked world, as well as its being the protocol for the Internet, intranets, and extranets. *TCP/IP and the AS/400* provides background for AS/400 professionals to understand the capabilities of TCP/IP, its strengths and weaknesses, and how to configure and administer the TCP/IP protocol stack on the AS/400. It shows TCP/IP gurus on other types of systems how to configure and manage the AS/400 TCP/IP capabilities. 362 pages.

THE A TO Z OF EDI AND ITS ROLE IN E-COMMERCE, SECOND EDITION

By Nahid Jilovec

E-commerce expert Nahid Jilovec gives you the practical details of EDI implementation. Not only does this book show you how to cost justify EDI, but it also gives you job descriptions for EDI team members, detailed criteria and forms for evaluating EDI vendors, considerations for trading-partner agreements, an EDI glossary, and lists of EDI organizations and publications. The second edition includes new information about EDI and the Internet, system security, and auditing. 221 pages.

VISUALAGE FOR RPG BY EXAMPLE

By Bryan Meyers and Jef Sutherland

VisualAge for RPG (VARPG) is a rich, full-featured development environment that provides all the tools necessary to build Windows applications for the AS/400. *VisualAge for RPG by Example* brings the RPG language to the GUI world and lets you use your existing knowledge to develop Windows applications. Using a tutorial approach, *VisualAge for RPG by Example* lets you learn as you go and create simple yet functional programs from start to finish. The accompanying CD offers a scaled-down version of VARPG and complete source code for the sample project. 236 pages.

ESSENTIALS OF SUBFILE PROGRAMMING AND ADVANCED TOPICS IN RPG/400

By Phil Levinson

Essentials of Subfile Programming and Advanced Topics in RPG/400 teaches you to design and program subfiles, offering step-by-step instructions and real-world programming exercises that build from chapter to chapter. You learn to design and create subfile records; load, clear, and display subfiles; and create pop-up windows. In addition, the advanced topics help you mine the rich store of data in the file information and program status data structures, handle errors, improve data integrity, and manage program-to-program communications. An instructor's manual is available. 260 pages.

DATA WAREHOUSING AND THE AS/400

By Scott Steinacher

In this book, Scott Steinacher takes an in-depth look at data warehousing components, concepts, and terminology. After laying this foundation, Scott presents a compelling case for implementing a data warehouse on the AS/400. Included on an accompanying CD are demos of AS/400 data warehousing software from several independent software vendors. 342 pages.

CONTROL LANGUAGE PROGRAMMING FOR THE AS/400, SECOND EDITION

By Bryan Meyers and Dan Riehl

This CL programming textbook offers students comprehensive knowledge of the skills they will need in today's MIS environment. Chapters progress methodically from CL basics to more complex processes and concepts, guiding students toward a professional grasp of CL programming techniques and style. In this second edition, the authors have updated the text to include discussion of the Integrated Language Environment (ILE) and the fundamental changes ILE introduces to the AS/400's execution model. 522 pages.

BUILDING AS/400 CLIENT/SERVER APPLICATIONS

Put ODBC and Client Access APIs to Work

By Mike Otey

Mike Otey, a leading client/server authority with extensive practical client/server application development experience, gives you the why, what, and how-to of AS/400 client/server computing, which matches the strengths of the AS/400 with the PC GUIs that users want. This book's clear and easy-to-understand style guides you through all the important aspects of AS/400 client/server applications. Mike covers APPC and TCP/IP communications as well as the underlying architectures for each of the major AS/400 client/server APIs. A CD with complete source code for several working applications is included. 505 pages.

DEVELOPING YOUR AS/400 INTERNET STRATEGY

By Alan Arnold

This book addresses the issues unique to deploying your AS/400 on the Internet. It includes procedures for configuring AS/400 TCP/IP and information about which client and server technologies the AS/400 supports natively. This enterprise-class tutorial evaluates the AS/400 as an Internet server and teaches you how to design, program, and manage your Web home page. 248 pages.

MASTERING AS/400 PERFORMANCE

By Alan Arnold, Charly Jones, Jim Stewart, and Rick Turner

If you want more from your AS/400 — faster interactive response time, more batch jobs completed on time, and maximum use of your expensive resources — this book is for you. In *Mastering AS/400 Performance*, the experts tell you how to measure, evaluate, and tune your AS/400's performance. From their experience in the field, the authors give you techniques for improving performance beyond simply buying additional hardware. 259 pages.

DATABASE DESIGN AND PROGRAMMING FOR DB2/400

By Paul Conte

This textbook is the most complete guide to DB2/400 design and programming available anywhere. The author shows you everything you need to know about physical and logical file DDS, SQL/400, and RPG IV and COBOL/400 database programming. Clear explanations illustrated by a wealth of examples demonstrate efficient database programming and error handling with both DDS and SQL/400. 610 pages.

Talk to Us!

Brought to you by iSeries NEWS!

iSeries Network